HISTORY OF THE POPES
VOL. XVII

PASTOR'S HISTORY OF THE POPES

THE HISTORY OF THE POPES. Translated from the German of LUDWIG, FREIHERR VON PASTOR. Edited, as to Vols. I.–VI. by the late FREDERICK IGNATIUS ANTROBUS, and, as to Vols. VII.–XXIV. by RALPH FRANCIS KERR, of the London Oratory, Vols. XXV.–XXXIV. by DOM ERNEST GRAF, of Buckfatt Abbey, and Vols. XXXV.–XXXVI. by E. F. PEELER.

Vols. I. and II.	A.D. 1305–1458
Vols. III. and IV.	A.D. 1458–1483
Vols. V. and VI.	A.D. 1484–1513
Vols. VII. and VIII.	A.D. 1513–1521
Vols. IX. and X.	A.D. 1522–1534
Vols. XI. and XII.	A.D. 1534–1549
Vols. XIII. and XIV.	A.D. 1550–1559
Vols. XV. and XVI.	A.D. 1559–1565
Vols. XVII. and XVIII.	A.D. 1566–1572
Vols. XIX. and XX.	A.D. 1572–1585
Vols. XXI. and XXII.	A.D. 1585–1591
Vols. XXIII. and XXIV.	A.D. 1592–1604
Vols. XXV. and XXVI.	A.D. 1605–1621
Vols. XXVII. to XXIX.	A.D. 1621–1644
Vols. XXX. to XXXII.	A.D. 1644–1700
Vols. XXXIII. and XXXIV.	A.D. 1700–1740
Vols. XXXV. and XXXVI.	A.D. 1740–1774

The original German text of the *History of the Popes* is published by Herder & Co., Freiburg (Baden).

THE
HISTORY OF THE POPES,

FROM THE CLOSE OF THE MIDDLE AGES

DRAWN FROM THE SECRET ARCHIVES OF THE VATICAN AND OTHER
ORIGINAL SOURCES

FROM THE GERMAN OF

LUDWIG, FREIHERR VON ·PASTOR

EDITED BY

RALPH FRANCIS KERR
OF THE LONDON ORATORY

VOLUME XVII
PIUS V. (1566-1572)

LONDON
ROUTLEDGE & KEGAN PAUL LTD
BROADWAY HOUSE: 68-74 CARTER LANE, E.C. 4.
ST LOUIS, MO.: B. HERDER BOOK CO.
15 & 17 SOUTH BROADWAY.
1951

First published in England 1929
Reprinted 1951

DEDICATED TO
HIS HOLINESS POPE BENEDICT XV.,
WITH PROFOUND VENERATION
BY
THE AUTHOR.

*Ubi Petrus, ibi Ecclesia, ubi Ecclesia,
ibi nulla mors, sed vita aeterna.*

(St. Ambrose, in Ps. 40, v. 30)

PRINTED IN GREAT BRITAIN BY
LUND HUMPHRIES
LONDON · BRADFORD

CONTENTS OF VOLUME XVII.

PAGE

Collections of Archives and Manuscripts referred to in
Volumes XVII. and XVIII. vii
Complete Titles of Books frequently quoted in Volumes
XVII. and XVIII. ix
Table of Contents xxvi
List of Unpublished Documents in Appendix . . xxxiv
Pope Pius XI. to Baron von Pastor xxxv

PIUS V. 1566–1572

The Conclave and Election of Pius V. 1
Previous Life and Character of Pius V. ; his first Measures
of Reform 46
Government of the States of the Church. Pius V. in
relation to Literature and Art 98
Reforming zeal of Pius V. Reform of the College of Car-
dinals, the Curia and the Roman Clergy . . . 136
Reform of the Church on the Basis of the Tridentine Decrees 192
The Reform of the Religious Orders 240
The Roman Inquisition preserves Religious Unity in Italy 288
The Trial of the Archbishop of Toledo, Bartolomé Carranza.
The Condemnation of Baius 344
Appendix of Unpublished Documents 383
Index of Names 427

COLLECTIONS OF ARCHIVES AND MANUSCRIPTS REFERRED TO IN VOLUMES XVII. AND XVIII.

ALESSANDRIA—Library.
ANCONA—Communal Archives.
AQUILA—Dragonetti Archives.
ASTI—Alfieri Archives.
AVIGNON—City Library.

BAMBERG—Archives.
BASLE—Library.
BERLIN—State Library.
BOLOGNA—State Archives.
BREGENZ—Museum Archives.

CARLSRUHE—Library.
CITTÀ DI CASTELLO—Graziani Archives.

DRESDEN—Library.

FAENZA—Library.
———— Landau Library.
FLORENCE—State Archives.
———— National Library.
———— Library of the Villa alla Pietra.
FRANKFURT A. M.—City Archives.

GENEVA—Library.

INNSBRUCK—Vice-regal Archives.

LONDON—British Museum.
LUCERNE—State Archives.

MANTUA—Capilupi Library.
———— Gonzaga Archives.
MILAN—Ambrosian Library.
———— Trivulzi Library.
———— Trotti Archives.
MODENA—State Archives.
MUNICH—State Library.

NAPLES—State Archives.
———— National Library.

PALERMO—State Archives.
PARIS—National Library.
PERUGIA—Library.
PISA—State Archives.

RAVENNA—Archiepiscopal Archives.
———— Seminary Archives.
———— Classense Library.
RIMINI—Gambalunga Library.

ROME—

(a) *Archives :*

Boncompagni.
Campo Santo.
Doria-Pamfili.
Gaetani.
Inquisition.
The Capitoline.
Ricci.
Sapienza.
Spanish Embassy.
Briefs.
Papal Secret Archives (Secret Archives of the Vatican).
State.

(b) *Libraries :*

Altieri.
Angelica.
Anima.
Casanatense.
Chigi.
Corsini.
Vallicelliana.
Vatican.

SALZBURG—Consistorial Archives.
SIENA—Library.
SIGNA—Bonelli Archives in the Villa La Selve.
SIMANCAS—Archives.
SPOLETO—Archiepiscopal Archives.
STOCKHOLM—Library.
STRASBURG—Departmental Archives.

TOULOUSE—Library.

TRENT—City Library.
TRÊVES—City Library.
TURIN—State Library.

VENICE—State Archives.
——— Library of the Correr Museum.
VERONA—Episcopal Archives.
——— Chapter Library.
VIENNA—State Archives.
——— Court Library.

WITTINGAU—Archives.

COMPLETE TITLES OF BOOKS QUOTED IN VOLUMES XVII. AND XVIII.

Abschiede, Die Eidgenössichen, ausdem Zeitraume von 1556-bis 1586 (Der amtlichen Abschiedesammlung, Vol. IV., part 2, Ed. by *Krütli*). Bern, 1861.

[*Acton*.] The massacre of St. Bartholomew ; The North British Review, new series, Vol. XII., London, 1870.

Adriani, G. B. Istoria de' suoi tempi, Vols. I., *seqq.*, Prato, 1822.

Albèri, E. Le relazioni degli ambasciatori Veneti al Senato durante il secolo decimosesto. 3 series. Florence, 1839-1855

Amabile, L. Il S. Officio della Inquisizione in Napoli, Vol. I., Città di Castello, 1892.

Ambros, A. W. Geschichte der Musik, Vol. II., 3rd Ed. by H. Reimann, Leipzig, 1891 ; Vol. III., 3rd Ed. by Otto Kade, 1893 ; Vol. IV., 2nd Ed., 1881.

Ancel, R. La disgrâce et le procès des Carafa d'après des documents inédits 1559 à 1567. Maredsous, 1909.

Angeli, D. Le chiese di Roma ; Roma, s.a.

Annovazzi, V. Storia di Civitavecchia. Roma, 1853.

Anquetil. L'esprit de la Ligue ou histoire politique des troubles de France pendant le XVIe et XVIIe siècle. Nouv. Edition, Vol. I., Paris, 1818.

Archivio della R. Società Romana di storia patria ; Vols. I. *seqq.*, Roma, 1878 *seqq.*

Archivio storico dell' Arte ; publ. per GNOLI ; Vols. I. *seqq.*, Roma, 1888 *seqq.*

Archivio storico Italiano ; 5 series ; Florence, 1842 *seqq.*

Archivio storico Lombardo ; Vols. I. *seqq.*, Milan, 1874 *seqq.*

Archivio storico per le provincie Napolitane ; Vols. I. *seqq.*, Napoli, 1876 *seqq.*

Armellini, M. Le chiese di Roma dalle loro origini sino al secolo XVI. Roma, 1887.

Armstrong, E. The French Wars of Religion ; London, 1892.

Arte, L'. Continuation of " Archivio storico dell' Arte ; Roma, 1898 *seqq.*

Astrain, A. (S.J.). Historia de la Compañia de Jesus en la Asistencia de España, Vols. I., II., Madrid, 1902-1905.

Atti e Memorie della R. deputaz. di storia patria per la prov. dell' Emilia ; Prima serie, 1-8 ; Nuova serie, 1 *seqq.*, Modena, 1863 *seqq.*

Aumale, Duc d'. Histoire des Princes de Condé ; 8 vols., Paris, 1869-1895.

Bain, Joseph. Calendar of State Papers relating to Scotland and Mary Queen of Scots, 1547-1603 ; Vol. II., Edinburgh, 1900.

Balan, P.   Storia d' Italia ; Vol. VI., Modena, 1882.
Baluze, St.   Miscellanea, Ed. MANSI ; 4 vols., Lucæ, 1761.
Baracconi, G.   I. Rioni di Roma. Terza ristampa ; Torino-Roma, 1905.
Bartoli, D.   Dell' istoria della Compagnia di Gesù : L' Italia, prima parte dell' Europa (opere, Vol. V.) ; Torino, 1825.
Bascapè (Carolus a Basilicapetri). De vita et rebus gestis Caroli S.R.E. Cardinalis tituli S. Praxedis archiepiscopi Mediolanensis libri septem ; Brixiæ, 1602 (also printed in " Acta ecclesiæ Mediolan. Vol. III., Brixia, 1603).
Bäumer, S.   Geschichte des Breviers ; Freiburg, 1895.
Baumgarten, H.   Vor der Bartholomäusnacht ; Strasburg, 1882.
Baumgartner, A.   Geschichte der Weltliteratur ; Vol. VI., Die italienische Literatur ; Freiburg, 1911.
Beccari, C. (S.J.).   Rerum Aethiopicarum Scriptores occidentales sæculo XVI. and XIX., Vols. V. and X., Rome, 1907, 1910.
Beiträge zur Geschichte Herzog Albrechts V. und der sog. Adelsverschwörung von 1563. Ed. by *W. Goetz* and *L. Theobald* (Briefe und Akten zur Geschichte des 16 Jahrhunderts mit besonderer Rüchsicht auf Bayerns Fürstenhaus, Vol. VI.), Leipzig, 1913.
Bekker, Ernst, Maria Stuart, Darnley, Bothwell. Mit einem Vorwort von M. Oncken (Giessner Studien aus dem Gebiet der Geschichte, Vol. I.), Giessen, 1881.
Bellesheim, A.   Geschichte der katholischen Kirch in Schottland von der Einführung des Christentums bis auf die Gegenwart. Vol. II., 1560-1878, Mainz, 1883.
—————— Geschichte der katholischen Kirche in Irland, Vol. II., 1509-1690, Mainz, 1890.
Belloni, A.   Storia letteraria d'Italia.   Il Seicento ; Milano, s.a.
Benrath, K.   Die Reformation in Venedig ; Halle, 1887.
Berga.   Pierre Skarga, 1576-1612 ; Paris, 1916.
Berliner, A.   Geschichte der Juden in Rom von den ältesten Zeiten bis zur Gegenwart. 2 vols., Frankfurt a. M., 1893.
Bertani, F.   S. Carlo, la bolla Coena Domini e Milano. Milan, 1888.
Berthier, J. J.   L'église de la Minerve à Rome. Rome, 1910.
Bertolotti, A.   Artisti Francesi in Roma nei secoli XV., XVI., e XVII. Ricerche e studi negli archivi Romani. Mantua, 1886.
—————— Artisti Lombardi a Roma nei secoli XV, XVI., e XVII. 2 vols. Milan, 1881.
—————— Artisti Modenese, Parmesi e della Lunigiana a Roma nei secoli XV., XVI., e XVII. Modena, 1882.
—————— Artisti subalpini in Roma. Mantua, 1885.
—————— Martiri del libero pensiero e vittime della santa Inquisizione nei secoli XVI., XVII., e XVIII. Roma, 1891.
—————— Repressioni straordinarie alla prostituzione in Roma nel sec. XVI. Roma, 1887.
—————— La schiavitù in Roma dal secolo XVI al XIX. Roma, 1887.
Biaudet, Henri.   Les nonciatures apostoliques permanentes jusqu'en 1648 (Annales Academice scientiarum Fennicæ, series B., Vol. II., 1). Helsinki, 1910.

Bibl. V. Die Organisation des evangelischen Kirchenwesens im
Erzherzogtum Oesterreich unter der Enns von der Erteilung
der Religionskonzession bis zu Kaiser Maximilians II. Tode
(1568-1576). In Archiv für österreichische Geschichte,
Vol. 87, Vienna, 1899, pp. 113 *seqq.*
—— Die Erhebung Herzog Cosimos von Medici zum Gross-
herzog von Toskana und die kaiserliche Anerkennung
(1569-1576). In Archiv für österr. etc., Vol. 103, Vienna,
1913.
—— Die Korrespondenz Maximilians II., Vol. I. Familien-
correspondenz 1564 Juli 26 bis 1566 August 11 ; Vienna, 1916.
Bicci, Marco Ubaldo. Notizie della famiglia Boccapaduli patrizia
Romana. Roma, 1762.
Blätter, Historisch–politische, für das katholische Deutschland.
Vols. 1 to 164, Munich, 1838–1919.
Blok, P. J. Geschichte der Niederlande. Vol. III., Gotha,
1907.
Bonanni, Ph. Numismata Pontificum Romanorum. Vol. II.,
Roma, 1699.
Bonnet, Jules. Aonio Paleario. Eine Studie über die Reforma
tion in Italien. Hamburg [1863].
Borgia, Sanctus Franciscus, quartus Gandiæ dux et Societatis
Jesu præpositus generalis tertius (Monum. hist. Soc. Jesu).
Vol. IV. (1565–1568), Vol. V. (1569–1572), Matriti, 1910–
1911.
Boverius, Zach. Annales seu sacræ historiæ Ordinis Minorum
S. Francisci qui Capucini nuncupantur. Vol. I., II., Lugduni,
1632–1639.
Braunsberger, O. Pius V. und die deutschen Katholiken. Frei-
burg, 1912.
Brognoli, V. de. Studi storici sul regno di S. Pio V. 2 vols.,
Roma, 1883.
Brom, G. Archivalia in Italie. Vol. I., s'Gravenhage, 1908.
Bromato, C. Storia di Paolo IV. P.M. 2 vols., Ravenna, 1748–
1753.
Brosch, M. Geschichte des Kirchenstaates. Vol. I., Gotha, 1880.
—— Geschichte Englands. Vol. VI., Gotha, 1890.
—— Geschichten aus dem Leben dreier Grosswesire. Gotha,
1899.
Bruzzone, P. L. Storia del commune di Bosco. 2 vols., Torino,
1861–1865.
Büdinger, M. Don Carlos' Haft und Tod. Vienna, 1891.
Bullarium Diplomatum et Privilegiorum Summorum Romanorum
Pontificum. Vol. VI., Aug., Taurin, 1860 ; Vol. VII.,
Neapoli, 1882.
Bullarium Ordinis Prædicatorum. *See* Ripoll-Brémond.
Bullarium Canonicorum Regularium Congregationis S. Salvatoris ;
Romæ, 1730.
Burckhardt, J. Die Kultur der Renaissance in Italien. 2 vols.,
10th Ed. by *L. Greiger.* Leipzig, 1908.

Calenzio, Generoso. Documenti inediti e nuovi lavori letterarü
sul Concilio di Trento. Roma, 1874.

Cambridge Modern History. Vol. III., The Wars of Religion. Cambridge, 1904.

Cancellieri, Fr. Storia dei solenni Possessi dei Sommi Pontefici detti anticamente processi o processioni dopo la loro coronazione dalla basilica Vaticana alla Lateranense. Roma, 1802.

Canisii, B. Petri. Epistulæ et Acta. Vols. I.–VI., Frib. Brisg., 1896–1913.

Cantù, G. Gli Eretici d'Italia. 3 vols., Turin, 1864–1866.

Capece, Galeota. Nunzii Apostolici di Napoli. Naples, 1878.

Carcereri, Luigi. Giovanni Grimani Patriarca d'Aquileia imputato di eresia e assolto dal Concilio di Trento. Roma, 1907.

Cardauns, Hermann. Der Sturz Maria Stuarts. Cologne, 1883.

Cardella, L. Memorie storiche de' Cardinali della S. Romana Chiesa. Vol. V., Roma, 1793.

Carinci, G. B. Lettere di Onorato Gaetani, Capitan generale della fanteria pontificia nella battaglia di Lepanto. Roma, 1870.

Carini, F. M. (S.J.). Monsignor Nicolò Ormaneto Veronese, vescovo di Padova, Nunzio apostolico alla corte di Filippo II. Rè di Spagna, 1572–1577. Roma, 1894.

Carmina illustrium Poetarum Italorum. Florence, 1719–1726.

Caruso, Giambatt. Discorso istorico-apologetico della Monarchia di Sicilia, pp. G. M. Mira. Palermo, 1863.

Catena, Girol. Vita del gloriosissimo Papa Pio quinto. Roma, 1586.

Cecchetti, B. La republica di Venezia e la corte di Roma nei rapporti della religione. 2 Vols., Venice, 1874.

Charavay, Et. Inventaire des autographes et documents historiques réunis par M. Benj. Fillon. 3 vols, Paris, 1879–1881.

Charpenne. Histoire d'Avignon. Paris, 1887.

Charrière, E. Négociations de la France dans le Levant (Collect. des docum. inéd. pour l'hist. de France, Vols. I., II.), Paris, 1848.

Chattard, G. P., Nuova descrizione del Vaticano. Vols. I.–III., Roma, 1762–1767.

Ciaconius, Alph. Vitæ et res gestæ Pontificum Romanorum et S. R. E. Cardinalium. Vol. III., Romæ, 1677.

Ciappi. Compendio della attioni e vita di Gregorio XIII. Roma, 1596.

Cibrario, L. Lettere di Santi, Papi, Principi, etc. Turin, 1861.

Clementi, F. Il Carnevale Romano nelle cronache contemporanee. Roma, 1899.

Colombo, Giuseppe. Notizie e documenti inediti sulla Vita di M. Giovanni Francesco Bonomi, vescovo di Vercelli. Turin, 1879.

Commemoriali, I libri, della Republica di Venezia. Regesti, vol. VI., Venice, 1903.

Conclavi de' Pontefici Romani. s.l., 1667.

Constant, G. Rapport sur une mission scientifique aux archives d'Autriche et d'Espagne (Nouv. Arch. des Missions scientif. et littér., vol. 18); Paris, 1910.

Contarini, Alvisi. Relazione di Francia 1502, in *Albèri,* Relazioni, I., 4; Florence, 1860.

Corpo diplomatico Portuguez . . . desde o seculo XVI., pp. Luiz Augusto Rebello da Silva. Vols. 6–10, Lisbon, 1886 seq.

Correro, Giov. Relazione di Francia, 1569, in Albèri, Relazioni, I., 4 ; Florence, 1860.

Correspondance du Cardinal Granvelle, publ. p. Poullet et Piot. 12 vols., Bruxelles, 1878–1896.

Correspondance de Philippe II. See Gachard.

Correspondencia de Felipe II. con sus embajadores en la corte de Inglaterra 1558 à 1584, vols. IV. and V. (Colección de documentos inéditos para la historia de España, vols. 91 and 92), Madrid, 1888.

Correspondencia diplomática entre España y la Santa Sede durante el pontificado de S. Pio V., por D. L. Serrano. 4 vols., Roma, 1914.

Cramer, L. La Seigneurie de Genève et la maison de Savoie de 1559 à 1603, 2 vols., Geneva, 1912.

Cupis, C. de. Le vicende dell' agricoltura e della pastorizia nell'agro Romano e l'Annona di Roma. Roma, 1911.

Cyprianus, E. Tabularium ecclesiæ Romanæ sæculi decimi sexti, in quo monumenta restituti calicis eucharistici totiusque concilii Tridentini historiam mirifice illustrantia continentur. Francofurti et Lipsiæ, 1743.

Daenell, Ernst. Die Spanier in Nordamerika, 1513–1824 (Historische Bibliothek, ed. by the Historische Zeitschrift, vol. 22), Munich and Berlin, 1911.

Dändlinker, K. Geschichte der Schweiz. 2 vols., 3rd Ed., Zurich, 1900–1904.

Degert, A. Procès de huit evêques français suspects de Calvinisme : Revue des Quest, Hist. ,vol. 76, Paris, 1904, pp. 61–108.

Dejob, Ch. De l'influence du Concile de Trente sur la littérature et les beaux-arts chez les peuples catholiques. Paris, 1884.

Dell'Acqua, C. Di San Pio V. Papa insigne fautore degli studi e degli studiosi. Milan, 1904.

Dengel, J. Geschichte des Palazzo di S. Marco, genannt Palazzo di Venezia. Leipsig, 1909.

Dengel, Ph. Nuntiaturberichte aus Deutschland. 2nd part, vol. V., fasc. 1, Vienna, 1920.

Depeschen, Venezianische, vom Kaiserhofe (Dispacci di Germania), ed. by the Historische Kommission der Kaiserlichen Akademie der Wissenschaften : vols. 1 to 3, ed. by Turba. Vienna, 1889–1895.

Desjardins, A. Négociations diplomatiques de la France avec la Toscane. Documents recueillis par Gius. Canestrini. Vol. I. seqq., Paris, 1859.

Diana, Ant. (O. Theat.). Litteræ, Decreta et Constitutiones recentiorum Pontificum, ad Tribunal S. Officii spectantes : in Diana, Opera, ed. by Martin de Alcolea. Vol. V., Lyons, 1687.

Dictionnaire de Théologie Catholique (Vacant-Mangenot). Vol. I. seqq., Paris, 1903.

Dierauer, Joh. Geschichte der Schweizerischen Eidgenossenschaft. Vol. III., 1516–1648 (Geschichte der europäischen Staaten. Ed. by *A. H. L. Heeren, F. A. Uckert, W. v. Giesebrecht* and *K. Lamprecht,* vol. 26). Gotha, 1907.

Documentos escogidos del Archivo de la casa de Alba, pp. la *Duquesa de Berwick y de Alba,* Madrid, 1891.

Döllinger, J. J. Beiträge zur politischen, kirchlichen und Kulturgeschichte der sechs letzten Jahrhunderte. Vols. II. and III., Regensburg, 1863–1882.

Döllinger, J. J. and H. Reusch, Die Selbstbiographie des Kardinals Bellarmin. Bonn, 1887.

Duhr, B. (S.J.). Geschichte der Jesuiten in den Ländern deutsche Zunge im 16 Jahrh. Vol. I., Freiburg, 1907.

Ehrenberg, H. Urkunden und Aktenstücke zur Geschichte in der heutigen Provinz Posen vereinigten ehemals polnische Landesteile. Leipzig, 1892.

Ehses, S. and S. Merkle. Concilium Tridentinum, vols. I. *seqq.* Frib. Brisg., 1901.

Eichhorn, A. Der ermländische Bischof und Kardinal Stanislaus Hosius. 2 vols., Mainz, 1854–1855.

Epistolæ P. Alphonsi Salmeronis Soc. Jes. ex autographis vel originalibus exemplis . . . nunc primum editæ. Vol. I., 1536–1565 ; Vol. II., 1565–1585, Matriti, 1906, 1907.

Escher, Conrad, Barock und Klassizismus. Studien zur Geschichte der Architektur Roms. Leipzig [1910].

Eubel, see *Gulik–Eubel.*

Faberi, Fr. S. Pio V. Studio storico. Siena, 1893.

Fea, C. D. Storia delle acque in Roma e dei condotti. Rome, 1832.

Feller, R. Ritter Melchior Lussy von Unterwalden. Seine Beziehungen zu Italien und sein Anteil an der Gegenreformation. 2 vols., Stans, 1906–1909.

Fillon, see *Charavay.*

Fleming, David Hay. Mary Queen of Scots from her birth to her flight into England. London, 1879.

Folieta, Ubert. De sacro foedere in Selimum libri quattuor. In *Grævius,* Thesaurus antiquitatum et historiarum Italiæ. Tom. I., pars II. Lugd. Batavorum, 1704.

Forbes-Leith, W. (S.J.). Narratives of Scottish Catholics under Mary Stuart and James VI. Edinburgh, 1885.

Forcella, V. Iscrizioni delle chiese e d'altri edifici di Roma dal secolo XI. fino al giorni nostri. 14 vols., Roma, 1869–1885.

Forneron, H. Histoire de Philippe II. Vol. I., Paris, 1881.

Fouqueray, H. Histoire de la Compagnie de Jésus en France. Vol. I. (1528–1575), Paris, 1910.

Frémy, E. Un ambassadeur libéral sous Charles IX. et Henri III. Ambassade à Venise d'Arnaud du Ferrier. Paris, 1880.

Frere, W. H. The English Church in the reigns of Elizabeth and James I. London, 1904.

Friedberg, E. Die Grenzen zwischen Staat und Kirche und die Garantien gegen deren Verletzung. Tübingen, 1872.

Friedländer, W. Das Kasino Pius IV. Leipzig, 1912.

Fumi, Luigi. L'Inquisizione Romano e lo Stato di Milano. Milan, 1910.

Gabutius, Joh. Ant. Vita Pii V. Romæ, 1605.

Gachard, L. P. Correspondence de Philippe II. sur les affaires des Pays-Bas. Vol. I., Brussels, 1848.

——— Relations des ambassadeurs Vénitiens sur Charles V. et Philippe II. Brussels, 1855.

——— Don Carlos et Philippe II. 2 vols., Brussels, 1863.

——— La bibliothèque des princes Corsini. Brussels, 1869.

——— Les bibliothèques de Madrid et de l'Escurial. Brussels, 1875.

Galluzzi, R. Istoria del Granducato di Toscana sotto il governo della Casa Medici. Nuova ediz. Vol. III., Florence, 1882.

Gams, P. B. Series episcoporum ecclesiæ Catholicæ. Ratisbon, 1873.

——— Die Kirchengeschichte von Spanien. 3 vols., 2nd ed., Ratisbon, 1879.

Garampi, G. Saggi di osservazioni sul valore delle antiche monete Pontificie, s.l., s.a. [Roma, 1766].

Gatticus, J. B. Acta cærimonialia S. Romanæ Ecclesiæ. Vol. I., Romæ, 1753.

Gaudentius, P. Beiträge zur Kirchengeschichte des 16 und 17 Jahrh. Bedeutung und Verdienste des Franziskaner-Ordens im Kampfe gegen den Protestantismus. Vol. I., Bozen, 1880.

Gaye, E. G. Carteggio inedito d'artisti dei secoli XV., XVI., e XVII. 3 vols., Florence, 1840.

Gennari, N. Della triplice santa alleanza di S. Pio V. contro Selim II., battaglia di Lepanto, e trionfo di Marc Antonio Colonna (Giornale Arcadico di Roma, 109, 1847).

Geuer. Die Kirchenpolitik L'Hospitals. Leipzig, 1877.

Giannone, P. Istoria civile del regno di Napoli. Vol. IV., Venezia, 1766.

Gindely, A. Rudolf II. und seine Zeit, 1600–1612. 2 vols., Prag, 1863–1865.

Giornale storico della letteratura Italiana. Vols. I. *seqq.*, Rome–Turin–Florence, 1883.

Gnoli, D. Vittoria Accoramboni. Florence, 1868.

Goetz, W. See " Beiträge."

Göller, Emil. Die päpstliche Pönitentiarie von ihrem Ursprung bis zu ihrer Umgestaltung unter Pius V. 2 vols. in 4 parts, Rome, 1907–1911.

González, Tomás. Apuntamientos para la historia del Rey Don Felipe segundo por lo tocante á sus relaciones con la reina Isabel de Inglaterra desde el año 1558 hasta el de 1576. In " Memorias de la R. Academia de la Historia," Vol. VII., Madrid, 1832.

Gori, F. Archivio storico, artistico, archeologico e letterario della città e provincia di Roma. Vols. I.-IV. Roma e Spoleto, 1875-1883

Gothein, E. Ignatius von Loyola und die Gegenreformation. Halle, 1895.
Gothein, M. Geschichte der Gartenkunst. Vol. I. Jena, 1914.
Goubau, F. Apostolicæ Epistolæ. Libri V. Antwerp, 1640.
Graevius, J. G. Thesaurus Antiquitatum Italia. 12 vols., Venice, 1732-1737.
Gratiani, Ant. Mariæ. Episcopi Amerini Epistolarum ad Nicol. Thomicium libri decem. in *Mai*, Spicilegium, Vol. VIII., Roma, 1842.
—— De bello Cyprio libri quinque. Roma, 1624.
Green, Mary Anne Everett. Calendar of State Papers. Domestic Series of the reign of Elizabeth. Addenda, 1566-1579. London, 1871.
Groen van Prinsterer, G. Archives ou Correspondance inédite de la Maison d'Orange-Nassau. 1st series, 9 vols., Leyden, 1841
Guglielmotti, Alb. Marc Antonio Colonna alla battaglia di Lepanto. Florence, 1862.
—— Storia delle fortificazioni nella spiaggia Romana. Roma, 1880.
Guidicini, Gius. Miscellanea storico-patria Bolognesi. Bologna, 1872.
Gulik-Eubel. Hierarchia catholica Medii Aevi. Vol. III., Monasterii, 1910.
Gurlitt, Cornelius. Geschichte des Barockstiles in Italien. Stuttgart, 1887.

Hammer, J. V. Geschichte des osmanischen Reiches. Vol. III. Pest, 1828.
Hartig, O. Die Gründung der Münchener Hofbibliothek durch Albrecht V. und Johann Jakob Fugger. Munich, 1919.
Hartzheim, L. Concilia Germanica. Vols. I.-X. Cologne, 1759.
Havemann, W. Das Leben des Don Juan d'Austria. Gotha, 1865.
Hergenröther, J. Katholische Kirche und christlicher Staat. Freiburg, 1872.
Herre, P. Europäische Politik im Cyprischen Krieg, 1570-1573. Leipzig, 1902.
—— Papsttum und Papstwahl im Zeitalter Philipps II. Leipzig, 1907.
Herzog. see : Real-Enzyklopädie.
Hilgers, J. (S.J.). Der Index der verbotener Bücher. Freiburg, 1904.
Hilliger, B. Die Wahl Pius V. zum Papste. Leipzig, 1891.
Hinojosa, R. de. Los despachos de la diplomacia Pontificia en España. Vol. I., Madrid, 1896.
Hinschius, P. System des katholischen Kirchenrechts. Berlin, 1869.
Hirn, J. Erzherzog Ferdinand II. von Tirol. Vols. I., II., Innsbruck, 1885, 1887.
Holzapfel, Heribert. Handbuch der Geschichte der Franziskanerordens. Freiburg, 1909.
Holzwarth, F. J. Der Abfall der Niederlande, 2 vols. Schaffhausen, 1865-1871.

Hopfen, O. H.   Kaiser Maximilian II. und der Kompromiss-katholizismus.   Munich, 1895.
Höpfl, Hildebrand (O.S.B.).   Beiträge zur Geschichte der Sixto-Klementinischen Vulgata.   (Biblische Studien, Vol. 18). Freiburg, 1913.
Hosack, John.   Mary Queen of Scots and her accusers.   Edinburgh, 1869.
Huber, A.   Geschichte Oesterreichs.   Vol. IV.   Gotha, 1892.
Hübner, P. G.   Le Statue di Roma.   Leipzig, 1912.
Hürbin, J.   Handbuch der Schweizer Geschichte.   Stans, 1900–1908.
Hurter, F.   Geschichte Kaiser Ferdinands II.   Vols. I.–VII. Schaffhausen, 1850.
Hurter, H.   Nomenclator litterarius recentioris theologiæ catholicæ.   Vol. I.   Oeniponte, 1892.

Intra, G. B.   Di Camillo Capilupi e de' suoi scritti.   Milan, 1893.
Inventario dei Monumenti di Roma.   Vol. I.   Roma, 1908–1912.

Jahrbuch, Historisches, der Görres-Gesellschaft.   Vols. 1–39. Münster and Munich, 1880–1919.
Janssen, J.   Geschichte des deutschen Volkes seit dem Ausgang des Mittelalters.   Vols. I.–IV., 19th and 20th Ed.   Freiburg, 1913–1917.
Jorga, N.   Geschichte des osmanischen Reiches.   Vol. III. Gotha, 1910.
Jurien de la Gravière.   La guerre de Chypre et la bataille de Lépante.   2 vols.   Paris, 1888.

Kallab, W.   Vasari-Studien.   (Quellen-schriften für Kunstgeschichte, N. F., Vol. XV.).   Wien, 1908.
Katholik, Der, Jahr. 1 seqq., Strasburg and Mayence, 1820–1919.
Keller, L.   Die Gegenreformation in Westphalen und am Niederrhein.   (1555–1585).   Leipzig, 1881–1887.
Kervyn de Lettenhove.   Les Huguenots et les Gueux (1560–1585).   6 vols., Bruges, 1883–1885.
Kervyn de Lettenhove.   Relations politiques des Pays-Bas et de l'Angleterre.   Vols. IV.–VI. (1564–1573).   Bruxelles, 1885–1888.
Kirchenlexikon oder Enzyklopädie der Kathol. Theologie . . . von *H. J. Wetzer* und *B. Welte.*   2nd Ed. by *Jos. Card. Hergenröther,* 12 vols., 1882–1901.
Korzeniowski, J.   Excerpta ex libris manuscriptis Archivii Consist. Romani 1509–1590 . . . collecta.   Cracoviæ, 1890.
Kraus, F. X.   Geschichte der christlichen Kunst.   2 vols.   Freiburg, 1908.
Kretzchmar, Joh.   Die Invasionsprojekte der katholischen Mächte gegen England zur Zeit Elisabeths.   Leipzig, 1892.

Labanoff, Prince Alex.   Lettres, etc. de Marie Stuart.   Vols. I.–VII.   Londres, 1844.
Laderchi, J.   Annales ecclesiastici, Vols. 35–37.   Bari Ducis, 1881–1883.

Lagomarsini. see *Pogiani.*

Lämmer, H. Zur Kirchengeschichte des 16 und 17 Jahrhunderts. Freiburg, 1863.

———— Meletematum Romanorum mantissa. Ratisbon, 1875.

Lanciani, R. Storia degli scavi di Roma. Vols. I.–IV. Roma, 1902–1910.

Laugwitz. Bartholomäus Carranza, Erzbischof von Toledo. Kempten, 1870.

Lavisse, É. Histoire de France. Vol. VI. Paris, 1904.

Lazzareschi, E. Le relazioni fra S. Pio V. e la Repubblica di Lucca. Florence, 1911.

Lechat, Robert (S.J.). Les réfugiés Anglais dans les Pays-Bas Espagnols durant le règne d' Elisabeth. Louvain, 1914.

Le Bret, Joh. Fried. Staatsgeschichte der Republik Venedig. Riga, 1775.

———— Geschichte von Italien ; in the " Haller Allegmeinen Welthistorie." Halle, 1786.

Legazioni di A. Serristori, ambasciatore di Cosimo I. a Carlo V. e in corte di Roma. Con note di *G. Canestrini.* Florence, 1853.

Lettere de' Principi. 3 vols. Venezia, 1570–1577.

Lettres de Catherine de Médicis, publ. par La Ferrière et Baguenault de Puchesse. Vols. IV. *seq.* Paris, 1891 *seq.*

Lettres de M. Paul de Foix archevêque de Toulouse et ambassadeur pour le Roi auprès du P. Grégoire XIII. escrites au Roi Henry III. Paris, 1628.

Lingard, John. A History of England. Vols. VII., VIII. London, 1838.

Litta, P. Famiglie celebri Italiane. Milano e Torino, 1819–1881.

Llorente, J. A. Histoire critique de l' Inquisition d' Espagne. Trad. par A. Pellier. 2 de Ed., Paris, 1818.

Longo, Fr. Successo della guerra con Selim Sultano Imperator de' Turchi e giustificazione della pace con lui conclusa, 1569–1573. (Archiv. stor. Ital., Appendice IV., n. 17). Firenze, 1847.

Lossen. see *Masius.*

Maffei, P. A. Vita di S. Pio V. Roma, 1712.

Maffei, V. Dal titolo di Duca di Firenze e Siena a Granduca di Toscana. Firenza, 1905.

Magistris, C. P. de. L'elezione di Cosimo I. de' Medici alla dignità di Granduca di Toscana nelle lettere dell' ambasciatore di Francia a Roma, 1569–1570. Torino, 1912.

Mai, A. Spicilegium Romanum. Vols. I.–X. Romæ, 1839–1844.

Manareus, O. (S.J.). De rebus Societatis Jesu Commentarius. Florence, 1886.

Manfroni, C. La Lega cristiana nel 1572. Con lettere di M. A. Colonna. (Archiv. d. R. Soc. Rom. di storia patria, vol 16). Roma, 1893.

———— Storia della Marina Italiana dalla caduta di Constantinopoli alla battaglia di Lepanto. Roma, 1897.

Marcks, E. Die Zusammenkunst von Bayonne. Strasburg, 1889.

———— Gaspard von Coligny. Vol. I., Stuttgart, 1892.

Margraf, J. Kirche und Sklaverei seit der Entdeckung Amerikas. Tübingen, 1865.
Marini, G. Degli Archiatri pontifici. Vols. I., II. Roma, 1748.
────── Lettera al ch. Mons. Muti Papazurri già Casali. Roma, 1797.
Marocco, G. Monumenti dello Stato Pontificio. Roma, 1833–1835.
Marx, E. Studien zur Geschichte des niederländischen Aufstandes (Leipziger Studien aus der Geschichte, Vol. III.). Leipzig, 1902.
Masius, Andreas. Briefe des A. M. und seiner Freunde (1538–1573), ed. by *Lossen.* Leipzig, 1886.
Mas Latrie, De. Histoire de l'Ile de Chypre, 3 vols., Paris, 1852–1861.
────── Trésor de Chronologie. Paris, 1889.
Mayer, J. G. Das Konzil von Trient und die Gegenreformation in der Schweiz. 2 vols., Stans, 1901–1903.
Mazzuchelli, G. M. Gli scrittori d'Italia. 2 vols., Brescia, 1753.
Meaux, De. Les luttes religieuses en France au XVI.e siècle. Paris, 1879.
Meister, A. Die Geheimschrift im Dienste der päpstlichen Kurie von ihren Anfängen bis zum Ende des 16 Jahrh. (Quelen und Forschungen aus dem Gebiete der Geschichte, vol. XI.). Paderborn, 1906.
Mélanges d'archéologie et d'histoire (Ecole française de Rome). Vol. I., Paris, 1881.
Merki, Ch. L'amiral de Coligny. La maison de Châtillon et la révolte protestante 1519–1572. Paris, 1909.
Merkle, S. Concilii Tridentini Diariorum, Pars I., II. Frib. Brisg., 1901–1911.
Meyer, A. O. England und die katholische Kirche unter Elizabeth. Vol. I., Rom., 1911.
────── [English transl. by *J. R. McKee,* Congr. Orat. presb., London, 1916.]
Michaelis, A. Geschichte des Statuenhofes im vatikanischen Belvedere (Jahrb. des Deutschen Archäol. Inst., vol. V.). Berlin, 1891.
Mignet. Histoire de Marie Stuart. Vol. I., II., Paris, 1885.
Mitteilungen des Instituts für österreichische Geshichtsforschung. Vols. I. seqq., Innsbruck, 1880 seqq.
Molitor, Raphael. Die Nach-Tridentinische Choral-Reform zu Rom., vol. I., Leipzig, 1901.
Molmenti, P. Sebastiano Veniero et la battaglia di Lepanto, Firenze, 1899.
Moran, Francis. Spicilegium Ossoriense. Vol. I., Dublin, 1874.
Moroni, G. Dizionario di erudizione storico-ecclesiastica. 109 vols., Venezia, 1840–1879.
Mullbauer, Max. Geschichte der katholischen Missionen in Ostindien von Vasco di Gama bis zur Mitte des 18 Jahrhunderts. Munich, 1851.
Müntz, E. Histoire de l'art pendant la Renaissance. I., Italie. 3 vols., Paris, 1889–1895.
────── et P. Fabre, La Bibliothèque du Vatican au XV.e Siècle. Paris, 1887.

Mutinelli.   Storia arcana d'Italia.   Vol. I., Venezia, 1885.

Nadal, H. (S.J.).   Epistolæ ab anno 1546 ad 1577.   4 vols.,
   Matriti, 1898–1905.
Narducci, H.   Catalogus codicum manuscriptorum in Bibliotheca
   Angelica.   Romæ, 1893.
Nau, Claude.   Maria Stuart von der Ermordung Riccios bis zur
   Flucht nach England (1566–1568).   Annotated by *H.
   Cardauns.*   Wurzburg-Vienna, 1885.
Nibby, A.   Roma nell' anno 1838.   Parte prima moderna,
   Roma, 1839.
Nicolai.   Memorie, leggi e osservazioni sulle Campagne e sull'
   Annona di Roma.   Roma, 1803.
Noailles, de.   Henri de Valois et la Pologne en 1572.   2 vols.,
   Paris, 1878.
Novaes, G. de.   Storia de' Pontefici.   Vol. VII., Roma, 1822.

Opitz, Theodor.   Maria Stuart.   2 vols., Freiburg, 1879.
Orano, Domenico.   Liberi pensatori bruciati in Roma dal XVI.
   al XVIII. secolo (Documenti inediti dell' Archivio di Stato
   di Roma, 1904.
Otto, K. v.   Geschichte der Reformation in Oesterreich unter
   Kaiser Maximilian II., 1564–1576 (Jahrbuch der Gesellschaft
   für Geschichte des Protestantismus in Oesterreich, vol. X.,
   Vienna, 1889).

Palandri, E. P.   Les Négociations politiques et religieuses entre
   la Toscane et la France (1544–1580), d'après les documents
   des Archives de l'Etat a Florence et a Paris.   Paris, 1908.
Paruto, Paolo.   Historia Venetiana.   Parte II.   Venezia, 1718.
Pastor, L. von.   Allgemeine Dekrete der Römischen Inquisition
   aus den Jahren 1555 bis 1597.   Freiburg, 1912.
Paulus, N.   Hexenwahn und Hexenprozess vornehmlich im
   16 Jahrh.   Freiburg, 1910.
Petramellarius, J. Ant.   Ad librum O. Panvinii de Summis Pontif.
   et S.R.E. Cardinialibus a Paulo IV. ad Clementis VIII.
   annum pontificatus octavum Continuatio.   Bononiæ, 1599.
Petrucelli della Gattina, F.   Histoire diplomatique des Conclaves.
   Vol. II.   Paris, 1864.
Pfleger, L.   Martin Eisengrein, 1535–1578.   Ein Lebensbild aus
   der zeit der katholischen Restauration in Bayern.   Freiburg,
   1908.
Philippson, M.   Philipp II. von Spanien und das Papsttum, in
   the "Hist. Zeitschrift," Munich, 1878, pp. 269-315, 419-457.
———— Westeuropa im Zeitalter Philipps II., Elisabeths, und
   Heinrichs IV.   Berlin, 1882.
———— Histoire du règne de Marie Stuart.   2 vols.   Paris,
   1891.
———— Die römische Kurie und die Bartholomäusnacht ; in the
   "Deutschen Zeitschrift für Geschichtswissenschaft."   Vol.
   VII., 1, Leipzig, 1892.
Phillips, Georg.   Kirchenrecht.   Vols. I.–VIII.   Regensburg,
   1845–1889.

Picot. Essai historique sur l'influence de la religion en France pendant le XVIIe siècle. Vol. I. Louvain, 1824.
Pierling, P. Rome et Moscou, 1547–1579. Paris, 1883.
———— La Russie et le Saint-Siège. Vol. I. Paris, 1896.
Piot. see Correspondance du Card. Granvelle.
Pirenne, H. Geschichte Belgiens. Vol. III. (1477–1567), Gotha, 1907.
Platner–Bunsen. Beschreibung der Stadt Rom von E. Platner, K. Bunsen, E. Gerhard, W. Röstell. 3 vols., Stuttgart, 1829–1842.
Platzhoff, W. Die Theorie von der Mordbesugnis der Obrigkeit im 16 Jahrh. (Historische Studien, 54). Berlin, 1906.
Pogiani, Julii. Sunensis Epistolæ et Orationes olim collectæ ab Ant. M. Gratiano, nunc ab Hier. Lagomarsinio (S.J.) adnotationibus illustr. ac primum editæ. Vols. I.–IV., Romæ, 1762.
Polenz, G. v. Geschichte des französischen Calvinismus. Vols. II., III., Gotha, 1859.
Pollen, John H. (S.J.). Papal Negotiations with Mary Queen of Scots during her reign in Scotland, 1561–1567. (Publ. of the Scottish Hist. Society, vol. 37). Edinburgh, 1901.
Pollen, John H. (S.J.). The English Catholics in the reign of Queen Elizabeth, 1558–1580. London, 1920.
Pometti, Fr. Per la storia della Marina Italiana. Roma, 1898.
Poullet. see Correspondance du Card. Granvelle.
Premoli, O. Storia de' Barnabiti nel Cinquecento. Vol I., Roma, 1913. Quartalschrift, Römische, für christliche Altertumskunde und für Kirchengeschichte. Ed. by *A. de Waal, H. Finke and St. Ehses.* I. *seqq.*, Rome, 1887 *seqq.*
Quartalschrift, Tübinger Theologische, I. *seqq.* Tübingen, 1819 *seqq.*
Quellen und Forschungen aus italienischen Bibliotheken und Archiven. Ed. by the " Preuss. Histor. Institut." I. *seqq.* Rome, 1898 *seqq.*
Quétif et Echard. Scriptores Ord. Prædicatorum. Paris, 1719.

Rachfahl, Fr. Wilhelm von Oranien und der niederländische Aufstand. 2 vols. Halle, 1906–1908.
Ranke, L. v. Französische Geschichte vornehmliche im 16 und 17 Jahrh. Vol. I., 2nd Ed. Stuttgart, 1856.
———— Englische Geschichte. Vol. I., Berlin, 1859.
———— Die römischen Päpste. Vols. I., III., 8th Ed., Leipzig, 1885.
Rasponus, C. De basilica et patriarchio Lateranensi libri V. Romæ, 1656.
Real-Enzyklopädie für protest. Theologie und Kirche. von *J. J. Herzog.* 3rd Ed. by *A. Hauck.* 23 vols. Leipzig, 1896–1909.
Reinhardt-Steffens. Die Nuntiatur von Giovanni Francesco Bonhomini, 1579–1581. (Nuntiaturberichte aus der Schweiz seit dem Konzil von Trient, par. I.). Solothurn, 1906.
Relacye, Nuncyuszów Apostolskich i innych osób o Polsce od roku 1548 do 1690. Ed. *E. Rykaczewski.* Vol. I., Berlin-Poznan, 1864.

Renazzi, F. M. Storia dell' università degli studi di Roma, detta la Sapienza. 2 vols. Roma, 1503–1804.

Renom de France, Histoire des troubles des Pays-Bas. Publ. par *Piot.* Vol. I. Bruxelles, 1886.

Reumont, A. Bibliografia dei lavori pubblicati in Germania sulla storia d' Italia. Berlin, 1883.

——— Geschichte der Stadt Rom. Vol. III. Berlin, 1870.

——— Geschichte Toskanas. Gotha, 1876.

Reusch, H. Der Index der verbotenen Bücher. 2 vols. Bonn, 1883–5.

Revue Historique. I. *seqq.* Paris, 1876 *seqq.*

Revue des Questions Historiques. I. *seqq.* Paris, 1866 *seqq.*

Rieger und Vogelstein. Geschichte der Juden in Rom. 2 vols. Berlin, 1895–6.

Riezler, S. Geschichte Bayerns. Vols. IV. and VI. Gotha, 1899.

Ripoll-Brémond. Bullarium Ord. Prædicatorum. Vol. V., Romæ, 1733.

Ritter, M. Deutsche Geschichte im Zeitalter der Gegenreformation und des Dreissigjährigen Krieges (1555–1648). Vol. I. Stuttgart, 1889.

Rocchi, E. Le piante iconografiche e prospettive di Roma del secolo XVI. colla riproduzione degli studi originali autografi di A. da Sangallo il Giovane per le fortificazioni di Roma, dei mandati di pagamento e di altri documenti inediti relativi alle suddette fortificazioni. Torino-Roma, 1902.

Rocco da Cesinale. Storia delle Missioni dei Cappuccini. Vol. I. Paris, 1867.

Rodocanachi, E. Les Institutions communales de Rome sous la Papauté. Paris, 1901.

——— Le Capitole Romain antique et moderne. Paris, 1904.

——— Rome au temps de Jules II. et de Léon X. La cour Pontificale ; Les artistes et les gens de lettres ; La ville et le peuple ; Le Sac de Rome en 1527. Paris, 1912.

Romanin, S. Storia documentata di Venezia. 10 vols. Venezia, 1853–1861.

Rosell, C. Historia del combate naval de Lepanto. Madrid, 1853.

Rosi, M. La riforma religiosa e l' Italia nel secolo XVI. Nota storica. Catania, 1892.

——— La riforma religiosa in Liguria e l' eretico umbro Bartolomeo Bartoccio (Atti della Soc. Ligure di storia patria, Vol. 24). Genoa, 1894.

Ruble, A. de. Antoine de Bourbon et Jeanne d' Albret. 4 vols. Paris, 1897.

Rundschau, Literarische. Vols. I.–VI. Aachen-Freiburg, 1875–1880.

Sacchinus, Fr. Historiæ Societatis Jesu, Pars tertia sive Borgia. Romæ, 1649.

Sala, A. Documenti circa la Vita e le gesta di S. Carlo Borromeo. 3 vols. Milan, 1857–1861.

——— Biografia di S. Carlo Borromeo. Milan, 1858.

Salmeron. see : Epistolæ P. Alph. Salmeronis.

San Carlo Borromeo nel terzo centenario della canonizzazione, 1610–1910. Periodico mensile, publ. dal November, 1908, al Dicembre 1910.
Santori, Giulio Ant. Card. di S. Severina, Autobiografia. Ed. by *G. Cugnoni* (Archiv. della Soc. Rom. di storia patria, Vol. 12 and 13), Roma, 1889–1890.
——— Diario concistoriale. Ed. by *P. Tacchi Venturi, S.J.* (Studi e documenti di storia e diritto, Vols. 23–25). Roma. 1902–4.
Sauli, Alessandro, S. Note e documenti. Milano, 1905.
Schellhass, K. Nuntiaturberichte aus Deutschland. Vol. III. (1572–85). Berlin, 1896.
Schiess, Traugott. Bullingers Korrespondenz mit den Graubündnern, 1566–1575 (Quellen zur Schweizer Geschichte, Vol. 25). Basel, 1906.
Schmidlin, J. Die kirchlichen Zustände in Deutschland vor dem Dreissigjährigen Kriege. Freiburg, 1908–1910.
Schwarz, W. E. Der Briefwechsel des Kaisers Maximilian mit Papst Pius V. Paderborn, 1889.
——— Die Akten der Visitation des Bistums Münster aus der zeit Johanns von Hoya, 1571–1573. Münster, 1913.
Segesser, A. Ph. v. Ludwig Pyffer und seine Zeit. 2 vols. Bern, 1880–1.
Sentis, F. J. Die " Monarchia Sicula." Freiburg, 1869.
Sereno, B. Commentario della guerra di Cipro e della Lega dei principi cristiani contro il Turco. Monte Cassino, 1845.
Serrano, L. La Liga de Lepanto entre España, Venecia y la S. Sede 1570–1573. Vols. I., II. Madrid, 1918–1920.
[*Serranus, J.*] Commentariorum de statu religionis et reipublicæ in regno Galliæ libri. 3 vols., s.l., 1571.
Serristori. see : Legazioni.
Sickel, Th. von. Römische Berichte. Vols. I.–V. Vienna, 1893–1901.
Skibniewski, St. L. Corvin v. Geschichte des Römischen Katechismus. Rome-Ratisbon, 1903.
Soldan, M. G. Geschichte des Protestantismus in Frankreich. Vol. I. Leipzig, 1855.
Sommervogel, C. (*S.J.*). Bibliothèque de la Cie de Jésus, 9 vols. Brussels-Paris, 1890–1900.
Soriano, Michele. Ritratto di Pio V. (*Albèri*, Relazioni, II., 4). Firenze, 1857.
Specht, Thomas. Geschichte der ehemaligen Universität Dillingen (1549–1804). Freiburg, 1902.
Spezi, P. Pio V. Roma, 1905.
Spicilegio Vaticano di documenti inediti e rari estratti dagli archivi e dalla bibl. della Sede Apost. Vol. I., Roma, 1890.
Spillmann, Jos. (*S.J.*). Die englischen Martyrer unter Heinrich VIII. und Elisabeth (1535–1583). 2 part., 2nd Ed. Freiburg, 1900.
Steinherz, S. Nuntiaturberichte aus Deutschland (1560–1572). Vols. I., II., IV. Vienna, 1897–1914.
Steinhuber, Andr. Geschichte des Kollegium Germanikum Hungarikum in Rom. Vol. I., 2nd. Ed. Freiburg, 1906.

Steinmann, E. Die Sixtinische Kapelle. 2 vols. Munich, 1901–1905.
Stimmen aus Maria Laach. I. *seqq.* Freiburg, 1871 *seqq.*
Streit, R. Bibliotheca Missionum. Monasterii, 1916.
Studi e documenti di storia e diritto (Publ. periodica dell' Academia di Conferenze storico-giuridiche : Vols. I. *seqq.* Roma, 1880 *seqq.*
Suau, P. St. François de Borgia. Paris, 1905.
Sudendorf, H. Regestrum ; (Notable Archives for German History). Berlin, 1851–1854.
Šusta, J. Die römische Kurie und das Konzil von Trient unter Pius IV. 4 vols. Vienna, 1904-1914.
Sylvain. Histoire de St. Charles Borromée. 3 vols. Milan, 1884.
Synopsis Actorum S. Sedis in causa Societatis Jesu, 1540–1605. Florence, 1887 (Private circulation).
Tacchi Venturi, P. Storia della Compagnia di Gesù in Italia. Vol. I., Roma, 1909.
Taja, Agostino. Descrizione del Palazzo Apostolico Vaticano. Opera postuma . . . revista ed accresciuta. Roma, 1750.
[*Tedeschis, Nic. Maria de.*] Istoria della pretesa Monarchia di Sicilia. Roma, 1715.
Tempesti, C. Storia della vita e delle gesta di Sisto V. 2 vols. Roma, 1866.
Theiner, Aug. Geschichte der geistlichen Bildungsanstalten. Mayence, 1835.
——— Annales Ecclesiastici, quos post . . . Baronium . . . ab An. 1572 ad nostra usque tempora. Vols. I.–III. Roma, 1856.
——— Vetera Monumenta Poloniæ et Lithuaniæ, etc., Vol. III., 1585–1696. Romæ, 1863.
Thompson, J. W. The Wars of Religion in France, 1559–1576 Chicago, 1909.
Thuanus, J. A. Historiæ sui temporis. Paris, 1604-1620.
Tiepolo, Paolo. Relazione da Roma in tempo di Pio IV. e di Pio V. (In : Albèri, Relazioni, II., 4, Firenze, 1857).
Tiraboschi, G. Storia della Letteratura Italiana. 10 vols. Modena, 1772.
Tomàssetti, Guiseppa. La Campagna Romana antica, mediævale e moderna. Vols. I., II. Roma, 1910.
Törne, P. O. v. Ptolémée Gallio Cardinal de Come. Helsingfors, 1907.
Turba. see : Depeschen, Venezianische.
Türke, Karl. Rom und die Bartholomaüsnacht. Chemnitz, 1880.

Ughelli, F. Italia Sarca. Editio II. 10 vols. Venetiis, 1717–1722.

Vaissette. Histoire de Languedoc. Vol. V. Paris, 1745.
Valensise, D. M. Il vescovo di Nicastro poi Papa Innocenzo IX. e la Lega contro il Turco. Nicastro, 1898.
Vasari, G. Le Vite de' più eccellenti Pittori, etc. Nuova Ediz. di G. Milanesi. Firenze, 1878 *seqq.*

Venuti, R. Numismata Romanorum Pontificum a Martino V. ad Benedictum XIV. Romæ, 1744.

Verancii, Ant. Epistolæ. In : Monum. Hungariæ historica. II. Scriptores, Vol. 25. Pest, 1871.

Verga, Ettore. Il municipio di Milano e l' Inquisizione di Spagna, 1563. (Arch. storico Lomb. Anno 24, fasc. 15). Milano, 1897.

Voinovich, L. Depeschen des Francesco Gondola (1570–1573). In, Archiv. für österreichische Geschichte. Vol. 98. Vienna, 1909.

Wadding, L. Annales Minorum. Vol. 20. Romæ, 1794.

Wahrmund, L. Das Ausschliessungsrecht (jus exclusivæ) bei den Papstwahlen. Vienna, 1889.

Weiss, Ch. Papiers d' état du Cardinal de Granvelle. Vols. I.–IV. Paris, 1841–1848.

Whitehead, G. Coligny. London, 1904.

Widmann, H. Geschichte Salzburgs. Gotha, 1907.

Wiedemann, Th. Geschichte der Reformation und Gegenreformation im Lande unter der Enns. Vols. I.–V. Prag, 1879 *seqq.*

Wirz, Kaspar. Bullen und Breven aus italianischen Archiven, 1116–1623. (Quellen zur Schweizer Geschichte, Vol. 21). Basel, 1902.

Wymann, Edward. Kardinal Karl Borromeo in seinen Beziehungen zur alten Eidgenossenschaft. Stans, 1910.

Yriarte, C. La vie d'un patricien de Venise au XVIe siècle. Paris, 1874.

Zaleski, K. S. Jesuici w Polsce. Vols. I. and IV. Lwów, 1900–1905.

Zeitschrift, Historische. Ed. by *Sybel.* Vols. I. *seqq.* Munich, 1859 *seqq.*

———— für katholische Theologie. Vols. 1–36. Innsbruck, 1877–1912.

———— für Kirchengeschichte. Ed. by *Brieger.* Vols. I. *seqq.* 1877 *seqq.*

Zinkeisen, J. M. Geschichte des osmanischen Reiches in Europa. 3 parts. Gotha, 1840 *seqq.*

Zivier, E. Neuere Geschichte Polens. Vol. I. Die zwei letzten Jagellonen, 1506–1572. Gotha, 1915.

TABLE OF CONTENTS OF VOLUME XVII.

CHAPTER I.

THE CONCLAVE AND ELECTION OF PIUS V.

A.D.   PAGE
1565 Rome completely quiet after the death of Pius IV.   .   .   1
     Preparations for the conclave.   1
     The state of the Papal treasury   2
     The principal candidates   3
     A long conclave probable   4
     The Cardinals go into conclave (December 19th)   .   5
     The number of the electors   6
     Parties in the conclave   7
     Strict observance of the enclosure   8
     Very little interference on the part of the princes and
          ambassadors   9
     The attitude of Cosimo de' Medici   .   .   .   10
     The policy of France   11
     The attitude of Philip II. of Spain   .   .   .   12
     The report sent by Requesens to the Spanish king   .   13
     His recommendations   15
     The influence of Spain upon the election of no great
          importance   16
     The Spanish Cardinals in the conclave   .   .   .   17
     The three party leaders : Borromeo, Farnese and
          Este   18
     Borromeo's attitude of reserve ; he refuses to use his
          influence at first   19
     The efforts of Este and Farnese   21
     The attempts of Este to secure the tiara for himself   .   22
     The influence of Borromeo   23
     Attempt to elect Morone   24
     This attempt is very nearly successful   .   .   .   27
     Morone's opponents   28
     The guidance of the conclave passes out of the hands
          of Borromeo   30
     Farnese's hopes of success   31
     His great popularity in Rome   33
     The candidature of Ricci   33
1566 The death of Gonzaga a blow to Farnese's hopes   .   34
     Various candidates put forward   35
     Rumour that Philip II. had nominated Ghislieri   .   36
     Borromeo once again takes a leading part, and puts
          forward Sirleto   37
     Borromeo comes to terms with Farnese, and secures
          the election of Ghislieri   39

A.D.   PAGE
The election of Ghislieri ; his acceptance of the
    dignity (January 7th)   40
He takes the name of Pius V.   40
Unexpectedness of the election   40
The decisive influence of Borromeo upon the election   43
General rejoicing among the Cardinals and in the city   44

CHAPTER II.

PREVIOUS LIFE AND CHARACTER OF PIUS V.   HIS FIRST MEASURES
OF REFORM.

1504 The birth of Michele Ghislieri ; his home and family   46
1521 He enters the Dominican Order   47
Ghislieri as a Dominican friar   47
Ghislieri as Inquisitor ; he is brought into contact
    with Cardinal Carafa   48
1551 He becomes Commissary-General of the Inquisition   49
1556 And Bishop of Sutri and Nepi   49
1557 Ghislieri created Cardinal by Paul IV. (March).   . 49
1558 And Grand Inquisitor of the Roman Church .   . 49
Cardinal Ghislieri not in favour with Pius IV. .   . 50
His personal appearance   52
1566 The character of Pius V.   53
His sense of the responsibilities of his office   .   . 54
His strict manner of life ; his great abstemiousness . 55
His health gives cause for anxiety 55
His great personal activity   57
His delight in prayer   58
His regular attendance at ecclesiastical functions   . 59
Visits to the Seven Churches   60
His great devotion to the Blessed Sacrament   . 61
" The Pope is a saint "   62
His great strictness recalls the days of Paul IV..   . 63
The opinion of the ambassadors 65
He has little experience of political affairs   .   . 66
Fears of the Pope's severity on the part of the Romans   67
The Pope's allocution to the Cardinals (January 12th)   67
He announces his policy : the extirpation of heresy,
    peace among the princes, and war against the
    Turks 68
His spirit of independence   68
The Pope's popularity rapidly increases .   .   . 69
His coronation (January 17th)   69
First reform measures ; the Dataria and Segnatura . 72
His zealous attendance at the Congregations   .   . 72
The influential Cardinals   73
The Pope and his relatives   74
Michele Bonelli created Cardinal (March 6th) .   . 77
The Pope puts all his trust in spiritual arms   .   . 79
Cardinal Bonelli's powers very restricted   .   . 80

A.D. PAGE

Pius V. and the Cardinals 81
The Pope and Cardinal Bonelli 83
1567 Paolo Ghislieri made Governor of the Borgo . . 84
His banishment 85
Ruthless severity of the Pope in offences against
    morality 86
The restriction of luxury 87
Strict rules for physicians 88
The Pope's war against public immorality . . 89
The prostitutes banished from Rome . . . 90
Severe ordinances against adultery ; the death penalty
    threatened 93
The Pope's strict watch over his household ; the Swiss
    Guard 95
Religious instruction in Rome 96
Rome becomes " a world-wide monastery " . . 97

CHAPTER III.

GOVERNMENT OF THE STATES OF THE CHURCH. PIUS V. IN RELATION TO LITERATURE AND ART.

Pius V. as a temporal sovereign 98
Reform of the administration of justice . . . 98
Revision of the trial of the Carafa . . . 99
Many executions in the Papal States . . . 101
The Pope and brigandage 102
Repression of feuds and factions 103
The financial administration of Pius V. ; his personal
    economy 104
But new taxes are forced upon him . . . 105
The Pope's lavish almsgiving 106
Charitable works in Rome 107
Protection of agriculture ; the price of bread . . 109
Pius V. in relation to Art 110
The Belvedere collection 111
The Pope and the treasures of antiquity . . 112
But he can in no sense be called the enemy of antiquity 114
Though his interests lie entirely in religious matters . 115
Restoration of the Sistine Chapel 117
The Torre Pia at the Vatican built by the Pope . 118
Building operations in the city ; restoration of
    churches 121
Pius V. and the building of St. Peter's . . . 122
Jacopo Vignola 123
Buildings at Loreto and Assisi 124
The water supply of Rome 125
Fortification works in the Papal States . . . 126
Painters employed by Pius V. 127
Pius V. and Literature 128
His interests entirely ecclesiastical ; the works of St.
    Thomas and St. Bonaventure 129

A.D.   PAGE

Biblical studies 130
The Vatican Library 132
The Papal Archives 133
The Roman University 133
A changed spirit in Rome 135

CHAPTER IV

REFORMING ZEAL OF PIUS V. REFORM OF THE COLLEGE OF
CARDINALS, THE CURIA AND THE ROMAN CLERGY

The Pope's zeal for reform 136
The court officials 137
Pius V. and Cardinal Borromeo 138
Niccolò Ormaneto 139
The reform of the Papal household . . . 140
The reform of the court 141
The Pope urges the Cardinals to simplicity of life and
   the imitation of Christ 144
He complains of electoral intrigues among them . 147
The Cardinals and the duty of residence . . 148
Cardinalitial rights of presentation restricted . . 149
Cardinal Innocenzo del Monte 150
Pius V.'s consideration for the Cardinals . . 152
His condemnation of intrigues concerning the Papacy 153
Plans for a renewal of the Sacred College . . 154
1568 Four new Cardinals appointed (March 24th) . . 156
Diego di Espinosa 157
Jerôme Souchier 158
Paolo della Chiesa and Antonio Carafa . . . 159
Further creations expected 160
The princes and the Sacred College . . . 161
1570 Sixteen new Cardinals created (May 17th). . . 162
The new Cardinals 163
1571 General fears of a " terrible " reform . . . 170
The reform of the Curia 170
The Dataria : " cessioni " and " renunzie " . . 172
Reform of the Penitentiaria 175
The College of Penitentiaries 178
The Segnatura, Cancelleria and Apostolic Camera . 178
The Pope in person begins a visitation of Rome . 179
Reform of the Roman clergy ; the Apostolic Visitors 181
They discharge their duties very strictly . . 183
Examination of confessors ; sacerdotal conferences. 184
Ecclesiastical dress 185
The duties of parish priests 186
The duty of residence 187
The Pope returns to this question again and again . 189
Visitation of the Papal States 190
Plan of a provincial synod for the whole of Italy . 191

A.D.   PAGE

CHAPTER V.

REFORM OF THE CHURCH ON THE BASIS OF THE TRIDENTINE DECREES

The Tridentine decrees the Pope's guide in all his
work of reform 192
The Roman Catechism 192
It is translated into several languages . . . 193
Reform of the Breviary 194
The Breviary of Pius V. 195
The Vulgate 198
Canon Law 199
1567 St. Thomas Aquinas declared a Doctor of the Church
(April) 200
Pius V. in relation to science and literature . . 202
Hagiography and historical criticism . . . 203
The Congregation of the Index 203
Pius V. and questions of dogma 204
The Immaculate Conception; the chalice for the
laity 205
The question of bull-fights in Spain . . . 206
Church Music 208
The Pope's great zeal for the Council of Trent . . 209
The establishment of seminaries 211
Provincial synods 214
The duty of residence 216
Diocesan visitations 218
Apostolic Visitors sent throughout Italy . . 219
Pius V. and the bishops 220
Confraternities of Christian Doctrine . . . 223
Regulations concerning divine worship . . . 224
Superstitious practices condemned 225
Caste prejudice in Spain 226
Reverence for the Blessed Sacrament . . . 226
Pious confraternities 227
Pius V. and simony 229
" Confidential simony " 231
The alienation of ecclesiastical property . . 233
The right of presentation 235
The efforts of the Pope supported by the presence of
many saints; Philip Neri, Charles Borromeo and
Peter Canisius 236
Juan de Avila and Alessandro Sauli . . . 237

CHAPTER VI.

THE REFORM OF THE RELIGIOUS ORDERS.

Earlier attempts at the reform of the religious Orders
in the XVth and XVIth centuries . . . 240
Nevertheless the Council of Trent a turning point in
their history 241

A.D.   PAGE
        Reform of the Cistercians ;   a general visitation begun   241
        Deplorable state of their houses in Italy   .   .   243
        The Order of the Humiliati .   .   .   .   .
        Borromeo attempts the work of reforming the Order   245
        Attempted assassination of the Cardinal   .   .   246
1571 Suppression of the Order (February 7th)   .   .   247
        In many cases Pius V. combines the various branches
            of the Orders   248
        The religious Orders in Spain ;   the Order of Calatrava   249
        The co-operation of the civil authorities in Spain
            necessary but dangerous   250
        Decadent state of the Spanish Conventual Franciscans   251
        They are placed under the Observants .   .   .   252
        The same done in the case of other Orders .   .   252
        Difficulties with the civil power in Spain   .   .   255
        The religious Orders in the Low Countries and Portugal   256
        General reform of the Conventual Franciscans   .   256
        The Third Order of St. Francis   257
        Many other Orders reformed by the Pope   .   .   258
        The Military Orders in Portugal   259
        Reform ordinances of Pius V. for the religious Orders   260
        He regards the vow of poverty as their foundation
            stone   263
        Abuses in the Orders ;   monks living outside their
            houses   265
        The enclosure of nuns insisted upon ;   prevalent
            laxity in this respect   266
        Cardinal Borromeo and the nuns of Milan   .   267
        The organization of the great Orders necessitates
            exceptions to the decrees of Trent .   .   .   268
        Difficulties experienced by the Mendicant Orders in
            relation to episcopal jurisdiction .   .   .   269
        Several further Orders declared to be true Mendicants   270
        The Pope's high esteem for the Mendicant Orders   .   271
        His favours to the Dominican Order .   .   .   272
        A great impulse given to the Benedictine Order.   .   273
        New and stricter Congregations forming themselves in
            the Orders   275
        Peter of Alcantara   275
        Teresa of Jesus   277
        The question of solemn vows ;   the Pope does not look
            with favour upon religious with simple vows   .   278
        This affects the Society of Jesus ;   the Pope's attempts
            to change their Constitutions   278
        The decree making solemn vows necessary for ordin-
            ation   280
        But the Pope was in no sense hostile to the Society .   282
        He pays a glowing tribute to their work   .   283
        New constitutions given to the Somaschi, Theatines
            and Barnabites   284
        John of God and the Fatebenefratelli .   .   285
        The Pope's unflagging zeal for the Tridentine decrees   286

A.D.   PAGE

CHAPTER VII.

THE ROMAN INQUISITION PRESERVES RELIGIOUS UNITY IN ITALY

The plans of Pius V. for a new palace of the Holy
Office 288
The first stone of the new building ; its completion . 289
The Pope's great zeal for the work of the Inquisition 290
New Congregation of the Inquisition . . . 292
Many stern edicts concerning the Inquisition . . 294
The Pope convinced that stern measures alone will
save Italy from Protestantism 297
The underground methods of Protestantism in Italy 299
Many public autodafés held in Rome . . . 300
The case of Pietro Carnesecchi 302
The heretics for the most part make their abjuration 305
Bartolomeo Bartoccio 306
The case of Paleario 307
Autodafés less common in the second half of the
pontificate 311
The Inquisition in the Papal States . . . 312
Heresy at Faenza 313
But heresy takes very little real root in Italy . . 314
Great vigilance of the Inquisition 315
The Inquisition in Venice ; difficulties with the Senate 316
The Inquisition at Genoa 318
And at Lucca 319
Fear of the Spanish Inquisition in Milan . . 320
Opposition to the Inquisition at Mantua . . 321
Intervention of Cardinal Borromeo . . . 324
Revolutionary tendency of heresy in Italy . . 325
The vigilance of the Pope 326
The Italian princes and the Inquisition . . . 328
Protestant students at the universities . . . 330
The Pope's ruthless measures against sodomy . 331
Sorcery and witchcraft 333
Pius V. and the Jews : their responsibility for many
crimes leads to severe edicts 334
Pius V. reverts to the laws of Paul IV., for the most
part abrogated by Pius IV. 336
1569 Edict of expulsion of the Jews from the Papal States
(February 26th) 338
The Pope's efforts to convert the Jews . . . 340
Notable converts from Judaism 341
Personal part taken by the Pope in the work of the
Inquisition 342

CHAPTER VIII.

THE TRIAL OF THE ARCHBISHOP OF TOLEDO, BARTOLOMÉ CARRANZA.
THE CONDEMNATION OF BAIUS.

1566 Pius V. successful in getting the trial of Carranza
transferred to Rome (December) . . . 344

A.D.   PAGE

The arrival of the archbishop in Rome . . . 345
The composition of the tribunal 345
1567 The trial begun (June) 346
Public opinion in Rome favours Carranza . . 348
An early end of the trial expected . . . 348
Nevertheless, the case drags on year after year . 349
Reasons for this delay ; efforts on the part of Spain
    to avert an adverse decision 350
Philip II.'s letter to the Pope ; his instructions to
    Zuñiga 351
The Pope accused of being predisposed in favour of
    Carranza 352
Pius V.'s determination to be guided by justice alone 353
Arrogant pretensions of the Spanish Inquisition . 354
And of Philip II. 355
His characteristic letter to the Pope . . . 357
Pius V.'s courteous but firm reply . . . 358
His warning to the king 360
The minute attention given to the case by the Pope. 361
The unfair methods of the Spanish theologians . 362
In spite of everything the Pope remains perplexed
    about the case 363
His labours and anxiety injure his health . . 364
And undoubtedly hasten his death . . . 365
The Pope's sternness prompted by his conviction of
    the necessity for strong measures against heresy. 365
His strong sense of duty ; in the second half of his
    reign his severity considerably relaxed . . 366
A new form of heresy in the Low Countries . . 367
The beginnings of Baianism 368
The doctrines of Baius 369
Baius and the University of Louvain . . . 370
The spread of Baianism ; the mission of Commendone 371
Silence imposed upon the disputants . . . 372
Baius republishes some of his works ; Philip II.
    appeals to the Pope for a decision . . . 373
1567 Seventy-six of the propositions of Baius condemned
    (October 1st) 374
Baius, however, is not named in the bull, nor is the
    bull publicly posted 374
Submission of Baius ; apparent end of the controversy 375
Baius, nevertheless, continues to defend his doctrines,
    and addresses an apologia to the Pope . . 376
1569 Abjuration of Baius 377
He once more defends his opinions ; the bull of con-
    demnation is published and accepted . . . 379
Pius V. and Italian Protestantism 380
Beneficial effects upon Italy of the Pope's severe
    methods 381
He undoubtedly saved his country from revolution
    and civil war 382

LIST OF UNPUBLISHED DOCUMENTS IN APPENDIX.

PAGE

1 The Conclave of Pius V. according to the Diary of
Cornelius Firmanus 383
2 Francesco Tosabezzo to the Duke of Mantua . 387
3 Avviso di Roma of January 12, 1566 . . . 389
4 Cornelius Firmanus on the Coronation of Pius V.. 391
5 Niccolò Cusano to the Emperor Maximilian II. . 392
6 Johannes Sambucus to Cardinal G. Sirleto . . 392
7–8 Camillo Luzzara to the Duke of Mantua . . 393
9 Avviso di Roma of April 13, 1566 . . . 393
10–15 Buildings of Pius V. at Bosco 394
16–25 Purification of morals in Rome, 1566 . . . 395
26 Bernardino Pia to Camillo Luzzara . . . 398
27 Pope Pius V. to the Governor of the Campagna and
Marittima 399
28–34 Avvisi concerning the purification of morals in
Rome in 1567 399
35–47 Extracts from the "Diarium" of Cornelius Firmanus concerning the activity of the Roman
Inquisition, 1566–1568 400
48 Pope Pius V. to the Duke of Mantua . . 404
49 Avviso di Roma of May 29, 1568 . . . 405
50 Bernardino Pia to Camillo Luzzara . . . 405
51 Death of Cardinal Vinc. Vitelli (November 19,
1568) 405
52 Niccolò Cusano to the Emperor Maximilian II. . 406
53–57 Avvisi concerning the purification of morals in
Rome in 1568 406
58 Niccolò Cusano to the Emperor Maximilian II. . 407
59 Avviso di Roma of April 2, 1569. . . . 407
60–65 Avvisi concerning the purification of morals in
Rome in 1569 407
66 For the History of the Church of St. Peter's under
Pius V. 408
67 Cardinal Santori and his Audiences with Pius V. . 409
68 The Briefs of Pius V. and the Archives of Briefs . 413
69 The Biographers of Pius V. 420

POPE PIUS XI. TO BARON VON PASTOR

PIUS PP. XI.

DILECTE Fili, salutem et apostolicam benedictionem.—Cum, exeunte hoc mense, integris, mentis corporisque viribus septuagesimum acturus sis natalem tuam, quos in Oenipontana studiorum Universitate habuisti olim vel discipulos vel in docendo conlegas, ii parant, ut nuperrime accepimus, conspirantibus quidem ceteris quorum tibi amorem admirationemque conciliasti, praecipuis te venerationis laetitiaeque suae honestare testimoniis. Qua in meritorum tuorum commemoratione num Romanum Pontificem, num Nos, qui tanti te laboresque tuos facimus et vetere tecum necessitudine coniungimur, silere deceat aut primas partes cuiquam cedere ? Praedicent quidem ii omnes, quotquot te quondam in celebri Athenaeo multos annos audierunt, summam illam tuam rerum gestarum cognitionem cum peracuta iudicii subtilitate incorruptoque veritatis studio coniunctam, seque beatissimos putent quod idem studium eandemque vestigandarum existimandarumque rerum rationem, ductu tuo, hauserint ac veluti imbiberint. At vero opus tuum princeps omnibusque expletum numeris, quod est *Historia Romanorum Pontificum*, Apostolica Sedes, hac opportunitate data, per Nos publice dilaudat atque extollit veluti iure suo et tamquam rem suo fotam gremio, quandoquidem immortalis memoriae decessor Noster Leo XIII. Tabularium tibi primo patere iussit, unde litterarum monumenta paene infinita in lucem eduxisti, quibus narratio tua niteretur. Tu autem, Dilecte Fili, ad tam grande opus aem attulisti ingenii aciem exquisitaeque doctrinae copiam, ut nullus fortasse unquam instructior paratiorque ad eius generis laborem accesserit. In iis enim voluminibus, quae ad hunc diem aliud ex alio edidisti, praeterquam quod omnia, vel minima, ad tabularum auctoritatem fidemque exiguntur, certa tutaque causarum consecutionumque indagatione eventa quaelibet penitus dispicis et, si qua eorum dubia aut in controversiam deducta, recte acuteque interpretando explanas. Quid, quod singulares ac proprias uniuscuiusque aetatis notas complexu tam miro proponis, ut quasdam quasi tabulas plenas veritatis, plenas artis depingas ? Factorum praeterea expositionem iis verborum sententiarumque luminibus exornas, ut unum aliquid inde exsistat absolutissimum, quod in sui admirationem studiosorum legentiumque animos convertat ac rapiat. Nec profecto ignoramus, adeo immensam tibi adesse, ex aliis quoque paene omnibus Europae bibliothecis atque archivis, materiam, ut haec tibi cotidie crescat, et crescant item praeter exspectationem, scribendo, volumina. Quid igitur tibi, Dilecte Fili, fausta hac occasione cupiamus, nisi ut Ille, cuius vice fun-

gimur, prorogata tibi aetate diutissime, ingenii corporisque tui
vires confirmet, immo etiam exacuat, ne totius operis conficiendi
facultas te spatiumque deficiat ?   Quod quidem opus quo magis
procedit, eo clarius, rebus pro veritate exploratis, divina Ecclesiae
virtus elucet ac splendet.   Quamobrem perge, invicta qua soles
alacritate, laboriosissimum persequi utilissimumque inceptum,
cui nec Noster bonorumque omnium plausus nec caelestium
deerit remuneratio gratiarum.   Quarum interea auspicem pater-
naeque benevolentiae Nostrae testem, tibi, Dilecte Fili, apostolicam benedictionem peramanter impertimus.

Datum Romae apud Sanctum Petrum die VIII. mensis Ianuarii
anno MCMXXIV., Pontificatus Nostri secundo.

PIUS PP. XI.

Dilecto Filio Ludovico baroni de Pastor
Legato apud Nos Extraordinario at-
que Administro cum liberis mandatis
Reipublicae Austriacae.

CHAPTER I.

THE CONCLAVE AND ELECTION OF PIUS V.

IN the December of 1565, after a pontificate of less than six
years, the dreaded time of a vacancy in the Holy See had once
again come. This time, however, in strong contrast to what
had occurred at the death of Paul IV., the quiet of the Eternal
City remained undisturbed. No wild demonstrations of joy
disturbed the streets, and no hand was raised to destroy the
traces of the dead Medici Pope, whose body peacefully awaited
in the Pauline Chapel its removal to St. Peter's.[1]

The usual accommodation for the conclave was prepared,
with the addition of the apartments of Borromeo in the
Borgia Tower.[2] Five companies of infantry, under the command of Hannibal von Hohenems, were held in readiness for
the protection of the Cardinals, and after the daily mass for
the repose of the soul of Pius IV., the Cardinals met in consultation each day for five hours.[3] Everything proceeded
smoothly, and Pasquino could find scarcely any material for
his spiteful comments.[4] It was said that never in the memory
of man had there been so peaceful a vacancy in the Holy See,
so that men hardly seemed to realize that the Pope was dead.[5]

[1] *Fr. Tosabezzo to the Duke of Mantua, December 10, 1565,
Gonzaga Archives, Mantua.

[2] *Avviso di Roma of Dec. 15, 1565, Urb. 1040, p. 152b, Vatican
Library. Artists such as Ant. Labacco and Giac. Barozzi da
Vignola took part in the preparation of the conclave ; see
BERTOLOTTI, Art. Mod. 20.

[3] *Avviso di Roma of December 15, 1565, loc. cit.

[4] Ibid. p. 153.

[5] *" Per Roma non si fa strepito nissuno, et vanno le cose
tanto quiete, che dal no esserci la persona di Papa, in poi non par
che il Papa sia morto " (loc. cit. p. 152b). *" Le cose passano
quiete più che mai in sede vacante a memoria di huomo," wrote
Girolamo Oltramari on December 12, 1565. State Archives,
Modena.

In order to ensure the good behaviour of the populace strict
regulations were issued ; no one was to enter Rome from
outside, all disputes were to be stopped, and anybody who
drew his sword was to lose his hand.[1] The procurator-fiscal,
Pallantieri, and Francesco Guarini, Bishop of Imola, for the
Borgo, were to act as governors for the maintenance of order.[2]
The result was that the peace of the city was not broken during
the whole period of the conclave.[3]

The College of Cardinals was suddenly called upon to deal
with the pressing question of rendering assistance to Malta,
which was menaced by the Turks.   Count Broccardo asked
for the payment of the 10,000 ducats promised by Pius IV.
The Cardinals were hesitating whether their powers would
allow them to accede to this demand, when all at once Ippolito
d'Este, as the representative of the Knights of Malta, came
forward and declared that, should the new Pope not confirm
the gift, he would be ready to guarantee the sum from his
private means.[4]   The State Treasury, which was far from
possessing the large sums which it was supposed to contain,
had already been called upon to provide 20,000 ducats,
including 300 for each of the poorer Cardinals ;[5] at the death
of Pius IV., there was not more than 205,000 scudi in cash,
and 300,000 in securities, at the Castle of St. Angelo.[6]

[1] *" Chi pone mano all'armi, ne vadi la mano." Avviso di
Roma, December 15, 1565, *loc. cit.* p. 153.

[2] *Avviso di Roma, December 15, 1565, Urb. 1040, p. 153.
Vatican Library.

[3] *" Roma sta quietissima " wrote Federigo Cataneo to Mantua,
December 22, 1565, Gonzaga Archives, Mantua.

[4] *Avviso di Roma of December 15, 1565, *loc. cit.* p. 153.   Immediately before the closing of the conclave Cardinal Pacheco
recommended Malta to the protection of Philip II.   Letter of
December 20, 1565, in Corresp. dipl. I, 54.

[5] *Avviso di Roma of December 15, 1565, *loc. cit.* p. 153b.

[6] *" Si sono trovati in Castel S. Angelo ducento e cinque mila
scudi in contanta solamente, et crediti per trecento mila, in
pollici ; oltre i cinquanta mila scudi che si levarono già di Castello
ne se sono anco levati altri 25 mila." Fr. Tosabezzo to the Duke
of Mantua, December 13, 1565, Gonzaga Archives, Mantua.

In the meantime Rome was giving itself up to speculation as to the result of the coming conclave. " Many are hoping for the tiara," Arco wrote on the day of Pius IV.'s death, " but generally speaking only eight or nine names are commonly mentioned, namely, the two religious, Dolera and Ghislieri, Morone, Ippolito d'Este, Ricci, Ferreri, Boncompagni, Sirleto and Grasso ; it is the general opinion that whoever is supported by the nephews of the dead Pope and the Duke of Florence will be the successful candidate."[1] Andrea Caligari[2] gives the same names, but adds five others, Farnese, who was working for his own election, Mula, Scotti, Saraceni and Crispi, each of whom had several supporters. A few days later Caligari gives a longer list,[3] adding to the above named Pisani, Cristoforo Madruzzo, Reumano and Salviati as aspirants to the tiara ; he could feel fairly sure of having hit the mark, since his list of eighteen names included all the possible candidates. He says of Ghislieri that many well informed persons entertained great hopes of his success, for secret reasons which he had not been able to fathom.[4] Caligari himself places Boncompagni, the Cardinal of Bologna, first ; all eyes are upon him, he says, and nothing but the fact of his absence in Spain stands in his way ; his compatriots of Bologna have therefore sent messengers to recall him with all speed, and are prepared to pay all the expenses of his journey.[5] In other letters

---

[1] *" Molti aspirano al pontificato, ma quelli che sono più nominati sono otto o nove, i due frati Araceli et Alessandrino, Morone, Ferrara, Montepulciano, Ferereo, Buoncompagni, Sirleto et Crasso." Arco to the Archduke Ferdinand, Dec. 9, 1565, State Archives, Innsbruck, Ambraser Akten.

[2] *Letter to Commendone of December 12, 1565, Lettere di princ. XXIII 56 (now 121), Papal Secret Archives.

[3] *Letter to Commendone of December 19, 1565, ibid. 61 (now 131).

[4] *" Alcuni homeni di giudicio fanno gran caso di Alessandrino per certi rispetti occulti che io no ho potuto sapere." Caligari to Commendone, December 12, 1565, ibid.

[5] Among the friends of Borromeo* " viene messo in gran consideratione Boncompagno ; ma perchè è absente, si dubita.

Caligari says that Morone is in much favour, and that his name is often mentioned.[1]

It is, however, very significant of the general uncertainty which existed that, in addition to the above-mentioned names, several others appear in some of the dispatches of the time. Thus Nosti Camaiani names among others the Cardinal of Lorraine and Simonetta.[2] Guido Ferreri names Corgna and Cicada among the older Cardinals ; the Cardinals created by Pius IV. would have liked their leaders, Borromeo and Mark Sittich von Hohenems, to work for the election of one of their own number, such as Crivelli, Sirleto, Paleotto, Boncompagni, Commendone or the elder Ferreri.[3] In the general uncertainty, one thing seemed fairly clear, namely that the conclave would be a long one, and that a decision would only be reached after many differences of opinion. The Bishop of Viterbo, Sebastiano Gualterio, circulated a memorandum in which he gave expression to these views. He was of opinion that, on account of the many different parties in the conclave, they should not attempt to form any preconceived ideas as to the person of the future Pope, since, even if two of the parties were to act in concert, they would not be in a position to secure the election of their candidate.[4] Caligari wrote that the general opinion was that the conclave would last for six months ;[5]

I signori Bolognesi, dice il publico, volendo torre via questo obietto, per quanto ho inteso di bonissimo loco, hanno spedito corrieri a richiamarlo con ogni celerità, volendo essi pagare tutti le spese del viaggio." *Ibid.*

[*] To Commendine, December 8 and 15, 1565, *ibid.*

[2] Dec. 5, 1565, in PETRUCELLI, 179.

[3] On Dec. 20, 1565, to the Duke of Savoy, *ibid.* 181 *seq.* *Cf.* on this matter HILLIGER, 90 n.

[4] *Caligari to Commendone on December 19, 1565, *loc. cit.*

[5] *" La comune opinione è che'l conclave habbia a durare sei mesi o poco manco et habbia ad esser molto garbuglioso per molti baroni che vi sono et di diversi pareri " (Caligari, December 12, 1565, *loc. cit.*). *" Vanno in conclave domani mattina," wrote Lionardo Conosciuti, December 19, 1565, " et si tien per fermo che v'habbino a stare un gran pezzo " because there are many disagreements (State Archives, Modena). *" Quelli che più sono

Pacheco thought that Este would be able, by his scheming, to keep the electors in conclave for a whole year.[1] The Venetians therefore took advantage of their audience on December 28th to urge the hastening of the election by calling attention to the ever increasing Turkish danger and the approaching Diet in Germany.[2]

In spite of these anxieties the question was debated in the College of Cardinals whether they ought not spontaneously to postpone the beginning of the conclave, and with it any prospect of completing the election, so that the French Cardinals might have time to be present. Only a short time before, Pius IV. had confirmed the old regulation which ordered that the Cardinals should enter the conclave ten days after the death of the Pope, and Cardinal Borromeo successfully resisted the proposal to make an exception to this rule on the very first occasion that offered.[3]

The solemn funeral offices for Pius IV. were completed on Wednesday, December 19th ; they had been celebrated with greater magnificence than for any Pope since the time of Paul III.[4] In the evening the electors went into conclave, which, however, was not yet closed.[5] On Thursday, December 20th,

in considerazione al Papato sono Morone, Ferrara, Araceli, Montepulciano, Ferrerio et Buoncompagno et alcuni vi aggiungongo anco Pisani et Trani, et si stima, che si tardara ad havere il Papa." (Avviso di Roma of December 15, 1565, loc. cit. p. 153b). *Tosabezzo expected a long conclave, especially on account of the number of Cardinals (to the Duke of Mantua, December 10, 1565. Gonzaga Archives, Mantua).

[1] Corresp. dipl. I 54.

[2] Requesens on December 30, 1565, ibid, 67.

[3] HILLIGER, 110.

[4] *Avviso di Roma of December 22, 1565, loc. cit. p. 156. *Giov. Amadori, December 19, 1565, State Archives, Modena. *Spesa per il funerale . . . fatta nella sede vacante di Pio IV, Papal Secret Archives, Arm. XXXV., 79.

[5] *" Ali XIX di decembre 1565 à hore XXII entrarono in conclave 48 cardenali." On the 20th, as the infirm Cardinal Pisani was unable to do so, Cardinal Morone said the Mass of the Holy Ghost, which was followed by the reading of the various bulls

1565, High Mass was celebrated in St. Peter's, and in the
evening the Cardinals assembled in the Pauline Chapel, where
the conclave bull of Pius IV. was read, and was sworn to by
those Cardinals who had not been present at the first congregation after the death of the Pope.   After this the ambassadors
swore to guard the conclave and to observe the regulations
of the bull, and the same was done by the two governors of the
city, the auditors of the Apostolic Camera, the auditors of the
Rota, the caporioni, and lastly by Count Hannibal von
Hohenems as Captain General of the Church, and by Gabrio
Serbelloni as Captain of the Guard.   The Cardinals then went
in procession into conclave, though they afterwards left it
for supper, and came back one by one.   About midnight the
conclave was closed and walled up.[1]

The number of Cardinals was at first forty-eight.[2]   Only

and then the first scrutiny.   Thus state the introductory remarks
to the list of the scrutinies for Maximilian II. in the State Archives, Vienna, " Romana," Hofkorrespondenz fasc. 6, 1564-
1567.   For the conclave of Pius V, cf. above all, the useful monograph of HILLIGER, published in 1891, where, p. 107, n. 1, there
is a good review of the sources, which, in our account, have been
added to from a number of unpublished reports, among which
special mention must be made of the *Diarium of Cornelius
Firmanus and the *Report of Francesco Tosabezzo (see App.
nn. 1 and 2).   The account in Conclavi de' Pontefici, which HILLIGER
attributes to Cardinal Galli, more probably came from the pen
of a confidential conclavist of that Cardinal.   Besides HILLIGER
cf. HERRE, Papsttum, 103 seqq.

[1] *Avviso di Roma of December 20, 1565, Urb. 1040, p. 155
seq., Vatican Library.

[2] *List in the report of the Cardinals to Maximilian II., State
Archives, Vienna.   This list may be checked by the lists of the
Cardinals present on Dec. 24 and Jan. 7 in Cornelius Firmanus,
*Diarium, Arm. XII of the Miscell. 31, p. 25b, 35, Papal Secret
Archives (cf. App. n. 1).   In the first instance Firmanus gives
51 Cardinals, but the Vatican copy only names 50 ; Castiglione
is missing, whose arrival was announced on the preceding day.
Incorrect lists are given by CIACONIUS, III., 992 (Sirleto is left
out !), PETRAMELLARIUS, 131 (S. Croce is given as present and
Este as absent) and ALBÈRI, II., 4, 165 seq. (only 51 Cardinals
are given as taking part in the conclave instead of 53).

one of them, the Cardinal Dean, Francesco Pisani, had been created by Leo X., the other Cardinal Bishops who were present, Morone, Cristoforo Madruzzo, Farnese and Crispi, had received the purple from Paul III., as had the Cardinal Priests, Savelli, Gaetani, Ippolito d'Este, and the Cardinal Deacon, Rovere. Ten years had not passed since the days of Julius III., but there were only eight of his Cardinals still living, seven of whom entered the conclave on December 20th, namely, Corgna, Saraceni, Ricci, Cicada, Cornaro, del Monte, and Simoncelli. Death had also carried off many of the Cardinals of Paul IV., and only six took part in the election of his second successor; these were Rebiba, Reumano, Capizuchi, Ghislieri, Dolera and Vitelli. All the other electors owed the purple to the late Pope. No less than twenty-four Cardinals created by the Medici Pope went into the conclave on the evening of December 20th, namely, Serbelloni, Salviati, Simonetta, Pacheco, Mula, Gambara, Gesualdo, Gonzaga, Avalos, Colonna, Galli, Delfino, Bobba, Sforza, Orsini, Guido Ferreri, Lomellini, Sirleto, Grasso, Luigi d'Este, Luigi Madruzzo, Medici, Alciati and Paleotto.[1] During the days and weeks that followed there arrived Niccolini,[2] Luigi Pisani and Castiglione[3], Correggio[4], and Pier Francesco Ferreri[5], who had all received the purple from Pius IV. Thus the number of

---

[1] Thus the list prefixed to *that of the scrutinies prepared for Maximilian II.

[2] *" Si fece poi il primo scrutinio et dopo pranzo arrivò il card. Nicolino, il quale portò l'intiero de la mente del S. Duca di Fiorenza, et fece unire il card. de Medici col card. Borromeo. Report of the conclave for Maximilian II.

[3] They arrived during the night between Dec. 22 and 23, 1565. Firmanus, *Diarium p. 25, Papal Secret Archives.

[4] He was present on the night of December 24; *ibid.* p. 25b. According to Camillo Luzzara (*letter of December 26) Gonzaga only arrived on that day. Gonzaga Archives, Mantua.

[5] He arrived January. 2, 1566 (*Avviso di Roma of January 5, 1566, Urb. 1040, p. 161b, Vatican Library). Crivelli appeared only a quarter of an hour after the election had taken place. Requesens on January 7, 1566, Corresp. dipl., I., 98.

Cardinals had risen to fifty-three, which was again reduced when Gonzaga died on the eve of the election.

On this occasion the closure and walling up of the apartments set aside for the conclave was no mere formality. Even before the Cardinals entered the conclave, wrote Pacheco, they were firmly resolved to observe the rule of isolation from the outer world more strictly than ever before, since the bull of Pius IV. had closed the conclave in such a way and under such strict penalties, including that of excommunication, that no one would dare to receive even a note from outside or to enter into any written communication with the outside world.[1] Pacheco's estimate was verified. The entrances to the place of election were strictly guarded,[2] and even though it was impossible to prevent stray items of information passing the barriers, it caused a considerable stir when on one occasion the guard discovered a note containing forbidden information in the cloak of Cardinal del Monte.[3] This time, too, the Cardinals' servants were much more severely restricted in their opportunities of receiving communications.[4]

As a natural consequence of this strict isolation the ambassa-

[1] " Ençerrandonos oy en el conclave, muy determinados que sea mas estrecho que fuè jamàs." (To Philip II., December 20, 1565, Corresp. dipl., I., 52). " La Bula del Papa Pio çierra de manera el conclave y pone tan abominables excomunicaciones que ninguno osará tomar poliça ni corresponderse con hombre de fuera (*ibid.* 53).

[2] *" Benche le cose vadino con molta stretezza, et che alle porte si facci per li deputati esatissima diligenza, perche non vi entrino ne eschino avisi di quel che passa, nondimeno hoggi si è detto che tutta questa notte havevano veghiato." Avviso di Roma, Urb. 1040, p. 155b, Vatican Library.

[3] *Avviso di Roma of January 5, 1566, *ibid.* p. 161b.

[4] *We manage to learn very little, wrote Camillo Luzzara to Mantua, December 29, 1565, "essendo i nostri conclavisti scrupulosi tanto, che non osano ne di aprir la bocca, ne di scriverci due parole." Gonzaga Archives, Mantua. Nevertheless Requesens says that all the same they knew what was happening in the conclave more than was right, but that the isolation was stricter than ever before, and that therefore he thought that many of

dors of the foreign powers could not on this occasion exercise
that influence upon the election which they had brought to
bear at the elevation of Pius IV. Besides this, the princes
themselves had become less inclined to interfere than in former
days. It is true that the question of the most suitable candidate for the tiara was freely canvassed in the correspondence
of the ambassadors, but no definite policy was arrived at, nor
was any actual interference attempted. Duke Alfonso of
Ferrara, indeed, immediately after the death of Pius IV., sent
Paolo Emilio Bernieri to the Emperor Maximilian II. to try
and obtain the election of his uncle, Cardinal Ippolito d'Este,[1]
it being, in his opinion,[2] very advisable to secure the tiara for
a Cardinal of princely birth, after the disastrous experiences
they had had, under recent Popes, of upstarts and ambitious
relatives ; the Emperor should therefore, said Duke Alfonso,
write to the leading Cardinals, and to the whole Sacred
College, to the Duke of Florence and Philip II., to support
the candidature of Este.[3] Maximilian, however, replied[4]
that, following the example of his father, who had not wished
to interfere with the Papal election, he had contented himself
with urging the Sacred College to make a wise choice, and that
he could not now act in a different sense by espousing the cause
of any definite candidate.

As a matter of fact the Emperor had not been quite as
neutral as he pretended. He had already, during the later
days of Pius IV., asked Cosimo de' Medici to tell him which
Cardinals were looked upon as probable candidates for the
tiara,[5] and after the Pope's death he had announced that he

the items of news which were supposed to have leaked out of the
conclave were false. Letter to Philip II. of December 30, 1565,
Corresp. dipl., I., 61.

[1] BIBL, Korrespondenz, I., 339. Instructions of Bernieri of
December 15, 1565, *ibid.* n. 300 *seq.*, p. 339 *seq.*, 341 *seq.*

[2] Instructions for Bernieri, *ibid.* 340.

[3] *Ibid.* 341 *seq.*

[4] December 24, 1565, *ibid.* 351.

[5] *Cf.* the reply of Cosimo of December 2, 1565, in WAHRMUND
265 ; HILLIGER, 96 ; BIBL, Korrespondenz, I., 331.

intended to take a strong and decided interest in the election.[1]
However, except for Delfino, Maximilian could scarcely count
upon a single reliable supporter in the Sacred College.[2]   He
could indeed name, though as a profound secret, either through
the Duke of Florence,[3] or through his ambassador, Arco, four
Cardinals, namely, Boncompagni, Grasso, Niccolini and Ricci,[4]
as being acceptable to him, but to promote the actual election
of any one of them Arco had to turn to the Duke of Florence
for help.[5]   Perhaps the reason why he made no mention of
Morone was that he was not in favour with the Duke, though
he would have been most acceptable to the Emperor, who
hoped to obtain from him the concession of the marriage of
priests.[6]

Cosimo de' Medici did his utmost to obtain a decisive
influence upon the course of the election. In order to strengthen
the hand of his ordinary ambassador in Rome, Serristori, he
sent thither the crafty Bartolomeo Concini,[7] while another
of his agents, Nosti Camaiani, managed to make his way into
the conclave in the guise of a conclavist.[8]   Cosimo could also
count upon his young son, Cardinal Ferdinando de' Medici,
and upon Niccolini, who had undertaken to promote the

[1] Giulio Ricasoli to Cosimo, December 14, 1565, in PETRUCELLI,
173.

[2] In a report of December 15, 1565, Arco says that among the
Cardinals there were " Imperiales 6, Re Filippo 10, Re di Francia
10, Duca di Firenze 8." But among these are counted the absent
Cardinals (WAHRMUND, 265). For the attitude of Maximilian
II. towards the conclave cf. also G. WOLF in Göttinger Gel. An-
zeigen, CLXXX. (1918), 442.

[3] December 21, 1565, in BIBL, Korrespondenz, I., 347.

[4] This secrecy was impressed a second time on Dec. 24, 1565,
BIBL, Korrespondenz, I., 354.

[5] HILLIGER, 105 ; cf. 89. The letter from the Emperor to
Arco was of December 21 and reached Rome on the 31 ; ibid.
106.   Cf. BIBL in Archiv für österr. Gesch., CIII., 21.

[6] Requesens, December 30, 1565 Corresp. dipl., I., 67.

[7] PETRUCELLI, 176. HILLIGER, 95. Cosimo to Borromeo,
December 11, 1565 in SALA, Docum., III., 370.

[8] PETRUCELLI, 176.

Duke's wishes. The leader of the Florentine party in the conclave was undoubtedly Sforza. Cosimo had strongly dissuaded the Emperor from giving his support to any Cardinal of princely family, or to one of any great distinction, such as Este, Farnese, Madruzzo, or Morone, on the ground that such men, as experience had shown, were likely, if they became Pope, to sacrifice everything so as to enhance the splendour of their own family. Several others, in the opinion of the Duke, were not to be supported, Pisani and Mula, because they were Venetians, Reumano because he was a Frenchman, and Ghislieri because he was obstinate and unbending, though he was a man of exemplary life. On the other hand he recommended to the Emperor, Cardinals Cicada, Dolera, Boncompagni, Niccolini, Grasso, Ricci and Ferreri,[1] though later on, in more particular negotiations with Arco, he decided in favour of Ricci, the Cardinal of Montepulciano.[2] Of the other Italian princes, the Duke of Urbino worked against Ricci, and the Duke of Savoy on behalf of the Cardinal of Vercelli, Pier Francesco Ferreri, as well as for Morone.[3]

French policy was not more likely to exercise much influence over the conclave than that of the Emperor. It is quite true that the power of France in the Eternal City had considerably increased under Pius IV. ;[4] proof of this may be found in the controversy as to precedence between the French and Spanish ambassadors, which the Pope had decided in 1564 in favour of France, and had thereby caused the departure of the Spanish ambassador, Requesens, who had already pointed out to his sovereign that he would have to take serious steps

---

[1] Bibl, Korrespondenz, I., 331 seqq.

[2] Bibl, Korrespondenz, I., 333, 366. *Cardinal Gonzaga sent news to Mantua that the Duke favoured Ricci, Dolera and Niccolini ; that the last named was really the most pleasing to him, but that Ricci was " più riuscibile " (Fr. Tosabezzo to the Duke of Mantua, December 15, 1565, Gonzaga Archives, Mantua). *" Non vorria [Cosimo] ne Morone ne Farnese." Cardinal Gonzaga in Tosabezzo, loc. cit.

[3] Requesens, December 30, 1565, Corresp. dipl., I., 67.

[4] Corresp. dipl., I., 66 seqq.

if Spanish influence in Rome was not to disappear,[1] while
during the illness of Pius IV. in 1563, the leader of the French
party among the Cardinals, Ippolito d'Este, had been in a
position to aspire quite openly to the tiara, and had dared to
say that this time his efforts would not be unsuccessful.[2]
Catherine de' Medici would certainly have been quite satisfied
with a Pope like Este,[3] but the Queen Regent lacked the means
of carrying her wishes into effect since, of the French Cardinals,
only Reumano took part in the conclave. Catherine's
daughter, however, Queen Elizabeth of Spain, tried to influence
her husband in accordance with French policy.[4]

In spite of his many shortcomings Philip II. still had greater
influence in the Sacred College than any other prince in
Christendom,[5] but he refused to make any use of it in the
election of the new Pope. He had, however, on December
18th, 1562, sent to his ambassador, Luis de Requesens, certain
instructions in which the election of the Pope was touched
upon, and in which he stated that the one thing necessary
was to elect a Pope who should be pious and a lover of peace,
or in other words a Pope who would not make political com-
plications for the Spanish king, and who would have the reform
of the Church at heart.   The election of Carpi, Puteo, Morone,

---

[1] *Ibid.* 62 *seqq.*

[2] " . . . Ferrara, il quale, per quanto intendo, si lasciava
intendere di tenersi per certo il Papato ; è però S. S. Illma persona
da conscere, se non in tutto, in parte almeno, le difficultà che ci
haria, ma penso che lo faccia giudicando con questa opinione farsi
favore, et mettere a qualcuno il cervello a partito.   Intendo
havere fatto anco professione che si creda che la riforma dispiaceva
più a lui che alcuno altro, et se ne è lasciato intendere, et tutto
giudico sia fatto per piacere ai cardinali giovani et perchè sperino
nella larghezza sua." *Serristori on December 3, 1563, State
Archives, Florence, Medic, 3283, p. 171.

[3] Desjardins, III., 521 ; Hilliger, 79.

[4] *Cf.* Douais, Les dernières années d'Élisabeth de Valois,
reine d'Espagne, Toulouse, 1896.

[5] " V.M., a quien oy se tiene mas respecto en el colegio que a
ningun principe christiano." Cardinal Pacheco to Philip II.,
December 20, 1565, Corresp. dipl., I., 51.

Ricci and Dolera might be furthered, while the Cardinal of Ferrara and all Frenchmen must be excluded.

When Pius IV. decided the quarrel about precedence between the French and Spanish ambassadors against Spain, Philip II. recalled his ambassador, but kept him at Genoa, and told him to draw up a statement on the next Papal election, and the prospects of all the Cardinals. Requesens complied with these instructions by giving a sketch of the whole College of Cardinals in a lengthy document.[1] The outstanding personality, in his opinion, was undoubtedly Morone. Requesens describes him as a vigorous man, of but fifty-seven years of age, and he adds the following remarks : " Morone is a man of agreeable character and wide experience, and for thirty years the most difficult missions have been entrusted to him ; if he were Pope he would do honour to his office, as no one else could do. On the other hand he is quite inscrutable, and no one can say whether in his heart he is well disposed towards the Spaniards, besides which, he lies under the reproach of having been in the hands of the Inquisition.[2] Another very distinguished Cardinal, Alessandro Farnese, must be regarded with suspicion as far as Spain is concerned, on account of the whole history of his family. He is not more then forty-six, but has already some grey hairs ; he is already one of the six Cardinal Bishops, has many friends, and a great gift of making new ones ; thus the hope which he entertains of gaining the tiara is well founded. Ricci, too, who is already seventy, but very vigorous, has good prospects, since he is old and much liked, and has the support of the Duke of Florence. He has had much experience of Rome, is very prudent, and would be a friend to Spain.[3] On the other hand, the Cardinal of Ferrara, Ippolito d'Este, who is clever and well versed in politics, is altogether on the side of France. He will never give up his attempts to obtain the Papacy, of which

---

[1] Letter of January 5, 1565, in Döllinger, Beiträge, I., 571-588.

[2] *Ibid.* 573 *seq.*

[3] *Ibid.* 578.

indeed he is by no means worthy, though his chances are now
greater than they have ever been, now that his old rival,
Carpi, is dead.   Five Cardinals are related to him, and there
are others in the Sacred College who would be generously
helped by him in their poverty ; he will be a source of much
anxiety to the representatives of Spain at the next conclave.
It would only be as a measure of desperation that the aged
Pisani would be elected, since he is bound to die before long,
and if he were Pope he would have to entrust the direction of
affairs to others.[1]   There are others, such as Madruzzo and
Corgna, who think they have a chance, but this is not really
the case.[2] Cicada has just as little chance, though he might
be put forward as a Spanish candidate for the sake of the
honour.[3]   Paul IV. bestowed the purple on several men who
might very well attain to the supreme dignity.   Rebiba, for
example, is a good theologian, a distinguished man, and full
of zeal for the cause of religion."[4]   Requesens accords similar
praise, in an even higher degree, to Cardinal Ghislieri.[5]   In
his opinion, Rebiba would be a very good Pope, but Ghislieri
would be the Pope called for by the times.[6] Requesens,
however, thought that these two would not receive any votes.
He speaks less disparagingly of the prospects of the Franciscan,
Dolera, whom he describes as learned and exemplary, the only
objection to whose election might be the fact that a religious
was not likely to be chosen.[7]   Of the Cardinals created by

[1] *Ibid.* 572 *seq.*

[2] *Ibid.* 575, 577.

[3] *Ibid.* 578.

[4] *Ibid.*

[5] *Ibid.* 579.   It is also stated in a letter from Cosimo to Maximilian II. of December 2, 1565 : " L'Alessandrino è di vita
esemplare, non di meno ha del cervicioso e del rigido " therefore
Ghislieri is placed among the " sospetti " whose election is not to
be favoured. BIBL, I., 331.

[6] " Es teologo y muy buen hombre y de vida muy exemplar
y de gran celo en las cosas de la religion, y a mi juicio es el Cardenal
que en los tiempos de agora mas convendria que fuese Papa."
DÖLLINGER, *loc. cit.*, 579.

[7] *Ibid.* 579.

Pius IV., Mula and Correggio would have to be reckoned with. Mula, trained as a humanist, a man of prudence and experience of public affairs, is wished for by the nephews of Pius IV. ;[1] Correggio is not personally known to the ambassador, though he has never heard anyone so highly spoken of by the world in general ; if Farnese should be unable to effect his own election at the next conclave, he will put forward Correggio.[2] It is necessary, too, to keep a watchful eye upon Vitelli, appointed by Paul IV. ; his youth precludes him from aiming at the tiara himself, but he is a clever man, who knows how to make himself agreeable everywhere, has unbounded energy and possesses many friends. He will have to be reckoned with at the next conclave. Philip would do well to try and win him over, the more so as he is much courted by the French.[3] The remaining Cardinals need not be taken into consideration, either because they are too young, or for some other reason.

As the result of this review of the Cardinals, Requesens advises the king to recognize as acceptable candidates, Morone, who cannot be omitted from the former list without offence, Ricci, Ghislieri, Dolera, Farnese, Madruzzo, Cicada and Correggio, or, if this be too many, to omit the last three names. Among them Philip should really exert himself on behalf of none but Ricci, Ghislieri and Dolera,[4] though the ambassador himself was of opinion that it was impossible to effect anything in the case of Ghislieri.[5] Only Ferrara and the Frenchmen should be excluded. Philip would do well to send Cardinal Granvelle to Rome to act as the leader of his party.[6]

Granvelle received orders to proceed to the Eternal City,[7]

---

[1] *Ibid.* 581.

[2] *Ibid.* 584 *seq.*

[3] *Ibid.* 583 *seq.*

[4] *Ibid.* 586.

[5] " . . . Alejandrino, aunque salir este postrero lo tengo por imposible." *Ibid.* 586. *Cf.* 579 : " Pienso que no tendra voto para ello, porque lo tienen por riguroso."

[6] *Ibid.* 586 *seq.*

[7] October 22, 1565, in HILLIGER, 75.

though he arrived too late for the conclave, since he only started on December 31st.[1] Requesens' lengthy recommendations were without result in other ways as well. Philip delayed in making up his mind, and when various letters of December 5th, 1565, warned him that the death of Pius IV. was at hand, and that he must not delay any longer, even then he did not send any names to his ambassador.[2] As had been the case at the last conclave, so on this occasion he declared that his only wish was to see a Pope elected who was filled with zeal for the honour of God, and who would think of the general good of Christendom, the ending of the religious differences, the reform of the Church, and the preservation of peace among Christian princes, especially in Italy. He did not wish to point out any Cardinal in particular as acceptable to himself, because, as experience had shown, such a course would only lead to discord in the Sacred College, while he himself would be satisfied with any Pope whose election would be for the good of the Church. If Pacheco and Granvelle had already arrived in Rome they could see to it that votes were not wasted. The ambassador ought to keep in close touch with Farnese and the Duke of Florence. Personal letters to Mark Sittich and Serbelloni were enclosed. Vitelli had offered his services to the king ; the Cardinal would have an opportunity of giving expression to his good will at the coming election. Ferrara and all the Frenchmen must be excluded. A private letter from the king urged the ambassador to act very circumspectly with regard to Morone ; it would perhaps be wise to close the way to the Papacy in his case.[3]

Philip's letter did not arrive till ten days after the beginning of the conclave ; until then the Spanish Cardinals might in any case have felt themselves free to follow their own judgment

---

[1] *Ibid.*

[2] Letter of December 21, 1565, Corresp. dipl., I., 55 *seqq.* Arco nevertheless claims to know that the ambassador had secret instructions to work on behalf of Ghislieri and Dolera To Maximilian II. on December 22, 1565, in WAHRMUND, 267.

[3] Corresp. dipl., I., 57 n.

without scruple, but the medieval ideas of loyalty to the
sovereign were so deeply rooted in the men of that time, that
the Cardinals hardly dared to use their liberty, and sought
by every means to learn the king's wishes.   Pacheco, who was
in Florence at the time of the death of Pius IV., wrote at once
to Philip when he heard the news to send Requesens to Rome.
When Pacheco arrived in Rome, the other Spanish Cardinals
had already sought information from Pedro de Avila as to
the king's wishes, and they now asked for further instructions
from Pacheco ; since they both had to admit their ignorance
on the subject, they anxiously wrote to Requesens, who could
not possibly arrive before the beginning of the conclave, to
send them in writing the information which they would no
longer be able to receive orally once the Cardinals had gone
into conclave.[1]   In his letter to the king[2] Pacheco went so
far as to say : " Among the chastisements with which we are
threatened by God is the fact that it has seemed good in the
eyes of your Majesty and the royal council to leave us our
liberty, since, if a Pope were to be chosen who was unworthy
and not sincerely Christian, I am convinced that all that
remains of Christendom would fall to pieces." Since Requesens
was unable to give any definite information, they held to the
former royal instructions which the ambassador had left behind
him in Rome on his departure in 1564, by which Carpi, who
was since dead, Ricci and Dolera were named as candidates.[3]

Requesens arrived in Rome on December 21st,[4] and on the
23rd he had an audience at the doors of the conclave, at which,
in a long speech, he exhorted the Cardinals to choose a good
Pope.[5]   He was able, by means of Correggio, who arrived
late, and with whom he spoke in Florence, and again in Rome,
to inform Borromeo and Mark Sittich of the exclusion of

[1] To Philip II., December 20, 1565, Corresp. dipl., I., 51 *seq* ;
cf. 60 *seq*.
  [2] *Ibid.* 54.
  [3] *Ibid.* 52.
  [4] Requesens to Philip II., Dec. 30, 1565, *ibid.* 60.
  [5] *Ibid.* 62 *seq*.

Ferrara.[1] By December 30th it was no longer possible to
send any news into the conclave or to receive any communications from within.[2] As a matter of fact, the agents of the
Italian princes were quite unable to give much information
as to what was happening in the Vatican. In these straits
Camillo Luzzara had to console himself with setting forth the
reasons why the election was bound to be a long one ;[3] he
succeeded in finding eighteen such reasons, based on general
principles,[4] and eleven more which he based upon the character
of individual Cardinals, and the like.

Thanks to the strict enclosure of the conclave, and the
attitude of reserve maintained by the foreign powers, the
Cardinals on this occasion found themselves less subject to
external influences than had ever been the case in the memory
of man. Goings and comings such as Vargas had contrived
at the previous conclave were out of the question now, and the
decision lay entirely in the hands of the electors, and of the
three party leaders, Borromeo, Farnese and Ippolito d'Este.

Another circumstance of good augury lay in the great
influence which Borromeo was likely to exercise as the leader
of his party. It was customary that the Cardinals created
by the late Pope should submit themselves in the conclave
to the judgment of the nephews.[5] If Borromeo, the most
important nephew from the spiritual point of view, had taken

---

[1] *Ibid.* 63.

[2] *Ibid.* 67.

[3] *To the castellan of Mantua, Dec. 29, 1565, Gonzaga Archives,
Mantua. Requesens sent the same or exactly similar information
to Philip II. (December 30). Corresp. dipl., I., 69.

[4] " The number of the electors is large, and each of the parties
among them is small ; some of the Cardinals are old, others
are noble ; some are rich, others are poor ; some are hostile,
others friends. All these things are to him reasons which support
his contention ; every foreign Catholic power and every Italian
prince affords him a further reason." *Loc. cit.*

[5] " Se tiene por muy mal que en la primera elecçion de Papa
no acudan las creatures a sus sobrinos." Pacheco to Philip II.,
Dec. 20, 1565, Corresp. dipl., I., 53.

advantage of this, he could have commanded more than twenty votes, which was enough to prevent the election of anyone he did not think suitable, but, as was only to be expected from a man of his character, he would only make use of this power for the good of the Church even at the cost of his personal predilections. It is very doubtful, however, taking into consideration his holiness and his strict conscientiousness, whether he would have made use of this power, and whether he would not have felt bound to leave the electors free to follow their own consciences.[1] Pacheco foresaw this risk,[2] and he therefore, before the conclave, urged Borromeo to be careful, above all things, to see that a good Pope was elected, saying that he would gain more merit in the sight of God by so doing than by giving himself up to fasts and disciplines for the rest of his life.[3] It is clear that Borromeo did not follow this advice in the sense intended by Pacheco. Before the beginning of the conclave, he consulted several Jesuit theologians as to whether he could with a good conscience use the votes of his Cardinals in the customary way, and he received in reply the written opinion that he must exactly follow the bull of Pius IV. which forbade any such party action.[4] It would seem that in practice he left it free to the Cardinals to follow him or not as they pleased, and it is very difficult to explain in any other way the

[1] * Pare che il card. Borromeo non si vogli impacciar de voti, et che concorrerà a persona idonea et buona." (Avviso di Roma of Dec. 15, 1565, Urb. 1040, p. 153b, Vatican Library). *" S'intende che il S. card. Borromeo vuole hora, contra quello che fu detto prima, attendere a fare il nuovo pontifice, et per ciò aspetta tutte le sue creature et in particolare Buoncompagno " Fr. Tosabezzo to the Duke of Mantua, December 13, 1565, Gonzaga Archives, Mantua.

[2] " Desde Florencia escrevi a V.M. que temia que Borromeo por sus escrupulos se havia de encoger en esta elecçion y dexar ir a sus creaturas adonde quisiessen." Corresp. dipl., I., 53.

[3] Pacheco, loc. cit.

[4] False reports concerning the reply of the Jesuits were spread at Naples, for which reason Borgia published the whole matter in a letter to Salmeron of Dec. 30, 1565. SALMERON, Epist., II., 60 n. 9.

want of unanimity among his party. At the beginning of the conclave he actually made over the duty of leading the Cardinals of Pius IV. to Mark Sittich, though he resumed it when Morone pointed out to him that this would result in the election of Farnese or Este.[1]

On his death-bed Pius IV. had advised his nephew to procure the election of one of the Cardinals created by himself ; if this should prove impossible he should give his support to those recommended by the Duke of Florence, and in that case he should lean in the first place to Morone, then to Ricci, and lastly to Dolera.[2] As a matter of fact, as he said in a conversation with Pacheco before the beginning of the conclave, Borromeo would gladly have seen one of the Cardinals to Pius IV. elected Pope,[3] probably because for the most part he saw in these younger members of the Sacred College more pious dispositions than in the older ones. In this conversation

---

[1] *" Egli ha represo l'assonto et il maneggio dei voti in se, i quali havea già renonciato ad Altemps, et questo per la coscienza glien'ha fatto Morone, dicendo che sarebbe causa, che come pecore smarrite si venderebbero a Ferrara o a Farnese, a chi più de loro offerisce." Federigo Cattaneo to the castellan of Mantua, December 29, 1565, Gonzaga Archives, Mantua. The same report is also substantially found in the *Avvisi di Roma, January 19, 1566, Urb. 1040, p. 167b, Vatican Library. " [Morone] ha rivolto Borromeo a ripigliar li suoi voti, li quali pareva che havesse posti in sua libertà, con mostrarle che altramente questo era un tirarsi sopra le spalle il Pontificato di Farnese o Ferrara, offesi l'un l'altro dal Papa suo zio, del quale egli poi portarebbe sopra di se gli odii et le inimicitie." *Avviso di Roma of December 20, 1565, Urb. 1040, p. 155b, Vatican Library. Cf. HILLIGER, 116.

[2] *" Perchè finalmente il Papa nell'ultimo della sua morte ha lasciato per ricordo a Borromeo, che non potendo far venire al Pontificato niuna delle sue creature, debba concorrere con cui vorrà il duca di Firenze et confidarsi nelle promesse di S. Eccellenza." *Avviso di Roma of December 22, 1565, Urb. 1040, p. 167b, Vatican Library.

[3] Pacheco to Philip II., December 20, 1565. Corresp. dipl., I., 53.

he suggested Boncompagni, Mula and Commendone, of whom, it would seem, Mula was the one wished for by Pius IV.[1] Pacheco was doubtful whether any of the younger Cardinals would have any chance of success, and said that in the event of Borromeo's chosen candidate meeting with insuperable difficulties, the wishes of Philip II. should be taken into account, pointing out at the same time that it would be easier to get votes for Dolera than for Ricci.[2]

We may question whether Borromeo let Pacheco fully into the secret of his own wishes. Later on his friends learned from him that he had from the first thought of the man who was actually elected, but that he had never made his idea known to anyone ; he also said that he had at first, in order to show them honour, put forward the names of those to whom he or his party were under an obligation. It was only later that he directed all his efforts to the election of a Pope of holy life and profound theological learning.[3]

The decision, however, was by no means entirely in the hands of Borromeo ; there were opposed to him Este and Farnese, who both surpassed him in experience and political skill, and without whose help he could not attain his ends. The Floren-

[1] Giac. Soranzo, October 30, 1565, in ALBÈRI, II., 4, 157. HILLIGER, 115.

[2] Pacheco, loc. cit.

[3] " Antequam ingrederetur conclave, plures ille quidem animo sibi proposuit, qui viderentur pontificatu digni, neque eum, qui postea electus est, ut eius intimi deinde cognoverunt, praetermisit, sed tamen mentem suam patefecit nemini." (BASCAPÈ, I., 1, c. 9, p. 21). It cannot be established whether Bascapè, who was one of Borromeo's confidants, includes Morone among the number of those proposed, merely for the sake of the honour. For the rest it was very soon understood in Rome that Borromeo was bound to feel drawn to Ghislieri. Lionardo Conosciuti *wrote on December 19, 1565, to Modena that in all probability Borromeo will make a " mina fratesca " that is to say either for Dolera or Ghislieri, " li quali ancorachè si creda che non siano per giungere al segno, si tien per fermo almeno che darano da sospicare alli degni di questo grado." (State Archives, Modena).

tine party under Sforza, and that of the Cardinals of Paul IV.
under Vitelli, had also to be reckoned with.   He could, however, with the help of the twenty votes and more of his own
followers, at least exclude anyone who did not seem to him
worthy of the supreme dignity in Christendom.   The result
was that several who aspired to the tiara, and who were much
spoken of at the time, really had very little chance.   Ippolito
d'Este who, before the conclave, to the scandal of all Rome,
openly tried to obtain the votes of the Cardinals, and boasted
that he had already secured twenty,[1] giving it to be understood
that through the influence of Catherine de' Medici and the
French ambassador, even Philip II. had given up his opposition
to him,[2] had vainly tried to win over Borromeo to his side,
and for this purpose had summoned his cousin Cesare Gonzaga
to Rome.[3]   The partisans of Este imagined that a close understanding had been arrived at between their leader and the
strict nephew,[4] but it was *a priori* impossible that Borromeo
should lend his support to the worldly Cardinal.   Altogether
apart from the veto of Philip II. and Cosimo, Este's candidature was thus doomed to fail.   The same was true in the
case of the Cardinal of Montepulciano, Giovanni Ricci ; he
was a man of great ability, and he had Spain and Florence

[1] Pacheco to Philip II., December 20, 1565   Corresp. dipl.,
I., 52. *Cf.* also the *report of L. Conosciuti of December 19,
1565, *loc. cit.*

[2] Requesens, December 30, 1565, Corresp. dipl., I., 61.

[3] *" Il signor card. di Ferrara ha mira d'esser Papa, et perciò
desidera il signor Cesare eccellentissimo se ne venga a Roma
per aiutarlo col mezzo del signor card. Borromeo, et a questo
fine Ferrara spedisce hora il Cortese a Mantova per le poste et
non vuole che si sappia parola di questo suo disegno." Franc.
Tosabezzo to the Duke of Mantua, December 8, 1565, Gonzaga
Archives, Mantua.

[4] On December 19, 1565, *Giovanni Amadori was of opinion that
Este might easily become Pope on account of the " stretta in-
telligenza che dicono aver fatto con Borromeo et Altaemps."
Este arrived on Sunday evening (December 16) ; the first cell was
allotted to him which was a good omen (State Archives, Modena).

on his side, but his hopes were bound to be disappointed, since Borromeo could not lend his support to a candidate whose ideas were so unecclesiastical.[1]

The great influence over the election which was generally attributed to Borromeo is shown in a report which Cardinal Gonzaga caused to be sent to the Duke of Mantua before the conclave, dealing with the prospects of the various candidates.[2] In the case of almost every candidate Gonzaga mentions the attitude towards him adopted by Borromeo, and in many cases he looks upon this attitude as a decisive factor. He speaks especially of three Cardinals, Morone, Farnese and Ferreri. Morone stands first among those whom Borromeo does not wish for any more than he does, but if the French have not time to arrive before the election, and Este is unable to exclude him, there is great reason to fear that he will be successful. In order to gain time Gonzaga tried to persuade Borromeo that he would be well advised to await the arrival of those Cardinals of Pius IV. who were still absent, Boncompagni, Crivelli, and Commendone. Farnese is popular with the poorer Cardinals on account of his wealth ; nevertheless Gonzaga hopes to be able to keep Borromeo and Mark Sittich from supporting him. In the opinion of Gonzaga, Ferreri has the support of Borromeo, and therefore has a good chance, though the older Cardinals look upon him as a man of but small importance and learning.

In Gonzaga's opinion a large number of other candidates are far less to be reckoned with than the three already named. Farnese is supporting Ghislieri, not in order that he may become Pope, which would be difficult to bring about, but in order to open his own way to the Papal throne. So far Ippolito d'Este had no chance, since Borromeo will not support him on any terms. He will therefore have to wait for help

[1] " Montepulciano sarebbe Papa, si Borromeo lo volesse, ma lo abhorrisce come la peste." Opinion of Cardinal Gonzaga sent to the Duke of Mantua by Fr. Tosabezzo on December 15, 1565, Gonzaga Archives, Mantua.

[2] *By means of Tosabezzo, December 15, 1565, *ibid.* ; see App. n. 2.

from France, and see to it that Borromeo is involved in endless delays.   In spite of the support of Cosimo, Dolera can hardly become Pope, and the same is true of Scotti, in spite of Farnese's favour, since before his death Pius IV. recommended the Cardinal nephews not to elect a Theatine, which Scotti is, and still less any of the Cardinals of Paul IV.   Mula would certainly have the support of Borromeo, but he is by no means in favour with the whole of the Sacred College.   The Duke of Florence favours Ricci, Dolera and Niccolini ; he is working for Ricci because he has the best prospects, though he himself prefers Niccolini ; he will have nothing to do with Morone and Farnese.   In order to exclude those not acceptable to the house of Gonzaga, an attempt will be made to support one of Borromeo's candidates, either Boncompagni, Commendone, or Crivelli.   Borromeo prefers Commendone, but Boncompagni would be better for the house of Gonzaga ; the Duke of Florence also wishes for him.   Ricci could be Pope if Borromeo were willing, but the latter detests him like the plague.   " In a word," the report ends, " everything is upside down, and nobody knows which party to support."

It appears that Gonzaga was right in thinking that an attempt would be made to elect Morone suddenly, and without formal voting ; even before the conclave began rumours of this had been current.[1]   On December 19th, and during the following night Cardinal Simonetta went in secret to the followers of Borromeo and proposed to them that on the following morning, and therefore before the formal closure of the conclave, there should be an assembly in the chapel in order to pay homage to Morone as Pope.   He got together thirty votes, but Ghislieri discovered the plan, Ippolito d'Este, Farnese and the Cardinals of Paul IV. declared themselves against it, while the French ambassador entered a strong protest, and thus Borromeo's intentions were frustrated.   Delfino in particular had supported Morone ; he claimed that in passing through Florence he had won over the Duke to his cause, and had

[1] *Avviso di Roma of December 22, 1565, Urb. 1040, p. 156b, Vatican Library.

written to the Emperor, by whose help he hoped to obtain
seven or eight more votes.[1] Ghislieri, on the other hand,

[1] " *L'istessa notte [from December 19 to 20] uscì voce che
Borromeo pensava di far papa la mattina seguente il cardinal
Moron. Ma Ferrara et Farnese offersero al incontro tutti li voti
loro per il cardinal d'Araceli, et in questo modo fu sedata la
pratica " (List of the scrutinies for Maxmilian II., State Archives,
Vienna). *" Mercordì [December 19] il giorno e la notte Simonetta
andò segretamente a tutti li cardinali Borromeisti, et ordinò loro,
che il giovedì mattina [December 20] in Capella andassero ad
adorar Morone in quel punto che ci sarebbe andato Borromeo, e se
questa pratica non fosse stata scoperta da Ferrara, e fatta impedire
tutta quella notte dell'ambasciatore di Francia, che fece protesti et
il diavolo per romperla, certamente Morone giovedì mattina, inanzi
che si fossero chiusi in Conclave, riusciva Papa ; pure passò quella
furia ne la mattina di giovedì ne tutto il giorno infino alle 7 di
notte; che all' hora si chiusero dentro tutti i cardinali fu fatto
altro ; si è bene inteso, che il venerdì mattina (December 21), e piu
il venerdì sera è stata rinforzata la medesima pratica di Morone,
che hà havuto (December 22) a 29 voti . . . e questo e tutto quello,
che s' è inteso hoggi, che è sabbato li XXII. del presente e stasera
alle 2 di notte è fama che questa notte sono per far gran rumore,
come l'avisano particularmente di man in mano alla giornata "
(Report of December 22, 1565, inserted in the Avvisi di Roma of
January 19, 1566, *loc. cit.* p. 167). " *Dicono che Alessandrino
scoperse una prattica di forsi 30 voti, che voleano adorare Morone
nella prima congregatione che si fà in capella post ingressum
conclavis cantata missa Spiritus Sancti,et scoperta,fù disturbata da
Ferrara et Farnese, che non ci vanno con molti altri et in particolare
le creature di Paulo IV. In questi 30 voti era Borromeo con
tutti i seguaci et alcuni altri, in particolare il Delfino, che dicono
fà cose grandi per Morone et, passando per da Fiorenza, ha
messo il cervello a partito al duca et ha scritto all' imperatore,
et spera per suo mezzo di farsi patrone di 7 o otto voti, purche
habbia spacio che venga la risposta dall' Imperatore, il quale
spera haver a sua devotione, per quanto si dice qui, che potrebe
esser falso, Trento, Mondovi, Augusta, Altaems, et quei di Fiorenza." Caligari to Commendone on December 27, 1565, Lett. di
princ. XXIII. 65 (now 140), Papal Secret Archives. Cf. Delfino
in HILLIGER 121 n.

declared that he could not understand how anyone could
support Morone with a clear conscience, knowing that he had
been brought to trial for heresy. If some of the matters of
the accusation were carefully examined he would not be
acquitted so completely as had been done by Pius IV.; in
any case the mere suspicion of heresy was enough to exclude
him from the Papacy.[1]

The attempt to elect a Pope by a bold stroke of this kind
was therefore frustrated. Borromeo thought that he had the
electors in his own hands, but it now appeared that not all the
Cardinals of Pius IV. were prepared to follow their leader.[2]

[1] " *. . . che non vedeva, come con buona conscientia si
potesse aplicar l'animo a Morone, sapendosi che contro di lui
vi era un processo di heresia, nel quale non mancano alcuni
capi, che quando fossero stati ben ventillati, et che si fosse havuta
debita cognitione della causa, non sarebbe stato così facilmente
assoluto, come precipitosamente fu nel principio di questo Pontificato passato, et che l'esser stato solamente sospetto di heresia,
questo bastava di ragione per escluderlo del Pontificato, sicome
si offeriva di mostrare con i libri in mano et con il processo, che
diceva di haver altre cose che haverebbe da dire; et perche li fu
detto, che Paolo IV. l'haveva processato perche li voleva male,
rispose che se Paolo IV. l'haveva inquisito d'heresia, per male,
che li voleva, Pio IV. l'haveva an co assoluto nulla habita causae
cognitione perche li voleva troppo bene, onde si stima, che questo
habbia molto debilitato li dissegni et le speranze di Morone, se
però non siano ciancie sparse da malevoli come facilmente occorse
in simili pratiche (Avisi di Roma loc. cit. p. 157). Lionardo
Conosciuti *writes on December 22 to Modena that Ghislieri is
very hostile to Morone, remembering the trial " quel si tien per
fermo che porti continuamente nella sacchozza." Whether this
is true or not, all Rome is talking of it. State Archives, Modena.

[2] " El cardenal Borromeo entró en el conclave con el mayor
sequito de cardenales que nunca tuvo sobrino de papa, porque
los presentes, hechos de su tio, pasavamos de XXX. Ymaginóse
que estava en su mano el hacer pontifice. . . . Quedó (in the
attempt on behalf of Mula) con quexa de algunos de los suyos
de no havellos visto tan dispuestos a su voluntad como quisiera."
Pacheco to Philip II. on January 22, 1566, Corresp. dipl. I. 95.

Borromeo then fell back upon his own wish, of securing the success of one of his uncle's Cardinals. For this purpose he had conferences with each of the electors, at first naming Mula and Boncompagni as his choice,[1] but afterwards, out of consideration for the older Cardinals, who wished to see one of their own number elected, Morone, Mula, Boncompagni and Sirleto.[2] But Farnese at once gathered twenty-seven votes against Mula, which meant that he was cut off from any chance of success.[2] On account of his absence Boncompagni had but little prospect of being elected, while Sirleto was not very popular. Nothing remained, therefore, but to make another attempt on behalf of Morone.[4]

During the night between December 22nd and 23rd they worked feverishly in the conclave both for and against Morone.[5] Nobody thought of going to bed and rumours and excitement were rife throughout the enclosure. The Cardinals forgot to have torches carried before them by their conclavists, and themselves ran from one to another with candles in their hands, and only half dressed. An eye-witness, Cornelius Firmanus, says that the excitement passed belief, and that such behaviour had never been seen before on the part of any Cardinal. If, during that night, Morone had been taken to the chapel to receive homage, he would have become Pope, as his opponents were so taken by surprise and fear that their faces were white as sheets, and they did not know what to do. Many, as it were against their will, and on the verge of tears, went towards the chapel, thinking it impossible to prevent the election.

As the opportunity was not seized at once, however, Morone's opponents plucked up courage. Este in particular

---

[1] Delfino in HILLIGER, 121 n.

[2] *Ibid.* Pacheco, *loc. cit.*, Corresp. dipl., I., 95. Conclavi de' Pontefici, 170.

[3] HILLIGER, 123.

[4] *Ibid.* 124.

[5] See in App. n. 1, the *report of C. Firmanus, Papal Secret Archives.

worked like ten men to secure Morone's exclusion.[1]   Sermoneta, Rovere and others were equally active, and they were
successful in collecting the needful number of votes against
Morone.

Before day dawned the business of the election was recom-
menced.   Many insisted that the Master of Ceremonies should
ring the bell for mass at once, so that they might get to the
voting and finish the election as quickly as possible, but the
Cardinals in charge of such matters protested, and mass was
accordingly celebrated at the usual hour, and the voting then
took place.   It was soon obvious that Borromeo was mistaken
in thinking that he could count on thirty-nine votes.[2]   Only
twenty-six electors declared themselves for Morone, nor did
it make any difference when Sforza, Orsini, and Guido Ferreri
successively gave their *accessus*, for five votes were still
wanting, since, with fifty-one electors, the two-thirds majority
was thirty-four votes.

The principal opponents of Morone were the two Este and
their friends, all those who had received the purple from
Paul IV., Morone's great enemy, some of Borromeo's Cardinals, and lastly, though Farnese himself gave his vote to
Morone, *titulo honoris*, Farnese's party, some of whom were
actuated by personal dislike, others because they would not
give up their own hopes of the tiara, and others on account of
religious scruples, and their recollection of the trial of Morone
before the Inquisition.[3]   Twenty-one votes were thus cast
against Morone, whereas eighteen were sufficient to exclude
him.[4]   Morone bore the shipwreck of his hopes with so much

---

[1] This refers to the young Luigi d'Este, " qual'oltre l'ardir del
sangue si faceva pronto per gli ammaestramenti del cardinal di
Ferrara suo zio " (Conclavi de' Pontefici, 172).   The elder Este
was lying ill in bed.

[2] Pacheco, *loc. cit.*, 96.

[3] *Ibid.* HILLIGER, 125 *seq.*

[4] *" A l'esclusione di Morone sono corsi questi : Ferrara, Man-
tova Este, Savello, Pisa, Urbino, Crispo, Gambara, Correggio,
Reumano, Padova, Simoncello, Capisucco, Saraceno, Alessandrino,
Cornaro, Vitello, Araceli, Salviati, Aragona.   Ritirati da Morone :

calmness and dignity, that it could not fail to increase the
respect in which he was held.[1] What had been most harmful
to him was undoubtedly his trial before the Inquisition. " If
his reputation had not been thus tarnished," says Requesens,
" he would have had a greater following than any other
Cardinal. I do not know how this can be, everyone admits
Morone's great qualities, yet when an attempt was made to
elect him there was general uneasiness, and much joy when
he was excluded."[2] The hostility of the Duke of Florence
was very disadvantageous to him, and the Spanish ambassador
was of opinion that Morone would have become Pope if the
adherents of Cosimo had supported him.[3]

At first Borromeo tried to hold to the candidature of
Morone, and to gain for him the votes still required. He was
not successful in this, but even lost some of his twenty-nine

Farnese, Trento, Madruzzo." (Letter of Camillo Luzzara to the
Duke of Mantua, December 29, 1565, Gonzaga Archives, Mantua).
In HILLIGER, 128, a list of the conclave adds to the twenty names
given by Luzzara that of the elder Pisani. Cf. Concini, December
29, 1565, in PETRUCELLI, 191 seq., where Crispi is missing and the
name of Sermoneta is given instead of Saraceni, and Reims (!)
instead of Reumano. In his *reports to Commendone Caligari
states (December 29, 1565) that there were 22 steady votes against
Morone, among whom were all the Cardinals of Paul IV., and
especially Ghislieri. Simonetta, Cicada and Delfino were steadily
for Morone. In the meantime everything will drag on because
Farnese and Este are waiting for replies from Spain and France
(Papal Secret Archives). After December 26 *Caligari states
that Morone's success was impossible ; " La cosa è più intrigata
che fosse mai " (ibid).

[1] *" Mostrò Moron is questa attione constantia notabile et si
portò talmente che fu giudicato virtuosissimo " (anonymous report to Maximilian II. of January 5, 1566, State Archives, Vienna).
" El lo pasó todo con grandissima prudencia ye disimulaçion sin
mostrar gana de ser Papa, antes de lo contrario." Pacheco,
loc. cit., 96.

[2] Requesens to Philip II., December 30, 1565, Corresp. dipl.,
I., 65.

[3] Ibid.

followers as the days went by. He then found himself in great difficulties in choosing another candidate, since, if he decided upon one of the younger Cardinals, he would offend the older ones, while among the latter there was not a single one who seemed suitable both to him and to the other electors. He therefore asked the Dean of the Sacred College, Pisani, to call together Cardinals Farnese, Cristoforo Madruzzo, Este, Corgna, Pacheco and Vitelli, and asked them to nominate a suitable candidate from their point of view, promising that, if his conscience permitted, he would support him with all his party.[1]

Borromeo's proposal was received with suspicion. They feared that he was not in earnest, and that he only wished to lay the responsibility for the long duration of the conclave upon the shoulders of his colleagues, or else that he would only pretend to support the candidate thus nominated, and thus weary the electors, leaving the way open for his own supporters.[2] Corgna, however, nominated Saraceni, Ricci, and Cicada, while Vitelli put forward the Franciscan, Dolera.

Borromeo rejected Ricci on the spot, and, in spite of the remonstrances of Delfino, persisted in so doing. He would have allowed himself to be won over to the candidature of Dolera, but Mark Sittich, whose views had to be respected as a nephew of Pius IV., flatly declared that he did not want a religious.[3] Neither Saraceni nor Cicada seemed suitable to Borromeo, and thus the conference in Pisani's cell had no results as far as choosing a candidate was concerned.

Thus the position of the man who had so far been the leading personality in the conclave was completely changed. Until now it had been Borromeo who put forward the proposals, while the others had been content to give their opinion as to their value, or to take steps to frustrate them. But now

---

[1] HILLIGER, 129 seq.

[2] *" Fu sospettato da qualch'uno deli detti cardinali che Borromeo havesse fatto questo officio per mostrare che per ipsum non stabat quin pontifex eligeretur." Report of the conclave to Maximilian II. of January 5, 1566, State Archives, Vienna.

[3] HILLIGER, 133.

the leadership had passed to the other parties, and it was they who put forward the candidates, and if the proposals of another party were displeasing to him, he had no other course open to him than to take the defensive and work for their exclusion.

Farnese thought that his time was come at last.[1] He made great efforts to win over Borromeo, but in vain. Nor were the Spaniards favourable to him, and it was even rumoured, and it would seem that Pacheco lent his support to the rumour,[2] that the Spanish ambassador had handed in a veto against him. It is true that Requesens denied the rumour, and sent for Farnese's secretary to tell him that he was ready to declare it false in a public audience in the presence of the whole conclave,[3] but when the Florentine agents called upon him, and pointed out to him that, as was only to be expected from the whole history of his house, Farnese could not be an acceptable candidate to Spain, he asked his king for exact instructions as to the attitude which he was to adopt, saying that, though he was bound to support Farnese in public, he could not be blind to the fact that his election to the Papacy would give very little guarantee of peace for Italy.[4] Requesens seems to have let himself be frightened by fictitious statements as to the great number of votes which Farnese and others were supposed to have obtained in the scrutinies.[5] Moreover,

[1] *L. Conosciuti reported concerning his efforts on December 19, 1565, adding that Farnese's hopes were vain. State Archives, Modena.

[2] Diary of Delfino, December 30, 1565, in WAHRMUND 267; HILLIGER 133, n.2.

[3] Requesens to Philip II., December 30, 1565. Corresp. dipl., I., 66.

[4] Requesens to Philip II., December 31, 1565. Corresp. dipl., I., 72 seq.

[4] Including the accessi the following figures were supposed to have been reached: Farnese, 32 votes; Ippolito d'Este in the same scrutiny, 26; Morone, 28; Ricci, 29; Pisani, 30; Dolera, 31; Corgna, 25; Saraceni, 23 (Corresp. dipl., I., 72). An *Avviso di Roma of December 29, 1565, gives similar figures (Urb. 1040, p. 160, Vatican Library): Farnese and Morone, 24 each,

the rumour of the exclusion of Farnese by Spain, which he had at first thought it his duty to deny so vigorously, Requesens later on stated to have probably originated from Farnese himself, with the idea of winning the support of France.[1]

Two days later the credulous ambassador had a fresh move to report, which had reached him from Cardinal Vitelli, through Marcantonio Colonna. He reports as follows : The adherents of Farnese are determined to make their leader Pope at all costs. If they can get twenty-eight or thirty votes for him their plan is to place him on the Papal throne in the chapel, and to keep him there till everyone has paid him homage, even if it takes two days. In view of Farnese's strong prospects no one would like to be the last to declare himself for him, and thus he would win over all the electors by degrees. In

and 4 *accessi* ; Ricci, 22 and 7 *accessi* ; Dolera, 25 and 7 *accessi*. Obviously this series of votes, rising with so great regularity, was intended to deceive the curious ambassadors and frighten them. According to the *report of the conclave for Maximilian II. (State Archives, Vienna) the true figures for the principal candidates from December 22, 1565, to January 5, 1566, were as follows :

	DECEMBER										JANUARY				
	22.	23.	24.	25.	26.	27.	28.	29.	30.	31.	1.	2.	3.	4.	5.
MORONE	11	17	29	11	10	10	12	10	12	12	14	12	15	12	10
FARNESE	10	7	7	7	14	13	10	12	9	12	13	13	12	16	11
RICCI	7	8	1	5	10	13	11	11	12	10	10	10	10	12	12
GHISLIERI	8	10	9	17	8	8	9	10	8	9	12	13	15	16	16
DOLERA	5	2	—	9	10	13	11	16	9	9	9	7	11	12	6
BONCOMPAGNI	6	8	—	5	5	6	5	8	6	7	7	4	3	4	3
ESTE	5	5	—	2	4	4	5	5	4	4	3	6	7	4	10
SIRLETO	12	4	—	4	4	8	5	8	6	6	8	7	8	7	8

Cristoforo Madruzzo reached his highest figures on January 3 and 4, with 10 and 12 votes ; Ferreri obtained 14 votes on January 4 ; Cicada reached 13 and 10 on December 31 and January 1 ; Corgna 11 and 10 on December 27 and January 5 ; Saraceni 10 on both December 26 and 27.

[1] Requesens to Philip II., December 30, 1565, Corresp. dipl., I., 71.

order to bring still greater pressure to bear upon the Cardinals, the Roman people were to take up arms on the appointed day and, after making a little disturbance acclaim Farnese as Pope.[1] It is a fact that during the night following January 4th such cries were to be heard in the streets of Rome.[2] The munificent Farnese was indeed very popular in Rome, and on his return from Parma after the death of Pius IV. he had been publicly hailed by the people as the next Pope.[3]

Cusano, the not very reliable Imperial agent, claims to have learned that Farnese was not very far from attaining his end, and that he only lacked two votes ; in order to frustrate him, he says, the Florentines set to work on behalf of Ricci,[4] whose hopes had run very high from the first. Requesens, too had for some time been recommending Ricci, who was not learned, but very capable, to Borromeo, besides the two religious, Dolera and Ghislieri.[5] On the evening of December 30th there was much activity on behalf of Ricci,[6] and even many of Borromeo's Cardinals, especially Mark Sittich, would have declared themselves in his favour,[7] if their leader had allowed them to do so. It now appeared, however, that in spite of his piety and gentleness, Borromeo could be severe, when he deemed it necessary. He spoke openly of Ricci's defects, and injured his chances of election considerably.[8] In order

---

[1] Requesens, January 3, 1566, *ibid.* For the rest Requesens adds that it must be admitted that Colonna had been deceived; *ibid.*

[2] *Avviso di Roma of January 5, 1566, Urb. 1040, p. 161. Vatican Library.

[3] " Il popolo alla prima vista l'ha cridato publicamente per Papa " Cusano to Maximilian II., December 22, 1565, in HILLIGER, 86, n. 2.

[4] *Cusano to Maximilian II., January 5, 1566, State Archives, Vienna.

[5] Requesens to Philip II., January 22, 1566, Corresp. dipl., I., 96.

[6] Corn. Firmanus ,*Diarium XII., p. 28b, Papal Secret Archives.

[7] *Anonymous report on the conclave to Maximilian II., January 5, 1566, State Archives, Vienna.

[8] Requesens, *loc. cit.*, 96. Ricci left an illegitimate son ; see ZUÑIGA in *Nueva colección de docum. inéd.*, II., 243.

to satisfy Mark Sittich, he promised him that he would not, for his part, work for either Dolera or Ghislieri. In spite of this, however, even without Borromeo's help, Ricci succeeded in collecting thirty votes for himself,[1] and if he had had two days longer he might perhaps have attained the goal of his ambitions. In the meantime Farnese had not given up hopes of winning the tiara. He sent a courier to Mantua in order to arrange a matrimonial alliance between his house and the Gonzaga and Este, and thus win votes.[2] On January 3rd, 1566, he sent Cardinals Orsini and Paleotto officially to Borromeo to beg his support in the election, but on the next day he received a reply from Borromeo and Mark Sittich that they considered it quite impossible to accede to his request.[3]

If Farnese had hoped by means of his matrimonial plans to win over to his side Cardinal Gonzaga, who had been opposed to him so far, he was soon to be undeceived. Gonzaga had been very ill since the beginning of the conclave, and at the end of 1565 his condition became so critical that on December 31st he received the last sacraments.[4] On January 6th, 1566, though he was only twenty-eight years of age, he was dead.[5] During the last days of his illness the election proceedings were almost entirely suspended, out of respect for the dying man.[6]

Borromeo could hardly feel any more enthusiasm for his cousin, the Cardinal of Vercelli, Pier Francesco Ferreri, than

---

[1] Requesens, *loc. cit.*, 96. *Cusano, *loc. cit.* speaks of 19 votes and 13 *accessi.*

[2] Cusano, *loc. cit.*

[3] *Report of the conclave to Maximilian II., January 5, 1566, *ibid.*

[4] Requesens, January 3, 1565, Corresp. dipl., I., 74. The rumour that he had been poisoned was of course spread abroad. *Arco, January 5, 1566, State Archives, Vienna.

[5] Corresp. dipl., I., 74 n.

[6] *" Le cose del conclave sono state assai quiete per dui o tre giorni attesa l'indispositione di Mantova, nella quale è stato molto assiduo Buorromeo." Serristori, January 2, 1566, State Archives, Florence, Medic. 3285, p. 3.

he had for Ricci and Farnese.   Ferreri had arrived in Rome on January 1st, 1566, and went into the conclave with the highest expectations, based on the support of the Duke of Savoy, who, he believed, had already won over France to his support, and would do the same with Spain.[1]   But Ferreri did not satisfy Borromeo's determination to have a holy Pope, while he found an enemy in Vitelli, who very soon succeeded in collecting thirty-two votes against him.

The finding of a new candidate had now become a very serious problem, and attention was now turned to those Cardinals who had not been able to be present at the conclave.[2] Thus the Theatine, Scotti, who would have been very acceptable to Borromeo, was spoken of,[3] while the praises of Boncompagni were also sung, and it was thought that he would certainly have become Pope if he had been present ;[4] many deplored the fact that Crivelli, like Boncompagni, had not returned from his mission to Spain.[5]   When, on January 2nd, 1566, the Imperial ambassador delivered to the Cardinals his master's letter of December 21st, together with the usual exhortation to them to make a speedy and a wise choice, attention was once again drawn to the Imperial candidate, Morone.[6]

---

[1] Requesens to Philip II., January 3, 1566.   Corresp. dipl., I., 76. Delfino to Maximilian II., January 4, 1566, in HILLIGER, 140.

[2] HILLIGER, 137.

[3] Requesens to Philip II., December 30, 1565, Corresp. dipl., I., 68.

[4] " A Boncompagno tienen aqui por buen hombre ; y todos affirman que si estuviera presente, tuviera mas parte que ninguno." Requesens to Philip II., January 3, 1566, ibid. 76.

[5] HILLIGER, 137.

[6] Requesens to Philip II., January 3, 1566, Corresp. dipl., I., 77. Arco gives an *account of his audience of January 5, 1566, and adds that Morone, Ricci and Dolera " multorum in se animos convertunt.   Ferunt autem regem catholicum pro card. Alexandrino vehementer laborare." (State Archives, Vienna).   A list of the conclave which is attached, however, professes to show that Madruzzo, Este, and Farnese have been able to secure the exclusion of Cardinal Ghislieri.

But Farnese now definitely declared himself against him, and thus rendered his election impossible.[1]

There was great excitement when, on January 4th, a Spanish courier arrived, and the rumour spread throughout Rome that Philip II. had nominated one Cardinal alone as acceptable to him, namely Ghislieri.[2] According to Requesens Este's party had spread this rumour in order to stir up feelings of resentment against Spain among the more influential Cardinals : with Borromeo, because his uncle had not been a special friend of the Dominican Cardinal ; with Morone, because Ghislieri had opposed him in the conclave ; with Ferreri and the older members of the Sacred College, because they thought they had a better right than one of the younger Cardinals.[3] At the same time the rumour was prevalent that the King of Spain, in accordance with the advice of his ambassador in Rome and the Viceroy of Naples, preferred a man who had been Grand Inquisitor, because he was himself thinking of introducing the Inquisition into all his kingdoms ; for this reason the three or four Neapolitan Cardinals took great alarm,

[1] HILLIGER, 140. The efforts that were being made on behalf of Morone, however, caused a Florentine agent much anxiety, so much so that he even advised the support of Morone. *Serristori, January 2, 1566, State Archives, Florence, Medic. 3285, p. 3.

[2] Requesens to Philip II., January 11, 1566, Corresp. dipl., I., 82 seq. According to *Arco " è stato detto, che porta commessione al commendatore [Requesens] perchè favorisca Alessandrino et Araceli, ma il commendatore nega et dice che'l rè catholico non vuole raccomandar alcuno. Nondimeno si sa che procura quanto può di parlare al card. Borromeo." To Maximilian II., January 5, 1566, State Archives, Vienna.

[3] Requesens, loc. cit. *" Le brigate tutte stupiscano che Alessandrino sia nominato et questa cosa ha messo il cervello a partito a molti." Este saw with satisfaction the disunion among the adherents of Borromeo, as showing how little Philip II. took them into consideration. Farnese thought otherwise, " il quale è stato con Ferrara più d'un hora et di mesto che vi entrò ne usci lieto assai, essendosi visto più lieto di lui Ferrara." List of the conclave of January 4, attached to a *letter of Arco of January 5 1566, State Archives, Vienna.

and Requesens thought it necessary to ask an audience of the conclave and to make a public declaration that Philip II. had not nominated any Cardinal.[1]

In the meantime the choice of possible candidates had become so restricted that Borromeo thought the time had come when he must throw aside all reserve, abandon the defensive attitude, which he had so far adopted, and once again take into his own hands the management of the election. On the morning of January 5th he put forward the name of Sirleto as the man whose election should be attempted.[2] This caused great excitement among the electors. Borromeo's suggestion met with approval in some quarters, but Ricci, for whom many were still working energetically, tried to exclude Sirleto. This time Borromeo again failed; it was a disadvantage to him that he had omitted to give notice of his proposal to at least the party leaders. Sforza, the head of the Florentine party, was so annoyed that he openly informed Borromeo that he would not have co-operated with him, even though Sirleto was his friend, and worthy of the tiara. He immediately, however, gave solid proof of this friendship, for when Borromeo asked him at least to allow Cardinal Medici to support Sirleto, he at once gave his consent. In spite of this Medici's vote was lost, since, when Vitelli went to him to tell him that the Pope was already elected, and that Medici must come and pay him homage, he received the angry reply that it was no use trying to effect the election by such fictions, and he refused to go at all. Not even Farnese had been told beforehand of the efforts which were being made for Sirleto. Borromeo now went to him with fifteen Cardinals and begged him to accompany them to the chapel, and to elect Sirleto by paying him homage. Farnese replied that he must first consult his party, and suggested that a ballot would be the better way. Sirleto himself, who was ill in bed during these negotiations, showed no desire for the supreme dignity; he even begged to be spared the burden of the

[1] *Loc. cit.* 83.

[2] Corn. Firmanus, *Diarium, XII., p. 32-32b, Papal Secret Archives.

Papacy, saying that his shoulders were not broad enough for it. In this connexion Cornelius Firmanus remarks : " I am convinced that he was speaking from his heart when he said this, for he was ever a man of exemplary life, a great lover of poverty, and living almost in penury ; he had no pride, was very courteous in manner, and was, in a word, a man of very holy life."[1]

This first failure with Sirleto did not discourage Borromeo, but it led him to take a definite step as far as Farnese was concerned.[2] In the afternoon of January 7th, he convinced

[1] *Diarium, p. 32b, Papal Secret Archives.

[2] *" Borromeo fece sapere a Farnese, che non s'aggirasse più il cervello in voler esser Papa, perche era risoluto di non lo voler questa volta, che però l'essortava come christiano a risolversi in far un altro. Farnese rispose, che non lo credeva cosi ingrato, che pensava si ricordasse che Pio IV. era stato fatto cardinale dall'avolo suo et che esso l'haveva aiutato a far Papa, dal che era nata tutta la grandezza d'esso Borromeo, mà poiche si mostrava tal per non tener piu sospeso il mondo proponeva, 4, Trani, Araceli, Alessandrino et Montepulciano. Borromeo accettò Alessandrino perche Montepulciano era stato offeso da esso gravemente ; Araceli era nemico d'Altemps et Trani era absente ; cosi non passorno 2 hore del tempo che la prattica cominciò, che d'accordo quei 2 con le loro sequele chiamorno tutti gl'altri et condussero Alessandrino dalla sua cella nella capella, et l'andororno Papa poi lo vestirno et lo portorno in chiesa la medesima sera rompendo il conclave " (Avviso di Roma of January 12, 1566, Urb. 1040 p. 163, Vatican Library. *Dipoi s' è inteso, chel cardinale Borromeo fece intendere al cardinal Farnese, che non pensassi al papato, perchè non era tempo ancora che facessi questi disegni, et che doveva più tosto pensare a convenire seco in un buono subiecto, che tener il mondo sospeso con tanto danno . . . " [What follows is in complete agreement with the Avviso quoted.] Cosi il card. Borromeo convenne in Alessandrino, perchè Trani non era in Roma, Montepulciano era stato offeso da esso [on account of his public statement that Ricci was an ignorant man and had led a rather immoral life], Araceli era in odio ad Altaemps [on account of the suspicion that he had come to an understanding with Cardinal Cesarini, with whom Altemps had been quarrelling about a rich Abbey](Arco on January 12, 1566,

him, through Alciati, that he must abandon all hopes of the
Papacy on this occasion, since he, Borromeo, was determined
to refuse him his support.   Instead of keeping the whole world
waiting, to its great injury, let him rather act in a Christian
spirit, and join forces with Borromeo for the election of a good
Pope.   In his reply to this the grandson of Paul III. referred
to the services rendered by the Farnese to the Borromeo ; it
was thanks to his grandfather that Pius IV. had been made a
Cardinal, and he had become Pope by the personal help of
Farnese himself ; the present greatness of the Borromei was
the result of the pontificate .of Pius IV.   Since however the
Cardinal nephew was determined to make no recompense for
these services, he proposed four Cardinals, for whose election
he promised his support ; these were Ricci, Scotti, Dolera
and Ghislieri.[1]   Borromeo decided upon the last named, and
thus was Ghislieri assured of the necessary majority, and
more was accomplished in the two hours that followed than
had been effected so far in three weeks' hard work.[2]

In the evening the Cardinals went to Ghislieri's cell, and
almost by force and against his will, led him to the Pauline

State Archives, Vienna).   *" Havendo Borromeo mandato hoggi
Alciato a Farnese instandolo che si risolvesse al fare del Papa ;
egli rispose, Borromeo si risolvesse di ellegersi uno ch'egli gli
haveva nominato, et che di questo modo il Papa si saria fatto.
Nominò Farnese : Montepulciano, Araceli, Crispo et Alessandrino
et a questo si attacò Borromeo, et con tutto che si creda certo
che il disegno di Farnese fosse di voler balzare anco questo card[le]
pure il fatto è andato di modo che egli è riuscito Papa.   Più
oltre non so per hora, ne in questi tumulti posso sapere più oltre,
ma domani spererò di saper meglio il fatto."   Camillo Luzzara
to the Duke of Mantua, on January 7, 1566, Gonzaga Archives,
Mantua.

[1] Other reports also include Pisani (HILLIGER, 143 n.   ).
The three names of Ricci, Dolera, and Ghislieri appear in all the
reports ; otherwise there is great diversity.

[2] According to *Arco fear of the election of Ricci united Farnese
and Borromeo ; before that they had left their adherents at
liberty under the impression that they had excluded Ghislieri.
To Maximilian II., January 12, 1566, State Archives, Vienna.

Chapel. At first there was considerable excitement and dispute as to the manner in which the election was to be effected. Some maintained that they should be provided with black and white ballot balls, and vote with them; others desired that the chapel should be arranged in the usual way for the scrutiny, while others again wished that the Cardinals should merely declare themselves one after another and openly for Ghislieri. This last proposal met with general approval. When the excitement had abated, all took their seats in their accustomed places, when Pisani rose and said: " I, Cardinal Francesco Pisani, Dean of the Sacred College, elect as Pope my most reverend lord Michele, known as Cardinal Alessandrino." Morone followed, and gave his vote in similar terms, and then all the rest in their turn. Luigi d'Este and Guido Ferreri voted in the names of their sick relatives, Ippolito d'Este and Pier Francesco Ferreri. All then rose and approached the newly-elected Pope. When Pisani asked him if he accepted the election, Ghislieri stood for a moment in silence, while the Cardinals waited for his reply. At length he answered with the simple words: " I am willing."[1] It would have been natural that he should have taken the name of his patron, Paul IV., but out of consideration for Borromeo he took the name of the dead Pope,[2] even though he had met with little favour during the late pontificate. By this magnanimous act the new Pope displayed a forgetfulness of self not unlike that of Charles Borromeo.

The election was generally unexpected.[3] Only a few days before the Spanish ambassador had written that, save for a miracle, the conclave would be indefinitely protracted, especially as the arrival of the French Cardinals was imminent.[4] This was also the general opinion in the city, where Crispi

---

[1] *" Mi contento sù " Corn. Firmanus, *loc. cit.*, p. 35b.

[2] Requesens to Philip II., January 7, 1566, Corresp. dipl., I., 78. CATENA, 22.

[3] " Cosa que no se pensó," Requesens, *loc. cit.* 77 ; " inaspettatamente " Serristori, January 23, 1566, Legaz. di Serristori, 420.

[4] Requesens to Philip II., January 3, 1566, Corresp. dipl., I., 73.

was looked for as the next Pope.[1] The Florentines, on the
other hand, thought that they had skilfully arranged everything for the election of Ricci,[2] when suddenly and
unexpectedly they began to work for Ghislieri, whom they
like many others among the electors, had passed over.[3] Pacheco
wrote that the election was evidently the work of the Holy
Ghost, since many who, at their entry into the conclave, would
have cut off their feet rather than support Ghislieri, had been
the first to agree to his election.[4] Among these was Mark
Sittich, who had previously so brusquely rejected the idea of
the election of a friar, but who now was all on fire for the
elevation of the Dominican.[5]

[1] *" Et cosi sono in tal disordine et discordio [after the failure
with Sirleto], che per un pezzo non haveremo Papa, massime con
la venuta de' Francesi " (Avviso di Roma of January 5, 1566, Urb.
1040, p. 161b, Vatican Library). *Ibid.* 161 : Crispi has the best expectations, since Dolera and Ricci, who were proposed together with
him to Cardinal Borromeo by Farnese have not attained success.

[2] *" Quando noi pensavamo d'haver condotto le cose in buon
termine per la persona di Montepulciano, è venuta grida di palazzo
che Alessandrino è stato adorato Papa in questo punto, et l'effetto
è certissimo, perchè di già card. Capizucca di conclave è sceso
in s. Pietro a render gratie a Dio. . . ." Serristori and Concini
to the Duke of Florence on January 7, 1566, " hore XXXIII. (!),"
State Archives, Florence, Medic. 3285 p. 9.

[3] Card. Sforza to the Duke of Tuscany, on January 8, 1566,
State Archives, Florence.

[4] " Nos llevó el Spiritu Santo sin padecerse presion, como se a
visto oy en muchos hombres, que quando entraron en conclave
antes se cortaran las piernas que ir a hacer papa á Alexandrino,
y corrieron a hazerle los primeros." Pacheco to Philip II. on
January 7, 1566, Corresp. dipl. I. 80.

[5] CATENA 20. HILLIGER 145. P. Tiepolo adduces the election
of Pius V. as an example of the way in which a Papal election
often takes the most unexpected turn : " quasi usciti da loro
medesimi vanno dove mai non averiano creduti . . . corrono
come persone prive di consiglio, dubitando ciascuno d'esser
ultimo ; et però si vede bene spesso riuscir pontefice chi meno
si era creduto, come è successo nel presente." Report of 1569,
in ALBÈRI II. 4, 185.

Ghislieri himself can hardly have expected his election ;[1] later on he confessed that he had only accepted it because otherwise the Papacy might have fallen to Morone, a thing which might easily have been harmful to the Holy See.[2] In other respects, however, he had, even during the conclave, held out the hand of friendship to his former adversary.[3] That Ghislieri had all the necessary qualities for a distinguished Pope had often been recognized, but it had not been thought that he would ever obtain the necessary votes ;[4] what had been especially feared was the opposition of Borromeo, for it was hardly to be expected that the nephew of Pius IV. would ever give his support to a Cardinal upon whom his uncle had never looked with favour.[5] As a matter of fact, as he wrote to Philip II., ever since the death of Pius IV., Borromeo had had Ghislieri in mind, among others, as a suitable Pope ;[6] if he had not at once declared

[1] " Trovandosi il Papa posto in questa Sede inaspettatamente, credo senza averci mai prima pensato." Serristori, January 23, 1566, Legaz. di Serristori 420.

[2] " Lo avrebbe volontieri ricusato, e lo avrebbe fatto, se avesse pensato che fosse potuto cadere in una persona ragionevole, ma vedeva le cose disposte in modo che dubitava non venisse in persona di Morone o qualche altro soggetto, con molto danno di questa Santa Sede." *Ibid.* 422.

[3] *Cf.* the *report on the conclave of Clement VIII., Archives of the Spanish embassy in Rome.

[4] *Cf. supra* pp. 3, 14, 21, 32, and HILLIGER, 62, 65, 73.

[5] *" Convenne dunque Borromeo in Alessandrino, et in spatio di due hore contro l'opinioni si può dire di tutti fu creato papa, perchè pochi volevano credere, che Borromeo fosse mai per andare in una creatura di Paolo quarto et in uno ch'era stato offeso non poco da papa Pio." Arco to Maximilian II., January 12, 1566, State Archives, Vienna.

[6] " Io in questa attione ringratio infinitamente Dio che mi ha fatto gratia di attendervi da di de la morte di Pio IV. sino a quest'hoggi, spogliato d'ogni privata passione e rispetto, con la sola mira del servitio e gloria di Dio." (Borromeo to Philip II., January 7, 1566, Corresp. dipl., I., 79). *" Con determinata volontò mi diedi a far tutto quello che m'era possible per veder

himself in his favour, this was undoubtedly because, in so
doing, he would have rendered him a very doubtful service.[1]
In any case the election of Pius V. must be attributed to him,
and that not only in the sense that he succeeded in thwarting
the artifices of Farnese and Este, and thus at length united
all votes for Ghislieri. The Spanish ambassador[2] and the
astute Florentines[3] had no great opinion of Borromeo's powers
of dealing with tricks and subterfuges, and his confidant,
Bascapè,[4] expresses the same opinion ; in the matter of the
election of Pius V., as had so often happened to him before,
his secret desires seemed to be fulfilled of their own accord,
and from the force of circumstances. Borromeo's great merit,
however, lay in the fact that he looked beyond the petty
considerations of a short-sighted family policy,[5] that he waited

la sua esaltatione." (Borromeo to Philip II., January 27, 1566,
Ambrosian Library, Milan, F.37, Inf. p. 7). *Cf.* Borromeo to
King Sebastian and Cardinal Henry, February 25 and 26, 1566,
in BALUZE-MANSI, III., 529.

[1] *Cf. supra* p. 36.

[2] " El negocio de Moron y de Sirletto estuvo tan çerca que
qualquiera dellos fuera Papa, si Borromeo supiera darse buena
maña." To Philip II., January 11, 1566, Corresp. dipl. I. 84.

[3] *" Basta che siamo fuori delli scogli, i quali si sono schifati
non già per il buon governo di Borromeo." Serristori and Concini,
January 7, 1566, *loc. cit.* (*cf. supra* p. 19, n. 1).

[4] " Minus sagaciter vel etiam prudenter eum curasse aliquid
et ideo non obtinuisse putamus interdum, qui sibi aequo animo
passus id fuerit eripi ; contra nec opinantem et pene coactum
admisisse, quod consulto sit secutus ac non libenti solum, sed
gaudenti etiam animo acceperit " (l. 1 c. 9 p. 21). In his report
for 1569, Tiepolo gives the following description of Borromeo
as the leader of the party : " sebbene nel conclave passato dasse
a'cardenali malissima sodisfazione, e si governasse in modo che
perdesse assai dell'amor loro." ALBÈRI II. 4, 184.

[5] " El cardenal Borromeo y Alteps an hecho a este, siendo
mal tratado de su tio ; digo que le an hecho, porque estava en
su mano el excluylle, y sino vinieran en él, fuera imposible sello ;
es action con que Borromeo a dado muy buen exemplo al colegio "
(Pacheco to Philip II. on January 7, 1566, Corresp. dipl. I. 80).

for the right moment, and when that time came made his decision in favour of Ghislieri.

Once the election was an accomplished fact there was general rejoicing among the Cardinals that they had given to the Church the very Pope called for by the times.[1] In the Eternal City men learned with satisfaction of the unexpected elevation to the throne of St. Peter of a Cardinal of such holy life. As Caligari said, just as the rules of the Church had not been so strictly observed for many years past, so it was the general opinion of all good men that the election would bring about in a high degree the glory of God and the exaltation of the Holy See.[2] Others, on the contrary, were much alarmed, because they knew they must expect little from the well known strictness of the newly elected Pope, and it would seem that for some time this was the prevailing opinion among most of the Roman people. The new Pope was not the man to allow himself to be turned from his purpose, but he said that with the help of God he hoped to govern in such a way

" Fu fatto dal card. Borromeo davero, che altri l'havevano proposto de burla per escludere Sirletto. . . . Questo è notorio a tutto il mondo, che in mano del card. Borromeo era l'esclusione de tutti ch'erano in conclave " (C. Borghese to Cesare Borromeo on February 2, 1566, Arch. stor. Lomb. 1903, 360 f).

[1] " Todos salimos los hombres del mundo mas contentos de ver en esta Silla una persona tan exemplar como los tiempos en que estamos lo requieren." Pacheco to Philip II. on January 7, 1566, Corresp. dipl. I. 79.

[2] *" Questa elettione, si come è stata la più canonica et legitima che sia stata fatta molti anni sono, così dà speranza di dovere resultare in grandissimo servitio di Dio et esaltatione di questa Sta Sede ; et così credono et tengono per fermo tutti i boni. Bene è vero che molti licentiosi ne restano sbigottiti, in particolare l'amico, al quale in questo non potrà cadere cosa più contraria a suoi disegni, li quali a che fine mirino V. S. Illma lo sà meglio di tutti." To Commendone on January 9. 1566, Lett. di princ. XXIII. 160^b—161, Papal Secret Archives.

that the grief felt at his death would be greater than that which was felt at his election.[1]

[1] CATENA, 24. When on January 15, 1566, the Emperor Maximilian II., from a letter of Cosimo de' Medici, learned of the election of a monk, he jeered at the news (DENGEL, Nuntiaturberichte, I., 33). The Viceroy of Naples, on the other hand, showed extraordinary joy (excessiva consolación) at the election, and celebrated it with fireworks and salvos of artillery, such as had never been known at Naples at the election of a Pope. Salmeron to Borgia, January 13, 1566, in SALMERON, Epist., II., 63.

CHAPTER II.

PREVIOUS LIFE AND CHARACTER OF PIUS V. HIS FIRST MEASURES OF REFORM.

IT is easy to describe the previous life of the new Pope.[1] He was born on St. Antony's Day (January 17th), 1504, at Bosco, near Alessandria, in the Duchy of Savoy, and he had received the name of that saint in baptism. His family had been settled in that place since 1366,[2] but had afterwards fallen into great poverty. The humble house in which the future Pope first saw the light is still preserved at Bosco.[3] From his early youth it was Antony's wish to give himself entirely to God. His father, Paolo, and his mother, Domenica Augeria, put no obstacles in his way, though they had not the means to educate their son, whose duty it became to tend the flocks. But a certain Bastone came to their aid, and he sent little Antony, together with his own son Francesco to the Dominicans at Bosco.[4] The friars soon recognized the boy's

---

[1] Of the biographies (*cf.* App. n. 69) see especially CATENA, 2 *seq.* *Cf.* also P. TIEPOLO, 169 *seq.*

[2] See BRUZZONE, Storia del comune di Bosco, II., Turin, 1863, 265. *Cf.* the Roman periodical, *Cosmos illustr.*, 1904, 59 *seq.*; *ibid.* 1903, 138 *seq.*, proof of the branch of the family at Pinerolo. The view held by all the older biographers, that the Ghislieri of Bosco went there in 1445, after their expulsion from Bologna, seems to be hardly tenable. It was only after the elevation of Michele to the Papal throne that the Bologna family thought itself honoured in recognizing him as a descendant of the same family. *Cf.* CLARETTA in *Arch. stor. Lomb.*, X., 710; *Riv. di Alessandria*, X., 3 (1901), 69; SPEZI, 12 n. 1.

[3] See BRUZZONE in *Cosmos illustr.*, 1904, 56 *seq.*; *ibid* 36 a reproduction of the house where Pius V. was born.

[4] This hitherto unknown episode of the youth of Pius V. is related by Cusano in a *letter of February 2, 1566 (State Archives, Vienna), printed in App. n. 5.

46

abilities, and since the regulations of the Council of Trent were not yet in existence, Antony was able, when he was only fourteen years old, to enter the Dominican convent at Voghera,[1] where he received the name of Michele. His superiors first sent him to Vigevano,[2] where he was professed on May 18th, 1521,[3] and afterwards to Bologna for his scientific training, and lastly to Genoa, where he was ordained priest in 1528.

For many years Fra Michele of Alessandria, as he was called, was lecturer in philosophy and theology in the convent of his Order at Pavia.[4] During this period of teaching, a duty which he discharged most conscientiously, he distinguished himself at the General Chapter held at Parma in 1543 by his defence of certain theses which boldly proclaimed the authority of the Holy See. Fra Michele was also commissary of the Inquisition in the city and diocese of Pavia, as vicar of his fellow Dominican, Sante of Padua.[5] He acquitted himself of all these offices so well that men compared him to St. Bernardine. The least rule of his Order was sacred to him ; he never travelled except on foot, with his wallet on his shoulder. He was a shining example to all his brethren by his great humility, his strict observance of poverty, his unwearied activity and his spotless purity of life. He could not avoid being twice elected Prior, but accepted the dignity most unwillingly, and this was still more the case when the

---

[1] When he was Pope Ghislieri showed his gratitude to this convent ; see A. CAVAGNA SANGIULIANA, Dell'abbazia di S. Alberti di Butrio e del monastero di S. Maria della Pietà in Voghera 1865.

[2] His cell is still shown : see C. CLERICI, Vigevano, 1880, 82.

[3] See the attestation in manuscript in GRANELLO, Fra Michele Ghislieri, I., Bologna, 1877, 25.

[4] See MAJOCCHI, La chiesa e il convento di S. Tommaso in Pavia, Pavia, 1895, 82 *seq.* ; *cf.* DELL'ACQUA, 33 *seq.* ; An incunabulum (PEROTTUS, Cornucopiae seu Comment. linguae latinae, Venetiis, 1490) with annotations in the hand of Ghislieri was put up for sale in 1899 by the Roman antiquarian B. Benedetti (Catalogue 61, Nov. 1899, n. 2099).

[5] See *Riv. di scienze storiche*, IV., 1, Pavia, 1907, 62 *seq.*

provincial chapter of Lombardy elected him Definitor, the office next in importance to that of Provincial.

In every way Ghislieri was the model of the true religious ; he refused to wear a mantle because he thought that one who belonged to a mendicant order should be content with his cowl. He was a great lover of cleanliness, and used to say that he had ever loved poverty, but never dirt. He allowed nothing to interfere with the performance of his duty, and when, as Prior of Alba, he found himself obliged, for the safety of his convent, to oppose the Count della Trinità, who threatened to have him thrown down a well, Ghislieri replied : " What God wills will be done."[1]

Ghislieri entered upon a very difficult task with his appointment as Inquisitor of the diocese of Como, which, on account of its proximity to Switzerland, was likely to be infected with the new religious ideas. When, in 1550, he confiscated twelve bales of heretical books, the booksellers affected managed to win over the bishop's vicar-general and the chapter, which obliged Ghislieri to appeal to the Inquisition in Rome. This tribunal summoned the accused before them, which caused so great a tumult in the city that Ghislieri was obliged to seek protection from his friend Bernardo Odescalchi. His position became even more perilous when the governor of Milan, Ferrante Gonzaga, took the part of his enemies. In order to clear up the affair, Ghislieri, at the end of 1550, betook himself to Rome, where he was brought into contact with the Cardinals of the Inquisition, and especially with Carafa, who was quick to recognize in the Lombard a kindred spirit, and one who was prepared to maintain the purity of the faith with unbending firmness.

As time went on, no threats and no dangers held any terrors for Ghislieri when it was a question of doing his duty. When he was given a mission to Coire, it was suggested to him that he would do well to travel through the heretical canton of the Grisons in disguise, but he vigorously refused, saying that he

---

[1] See CATENA, 150. The incident is related somewhat differently by Tiepolo in MUTINELLI, I., 51.

would be glad to die as a martyr dressed in the habit of St. Dominic. Twice Ghislieri acted as Inquisitor at Bergamo, a very difficult office.[1] In 1551, at the recommendation of Carafa, Julius III. summoned him to Rome as commissary general of the Inquisition. In this office he displayed the greatest zeal, and had many dealings with Marcello Cervini,[2] who, after the death of Julius III., ascended the Papal throne as Marcellus II. After the death of the latter, which followed almost immediately,[3] his patron Carafa became Pope, and he confirmed Ghislieri in his office of commissary general of the Inquisition, and on September 4th, 1556, appointed him Bishop of Sutri and Nepi, taking care at the same time that this indefatigable man should not be altogether removed from his previous activities, by making him Prefect of the Palace of the Inquisition.[4]

Michele fought hard against accepting the episcopal dignity, but Paul IV. thought it well to attach a chain to his feet, lest he should again think of retiring to his convent.[5] How highly the Pope esteemed the humble Dominican is shown by the fact that on March 15th, 1557, he appointed him Cardinal, and on December 14th in the following year Grand Inquisitor of the Roman Church.[6] Ghislieri received as his

---

[1] See P. TIEPOLO, 191 ; CATENA, 9 seq., 148 ; GABUTIUS, 9 seq. Cf. Vol. XIII. of this work, p. 219.

[2] Cf. Vol. XIII. of this work, pp. 220, 222 ; XIV., 269 seqq.

[3] A letter of Fra Michele Alessandrino to G. B. Brunatello in Venice, dated Rome, June 8, 1655, refers to the trial of the surgeon of Marcellus II., who was accused of having poisoned the Pope ; see FILLON, n. 2447.

[4] See Vol. XIV. of this work, p. 271. Cf. MORONI, LXXI., 118. In the episcopal palace of Sutri, the door through which Ghislieri was accustomed to pass has been walled up, so that no one should use it any more. The episcopal archives at Nepi were destroyed during the French occupation. In the episcopal palace there nothing but a picture (Pius V. in prayer before the crucifix) tells of the former occupant of the see.

[5] See ALBÈRI, II., 4, 200 seq.

[6] See Vol. XIV. of this work, pp. 262, 271.

titular church S. Maria sopra Minerva, which later on, in
1561, he exchanged for S. Sabina.

During the campaign of Paul IV. against heretical books,
Cardinal Alessandrino, as Ghislieri was called from his native
place, had repeatedly dissuaded his subordinates from too
severe or hasty action.   Towards the end of the reign of Paul
IV. he had to face bitter reproofs from the Pope, who was
daily becoming more gloomy and violent, on account of
his conduct in the affair of the Spanish archbishop,
Carranza.[1]

Ghislieri's position became even more difficult under
Pius IV., whose more worldly outlook was in strong contrast
to his own rigid views.[2]   Several times the Cardinal, who
since 1560 had been Protector of the Barnabites,[3] and Bishop
of Mondovì, where he laboured alike for reform,[4] the promotion
of learning,[5] and ecclesiastical liberty,[6] boldly addressed
severe rebukes to Pius IV., especially when, at the beginning
of 1563, two sons of princes were about to be nominated to
the Sacred College.   Ghislieri was not able to prevent these

[1] See Vol. XIV. of this work, p. 315 seqq.

[2] See the characteristic letter of Ghislieri to his nephew in
MAFFEI, Pio V., 47 seq. ; BRUZZONE, Bosco, I., 139 seq.   That
Ghislieri's nickname " fra Scarpone " (SANTORI, Autobiogr., 371)
does not mean " scorpion " as HERRE (p. 204) thought, has been
proved by ŠUSTA (Mitteil. des österr. Instituts, XXX., 546) and
SCHELLHASS (Zeitschrift für Kirchengesch. XXX., 143 n. 2).

[3] See PREMOLI, Storia dei Barnabiti nel cinquecento, Rome,
1913, 181.   Cf. ibid., 24, for the early relations of Ghislieri with
the Barnabites.

[4] See CATENA, 15.

[5] By the erection of a university ; see DELL'ACQUA, 38 seq.,
where there are also some particulars as to the traces of Pius V.
preserved in the cathedral at Mondovì.   Cf. GRASSI, Mem. della
chiesa di Monteregale in Piemonte, I., Turin, 1789, 87.   The
Library at Alessandria still contains a beautiful choir-book of
Pius V.

[6] Cf. the characteristic letter of Ghislieri to Emanuele Filiberto,
Duke of Savoy, dated Mondovì, October 1, 1561, in Bollett. Subalp.
VI., 255 seq.

appointments, any more than he could the limitations set upon his powers as Grand Inquisitor by Pius IV.[1]

Since he was manifestly out of favour with Pius IV.,[2] it can easily be understood that Ghislieri seriously thought of returning to his bishopric of Mondovì, in order to complete the reforms which he had begun there in 1560. Moreover, he was so seriously attacked by stone in 1564 that he caused his monument to be set up in S. Maria sopra Minerva.[3] It is certain that no one in Rome at that time anticipated his elevation to the Papal throne, and least of all, in his simplicity and humility, the Cardinal himself, who, when he found himself faced with the fact of his election, which took him altogether by surprise, hesitated for a moment before he accepted it. The very sense of responsibility, which had always made him shrink from any dignity, was what at length decided him to obey the call of the Sacred College, for he dared not withstand the voice of God.[4]

Sprung as he was from a poor and obscure family, Pius V.

[1] Cf. Arch. stor. Ital., IV., 6, 372.

[2] In his report on May 17, 1572, of the election of Gregory XIII., Cusano, speaking of the way in which Bonelli had gone over to the side of Boncompagni, remarks : *" a lui è intervenuto come al card. Borromeo, il quale fece Papa Pio V., che era in tutto naturale di Paolo IV. et non v'era cardinale in questo conclave di questo tempo che fosse stato più dispregiato et vilipeso da Pio IV. suo zio che la manca parola che dicesse contra di esso di frate scarpone [see supra p. 50, n. 2] et che farebbe rotornar al refettorio, et non ostante questo elesse in pontefice come ha fatto l'Alessandrino." State Archives, Vienna.

[3] See the inscription in CATENA, 18 ; cf. DELL'ACQUA, 37. As Cardinal, Ghislieri lived in lodgings in the Borgo ; see AVVISO DI ROMA of Feb. 22, 1567 : *" Il Papa ha comprata la casa, nella quale stava quando era cardinale et dice voler che la goda il card. Alessandrino mentre vive et dopo la sua morte sarà dei suoi parenti." (Urb. 1040, p. 363b, Vatican Library.) Cf. LANCIANI IV., 22 seq. For the famiglia of the Cardinal see the Rotulo in MORONI, XXIII., 76 seq.

[4] See Legaz. di Serristori, 421-422. Cf. *Avviso di Roma of January 23, 1566, Urb. 1040, Vatican Library.

had, so to speak, passed through every grade of the Church's army. It had not been on account of his birth, nor by the favour of princes, nor by intrigue, but merely in virtue of his zeal in the service of the Church, that the strict religious had become in turn Prior, Inquisitor, Bishop, Cardinal, and at last Pope. His life, spent in unwearied labours, and amid penances and privations of every kind, had left its manifest traces upon his bodily strength. Although he was only sixty-two, his emaciated figure, with bald head and his long white beard, gave the impression of an old man. He was of middle height, with small eyes, but a keen sight, an aquiline nose, clear and healthy complexion, and strongly marked features.[1] The general impression of asceticism, which made

---

[1] For the physical appearance and natural characteristics of Pius V., see the famous description by Tiepolo in 1566 (*Relazione*, 169 *seq.*) according to which the new Pope stands out in contrast to the dead Pius IV. " in luminoso contrasto e meravigliosa richezza " (ANDREAS, 106), though his great spirituality seems exaggerated in more than one respect. *Cf.* also the Ritratto di Pio V. of M. Soriano (ALBÈRI, II., 200 *seq.*), the " Informatione delle qualità di Pio V. e delle cose che da quello dipendono," written in November, 1566, and July, 1567, and published by VAN ORTROY in *Anal. Bolland.*, XXIII. (1914), 192 *seq.*, and in App. nn. 7 and 8 the *report of C. Luzzara of Mar. 27, 1566, Gonzaga Archives, Mantua. The markedly ascetic traits of Pius V.'s features are clearly shown in his medals, especially that of Giov. Antonio Rossi (see VASARI, V., 387 ; ARMAND, Médailleurs ital., Paris, 1879 ; MÙNTZ, III., 242 ; MORTIER, S. Maria della Quercia, 161). For two other medals of Pius V. see DE FOVILLE, Médailles de la Renaissance in the *Revue numismat.*, XVIII. (1914), 1. There is a beautiful cameo of the head of Pius V. in the Museo Cristiano at the Vatican. Of the many engravings on copper, which depict Pius V., special mention may be made of those by Beatrizet (*cf.* HÜBNER, Le statue di Roma, I., 35), by Niccolò Nelli (Pius V. aetat. LXIII. A. 1567 ; a copy in the collection of engravings in the gallery at Munich), that by Philippus Soius (Soye, died 1567) made for O. Panvinio, that of Moncornet and F. van Hülsen (good copies in the Imperial Familien-Fideikommiss library at Vienna). The engraving in the " Imagines " of F. Zenoi

him look, as an ambassador wrote, as if he were but skin and
bones,[1] inspired awe. Everyone felt that he was in the
presence of a man of unshakeable firmness, and of a profound
seriousness, which, far removed from anything of this world,
was fixed entirely upon spiritual things.

Pius V. was so imbued with the responsibilities of his office
that he looked upon it as an obstacle in the way of his salvation.
It was, indeed, obvious how much his new dignity weighed
down this man, who would have wished above all things to
have remained a friar.[2] It was only in the quiet of his convent,
he would say with many sighs, that he had known real peace
of conscience, and that already before this, his dignities, both

(Venice, 1569), is in MÜNTZ, III., 33. Rome is very rich in oil
paintings of Pius V. They are to be seen at S. Silvestro al Quirin-
ale, at SS. Domenico e Sisto (first altar on the left, and probably
from the monastery founded by Pius V. ; see NIBBY, I., 209),
in the Vatican Library and in the palace of the Holy Office. The
best of these portraits, which shows a full length figure of the
Pope, who is seated, is by Scipione Pulzone, and is in the Colonna
Gallery, Rome. Another copy is in the Collegio Ghislieri at
Pavia (reproduced in DELL'ACQUA, Pio V, Milan. 1904), and a
third in the convent of the Dominicans in Milan. In BARGELLINI,
Etruria merid., Bergamo, 1909, 132, there is a reproduction of the
fairly good portrait in the Cathedral at Sutri. The well known
portrait of Pius V. by Dom. Muratori only dates from the beginning
of the XVIIIth century ; the original is in his cell at S. Sabina ;
see Cosmos illustr., 1904, 3. The marble bust of Pius V. at the
Trinità dei Monti on the tomb of Cardinal Carpi, erected by the
Pope in 1568 (see FORCELLA, III., 125) is no longer in existence.
The statue at S. Croce at Bosco (see DELL'ACQUA, 44) represents
the Pope kneeling ; the seated figure on his tomb in S. Maria
Maggiore is the work of Lionardo da Sarzana. A later, but
excellent, portrait of Pius V. in profile (Italian work) is in the
Museum at Copenhagen. For the arms of Pius V. see PASINI-
FRASSONI, Armorial des Papes, Rome, 1906, 38.

[1] Report of Cusano of January 26, 1566. State Archives,
Vienna.

[2] See the *letter of Cusano of March 2, 1566. State Archives,
Vienna. Cf. POLANCI Epist. in Anal. Bolland., VII., 46.

as bishop and cardinal, had sadly disturbed it ; this was now the case more than ever when he remembered the account which, as Pope, he would one day have to render to Almighty God.[1] The supreme dignity seemed to him a heavy cross, under which he feared to fall. In a letter to the Grand Master of Malta he confessed that he had had thoughts of renouncing the tiara, and that the only thing which had held him back from such a step was his firm trust in the help of the Almighty.[2] Both in public and in private he begged people to pray much for him,[3] while at the same time he redoubled his accustomed exercises of piety and mortification.

Pius V. made it plain that now that he was Pope he still intended to remain the strict mendicant friar that he had been all his life, for he refused to lay aside his rough shirt,[4] and as far as possible continued his former manner of life. He went early to bed so as to be able to rise early in the morning. He said mass every day,[5] after which came prayers and meditation ; he also recited the Rosary every day.[6] Immediately after he had broken his fast he devoted himself to the affairs

---

[1] See TIEPOLO, 201 ; CATENA, 31 seq. ; GABUTIUS, 226–227. Cf. the saying of Pius V. related by Tiepolo, in MUTINELLI, I. For the meaning of similar expressions see LADERCHI, 1566, n. 6.

[2] See the beautiful letter to Pietro di Monte of December 8, 1570, in CATENA, 290 seq.

[3] See CATENA, 35 ; GABUTIUS, 199.

[4] *" Sotto ai panni pontificii porta la camiscia di rascia come facea quando era frate et essendogli portata rascia fina et sottile per far camiscie, ne ha fatto pigliar della più grossa dicendo che non vuol mutar quello che non si vede dal vulgo." Avviso di Roma of January 19, 1566, Urb. 1040, p. 166b. Vatican Library.

[5] According to TIEPOLO, 172, it might be supposed that he only celebrated mass frequently, but Arco, on January 12, 1566, expressly states : *" Ipse bene valet et quotidie sacris privatim operatur." (State Archives, Vienna.) The same thing is stated in the *Avviso di Roma of January 12, 1566, printed in App n. 3, as well as in other reports, e.g. POLANCI Epist., in Anal. Bolland., VII., 51, and the letter of Requesens of March 18, 1566, Corresp. dipl., I., 161.

[6] CATENA, 35.

of state and granted audiences. He was indefatigable in this latter respect, and even when Rome lay under a heavy scirocco, he would not allow himself any rest.[1] He said that the best cure for the oppressive heat was to eat and drink very little. The small quantity of food and drink that sufficed him was extraordinary. At noon he took some bread-soup with two eggs, and half a cup of wine, and his supper in the evening generally consisted of some vegetable broth, salad, shell-fish, and cooked fruit. Only twice a week did meat appear at his table. Before and after the meal long prayers were recited, and during part of it a book was read, after which he and his guests maintained a monastic silence.[2] Nor did he act differently all through the day ; only rarely did he allow himself any recreation, yet in spite of this he was of a naturally lively disposition, as Bernardo Cirillo, his majordomo, often had occasion to remark.[3]

The health of Pius V. had for many years suffered from stone ;[4] the doctors and diplomatists therefore thought that he would not live very long.[5] Although he often felt very

[1] *Cf.* the *report of C. Luzzara of March 27, 1566, Gonzaga Archives, Mantua, the *letter of Requesens, *supra* p. 54, n. 5, and the *letter of Arco of August 31, 1566, State Archives, Vienna.

[2] See Tiepolo in MUTINELLI, I., 55 *seq.* (where instead of *fortaia* is found *tortaia*). *C .* MARINI, II., 320 ; CATENA, 27 *seq.* On November 18, 1567, Arco *states that the Pope has still further reduced his table, on which he only spends three and a half scudi a day. State Archives, Vienna.

[3] See the " Informatione delle qualità " in *Anal. Bolland.*, XXXIII., 195.

[4] See TIEPOLO, 181 ; MARINI, II., 318 *seq.* and the *report of Arco on September 7, 1566, State Archives, Vienna.

[5] See the letter of Granvelle of March 10, 1566 (Corresp., ed. PIOT, I., 155) and the *report of C. Luzzara of June 12, 1566 : *" La maggior parte di questi medici del Papa intendo che conchiudono che S.Stᵃ habbia la pietra et grossa, et che facciano mal giuditio de la vita sua, aggiunto a questo la magrezza et attinuatione ne la quale è, che non può essere maggiore." Gonzaga Archives, Mantua.

unwell,[1] the Pope would not hear of sparing his strength,[2] all the more so because on the whole his health was better as Pope than it had been when he was a Cardinal.[3] He continued his former practice of taking a great deal of exercise, and when, in November, 1566, he went to the sea coast to inspect the works of fortification, he made very little use of his litter. He generally went about on foot, and in spite of all his labours, never slept more than five hours.[4]

As time went on all those who had hoped for the early death of the Pope were disappointed. As a remedy for the stone Pius used asses' milk, and though the physicians feared lest he should weaken his stomach, he persisted in the use of this remedy, which he had often found useful before.[5] Speaking generally, his state of health was fairly satisfactory, even in 1567. " He flourishes like a rose tree, and will live a long

[1] See the *report of Arco of May 25, 1566, State Archives, Vienna and the *letter of C. Luzzara of June 1, 1566 : *" E voce pubblica per Roma che il Papa sia molto debole et ch'egli medesimo diffidi de la vita sua." (Gonzaga Archives, Mantua). See also the *report of Serristori of November 1, 1566 (State Archives, Florence).

[2] See the *report of Cusano, February 16, 1566, State Archives, Vienna, and *that of Babbi, November 1, 1566, State Archives, Florence.

[3] With the reports of Tiepolo in MUTINELLI, I., 39 seq., 47 seq., cf. the *letter of Serristori, April 1, 1566, State Archives, Florence, and the letter of July 13, 1566, in MASIUS, Briefe, 374. Cf. the *letter of Caligari to Commendone, September 21, 1566, Lett. di princ., XXIII, Papal Secret Archives ; *Avviso di Roma of December 28, 1566 (Urb. 1040, p. 330b, Vatican Library) ; *report of B. Pia of May 31, 1567 (sta tanto bene quanto si stesse mai), Gonzaga Archives, Mantua.

[4] *Avviso di Roma of November 23, 1566, Urb. 1040, p. 305, Vatican Library.

[5] Cf. Tiepolo in MUTINELLI, I., 45 seq., the *report of C. Luzzara of May 29, 1566 (Gonzaga Archives, Mantua), and the *Avvisi di Roma of June 29, 1566 and June 19, 1568, Urb. 1040, p. 248, 526b, Vatican Library.

time," wrote Serristori on March 15th, 1567.[1] Even during
the summer of the same year the reports continue to be
favourable,[2] and during the procession of Corpus Domini in
1567 the Pope seemed more vigorous than any of the Cardinals.[3]
In the December of the same year they wrote from Rome that
though the Pope fasted and prayed during Advent like a monk,
he looked very well.[4] He continued his great activity ; often
he walked eight miles in spite of the heat of summer, and they
were afraid that he was doing too much for his age.[5] In the
autumn he went almost every morning to his little villa outside
the Porta Cavalleggieri. In his visits to the churches, which
he often made on foot, he tired out those who accompanied
him.[6] During the Holy Week of 1568 he fasted so strictly
that he brought on a serious giddiness.[7] It was only the advice
of a new doctor which was successful in the following year in
persuading him to have more consideration for his health and
his age,[8] to sleep longer and to restrict his fasts to some extent,
though he insisted in this last respect on doing as much as
possible. He ordered the cook, under pain of excommunication, not to put anything forbidden into his soup on days

[1] See the *letter in the State Archives, Florence, Medic. 3287,
p. 77.

[2] See the *report of Arco of June 15, 1567, State Archives,
Vienna and the *letter of Caligari to Commendone of July 16,
1567, Lett. di princ., XXIII., Papal Secret Archives.

[3] See the *report of Arco of May 24, 1567, State Archives,
Vienna.

[4] *" Con tutto che osservi l'advento alla fratesca con digiuni et
celebratione ha una buona ciera." Avviso di Roma of Dec. 13.
1567, Urb. 1040, p. 460, Vatican Library.

[5] See the *Avvisi di Roma of May 22, and August 21, 1568, Urb.
1040, p. 520,567, Vatican Library. Cf. the *reports of Arco of
June 21 and July 5, 1567, State Archives, Vienna.

[6] See the *Avvisi di Roma of October 2, 1568, and October
5, 1569, Urb. 1040, p. 590 ; 1041, p. 158b, Vatican Library.

[7] See *Avviso di Roma of April 17, 1568, Urb. 1040, p. 503b,
ibid.

[8] See *Avviso di Roma of December 17, 1569, Urb. 1041
p.198b, ibid.

of abstinence,[1] and on Good Friday he would take nothing cooked at all.[2]

The Pope found his chief delight in prayer, and his fervour often moved him to tears.[3] Every time that he had to come to an important decision he prayed with special fervour.[4] As soon as he had concluded his official duties he returned to his spiritual exercises,[5] and during Holy Week he retired altogether, so as to give himself up entirely to meditation on the Passion of Christ,[6] and since his special devotion was to the Crucified,[7] Pius V. is represented in most of his pictures with a crucifix in his hands.

[1] " *Il Papa fa grand' astinentia, fa la quaresima et digiuna ogni giorno et ha comandato espressamente a quelli, che hanno cura della bocca sua, che guardino per quanto hanno cura la sua gratia de non alterarli li brodi con istilati o altro, publicando che saranno escomunicati oltre le pene arbitrarie se uscirano del suo comandamento " (Avviso di Roma of February 22, 1567, Urb. 1040, p. 362b, Vatican Library). Cf. the *report of B. Pia of December 20, 1567, Gonzaga Archives, Mantua. See also MARINI, II., 319. As Pope, Pius V. kept the cook whom he had had as Cardinal ; see MORONI, XXIII., 77. The title of " cuoco segreto di Pio V." was also borne by Bartolomeo Scappi, who, since he had no opportunity of putting his office to practical use, used his skill theoretically in a very widely sold cookery book (Opera, Venice, 1570, 1596, 1605). Cf. HÜBNER, Sixtus V., II., 138 seq. ; RODOCANACHI, Rome, 48.

[2] See in App. n. 9 the *Avviso di Roma of April 13, 1566, Vatican Library.

[3] TIEPOLO, 172. POLANCI Epist. in Anal. Bolland., VII., 46.

[4] See GRATIANI Epist., 379.

[5] Cf. the *Avviso di Roma of January 26, 1566, Urb. 1040, p. 170b, Vatican Library.

[6] Cf. Tiepolo in MUTINELLI, I., 40.

[7] " *S. Pius V. una cum S. Carlo Borromeo coemiterium visitare et ante crucifixi imaginem, quae in capella Campi Sancti summa ab antiquis temporibus veneratione colitur, preces fundere consuevisse vetera confraternitatis monumenta tradiderunt," reports the Historia Campi Sancti, MS. in the Archives of that Confraternity.

It is said of him that throughout his pontificate Pius V.
never failed to be present at any of the ecclesiastical functions
prescribed by the ceremonial, even when he was ill.[1] He
gave everyone a striking example by the recollection and piety
he displayed on those occasions.[2] At Christmas he first
assisted at matins and mass, then said two low masses, after

[1] TIEPOLO 172. C. FIRMANUS, *Diarium XII., 31 p. 154 :
" S^mus Dominus N^r a die sue assumptionis ad pontificatum usque
ad hanc diem (Cf. February 20, 1567) semper celebravit missas
et solum per undecim dies cessavit ; nunquam reliquit aliquam
capellam nisi in cathedra S^ti Petri in die subsequenti suam
coronationem, quam reliquit pro cardinalium commoditate, et in
anniversario coronationis et cathedra S^ti Petri precedenti propter
maledictam differentiam precedentiarum ut supra " (Papal Secret
Archives). Cf. the *report of Cusano of January 8, 1569, and *that
of Arco of February 5, 1569 (the Pope often in the ceremonies
"maximo cum labore et incommodo,quod tamen iucunda admodum
facie et hilari animo pertulit "), State Archives Vienna. Sometimes
he did more than he was obliged to do. For example, he attended
the funeral offices for the Cardinals. When the master of ceremonies reminded him that the Popes were not accustomed to
attend such ceremonies, he said : " Anco i monaci mal volontiere
vedono l'abate in coro, ma noi vogliamo venire seben non è
usanza, et così si andò " (Urb. 1040, p. 317, Vatican Library). See
also the *Avviso di Roma of December 28, 1566 : *" Questi altri
giorni sempre s'è trovato alle capelle con tanta sollecitudine che
i cardinali son stati sforzati levarsi avanti il giorno." (Urb. 1040,
p. 330b ; cf. ibid. 338, *Avviso of December 8, 1566 : *" Passerà
questo tempo con solitaria devotione ne resta mai di venir alle
solita capelle dell'Advento et altre et digiuna ogni giorno et dice
messa e fa chel card. Alessandrino faccia il medesimo ") ; also the
*Avvisi of April 5, 1567, Urb. 1040, p. 375b, and of December 9,
1570, Urb. 1041, p. 380b, Vatican Library.

[2] See Tiepolo in MUTINELLI, I., 40. An *Avviso di Roma of
April 17, 1568, refers to the reading of the Passion, " stete sempre
in piedi con gran devotione come ha anco fatto in tutti li altri
officii di questa settimana santa " (Urb. 1040, p. 502b, Vatican
Library). Cf. the *report of Cusano of March 9, 1566, State
Archives, Vienna.

which he celebrated High Mass in St. Peter's.[1] He also
assisted regularly at the sermons in the Vatican.[2] Sometimes
the Pope himself preached in St. Peter's, at S. Maria sopra
Minerva, and at the Lateran.[3] At Easter time, or when a
jubilee had been proclaimed, he liked to give communion
himself to his household.[4] On Ash Wednesday he would
give it for perhaps three hours to many of the faithful,[5] and
during Lent he liked to visit the church of S. Sabina on the
Aventine.[6]

A pious exercise which was very ancient, and which Pius V.
and Philip Neri especially revived,[7] was the visit to the seven
basilicas. At least twice a year, generally in spring at the
time of the Carnival, when reparation for excesses seemed
to be especially called for, and in the autumn, the Pope made
this long and fatiguing pilgrimage,[8] and in doing this, as was
always his custom when he went about, he was accompanied
by a small retinue, and distributed alms to the poor with his

---

[1] *Avviso di Roma of December 28, 1568, Urb. 1040, p. 330b,
Vatican Library.

[2] *" Ogni mattina S.S. va alla predica in palazzo dove predica
il prior di S. Sabina " (Avviso di Roma of February 22, 1567, Urb.
1040, p. 362). The Pope was always to be seen at the sermons
of P. Benedetto (*Avviso di Roma of January 1, 1569, Urb. 1041,
p. 1, Vatican Library). Cf. the *report of Cusano of March 16,
1566, State Archives, Vienna, and POLANCI Epist. in Anal Bolland.,
VII., 51.

[3] See POLANCI Epist. in Anal. Bolland., VII., 65.

[4] See C. Firmanus, *Diarium, August 3, 1566, Papal Secret
Archives.

[5] See the *letter of Arco of March 6,1568, State Archives,
Vienna.

[6] See *Avviso di Roma of February .15, 1567, Urb. 1040,
p. 355, Vatican Library.

[7] Cf. MESCHLER, Die Fahrt zu den sieben Kirchen in Rom, in
Stimmen aus Maria-Laach, LVIII., 20 seq.

[8] See C. Firmanus, *Diarium, April 8 and October 10, 1566,
April 3 and November 5, 1567, March 2, April 12, and October 29,
1568, Papal Secret Archives ; *report of Zibramonti of March 4,
1571, Gonzaga Archives, Mantua.

own hands.[1] No Pope had ever been known to make so
wearisome a pilgrimage during the whole period of the Renaissance, and it was therefore looked upon as something quite
new.[2] But, as was the case with other things, Pius V. soon
found imitators in this, and at Easter, 1571, it is reported
that the Cardinals and almost all the prelates of the court
made the visit of the seven basilicas.[3]

Pius V. always showed a great devotion to the Blessed
Sacrament ; this was especially evident at the feast of Corpus
Domini. In the first year of his reign he was one of the first
to arrive for the function, and so early that they had to light
lamps in order to see. First of all the Pope said a low mass,
preceded and followed by long prayers and meditation. At
the procession previous Popes had made use of a litter, and
had worn a precious tiara, but he went on foot, carrying the
eucharistic Saviour with bare head and the greatest devotion.
With eyes fixed on the Blessed Sacrament, and with unceasing
prayer, Pius V., in spite of the great heat, made the whole
procession, which passed through the Borgo, which was all
decorated for the feast ; men noticed his compunction, as
well as the fact that he frequently burst into tears.[4] In the
years that followed the ambassadors could never say enough
of the Pope's deep recollection, especially at the feast of
Corpus Domini.[5] It can clearly be seen from their letters

---

[1] See the *Avviso di Roma of April 13, 1566, in App. n. 9 ;
Tiepolo in MUTINELLI, I., 40 ; *report of Cusano of April 13,
1566, State Archives, Vienna ; *letter of C. Luzzara of
November 19, 1566, Gonzaga Archives, Mantua.

[2] See the *report of Arco of April 13, 1566, State Archives,
Vienna.

[3] See the *Avviso di Roma of April 14, 1571, Urb. 1042, p. 46,
Vatican Library.

[4] See the report of Tiepolo of June 15, 1566, in MUTINELLI
I., 47 seq. and POLANCI Epist. in Anal. Bolland, VII., 63.

[5] Cf. the *report of B. Pia of May 31, 1567, Gonzaga Archives,
Mantua ; *Avviso di Roma of June 19, 1568 : *" Andò .in
processione con il Corpus Domini in mano et testa tutta scoperta
con gl'occhi sempre affissi nel santissimo sacramento con molta

what a deep impression his piety made.[1] His behaviour,
as even a man so given to criticism as Galeazzo Cusano admits,
was faultless, and worthy of the successor of St. Peter.[2] In
1566 so cold a diplomatist as the Spaniard, Requesens,
gave it as his opinion that the Church had not had a
better head for the past three hundred years.[3] In the
reports we constantly find the words : " The Pope is a
saint."[4]

" In consequence of his mortification," we read in an account

devotione " 34 bishops and 26 cardinals took part in the procession
(Urb. 1040, p. 526b, Vatican Library) ; *Avviso di Roma of
June 11, 1569 : *" N.S. sotto il baldachino a piedi con il capo
scoperto con una grandissima devotione." (Urb. 1041, p. 91b,
ibid) *Arco on June 15, 1566, reports concerning the part taken
by the Pope in the procession on Corpus Domini that he went
on foot with his head uncovered " humiliter et sancte, quod
multo ex tempore nullos ex Pontificibus alios fecisse constat."
State Archives, Vienna.

[1] *Cf*. Corresp. de Granvelle, éd. POULLET, I., 124 and the letters
of Giov. Polanco published by DELPLACE in *Anal. Bolland.*, VII.,
46 *seqq.*, which to some extent had appeared in a translation
and somewhat altered in " Epistolae . . . ex urbe ad Germaniae
principes quosdam et alios primarios viros scriptae de gestis
Pii V. P. M., Coloniae, 1567 ; see *Anal. Bolland.*, XV., 77 *seq.*
where, however, the earlier edition (catalogued by PFLEGER,
Eisengrein 127) of M. Eisengrein is forgotten, " Nova fide digna
de rebus hoc anno a R. P. Pio V gestis ex epistolis doctor. quorun-
dam excerpta, Ingolstadt, 1566."

[2] *Letter of April 20, 1566, State Archives, Vienna.

[3] Corresp. dipl., I., 203.

[4] " The Pope appears to me every day more holy," is the judgment of so coldly calculating a diplomatist as Granvelle, on March
10, 1566 (Corresp. éd. POULLET, I., 147 ; *cf*. 124, 345). *Cf*. the
*Avviso di Roma of January 26, 1566, Urb. 1040, p. 170b,
Vatican Library ; Tiepolo in MUTINELLI, I., 53. On April
1, 1569, B. Pia wrote : *" Dio benedetto sia lodato che
dadegno di voler sotto questo santo papa aiutar la sua
navicella nel più tempes-toso mare." Gonzaga Archives,
Mantua.

based upon close personal observation,[1] " Pius V. is almost entirely free from passions, and in this stands out in strong contrast to all other men. Nothing is so near to his heart as the wish to restore the Holy See to its former greatness and its ancient splendour, by the improvement of morals and the rooting out of abuses. When it is necessary, no trouble is too great for him, and no measures are too strict. Even when he grants a favour, like a good confessor, he adds thereto some good advice. As soon as he detects anything in the nature of a profanation of holy things he is seized with a righteous anger, his countenance is inflamed, and the culprit has to listen to many stern rebukes, though his heat disappears as soon as he sees signs of repentance. He is quite inexorable in the case of the smallest offence against the divine law, or against the precepts and teaching of the Church."[2]

Pius V.'s strictness in all that concerned reform, the administration of justice, and the Inquisition, recalled the days of Paul IV. Himself as pious as he was humble, and as grave as he was severe, Pius V. expected much from others. Above all, he insisted on absolute truthfulness; the man who had once told him a lie lost his favour for ever.[3] He liked people to speak frankly to him and to tell him of his mistakes, but he had no opinion of those who always agreed with him or

[1] See the " Informatione delle qualità di Pio V." in *Anal. Bolland.*, XXXIII., 192. When the secretary of State, Bonelli, was ill, an *Avviso di Roma of July 12, 1570, reports with what calm Pius V. bore adversities. Urb. 1041, p. 304, Vatican Library.

[2] See the Informatione, etc., *loc. cit.* 193 ; TIEPOLO, 175 *seq.* ; SORIANO, 200 ; CATENA, 28 *seq.* *" Il papa " Serristori reports to Florence on February 7, 1567, " è di natura molto sensitiva et in un' tratto si accende et viene in collera, poi facilmente, come vede V.E., si lascia piegare de un poco di humiltà et submissione." (State Archives, Florence, Medic. 3287, p. 40). *Cf.* also the *reports of C. Luzzara of May 15, and June 12, 1566, Gonzaga Archives, Mantua, the *report of Arco of May 18, 1566, and *that of Strozzi of September 28, 1566, State Archives, Vienna.

[3] SORIANO, 201. CATENA, 31.

flattered him ;[1] he often gave proof that he was always ready
to hear the truth, even when it was bitter.[2]   He was exceedingly condescending to the poor and those of low estate, and
plainly showed his disappointment when he was unable to
grant any request.   His charity towards the needy, and
his generosity to those who served him well, were very great,
indeed too great in the opinion of many.[3]

Pius V. did not allow himself to be led away by first impressions, but once he had formed a definite opinion on any
subject, it was almost impossible to shake him.   He was
quicker to form a bad opinion of anyone than a good one,
especially in the case of people he did not know well.[4]   Neither
worldly considerations nor violent threats could move him
from what he thought to be right.   He once said that he
would rather retire into privacy at the Lateran with two
chaplains than allow anything he considered wrong.   The
Venetian diplomatist, Soriano, was of opinion that it was
necessary to know such a Pope in order to understand how it
was possible for a man who had sprung from such lowly circumstances to feel so sure that he could forego all human
considerations.[5]

[1] For example, Arco, on August 31, 1566, *reports that when,
sometimes, in a question of a dispensation, an appeal was made
to the opinions of theologians, Pius V. replied " che molti theologi
et canonisti erano adulatori de pontefici." (State Archives,
Vienna).   Cf. also CIACONIUS, III., 1014.   On November 25, 1567,
B. Pia *reports that the Pope paid no attention to *dottori* (jurists)
and that he governed his actions by his *massime theologiche*
(Gonzaga Archives, Mantua). See also SANTORI, Autobiografia, XII., 340.

[2] See the episode related by Cusano in his *letter of April 6,
1566.   State Archives, Vienna.

[3] See the " Informatione delle qualità," etc., 193 *seq.* Cf.
Tiepolo in MUTINELLI, I., 58.

[4] See *ibid.*

[5] SORIANO, 202.   Cf. POLANCI Epist. in *Anal. Bolland.*, VII.,
57 ; CATENA, 32.   It is certain that several of the diplomatists
were led by Pius V.'s great conscientiousness to think that he
was very timid : thus *Khevonhüller on March 30, 1566, and

Even those who judged merely in the light of worldly considerations paid tribute to the merits of Pius V.   The ambassadors, who were bound to look at everything from a prejudiced point of view, and always to keep before their eyes the frequently excessive demands of their masters, mention as weaknesses in the Pope his readiness to believe bad tidings, his great scrupulosity, which they attribute to his sensitive conscience, the obstinacy with which he clung to any idea which he had formed, and especially his tendency to distrust people.[1] Requesens is right in saying that the bitter experience which Pius V. had had of the selfishness of certain Cardinals was the reason why he did not dare to trust more than a few people.[2] But above all the ambassadors lament the Pope's lack of experience in political matters.

It is true that Pius V. had had as little to do with politics hitherto as with the affairs of the court, and he was certainly at a disadvantage in both respects, and that not only from his want of knowledge of men and of the world, but also

---

*Cusano on February 2, in the same year.   Arco's view was more correct ; on September 7, 1566, he expressed the opinion that the Pope would make further mistakes " perchè è troppo fermo nelle sue opinioni et mostra di curare poco delli principi."   State Archives, Vienna.   On April 28, 1567, Vincenzo Matuliani wrote : *" La natura di questo principe è di non voler fare cosa a requisitione di persona che viva se non quello che viene dalla sua volontà governata con molta prudenza e retta da una mente santissima."   State Archives, Bologna.

[1] See TIEPOLO, 175 ; cf. SORIANO, 202. On May 16, 1566, Serristori complains : *" Non si fida di huomo del mondo et quello che è peggio fuori di queste cose della religione S.S^tà non intende punto delle cose del mondo et manco di quelle della corte ; non si fida d'huomo che viva, non ha ministri che intendino, dall' che le cose di qua vanno a mal camino."   (State Archives, Florence, Medic. 3592). *" Il papa non si fida d'alcuno " reports Khevenhüller March 30, 1566, State Archives, Vienna.

[2] Corresp. dipl., I., 161.

because he had not had the necessary experience.[1]   The consciousness that God had called him to the supreme dignity, and that he was ignorant of these less important matters, often led him to act, even in worldly affairs, with a determination that was quite wanting in consideration for others, and which refused to listen to any arguments suggested by human prudence.   Starting from this idealistic standpoint, and looking at everything merely from the supernatural point of view, it was natural to him to pay too little attention to the actual conditions with which he was faced.

Pius V. was no diplomatist, nor did he profess to be one. He was as sharply marked off from his predecessor, Pius IV., by his complete indifference to political considerations as he was by the strictness of his own life.   It has rarely happened in a Pope that the sovereign has been so subordinated to the priest, as was the case with this son of St. Dominic, who now sat on the throne of St. Peter.   One thing alone was dear to his heart, the salvation of souls ; to this he devoted all his energies, and he estimated the value of every institution and every act in accordance with its usefulness for that purpose.

The reputation for ruthless severity which attached to Pius V. as a former Grand Inquisitor, roused the fear of the Romans during the days that followed his election, lest they should be entering upon a pontificate like that of Paul IV.   The Pope, who fully realized this feeling with regard to himself, sought to calm men's minds by declaring that he knew very well that he had to deal with men and not with angels.[2]   The generosity which the Pope displayed during the first days of

---

[1] With the " Informatione," etc., loc. cit., 194, cf. especially TIEPOLO, 179 and SORIANO, 202.   See also Corresp. de Granvelle, éd. POULLET, I. 519, 595 ; Corresp. dipl., I., 161, and the *letter of Serristori of May 16, 1566, quoted supra p. 65, n. 1.

[2] See the *report of Arco of January 12, 1566, State Archives, Vienna, the *Avviso di Roma of January 12, 1566, Vatican Library (see App. n. 3), and CATENA, 24.   Cf. also the *letter of Babbi of January 8, 1566, State Archives, Florence.   P. PASCHINI, Note per la biografia del card. G. Sirleto. Naples, 1918, 56 seq.

his reign also helped to allay these fears. The conclavists and auditors of the Rota received gifts of money, as did the poorer Cardinals, among whom 20,000 scudi were distributed. Hannibal von Hohenems, to whom Pius IV. had promised 100,000 scudi before he died, received at least half that sum, and was confirmed in the offices which he had held.[1]

If, in spite of all this, the fears of the Romans were not quite allayed, the reason lay in the fact that, side by side with these proofs of his benevolence, Pius V. also displayed great severity. He refused all the petitions presented for his signature after his election;[2] the Conservatori were not allowed to kiss his foot, because, during the vacancy they had taken from Paulus Manutius the house which contained his printing press. The fact that, at the distribution of offices, the friends of Paul IV., and not those of Pius IV., were selected, also pointed to increased severity.[3]

The allocution which the Pope addressed to the Cardinals at the first General Congregation on January 12th, 1566, was full of significance ; he said that he did not intend to treat them as his servants, but as his brethren, remarking at the same time that the evil life led by many ecclesiastics had played no small part in the beginning and spread of heresy. He exhorted them to reform themselves and their households ; if they would do that he would repay them by his favour and his confidence. He declared that it was his intention to carry

[1] *Cf.* the *report of Cico Aldrovandi of January 9, 1566 (liberalità degna di principe), State Archives, Bologna ; the *letter of Serristori of January 11, 1566, State Archives, Florence, and the *report of Arco of January 12, 1566, State Archives, Vienna. The *confirmation of the gift to Hannibal von Hohenems, of January 11, 1566, in the Archives of the Museum at Bregenz, n. 109.

[2] *" Electus noluit signare ullam supplicationem." C. FIRMANUS, Diarium, in Miscell., Arm. XII., 31, p. 36, Papal Secret Archives.

[3] See the two *reports of Arco of January 12, 1566 (in Latin and Italian), State Archives, Vienna. For the question at issue between the Romans and P. Manutius see RODOCANACHI, Capitole, 118 *seq.* ; *cf. Mél. d'archéol.*, III., 269 *seq.*

out the decrees of the Council to the letter, and especially
the duty of residence.   Turning to the Cardinals who were
the Protectors of the various countries, the Pope said that they
must seek for nothing for themselves or their relatives, but
must be willing to meet the wishes of the princes in so far as
they did not run counter to the Council and the work of
reform.   His own policy would be directed to nothing but
the maintenance of peace among Christian princes, the
extirpation as far as possible of heresy, and the obtaining
of help against the Turks.   Pius V. then listened patiently
to the petitions of all the Cardinals, and granted them as far
as possible, though he observed that it was not in keeping
with the dignity of Cardinals that they should approach the
Pope ten at a time ; they should seek an audience singly, and
he would willingly receive them at any hour.   The poorer
Cardinals must come to him for help without any hesitation.[1]

From the first the new Pope gave signal proof of his independence in spiritual matters.   His former brethren in religion,
who made frequent appearances at the Vatican, were informed
that they must remain in their own convents ; if his Holiness
had need of them, he would send for them.[2]   Pius V. showed
in like manner that he intended to be free from the influence
of the Theatines and the Jesuits.[3]   He told the Imperial
ambassador, Arco, that he would gladly give help to Maximilian II. against the Turks, but that the Emperor must spare
him any requests for concessions to the apostates, such as
he had made to Pius IV.   The Pope definitely refused the
request of the ambassador that he would confer the red hat

[1] With the report in Legaz. di Serristori 420, *cf.* the * letter
of C. Aldrovandi of January 12, 1566 (State Archives, Bologna),
also *report of Arco of January 12, 1566, and that of G. Cusano of
January 19, 1566 (State Archives, Vienna).   LADERCHI (1566, n.
28), wrongly describes this meeting as a *consistorium* ; the wrong
date given by him (January 11) is taken from the *Diarium of
Firmanus (*loc. cit.*) p. 39b, Papal Secret Archives).

[2] See the two reports of *Arco of January 12, 1566, *loc. cit.*

[3] See in App. n. 3 the *Avviso di Roma of January 12, 1566,
Vatican Library.

on Diego Lasso at the first consistory, saying that his predecessor had already increased the number of the Sacred College overmuch, and had thereby lowered its dignity ; he added that he was not thinking of making any new Cardinals.[1]

When he heard that Paulus Manutius had received back his house, Pius V. at once extended his favour to the Conservatori, and promised that he would not burden the people with extraordinary taxation, since he himself could manage with very little, when a piece of bread and two eggs were enough for him. On January 12th, 1566, the Pope's intention of naming three Cardinals to attend to political affairs was announced, for he wished to devote himself as far as possible to spiritual matters. From motives of economy, and because he was convinced that the Popes would always be protected by the hand of God, he gave orders for the disbanding of the light cavalry, with the exception of two companies ; his arms, he said, were the Holy Scriptures, and his defenders the sons of St. Dominic.[2] He would have liked to have done without any troops at all.[3]

Popular opinion, at first so unfavourable, soon changed completely. At a public meeting of the senate, it was resolved that all the civil officials should receive festal robes for the Coronation, which was fixed for the feast of St. Antony, the Pope's sixty-second birthday. In the procession on this occasion, from which the Spanish ambassador and Marcantonio Colonna were absent on account of the dispute about precedence, the Caporioni carried the Pope to the crypt of the

[1] See the two *reports of Arco of January 12, 1566, loc. cit.

[2] See the *letter of Cusano of January 19, 1566 (State Archives, Vienna), cf. *Avviso di Roma of January 19, 1566, Urb. 1040, p. 166, Vatican Library. The complete disbanding of the light cavalry, however, had to be suspended on account of the disturbances at Ascoli and the Turkish peril (*report of Cusano of January 26, 1566, State Archives, Vienna) ; cf. the *Avviso di Roma of February 2, 1566, Urb. 1040, p. 173, Vatican Library (see infra p. 103, n. 1).

[3] See the *letter of Arco of January 22, 1566, State Archives, Vienna.

Prince of the Apostles.   The coronation was performed by
Cardinals Rovere and del Monte in front of St. Peter's, upon
a tribune in full view of the great crowds of people, and which
had been adorned with allegorical pictures.   Filled with
enthusiasm, the people cried : " Viva Pio V. ! "   The ceremony was so long that night was falling when the Cardinals
went to the coronation banquet, which had been made ready
in the apartments of Innocent VIII.   The banquet was on a
splendid scale, but not unduly lavish ; indeed the service
and arrangements were somewhat deficient considering the
number of the guests.   The Pope himself ate as little as if he
had been in the refectory of his own convent.   " God grant,"
so runs a report from Rome, " that he may be preserved to
us, because so far he has shown himself to be a true Vicar
of Christ."[1]

At the coronation of Pius IV., several persons had been
crushed to death in the crowds ; the new Pope, therefore,
did not have money scattered among the people, but sent
instead large alms to the poor and the religious houses.   His
first act after his coronation, and one which was in itself a
sign of his strict views, was to give orders for the dismissal
from the Vatican of Doctor Buccia, the court jester of Pius
IV.[2]   In 1567 the custom of celebrating the anniversary of
the coronation by a state banquet was abolished, and the
money which would have been spent was distributed to the
poor.[3]

" The Pope," thus begins an account of the solemn ceremony

[1] *Avviso di Roma of January 19, 1566, Urb. 1040, p. 166b-167,
Vatican Library, and C. FIRMANUS, *Diarium, in Miscell., Arm.
XII., 31, p. 40b seq., Papal Secret Archives, Cf. App. n. 4.

[2] See the *report of Cusano of January 19, 1566, State Archives,
Vienna.   According to the *Avviso di Roma of January 19, 1566
(Urb. 1040, p. 166, Vatican Library), Buccia was a schiavone.
For his life see CONSTANT, Rapport, 222 seq.   Naturally Pius V.
did not wish to have anything to do with actors ; see Giorn. d.
lett. Ital., LXIII., 298 seq.

[3] *Avviso di Roma of January 18, 1567, Urb. 1040, p. 350,
Vatican Library,.   Cf. CANCELLIERI, Possessi, 110.

of taking possession of the Lateran, which took place on January 27th, 1566, " perseveres in his holy life, and shows himself a true Vicar of Christ. The Romans love him as a father. On his way to the Lateran they hailed him with such manifestations of joy as have not been seen for ten pontificates." The news went round that as he was leaving his apartments he had patiently stopped to listen to a man who was seeking justice, saying that such simplicity delighted him. When, during the procession, he caught sight of his old school-fellow, Francesco Bastone, who had come from Alessandria, Pius V. called him to his side, and in grateful memory of the help which his father had once given him, appointed him Keeper of the Castle of St. Angelo. This act showed all Rome from what a lowly family the Pope had come. It is a wonderful thing, wrote a diplomatic agent of the Emperor, that this man, who once tended the flocks, should now have become the chief shepherd of Christendom."[1]

Four days before the taking possession of the Lateran, a consistory had been held, at which the Pope announced certain reforms for the clergy and people of Rome. A special commission of Cardinals was appointed for the reform of the secular clergy ; this was composed of Borromeo, Savelli, Alciati and Sirleto, and they were to inquire into the learning, life and morals of all priests. On this occasion the Pope exhorted the Cardinals to watch carefully over their households, and told them that he had abolished the right of sanctuary, since justice must be able to lay its hand upon the guilty everywhere, even in the Apostolic Palace. The bishops were reminded of the duty of residence, from which only those were to be exempt who, like the Datary, were directly employed

[1] See in App. n. 5 the *letter of Cusano of February 2, 1566, State Archives, Vienna. Cf. the *Avviso di Roma of February 2, 1566, Urb. 1040, p. 172, Vatican Library ; Firmanus in CANCELLIERI, III, seq. ; RODOCANCHI, St. Ange, 170, and Capitole, 113 ; BRUZZONE in Riv. di Alessandria, XIV. (1905), 378 seq., where there are other instances of favours conferred by Pius V. on his compatriots.

at the Papal court.[1] The Pope had reformed the Dataria immediately after his election.[2] At the beginning of February he also undertook the reform of the Signatura, the personnel of which was substantially reduced.[3] Since no record could be found of many of the expenses of Pius IV., the late Pope's treasurer, Minale,[4] was called to account, and being found guilty, was condemned to the galleys for life.[5] Under pain of excommunication, a *motu proprio* demanded from all the Cardinals a list of the revenues and benefices which they had received from Pius IV., since, so the new Pope declared, he did not wish to help rich Cardinals.[6]

The zeal with which Pius V. devoted himself to the sittings of the congregations, especially that of the Inquisition, and to giving audiences, knew no bounds.[7] Every Sunday and Thursday he gave public audiences, when the poor people were given precedence. The patience which the Pope showed in listening to their complaints restrained the officials from any act of injustice, while it inspired the Romans with enthusiasm. It is said that on these audience days the Pope would listen to the people who presented themselves, without leaving his

[1] See the *report of Arco of January 16, 1566, and *that of Cusano of January 26, 1566, both in State Archives, Vienna.

[2] See in App. n. 3 the *Avviso di Roma of January 12, 1566, Vatican Library.

[3] See the *letters of Cusano of February 2 and 16, 1566, State Archives, Vienna.

[4] See the *report of Cusano, March 16, 1566, State Archives, Vienna.

[5] See the *Avvisi di Roma of September 27, 1567. June 19 and Sept. 25, 1568, Urb. 1040, p. 442, 527, 584, Vatican Library, and the *report of Arco of November 29, 1567, State Archives, Vienna. Minale died in prison at Ostia ; see *Avviso di Roma of July 13, 1569, Urb. 1041, p. 109, Vatican Library.

[6] See the *reports of Arco and Cusano of February 16, 1566, State Archives, Vienna.

[7] Concerning these audiences Arco wrote on February 23, 1566, that Pius V. granted them *" omni studio omnique conatu etiam supra vires " State Archives, Vienna.

throne, for ten hours at a time.[1]   He earnestly impressed upon
the Conservatori the duty of seeing to a regular supply of
provisions, and promised them every assistance in this respect,
saying that if it were necessary he was ready to give them
an audience at any time.   He showed special marks of
honour to the Cardinals, and when they came for an audience
he made them remain covered, and begged them to be
seated, which had not been customary in the time of Pius
IV.[2]

At first the Cardinal who had the greatest influence was
Alessandro Farnese, who had effected the election of Pius V.,
and was specially experienced in political affairs.   As it was
precisely in this respect that Pius V. lacked knowledge, he was
all the more ready at the beginning of his pontificate to avail
himself of that of Farnese ; it was thought that the latter
would in this way pave the way for himself to the supreme
dignity.[3]

Besides Farnese, Pius V. entrusted the direction of political
matters to Cardinals Vitelli, Rebiba and Reumano, the
administration of justice to Capizuchi, Niccolini and Gambara,
and matters connected with benefices to Scotti, Rebiba and
Reumano.   Archbishop Marcantonio Maffei was appointed
Datary.[4]   Of those who obtained positions of influence and

[1] *Cf.* the *letter of Cusano of January 26, 1566, State Archives,
Vienna, and the *Avviso di Roma of February 24, 1566, Urb.
1040, p. 183b, Vatican Library.   See also CATENA, 28.

[2] See the *report of Cusano of January 26, 1566, State Archives,
Vienna (*infra*, p. 152).

[3] The Pope, *wrote Serristori on January 8, 1566, hands over
all memorials to Cardinal Farnese " essendo quello che adesso
governa tutto " (State Archives, Florence, Medic. 3591).   Farnese,
*reports Cusano on January 26, 1566, has a say in all important
matters *" e in vero S.S.Ill^me è quella che dà la norma a tutti
come meglio instrutta delle cose di governo di stati ch'ogno'altro
cardinale et fino a qui tutto si è fatto con sua consulta." (State
Archives, Vienna).   *Cf.* Legaz. di Serristori, 421.

[4] See the *Italian report of Arco of January 12, 1566, State
Archives Vienna.

authority, the majority were men belonging to the school of Paul IV.[1]

At first Pius V. was unwilling to have a Cardinal nephew to assist him. In the place of Tolomeo Galli, who had been very influential during the last year of Pius IV., he appointed as *segretario intimo* his former secretary, Girolamo Rusticucci,[2] whom he knew and valued as a man of few words, a retiring disposition, and entirely devoted to him.[3] He entrusted the direction of his correspondence, and the carrying out of his orders, which was equivalent to making him Secretary of State, to a man of the strict school of Carafa, Cardinal Reumano,[4] who occupied Borromeo's apartments in the Borgia Tower,[5] but the Pope retained the real control of the government in his own hands. His consciousness of his great

---

[1] *" Et in questi principii tutte le creature di Paolo IV. pretendono assai et si vede chiaramente che N.S^re le abbraccia." Caligari to Commendone from Rome, January 9, 1566, in Lett, di princ., XXIII., p. 73b, Papal Secret Archives. The majordomo, B. Cirillo, was also a " creatura di Paolo IV " ; see *report of Serristori of January 8, 1566, State Archives, Florence, Medic.3591.

[2] See TÖRNE, Pt. Gallio, 48 *seq.* With Rusticucci were associated the two secretaries of briefs, Cesare Glorierio and Antonio Fioribello, as well as the secretary for cyphers, Trifone Bencio. Fioribello retired in October 1568, and, since Giulio Poggiani had died on November 5,1566, was succeeded by Tommaso Aldobrandini (November 30, 1566). *Cf. Mitteil. des österr. Instituts*, XIV., 562, 585 *seq.* ; RICHARD in *Rev. d'hist. ecclés.*, XI., 521 *seq.* ; MEISTER, Geheimschrift, 51. For the collection of the briefs of Pius V. and the Archives for Briefs see App. n. 68. Pius V. was the first to introduce a fixed salary for nuncios ; see BIAUDET, 27, 75.

[3] See " Informatione delle qualità," *loc. cit.* 198. The influence of Rusticucci steadily increased. An *Avviso di Roma of November 6, 1568, speaks of him as ". più favorito che mai " (State Archives, Vienna). Later on he was replaced by Bonelli as Secretary of State (*cf.* PALANDRI, 130, n. 2) ; see Vol. XVIII. of this work.

[4] See the report of Serristori of January 19, 1566, in TÖRNE, 48 ; *cf.* Corresp. dipl., I., 123. For Reumano *cf.* Vol. XV. of this work, p. 23.

[5] See the *letter of Caligari to Commendone, January 22, 1566, in Lett. di princ,. XXIII., p. 79. Papal Secret Archives.

position, and of the fact that he had never had any ulterior ends, gave Pius V. a great freedom of action, which from time to time showed itself in altogether unexpected decisions. And since this only came to be understood by degrees,[1] the diplomatists at first tried to guess which of the Cardinals would attain to the greatest influence.[2] For their part the Cardinals were filled with the deepest jealousy of Reumano.

Pius V. was accustomed to give his confidence only to those who sought nothing for themselves.[3] He very soon discovered that the ambitious Farnese thought more of his own interests than of those of the Church,[4] and his opinion of the disinterestedness of Vitelli, whom he still trusted at the beginning of February,[5] was also soon destroyed, and therefore Pius V.

---

[1] From a *report of Serristori of February 7, 1567, (State Archives, Florence, Medic. 3287, p. 40), it is clear with what dislike the Cardinals viewed the independence of Pius V. On June 19, 1568, Cusano *reports that the Cardinals were complaining of the strictness of the Pope ; on July 10 he *announces that the Pope decides all important matters himself, and that only matters of small importance are raised in the consistory (State Archives, Vienna). In an *Avviso di Roma of January 4, 1570, we read : *" Le resolutioni così repentine del Papa fanno suspettare tutta la corte che si habbia da fare una promotione all'improviso senza saputa d'alcuno." Urb. 1041, p. 204b. Ibid. an *Avviso di Roma of May 13, 1570 : *" L'impenetrabil mente del Papa " causes the most divergent rmours in the court concerning a nomination of Cardinals. Vatican Library.

[2] When Cardinal Scotti was assigned apartments in the Vatican, Cusano (*letter of March 2, 1566, State Archives, Vienna) was of opinion that he would attain to the most influential position. The Florentines were afraid of the influence of Farnese, and were working against him ; see Legaz. di Serristori, 421, 423 seq. HILLIGER, 151.

[3] See the *letter of Caligari to Commendone of February 2, 1566, in Lett. di princ., XXIII., n. 88, Papal Secret Archives.

[4] *" S'intende che Farnese s'andava apparechiando la via al papato il che venuto alle orechie del Papa ha detto che fa male et che ce lo farà intendere." Arco on February 16, 1566, State Archives, Vienna.

[5] See the *letter of Caligari mentioned in n. 3.

found himself constrained to call to his assistance one of his relatives, in whom he thought that he could put absolute confidence. To have done this must have cost him a considerable effort, for he hated nothing so much as any kind of nepotism. When, during the first days of his reign, he was reminded that he ought to promote his relatives, he had replied : " God has called me to be what I am, in order that I may serve the Church, and not that the Church might serve me."[1] He sent word to one of his relations, who had come to Rome without his knowledge at the end of January, that he must go away at once.[2] Two sons of Domenica Bonelli, the daughter of the Pope's sister, Gardina Bonelli, were inmates of the Germanicum, and studying under the Jesuits ;[3] Pius V. sent them word through the rector that they were to go on with their studies, and that he would take care of them if they remained hidden and humble, but that they must not expect great things from him.[4]

While he was still a Cardinal, Pius V. had sent yet a third

[1] *Avviso di Roma of January 19, 1566, Urb. 1040, p. 166, Vatican Library. Cf. Caraccia in LADERCHI, 1566, n. 34.

[2] See *Avviso di Roma of January ,1566, Urb. 1040, p. 170b, Vatican Library, and the *letter of Caligari of January 26, 1566, loc. cit., Papal Secret Archives.

[3] Gardina married first Marcantonio Manlio, and secondly Bartolomeo Gallina. She died in 1548. Cf. BRUZZONE in Riv. di Alessandria, X., 2 (1901), 27. See also *Diversi appunti e notizie d. famiglia Bonelli, in the Bonelli Archives in the Villa Le Selve near Signa (Tuscany). In these archives, of which Prof. Dengel was the first to make use, the acta from the earlier Bonelli archives in Rome are not to be found, as was to have been expected from the date of Laderchi and Garampi. [In the Barberini Library (now in the Vatican Library), not only the codices 3615 and 3638 (see SERRANO, Corresp. dipl. I., XXIX., but also 3613, 3614, 3635, 3636, 3637, come from the Archives of Cardinal Michele Bonelli, and the numbers by which LADERCHI quotes them are still visible, though very imperfectly.]

[4] See *Avviso di Roma of February 24, 1566, Urb. 1040, p. 185b, Vatican Library. Cf. POLANCI Epist., in Anal. Bolland., VII., 61 ; STEINHUBER, I[2], 62.

son of Domenica Bonelli, named Antonio, to study at the
Germanicum. This man had followed in his uncle's footsteps,
and had entered the Dominican order, taking the name of
Michele. At the time of the Pope's election this great-nephew,
who was then twenty-five years of age, was studying at
Perugia. At the very commencement of the pontificate it
was said in Rome that Michele Bonelli would be made a
Cardinal,[1] and indeed, on March 6th, 1566, he was received
into the Sacred College.[2] The Pope had only allowed himself
to be persuaded to take this step at the urgent request of all
the Cardinals and the Spanish ambassador, who pointed out
to him the necessity of the appointment of a trustworthy
confidant for the carrying out of his many duties.[3]

Cardinal Alessandrino, as Bonelli was called, remained,

[1] *Avviso di Roma of January 12, 1566, Vatican Library. See
App. n. 3. In his *report of February 27, 1566, C. Aldrovandi
describes Michele Bonelli as " giovane di buoni costumi." State
Archives, Bologna.

[2] At first Bonelli stayed for some days in secret in the Dominican
convent at the Minerva ; he presented himself at the Vatican for
the first time on March 2 ; see the *letter of Cusano of March 2,
1566, State Archives, Vienna, and the *Avviso di Roma of March
2, 1566, Urb. 1040, p. 187b, Vatican Library. Ibid. 185b, an
*Avviso di Roma of February 24, 1566, according to which the
envoy from Alessandria asked for the promotion of the Pope's
nephew. The college of jurists at Alessandria also sent a special
mission ; see Riv. d'Alessandria, XV., 483.

[3] For the nomination of Michele Bonelli on March 6, 1566, cf.,
besides Legaz. di Serristori, 424, and Tiepolo in TÖRNE, 241 seq.,
the *reports of Babbi of March 5 and 7, 1566 (State Archives,
Florence), the P.S. to the *report of Arco of March 5, with the
account of the consistory of March 6, 1566 (State Archives, Vienna),
and the report of F. Borgia to the Jesuit rector at Genoa on
March 8, 1566, in SUAU, II., 129 seq. See further Corresp. de
Granvelle éd. POULLET, II., 154 ; CIACONIUS, III., 1029 seq. ;
LITTA, 80 ; MAZZUCHELLI, II., 3, 1593 ; GULIK-EUBEL, 47 ;
CARDELLA, V., 110 seq. For the tomb of Bonelli see BERTHIER,
Minerve, 259 seq. His portrait by Scipione Pulzone in Cosmos
illustr., 1904, 25.

by the Pope's desire, a member of the Dominican order ; he was given as his titular church, that of the Order, S. Maria sopra Minerva, with apartments in the Vatican,[1] where he was very soon initiated into official business.[2] It was his duty to direct the affairs of the Pontifical States,[3] but Cardinals Reumano and Farnese were associated with him as his advisers in matters concerning the foreign princes, though in such a way that they were to work under his orders.[4]

Reumano fell ill at the end of April, and, to the Pope's great sorrow, he died on the 28th of that month,[5] so that the sole charge of affairs fell upon the shoulders of Bonelli, all the more so as since March, Farnese and Vitelli had gradually fallen into the background.[6]

[1] The " Stanze nella galeria di Belvedere " reports an *Avviso di Roma of March 9, 1566, which also states " fra pochi dì farà facende come nepote." (Urb. 1040, p. 191, Vatican Library). Afterwards Alessandrino moved to the apartments of Borromeo ; see the *report of Arco of May 5, 1566. State Archives, Vienna.

[2] Alessandrino, *reports Arco on March 16, 1566, has begun to attend the Consulta and the congregations ; he signs many letters ; it is thought that he will shortly have the government in his hands ; he has, however, only received 1000 scudi as salary (State Archives, Vienna). Cf. Serristori in Törne, 50, *Avviso di Roma of March 16 and 23, 1566, Urb. 1040, p. 194b, 197 (Vatican Library), and the *report of Arco of March 23, 1566, which makes mention of a brief giving the nephew power to take charge of the affairs of the Papal States. Alessandrino, *says Cusano on March 30, 1566, takes part in everything, although he has not got the same authority as has previously been enjoyed by the Pope's nephews. State Archives, Vienna.

[3] See the *report of Arco of March 23, 1566. State Archives, Vienna.

[4] See the postscript to the *report of Francis von Thurm, dated Venice, April 6, 1566 (State Archives, Vienna), and the *Avviso di Roma of April 6, 1566, Urb. 1040, p. 203, Vatican Library.

[5] With Corresp. dipl., I., 217n. cf. the *report of Cusano of May 4, 1566, State Archives, Vienna.

[6] *" Farnese e Vitelli hanno perduto in fatto l'autorità " writes Serristori on April 1, 1566, State Archives, Florence, Medic. 3592. On March 27, 1566, C. Luzzara reports : *" Il card. Alessandrino

Vitelli had become troublesome to the Pope because he wished to interfere in everything, and also because he was too intimate with Cardinal Bonelli.[1] He and Farnese were both of them too different in character from the Pope ever to be trusted advisers ; an example of the great divergence of their points of view may here be given.

At the beginning of his pontificate Pius V. understood in such a literal sense the protection which Our Lord had promised to his Vicar on earth, that he would have liked to have done away with all human means of defence. When Vitelli and Farnese pointed out to him that a fortress of such importance to the safety of the Papal States as Anagni ought to be put into a better state of repair, the Pope replied that the Church had need of neither cannon nor soldiers. Her arms were prayer and fasting, tears, and the Holy Scriptures, and he would prefer to follow in the footsteps of those Popes who had defended the dignity of the Holy See by spiritual arms. Moreover, there was no reason to fear that the Spaniards would seize Anagni, since Philip II. was allied to both the Emperor and France, and all three would defend

comincia ad havere tutte le facende o poco manco." (Gonzaga Archives, Mantua). *Cf.* as to this the already quoted *report of Serristori, of April 1, 1566. *" Il card. Alessandrino fa hora le facende come fanno li nepoti de Papi et è in capite et il card. Reumanio sta mal alla morte." (Avviso di Roma of April 27, 1566, Urb. 1040, p. 218b, Vatican Library). Bonelli received a monthly stipend of 100 ducats (see *ibid.* p. 235b.). Later on his revenues were greatly increased, so that he was able to help his brothers, towards whom the Pope showed himself very reserved (see TIEPOLO, 177). On Decemb r 12, 1568, Bonelli became camerlengo, but resigned the office on May 10, 1570, in favour of L. Cornaro for 70,000 scudi, which Pius V. seized for the Turkish war ; the nephew was compensated with the abbey of S. Michele at Chiusi, and the priorate of the Knights of Malta. See CARDELLA, V., 111 ; *cf.* GARAMPI, 269.

[1] Thus *reports Cusano on March 16, 1566, State Archives, Vienna. When, a year later, Vitelli's schemes to obtain the tiara for Este were discovered, Vitelli fell into complete disgrace ; see the *report of Arco of May 3 and June 7, 1567, *ibid.*

the rights of the Apostolic See. Neither would Pius V. hear of keeping up the artillery, leaving this matter to the care of the citizens of Anagni. After this the Cardinals, as Cusano wrote, were convinced that if the Pope lived a long time he would get rid of all his troops, and would even do away with the Swiss Guard.[1]

Pius V. was but ill-satisfied with the way in which the Commission of State, which was at first composed of Farnese, Reumano, Rebiba and Vitelli, carried out its duties, and he added Granvelle to their number, which did not at all please the other four. Vitelli at once resigned, and Farnese thought of doing likewise ; it was generally thought that he would leave Rome so as to avoid an open quarrel.[2]

The importance of Bonelli's position was externally manifested by the fact that in May, 1566, he took possession of the apartments in the Borgia Tower vacated by the death of Reumano, and which were usually occupied by the Cardinal nephew.[3] Cardinal Bonelli familiarized himself with his duties more quickly and far better than most people had expected.[4] He was not, however, a personality of any great weight, for which reason the Pope did not allow him to do anything of importance without his consent.[5] The same thing held good throughout the pontificate. The influence of the Cardinals tended to grow less as Pius V. realized that many of them were dependent upon the princes, and were

---

[1] *Report of Cusano of March 23, 1566, *ibid.* *Cf. supra* p. 69.

[2] *Reports of Cusano of March 30 and June 15, 1566, State Archives, Vienna. For the complete disgrace into which Vitelli fell, see HERRE, Papsttum, 152 *seq*.

[3] See the *report of Cusano of May 11, 1566. State Archives, Vienna.

[4] According to the *report of Cusano of March 2, 1566 (State Archives, Vienna), Pius was in doubt, even then, whether Bonelli was fit for the duties of Secretary of State. *Cf.* TÖRNE, 50.

[5] See TIEPOLO, 175–176 ; *cf.* Corresp. dipl., IV., 377. According to the *report of Strozzi of November 15, 1566, Bonelli said in complaint : " gli altri [nipoti] havevano autorità dal Papa et io non n'ho alcuna." State Archives, Vienna.

working for their own selfish ends ; his want of confidence in them became so great that he often acted in direct contradiction to their advice.[1]

In spite of his spirit of independence,[2] Pius V. did not altogether despise good advice, though he only made much account of those who belonged to the strict school, such as Scotti, Rebiba, Sirleto, Capizuchi, Mula, Dolera, Simonetta, Alciati,[3] and Commendone, who for a time held the first place among the Pope's confidants.[4] Granvelle, too, counted for a good deal from the first.[5] Later on Cardinal Chiesa took an important share with Bonelli in the work of administration.[6] The advice of Morone was especially sought

[1] See Tiepolo in MUTINELLI, I., 87.

[2] *" Vuol intendere tutte le cose Lei," wrote Serristori on April 1, 1566. State Archives, Florence, Medic. 3592.

[3] These had apartments in the Vatican ; see *Nota di tutte le stantie de Palazzo et chi l'habita questo dì 3 de Marzo, 1566, Varia Polit., LXXIX., 218 seq., Papal Secret Archives. A *letter from Rome of September 28, 1566, names Morone, Dolera, Rebiba, Gambara and Bonelli as the Cardinals of the greatest influence (State Archives, Vienna). Cf. the *letter of Strozzi of October 5, 1566, concerning Pius V.'s leaning to Sirleto (ibid). The influence of Rebiba is again mentioned in May, 1570 ; see VOINOVICH, 554.

[4] *" Commendone è hoggi il primo cardinale della corte et quello a cui il Papa crede più che ad alcun altro " says B. Pia in a *letter from Rome on February 7, 1567,Gonzaga Archives,Mantua. Cf. SCHWARZ, Briefwechsel, 48, and the *report of Strozzi of February 8, 1567 (" Ha [il Papa] per molto favorito il card. Commendone," and often calls for his advice), State Archives, Vienna. After the nomination of Chiesa as Cardinal *Cusano states on May 1, 1568, that Commendone was " caduto assai del favor del Papa." Ibid.

[5] *" Il card. Granvella è stimato assai dal Papa et è chiamato a tutte le consulte per le cose di Germania." Arco, March 30, 1566, State Archives, Vienna.

[6] See *Avviso di Roma of April 3, 1568, Urb. 1040, p. 499b, Vatican Library.

in political affairs,[1] as well as in matters of reform, in the
carrying out of which Pius made use of such distinguished
men as Ormaneto and Giovanni Oliva.[2] For the conduct of
all political affairs which concerned the princes, he appointed
a congregation at the beginning of November, 1566, composed
of Cardinals Morone, Farnese, Mula, Granvelle and Commendone.[3] The Pope had also a high opinion of the Datary,
Maffei.

At the end of 1566 a well-informed correspondent gave it
as his opinion that anyone could get an introduction to the
Pope through his more intimate friends, but that to get
any important business transacted it was necessary to have
recourse to Cardinal Bonelli and the secretary, Rusticucci,
through whose hands all business passed.[4] Yet Pius V.
was not altogether dependent upon them ; in order to make
it quite clear that his nephew did not exercise any undue
influence over him, the Pope often found fault with him,

[1] The *Avviso di Roma of March 23, 1566, relates that the Pope
had kept Morone in Rome because he thought " haver bisogno
de pari suoi qua et lo stima et honora assai " (Urb. 1040, p. 197,
Vatican Library). In his *report of May 29, 1566 (Gonzaga
Archives, Mantua), C. Luzzara remarks how much weight Morone
had with the Pope. Zuñiga also, in his letter of December 29,
1570, witnesses to Morone's influence in political matters, Corresp.
dipl., IV., 156. Cf. also on this point the *Avviso di Roma of
July 7, 1571. State Archives, Naples, C. Farnes, 763.

[2] See the " Informatione," etc., in Anal. Bolland., XXXIII.,
188 seq., 194 seq.

[3] *" Creò una congregazione di 5 cardinali che attendano alle
cose con li principi che sone," etc. *Avviso di Roma of
November 9, 1566, Urb. 1040, p. 318b, Vatican Library.

[4] See " Informatione," etc., loc. cit. which brings out very fully
the distinction between the old and the new confidants of the
Pope, which continued to exist (see Mitteilungen des österr. Instit.,
XIV., 544), and their relative position. Rusticucci obtained the
rights of Roman citizenship (see LANCIANI, IV., 23) and even
though he accepted gifts, he managed to keep in favour with
Pius V. (see TIEPOLO, 175). For the majordomo of Pius V.,
Franc. de Reinoso, cf. Corresp. dipl., IV., li. seq.

and especially exhorted him to a strict and retired life. When he heard that the Cardinal often went out to the vigna, though in a perfectly innocent way, and in the company of ecclesiastics, he reproached him, and held up before him as an example his own conduct when he was a young man.[1] He himself selected the members of Bonelli's household, and limited their number, and he expressly forbade his nephew the use of silk attire and silver plate.[2] In a letter to Hosius on November 2nd, 1566, Francis Borgia relates how the Pope, when making a chance visit to Bonelli's apartments, noticed some silk hangings, and ordered their immediate removal. Later on he desired his nephew to live, not as a Cardinal but as a religious.[3] From the first the stipend allotted to Bonelli was very small, and when the Cardinal asked the Pope to allow him some of the *spoglie* from Spain, Pius V. was very angry, and his wrath was even greater when he learned that it was Cardinal Vitelli who had given him this advice ; the Pope then forbade his nephew to have anything whatever to do with the said Cardinal. The scene was such a violent one that Bonelli was made quite ill by it.[4]

[1] *" Havendo il Papa inteso che il card. Alessandrino andava troppo speso alle vigne et parendoli vita troppo licentiosa, gli ha commesso che non parta più di Palazzo et che piglia esempio della vita de S.Stà quando anco era giovane." (*Avviso di Roma of June 22, 1566, Urb. 1040, p. 245b, Vatican Library). *Cf.* the *report of Cusano of June 8, 1566, State Archives, Vienna, and the *letter of Caligari to Commendone of July 13, in Lett. di princ., XXIII., n. 12, Papal Secret Archives, and that of July 20, 1566, in *Anal. Bolland.*, XXXIII., 210, n. 1.

[2] See LADERCHI, 1566, n. 37 ; *cf.* the *report of Babbi, March 13, 1566, State Archives, Florence, and the *Avvisi di Roma of September 28 and October 26, 1566, Urb. 1040, p. 289b, 311b, Vatican Library.

[3] See SUAU, II., 130 ; *cf.* MUTINELLI, I., 50. See also *Avviso di Roma of May 3, 1567, Urb. 1040, p. 390, Vatican Library.

[3] See the *reports of Arco and Cusano of May 18, 1566, State Archives, Vienna. *Ibid.* a *report of Cusano of December 2, 1568, according to which Bonelli's revenues, which at first only amounted to 3,000 to 4,000 scudi, were considerably increased.

His other relations were treated with equal severity.
Bonelli's father, who came to pay a visit to this son of his
who had climbed so high, received orders to go back home
as quickly as possible.[1] The Cardinal's mother was only
able to go to him at night, for Pius V. would not hear of such
vanities as a public reception.[2] When Bonelli's sister married, she only received a small dowry, and in the same way
all his other relatives, whose hopes had run high, were completely disillusioned. The Pope saw to it that they had a
modest competence and could live decently ; he educated
their sons with the Jesuits, but he did no more for them,
and kept them at a distance as much as possible.[3]

Pius V. made an exception in the case of Paolo Ghislieri,
his brother's son, whom he redeemed from captivity with the
Turks, and first sent back to his own country, but afterwards,
since he was a capable soldier, summoned to Rome, and in
May, 1567, appointed Captain of the body-guard, and
Governor of the Borgo.[4] Paolo had already several times
drawn down upon himself the severe censure of the Pope for

[1] *Avviso di Roma of October 5, 1566, Urb. 1040, p. 295,
Vatican Library.

[2] *Avviso di Roma of October 4, 1567, Urb. 1040, p. 445, *ibid.*

[3] See in App. n. 3 the *Avviso di Roma of January 12, 1566,
ibid. ; the *report of Cusano of March 30, 1566, State Archives,
Vienna ; the *letter of C. Luzzara of August 3, 1566, Gonzaga
Archives, Mantua. *Cf.* TIEPOLO, 178 ; Corresp. de Philippe II.,
I., 596 ; POLANCI Epist. in *Anal Bolland.*, VII., 52 *seq. ;* MORONI,
XXX., 193 ; BRUZZONE, Bosco, 140 *seq.* and *Riv. di Alessandria*,
XIV. (1904), 382. Girolamo Ghislieri, who felt no vocation to
the ecclesiastical state, had to go back to his brother Michele
(*cf.* STEINHUBER, Collegium Germanicum, I., 62) and later on
became governor of the Borgo ; see *Avviso di Roma of November
6, 1566, Urb. 1040, p. 596, Vatican Library. For the subsequent
fortunes of the Pope's family, see the detailed accounts in *Riv. di
Alessandria*, X., 3 (1901), XIV. (1904), 396 *seq.*

[4] With Tiepolo in MUTINELLI, I. 54, *seq., cf.* the *Avvisi di Roma
of October 5 and 12, 1566, April 19 and May 3, 1567 (Vatican
Library) and the *letter of Arco of May 3, 1567, State Archives,
Vienna. *Cf.* also GABUTIUS, 230.

the pomp which he displayed,[1] but when Pius V. caught
him in a lie, he very nearly banished him in disgrace, and the
young man had the greatest difficulty in appeasing the angry
Pope.[2] His displeasure was again aroused when Paolo, by
his display of pomp, offended against a recently issued edict
for the reduction of luxury. Not only did Pius V. punish
the offence, but he forbade his nephew, since he could no
longer trust him, to leave the Vatican after the Ave Maria.[3]
When, later on, it was discovered that Paolo was leading an
immoral life, his fate was irrevocably sealed ; the Pope had
him called before him in a civil court, and then, without
looking at his nephew, caused his sentence to be read aloud,
which ran as follows : Paolo Ghislieri is to forfeit all his goods
and revenues, and under pain of death is to leave the Vatican
within two days, the Borgo within three, and the Papal States
within ten.[4] Every attempt to get the sentence of banishment revoked was in vain, although several very distinguished
persons intervened on his behalf, and the Pope absolutely
refused to send any help to the outlaw, as he wandered about
from country to country.[6]

[1] Tiepolo, September 21, 1566, in MUTINELLI, I., 56 *seq.* *Avvisi
di Roma of June 14 and 21, 1567, Urb. 1040, p. 403, Vatican
Library.

[2] See the *Avvisi di Roma of April 17 and May 1, 1568, Urb.
1040, p. 502b, 510, Vatican Library.

[3] See *Avviso di Roma of September 11, 1568, Urb. 1040,
p. 579b, Vatican Library, and the *report of Arco of the same
date, State Archives, Vienna.

[4] See C. FIRMANUS, *Diarium, October 22, 1568, Papal Secret
Archives, the *Avvisi di Roma of October 20 and 26, 1568, Urb.
1040, p. 587b, 588b, Vatican Library, and the *report of Arco
of October 28, 1568, State Archives, Vienna.

[5] See the *Avvisi di Roma of December 18, 1568, Urb. 1040,
p. 616 ; February 5, July 23, August 24, and October 8, 1569,
Urb. 1041, p. 19b, 117b, 138, 162, Vatican Library. In 1571
Paolo took part in the Turkish war. When he came back after
the battle of Lepanto, he could not remain in Rome, nor did he
receive any assistance from the Pope. In February, 1572, we
find him in Naples, where he was assisted by Don Juan ; see

The Romans had many other opportunities of realizing with what ruthless severity Pius V. punished moral offences. As early as January 19th, 1566, Caligari informed his friend Commendone of the publication of a stern edict against the immorality prevalent in Rome.[1] At the consistory of January 23rd the Pope spoke, not only of the need of reform among the clergy, but also of his intention of taking action against blasphemy and concubinage.[2] To give effect to this intention he issued, on April 1st, 1566, an edict which imposed the severest penalties for the disturbance of divine worship, the profanation of Sundays and festivals, simony, blasphemy, sodomy and concubinage.[3] In July, 1566, an ordinance was issued for the limitation of luxury in dress and of excessive lavishness in banquets,[4] which was followed

*Avviso di Roma of February 23, 1572, Urb. 1042, p. 41, *loc. cit.* That the Pope's severity was justified is shown by the condemnation of Paolo to death for homicide in 1577. He died in 1596. See BRUZZONE in *Cosmos illustr.*, 1903, 141 ; 1904, 61.

[1] *Lett. di princ., XXXIII., n. 77, Papal Secret Archives. A copy of the *Bando generale concernente il governo di Roma, dated January 15, 1566, is in the State Archives, Vienna, Varia 3.

[2] *Report of Arco of January 23, 1566, State Archives, Vienna.

[3] See Bull. Rom. VII., 434 *seq.* The edict ordered also " ut cadaverum capsae in ecclesiis super terram existentes amoveantur " a thing which had already been ordered by Paul IV. The penalties were quite in the draconian spirit of the Carafa Pope ; *cf.* Vol. XIV. of this work, 259 *seq.*

[4] In the collection in the Papal Secret Archives and in the Casanatense Library in Rome there is no copy of the " Bando e riforma sopra le immoderare spese et pompa del vestire et de' conviti " which is spoken of in the *Avviso di Roma of May 25 and June 1, 1566 (Urb. 1040, p. 220. 231b, Vatican Library) ; the same is true of the Bando of January 15, 1566 (see *supra* n. 1). A copy is preserved in the State Archives, Vienna, Varia 3, and bears the date June 28, 1566, but according to the *report of Cusano of July 6, 1566 (State Archives, Vienna) it was only published at the latter date.

in October, 1566, by another edict concerning dress.[1] In June, 1567, there came a special law against excessive pomp at marriages, and the ruinous inflation of marriage dowries and settlements.[2] Special regulations were made against games on festival days,[3] and against the spreading of reports that were libellous and treasonable by means of written broadsheets.[4] Scandal-mongers, Pius V. said, ought to be punished

---

[1] See " Bando sopra la reforma del vestire," dated October 4, 1566, Editti in Miscell., Arm. V., 60, p. 229, Papal Secret Archives ; cf. *Avviso di Roma of October 5, 1566, Urb. 1040, p. 294, Vatican Library. On November 9, 1566, Strozzi reports as to its rigorous carrying out ; *" Gli sbirri sono andati nella contrada del Pellegrino, ch'è delle principali di Roma, et hanno spogliato le botteghe degli orefici di lavori d'oro, di gioie et di perle dicendo che sono contro la pragmatica." (State Archives, Vienna.) See also the *Avviso di Roma of June 14, 1567, Urb. 1040, p. 403b, Vatican Library. CALVI in N. Antologia, 142 (1909), 593, speaks of a tax of 1568 on the use of carriages by ladies.

[2] Bull. Rom., VII., 596 seq. Cf. RODOCANACHI, Institutions, 277.

[3] *" Ha fatto andar un bando sotto pene gravissime che veruno non giuochi queste feste." Strozzi on December 21, 1566. He also *reports on December 28, 1566, an order to " dar corda " to certain persons for having gamed on a feast day. State Archives, Vienna.

[4] As early as October 27, 1566, Carlo Stuerdo reports from Rome to the Duke of Parma : *" Qua vien minacciato di carcere quelli che scrivono a Venetia mille baiate." (State Archives, Naples, C. Farnes. 763). The severe constitution of March 17, 1572, in Bull. Rom., VII., 969 seq. Cf. Arch. stor. d. Soc. Rom., I., 406, 408 ; Hist.-pol. Blatter, XXXVII., 574 seq. ; CIAMPI. Innocenzo X., p. 254 ; BERTOLOTTI, Giornalisti, astrologi, e negromanti in Roma, Florence, 1878, 1. The partisan work of PICCA, I martiri del giornalismo nella Roma papale, Rome, 1912 ; the author is ignorant of the celebrated collection of Avvisi in the Vatican Library. There (Urb. 1041, p. 316b) an *Avviso di Roma of July 22, 1570, states : * ' Il papa è in colera con alcuni che hanno fatte alcune pasquinate contro alcune persone da bene : " it will go badly with them.

as murderers.[1] That long-established pest of Rome, the
beggars, was to be dealt with,[2] and in 1567 all vagrants[3]
and gypsies[4] were banished from the Papal States. The
amusements of the Carnival were purged of all unseemliness,
and no one was allowed to dress up as a woman or a religious.
Bull-fights were altogether prohibited, and the races restricted
to the Corso, because such things seemed unfitting in the
Borgo, where the head of the Church resided.[5] To what
an extent these ordinances went into detail is shown among
other things by the fact that shop-keepers and artisans
were forbidden to make use of the images of the saints as
signs.[6]

The Fourth Council of the Lateran had already laid upon
physicians the obligation of immediately urging the sick
to receive the Sacraments, but this very necessary and well
meant law had been but little observed.   For this reason

[1] See the *Avviso di Roma of January 1, 1569, Urb. 1040,
p. 1, Vatican Library.

[2] The Pope wishes *" ridur i poveri mendicanti della città in 4
quartieri con farli proveder di vitto necessario acciò non vadino
vagabondi e disturbando, per le chiese le orationi et che i curati si
piglino fatica di ammaestrarli a viver christianamente et a darli
li s. sacramenti a tempi debiti " (*Avviso di Roma of March 12,
1569, Urb. 1041, p. 41, Vatican Library. Cf. Bull. Rom., VII.,
436, and TACCHI VENTURI, I., 394.

[3] See *Avviso di Roma of June 12, 1567, Urb. 1040, p. 421,
Vatican Library. Cf. the *report of Arco of January 24, 1568,
State Archives, Vienna.

[4] See *Avviso di Roma of September 20, 1567, Urb. 1040,
p. 437. Cf. *Avviso di Roma of June 14, 1570, Urb. 1041, p. 290b,
according to which some gipsies were also sent at that time to the
galleys. Vatican Library.

[5] See in App. n. 26 the *report of B. Pia of January 22, 1567,
Gonzaga Archives, Mantua. For the action taken by Pius V.
against actors see CATENA, Lettere, 481. This evidence has been
missed by E. RE in his article Commedianti a Roma nel sec.
XVI., in Giorn. stor. d. lett. Ital., LXIII., 298 seq.

[6] See *Avviso di Roma of June 28, 1567, Urb. 1040, p. 407,
Vatican Library.

several provincial synods had made strict regulations on the subject. A synod held at Ravenna in 1311 had ordered doctors to withhold their services from the sick to whom they were called until they had first seen to the salvation of their souls. A synod held at Tortosa in 1429, and the provincial synod held by Charles Borromeo at Milan in 1565 had made similar laws. Fired with zeal to promote in every possible way, and by every possible means, the spiritual welfare of all Christians, Pius V. returned to the attack, and on March 8th, 1566, issued a constitution which laid down that every physician who was summoned to a sick person who was confined to his bed was before everything else bound to exhort him to receive the sacrament of penance, and to suspend his visits after three days unless a confessor had attested in writing that the confession had been made, or else that for some good reason an extension of the time had been allowed.[1] In spite, however, of the severe penalties imposed for the non-observance of this regulation, it did not meet with much success.[2]

It is not surprising that so strict a Pope should have waged war against public immorality in Rome, and should have

---

[1] Bull. Rom., VII., 430 seq. ; cf. KOBER in Tüb. Theol. Quartalschrift, LV., 660 seq. The extract in RANKE, Päpste, I³, 233, is partly inexact. An *Avviso di Roma of March 19, 1569, records the severe ordinance against doctors who gave persons in good health permission to eat meat on fasting days (Urb. 1040, p. 37b). Cf. in Urb. 1042, p. 29b, the *Avviso di Roma of February 24, 1571, Vatican Library.

[2] Theologians and canonists of repute maintained the view that the rigorism of the ordinaces of Pius V. went too far, and they accordingly declared that when the malady was dangerous the doctor was not obliged to suspend his care and aid, and that in such a case the ordinance was not binding. Other theologians made yet another limitation ; namely that the doctor was bound to make his exhortation to the reception of the sacraments, not in every illness, but only in the case of those which were dangerous, or where the issue was doubtful. See BENEDICT XIV., Instit., XXII. ; KOBER, loc. cit., 666 seq.

tried to put an end to the evils of prostitution.[1] As a first step, at the end of June, 1566, all women of ill-fame were driven out of the Borgo by the police, and the Conservatori were ordered to find some segregated locality for the others who lived in various parts of the city. The Trastevere was thought of as a place for this purpose. An edict published on St. Mary Magdalen's day, July 22nd, 1566, ordered that the more notorious prostitutes (cortegiane) were to be expelled from Rome within six days, and within a further period from the Papal States, unless they preferred to marry or enter the convent delle Penitenti. This edict caused great anxiety in Rome ; many complained that such rigour would depopulate the city, and that many tradesmen, who had supplied goods to these people on credit, would suffer seriously. The customs authorities asked for a reduction of their tax by 20,000 ducats, on the ground that the expulsion of these people would mean a great reduction in the importation of dutiable goods.[2] The city council met and decided

---

[1] The police measures, as far as morals were concerned, which were taken by Pius V., dealt principally with the increase of prostitution dating from the XVth century ; as to this see what has been said in Vol. V. of this work 98 seqq. With GRAF (Attraverso il Cinquecento, Turin, 1888, 269 seq., 281) and RODOCANACHI (Courtisanes et Bouffons, Paris, 1894, 82 seq., 174) BERTOLOTTI has treated of the matter specially fully (Repressioni straordinarie della prostituzione in Roma nel sec. XVI., Rome, 1887) ; he has published valuable reports from Mantua, but has been as little fair to Pius V. as BROSCH (I., 242 seq.). Altogether apart from the undignified treatment of so serious a matter, the reproaches which they both make against Pius V. are quite unjustified. It may be admitted that the means adopted by Pius V. did not altogether attain the end in view, but it must be remembered that our age is still in as great a state of perplexity as to how to deal with the evil of prostitution, and it is still a matter of dispute whether the means finally adopted by Pius V. were right or wrong. That the Church has the right to work for the extirpation of prostitution *by every means* is brought out by PENCK in the Handwörterbuch der Staatswissenschaften, V., 296.

[2] *Cf*. the *Avvisi di Roma in App. nn. 16 to 25 Vatican Library.

to send to the Pope a deputation of forty citizens to ask
for the recall of the decree, which had already been put into
force. The deputation—and they could have expected
nothing else—met with a stern refusal. Such shame, the
Pope said, could not be tolerated in holy Rome ; he would
rather change his residence to some other less tainted place.
A written protest[1] was equally unsuccessful, nor was even
the intervention of the ambassadors of Spain, Portugal and
Florence of any avail.[2]

Pius V. remained inexorable on the subject of the expulsion of the more notorious courtesans. By August 10th
most of them had already left Rome, and others were preparing to do so, though many had been converted. The fact
that some of those who had been expelled had been killed
by highwaymen told in favour of those who were still in Rome.
These were accordingly not expelled, but had to put a stop
to their public disorders, and a segregated quarter was
assigned to them near the Ripetta, which they were not to
leave either by day or night under pain of a public whipping.
By this severity Pius V. hoped to induce them either to
leave Rome or to be converted. For this purpose special
sermons were arranged for them, as was also done in the case
of the Jews. On September 5th, 1566, a fresh order for the
expulsion of those who were quite incorrigible was issued.[3]

---

[1] See *ibid.* There are many copies in manuscript (Berlin,
Royal Library ; Inf. polit., XII., 230 *seq. ;* Paris, Bibliothèque
Nationale [see MARSAND, I., 630, 757 *seq.*], Mazarin Library,
Cod. 1779, p. 220 *seq.*) of an " Epistola a N.S^{re} P. Pio V. nella
quale si esorta S.S^{tà} a tolerare in Roma gl'Hebrei et le cortegiane,"
dated August 13, 1566, printed in *Rev. des études juives*, July, 1892,
which among other things elaborates the argument that, by
driving out the aforesaid persons " V.S^{tà} non havra poi chi
ridurre al bene ne che punire al male." If he drives them out
now, they may all be lost, whereas it might be possible to convert
them if they remained !

[2] See the *letter of Arco, August 3, 1566, State Archives,
Vienna.

[3] See *Avvisi di Roma in App. nn. 16 to 25, and in BERTOLOTTI,

How deep seated this evil was is clear from the fact that during the whole of his reign Pius V. was forced to take action against it year after year. Prostitutes who had left their quarters were constantly whipped, and others expelled. A proof of the anxiety which the Pope felt for the conversion of these fallen women is to be found in the fact that in August, 1567, he persuaded six elderly ladies to devote themselves to this difficult task.[1] Those who returned to a better manner of life received large alms, so that they might not relapse into their former state. The segregation of the incorrigibles was made even more complete in the autumn of 1569 by the erection of walls and gates round their quarter, like the Ghetto.[2] Lodgings were subjected to a very strict police supervision, and since this constantly gave rise to inconvenience, in 1570 all women under forty years of age, even though married, were forbidden to let rooms.[3]

The Pope watched over the sanctity of family life very carefully and nothing escaped his attention. Thus he forbade young girls from being employed as servants,[4] while an

loc. cit., 10–11. In his *Diarium (Miscell., Arm. XII., 31, p. 143) Firmanus states : *" Die dominica 24 [Novembris] fuit praedicatum in multis ecclesiis Urbis, vicinis habitationibus meretricum, de ordine rev^{mi} vicarii Suae S^{tis} , et solum meretrices iverunt et non aliae personae." Papal Secret Archives.

[1] See the *Avvisi di Roma of 1567–1569 in App nn. 28-34, 53-57, 60-65, Vatican Library. For the last years cf. BERTOLOTTI, loc. cit. 13 seq., where, however, the dates are often wrong (p. 13 the Avviso di Roma of May 19 belongs to 1571, as does that of July 14 on p. 14.).

[2] See the *Avviso di Roma of October 17, 1569, in App. nn. 60-65, Vatican Library.

[3] *Avviso di Roma of September 9, 1570, Urb. 1041, p. 339 ; ibid. 342b and *Avviso of September 20, 1570 : " 20 donne " who kept " camere locande," are imprisoned (Vatican Library). According to an *Avviso of September 9, 1570, in the State Archives, Vienna, it was ordered that the married women who let rooms must be at least 50 years of age.

[4] See *Avviso di Roma of June 5, 1568, Urb. 1040, p. 525. According to an *Avviso of July 12, 1567, the following edict was

edict published in the autumn of 1566 forbade, under severe penalties, all Romans who had houses of their own to frequent taverns.[1]

The many cases of adultery which occurred in Rome filled Pius V. with indescribable grief, and ever increasing indignation ; from the beginning of his reign he did all he could to bring about a change in this respect. The many difficulties which he met with[2] forced him to take more and more strict measures. A report of August 25th 1568 states : " The threat of the death penalty for adultery is expected, so that everyone will either have to become moral or leave the city."[3] People were constantly imprisoned without consideration of rank.[4] In September, 1568, a noble Roman lady who had been found guilty of adultery was imprisoned for

issued : no young married woman may keep " camere locande " ; *ibid.* p. 418b, Vatican Library.

[1] " Bando che niuno habitante in Roma et borghi possa andare all' hostaria con la prohibitione delli giuochi, baratterie et altre cose illecite," a very rare pamphlet of Ant. Bladus, Rome, 1566. The exact date of this order is seen from the *Diarium of Firmanus (October 3, 1566), Miscell., Arm. XII., 31, p. 130b, Papal Secret Archives. *Cf.* *Avviso di Roma of October 5, 1566, Urb. 1040, p. 294, Vatican Library. According to the *letter of Arco of September 14, 1566, the Pope had spoken of the matter in consistory on the 14th. State Archives, Vienna.

[2] *" Il continuo metter prigione le donne in questa città causa errori grandi," one has committed suicide. *Carlo Stuerdo to the Duke of Parma from Rome, October 27, 1566, State Archives, Naples, C. Farnes. 763. *Cf.* also BERTOLOTTI, *loc. cit.* 11.

[3] *" Qui s'aspetta de dì in dì con gran terrore, che esca una bolla contra li adulteri, la qual si dice sarà terribilissima, et che le pene saran capitali, si che sarà necessario, ch'ogn' huomo diventi buono ò se risolva abbandonar questa patria." Urb. 1040, p. 570b. *Ibid.* 440b an *Avviso di Roma of September 13, 1567, according to which such a bull was already expected. Vatican Library.

[4] *Avviso di Roma of September 17, 1568, State Archives, Vienna ; another of August 13, 1569, in App. nn. 60-65.

life.[1]   One of the richest and most respected bankers in Rome,
the Sienese de Vecchi, having been convicted of adultery, was
publicly whipped in December, 1568, " as a salutary example
for the nobles," says the chronicler.[2]   In the following year
it was rumoured that the Pope intended to expel from Rome
all married women who fell into this sin[3], and this penalty
was often inflicted after the culprit had been whipped for
the first offence.[4]   In June, 1570, the Governor of Rome
had great difficulty in dissuading the Pope from inflicting
the death penalty for adultery, but at length Pius V. agreed
that adulterers should be punished by whipping, imprisonment, or banishment.[5]

The Pope watched over the morals of his own servants
with a special strictness.[6]   The Governor of Anagni was be-

---

[1] *Avviso di Roma of September 25, 1568, Urb. 1040, p. 585
Vatican Library.

[2] *" Dicta die [veneris 3 decembris] fuit fustigatus per Urbem
nobilis Senensis dominus de Vecchiis, qui fuerat ditissimus et
superbissimus bancherius, postea decoxerat et propter quaedam
adulteria fuit carceratus per multos dies et tandem favoribus non
suffragantibus, sic mandante S^{mo} D^{no} N^{ro}, ad exemplum delin-
quentium nobilium, fuit, ut dixi, per loca solita fustigatus."
(FIRMANUS, *Diarium, loc. cit., p. 272b.   Papal Secret Archives).
Cf. BERTOLOTII, loc. cit, 11.

[3] Tiepolo in MUTINELLI, !., 80 seq.

[4] Soriano in BROSCH, I., 243.   In the face of Pius V.'s strong
sense of justice, one can only treat as uncalled for Brosch's remark,
" We do not know what sort of proofs of this crime were obtained.'

[5] See the report of Capilupi of June 26, 1570, in BERTOLOTTI,
loc. cit. 12.   Cf. *Avviso di Roma of June 28, 1570, Urb. 1041,
P. 296 Vatican Library.

[6] Giulio Orsini for example was forced to send away his con-
cubine ; see the *reports of Arco of March 30 and April 4, 1566,
State Archives, Vienna :   *" Die XV. dicti mensis [ianuarii]
pontifex creavit magistrum capelle r^{dum} dominum sacristam, qui
eius pedes fuit osculatus, cui mandavit ut reformaret cantores,
inter quos sciebat esse aliques concubinarios et discolos ; et
verum dicebat."   C. FIRMANUS, *Diarium in Miscell., Arm. XII.,
31, p. 40, Papal Secret Archives.

headed in 1571 for violation.[1] The Swiss Guards were forced
to marry their concubines or leave them,[2] and in order to
effect a radical change among these old soldiers, Pius V. had
sermons preached to them and their servants in their own
language by a Jesuit.[3] The cavalry were obliged to receive
the sacraments regularly,[4] and they were not allowed to go
out in the evening without the permission of their captain.
A list was kept of all who left the Vatican after dusk, and this
the Pope caused to be submitted to him regularly.[5] Women
were not allowed to set foot in the Belvedere.[6]

Even unfriendly judges have recognised that Pius V. was
actuated by the best intentions in his efforts to root out the
moral evils of the day.[7] Very often his strictness was excessive, because he punished with great severity, not only
grave offences, but also smaller transgressions,[8] so that the
prisons were overcrowded.[9] Moreover, looked at from the
point of view of the evils that were actually stamped out,
the results were far from satisfactory. This was due, among

---

[1] See the *report of Arco of August 18th, 1571, State Archives,
Vienna.

[2] See the *Avviso di Roma of June 5, 1568, Urb. 1040, p. 525,
Vatican Library, and the *report of Arco of June 5, 1568, State
Archives, Vienna.

[3] POLANCI Epist., in *Anal. Bolland.*, VII., 51.

[4] See the *report of Arco of May 17, 1567, State Archives,
Vienna.

[5] See *Avviso di Roma of September 25, 1568, Urb. 1040,
p. 585, Vatican Library.

[6] *Avviso di Roma of June 12, 1568, *ibid.* 534.

[7] See LE BRET, VIII., 223.

[8] See the *Avviso di Roma of October 20, 1568, Urb. 1040,
p. 589, Vatican Library.

[9] According to an *Avviso di Roma of August 31, 1566, the
prison at Tor di Nona had already had to be enlarged on account
of the number of prisoners (Urb. 1040, p. 278, Vatican Library).
An undated *report of B. Pia in 1568 states that there were 1200
persons in the prisons of Rome and " infinite donne." Gonzaga
Archives, Mantua.

other things, to the peculiar character of Rome itself, as an international city, and one filled with foreigners.[1]

Knowing well that if any definite success was to be obtained the rising generation would have to be trained on better lines, Pius V. above all devoted himself to seeing that the young received systematic and easily mastered instruction in the truths of the Christian religion. In 1568 the parish priests of Rome were instructed to make it known to the faithful that they were bound, under grave penalties, to send their children on Sunday afternoons to the church for instruction in Christian doctrine, as had been laid down by the Council of Trent.[2] When, later on, special associations were formed to assist the priests in this work, the Pope in 1571 formed them into a regular confraternity called " della dottrina cristiana " enriched it with indulgences, and asked the bishops to set up similar confraternities everywhere.[3] In this way a real improvement in moral conditions was bound gradually to be effected, and there is good evidence to show that this took place even during the life of Pius V.[4]

[1] P. Tiepolo brings out this aspect of Rome in the introduction to his *report of 1569 ; see Cod. 6624, p. 317, Court Library, Vienna.

[2] See the *report of Arco of July 17, 1568, State Archives, Vienna.

[3] See Bull. Rom., VII., 945 *seq.*

[4] P. Tiepolo, who says : " gli uomini, se non sono, almeon paiono migliori " (p. 172), also recognizes the change in Rome. This was already clearly to be seen in 1566 (see PFLEGER, Eisengrein, 50 *seq.* ; BRAUNSBERGER, Pius V., 108 *seq.*) *" Le feste " reports an *Avviso di Roma of January 3, 1568, " si non passate con prediche et altre divotioni, non s'è giocato in loco alcuno, prohibite le mancie, livree et ogni altra vanità." Urb. 1040, p. 446b. *Ibid.* December 4 : the greater part of the people gained the Jubilee. Urb. 1041, p. 1, January 1, 1569 : *" Bandi sopra il gioco in queste feste assai ben osservati." In Urb. 1042, p. 48 (April 14, 1571) there is mention of the extraordinary zeal with which the people frequented the churches in Holy Week (Vatican Library). Giulio Gabrielli of Gubbio (died March 12,

Under the strict regime which had now been set on foot the Eternal City began to assume that peculiar character, which has been given the name of the " world-wide monastery."[1]

1579) gave the following judgment : " Quis enim non videat, postquam ecclesiae gubernaculo Pius V. P.M. praepositus est, tantam et in urbe Roma et in aliis suae dictionis oppidis factam esse morum mutationem, ut libido in pudicitiam, luxuria in temperantiam, impietas denique, ipsius nomen sequuta, in pietatem versa videatur ? " (S. Gregorii Naz. Orationes tres, Antwerp 1573, 163). Gianfrancesco Lombardo expresses himself in similar terms in a letter of November 11, 1568 ; see CYPRIANUS, 484 seq.

[1] The supposed intention of Pius V. to change Rome into a convent, was discussed by his contemporaries very shortly after his election ; see MASIUS, Briefe, 374.

CHAPTER III

GOVERNMENT OF THE STATES OF THE CHURCH. PIUS V. IN RELATION TO LITERATURE AND ART.

A MAN of such strictness, such untiring energy, and such stainless character as Pius V., was pre-eminently fitted for the task of introducing into the life of the Church the reform decrees of the Council of Trent, and thus to set the seal upon the labours of his predecessor. For this reason his pontificate is of the highest importance, while only less important were his unflinching struggle against the new doctrines, and his energetic revival of the old idea of a Crusade against the Turks in defence of the Christian faith and European civilization.

In comparison with this threefold activity, which was to a great extent crowned with success, the work of Pius V. as the ruler of the Papal States[1] falls into the background, all the more as in this respect he was upon ground that was unfamiliar to him, and which to a great extent remained so to the end. He certainly had the will to remove abuses and to restore good order, though he lacked practical experience and did not know how to temper his severity.

During the latter days of Pius IV. no branch of the temporal administration had been in such a bad state as that of justice. The exhortation which Pius V. addressed to the assembled judges in the Hall of Constantine on October 30th, 1566,[2]

---

[1] A *list of the provinces of the Papal States, with particulars of the officials, revenues and troops in the time of Pius V., is in Varia Polit. 79 (now 80), p. 253 seq., Papal Secret Archives. Cf. also the introduction, not printed in Albèri, to the *report of P. Tiepolo of 1569, which is to be found in many collections of codices (Libraries at Avignon, Berlin, Gotha, Munich, Venice, Vienna, Vatican, etc.).

[2] See *Urb. 1040, p. 313, Vatican Library.

made it plain that he considered it his sacred duty to provide
for a strong and impartial administration of justice.   It now
became as difficult for culprits to escape by means of bribery
as it had been easy under his predecessor, and it was above all
to seeing that the poor and the helpless should have justice
that Pius V. directed his efforts.   When a poor baker complained to him that Cardinal Simoncelli had owed him 36
scudi for bread for six years, the nephew of Julius III. was
forced to make immediate payment.   On the last Wednesday
of every month Pius V. held a public audience at which all
were at liberty to make their complaints about the courts
of justice.   The Pope also turned his attention to the reform
of the legal fraternity.[1]   What a deep respect he had for
justice is certainly best shown by the revision of the trial of
the Carafa which he caused to be made, and which ended on
September 26th, 1567, in the annulment of the sentence
pronounced by Pius IV., and the restoration of the house of
Carafa.[2]   By such procedure as this Pius V. showed that he
did not hesitate to act in direct opposition to all the rules of

[1] See the *report of Arco of April 26, 1567, State Archives,
Vienna, and the *Avvisi di Roma of February 14 and December 18,
1568, Urb. 1040, p. 486, 616, Vatican Library.   Cf. TIEPOLO, 173 ;
CATENA, 136 seq. ; GABUTIUS, 218 ; LADERCHI, 1566, n. 113 seq.
Pius V. took great trouble to secure a good administration of
justice even in the provinces.   An *Avviso of March 9, 1566,
relates that power over criminal cases was withdrawn from
Cardinal Mark Sittich at Terni, in consequence of which the
Cardinal resigned civil cases as well, and went away " et nell'universale li nipoti et parenti di Pio IV. par che restino mal sodis-
fatti del Papa."   Urb. 1040, p. 190b, Vatican Library.

[2] Cf. the authoritative account by ANCEL, Disgrâce, 169–181,
who makes it clear that the new trial, the acts of which have not
so far been found, seems to have dealt almost entirely with the
crimen laesae maiestatis, and that the assassination of the Duchess
of Paliano was not again brought under consideration.   That
Pius V. did not consult any Cardinal before coming to his decision
(ANCEL, 178) is also attested by Arco in his *report of September 27
1567, State Archives, Vienna.   See also Corresp. dipl., II., 218
seq., 224.

prudence, or to compromise the reputation of his predecessors, even in the case of Paul IV., whom he had so revered ; he was also ready to trample on the interests of people whose assistance might be very useful to him.[1]   Even Alessandro Pallantieri, the procurator-fiscal in the Carafa trial, did not escape punishment. He had become governor of the March of Ancona at the beginning of 1567,[2] and it seemed as though his great severity had won the Pope's favour to such an extent that men were prophesying the cardinalate for him,[3] when all of a sudden, on September 17th, 1569, he was imprisoned by the Inquisition[4] on the charge of having, in the time of Julius III., obtained by bribery the release from prison of a relapsed heretic of Faenza, of having retained a considerable part of the Carafa property in spite of the order for restitution made by Pius V., and of having paid no attention to the excommunication which he had incurred by so doing.[5]   The investigation of these charges brought to light the part which Pallantieri had played in the conduct of the Carafa trial.[6] The trial of Pallantieri ended in his being condemned to death, and on June 7th, 1571, the sentence was carried out on the very spot where the Duke of Paliano had been beheaded.[7]

[1] See ANCEL, loc. cit. 181.

[2] See GARAMPI, Sul valore, 293. ·

[3] See the *Avviso di Roma of June 9, 1571, Urb. 1042, p. 70, Vatican Library.

[4] See MARINI, I., 428.

[5] See *Avviso di Roma of September 27, 1569, Urb. 1041, p. 155b, Vatican Library.

[6] According to the *Avviso di Roma of October 8, 1569 (loc. cit. 159) all the acts of the Carafa trial were then taken to the Inquisition ; it is in those archives, therefore, that search must be made for the acts of the revision held by the orders of Pius V.

[7] See *Avviso di Roma of June 9, 1571, loc cit. and the *report of Arco of June 9, 1571. The latter *relates on May 19, 1571, that on the Thursday the case of Pallantieri was considered in the presence of the Pope, who for three hours heard pro et contra. State Archives, Vienna. Ibid. an *Avviso of March 17, 1571, according to which Pallantieri tried to save himself by paying 30,000 scudi.   In the opinion of Pallavicini, Palantieri deserved

38987

Pius V.'s interference with questions of justice, however, was not always just or reasonable ; he sometimes pronounced hasty sentences which he afterwards had to revoke.   Tiepolo says that the Pope never tempered a criminal sentence with mercy, and that generally he would have liked to have made it more severe.[1] No rank or dignity could obtain any mitigation of the punishment. A noble Roman lady who had committed homicide was executed, and that publicly, which was quite unusual, in spite of the intercession of the Conservatori and many Cardinals.[2] A circular addressed to the governors of the Papal States in August, 1568, urged them to employ nothing but severity, and to show no mercy. It was estimated that more executions took place at that time in a single month than in four years under Pius IV.[3] Many, including light offenders, took to flight before this excessive severity, with the result that the bands of robbers who infested some parts of the Papal States, and especially the mountainous districts towards Naples,[4] were constantly on the increase, which was one of the reasons why the Pope's praiseworthy efforts to deal with this pest were only partially successful.[5]

the death sentence. Cf. PASTOR, Dekrete, 16, n.   See RODO-CANACHI, St.-Ange, 173. Ibid. 175, the trial of Matteo Minale.

[1] TIEPOLO, 173. From FIRMANUS, *Diarium (Miscell., Arm. XII., 31 in Papal Secret Archives) it is evident how frequent death sentences were.

[2] See Tiepolo in MUTINELLI, I., 78–79.

[3] See the *report of Cusano from Rome, August 17, 1568, State Archives, Vienna. Cf. MUTINELLI, I., 92.

[4] A *letter from Cardinal Bonelli to Francesco Ghislieri, governor of Ascoli, dated Rome, April 17, 1566 (in 1911 in the possession of the antiquarian Luzzietti) deals with the bandits who had taken refuge in the Abruzzi. For the bandits at Teramo, see Riv. Abruzzese, XXVII., (1912) 458 seq.

[5] In his *report of June 7, 1567 (State Archives, Vienna) Arco tells of an expeditionary force against the bandits. For the outbreak of brigandage in 1570, see HIRN, Erzherzog Ferdinand II. von Tirol, I., 505 n. 1. For the whole subject cf. LADERCHI, 1566, n. 122 seq.

Another reason was to be found in the fact that the very proper attempts to act in concert with the neighbouring states in putting down brigandage led to frequent and bitter disputes with Naples.[1] The bull which was issued on July 13th, 1566, against those who harboured murderers and bandits, was made even more severe on August 15th, and enacted that the death penalty was to be inflicted on the offenders, and that of banishment on their relatives.[2] In order to stamp out brigandage, the Pope, in 1567, ordered the destruction of the forests in the neighbourhood of Rome,[3] a thing which led to the spread of malaria, and contributed in no small degree to the deterioration of the healthiness of the Compagna, so that every year a large number of the foreign labourers who had come for the harvests died of fever.[4]

Public safety in the Papal States was threatened, not only by the brigands, but also by the long established feuds between the cities, and among the nobles. At Ascoli, Anagni, Città di Castello, Sassoferrato, Perugia, and elsewhere, disturbances broke out which caused the Pope much anxiety, and several times obliged him to send armed forces against them, a thing which was especially galling to him, whose high ideals would

---

[1] *Cf.* TIEPOLO, 173 ; CATENA, 51 *seq.* ; BROSCH, I., 238 *seq.* See also Corresp. dipl., II., 368. An *Avviso di Roma of March 26, 1569, relates that two days previously at the Bridge of S$_t$. Angelo had taken place the execution of " Cecone da S. Lupidio, cappo de'banditi della Marca." Urb. 1041, p. 47, Vatican Library.

[2] See Bull. Rom., VII., 452 *seq.*, 456 *seq.*

[3] An *Avviso di Roma of April 26, 1567, relates that between Porta Prima and Romana the Venetian courier had been attacked and robbed, that the Pope had ordered him to be compensated, and had further enacted " che si levino et abbrugino tutte quelle machie sino a Prima porta " (Urb. 1040, p. 385, Vatican Library). *Cf.* the *brief of December 5, 1567, Papal Secret Archives ; *cf.* App. n. 27.

[4] 9 Sreports Tiepolo in the unpublished part of his *report for 15.60 Cod. 6624, p. 319, Court Library, Vienna.

rather have led him to disband all his troops.[1] The rival
factions made use, not only of those who had fled from Rome
or been exiled, but also of soldiers who had deserted and of
unworthy monks who had come into conflict with the reforming
activities of Pius V., and even, in some parts of the March
and in the Romagna, of heretics. When the Pope learned
that Faenza was full of heretics, he thought of proceeding to
the very limits of severity ; he wished to destroy the city,
and transfer the inhabitants to some other place.[2] At the
end of the pontificate, however, there was for the most part
greater tranquillity in the Papal States than there had been
before.[3]

On February 12th, 1572, the orders which Pius IV. had
issued against the carrying of arms, and which applied to

[1] From the *report of Cusano of January 26, 1566 (State
Archives, Vienna) it is clear how unwillingly the Pope made up
his mind to take proceedings against Ascoli. In an *Avviso di
Roma of February 2, 1566, it is stated that Pius V. had disbanded
the cavalry with the exception of two companies, *" et dice che i
pontefici sono guardati dalla man di Dio et non da archibugi.
Non vuol guaidia o cavalleria per esser necessitato a pagarli
metter impositione of popolo." (Urb. 1040, p. 173) ; cf. supra
p. 69. But as early as February 9, Torquato Conti had to be
sent to Ascoli with " 150 fanti " to suppress the rising (ibid., 169,
Vatican Library). Cf. BROSCH, I., 241 for the disturbances at
Città di Castello. For others at Anagni, see *Avviso di Roma
of May 11, 1566, Urb. 1040, p. 225. Ibid. 1041, p. 127b, an
*Avviso of August 27, 1567, on the disturbances at Perugia, which
annoyed the Pope very much. For Ascoli, see Saggio di cose
Ascolane, Teramo, 1766, App. ccxcvi. On January 24, 1567,
*" Alex. Pallanterius, gubernator Marchie," obtained " facultates
contra bannitos Asculi et Firmi." Archives of Briefs, Rome.

[2] See Tiepolo · in MUTINELLI, I., 79 ; cf. infra p. 313 seq.
An *Avviso di Roma of September 19, 1571 (Urb. 1042, p. 117b.
Vatican Library) reports the banishments which had taken place
in the territories of Cardinal Farnese.

[3] This is proved from *Tiepolo in 1569 ; see Cod. 6624, p. 320,
Court Library, Vienna.

Rome and the whole of the Papal States, were renewed, and made more severe.[1]

The bull of March 29th, 1567, concerning the inalienability of the territory of the Roman Church, has attained great notoriety.[2] It was aimed at putting an end to nepotism, which had had such disastrous effects upon the Church.

Pius V.'s financial administration of the Papal States calls for particular notice. Immediately after his election he abolished the duty on wine in Rome,[3] revised the other taxes, and caused the expenditure to be carefully examined.[4] In the Patrimony he abolished the duty on flour in consideration of the payment of a sum of money, to be made once for all.[5] The Pope hoped that his great personal economy[6] would make it possible for him to give relief in other ways as well. To a bishop who submitted to him a scheme for improving the finances he replied that he had better help the Church by his prayers and his good life, and that she had no need of wealth ;[7] a sentiment which, though very idealistic, scarcely met the

---

[1] Bull. Rom., VII., 965 seq.

[2] See ibid. 560 seq.; cf. Freiburg Kirchenlexikon VII., 599. Further particulars infra p. 233 seq.

[3] The import duty was " 4 giulii per barilla ; " see *Avviso di Roma of January 19, 1566, Urb. 1040, p. 166. Vatican Library.

[4] *" Questo fa che la plebe ama molto S.Stà " says the *Avviso di Roma of March 16, 1566, ibid. 194.

[5] See Tiepolo in BROSCH, I., 245, n. 1.

[6] Thus for example the Vigna di Giulio III. was given " in governo " to the Cardinal of Aragon *" e così viene ad esser desobligato di recever gl'ambasciatori e fare spesa, come si usava prima." (*Avviso di Roma of May 4, 1566, Urb. 1040, p. 220b, Vatican Library). For the reduction of expenditure on the troops see Quellen u. Forschungen, VI., 84.

[7] *Avviso di Roma of January 19, 1566, Urb. 1040, p. 166. The Pope does not wish for taxes, even indirect ones, says an *Avviso of March 30, 1566, Urb. 1040, 199b, Vatican Library. The Florentine, Bartolomeo Bussoti was Thesaurarius of Pius V. ; see FIRMANUS, *Diarium in Miscell., Arm. XII., 31, p. 47. Papal Secret Archives.

needs of the times. As early as November, 1567, the Pope
found himself in great financial difficulties ;[1] he set himself
to devise a way of meeting them without overburdening his
subjects,[2] but since he could not avoid having to give assistance
to the French Catholics, to his great grief he at length found
himself obliged to impose some extraordinary taxes upon his
subjects,[3] though he took care that they should fall principally
upon the wealthy, and that the clergy should make a suitable
contribution.[4]

Since the revenues steadily continued to decline—it was
calculated in 1570 that the falling off since 1538 was as much
as 400,000 scudi[5]--while the wider interests of the Church,
the helping of the oppressed Catholics, especially in France,
and the Turkish war, demanded ever greater and greater
sacrifices, the Pope, in 1569, found himself obliged to impose
a further extraordinary tax of 500,000 scudi upon imports, a

---

[1] See the *brief to the " dux Nivern." of November 15, 1567 (in
summa fisci nostri inopia), Arm. 44, t. 13, n. 73b, Papal Secret
Archives.

[2] *" Die noctuque cogitat quonam pacto pecunias reperire
possit minimo cum populorum et plebis damno." (Arco on
November 8, 1567, State Archives, Vienna). In the interest of
his subjects Pius V. also issued severe enactments against the
acceptance of presents by the state officials ; see *Studien und
Mitteilungen aus dem Benediktiner- und Zisterzienserordens*, I.,
3, 213.

[3] The hopes which had been built upon the recovery of ancient
coins at Civitavecchia were not fulfilled. (*Cf.* *Avviso di Roma
of March 22, 1567, Urb. 1040, p. 372, Vatican Library ; *cf.* on
this matter *Spicil. Vatic.*, 83 *seq.*) ; see GRATIANI Epist., 277.
For the taxes *cf.* the *reports of Arco of November 8 and 15, 1567.
State Archives, Vienna.

[4] See LADERCHI, 1567, n. 141 *seq.*, 146 *seq.* ; *cf.* GUILLAUME,
L'abbaye de Cava, Cava de' Tirreni, 1877, 320. In order that it
might be able to pay the tax, Ancona in a *brief of February 8,
1568, obtained permission to increase the tax on slaughtering.
Communal Archives, Ancona.

[5] See SERENO, 398.

thing which occasioned much surprise.[1]   Besides this, during
the later years of his reign the permanent public debt was
quadrupled by the establishment of the Monti.[2]

Although he was so parsimonious, the Pope nevertheless
practised almsgiving on a grand scale.[3]   He not only freely
assisted the poorer Cardinals, and the bishops who had been
driven from their sees, but also his needy servants.   In Rome
he contributed largely to the hospitals, especially that of
S. Spirito, to which he gave 20,000 scudi, and several times
personally visited the sick.   When, in the summer of 1566,
the city was visited by a pestilence brought on by the excessive
heat, he dealt with the emergency in every possible way, sent
for doctors, and especially concerned himself in relieving the
poor by the help of the religious.[4]   The same thing happened
when the pestilence recurred during the summer of 1568.
The parish priests were instructed to draw up lists of the sick,

[1] See TIEPOLO, 174.   In his *letter of January 22, 1569 (State
Archives, Vienna) Cusano shows how difficult it was to obtain
money.   In order to ease the finances in June, 1569, all the
notariships in the Papal States were sold, bringing in a sum of
70,000 scudi (*Avviso di Roma of June 11, 1569, Urb. 1040 p. 91b).
The *Avvisi of June 29 and July 9, 1569, Urb. 1040, p. 101, 107b,
Vatican Library, mention other financial schemes.

[2] Namely the Monti Novennale, Giulio, Religione and Provincia ; see COPPI, Sulle finanze dello Stato pontificio, Rome,
1855.   Cf. MORONI, LXXIV., 291 ; SANTORI, Diario XXIII.,
330 ; XXIV., 106.   According to Cerasoli Pius V. deposited
467,000 scudi in the Castle of St. Angelo, and drew out on various
occasions 288,000.   Cf. Studi e docum., XIII., 305, as well as
SERAFINI, Le monete e le bolle plumbee nel medagliere Vaticano,
I., Milan, 1910.

[3] Cf. CATENA, 25, 136, 149 ; GABUTIUS, 204 seq. ; LADERCHI,
1568, n. 48 seq. ; the periodical Caritas, 1898, n. 7.

[4] See CATENA, 50.   For the cause of the pestilence in the summer
of 1566 (heat " con un vento sirocale che abbruggiava il dì et la
notte ") see *Avviso di Roma of August 31, 1566, Urb. 1040,
p. 278.   Ibid. 284 and 287, *Avvisi of September 14 and 21,
1566 : *" Il Papa continua tuttavia in far visitar gl'infermi et
sovenirli."   Vatican Library.

and to send them to the Jesuits, whose duty it was to visit
them and succour them with means furnished by the Pope.[1]
He increased the dowries for poor girls at the Minerva, and
the Monte di Pietà received in January, 1567, a gift of 10,000
scudi, so that the institution might be able to advance loans
without interest, and at the same time it was ordered that the
things pledged were not to be sold before 18 months had
elapsed.[2] The Pope was also indefatigable in ransoming and
helping the unfortunate people who had been enslaved by
the Turks.[3]

It was the unanimous opinion in Rome that no Pope for a
long time past had been so active in works of charity as Pius
V.[4] The abolition of the excessive levy of duty at the city
gates met with universal approval,[5] as did the Pope's efforts
to promote industries in Rome, as for example, the weaving

---

[1] See the *report of Arco of August 28, 1568, State Archives,
Vienna. Cf. *Avvisi di Roma of August 14 and September 4,
1568, Urb. 1040, p. 562–573, Vatican Library ; C. FIRMANUS,
*Diarium, in Miscell., Arm. XII., 31, p. 253. Papal Secret
Archives. A *brief to Girolamo Mercuriani of November 10,
1569, recalls him from Padua to Rome, where there was a lack
of doctors ; see Arm. 44, t. 14, n. 287 and 288, ibid.

[2] Cf. with GABUTIUS, loc. cit. cf. the *report of Strozzi to Maximilian II. from Rome, January 18, 1567, State Archives, Vienna,
and the *Avviso di Roma of March 8, 1567, Urb. 1040, p. 367b,
Vatican Library.

[3] See GABUTIUS, loc. cit. The other day, reports an *Avviso di
Roma of August 10, 1566, the Pope received in the Sala grande of
the palace of S. Marco 100 Christian slaves set free by Doria ;
each received " 1 scudo, buon pranzo, camisa nova, capello et
paio di scarpe." Urb. 1040, p. 269. Cf. ibid. 399 *Avviso di
Roma of May 31, 1567 and Urb. 1041, p. 4 the *Avviso of January
4, 1569. Vatican Library. See also LADERCHI, 1569, n. 347 ;
SANTORI, Autobiogr., XII., 346, and in App. n. 67 the *audiences
of Santori with the Pope. Papal Secret Archives.

[4] *" In effetto in operibus pietatis da un gran tempo in qua non
è stato maggior Papa di lui." *Avviso di Roma of May 10, 1567,
Urb. 1040, p. 392b, Vatican Library.

[5] See *Avviso di Roma of September 28, 1566, ibid. 290.

of cloth.[1] Trade was also protected by special constitutions
against usury on the exchange market, and against fraudulent
banking.[2] A special constitution was directed against the
robbery of shipwrecked mariners.[3] The death penalty,
already in existence for the crime of clipping the gold coinage,
was extended in 1570 to the silver coinage as well.[4]

Just as in Rome itself efforts were made to improve the
unhealthy districts, and steps were taken to prevent the
pollution of the Tiber, which was generally used for drinking
purposes,[5] so Pius V. also directed his attention to the draining
of the marshes in the Campagna[6] and in other parts of the
Papal States, as for example, in the neighbourhood of Ravenna
and Foligno.[7]

[1] See Bull. Rom., VII., 612 seq. ; cf. the *Avvisi di Roma of
September 27, 1567, Urb. 1040, p. 442, Vatican Library, and
July 3, 1568, State Archives, Vienna. In the first of these *Avvisi
the subsidy for the weaving of cloth from the Pope is given as
10,000 scudi (the 100,000 in CATENA, 128 seq. is an exaggeration).

[2] Bull. Rom., VII., 862 seq. ; cf. DE CUPIS, 158.

[3] See LADERCHI, 1566, n. 142 seq.

[4] See Bull. Rom., VII., 861 seq.

[5] See CATENA, 50 ; LANCIANI, II., 26 ; IV., 13 seq., 24 seq., 28.
In his *letter of April 27, 1566, Cusano (State Archives, Vienna)
speaks of the order that the Cardinals must pave the street before
their palaces. Cf. in App. n. 50 the *report of B. Pia to Luzzara
of July 10, 1568. Gonzaga Archives, Mantua. An *Avviso di
Roma of August 21, 1568, also states that a monthly tax of " 3
giulii " was imposed for the keeping clean of the streets on every
possessor of a carriage (Urb. 1040, p. 567b, Vatican Library).
In the inundation of the Tiber in January, 1567, when part of the
passage between the Vatican and the Castle of St. Angelo fell in,
Pius V. gave all the assistance that he could. See the *report
of Strozzi of January 4, 1567, State Archives Vienna. See also
BACCI, Del Tevere, Rome, 1576, 369 seq.

[6] See the motu proprio " Dei nostri almae urbis." Cf. DE
CUPIS, 149 and LANCIANI, IV., 14.

[7] See the *brief to " Franc. episc. Imolae, Romand. gubern."
of March 21, 1566 (Ravenna) and the *other, to " Ioh. Bapt.
Garganus, civis Rom., commiss. noster," of November 2, 1567
(Foligno), Archives of Briefs, Rome.

The greatest credit is due to the Pope for the improvement effected in agriculture in the Campagna, and the establishment of granaries in Rome. After he had, in September, 1566, set up the tribunal of agriculture, he issued, on October 11th in the same year, a constitution which has deservedly become famous, which afforded protection and support of all kinds to agriculture in the Campagna, secured the importation of grain into Rome, and strictly forbade every kind of monopoly. Anyone who offended in this respect, be he baron, bishop, or even Cardinal, was subject to the severest penalties. In his care for the well-being of his subjects, the Pope constantly saw to it that the officials in charge of the supply of grain, who were partly municipal and partly subject to the Apostolic Camera, and who fixed the price of grain, should always supply it to the bakers at the same fixed price, however high might be the price at which it was purchased.[1] Especially in times of famine, as for example in 1568 and 1569, the Pope made unwearied efforts to meet the scarcity, and to prevent any kind of usurious profit being made out of the crisis. The people must have bread at a fair price, since, as he was accustomed to say, it is written in the Bible : *qui abscondit frumenta, maledicetur in populis.* (Prov. xi 26.)[2]

---

[1] *Cf.* CATENA, 53 *seq. ;* GABUTIUS, 206 *seq.* For these two ordinances see Bull. Rom., VII., 481 *seq.*, 484 *seq.* Besides NICOLAI, II., 37 *seq.*, see also DE CUPIS, 151 *seq.*, 153 *seq.*, and the same author's Saggio bibl. degli scritti e delle leggi sull'agro Romano, Rome, 1903, 146, and Usi civili nell'agro Romano, Rome, 1906, 21 *seq. ;* also ARDANT, Papes et paysans, Paris, 1891, 147 *seq. ;* TOMASSETTI, I., 215 ; RODOCANACHI, Institutions, 280. An *Avviso di Roma of July 6, 1569, announces that on the previous day the Pope had taken 30,000 scudi from the Castle of St. Angelo for the " abondanza," and had sent 20,000 to the Marches for grain. Urb. 1041, p. 106, Vatican Library.

[2] *Cf.* CATENA, 53 *seq.*, and the *Avvisi di Roma of August 17 and September 24, 1569, August 12, 1570, and September 12, 1571, Urb. 1040, p. 133, 146 ; 1041, p. 318 ; 1042, p. 112, Vatican Library. See also Bull. Rom., VII., 848 *seq.*

Unfortunately, his subordinates did not always act up to
the noble aims of the Pope,[1] who, moreover, was not always
very happy in the steps he took in his capacity of temporal
ruler. For example, an edict concerning the coinage which
he issued in July, 1571, caused great consternation.[2] His
true sphere was to be found in his care for spiritual matters,
and, like Cardinal Bonelli, he was, in view of all that had to
be done in that direction, unable to devote sufficient attention
to the temporal administration. Therefore, in April, 1568,
Cardinal Chiesa was appointed to assist the Cardinal nephew,
and in the January of the following year, Cardinals Alciati
and Paleotto were likewise appointed.[3] In July, 1570, it was
rumoured that the Pope intended to withdraw altogether
from temporal affairs, and leave them to these four Cardinals.[4]

The attitude of Pius V. towards art has been misjudged in
more than one respect. He laid himself open to this by an
enactment by which he placed himself in direct opposition
to the Popes of the age of the Renaissance. On February 10th,
1566, it was learned in the city that the Pope had made over
to the Roman people all the antique statues which were in the
theatre of the Belvedere and its surroundings, and had
charged some of the nobles to have them moved to the Capitol.
It was further said that the priceless treasures which stood in
the cortile of the Belvedere, and which had been protected
from rain and risk of injury by screens in the time of Pius IV.,
were to share the same fate. The Pope's reason for this was
that it was unfitting that the successor of St. Peter should

---

[1] *Cf.* RODOCANACHI, Institutions, 280.

[2] See *Avviso di Roma of July 18, 1571, Urb. 1042, p. 90,
Vatican Library.

[3] See the *Avvisi di Roma of April 3, 1568, and January 15,
1569, Urb. 1040, p. 479, and 1041, p. 4, Vatican Library.

[4] An *Avviso di Roma of July 8, 1570 (Urb. 1041, p. 307,
Vatican Library) reports : " S'è sparso voce per la corte chel
Papa non voglia più intervenire alli negotii profani et secolari,
ma deputarvi sopra 4 cardinali cioè Cesi, Thiano, Montalto et
Piacenza, et che Sua S^{tà} voglia attender solamente alle cose
spirituali et dell' inquisitione."

have pagan images in his palace. In view of the enthusiasm for sculpture then prevalent in Rome it is not surprising that this proposal of the Pope should have aroused much opposition, even from many of the Cardinals, and it was due to their remonstrances that the famous antiques of the gallery of statues in the Belvedere were retained in the Vatican. Pius, however, gave way to the entreaties of the Cardinals on condition that the collection should remain closed to the public.[1]

An inventory, compiled on February 11th, 1566, of the antiques which were to be made over to the Roman people, includes 127 pieces, among which, it is worthy of note, was even the statue of St. Hippolytus. On February 27th a further list of about twenty busts and statues was added.[2] The

[1] See the *report of Cusano of February 16, 1566 (which escaped the notice even of Michaelis, the best authority on this matter), according to which the words used by Pius V. were : " che non conveniva a chi era successore di Pietro tener simili idoli in casa . . et perchè ve ne sono alcune servate delle più rare par pur' che ad instantia di molti cardinali che glielo chiesero in gratia speciale S. Stᵃ si sia contentata ci restino ma con fatto stiano sempre chiuse." Cusano goes on to relate that when Cardinal Farnese pointed out to the Pope that it would be desirable to give to the Emperor the 12 busts (che sono per moderni cosa rarissima) which had been copied in the time of Pius IV. from antique busts of the Emperors, Pius V. assented (State Archives, Vienna). The letters of Arco on this subject were published by MICHAELIS (Statuenhof, 63) ; his doubt as to whether the last letter, which tells how the busts had been sent to Spain, belongs to 1568 or 1569, is settled by an *Avviso di Roma of January 24, 1568, which states : *" Li 12 imperatori, che con tanta diligentia erano custoditi in Belvedere da Pio IV., sono stati tutti incassati et si mandono per ordine del Papa a donare al re catholico." Urb. 1040, p. 479b, Vatican Library. Ibid. 169b, an *Avviso of February 9, 1566, with the notice : *" Il papa ha donato tutte le statue di Belvedere al popolo Romano con non poco dispiacere delle creature di Pio IV."

[2] These lists in BICCI, Boccapaduli, 115 seq., from which is taken the new edition of MICHAELIS, Statuenhof, 60 seq., with a note of those which were sent to the Capitol, and of those sent to Florence.

senate and people of Rome at once took steps to take possession
of this precious gift, and ordered that a mass of thanksgiving
should be celebrated at the Minerva on St. Antony's day.[1]
They first received 17 statues and statuettes, a small group
with putti, and 12 busts, which did not include any works of
great importance, and which came for the most part from the
stairs leading to the Belvedere, and from one of the rooms
in the Vatican. In the meantime the Cardinals of Pius IV.
were successful in dissuading the Pope from sending the
remaining statues. The Romans, however, did not give up
hopes of acquiring them, and in February, 1570, they made
a claim for them, though without immediate success.[2]

The news that the Pope intended to purge his palace of
antiques aroused in the mind of so great a connoisseur as the
Emperor Maximilian II. the desire to obtain possession of
some pieces for his own collection. Since, however, Pius V.
had in the meantime made a present of some of the statues
to the Cardinals, it was not easy to find any which would
suit the Emperor's purpose. In July, 1569, two more than
life-size statues were sent to him, a Hercules and an Aphrodite,
which were followed some years later by three statues from

---

[1] '*Le statue del Belvedere già si levano e le conducono in
Campidoglio per haver il Papa fattone gratia al popolo Romano,
et perciò s'obligano in perpetuo far celebrar una messa nella
Minerva nella capella di S. Tommaso d'Aquino il giorno di S.
Antonio e dare un calice con 4 torcie bianche ogn'anno, e mercordi
cominciorno, ove furono tutti i cardinali Rom." (Avviso di Roma
of February 16, 1566, Urb. 1040, p. 182. Vatican Library; cf.
FIRMANUS, *Diarium, in Miscell., Arm. XII., 31, p. 56b, Papal
Secret Archives). On March 2, 1566, Cusano *reports that the
deputies of the city of Rome had been during the whole week
transporting statues from the Belvedere to the Capitol (State
Archives, Vienna). Of the inscriptions of thanks at the Capitol,
one mentions no definite number, and the other mentions 30 ;
see FORCELLA, I., 61–62.

[2] *" Li conservatori hanno dimandato in gratia al Papa le
statue di Belvedere per metterle nella bella fabrica di Campidoglio," the Pope has postponed " il levarle." *Avviso di Roma of
February 4, 1570, Urb. 1041, p. 231b, Vatican Library.

the Villa Giulia.[1] Several pieces from the same place were also sent to Florence, as a gift to Francesco de' Medici, the eldest son of Cosimo. The agent of the Medici in Rome obtained from the Pope in March, 1569, the gift of no fewer than 26 statutes taken from the villa of Pius IV.[2]

This generosity of the Pope, which had stripped the villas of Julius III. and Pius IV., aroused the fear in Rome that Pius V. intended to make a clean sweep of all pagan remains. In the spring of 1569 the Imperial agent, Cusano, announced to his master that the Pope intended not only to destroy the theatre of the Belvedere, but also to lay hands on the Colosseum and the triumphal arches, in order to remove the temptation from visitors to Rome to pay more attention to pagan than to Christian things. The fear was expressed, as had been the case in the time of Adrian VI., that, in order to obtain the material for the restoration of the churches, Pius would make an onslaught on the grandest monuments of Roman antiquity and reduce the statues to lime,[3] though it was soon realized that these fears were exaggerated. The changes in the theatre of the Belvedere were limited to the removal of the tiers of seats, so that there might be no more public performances

---

[1] See the reports of Arco in MICHAELIS, Statuenhof, 63 *seq.*, to complete which use may also be made of the *report of Monti from Rome, July 28, 1569, which mentions the statues of Hercules and Aphrodite (8–9 palms in height) presented to the Emperor, " et sono stimate assai per la loro bellezza et antichità." State Archives, Vienna. *Ibid.* a *report of Arco, which escaped the notice of Michaelis, of March 19, 1569 : Cardinal Colonna has presented to the Emperor a bust of Socrates and one of Antoninus, Farnese a statue of Mercury. In Varia, fasc. 4 of the State Archives, Vienna, there is also a *letter from Fra Guglielmo della Porta to Maximilian II., of March 23, 1569 : he sends the Emperor a sketch for a crucifix.

[2] See MICHAELIS, Statuenhof, 43 *seq.*, 65 *seq.* ; *cf. Archäol. Zeitung*, XXXIV., 152.

[3] See in App. n. 58 the *letter of Cusano of March 26, 1569, State Archives, Vienna, and the *Avviso di Roma of April 2, 1569, Urb. 1041, p. 50, Vatican Library (App. n. 59).

there, a thing which, in the eyes of Pius V., was unseemly in the palace of the head of Christendom.[1] The Colosseum and the triumphal arches were quite unharmed, while much of the magnificent statuary with which the Renaissance Popes had enriched the Vatican remained to excite the admiration of future visitors ; this was especially the case with the famous gallery of statues which, though closed to the public, was placed under the care of the Pope's physician, Michele Mercati, who was director of the botanical garden established by Pius on the Vatican Hill.[2]

All this shows that the reproach which has been levelled against Pius V., that he was the declared enemy of antiquity, is unjust.[3] Granted his great strictness as to morals,[4] it was only to be expected that he would be scandalized at the many nude statues, as indeed had previously been the case with northern visitors to Rome,[5] but there is no evidence as to this,

---

[1] *" La destrutione del teatro di Belvedere si ridurà a questo che quelle scale si levino via tutte et che si facino stanze habitabili acciò non ci resti comodità di far spettacoli publici." *Avviso di Roma of April 16, 1569, Urb. 1041, p. 54b, Vatican Library.

[2] See MICHAELIS, Statuenhof, 44. That of Cosimo I. served as a model for the botanical garden ; see REUMONT, Toskana, I., 273.

[3] This has recently been set forth clearly by HÜLSEN (Götting. Gelehrte Anzeigen, 1914, n. 5, p. 271 n. 3).

[4] In this connexion mention may be made of the hitherto unnoticed, but highly characteristic, comment, which is found in a letter from Archbishop Olaus Magnus of Upsala to Hosius, dated Venice, June 8, 1552. In this letter the strict northerner blames the freedom of Cardinal Crescenzi : " mentre egli viveva io vidi nel suo palazzo a Roma fauni, satiri e nudità femminili, come se la carne ribelle non avesse forza sufficiente a indurre la debole natura umana in mille immagini e pericoli malvagi." HOSII Epist., II., 211.

[5] Cardinal Ricci obtained in August, 1569, the busts, statues and bas-reliefs hitherto preserved in the villa of Julius III. ; he sent them to Florence ; see *Avviso di Roma of August 6 and 13, 1569 (" Il residuo delle statue della vigna di Giulio III., che ha havuto il card. Montepulciano, si mandano a poco a poco al duca

and the very fact that the Pope presented such statues to
the Romans, as well as to the cardinals and princes,[1] to be
publicly exposed in their palaces, goes to show that he, in
common with almost all Italians, felt no scruples on the
subject.[2] If he had considered the exhibition of nude statues
in his palace dangerous for himself, he would certainly have
acted ruthlessly in the matter. All that can with truth be
said of his hostility for antiquity is that, to Pius V., whose
interests lay entirely in religious matters, the statues of
antiquity, which were, in the eyes, not only of the learned men

di Firenze et alcune sorte di pietre mischie bellissime "), Urb.
1041, p. 117, 131, Vatican Library. Since the gift had only
been made by word of mouth, Pius V. confirmed it in a *motu
proprio of September 27, 1571, Ricci Archives, Rome. Cardinal
Este also received presents before his quarrel with Pius V. (see
LANCIANI, III., 81 ; cf. WINNEFELD, Die Villa Hadrians bei
Tivoli, Berlin, 1895, 5) ; see in App. n. 52 the *report of Cusano
of December 18, 1568, State Archives, Vienna. The two examples
of the Pasquino group which had been found near the Mausoleum
of Augustus and outside the Porta Portese also went to Florence
in 1570. The most important discoveries of antiquities in the
time of Pius V. were the monuments and inscriptions of the
brothers Arvali which came to light in 1570 outside the Porta
Portese, and which for the most part went to the collection of
Fulvio Orsini ; see HENZEN, Acta (1874). An *Avviso di Roma
of October 25, 1569, relates the discovery of an antique which
had taken place in a rather curious way in the city : *" L'orso
del card. Orsino che sta legato appresso Pasquino graffiando
l'altro giorno la terra sotto quella pietra di marmo, dove è fermato
Pasquino cavò fuori moti giulii antichi et alcune medaglie d'oro
con una chiave d'argento." Urd. 1041, p. 169b, Vatican Library.

[1] Cf. supra p. 112 seq. In 1569 and 1570 Albert V. of Bavaria
also received from Pius V. presents of antique statues ; see
GOETZ, Beiträge, 508, n. 2, 733 n. 1. In BERTOLOTTI, Artisti
Venez., Venice, 1884, 27, a permit to M. Soriano of July 14, 1571,
to transport from Rome to Venice " 2 teste di marmo antiche."

[2] Since scandal was given at Bologna by the nudity of the
statue of Neptune on the fountain there, Pius V. approved of its
being covered up ; see PATRIZI, Il Gigante, Bologna, 1897, 62.

of the time, but also of princes of strict Catholic principles
" venerable relics of ancient days "[1] were either matters of
indifference, or else, as being idolatrous, unsuitable for the
adornment of his palace ; his point of view was very similar
to that of Adrian VI.[2]

Even though we may admit a want of understanding on his
part of the great educational value of such artistic treasures,
Pius V. was by no means indifferent, and still less, hostile,
towards the arts. There exists an authentic document
concerning the inventory made after his death of the objects
which adorned his private apartments ; this shows that they
were filled with all manner of works of art, bronzes, intarsia,
cameos, medals, paintings on wood, among them a Last
Judgment by Fra Angelico, miniatures by Giulio Clovio, and
other precious objects.[3] Since Pius V. did not allow himself
the smallest luxury—he went so far in his parsimony that
he at first used the robes worn by his predecessor before having
new ones made for himself[4]—one can only suppose that these
objects of art were for the most part presents. Some of
them, as for example the gifts of Requesens and Cardinal
Ricci,[5] and that of the Bishop of Portalegre, can even be

---

[1] In the *letter from Albert V. to his agent, Castellini, dated
Munich, April 27, 1568, we read : " Literas tuas, quarum dies
fuit 27 Martii, accepimus et ex iis pergratum nobis fuit intelligere
quid de statuis ac antiquitatibus illis egeris, nec dubitamus quin
rev. dom. card. Alexandrinus tantum officii ea in re in nostri
gratiam sit positurus, tu nulli labori parcens omni labore, studio
et diligentia in id totum incumbas, ut tandem etiam aulam
nostram *venerandae antiquitatis monumentis* secundum vota
nostra conspicuam havere possimus." Orig. in Cod. B. 34, p. 5,
Library at Faenza. For Castellini and the Duke's collection *cf.*
the article of CHRIST in the Papers of the Academy at Munich,
Phil.-hist. Klasse, X., 357 *seq.*

[2] See Vol. VII. of this work p. 7 *seq.*

[3] See LANCIANI, IV., 41 *seq.*

[4] See CATENA, 27.

[5] " *Il commendator di Castiglia ha dato a S. S^{tà} un panno
d' oro et di seta nel quale è ritratta l'historia de tre magi. Il
card^{le} di Montepulciano ha donato a S. B. una canna d'India

identified. In May, 1568, the Duke of Urbino presented Pius V. with some valuable majolica, which afterwards came into the possession of Cardinal Bonelli.[1]

The building operations of Pius V. in the Vatican must have cost 30,000 scudi.[2] First of all he had to undertake a restoration of the Sistine Chapel, in the ceiling of which serious cracks had appeared as early as October, 1565. The state of the chapel was so bad that none of the functions could be held there on January 18th, 1566, the feast of St. Peter's Chair. Pius V. at once took the work in hand with so much energy that the chapel was soon fit for use again. The pictures on the ceiling were saved, and skilfully restored by the Modenese painter, Domenico Carnevale.[3]

In the Vatican Palace Pius V. completed the works begun by his predecessor,[4] and he further erected a new building

d'altezza d'un huomo, i cui nodi sono cerchiati d'argento ne quali è scritta la vita di S. Pietro." Strozzi to Maximilian II. from Rome, January 4, 1567, State Archives, Vienna. *Cf.* *brief to Andreas de Noronha, August 22, 1569, Arm. 44, t. 14, p. 191, Papal Secret Archives.

[1] This gift of the " bellissima credenza de piati de maiolica historiata con figure " is noted in the *Avviso di Roma of March 13, 1568, Urb. 1040, p. 487b, Vatican Library. The gift to Cardinal Bonelli is related by Cipriano Saracinello in a *letter to Cardinal Farnese from Rome, March 6, 1568, State Archives, Naples, C. Farnes., 763. A majolica plate (Venetian work) with the cardinal's arms of the Ghislieri in the collection of R. Zschille is mentioned by O. v. FALKE in his Katalog der italien. Majoliken, Leipzig, 1899, n. 22, but in assigning it to the year 1550, he is certainly putting the date too early.

[2] *Cf.* CATENA, 135.

[3] See STEINMANN in *Kunstchronik*, N.S., XV. (1903–04), 570 *seq.* and SIXTINA, II., 779 *seq.* To the evidence there given must be added a payment of December 20, 1569, from the *Secondo libro d. Recettoria d. r. Camera Apost. del Aº 1567, State Archives, Rome.

[4] Arco on April 12, 1567, reports : *" S.Stà ha detto di voler far finire le fabriche principate da Pio IV. et principalmente quella

adjoining the Borgia apartments. The Torre Pia contains three chapels, one above the other, which were dedicated to St. Stephen the martyr, St. Peter Martyr, the Dominican, and St. Michael, and were richly adorned by Giorgio Vasari and Guglielmo della Porta.

The chapel of St. Stephen, on the ground floor, and now adjoining the store-rooms of the Vatican Gallery, still bears the arms of Pius V. on the door. The frescoes on the walls represent scenes from the life of the protomartyr ; his preaching, the healing of a cripple, his distribution of alms, and his burial. On the frieze, besides the date, 1571, may be seen the words of the saint in the Acts of the Apostles : " I see the heavens opened, and the Son of Man standing at the right hand of God. Lord, lay not this sin to their charge." The painting on the ceiling shows the heavens opened, with the most holy Trinity and the choirs of angels. The altar-piece, which is the key to the other paintings, represents the stoning of St. Stephen. This latter work of Vasari is now in the chapel of Nicolas V.[1]

The chapel dedicated to St. Peter Martyr, and adjoining

---

del Palazzo," and on October 4, 1567, *it seems that the Pope wishes to finish the " fabrica di Belvedere " (State Archives, Vienna). The arms of Pius V., among other things in the Cortile of the Belvedere, are noted in CHATTARD, II., 237, 242, 405, 407, 433. One is still preserved on the inside of the doorway of the Mint.

[1] Cf. VASARI, VII., 715 seq. ; TAJA, 95 seq. ; CHATTARD, II., XXVIII, 92 seq., 238 seq., 439 seq. ; LANCIANI, IV., 8 seq. In the *books of accounts of the " Deposit. gen. della Camera Apost." there are entered for the years 1570-1572 many payments for the " fabrica delle stanze nuove in palazzo apost. acanto a Torre Borgia," and of the " capelle " there. In spite of the description, which is very incomplete, which has been given by Taja, Chattard, and Moroni (IX., 156 seq.), these chapels are now almost entirely forgotten ; the first and the third are only accessible by special permission. For the chapel painted by Vasari with the help of his pupil, Zucchi, see also Voss, Die Malerei der Spät Renaissance in Rom und Florenz, II., Berlin, 1920, 292.

the Borgia apartments, is also in a good state of preservation. The walls and ceiling are decorated in a very rich style in stucco, gold, and fresco. The altar-piece, also the work of Vasari, represents the martyrdom of the champion of the faith against the Cathari, who came from the Dominican order. The frescoes on the walls, still quite intact, and executed by Vasari and his pupils, depict scenes in the life of the saint. On the right the saint is seen driving away the devil who had appeared in the market place of Florence to disturb his preaching ; on the left is another of his miracles. On the small wall to the right of the entrance is shown the presentation of standards with red crosses to those who went to fight the heretics, and on the left the saint in prayer before the crucifix. The ceiling shows the triumph of the Church over the heretics, together with allegorical figures of the cardinal virtues and portraits of Dominican saints ; first the founder with the lily, two Popes, probably Innocent V. and Benedict XI., and three writers, Thomas Aquinas, Albert the Great, and Vincent of Beauvais.[1] No less significant than the choice of subjects is the fact that the allegorical figures, which the artists would naturally have shown as naked, are clothed. It is also noteworthy that the builder of the chapel in his modesty has introduced nothing to record the fact.

The chapel of St. Michael, adjoining the Stanze, has been completely changed by later decoration.[2] The altar-piece, by Vasari, showed the Coronation of Our Lady, while in the dome was seen the expulsion of Lucifer and the rebel angels from heaven.

The chapel dedicated to St. Peter Martyr was intended for the use of the Pope himself, and the other two for his household, who were obliged to say or hear mass daily. For the same reason, a special little church, S. Martino e S. Sebastiano, decorated by Giulio Mazzoni, a

[1] *Cf.* CHATTARD, II., 303.
[2] The lunettes are completely destroyed, and the paintings are by modern hands.

pupil of Vasari and Daniele da Volterra, was erected behind
the bastion of Nicholas V. for the use of the Swiss Guard
at the Vatican.[1]

At the Villa Pia Pius V. only completed what was strictly
necessary. In a very different spirit from the rather pompous
way in which Pius IV. called attention to his own work, Pius V.
very modestly marked the part which was due to him with
a small tablet bearing the letters P.V.[2] He ordered his
physicians to grow palms and exotic shrubs in the garden
of the Villa, which rather interfered with the character of
the building.[3] During the summer of 1569 Pius V. often
dined at the Villa;[4] he only resided at the Palace of S. Marco
during the first summer of his pontificate.[5] Later on his only
recreation consisted in walks to his beloved convent of S.
Sabina on the Aventine,[6] and to the modest little villa which

---

[1] *Cf.* CHATTARD, III., 334, ARMELLINI, 463, LANCIANI, IV., 9.
The arms of Pius V. on the exterior are still preserved, but the
inscription mentioned by FORCELLA (VI., 79) is destroyed. The
frescoes over the altar represent God the Father, in the right hand
niche is St. Sebastian, and in the left one St. Martin. The altar-
piece is an Annunciation of the Madonna. On the right hand
wall near the altar recess Christ is depicted on the cross with
Peter and John, and on the left is the Madonna with St. Anne and
the Bambino.

[2] See FRIEDLANDER, 88, who has not made use of the *Avviso
di Roma of June 10, 1570 : *Pius V. brought a water supply from
the Vatican to the casino of Pius IV., which had been commenced
by his predecessor. State Archives, Vienna.

[3] *Cf.* A. GOTHEIN, Gartenkunst, I., 278.

[4] See *Avviso di Roma of July 6, 1569, Urb. 1041, p. 106,
Vatican Library.

[5] DENGEL, Palazzo di Venezia, 106 *seq.*

[6] According to a *report of Arco of June 21, 1567 (State Archives,
Vienna) the Pope visited the humble cell, which commands a
splendid view, and contains memorials of himself, and adds that
he had once lived there as a monk. The name of Pius V. occurs
several times in inscriptions in the convent ; see FORCELLA,
VII., 305.

he had built as Cardinal outside the Porta Cavalleggieri on‧ the Via Aurelia.[1]

Pius V. once declared that the Popes ought to rejoice the world, not so much by their buildings as by their virtues, and accordingly his building operations in the city were confined to what would either serve some religious purpose or would be for the public utility.[2]

To the former class belong the completion of S. Maria degli Angeli,[3] S. Maria in Traspontina,[4] and the ceiling of the Lateran basilica,[5] the building of SS. Domenico e Sisto and the adjoining convent of Dominican nuns on the southern slope of the Quirinal,[6] the Palace of the Inquisition,[7] the erec-

---

[1] There he sometimes recreated himself in the autumn with " caccia de tordi " ; see *Avviso di Roma of October 20, 1571, Urb. 1042, p. 135b, Vatican Library. For the " Casaletto di Pio V.," now a school of agriculture, see FEA, Storia delle acque, 37 ; NIBBY, Dintorni, I., 405 seq. ; LANCIANI, IV., 31 seq. ; Hist.-pol. Blätter, LXXXV., 137 seq. On the right of the entrance is the simple kitchen, then comes the garden, and lastly the villa, with a large court-yard. No inscription nor coat of arms recalls Pius V., whereas the arms of the subsequent owners, the Chigi, are still to be seen. For the neighbouring chapel of the Madonna del Riposo, see TOMASSETTI, II., 480.

[2] See GABUTIUS, 208. Here, as in CATENA, 132 seq., 135 seq., is a series of notes on the attitude of Pius V. towards art, which, however, could be added to in many ways.

[3] See the briefs of March 30, 1566, and February 7, 1568, in LADERCHI, 1566, n. 70 and 1568, n. 28 ; Corresp. dipl., I., 182 seq.

[4] See BONANNI, I., 320 seq. ; VENUTI, 130 seq.

[5] See RASPONUS, 16, 18 ; ROHAULT, 266, 519 seq. ; BERTO-LOTTI, Art. Lomb., I., 136 ; Art. Francesi, X. (1907), 134 ; THODE, V., 189 ; LAUER, 314 seq., 316, 318 seq. ; LANCIANI, IV., 28. Cf. Bibl. Corvisieri, II., Rome, 1901, 376. The constitution of Pius V. on the pre-eminence of the Lateran Basilica in LADERCHI, 1569, n. 48. An *Avviso di Roma of October 30, 1568, states : Pius V. visited at the Lateran " la fabrica che S. Stᵃ fa fare per li penitencieri di S. Pietro." State Archives, Vienna.

[6] See CATENA, 25 ; NIBBY, I., 209.

[7] Cf. infra, p. 288 seqq.

tion of a house for converted Jews near the church of the
SS. Annunziata in the ruins of the Forum of Augustus,[1] the
conversion of the monastery of S. Basilio into a place of
instruction for catechumens, the restoration of various
churches and monasteries,[2] and lastly the continuation of
the new building of St. Peter's.[3]

Pius V. rendered great service to the completion of the
basilica of the Prince of the Apostles by devoting large sums
of money to it.[4] The difficult question of the vaulting of
the dome, which had already been a matter of anxiety to his
predecessor, especially preoccupied him.[5] This matter,
together with others connected with the building, was discussed
in the spring of 1567, when, as the result of the pressing and
repeated invitation of the Pope, Giorgio Vasari came to Rome,
where he was given lodgings in the Vatican close to the Pope's

[1] See NIBBY, I., 100 ; ANGELI, Chiese, 49 ; LANCIANI, IV., 25.
On the gate of the convent (Via di Tor de' Conti, n. 1) may still
be seen the inscription " Pius V. Pont. Max." ; the coat of arms
which was above it has been destroyed.

[2] See ARMELLINI, 215,375 ; *ibid*, 298 *seq*. the assignment of
S. Maria Egiziaca to the Armenians. *Cf.* LANCIANI, IV., 12.
Payments for the restoration of S. Sabina in the *Terzo libro d.
Deposit. d. v. Cam. Apost. 1568, State Archives, Rome. On the
two side entrances, now walled up (facing the Via de'Penitenzieri)
of S. Spirito in Sassia may be read the name " Pius V. P.M." ; on
the façade of the church of the Minerva his arms may be seen.
On May 15, 1568, Arco reports : *on Monday the Pope went to
S. Sabina and ordered that the ruined church of the Priory on the
Aventine be restored ; on June 19, 1568, he reports : *the heirs
of Cardinal Salviati were ordered to pay 3,000 scudi, as Pius V.
wished " sgravar l'anima del cardinale con far riparare la chiesa
del priorato alla quale non haveva mai fatto beneficio alcuno "
(State Archives, Vienna), the arms of Pius V. on the Torre di
S. Andrea at Orvieto also undoubtedly tell of some work of
restoration.

[3] *Cf.* App. n. 66.

[4] See LADERCHI, 1569, n. 50 ; *cf.* J. C. VESPIGNANI, Compend.
privileg. fabricae S. Petri, Rome, 1676, 6 *seqq.*, 17 *seq.*

[5] *Cf. Jahrbuch der Preuss. Kunstsamml.*, XXXIII., 152 *seq.*

own apartments. Vasari takes to himself the credit of having determined Pius V. not to allow the smallest deviation from the plans of Michelangelo. Jacopo Vignola[1] was appointed architect in chief of St. Peter's, at first by himself, and later with his son, Giacinto.[2]

It was Jacopo Vignola who, in 1568 by the order of Cardinal Farnese, began the building of the magnificent church of the Jesuits, the Gesù, which was to attain to such importance, both from the artistic and the religious point of view.[3]

An especially beautiful trait of the character of Pius V. was his gratitude to all those who had ever conferred any favour on him. To this feeling of piety were due the monuments, so remarkable for their rich decoration in coloured marbles, which he erected to Paul IV. in S. Maria sopra Minerva, to Cardinal Alfonso Carafa in the Cathedral of Naples, and to Cardinal Ridolfo Pio di Carpi at the Trinità dei Monti.[4] For

[1] *Cf.* D. FREY, Michelangelo-Studien, Vienna, 1920, 111 *seq.*

[2] See *Frey* in *Jahrbuch der Preuss. Kunstsamml.*, XXXVII., Beiheft, p. 50 *seq.* The " Deputati della fabrica di S. Pietro," who confirmed the mandate published by Frey, *loc. cit.* were : " Fr. Ar. Senensis, P. Narniensis, Alex. Casalis and Alex. Riarius." From a Bando concerning " beni alienati " of June 15, 1571, bound up with the Privilegia, auct., facult., indulgentiae fabricae princ. apost. S. Petri de Urbe, Rome, 1559, Barberini Library (now at the Vatican), stamp. TTT, II., 16, it appears that the deputies at the time were : " A. Riarius, F. archiepisc. Senen., A. Casalius, Dom. Pinellus." It is therefore incorrect to describe, as does Frey, *Fr. Ar.* as *Arberinus ;* we must read *Fr*[anc.] *Ar*[chiep.] *Senensis,* that is Bandini, who was Archbishop of Siena from 1529 to 1588.

[3] See in App. n. 49 the *Avvisi di Roma of May 29 and June 3, 1568, State Archives, Vienna. In 1567 there arose near the Torre delle Milizie the church and convent of S. Caterina da Siena, in 1568 on the road leading to S. Paolo the chapel of the " Divisione degli Apostoli," and in the years 1566–1569 the façade of S. Maria dell'Orto ; see *L'Arte,* 1913.

[4] See CATENA, 54 *seq. ;* BERTOLOTTI, Art. Lomb., I., 100, 102 *seq. ;* FORCELLA III., 125 ; ANCEL, Disgrâce, 178, n. 2. For the tomb of Paul IV., see also Vol. XIV. of this work, p. 416. Pay-

his own tomb he chose Bosco, his native place, where he built
a richly endowed convent for the Dominicans. Vasari
received the order to supply for this church of S. Croce a great
high altar with a representation of the Adoration of the Magi ;
he sent the painting to the Pope in the spring of 1567. In
October 1568 Pius V. commissioned another sculptor, Gianantonio Buzi, to erect his own tomb. The monument is still
in a good state of preservation. Between two rows of colums
there is shown the risen Christ, with the Pope kneeling at his
feet. At the two sides, between pillars, are large statues of
Faith and Charity. The monument is completed above by a
niche surmounted by a cross, and containing a statue of the
archangel Michael slaying the dragon.[1]

His love for his own country, which also found liberal
expression in other ways,[2] did not lead Pius V. to forget such
venerated sanctuaries as Loreto and Assisi. At Loreto he
had four magnificent bronze doors cast for the marble casing
of the Holy House, while at Assisi, over the chapel where
St. Francis died, he gave orders for the commencement of
the great church of S. Maria degli Angeli, which is distinguished
for its grand simplicity, and the lofty dome which can be seen
for miles across the plain of central Umbria.[3]

ments for the tombs of Paul IV. and Carpi in *Secondo e terzo
libro d. Recett. d. r. Cam. Apost. 1567 and 1568, State Archives,
Rome.

[1] See DELL'ACQUA,' 44, where there is a good reproduction ;
CATENA, 133 seq. ; THIEME VI. 380. Cf. BRUZZONE, Bosco, I.,
131, 133 ; II., 164 seq. ; Riv. di Alessandria, 1902, and XIV.,
383, 395 ; LANCIANI, IV., 44 seq. ; Jahrbuch der Preuss. Kunstsamml., XXXIX., 194 n. 1 ; KALLAB, Vasari-Studien, 125, 129 ;
BRUZZONE in Cosmos illustr., 1914, 43 ; L. MINA, Della chiesa e
convento di Bosco Marengo, Alessandria, 1904. For the altar of
Vasari, cf. KRAUS-SAUER, II., 2, 683. For the buildings of Pius V.
at Bosco, see App. nn. 10-15.

[2] See BRUZZONE, Bosco, 1., 134 seq. ; DELL'ACQUA, 29.

[3] See BEISSEL, Das hl. Haus zu Loreto, Freiburg, 1891, 18 ;
LASPEYRES, Kirchen der Renaissance in Mittel-Italien, Leipzig,
1882, Pt. 2, p. 37 ; GURLITT, Gesch. des Barockstiles, 56 seq. ;

Rome also owes to Pius V. a number of foundations of great public utility ; an establishment for the manufacture of wool, the continuation of the University buildings, the erection of suitable quarters for sick prisoners near Tor di Nona, the construction of the Via Alessandrina, and the Via Bonelli, which still keep alive to-day his own name and that of his secretary of state, and lastly the restoration of the Acqua Vergine,[1] by means of which Pius V. could boast that he had restored to the city a good water supply.[2] At first the Pope would hear nothing of fortifications, but the Turkish peril

GUASTI, La chiesa di S. Maria degli Angeli, Florence, 1882, 76 ; CAVANNA, L'Umbria Francescana, Perugia, 1910, 2 seq. According to the researches of P. GIUSTO, it was not Vignola but Galeazzo Alessi who sketched out the plan for S. Maria aigli Angeli. See Corriere d'Italia, 1920, No. 185.

[1] With GABUTIUS and CATENA loc. cit. Cf. also FEA, Storie d. acque antiche, 12 seq. ; NIBBY, II., 14 ; Riv. Europ., 1880, 375 seq. ; LANCIANI, IV., 12 seq. An *Avviso di Roma of August 14, 1568 relates : *" S'è risoluto che la fabrica già cominciata da Pio. IV. per condursi qua l'acqua di Salone si finischi secondo il disegno a beneficio publico." On the following Friday there was a meeting of the street authorities and deputies under the presidency of Cardinal Ricci. Urb. 1040, p. 562b, Vatican Library. Ibid. 1041, p. 268, an *Avviso di Roma of June 20, 1570 : On Wednesday the Pope went to Salone to give orders " che quell'acqua sia tirata in Roma sino insu la piazza della Rotonda sicome è stato principiato da Pio IV." Ibid. 334b, an *Avviso di Roma of September 2, 1570 : The Pope went to the vigna and visited the acqua di Salone, which now goes to the fountain of Trevi. An *Avviso of September 9, 1570 (State Archives, Vienna) reports : " L'acqua di Salone è condotta in Roma alla fontana de Trevi e si tratta di condurla in piazza Navona."

[2] Cf. the poems of Ludovico Cavani in Carmina illustr. poet., III., 320 seq. Another project of Pius V.'s was not carried out ; Arco says of it in his *report of November 11, 1570 : *" Qui si tratta di far fontane su tutte le piazze et si fa conto che si spenderanno più di 40 mila scudi." State Archives, Vienna. Ibid. an *Avviso di Roma of August 26, 1570, concerning the fountain of Cardinal Ricci at the " Collis hortulorum " (Pincio).

soon made him change his mind. On account of this the city walls were repaired, the fortifications of the Borgo,[1] on which the Turks taken prisoner at Lepanto were made to work, was completed,[2] the Castle of St. Angelo was strengthened,[3] the sea coast of Latium was protected by towers,[4] and the works at Civitavecchia, Ancona, and Camerino were finished.[5] Cesare Guasco,[6]

---

[1] *Cf.* LANCIANI, IV., 10 *seq.*; *Inventario*, I., 317. Several coats of arms are preserved in the Via delle Mura, near the Porta Cavalleggieri, among them a large one of Pius V. of 1568.

[2] See the *letter of Arco of December 15, 1571, State Archives, Vienna.

[3] See RODOCANACHI, St.-Ange, 171, according to whom the expenses came to 50,000 scudi. Nevertheless, in the museum of the Castle of St. Angelo there is only one inscription of the modest Pius V. He applied himself at once to the fortification of the Borgo ; see the *Avviso di Roma of January 1, 1566, and the *report of Serristori of January 19, 1566, State Archives, Florence, Medic. 3285. An *Avviso of March 20, 1568, states that for the fortification of the Borgo, besides the 50,000 scudi taken from the treasure in the Castle, Pius V. intended to impose a fresh tax " alla mola ; " Mons. di Narni supervised the works, which the Pope was anxious to hurry forward (Urb. 1040, p. 490). An *Avviso of April 3, 1568, says · *" Si seguita la fortificatione di Borgo et Castello con tanta dilgenza che l'opera sarà finita per tutto Giugno." (*ibid.* 499). But even by May 14, 1569, an *Avviso says that Narni is still going on " a far fabricare la fortezza di Borgo (Urb. 1041, p. 76, Vatican Library). *Cf.* ROCCHI, Le piante icnografiche di Roma del sec. XVI., Turin-Rome, 1902. Reference to the same subject is also made in the *Discorso sopra la fortificatione di Castel S. Angelo et del Borgo di Roma l'anno, 1568, Stockholm Library, Ant. Coll. Donation, 1742, Fol. Nr. 8, p. 341 *seq.*

[4] See Vol. XVIII. of this work.

[5] See GABUTIUS and CATENA, *loc. cit.*, BERTOLOTTI, Art. Subalp., 72 *seq.*, and Vol. XVIII. of this work. The fortification of Castelfranco, which was begun for the defence of Bologna, was not completed ; see BOTERO, Relationi VI., Venice, 1618, 40.

[6] See BERTOLOTTI, Art. Subalp., 68 *seq.*

Torquato Conti,[1] and Paciotti[2] were the engineers employed by the Pope.   According to Catena Pius V.
spent 341,800 scudi upon his building operations.[3]   Of the
painters employed by the Pope, among whom was to be found
a Netherlander, Bartolomaeus Sprenger,[4] Vasari is the one
most frequently mentioned.   Towards the end of the pontificate of Pius V. he sketched the great mural paintings which
were to decorate the Sala Regia ; besides the pictures of the
return of Gregory XI. from Avignon to Rome, no less than
three paintings were to celebrate the victory over the Turks,
but only that of the Battle of Lepanto had been finished when
the Pope died.[5]

[1] See the *report of Cusano of May 18, 1566, State Archives,
Vienna.

[2] See the *brief of February 27, 1572.   Archives of Briefs,
Rome.   Payments to the " Cavalier Paciotto " in *Deposit.,
t. 157 (1572), State Archives, Rome.

[3] CATENA, 226.

[4] See *Jahrb. der Kunstsamml. der österr. Kaiserhauses*, XXVIII.
105 ; cf. JANSEN-PASTOR, VI., 15–16, 113.   *Bullett. de l'Institut
historique Belge à Rome*, I., Rome, 1919, 309.   Zuccaro fell a
victim to the plague which raged during the summer of 1566 ;
see *Avviso di Roma of September 7, 1566 ; the other day took
place the burial of " Thadeo pittore tenuto in tal stima che
l'hanno posto nella Ritonda vicino a Raffaello d'Urbino." (Urb.
1040, p. 282b, Vatican Library).   His exaggerated epitaph in
FORCELLA, I., 297.   In a *letter of May 29, 1569, Arco speaks of
a " dipintore chiamato Ulisse da Volterra (la sua professione
principale è di lavorare di stucho et di fontane) " whom he
recommends to the Emperor (State Archives, Vienna).   For the
lack of painters in Rome (1568) see GACHARD, Corresp. de Philippe
II., II., 51.   For the goldsmiths of Pius V. see *Arch. stor. Lomb.*,
1877, I., 295 *seq.* and *Kunsthistor. Jahrb. des österr. Kaiserhauses*,
XII., 153 *seq.*, where there is an illustration and reproduction of
the sword and hat (now in Vienna) sent in 1568 by Pius V. to the
Archduke Ferdinand of the Tyrol.   Payments to Giov. Ant. de
Rossi *supra* p. 52, n. 1) " intagliatore della Zecca," in *Deposit.,
t. 157 (1572 Exit., p. 16, 19, State Archives, Rome).

[5] See KALLAB, Vasari-Studien, 134 ; QRBAAN in *Jahrbuch der
Preuss. Kunstsamml.*, XXXIX. (1919), Beiheft, p. 7.

Pius V. also took steps to promote learning, although—a thing which in view of his whole character cannot be considered surprising—worldly and aesthetic considerations gave place entirely to those which were practical and ecclesiastical.[1]

The poetical effusions with which he was hailed immediately after his election,[2] and again and again later on,[3] certainly made no appeal to him, any more than did the laudatory panegyrics of the various embassies for the *obedientia*.[4] We do not know of any poets being rewarded by him, though it is recorded that one who had composed pasquinades was severely punished.[5]   It would appear that even the poets[6]

[1] While still a Cardinal Pius V. had been active in this sense with the Venetian academy or " della Fama," which elected him its protector ; see HARTIG, Münchner Hofbibliothek, 216 *seq.*

[2] See CES. SACHETTI, I tre conti per la nuova creatione di Pio V., Bologna, 1566. The Bavarian humanist, Johann Anspach, also acclaimed Pius V. ; see *Hist.-pol. Blätter*, C., 501 *seq.*

[3] See the poems of Girol. and Cornelio Amalterio, of Girol. Catena, Lodovico Cavani and Tommaso Correa in *Carmina illustr. poet.*, I., 136 *seq.*, 178 *seq. ;* III., 314 *seq.*, 317 *seq.*, 319 *seq.*, 330 *seq.*, 448 *seq.*   *Ibid.* many poems on the battle of Lepanto. *Cf.* Vol. XVIII. of this work.

[4] The " Oratio ad Pium V.P.M. nomine ducis Alfonsi II: habita in Roma A, 1566," of M. A. Muret was at once printed in Rome by de Accoltis.   Muret had also saluted Pius IV. in the name of Francis II. (Oratio, ed. Romae, A. Bladus, 1560).   The *discourse of Poggiano to Pius V. in the name of the King of Poland in the Graziani Archives, Città di Castello.

[5] A poet, relates an *Avviso di Roma of January 4, 1567, asked the Pope for a vacant office ; Pius V. had the matter gone into, [6] poi li disse per esser authore et compositore di pasquinate in loco di gratia vi priviamo delli beneficii che tenete indegnamente aggiungendo che mai ne possiate havere et così se lo levò davanti." Urb. 1040, p. 343, Vatican Library.

[6] A Caro was looked upon as the most eminent poet, on whose death FIRMANUS (*Diarium XII., 31, p. 142b) reports : " Die dominica 17 novembris [1566] obiit in via Julia . . . Hannibal Carus. . . . Hic erat poeta unicus illis temporibus in Italia, pulcherrimi aspectus, optimae vitae, exemplaris in omnibus suis actionibus et honor, decus ac principale ornamentum totius nostri Piceni." Papal Secret Archives.

who sang the praises of the part taken by the Pope in the victory of Lepanto remained without recognition.[1] The fact that in spite of his parsimony he gave 5,000 scudi for the reprinting of the works of St. Thomas and St. Bonaventure shows in what direction the real interests of Pius V. lay.[2] It is true that he never carried into execution the literary plan which he had once, while a simple religious, propounded to a learned German, namely, an edition of unedited Greek works,[3] but on March 5th, 1571, he appointed a commission composed of Cardinals Sirleto, Hosius, Maffei, Montalto, Colonna and Giustiniani to examine and refute in writing the Confession of Augsburg, and the attacks of the Centuriators of Magdeburg.[4] Clearly realizing the necessity of a solid defence against the attacks of the Protestants in the matter of Church history,[5] the Pope in 1567 charged the learned Jesuit Canisius to show in the first place, with examples, how the Centuriators had distorted historical events.[6] Since Pius V. died hardly a

[1] See the poems of G. B. Albano, H. Catena, Lud. Cavani, and Tommaso Correa in *Carmina illustr. poet.*, I., 456 *seq.* ; III., 316 *seq.*, 317 *seq.*, 448 *seq.* Of the many poems which were occasioned by the Battle of Lepanto (see Vol. XVIII. of this work) there was dedicated to the Pope the very rare " Canzone supra la vittoria ottenuta dall'armata de principi christiani contra la Turchesca," Venice, A. Muschio, 1571, on the title-page of which there is a vignette with the motto : " Roma et Italia resurgens." Perhaps its author was the Venetian, Ottaviano Maggi ; *cf.* MELZI, I., 171. Another very rare work is " Hier. Zoppio, Laude del santiss. et grandiss. Pio V.P. per la glorios. et felic. vittoria contra Turcho," Bologna, Aless. Benaccio, 1571.

[2] See CATENA, 136.

[3] See the *letter of Giov. Sambucus to Sirleto of February 20, 1566, Vatican Library ; see App. n. 6.

[4] See *Acta consist. card. S. Severinae*, XXIII., 322.

[5] The *Centenarius* of Wilhelm Eisengrein (Ingolstadt, 1566) of which Pius V. accepted the dedication, certainly gave the first impulse to this ; see PFLEGER in *Histor. Jahrbuch*, XXV., 782 *seq.; cf.* also BRAUNSBERGER, Pius V., 62 *seq.*, and *Corresp. dipl.*, II., 273.

[6] See CANISII Epist., V., 480 *seq. ; cf.* BRAUNSBERGER, Pius V., 64 *seq.*

year after the appointment of the commission, the plan of a
great and exhaustive refutation of the Centuriators could
not be carried out.[1] The Pope, however, saw the publication
of the new edition of the works of St. Thomas, which filled
seventeen folio volumes ; this had been prepared by the
Spanish Dominican, Tommaso de Manriquez, with the help of
his brethren, and was dedicated to Pius V.[2] A bull of April
11th, 1567, ordered that henceforth the day of the death of
the " angel of the schools," March 7th, should be kept
throughout the Church in the same way as the feasts of the
four great Doctors of the Church.[3] The most celebrated and
valuable work which was dedicated to Pius V. came from the
pen of the great Biblical scholar, Sisto da Siena, whose life
the Pope had saved when he was commissary-general of the
Roman Inquisition. This was the Bibliotheca Sancta, printed
at Venice in 1566, which has served as a rich mine to later
students of the Holy Scriptures.[4] The Dominican, Jacopo
Nacchianti, a fellow-student of the Pope, dedicated to him
his commentaries on the Epistles to the Ephesians and the
Romans.[5] A learned German, Doctor Georg Eder, also
dedicated to Pius V. a kind of introduction to the Holy
Scriptures.[6]

Certain other works dedicated to Pius V. are also characteristic. Besides a poem on the birth of Christ,[7] there is a dis-

---

[1] See Schmid in *Histor. Jahrbuch*, XVII., 83 ; Eichhorn, II.,
463 *seq.* *Cf.* also *Corresp. dipl.*, IV., lx. *seq.*

[2] See Quétif-Echard, II., 230, and *infra* p. 200.

[3] Bull. Rom., VII., 564 *seq.*

[4] *Cf.* Kaulen, Einleitung in die hl. Schrift, Freiburg, 1898,
9 *seq.*

[5] See Lauchert, 587 *seq.*

[6] For the " Oeconomia Bibliorum " of Eder, Cologne, 1568, see
Paulus in *Hist.-pol. Blätter*, CXV., 25 *seq.* For his Vite dei Santi
Surius received two briefs of praise. See Laderchi, 1570, n. 446 ;
1571, n. 39. Martin Eisengrein also was repeatedly honoured by
Pius V. ; see Pfleger, Eisengrein, 72 *seq.*, 79 *seq.*

[7] *Laevinii Torrentii, Hymni de partu Virginis ad Pium V., in
Cod. Ottob. 886, Vatican Library.

sertation by Lorenzo Belo, who defends, quite in accordance
with the mediaeval theory, the supreme power of the Pope
even in temporal matters.[1] There is also an Italian translation[2] of the description of the seven basilicas of Rome by
Onofrio Panvinio, an essay on the primacy of St. Peter by
the same writer, and a new edition of the Vite dei Papi by
Platina.[3] When the envoy of the Duke of Urbino presented
to the Pope in 1570 a work by Pandolfo Sansovino on the life
of Christ, he received a gift of 200 scudi ; on the other hand,
the Greek, Antonio Esparcho, who had been collecting manuscripts for the Vatican Library in his own country, and had
been receiving a pension granted by Paul III. and continued
by Paul IV. and Pius IV., tried in vain to secure the continut
ance of this help.[4] The reason why Paulus Manutius lef-

[1] *Laurentii Beli, De summa pontificia potestate creandi et
destruendi dignitates et potestates in toto terrarum orbe ad Pium
V., in Cod. Vatic. 5495 and Ottob. 815, Vatican Library ; also in
*Carte Strozz. State Archives, Florence. For Belo *cf.* MARINI,
Lettera, 55 *seq.* In Cod. Vatic. 1107 *Petri Pontii Consultatio
ad Pium V., quod super matrimonio rato Papa dispensare possit.

[2] Made by Marcus Ant. Lanfrancus Veronensis, in *Cod. Vatic.
6432, Vatican Library.

[3] O. PANVINIUS, De primatu Petri et apost. sedis potestate lib.
II. ad Pium V., in Cod. S. 8, 9 of the Angelica Library in Rome,
printed in a compendium at Verona, 1589, and several times
afterwards ; see NARDUCCI, Catal. Bibl. Angel., 528. For the
new edition of 1568, dedicated to Pius V., of the *Vite dei papi* of
PLATINA, see Vol. XV. of this work p. 421. The dedication
of a work on canon law in CIACONIUS, III., 1064. The Cod.
Vatic. 3944, p. 48 *seq.* contains, *Capizuchus, Ad Pium V. super
clericorum connubiis a Germanis petitis (Vatican Library). In
Cod. Urb. 1235 is to be found a *Trattato della quiete civile e della
sua causa da Niccolò Sergiusti Lucchese detto il Dirceo con lettera
a P. Pio V. Vatican Library.

[4] See *Mél. d'archéol.*, XIII., 290 *seq.*, an *Avviso di Roma of
July 17, 1568, announces that Mons. Foglieta, who was writing
the " Historia del mondo, s'è posto al servitio del card. Ferrara "
(Urb. 1040, p. 549, Vatican Library). *Cf.* " U. Folietae Tybur-
tinum H. Estii card. Ferrariensis " in GRAEVIUS, Thes., I., 2.
1228 *seq.* and *Atti Mod.*, V., 204.

Rome in 1570 was certainly not only his spiritual state, but
also his need of support.[1]   With the exception of works of an
ecclesiastical character,[2] Pius V. only showed any real interest
in those concerned with his favourite subject, the war against
the Turks.[3]

The use of the Vatican Library, of which Cardinal Sirleto[4]
was made librarian for life in 1572, was made more difficult,[5]
though on the other hand Pius V. tried to acquire for it the
famous   collection   of   manuscripts   belonging   to   Cardinal

[1] In his letters Paulus Manutius speaks in a confused and contra-
dictory manner of his departure ; see TIRABOSCHI, VII., 1, 165
seq.   The monograph which Mgr. Le Grelle is preparing will no
doubt throw full light upon this matter.   For the attitude of
Pius V. towards the mysterious G. Cardano, see Bollet. Pavese,
IV., 591 seq.

[2] Pius V. encouraged Girol. Muzio to compose his " Risposta
all' Apologia anglicana " ; see LAUCHERT, 665.

[3] POMETTI, 66 seq. enumerates a series of these from the codices
in the Papal Secret Archives.   The *Discorso a Pio V. and the
*Discorso of G. Selvago are also in Cod. Maggliabecch. XXIV.,
33, p. 258 seq., 226 seq. of the National Library, Florence.   Ibid.
XXX.-46 the discourse of P. Vettori.   This matter is also dealt
with by *Fr. Brochii civis Florent. Oratio de bello decernendo
contra Turcas ad Pium V. (Cod. Vatic. 6153, Vatican Library)
and Vinc. Negusantius (architect. Arbensis), Pro bello in Turcas
ad Pium V. oratio, Fano, 1595.

[4] The *brief " Tuorum magnitudo meritorum " of March 18,
1572, is in the Archives of Briefs, Rome.

[5] CIAN in Giorn. stor. d. lett. Ital., IX., 456, deals very well with
this matter.   G. Mercati is about to publish an article in Histor.
Jahrbuch on the prohibition, mentioned on the authority of an
*Avviso di Roma of April 29, 1570 (Urb. 1041, p. 269b) that
" niuno," under pain of excommunication, " possia copiare scritture nella libreria Vaticana."   This prohibition certainly only
refers to the use of codices which were under suspicion from the
ecclesiastical point of view by incompetent persons ; it is clear
among other things from the particulars in Histor. Jahrb., XVII.
81 ; XXV., 788, that learned Catholics, even Germans like William
Eisengrein, were allowed to work in the Vatican Library under
Pius V.

Vitelli,[1] and continued the transference of manuscripts from Avignon to Rome which had been undertaken by his predecessor.[2] In the spring of 1567 the Pope gave orders for the preparation of a place in the Vatican to serve as a secret archivium for the more important *acta*,[3] while a special provision of 1566 dealt with the preservation of ancient documents.[4] A motu proprio of August 19th, 1568, ordered the compilation of a full and detailed catalogue of all manuscripts relating to the Roman Church, but the plan, like that of Pius IV. of forming a central archivium, met with insuperable difficulties. Apart from the fact that the Church was at that time faced with more pressing undertakings, the necessary conditions and powers were lacking.[5]

On the other hand the efforts which Pius V. made on behalf of the Roman University were crowned with success. Although, at the end of the XVIIIth century, Pavia showed, by the erection of a monument, its gratitude for the foundation of the Collegio Ghislieri, which was founded to receive 24 students for the University there,[6] no outward sign records the services of Pius V. to the Roman institution, which,

[1] See the *report of Firmanus of November 19, 1568, Papal Secret Archives.

[2] See MUNTZ, La bibl. du Vatican, Paris, 1886, 115 *seq.*

[3] See LANCIANI, IV., 8.

[4] See ORBAAN, Een pauselijk verbod tegen het opgebruiken van handschriften, in *Tydschrift van boek en bibliotheekwezen*, 1907, Pius V. also insisted that the nuncios should keep a record of their dispatches ; see *Nunziat. di Polonia*, I., 18 (instructions of April 19, 1567). Papal Secret Archives.

[5] Opinion of SICKEL, Beiträge, I., 13 *seq.* ; 16 *seq.* ; II., 86 *seq.* ; MARINI, Mem. d. archivi, 25 *seq.* ; *Studi e docum.*, VIII., 12 ; Merkle, I., xix., civ.

[6] For the Collegio Ghislieri, which still exists to-day, though in a different form, see LADERCHI, 1571, n. 159 ; BONANNI, I., 295 ; VENUTI, 132 ; BRUZZONE, Bosco, II., 106 *seq.* ; 366 *seq.* ; *Riv. di Alessandria*, XIII., 61 *seq.* ; DEL GIUDICE in *Rendiconti del R. Istit. Lomb.*, 2ª Serie, XXIII. (1890) ; E. GALETTI, Il Collegio Ghislieri di Pavia, Pavia, 1890 ; *Bibl. Corvisieri*, II., 401 ; DELL'ACQUA, 51 *seq.*

however, are proved by the records in its archives.   He not only took care that the new buildings made good progress, but he also saw to it that the internal requirements of the University were met by efforts to remove the abuses by reason of which its financial affairs had fallen into a state of confusion. If he was not completely successful in this, it is beyond question that his ordinances laid the foundations for the subsequent development of the " Sapienza " just at the time when the other Italian universities were beginning to lose their former splendour.   The Pope showed what an interest he took in the affairs of the University by several times presiding in person at the meetings of the commission of studies formed by Julius III.[1]

The number of the professors at the Roman University, which had been 34 in 1536, was increased to 37 in 1568 ;[2] not a few of them were men of great distinction and repute, such as the jurists, Girolamo Pariseti and Camillo Plauto, the physicians, Francesco Ginnasi, Ippolito Salviano, and above all, Marc Ant. Muret and Silvio Antoniano.[1] What a change had taken place in men's ideas is characteristically shown by the decision of the commission of studies on October 16th, 1569, to substitute for the formula, *Quod bonum faustum felixque sit*, which had been placed at the head of the register in the time of Leo X., the words, *In nome della santissima e indivisibile Trinità.*[4]

The spirit which had become paramount in the Eternal

---

[1] *Cf.* *Avvisi di Roma of November 2 and 9, 1566, and October 2, 1570, Urb. 1040, p. 314b, 317 ; 1041, p. 357, Vatican Library ; MARINI, Lettera, 128 *seq.* ; RENAZZI, II., 140 *seq.* ; LADERCHI, 1566, n. 157 and the important contribution of POMETTI in Scritti vari di filologia dedic. a E. Monacı, Rome, 1901, 70 *seqq.*, 89 *seqq.*, where, however, no notice is taken of the " Rotulus " of 1568, published in *Il Muratori*, I., Rome, 1892, 77 *seq.*

[2] See in *Cod. H-III-62, p. 16 *seq.* of the Chigi Library, Rome, the catalogue of Carlo Cartari based upon the **Ruoli* in the Sapienza Archives.

[3] *Cf.* POMETTI *loc. cit.*, 90.

[4] See MARINI, Lettera, 17.

City under Pius V. is shown no less clearly in the inscription over the principal entrance of the Palazzo dei Conservatori : " The senate and people of Rome entrust the protection of the Capitol, once sacred to Jove, to the true God, to the author of all good, Jesus Christ, with a prayer for the common good.   In the year of salvation, 1568."[1]

[1] See BICCI, Notizie d. famiglia Boccapaduli, Rome, 1762, 132 ; FORCELLA, I., 38 ; POGATSCHER in *Repert. für Kunstwissenschaft*, XXIX., 500 *seq.*

CHAPTER IV.

REFORMING ZEAL OF PIUS V. REFORM OF THE COLLEGE OF CARDINALS, THE CURIA, AND THE ROMAN CLERGY.

EVERYONE who, even by repute, knew his fiery zeal, realized that with Cardinal Ghislieri the genius to reform and the spirit of the Council of Trent had ascended the Papal throne. The advocates of a radical ecclesiastical revival joyfully spread the news of the election of Pius V.,[1] and of his first reforms,[2] while, at the end of the first year of his reign, a correspondent summed up his impressions of him as follows : " The new Pope, for whom his ill-wishers predicted a short pontificate,[3] has strength for another ten years, and reform plans for another hundred or a thousand years."[4] Pius V. himself made no secret of his intentions. On July 1st, 1566, in imploring the Republic to abstain from any further plans of war, in order that no obstacles might be placed in the way of peace in Italy, and thus in that of an ecclesiastical revival, he wrote to Genoa that he wished to reform everything in the Church of God that stood in need of reform.[5] On March 2nd, 1566,

---

[1] Circular in the name of Francis Borgia to the provincials of the Jesuits, January 15, 1566, S. FRANCISCUS BORGIA, IV., 162-167.

[2] *Cf.* circulars of Polanco to the Society of Jesus, of January 25, April 30, June 17, and October 21, 1566, *Anal. Bolland.*, VII. (1888) 46 *seqq.* These letters were published with some editions at Cologne in 1567 ; *ibid.*, XV. (1896), 77 *seq.*

[3] CATENA, 21.

[4] *Ciregiola to Cardinal Medici, December 8, 1566 : " Non solo supera tutte le stravagante opinioni e umore e male mercantie di mercato nuovo, ma che haverà vita per dieci anni e riforme per cento a per mille." — State Archives, Florence.

[5] *[Reformare] sicut instituimus, in Ecclesia Dei quidquid reformatione indigere perspicimus. Brevia, Arm. 44, t. 12, n. 79, Papal Secret Archives.

Cardinal Granvelle declared that everything was changed in Rome.[1] The new officials who had been appointed during the first days of the pontificate, for the Apostolic Palace, the Dataria, the government of the Papal States, and other important offices, were all significant of the new methods which the Pope intended to adopt.[2] In affairs of State, the Spanish ambassador says, when giving a list of the new officials, he will make use of Farnese, but for the administration of the city, and for the carrying out of the Council of Trent, which, it is said, he intends to do with full rigour, Borromeo will be his right hand.[3]

[1] Corresp. de Granvelle, éd. POULLET, I., 247.

[2] *" Ha creato officiali : monsgr. Cirillo maestro di casa, msgr. Alessandro Casale Bolognese maestro di Camera ; governatore di Roma il vescovo d'Imola, segretario de brevi Fiordibello et msgr. Cesare segretario delle lettere si è detto del vescovo di Cesena, ma non è anco stabilito. Il datario andarà alla foggia di Paulo IV., assistendo Pisa, Trani et Reomano ; et questo datario seguitarà va per detto, tanto che sia stabilito l'altro : non si piglieranno compositioni. Ms. Giovanni Battista Pistone fiscale è stato confirmato et tuttavia si sta sul negotiare. Addesso de cardinali sono favoriti Farnese, Savello, Gambara, Correggio, Vitelli, Pisa, il quale si dice che haverà Bologna et forsi il carico de negotii." Caligari to Commendone on January 9, 1566, Lett. di princ. XXIII. 73^b (now 160^b–161), Papal Secret Archives. " Ha hecho un muy buen datario que es el arçobispo [of Chieti, later on Cardinal] Mafeo, y puesto por superintendentes de la dataria los cardenales Trani, Reumano y Pisa que ya lo fueron en tiempo de Paulo IV. ; y pienso que se proveeran los beneficios por examen, como en su tiempo se hazia. Ha encomendado la superintendencia del govierno y justicia criminal de todo el estado eclesiastico a los cardenales S. Clemente, Gambaro y Nicolino." Requesens to Philip Il., on January 11, 1566, Corresp. dipl. I., 86.

[3] " En todas las cosas de estado creo que se governará por el parescer del card. Farnes. como lo ha començado ; y creo que él y Vitello y Pisa seran los que mas podràn con Su Beatitud, y tambien creo que se servirà de Borromeo en lo que toca al govierno spiritual de esta çiudad y execucion de las cosas del concilio, el qual dizen que quiere guardar en todo rigor." *Ibid.*

In all his reform work Pius V. allied himself closely with
Cardinal Borromeo, who frankly made known to the Pope
his own ideas for the renewal of the Church, and of the things
that she chiefly stood in need of.[1]   There is no Cardinal holier
than he, said Pius V., in July, 1566, nor one who tells me the
truth more frankly than he does.[2]   The other Cardinals have
nothing but their own interests in view, whereas all Borromeo's
counsels are directed to the common good.   He wished him,
therefore, to return to Rome and to have him always by his
side.[3]   Indeed, in spite of his zeal for the observance of the
duty of residence on the part of the bishops, it was only very
unwillingly, and on the condition of his early return in the
autumn, that Pius V. at length gave the Cardinal of Milan
permission to go to his diocese in April, 1566,[4] and again later
on it was rumoured that in spite of his reluctance Borromeo
would be recalled to Rome.[5]

In order to make up for the absence of the Cardinal of Milan,
immediately after the latter's departure from Rome, Pius V.
summoned to his side the man who had so far been Borromeo's

[1] BASCAPÈ, I., 1, c. 9, 9. 22.

[2] *Ciregiola to Cardinal Medici, July 19, 1566, State Archives,
Florence.

[3] *Avviso di Roma of July 13, 1566, Urb. 1040, p. 243, Vatican
Library.   " Esso [Pius V.] poco si consiglia, dubitando quasi di
non poter trovar fedel consigliero, perciochè in Roma in vero si
parla a passione più che in qualsivoglia altra parte, etc." TIEPOLO,
179.

[4] BASCAPÈ, loc. cit.   " Il Papa fa difficoltà dare licentia al
cardinal de venire a Milano et lo ticne occupato ncle sue facende
et negotii et dic [ono] che egli è uno Angello . . . Et cardinale
Borromeo viene ogni giorno apresso questa corte in magior reputa-
tione, stimandolo che possa ciò che vuole dal Papa e così voresse
domandare come haveria, ma lui fa con questo come faceva ancora
con il suo passato."   Camillo Borromeo to Cesare Borromeo, in
Arch. stor. Lomb., 1903, 361.   Borromeo left Rome on March 11,
1566 (*Avviso di Roma of March 16, 1566, Urb. 1040, p. 194,
Vatican Library), and reached Milan on April 5 (SPROTTE, 2).

[5] *Avviso di Roma of November 12, 1569, Urb. 1041, p. 152,
Vatican Library.   Cf. San Carlo, 113, 224.

right hand in the reform of his archdiocese, Niccolò Ormaneto,[1] a priest of Verona who had been trained in the school of Matteo Giberti. After prolonged studies, especially in Canon Law, Ormaneto had at first had charge of the parish of Bovolone as archpriest. When he was sent as legate to England in 1553, Cardinal Pole chose this able man as his companion, and made use of his services for important missions to the Pope and the Emperor,[2] as well as for the reform of the English clergy and the University of Oxford.[3] After the death of Pole, Ormaneto might have received the archbishopric of Avignon, but he preferred to return to his post as a simple priest in his parish of Bovolone, though he was soon to exchange this quiet work for a field of wider activity. His bishop, Navagero, took him with him to the Council of Trent, and when it became necessary to restrain Albert V. of Bavaria from precipitate action in the matter of communion under both kinds, this thankless task was entrusted to Ormaneto, who carried it out with complete success.[4] As Valiero, Navagero's successor, attests, he next won considerable repute at the diocesan synod which was held at Verona after the conclusion of the ecumenical council. Cardinal Borromeo chose this prudent and experienced disciple of his master Giberti to hold the diocesan synod at Milan, and thus set on foot the work of ecclesiastical reform.

A yet wider and more important field of work opened before Ormaneto when, in June, 1566, he was summoned to the capital of Christendom.[5] Borromeo let him go most reluctantly ; I feel, he wrote,[6] as if my right hand had been cut off.

---

[1] Cf. F. M. CARINI, Monsignor N. Ormaneto, Rome, 1894. C. ROBINSON, Nic. Ormaneto, London, 1920.

[2] Cf. Vol. XIII. of this work, pp. 275, 278.

[3] CARINI, 6.

[4] Cf. Vol. XV. of this work, p. 331; ŠUSTA, IV., 23 seq. 28 118.

[5] For his arrival in Rome (July 8) and his first audience cf. VAN ORTROY in Anal. Bolland., XXXIII. (1914), 189.

[6] To Cardinal Alciati, June 5, 1566, Anal. Bolland., XXXIII., 194, n. 4. At first Ormaneto was only summoned for two years. Borromeo to Pius V., June 26, 1566, in BALUZE-MANSI, III., 531.

Following Borromeo's example, Pius V. had taken in hand, before everything else, the reform of his immediate entourage ; the moral revival which was to spread from the court was to extend, in the first place to the Cardinals, and by their example spread to the rest of the clergy, and so to the whole of Christendom.[1] He was therefore very particular in the choice of the pontifical household. It is true that at the beginning of his pontificate he had, as the result of pressure put upon him by important persons, to admit some whom he would not himself have chosen,[2] but it very soon transpired that he had limited his court to 500 persons, and that he did not intend to spend more than 50,000 ducats a year upon his household.[3] Anyone who wished to remain in his service had to make up his mind to lead a strict life ; almost every day a Dominican held a religious conference in the Apostolic Palace, at which the Pope himself and the Cardinals assisted. When an indulgence on account of the Turkish danger was published, Pius V. insisted that the court officials must gain it, and distributed Holy Communion to them with his own hands.[4] Even in the first year of his reign men wrote several times from Rome that the Apostolic Palace was like a monastery, and that there were no longer any traces of the old court life.[5]

[1] Polanco, January 25, 1566, *Anal. Bolland.*, VII. (1888), 47.

[2] *Ibid.*

[3] *" Ritenne solo cinquecento boche perchè non vuole si spenda l'anno nella casa sua più di 50,000 ducati." Cusano, January 26, 1566, State Archives, Vienna. *Cf.* Polanco, April 30, 1566, *Anal. Bolland.*, VII., 55.

[4] *Ibid.* 51.

[5] *" Nel palazzo del Papa non si vedono le gente se non in quel modo che si va alli monasteri de frati osservanti, niuna sorta di corte si vede." Camillo Borromeo to Cesare Borromeo, on February 23, 1566, Trivulzi Library, Milan. Cod. 551. *" Le cose de la corte passano in silentio al presente, et V. S. facia conto che il palazzo dal' audientia in poi che da il ill. cardinale Alessandrino la mattina, sia un convento quietissimo et solitario de frati." Luzzara to the Duke of Mantua, on August 10, 1566, Gonzaga Archives, Mantua.

" Only monks and Theatines go to the palace, and they think they can reform the world in a day," wrote the Imperial agent Cusano, in June, 1566,[1] yet at that time they were only in the first stages of the reform.

When Ormaneto had arrived in the Eternal City, even the Papal court was gradually brought under the watchful eye of that experienced reformer. On October 6th, 1566, the Pope himself addressed a stern allocution to his assembled household, exhorting them to lead exemplary lives, and giving them a number of rules, which were for the future to be binding upon the whole court. He ordered in the first place that a list should be made of all those employed about the court, showing their ecclesiastical rank, and the benefices enjoyed by each, so as to prevent an accumulation of benefices or the non-observance of the duty of residence.[2] The priests were bound to say mass at least three times a week, and the rest were to receive the sacraments every two weeks. The court clerics were forbidden to use dresses with collars and cuffs, and wide sleeves, or velvet or silk ; henceforward they were to wear the customary dress of clerics, made of plain cloth. In order that the court gentlemen and their servants should not waste a great part of their day in idleness, lectures were to be delivered at the palace on theological and philosophical subjects, and furthermore, books were to be provided so that the chamberlains and attendants might be able to occupy their time profitably. Ormaneto was given full authority to reprove and admonish the whole of the household, and to refer to the Pope if necessary. The maestro di camera, Cirillo, might dismiss all who were disobedient or incorrigible. In conclusion, the Pope pointed out that his duty as chief

[1] *Per palazzo non si vedono altri che frati et Chiettini, che pensono riformar il mondo in un giorno." On June 8, 1566, State Archives, Vienna.

[2] Polanco, October 21, 1566, loc. cit. 65. Cf. *Avviso di Roma of November 9, 1566, Urb. 1040, p. 318, Vatican Library. Later on Carniglia went back to all the Cardinals and prelates, exhorting them to urge their servants to residence. *Avviso of December 23, 1571, ibid. 1042, p. 167b.

shepherd constrained him to make these rules, and he again urged Ormaneto to watch over the carrying out of his orders unless he wished to bring down punishment upon himself.[1]

Ormaneto waited before taking any drastic steps until he had completely mastered the conditions obtaining in the apostolic palace. Then, following the example of Cardinal Borromeo, he began his reform of the court in June, 1567, by dismissing about 150 of the gentlemen and minor officials. Of the six physicians only three were retained, and of the 37 employed in the stable only 18. So that none should go away discontented the gentlemen received 200 scudi each, and the others 100. This reduction of the court personnel made possible a saving of 5000 scudi a year, which was devoted to the assistance of monasteries and pious foundations.[2]

---

[1] POLANCO, October 21, 1566, *loc. cit.* ; *cf.* MUTINELLI I., 57. *" Die dominica, 6 Octobris [1566] Papa fecerat intimari omnibus familiaribus suis quod hora 19 omnes reperirentur in aula Constantini, in qua convenerunt infiniti offici les, sed Papa, hoc forsan ignorans, hora 20ª in camera audientie fecit longum sermonem illis qui ibi reperiebantur circa morum reformationem, cum vellet Sanctitas Sua reformare mores depravatos aliorum, nemo posset dicere debuisse prius suos familiares deinde alios corrigere ; hortatus fuit omnes ad celebrandum sepe, dico presbiteros, et alios omnes quod communicarent saltem bis in mense. Dixit multa circa vestimenta ; prohibuit vestes de serico et de velluto et caligas frappatas ac calciamenta et multa similia " (FIRMANUS, Diarium XII. 31 p. 131, Papal Secret Archives). *Cf.* *Avviso di Roma of October 12, 1566, Urb. 1040 p. 300ᵇ, Vatican Library. *S. Stà per dar esemipo ad altri nella riforma, comincia sempre da se et dalla sua famiglia, et dicono che fa vestire tutti li suoi staffieri et officiali di negro simplicemente con le calce all'antiqua." Avviso of October 19, *ibid*, 306.

[2] *" Per principio di nova rifforma della casa, instituta da monsignore Ormaneto a imitatione di quella che fece già Borromeo, si sono licentiati delle 37 parafrenieri che S. Stà havea 19, et se gli sono prima dati cento scudi dono per ciascuno, a quelli che restano vuole S. Beatitudine che si proveghi in modo che tutti possino star in Palazzo, et questa spesa che si scema dei detti licentiati et altri che di mano in mano come più comodi si ripar-

While the court of Paul IV. had numbered 421 nobles and 313 lesser officials, or 734 in all, with 247 horses, and Pius IV. had increased this number to 533 nobles and 529 others, or in all 1062 persons, with 358 horses, under Pius V. in 1571 the total was 319 nobles and 282 others, or in all 601 persons, with 161 horses.[1]

In spite of all this he did not desist from his labours for the reform of the court in 1568 and 1569. We constantly hear either of an exhortation addressed by Ormaneto to the chamberlains in the Pauline Chapel,[2] or that he was employed in other ways on the reform of the court,[3] or that the curiosity of Rome on the subject of a secret consistory had led men to guess that it was concerned with the reform of the apostolic palace.[4] Further regulations were also issued ; thus at the beginning of 1568 the Pope insisted that all the members of his household should reside in the Papal palace, and that the gates should be shut at night.[5] Then came the order that

tarano, vuole che se ne aiutino i monasteri et luoghi pii " (B. Pia to Luzzara, on June 7, 1567, Gonzaga Archives, Mantua). " *La riforma della casa del Papa oltri li 19 parafrenieri si risolse in licentiar tre medici delli sei che servarano il Palazzo (B. Pia to Luzzara on June 7, 1567, ibid.). *Mons. Ormaneto ha reformata la famiglia del Papa, ha levato tra palafrenieri et gentilhuomini ca. 150 bocche et. il Papa per non mandarli malcontenti ha fatto donare alli palafrenieri 100 sc. per uno, alli altri 200 " (Avviso di Roma of June 7, 1567, Urb. 1040, p. 399b, Vatican Library ; cf. May 31, 1567, ibid. 389). On November 20, 1566 *C. Luzzara wrote from Rome that the Pope wished still further to reduce his household " perche non vuole maritate ne persone che habino benefici di residenzia al suo servitio." Gonzaga Archives, Mantua.

[1] Sickel in Mitteilungen des Instituts für österr. Geschichtsforschung, XIV. (1893), 569. About a sixth part of the household of Pius IV. continued under his successor ; ibid. 545.

[2] *B. Pia, May 22, 1568, Gonzaga Archives, Mantua.

[3] *Avviso di Roma of February 14, 1568, Urb. 1040, p. 487b, Vatican Library.

[4] *Avviso di Roma of December 14 1569 ibid. 1041 p. 196b.

[5] *Arco, January 17, 1568, State Archives, Vienna. *" S. Stà non vuole che donna di sorte alcuna si possa accostare al Belvedere." Arco, June 12, 1568, ibid.

all the doors of the palace should be walled up save two, and that of these two only one should be open at night, and that all the residents in the palace should be within by nightfall.[1] Thus, although the Pope was constantly called upon to deliver exhortations and make new rules, the reform of the court had nevertheless made great progress, and the abuses and liberties which had formerly existed had disappeared.[2]

Cardinal Borromeo kept in constant and confidential touch with Ormaneto from Milan. On December 18th, 1566, he wrote to him about the need for the reform of the College of Cardinals, " a thing which " Borromeo adds, " I have already proposed to the Pope."[3] During the course of the same year he sent his views on the subject to Ormaneto,[4] and in November, 1566, Pius V. sought the latter's aid in the difficult task of the spiritual renewal of the great princes of the Church.[5]

In his first consistory, a few days after his election, Pius V. had exhorted the Cardinals to a manner of life in keeping with

[1] *" Tutte le porte di Palazzo si murano ne staranno aperte se non quella che va in S. Pietro et quella de Svizzeri, et da 24 hore in su quella sola de Svizzeri, et chi abita in Palazzo havrà da ridurvisi alle 24." B. Pia to Luzzara, on August 21, 1568, Gonzaga Archives, Mantua. *Cf.* Arco, August 21, 1568, State Archives, Vienna.

[2] *On the Wednesday the Pope made a speech in the consistory, tuttavia più questa corte si va restringendo al ben oprare at lassare li abusi et la licentia del viver dannoso." (Avviso di Roma of March 5, 1569, Urb. 1041, p. 35. Vatican Library). On October 17, 1567 *Serristori wrote from Rome that the Pope had already reformed his palace and reduced the expenditure. State Archives, Florence, Medic. 3287.

[3] Ambrosian Library, Milan, F. 37, Inf. 475.

[4] 1566, without date of the day ; *ibid.* 356.

[5] *" Il Papa è ingolfato più che mai in queste sue riforme. Il principal ministro è un gentilhuomo Veronese mons. Ormaneto," lately vicar of Borromeo at Milan. " Hora si attende alla riforma de frati sfratati et de cardinali, delli quali si mettono in ordine le bolle." Avviso di Roma of November 16, 1566, Urb. 1040, p. 320, Vatican Library.

their position, so that the lower clergy might take their lead from them.[1]   What would have pleased the Pope most would have been if the princes of the Church would all have adopted a manner of life after the example of Borromeo.   In August, 1566, it is said that he expressed the view that the Cardinals should not have gold or silver plate at their tables, but only porcelain,[2] and on another occasion he urged them to have reading at their meals,[3] though there was no question of any precept on the subject being enjoined.   The Pope, however, took every opportunity of recommending to the princes of the Church poverty and apostolic simplicity, and he tried to influence them in that direction by his own example.   At one of his first consistories he had exhorted them to lead exemplary lives by pointing out that the heresies of the time had been brought into being for the most part by the evil lives led by ecclesiastics,[4] and, fourteen days later, he returned to the same subject ; it was his wish to abolish the right of sanctuary exercised by the Cardinals.   At the beginning of April he announced in consistory that it was his intention to reduce his own court for reasons of economy ; the Cardinals ought to follow his example, and be careful to lead exemplary lives, and wear ecclesiastical dress if they were in orders or in possession of benefices.[5]   When he conferred the purple on his nephew

[1] LADERCHI, 1566, n. 28. Serristori, January 12, 1566, Legaz., 420.

[2] *Avviso di Roma of August 17, 1566, Urb. 1040, p. 274b, Vatican Library.

[3] *Arco, January 19, 1566, State Archives, Vienna.

[4] Legaz. di Serristori, 420 (January 12, 1566).   Cf. supra, p. 67.

[5] *Arco, January 26 and April 6, 1566, State Archives, Vienna. Cf. *Caligari to Commendone, June 18, 1566, Papal Secret Archives ; *B. Pia, June 5, 1568, Gonzaga Archives, Mantua. The right of sanctuary in favour of the houses of the Cardinals and the foreign ambassadors had been revoked by the Pope on January 23 1566 (Acta consist. in GULIK-EUBEL, II., 47 n.).   A limitation of the right of sanctuary for assassins in Spain and Rousillon made by a brief of October 6, 1567, in Bull. Rom., VII., 617.

Bonelli, he turned in consistory to the newly-made Cardinal and spoke of the office and dignity of the cardinalate, making it clear that this high position called for a blameless manner of life ; let Bonelli, he said, look upon his undeserved dignity as an occasion for showing a greater gratitude to God, humility, meekness, fear of God, obedience, and charity to his neighbour. [1]

For the most part, it must be admitted, the lofty tone of these pontifical allocutions had in the end to be adapted to very everyday requirements. Thus, in 1566, Pius V. took the opportunity of the approach of Advent to make " a magnificent speech " urging his hearers who bore the purple to sanctify the time of preparation for Christmas by prayer and fasting, but he had to end by reproving them for gossiping and disputing in the churches to the scandal of the people.[2] He himself gave a shining example in the sanctification of Advent, and he insisted that Bonelli, and requested that the others, should do the same. As far as I know, wrote the Imperial agent, Pacheco and Gambara follow his example.[3] A little before Christmas he exhorted the consistory to the imitation of Christ, as He had shown Himself when He came upon earth, by their obedience, poverty, sound doctrine,

---

[1] " *[Die mercurii 6 martii fuit consistorium secretum]. . . . In fine dicti consistorii . . . [frater Michael Bonellus creatus cardinalis] . . . genuflexus audivit quedam que S^{tas} Sua dixit circa officium et dignitatem cardinalatus et viram inreprehensibilem quam agere debebat hortans eum ut eo magis Deo gratias ageret essetque humilis, mansuetus, Deo serviens ac hominibus obediens et gratus, quanto quod nullis ipsius concurrentibus meritis ad tam grande fastigium et tanti momenti dignitatem promotus fuisset, et alia similia." FIRMANUS, Diarium XII., 31, p. 63, Papal Secret Archives.

[2] * Ciregiola to Cardinal Ferdinand de' Medici, November 29, 1566, State Archives, Florence. *Strozzi, November 30, 1566, State Archives, Vienna. On November 30, 1567, when four of the Cardinals were gossiping during the mass of Advent, the Pope made them a sign ; see Firmanus, *Diarium, Papal Secret Archives, loc. cit.

[3] *Strozzi, December 7, 1566, State Archives, Vienna.

peace, charity to their neighbour, good example and holy life, but this time his speech wound up by complaints about the many intrigues being carried on about the next Papal election. " I have exact information," he said, " and I marvel at the indifference with which men view the things which are subject to excommunication. If many people desire my death, I conform myself to the will of God, but in the meantime I am quite prepared to go on living."[1]   He was unwearied, especially in Lent, in exhorting them to fervent prayer and the worthy reception of the sacraments.[2]   Pius followed up his exhortations by his example.   On the Monday in Holy Week in 1571 he visited the seven basilicas of Rome, going on foot for four miles, and accompanied by six Cardinals.   All the prelates of the court, and even the Cardinals, followed his example.[3]

The Pope was well aware of the difficulty of moving from a manner of life to which they had long been accustomed, a body of men of mature age, who all looked upon themselves as princes.[4]   In spite of this, however, he never ceased from his exhortations and requests.   In the August of 1568 he expressed to Cardinals Morone and Ricci his desire that the Cardinals should cut down the expenses of their households in order that they might save money to help the French Catholics.[5]   At the beginning of 1571 " the reformers " had

[1] *Ciregiola to Cardinal Medici, December 20, 1566, State Archives, Florence.

[2] Cf. *B. Pia, March 12, 1567, Gonzaga Archives, Mantua.

[3] " *Con l'esempio di questa divotione del Papa non ci resta cardenale, che non habbia visitato o che non sia per visitare le dette sette chiese, et il simile fanno tutti li prelati di questa corte." Avviso di Roma of April 14, 1571, Urb. 1042, p. 46^b, Vatican Library.

[4] Cf. the detailed *report of Serristori of January 17, 1567, State Archives, Florence, Medic. 3287.

[5] *Il Papa disse hieri a Morone et Montepulciano che voleva riformare la sua casa et che anco riformassero le loro i cardenali per dar quel che si spende nel superfluo de servitio a Francia per aiuto (B. Pia to Luzzara, August 28, 1568, Gonzaga Archives, Mantua).   Cf. *Cusano, August 28, 1568, State Archives, Vienna.

presented to the Pope their ideas as to the manner of life
of the Cardinals, suggesting that it was not seemly that they
should use silver plate at their tables, that their households
ought to wear clerical dress, and that they should maintain
a chaplain to administer the sacraments every month to their
households.[1]   It was certainly not the fault of the Pope if
these proposals were not made matters of strict precept,[2]
for he would even have liked to have simplified, as having
somewhat too worldly an appearance, the terms in which the
matter was laid before the Cardinals.[3]

Even in the case of the most exalted princes of the Church,
Pius V. did not always restrict himself to exhortations and
prayers, but spoke to them with all the authority of the Vicar
of Christ, and reminded them of the strictness of the Church's
laws.   At the beginning of his pontificate he very plainly
brought home to the bishops who were numbered among the
senate of the Church their duty of taking up their permanent
residence in their sees and among their own flocks.[4]   Many

---

[1] " *Si dice anco che li reformatori [i.e. Ormaneto and Bin-
arini] hanno detto al Papa che sarebbe bene riformare li cardenali
et le case loro, et non lasciare che magnassero in argento et che
facessero andare le loro famiglie vestite di longo et tenessero un
confessore in casa che ogni mese confessasse et comunicasse tutta
la famiglia loro " (Aurelio Zibramonti to the Duke of Mantua,
January 13, 1571, Gonzaga Archives, Mantua).   For Alfonso
Binarini, the companion of Ormaneto, who died Bishop of Camerino, cf. UGHELLI, I., 612.

[2] Cusano (*report of January 20, 1571, State Archives, Vienna),
claims to have heard " da buona fonte " of a strict reforming
regulation for the houses of the Cardinals, which was very shortly
to be issued.   On February 12, 1571, *B. Pia knew of a consistory
concerning the reform of the Cardinals and their households.
On February 9, 1572, he *announces that the Pope had exhorted
the Cardinals in consistory to live piously together with their
households especially during the time of the carnival, which
was then going on.   Gonzaga Archives, Mantua.

[3] They were only to be called *Reverendissimi*, and no longer
Illustrissimi.   *Arco, December 24, 1569, State Archives, Vienna.

[4] Arco, January 26, 1566, *ibid*.

of the Cardinals obeyed, and sooner or later left the Eternal City,[1] but the Pope often had to return to the subject and repeat his exhortations.[2] Pius V. himself, however, forbade some of the Cardinals to go to their dioceses, because their presence in Rome was necessary for the government of the Church.[3]

Up to that time the Cardinals had in various ways possessed the right of conferring parishes, convents and benefices at their pleasure, in such a way that the Pope found his hands tied when he wished to reward deserving men. On April 30th, 1567, Pius V. caused the Cancelleria to revoke all the Papal edicts on which these rights of the Cardinals rested,[4] in such

[1] E.g. Mula, Dolera and Bobba (*Avviso di Roma of March 23, 1566, Urb. 1040, p. 196b, Vatican Library), Sirleto (*Avviso of November 16, 1566, ibid. 320b), Santa Croce (*Arco, March 8, 1567, State Archives, Vienna), Guido Ferreri (*B. Pia, February 21, 1567, Gonzaga Archives, Mantua). On January 13, 1567, the Pope had exhorted the Cardinals to send their dependents into residence, and to do the same themselves. Firmanus, *Diarium, loc. cit. p. 152, Papal Secret Archives.

[2] Cf. *Arco, February 6, 1566, and December 20, 1567, State Archives, Vienna ; Serristori, December 20, 1566, State Archives, Florence, Medic. 3287 ; *Avviso of January 24, 1571, Urb. 1042, p. 12, Vatican Library. *" Par che li cardenali non sappiano trovar la strada di partir per la loro residentia, et che vi vadino mal volontieri a questi tempi," Avviso of February 7, 1568, ibid. 1040, p. 485.

[3] Thus to Cardinals Santori (see infra, p. 166) and Delfino (*Avviso di Roma of November 2, 1566, Urb. 1040, p. 314, Vatican Library). Farnese, who received the pallium on January 25, 1568, was exhorted to go to his bishopric of Monreale, but to come back shortly (*Avviso of January 31, 1568, ibid. 481b). For his departure cf. the *Avviso of February 14, 1568 (ibid. 486). In 1571 Sirleto wished to go to his diocese, but the Pope kept him (*Avviso of April 14, 1571, ibid. 1042, p. 47b). On June 12, 1568, *B. Pia announces the forthcoming departure of Commendone for Padua and Verona to his abbey, Gonzaga Archives, Mantua.

[4] Bull. Rom., VII., 571. Pius V. was planning this arrangement as early as October, 1566. *Strozzi, October 26, 1566, State Archives, Vienna.

a way that they were only able to exercise them in a very limited degree. This ordinance was of great importance, for the Pope thus took into his own hands the full disposal of a great number of benefices in every diocese, and at the same time very greatly limited the influence of the Cardinals.[1]

It must have been especially painful to the noble soul of Pius V. that even his nephew Bonelli was not able to stand, like another Borromeo, the sudden change from the sheltered walls of a convent to the possession of great power, and that he should have found himself called upon to make strict provisions even in his case.[2]

It was the unhappy Innocenzo del Monte, however, who gave the Pope the greatest trouble. On many different occasions it had been made evident how inexcusable had been the action of Julius III. when he had raised such a man to the purple.[3] Pius IV. had kept this man, who had been depraved from his youth, a prisoner in the Castle of St. Angelo for sixteen months,[4] and under Pius V., del Monte was again placed in the same prison on account of further charges,[5] though the

[1] *" Questa è stata una fatione notabilissima et tornarà a molto servito di questa corte, poi chè il Papa riterenà collatione de benefici in tutte le diocesi, si che puoco più havranno i cardenali dei vescovi ordinari." B. Pia to Luzzara on May 3, 1567, Gonzaga Archives, Mantua.

[2] Cusano, June 23, 1571, State Archives, Vienna. *Cf.* *Avviso di Roma of July 4, 1571, Urb. 1042, p. 78b, Vatican Library.

[3] *Cf.* Vol. XIII. of this work, p. 71.

[4] BRUZZONE published in the *Messagero*, an. XXXIII., no. 198, of July 18, 1911, the request for pardon made by del Monte, with a full confession of his guilt. *Cf.* GULIK-EUBEL, 35 ; RODOCAN-ACHI, St. Ange, 165. For the fresh punishment of del Monte see *Avvisi di Roma of August 4 and 14, 1566, Urb. 1040, Vatican Library.

[5] *Avvisi di Roma of May 7, 14, 18, 21, 25 and 28, 1569, Urb. 1041, p. 70, 76, 80, 81, 83, 84, Vatican Library. *Arco, May 25, 1569, State Archives, Vienna. *Cf.* the *citation of del Monte of January 28, 1568, for a scandal committed in the territory of Siena, in Brevia, Arm. 44, t. 13, p. 132, Papal Secret Archives : charge given on January 30, 1568, to the Jesuit Rodriguez to get

commission of Cardinals appointed to try his case decided that his guilt was not deserving of death or degradation.[1] In 1569 Pius banished him with some servants to Montecassino,[2] where two Jesuits were given the difficult task of trying to bring him to a better moral state.[3] At the end of July the abbot thought he could report an improvement in the Cardinal,[4] and later on del Monte was allowed to take up his residence in a monastery at Bergamo.[5]

The conduct of Pius V. in the case of del Monte was certainly not excessively stern, for it was evident that the unfortunate man could not be held accountable for the mistake by which, without any fault on his part, he had been placed in a position for which he was totally unfitted.

together information on the case, *ibid.* p. 134 ; *brief of February 21, 1568, to the Duke of Florence, who had interceded on behalf of del Monte, *ibid.* p. 156. The Duke attests that del Monte was not guilty of rapine, of which he had been accused. The Pope consequently agreed that the Cardinal should still remain in Tuscany, provided that the Duke would take charge of him and give him a Theatine to instruct him (*Arco, February 21, 1568, State Archives, Vienna). A severe exhortation from the Pope to del Monte (*Arco, February 28, 1569, *ibid.*). Prohibition to del Monte to return to Florence : *Avviso di Roma of December 11, 1568, Urb. 1040, p. 615, Vatican Library. A room was assigned to del Monte in the Vatican, and two Theatines were appointed to be his companions ; *Avviso di Roma of December 18, 1568, in the reports of Cusano, State Archives, Vienna.

[1] *Avviso di Roma of June 14, 1569, Urb. 1041, p. 90, Vatican Library.

[2] *Avvisi di Roma of June 11 and 16, 1568, *ibid.* 91, 95b. *Brief of June 13, 1569, to the abbot of Montecassino, Brevia Arm. 44, t. 14, p. 125, Papal Secret Archives ; *another of June 22, 1569, to the same (he is not to admit anyone to see del Monte who could interfere with his conversion), is in the Archives of Briefs, Rome.

[3] *Arco, May 11, 1569, State Archives, Vienna.

[4] *Avviso di Roma of July 30, 1569, Urb. 1041, p. 125, Vatican Library.

[5] *Avviso di Roma of March 17, 1571, in the reports of Arco, State Archives, Vienna.

In other respects Pius V. honoured the Cardinals as the greatest princes of the Church, and his natural advisers. " The Pope," writes Cusano, " informs them of everything that concerns the Apostolic See, he listens to their opinions, honours them, and shows that he values them greatly. At audiences he treats them with the greatest consideration. Unless things change very much," he adds, " Pius V. will be the best-loved Pope we have had for many years."[1] A few weeks after his election Pius V. said that the poorer Cardinals must turn to him for help without hesitation,[2] and at the end of January, 1566, he distributed forty purses, containing in all 20,000 scudi, to the poorest Cardinals.[3] All were made to hand in a list of their revenues, and those who had more than 6,000 scudi had to give up a fifth part for the benefit of their poorer colleagues and for ecclesiastical purposes.[4] The attempt on the life of Cardinal Borromeo gave the Pope an opportunity of making the constitution of Boniface VIII. against all acts of violence against a Cardinal more severe.[5] At the same time this zealous champion of the purity of the

---

[1] *" Buono che S. Stà è risoluta di far participi d'ogni cosa pertinente alla Sedia Apostolica alli cardenali con pigliar nelle risolutioni il voto loro, i quali honora et mostra tenerli in molta stima perche quando li vanno a parlar, li fa coprir et sedere, cosa ch'era stata messa in abuso da Pio IV, che li strapazzava come ogni altro huomo." Cusano on January 26, 1566, State Archives, Vienna, see *supra*, p. 53.

[2] *Arco, January 19, 1566, *ibid*. Cf. *supra*, p. 72.

[3] *Avviso di Roma of January 26, 1566, Urb. 1040, p. 171b, Vatican Library.

[4] *Avviso di Roma of February 6, 1566, *ibid*. 182b. Cf. *Arco, February 6, 1566, State Archives, Vienna. According to a *report of Arco of February 9, 1569, at the consistory of February 6, pensions of 1,000 scudi were granted to Santa Croce, Orsini, Lomellini and Boncompagni ; *ibid*.

[5] Bull of December 19, 1569, Bull. Rom., VII., 792 *seq*. For the motuproprio of 1567 revoking all enactments contrary to the " capitula conclavis iurata," see *Quellen und Forschungen*, XII., 227.

Church did not succeed, in spite of his affability and con-descension, in making them forget his strictness. As early as June, 1566, we hear of Cardinals who keep at a distance from the Pope, that he is very severe in matters of religion, that he has no respect for persons, and becomes more terrible every day.[1] At the end of 1569 it was rumoured in Rome that the Pope had complained in consistory that the Cardinals did not form a circle round him when he vested for a function, and thus plainly showed how little they cared for him.[2]

Even more painful to Pius V. than these manifestations of dislike were the things he heard, even within a few months of his ascending the throne, of intrigues among the Cardinals concerning the next Papal election. On account of the broken health of Pius V. it was thought that there must soon be another conclave ; Farnese looked upon himself as already Pope and was seeking the support of Spain, while Vitelli was at the head of a French party.[3] When the Pope heard of these intrigues, in May, 1566, in the first outburst of his just anger, he declared that he would show the Cardinals that there had not been a more terrible Pope for two hundred years than he.[4] He did not, however, carry this threat into effect, and when, about Christmas, 1566, he spoke on this painful subject in the consistory, he did so in all seriousness, but at the same time very gently ; all that he did was to keep a watch upon the correspondence of the Cardinals.[5] He adopted the same tone a few months later, when he had again to speak of electoral intrigues. At the consistory of June 4th, 1567, just about the time when he had so drastically cut down his own court, he reminded his hearers of the sublime dignity

---

[1] *Priorato to the Duke of Modena, June 19, 1566, State Archives, Modena.

[2] *" Si duolse S.S. con li cardinali che mentre lei si apparava non li facevano circolo intorno, come si conveniva, ma che demos-travano segno manifesto che poco lo stimavano." Avviso of December 17, 1569. Urb. 1041, p. 199, Vatican Library.

[3] HERRE, 138 *seqq.*, 151 *seqq.*

[4] *Cusano, May 25, 1566, State Archives, Vienna.

[5] *Arco, April 5 and June 21, 1567, *ibid.*

to which they had been called by God, and deplored the fact
that the thoughts of some of the Cardinals were directed to
nothing except intrigues to obtain the papacy either for themselves or their friends.   This did not grieve him so much in itself as the fact that any of them should treat so lightly the
bulls of Paul IV. and Pius IV. If they did but know how wrong
and displeasing to God it was, they would certainly not act in
such a way.[1] It is said that while he was speaking the Pope
kept his eyes fixed upon Cardinal d'Este.[2]   After the consistory Este several times asked the Pope for absolution from
the censures which he had incurred by his conduct.[3]   Cicada,
too, had taken part in the intrigues to obtain the tiara, a fact
which specially roused the indignation of the Pope, since
Cicada had been one of those who had been principally consulted in the drafting the the bull of Pius IV.[4]

It would seem that for a time Pius V. contemplated the
issuing of a bull for the reform of the conclave,[5] but it was
principally by taking care that there were worthy electors
that the Papal election was to be safeguarded, and therefore
the renewal of the College of Cardinals was one of the main
objects of the zealous Pope.   At a moment of physical illness,
a few months after he had ascended the throne, he said that
he felt his strength failing ; he regretted this, not for its own
sake, since he was ready to appear before God at any moment,
but because he would have to leave the College of Cardinals

[1] LAEMMER, Melet., 219.

[2] *Arco, June 7, 1567, State Archives, Vienna.

[3] *Arco, June 15, 1567, *ibid.*

[4] *Arco, June 21, 1567, *ibid.*   B. Pia as well (to Luzzara, June 7,
1567, Gonzaga Archives, Mantua) had information that *alcuni*
cardinals had asked pardon of the Pope, and had obtained it on
condition of amendment.   In another *letter of the same date
(*ibid.*), Pia says that in his discourse the Pope had named Este
and Vitelli.

[5] *Avviso di Roma of March 20, 1568, Urb. 1040, p. 490b,
Vatican Library.   The powers of the Camerlengo were to be
restricted, as well as the expenditure during a vacancy in the
Holy See.

filled with ambitious and unconscientious men, and that he had not been able to effect any change.[1]

Death, however, was not so near to the zealous champion of the purity of the Church as he supposed, and he was able to set his hand to the reform of the supreme senate of the Church, and that not in any hurried way, but after long consideration.

Pius V. had allowed two years of his pontificate to elapse without investing anyone with the purple, with the exception of his nephew, Bonelli. Attempts, however, to induce him to create new Cardinals had not been wanting. Those who knew the Pope's ideas, and the considerations which would have weight with him, pointed out to him into what unworthy hands the government of the Church might fall if he did no take steps in time to increase the number of the party of the Cardinals of strict ecclesiastical views by quickly making some appointments. But Pius V. refused to let himself be led into any hasty action, even by these considerations. Month after month went by, and men's expectations were still left unfulfilled.[2]

[1] *" Essendo apparecchiato ogni hora che Dio lo chiamasse, ma gli doleva, che lasciava il collegio pieno d'huomini ambitioso et di poca consciencia, al che havrebbe rimediato se Dio gl'havesse dato vita." Arco, May 25, 1566, State Archives, Vienna.

[2] *" Si presentono pratiche di fare card^{li} nuovi, et perchè l'humore del Papa non vi inclina, cercano di disponerlo con queste ragioni, et la pratica è giudicata da questi santocci et frati domestici del Papa, i quali vanno sforzandosi di dargli ad intendere che sapendo S. S^{tà} quai siano que card^{li} che fanno pratiche di papato, et in che male mani cascheria il governo de la chiesa quando egli toccasse ad uno di questi tali, è opera degna et debita di lei di provedere a questo pericolo et danno de la sede apostolica. El modo de provederci è di fare sei over otto card^{li} che impedissero queste pratiche presenti, di maniera che se quest'humore sarà pronto mosso et aiutato, o da la M^{tà} dell'imperatore o da altro principe, et massimamente dal re cattolico, si può tenere per fermo che a settembre, o poco più la si haveranno card^{li}, vivendo però il Papa, il che negano questi astrologi, i quali non vogliono che passi agosto." Luzzara to the Duke of Mantua May 25 1566, Gonzaga Archives, Mantua.

An addition to the College of Cardinals was looked for all
the more eagerly at Ash Wednesday, 1568, because the next
creation was likely to be of decisive importance at the next
Papal election. The fact that no less than six friars were
named among those upon whom his choice was expected to
fall is very significant of the idea which men had of Pius V.[1]
The rumours, however, came to nothing.[2] Ash Wednesday
had brought only disappointment, when suddenly, on March
24th, there came news of the nomination of four Cardinals ;
those chosen were the Spaniard, Diego de Espinosa, the
Frenchman, Jerôme Souchier, and the two Italians, Antonio
Carafa and Paolo della Chiesa.[3] The story was current in
Rome that the Pope had told none of them of his decision
but that only a few days before he made up his mind he had
ordered prayers in the churches and convents for an important
matter concerning the Church.[4] The unexpected step did not
fail to excite opposition ; Cardinal Mula made objections,
while the French ambassador at once went to the Vatican,
accompanied by Rucellai, to demand the withdrawal of the
nomination of Souchier. The Pope, however, rejected the
demand unhesitatingly, whereupon the French ambassador
withdrew with the remark that Pius V. was too partial to the

[1] *Avviso di Roma of February 7, 1568, Urb. 1040, p. 485,
Vatican Library. Corresp. dipl., II., lxxvii. seq. On January
10, 1568, Arco showed himself on the whole well informed as to
the candidates. For Germany, the Archbishop of Trêves or of
Salzburg, or Canisius, was to be nominated, for Spain Espinosa, for
France Souchier or Pellevé, for Rome Carafa, Chiesa, Cesi,
Melchiori (Bishop of Macerata). Peretti, Giustiniani, the General
of the Augustinians, Paolo d'Arezzo, and Pavesi (Archbishop of
Sorrento). On February 14 Arco added Aldobrandini and
Rusticucci to his list. CANISII Epist., VI., 731 seq.

[2] *Avviso di Roma of February 14, 1568, Urb. 1040, p. 487,
Vatican Library.

[3] *Avviso di Roma of March 27, 1568, ibid. 493. Arco, March
27, 1568, CANISII Epist., VI., 732.

[4] Graziani to Tomicio, March 27, 1568 in MAI, Spicil., VIII.,
379.

Catholic King.[1] Otherwise the Pope's choice was received with general satisfaction, the reform party in particular rejoicing that the supreme ecclesiastical dignity had been conferred on men of their own way of thinking.[2]

No less great was the satisfaction of Philip II. when, on Maundy Thursday, 1568, a special courier from Bonelli informed him that the red hat had been bestowed upon his trusted servant, the first minister of Spain, Diego de Espinosa.[3] Born in 1512 of a noble family which had fallen into reduced circumstances, Espinosa, after a distinguished course of studies in law at Salamanca, first received the post of judge in the court of appeals of the archiepiscopal curia of Saragossa, and afterwards, purely on account of his merits, passed from office to office until, at 43, he was appointed President of the Royal Council of Castille. Honour and position were heaped upon him, and the king's favour raised the President of the Royal Council to that of President of the Council of State and of the *camera di grazia ;* in 1558 he received the very rich bishopric of Siguenza, which had the enormous revenue of 36,000 ducats a year. Later on, Pius V. regretted that he had consented to the appointment of Espinosa as Grand Inquisitor, because this office, united to all his other dignities, made him almost a Pope in Spain. In 1567, Philip II. asked for the cardinalate for his favourite in an autograph letter, in order that, during the king's projected journey to Flanders Espinosa might act with greater authority as regent in Spain. When the cardinal's hat was sent to him at the Ascension, 1568, Philip honoured him in every way as a prince of the Church. When Espinosa went to consult him the king went to meet him in the ante-chamber, saluted him with uncovered head, and made him sit in a chair but little lower than his own. Espinosa retained his dignities till his death, but his health failed pre-

---

[1] *Arco, March 27, 1568, State Archives, Vienna.

[2] *Avviso di Roma of March 27, 1568, *loc. cit.* Graziani, *loc. cit.*

[3] For Espinosa *cf.* especially SERRANO in *Corresp. dipl.,* II., lxxv–lxxxiv. See also CIACONIUS, III., 1031 ; CARDELLA, V., 114 *seq.*

maturely under the heavy burden of his duties, and shortly after the death of Pius V. he, too, ended his life of labour on September 5th, 1572.

If Espinosa owed his elevation to foreign influence, that of Jerôme Souchier, the learned abbot-general of the Cistercians, came entirely from Pius V. himself, who had found in him a man after his own heart.[1] As had been the case with the Pope himself, learning and piety had been Souchier's only delight from youth. After he had entered the Cistercian Order, his superiors sent him to the University of Paris, whence he returned a doctor in philosophy and theology. His clear discernment and calm foresight brought him to the notice of the Cardinal of Lorraine, and through him to that of Henry II. and Charles IX. Having been made Abbot of Clairvaux he took part in the Council of Trent, where his learning and strong ecclesiastical views won for him the esteem of Cardinals Hosius and Borromeo. After his return from the Council he set to work to bring new life into his Order, as abbot-general of the Cistercians. The dignity of the cardinalate was not only unexpected by him, but was unwelcome, and he told the Pope that its weight would prevent him from labouring any more for his own Order, and that he did not possess the necessary qualifications for a prince of the Church. Pius V. succeeded in reassuring the humble religious on both these points ; he must leave it to the Pope, he was told, who could not forego the services of such men as he in the discharge of his apostolic office, to decide who was fit to be a Cardinal and who was not.[2] Souchier, however, did not bear the burden of the cardinalate for long. When the news of his death on November 23rd, 1571, was brought to the Pope, Pius V. said : " Would that I could die the death of this just man ! " and at the next consistory he lamented that a great light of the Church had been extinguished.[3]

[1] *Arco, December 24, 1568, State Archives, Vienna. CIACONIUS, III., 1033.

[2] Brief of May 8, 1568, in GOUBAU, 79 seq. CIACONIUS, III., 1032 seq.

[3] CIACONIUS, III., 1034. CARDELLA, V., 117.

Just as with Souchier a doctor of the Sorbonne and a representative of theological learning had entered the Sacred College, so with Giovanni Paolo della Chiesa there came a representative of the celebrated school of law at Padua. Della Chiesa, who was born at Tortona in 1521, had been married, and had only entered later into the service of the Church. A distinguished jurist, and the most skilful advocate in the whole of Milan, he defended the rights of the Duke of Terranuova against Philip II., and was afterwards made a senator of Milan. After the death of his wife he was sent to Rome to maintain the claims of the senate of Milan in their dispute with Cardinal Borromeo. Pius V. drew this able man into the service of the Church, conferred benefices on him, made him Cardinal Deacon and Cardinal Priest, and entrusted to him the Signatura Justitiae. Della Chiesa only lived 55 years, and died on January 13th, in the year of Jubilee, 1575.[1]

The fourth of the new Cardinals, the Neapolitan, Antonio Carafa, was distinguished in yet another branch of learning.[2] He had become a profound Greek scholar in the school of Sirleto, and in that capacity later on rendered great services to the Church under Sixtus V. and Clement VIII., especially by his emended edition of the Greek version of the Old Testament. Carafa only attained his thirtieth year the day after his nomination as Cardinal. He had already been destined for the Roman purple by Paul IV., but under Pius IV. he not only saw all hope of his promotion vanish, but he even lost his canonry of St. Peter's. Pius V. again reverted to the intention of Paul IV., obviously with the intention of restoring the good name of the Carafa Pope and his family in the person of Antonio Carafa.[3] The later life of the Cardinal proved how

---

[1] See CARDELLA, V., 118.

[2] See *ibid.* 119 *seq.*

[3] Albert V. of Bavaria showed his joy in a *letter to Castellini of April 27, 1568, Cod. B. 34, Library, Faenza. Many *letters of congratulation to Carafa on his cardinalate are in Cod. Barb. LXI., 40, Vatican Library. *Ibid.* 41–48, *Lett. orig. ad A. Carafa, 1568–1577.

happy the selection was.   All Rome was thrown into mourning
when, on January 13th, 1591, he succumbed to heart disease.
The master of ceremonies, Mucanzio, could hardly find words
to express the great qualities of the dead man, who had made
the Maronite College his heir, and had expressed the wish to
be buried without pomp and in silence.[1]

After this first creation of Cardinals more than two years
went by, and the Pope had taken no further steps to complete
the number of the senate of the Church by fresh nominations.
The state of expectancy at the Roman court grew greater and
greater at the prospect that once again, without any notice or
consultation, he would suddenly produce a new list of
Cardinals.[2]   Of the sixty-eight Cardinals at the beginning of
the pontificate eight had died by the end of 1567, and eight
more by 1569,[3] and it had become necessary to fill the places
of such eminent men as Reumano, Dolera, Scotti, Mula and
Cicada.   There was no lack of conjecture and rumour as to
those who had been chosen by the Pope, and it was said that
Pius V. had written to cause inquiries to be made in all the
countries of the world, in order to discover learned and blameless men, and that he would not give the preference to Italians
over those of other nationalities.[4]   The nomination of eight
Cardinals was looked upon as certain at Christmas, 1568, and

[1] *" Urbs tota et universa curia tanti viri iacturam moleste
admodum tulit, spectatae enim probitatis, integerrimae vitae et
sicuti a nonnullis audivi virgo habebatur, religione, caritate
animi, candore, humanarum rerum scientia, eruditione et usu
cunctis amabilis in magna fuit hominum veneratione et aesti-
matione ; eius etiam ultimum elogium quantus vir fuerit demon-
strat ; instituit enim haeredem collegium Maronitanum quod
paupertate laborabat et reliquit, ut eius corpus sepelliretur sine
pompa noctis tempore in ecclesia s. Sylvestri in monte Quirinali."
MUCANTII Diaria caerem., Bibliothèque Nationale, Paris.

[2] *Avviso di Roma of December 14, 1569, Urb. 1041, p. 196b,
Vatican Library.

[3] CIACONIUS, III., 1066.   For the death of Cardinal Vitelli, see
App. n. 51.

[4] Cusano, August 7, 1568, CANISII Epist., VI., 732.

men thought that they could name six of them.[1]   Still greater
expectations were raised at the Christmas of the following
year, because, in the middle of December, 1569, the Pope did
not give audience on matters of business for several days, and
had unexpectedly summoned a consistory, at which he appeared with a roll of paper in his hand, and admitted none
but the Cardinals.[2]   But even this conjunction of circumstances proved illusory, and men's curiosity was kept at
breaking point for yet another six months.   In the meantime
France and Spain[3] were naturally seeking to bring influence
to bear upon the next appointment.   Philip II. named several
possible candidates as indifferent to him, and others who
would be acceptable ;   his ambassador was instructed to
oppose the nomination of Burali and Santori, the former
because he was a Lombard, and the later because he was a
Neapolitan ;   either of them, if he became Pope, might create

---

[1] Cusano, November 13, 1568, *ibid.* " The name of Canisius has
again been put forward as a candidate, but he has made counter-
representations to the Cardinals." B. Pia too wrote on November
13, 1568, to Luzzara : *" N. Signore ha pensiero di far cardinale
uno della natione Tedescha, et ha in consideratione tre persone,
Treviri, et Salsburg Arcivescovi et il Canisio Giesuita. Ha anco
molta inclinatione al frate fratello del commendator mayor
ambasciatore di Spagna qui [Gaspare de Zuñiga], et per essere
molto edificato di lui et per rispetto del fratello, del quale S. Stà
fa gran conto. Francesi fanno instanza per un tale de Amiens
[undoubtedly Pellevé] . . . et da molte parti son fatte delle
mosse anco da chi crede di piacere a S. Stà così facendo, et seco
se nominano Ceneda [Mich. della Torre], Narni [Cesi], Macerata
[Girol. Melchiori], Datario [Pietro Ant. Maffei], et generale della
Minerva [Vincenzo Giustiniani]. Ma del Datario et generale se ne
crede puoco, l'uno per essere tanto creatura di Farnese et da vita
differente dall' humor de N.S., l'altro perchè entranto.   S.
Beatitudine a far il generale, par che pace non possa restare di
non far anco di altra religione, come di S. Agostino et S. Francesco.
et se non generale almeno frate." Gonzaga Archives, Mantua.

[2] *Avviso di Roma of December 14, 1569, Urb. 1041, p. 196b,
Vatican Library.

[3] *Cf. supra* n. 1, the *letter of B. Pia of November 13, 1568.

difficulties for the Spanish rule in Italy.[1]   Zuñiga pointed out
to his master the risk of any political interference ; he was of
opinion that under certain circumstances a Spanish recommendation might even prove absolutely fatal to the persons
recommended, because the Pope would suppose that they had
sought the intercession of the king, and would thus forfeit
the good opinion of Pius V.[2]   Had not Pius plainly said that
the Pope did not give his advice to the princes as to whom they
should appoint as their officials or generals, and that there
was, therefore, no reason for finding fault with him if he did
not entertain the suggestions of the princes in the nomination
of Cardinals ?[3]

After careful thought and inquiry Pius V. at last made up
his mind on the subject of his candidates in the middle of
May, 1570.   This time the actual nomination was not made
suddenly or without warning, for the Pope announced the
creation for the Wednesday after Pentecost, May 17th, and
revealed the names of the sixteen whom he had decided upon
on the previous Sunday, so that all might have time to submit
their difficulties and objections.[4]

The Pope's choice caused widespread amazement.   Men were
prepared for eight or ten, or at the most, twelve new Cardinals,
but to create sixteen at once seemed to many people to be
subversive of all precedent.   Many especially could not understand why the Emperor's candidate, Gianvincenzo Gonzaga,
Prior of Barletta, was not to receive the red hat.   In their
opinion a man of such noble birth, related to so many princely
German houses, and who had been so many times recommended by the Emperor, could not and should not be passed
over, all the more so as both Spain and France had been taken
into consideration in the nomination.   Arco, therefore, as
Imperial ambassador, Madruzzo and Otto Truchsess, as German Cardinals, and Urbino as a near relative, made incredible

---

[1] Corresp. dipl., III., 101 n. ; cf. 148.

[2] Letter to Philip II. of September 23, 1569, ibid. 147 seq.

[3] *Strozzi, December 7, 1566, State Archives, Vienna.

[4] *B. Pia to Luzzara, May 16–17, 1570, Gonzaga Archives,
Mantua.   SANTORI, Diario, 303.

efforts to get him nominated even at the last moment, but the day of the consistory arrived without their having met with any success.[1] The Spanish ambassador met with no more success in the objections which he made to some of the chosen candidates. Pius V. plainly said to him that he was appointing the Cardinals purely for their merits, and not on account of the recommendations of the princes, and he might rest assured that even the king would be satisfied by the choice which he had made.[2]

Immediately before the consistory of May 17th the Pope had to face a last attack. The Cardinals were admitted to his presence ten at a time, and for six hours they attempted to shake the Pope's determination. But Pius stood firm, and neither was the Prior of Barletta, nor any of the others who had been passed over, included in the list, nor were any names omitted.[3]

Although the recommendations of the Emperor and the King had not been allowed to weigh in the scales, the wishes of the princes had not been altogether disregarded. Of the two Frenchmen raised to the purple on May 17th, the Bishop of Le Mans, Charles d'Angennes de Rambouillet, who was the experienced counsellor of the French court in all the most difficult questions, and had been its envoy at almost all the courts of Europe, had been suggested by Charles IX.[4] Pius V., however, had had personal knowledge of him when he was ambassador in Rome, and had formed a high opinion of his loyalty to the Roman See.[5] The other Frenchman raised to

---

[1] *Ibid.*

[2] " Que él hace cardenales a los que lo merecen, no a supplicacion de principes." Corresp. dipl., III., 358 n.

[3] *B. Pia to Luzzara, *loc. cit.* SANTORI, *loc. cit.*

[4] CIACONIUS, III., 1047. CARDELLA, V., 134.

[5] " Dice [the Pope] que tiene hecha mucha experiencia del buen zelo deste ambaxador ; y a otros ha dicho que piensa tener en él otro cardenal Bordisera que le avisa de todo lo que passa en Francia sin perdonar a la Reyna ni a otro consistorio ninguno " (Zuñiga to Philip II., May 17, 1570, Corresp. dipl., III., 357). In the *brief of May 26, 1560, which announces to the King of France

the cardinalate, Nicholas de Pellevé, had owed his appointment as Bishop of Amiens, Archbishop of Sens, and lastly as Archbishop of Rheims, to the favour of the French kings, Henry II. and Charles IX.   Under Paul IV. he had been sent as envoy to Mary of Guise in Scotland, and had there done all he could to save the Catholic religion.[1]   Pellevé's zeal for the Catholic faith, his theological learning, and his blameless life,[2] clearly justified the honour now bestowed upon him.

Like France, Spain too was represented by two Cardinals among the new creations.   Of these, Gaspare de Zuñiga Avellaneda, the son of the Count of Mirandola, was a cousin of the Spanish ambassador in Rome, who was much in the favour of the Pope.   He had distinguished himself for his learning as professor of theology at Salamanca, and for the way in which he had governed his dioceses as Bishop of Segovia and Archbishop of Seville.   Zuñiga died before Pius V., on February 2nd, 1571, at Jaen.[3]   Gaspare Cervantes had also merited the red hat by the way he had discharged his duties as Archbishop of Tarragona.[4]   Like Pellevé, he had taken part in the Council of Trent ; it is significant of his zeal for the carrying out of the decrees of the Council that he immediately afterwards held a diocesan synod, being at that time Archbishop of Salerno,[5] and later on, at Tarragona, established a seminary for boys.   His friendship for the Jesuits is another proof of his ecclesiastical views ; in 1574 he established a noviciate for them at Tarragona, and when he had to go to Rome in connexion with the case of Carranza, he appointed a Jesuit, Alonso Román, as visitor of his diocese.[6]

Like France and Spain, the east may be said to have been

the elevation of the two French subjects, the assurance is given that there had never been a more trustworthy ambassador than Rambouillet. Brevia Arm. 44, 6. 15, p. 115b, Papal Secret Archives.

[1] BELLESHEIM, Scottland, I., 413.

[2] CIACONIUS, III., 1041.   CARDELLA, V., 125 seq.

[3] See CARDELLA, V., 123 seq.

[4] See ibid. 124.

[5] LADERCHI, 1566, n. 182.

[6] ASTRAIN, III., 41 seq.

also represented in the creation, since one of the new Cardinals, the General of the Dominicans, Vincenzo Giustiniani, a member of the well-known and celebrated Genoese family, had been born in the island of Chios, and had there entered the Dominican Order, attaining to its highest dignity by the time he was 38 years old. He, too, was at the Council of Trent with 18 bishops and 27 theologians of his Order. At the time of his nomination as Cardinal he was Papal envoy in Spain, where he defended the cause of the Pope and Cardinal Borromeo in the long Milanese controversy concerning jurisdiction, and at anyrate brought about " the beginning of the end " in that weary dispute. In the world of learning he had rendered great services in the preparation of the new edition of the works of St. Thomas.[1]

Besides Giustiniani, three others of the newly-appointed Cardinals belonged to the religious orders ; the first of these was the Dominican, Arcangelo Bianchi, who had long been the regular confessor of Pius V., his trusted companion when he was inquisitor, and who, when Ghislieri became Pope, had been made Bishop of Teano and Commissary General of the Inquisition.[2] Of the Franciscans, the purple was conferred on Felice da Montalto, the future Sixtus V., whom Pius V. had already made General of his Order. Pius V. also gave the newer Orders a representative in the Sacred College by the nomination of the Theatine, Paolo Burali of Arezzo, a man of extraordinary sanctity. Philip Neri lamented the death of Paolo as a misfortune for the whole of Christendom. His canonization was seriously contemplated, and his fellow Theatine, Andrew Avellino, who was himself raised to the altars of the Church, ranked him with St. Charles Borromeo. Burali had at first been an advocate, and afterwards a judge ; his impartiality and incorruptibility were especially remarkable, and it is related that in a certain trial, when he had to give judgment against a poor widow, he indemnified her out of his own means. He entered the Theatine Order at the age of

[1] See CARDELLA, V., 146 seq.

[2] See ibid. 135. The tomb of A. Bianchi, with a fine bust, at S. Sabina ; the inscription in FORCELLA, VII., 306.

forty, and would have wished to remain a simple lay-brother, if his superiors would have allowed him to do so. Later on he was offered several bishoprics, which he refused, until, after the death of Cardinal Scotti in 1568, Pius V. obliged him to accept that of Piacenza. As a bishop he continued to live as he had done as a Theatine ; he built schools for the poor, in which the instruction was given gratis, a seminary, an orphanage, a home for girls and widows, a refuge for penitents, a convent for the Capuchins, and another for the Theatines. The acts of the synod which he held in 1570 were printed.[1]

Among the new Cardinals, Giulio Antonio Santori stood out on account of his extraordinary nobility of soul.[2] A man of the greatest purity of life and vast learning, Santori led a life of great asceticism, slept very little, and did penance after the manner of the early saints ; his charity led him to expend, during the time of his cardinalate, 70,000 ducats on the poor, whose father he was called.[3] Like Burali, he had originally been an advocate, though he soon gave up his career in order to enter the priesthood, and was soon made vicar-general of the Bishop of Caserta. Since he worked with all his energies against the Protestant movement, which was very powerful in that place, he had to bear many calumnies and attacks, and was even in danger of his life.[4] In the autumn of 1563 he had to flee before his enemies, and retired to Naples, where he helped Cardinal Antonio Carafa. But the persecution broke out anew in that place, and after the death of the Cardinal, Santori went into retirement, and gave himself up to works of charity and his studies ; it was at this time that

---

[1] CIACONIUS, III., 1053. Biographies of Burali were written by G. A. CAGNANO, Rome, 1649 ; G. B. BAGATTA, Venice, 1698 ; G. BONAGLIA, Rome, 1732. Clement XIV. proclaimed Burali Blessed ; see brief of May 13, 1772, Bull. Rom. Contin., IV., Rome, 1841, 428.

[2] Cf. App. n. 67.

[3] He is styled " Promotor delle opere pie et padre dei poveri " by the author of the *Relatione fatta all'ill. sig. card. d'Este, in 1599, Cod. 6619, p. 89b, Court Library, Vienna.

[4] Cf. Vol. XIV. of this work, p. 285.

he wrote a book on the morals of the heretics.[1] His great learning and his zeal for the faith were the things that recommended him to Pius V.,[2] who summoned him to Rome, made him a consultor of the Inquisition, and Archbishop of Santa Severina. It was with great difficulty that Santori obtained from the Pope, in spite of the latter's zeal for the residence of bishops, leave to retire to his diocese, but he was still on his way thither when he received an order from the Pope to return, because Pius V. intended to make him a Cardinal, and employ him in the service of the universal Church. Santori was a scholar of great attainments, especially on all liturgical matters ; he read much, and remembered all that he read. He especially applied his learning to the reform of the Roman Ritual. Strict with himself, he was also strict with others,[3] and in his zeal for the reform of discipline and for the purity of the faith, he was a kindred spirit to Pius V.

Like those already named, so were all the others men on whose worth the Pope thought that he could rely, since for the most part he had himself known them for a long time. Thus Girolamo Rusticucci had been his secretary for nine years.[4] Ghislieri had made the acquaintance of Giovanni Girolamo Albani, who, after distinguished studies in law had risen to a high military position in the service of Venice, when he was Inquisitor at Bergamo. After the death of his wife, this man, who was clever, and of quick and sound judgment, was summoned to Rome by the Pope, and employed in the administra-

---

[1] See SANTORI, Autobiografia, XII., 339.

[2] *Cf.* BENTIVOGLI, Memorie, Amsterdam, 1648, 62.

[3] See the *Relatione, p. 90, cited *supra* p. 166, n. 3.

[4] *Cf. supra*, p. 74. For Rusticucci see the information in CARDELLA, V., 148 *seq.* The author of the *Relatione cited *supra*, p. 166, n. 3, describes Rusticucci thus : " d'ingegno posato, ma sagace, di moto tardo, ma diligente, di buoni sentimenti, ma di tardissima espressione. . . . Ha più prudenza che dottrina. . . . È officioso, amorevole." It is further stated : " Servì con molto amore per sottosegratario il card. Alessandrino, al quale ancora in una sua necessità provedde di non so che picola somma de denari." *loc. cit.* 91.

tion of the Papal States.[1] Giovanni Aldobrandini had made
a great name for himself as Bishop of Imola, and later as
Grand Penitentiary ; Marcantonio Maffei, Archbishop of
Chieti, had done the same as head of the Dataria, and Carlo de
Grassis, Bishop of Montefiascone and Corneto, as Governor of
Rome.[2] The Roman, Pietro Donato Cesi, Bishop of Narni,
of whose diplomatic skill the Pope made use later on, had
been Prefect of Ravenna, and vice-legate of Bologna. His
love for the poor was justly celebrated, and in a time of famine
he looked after them like a father ; he also constructed an
aqueduct, so as to obtain fresh water from the mountains.
Later on Ravenna asked him to come and act as arbitrator
in order to settle its disputes by his skill and sense of justice.[3]
All those mentioned were made Cardinal Priests. Giulio
Aquaviva, who was only twenty-four years of age, a scion of a
princely house, and a man of great piety, was made Cardinal
Deacon.[4] Of Giulio's six brothers, three entered the eccles-
iastical state ; Ottavio also became a Cardinal, Orazio a
Cistercian and a bishop, while Ridolfo entered the Society of
Jesus, and died a martyr in India.

The creation of Cardinals of 1570 was naturally viewed in
many different lights in Rome.[5] The Spanish ambassador,
Zuñiga, whose advice upon the question had been so often
rejected by Pius V., was of opinion that the nomination had
undoubtedly been made " somewhat hastily " and that persons
of greater eminence and deeper learning should have been
appointed,[6] but such remarks only show how much public
opinion had lost sight of the qualities required in a prince of

[1] See CARDELLA, V., 151 seq.

[2] Ibid. 122 seq., 133 seq.

[3] Ibid. 131 seq.

[4] Ibid. 150 seq.

[5] *Avviso di Roma of May 20, 1570, Urb. 1041, p. 281, Vatican
Library.

[6] " No ay deffecto notable en los italianos ; pero deviera S.S.
escoger mas raros subyectos y mayores letrados, porque no se
puede negar sino que la promocion es algo desbaratada." To
Philip II., May 17, 1570, Corresp. dipl. III., 357 seq.

the Church, though, in other things he says, Zuñiga justifies
the Pope's choice in the most surprising way. Even at the
last moment he had raised objections to Aquaviva and Cervantes, though he himself says of the latter that he had never
seen a man of less ambition or more exemplary life ;[1] he
speaks of Aquaviva as a virtuous young man, of good scholarly
attainments.[2] According to the instructions of his master,
he would, if it had been possible, have excluded Burali and
Santori as well from the cardinalate, but when in 1570 there
arose the question of appointing a legate for Germany, Zuñiga
wrote that they ought to choose a man of exceptionally
virtuous life, and recommended Burali as one who had a great
reputation in this respect, and who would be much esteemed
in Germany.[3]

Pius V. was well aware of all this, because he had so long and
so carefully sought for suitable Cardinals, and, in spite of every
attack, had so firmly insisted upon the men whom he had
chosen. If the Council of Trent had exhorted the chief shepherd
of the Church to include in the ranks of its supreme senate none
but the most eminent men, and if, in so doing, as well as in the
appointment of distinguished bishops, it had put its finger
on the thing most needed for the reform of the Church,[4]
Pius V. had done his best to act up to that exhortation. The
next Papal election seemed to be assured ; if the next Pope
should walk in the ways of his predecessor, no longer would
those scandals which had so often placed their best weapons
in the hands of the enemies of the Holy See be found in the
senate of the Church. For this reason the renewal of the
Sacred College of 1570 was, in the best sense of the word, a
great act of reform.

The Pope, wrote Tiepolo on October 19th, 1566, does nothing
but reform ;[5] on the same day Strozzi states that on the
Monday there had been a meeting of the Congregation of the

[1] Zuñiga to Philip II., May 15, 1570, Corresp. dipl., III., 358 n.
[2] Ibid. 357 (May 17, 1570).
[3] Ibid. 363 seq. (May 19, 1570).
[4] Sess. 24, de ref., c. 1.
[4] MUTINELLI, I., 57.

Council, on the Tuesday a meeting about the new scheme of
studies, on the Wednesday one about the reform of the Breviary, on the Thursday before dinner one about the Inquisition,
and in the afternoon one about the reform of the clergy, and
that the Pope had busied himself about all these matters.[1]

Since 1566, by the Pope's orders, a great scheme of reform
of all the tribunals and officials of the Curia had been in preparation.[2] About Christmas, 1568, the reform commission
was able to present its report,[3] which the Pope went into
very fully on January 5th, 1569. For four hours it was reported in Rome, the Pope listened to the reading of the report,
and even then only a third part of the lengthy document was
got through. But, just as had been the case when the scheme
was first mooted, so now the head of the Church did not seem
inclined to put it into execution forthwith. Pius V. had said
that he did not wish to embitter the whole court against him,
and therefore men comforted themselves in Rome with the
hope that the reform which they all dreaded would not be so
terrible after all.[4] Fear, however, was by no means allayed
in those circles which were the first to be attacked. In June,
1569, it was reported that Abbot Bonhomini, the agent of
Cardinal Borromeo, had arrived with a thick volume of reform
proposals. At the beginning of March, 1571, men once more
expected a " terrible reform."[5] At the same time, however,

[1] *" tal che s'occupa tutto in questi essercitii." State Archives,
Vienna.

[2] *Avviso di Roma of December 25, 1568, Urb. 1040, p. 619,
Vatican Library.

[3] *Ibid.* For the nomination of the five deputies for the reform
of the tribunals see *Avviso di Roma of August 2, 1567, *ibid.* 426.
A *motu proprio (undated) " super reformatione taxarum,
officiorum et tribunalium urbis " in Bandi V., 36, p. 10, Papal
Secret Archives. *" Facultates concessae per Pium V. deputatis
ad reformationem tribunalium et officiorum Urbis," *ibid.* p. 12.

[4] *Avviso di Roma of January 8, 1569, Urb. 1041, p. 624,
Vatican Library.

[5] *Avvisi of June 11, 1569, and March 1, 1571, *ibid.* 1041, p. 92 ;
1042, p. 23b.

there was no secret in Rome as to the difficulties which seemed to make any radical change of the existing conditions almost impossible.[1]

The chief obstacle in the way of any complete change in the Curia lay in the fact that for a long time past many of the offices therein had been sold for money.[2] More especially since the time of Sixtus IV. the Popes had often found themselves in great financial difficulties, and in order to provide a remedy the number of official positions which were sold for large sums was increased ; for example, the position of clerk, which under Callixtus III. had been obtainable for 1000 gold florins, had cost twice that sum under Julius II., and three times as much under Leo X.[3] Anyone who had thus obtained a post to which an income was attached, naturally sought to administer it in such a way as to enrich himself ; complaints that there were no limits to the venality of the Roman officials, or to the corruption of the clerks, and indeed of the whole Papal court, were the inevitable consequence of such a state of affairs, which even the Popes deplored as intolerable, but which they were unable to remedy at a single blow.[4] Once so many clerks, procurators, etc., had bought their offices in good faith they could not be dismissed without suitable compensation. But whence was to come the means for suitably compensating a whole army of officials ?[5]

Pius V. had wished from the first to put an end to this unseemly state of affairs at all costs. The holy severity which animated him found almost ruthless expression when he replied in 1569 to the complaints of some officials who had

[1] * Avviso of July 30, 1569, *ibid.* 1041, p. 125.

[2] *Cf.* GÖLLER, II., 1, 91 *seq.*

[3] *Ibid.* 92 n.

[4] For the attempts at reform in this respect, especially in the case of the Penitentieria, see GÖLLER, II., 1, 97 *seqq.*, 145 *seqq.*

[5] *Cf.* GÖLLER, II., 1, 94. In the time of Pius IV. we may learn from the notes on the draft of his bull for the reform of the Penitentieria that several persons had sacrificed their whole property in order to buy a post in that department ; *ibid.* 128 and II., 2, 134. *Cf. ibid.* 103 a note from the time of Alexander VI.

been dismissed from the Penitentiaria : It is always better, he said, to die of hunger than to lose one's soul.[1]   In reality he had no intention of condemning anyone to die of hunger, and therefore, in spite of his zeal, he had to proceed step by step.

In the first months of his reign, Tiepolo wrote that the Pope was watching the Dataria very closely, and that he would no longer tolerate the slightest suspicion of simony.[2]   Immediately after his election he had set a very distinguished president over this department in the person of Archbishop Maffei, and had placed it under the care of Cardinals Scotti, Reumano and Rebiba,[3] ordering that for the future money was no longer to be taken for compositions.[4]   A constant source of scandal and simoniacal intrigue were the many *cessioni* from benefices, made to the Pope, not unconditionally, however, but in favour of some third party.[5]   Pius V. forbade all such arrangements ;[6] the Datary must submit to him all requests for such resignations, so that he might be sure there were no unjust conditions attached to them.[7]   In 1566 he appointed several Cardinals to examine into the question how far such resignations could

[1] *Arco, February 19, 1569, State Archives, Vienna.

[2] May 25, 1566, in MUTINELLI, I., 45.

[3] See SALMERON, Epist., II., 60.

[4] Requesens, January 11, 1566, Corresp. dipl., I., 86.

[5] *" [le renoncie], dalle quale procedevano infiniti scandali di simonie et altri errori " *Avviso di Roma of September 28, 1566, Urb. 1040, p. 291b, Vatican Library.

[6] " *Nella medesima signatura ordinò al datario che non passasse più suppliche di quelle che parlano di rinuntie de benefici in mano del Papa, ma però in favore di tale, perciochè pare a lui che questo sia modo di appropriarsi troppo lungamente beneficii ecclesiastici et in se stesso non può patire questa cosa, con tutto che per tanti et tanti anni sia stata accettata et usata dai pontefici et da la corte.   Di modo che da qui innanzi chi vorrà rinuntiare in mano del Papa bisognerà rinuntiare liberamente, et non più in favore di persona."   Luzzara to the Duke of Mantua, May 15, 1566, Gonzaga Archives, Mantua.

[7] *Avviso di Roma of May 18, 1566, Urb. 1040, p. 229, Vatican Library.   These " profane conditions " might be, for example, the various forms of confidential simony.

be allowed without sin,[1] and in the following year theologians
and canonists were appointed to discuss the matter.[2] The
conditions under which such resignations or *renunzie* were
lawful were laid down in detail, and were to be expressed in
accordance with a definite formula in the briefs which granted
them ;[3] only in certain very limited cases could the bishops
receive such permission ;[4] nobody who was not in major
orders could renounce his benefice without making restitution
of the fruits he had already enjoyed.[5] In dealing with offices
with a cure of souls attached to them, the Datary was not to
allow the resignation of such an office except on the grounds
of old age or illness.[6]

Pius V. not only issued these orders for others, but con-

[1] *Arco, May 25, 1566, State Archives, Vienna.

[2] *Avviso di Roma of February 22, 1567, Urb. 1040, p. 362b,
Vatican Library.

[3] Motu proprio of May 13, 1567. Bull. Rom., VII., 552 *seqq.*
The resignations, *states Arco on February 22, 1567, were allowed,
but there must be no admission of unworthy candidates, or of such
as had given rise to the least suspicion of simony (State Archives,
Vienna). The acceptance of such resignations had been forbidden
to the Roman authorities and to the ordinaries pending a definite
regulation of the question. Bull of August 8, 1567, in LADERCHI,
1567, n. 4.

[4] Bull of April 1, 1568, Bull. Rom., VII., 664 *seqq.*

[5] *" S. B^ne ha prohibito al datario le resignationi di quelli che
hanno beneficii et non sono in sacris, et vogliono lasciarli, volendo
che col lasciarli restituiscono anco i frutti percepti accioche a
piacer loro non habbino di quei della chiesa o fatto acquisto et
pensino hora di scaricarsene." B. Pia to Luzzara, Rome, May,
1568, Gonzaga Archives, Mantua.

[6] *" S.S continua a restringere anco un poco più le cose della
riforma et particularmente nella Dataria, non volendo che si
possi più far resegni de beneficii curati per qual causa che sia, non
amettendo nè vecchiezza nè infirmità " (Avviso di Roma of
November 3, 1571, Urb. 1042, p. 145b, Vatican Library). Age
and illness are naturally recognised as a judicial reason for a
resignation ; see Bull. Rom., VII., 665, 3. The *Avvisi frequently
insist upon the Pope's strictness in the granting of matrimonial

sidered himself bound by them as well. Through his ambassador, the Duke of Florence had asked for his approval
of the compulsory resignation of the aged Bishop of Pistoia
in favour of Alessandro Pucci. Without a moment's hesitation Pius V. definitely refused the request, on the
ground that such resignations made the bishops rulers
of their dioceses even after their death.[1] On account of
the position of the Church in Germany, however, he was
at last forced, after long resistance, to allow the resignation of the Bishop of Freising in favour of the young
Bavarian Duke Ernest.[2]

Even during the first year of the Pope's reign certain remarkable effects of these strict measures had made themselves
felt. In September, 1566, the abbreviators presented . a
petition asking for compensation for the emoluments which
they no longer received from the *renunzie*.[3] In the October

dispensations. The Spanish ambassador offered him 12,000
ducats as a fee for such a dispensation ; Pius V. replied : *" che
non ne vuole far altro a modo alcuno et che non era licito."
(August 10, 1566, *loc. cit.*, 1040, p. 271b). Dispensations in the
second and third degrees of kindred were done away with except
in the cases of great lords (November 22, 1570, *ibid.* 1041, p. 373b ;
cf. Conc. Trid., sess. W4, c.5). Dispensations in the second degree
which approached the first were refused by Pius V. even to these
latter, as for example to Count Ferrata di Ladrone, who was
recommended by the Emperor (*Arco, February 16, and August 3,
1566), to the Marquis of Veles (*Arco, July 5, 1567, State Archives,
Vienna). When it was said to the Pope that according to
theologians and canonists he could grant such dispensations, he
replied that many of these had been flatterers of the Popes
(*Arco, August 3, 1566, *loc. cit.*). No dispensation was granted
without the attestation of the bishop (*Avviso of March 5, 1569,
Urb. 1041, p. 34, Vatican Library). *Cf.* Schwarz, Briefwechsel,
I., 63, 72.

[1] " Risposemi risolutamente senza pensarci punto ; non lo
volere acconsentire." Legaz. di Serristori, 447.

[2] Laderchi, 1566, n. 263 *seq.*

[3] *Avviso di Roma of September 28, 1566, Urb. 1040, p. 291b,
Vatican Library.

of the same year the complaint was made that the Dataria had not received a quarter of its usual revenue, because the Pope had entirely done away with compositions, namely those fines which had been customary in connexion with the absolution of certain offences, and that various other sums which had come to the Dataria under other pontificates had also been lost.[1] These fines, however, were not in the least simoniacal, and thus it is easy to see why the Pope gave two Cardinals leave to impose such fines in connexion with certain offences in order to raise money for the league against the Turks.[2] The administration of the basilica of St. Peter's also received similar powers.[3]

Even more than the Dataria the Pope had at heart that tribunal which, according to its original purpose, dealt expressly with matters of conscience, or for the peace of men's consciences, and which, for the most part, did its work in the confessional, the Apostolic Penitentiaria. This had come into being at the end of the XIIth century, principally to meet the need felt in Rome for a body of confessors who should be able, by Papal authority, to absolve from all reserves those penitents who flocked to the tombs of the Princes of the Apostles.[4] In course of time the Penitentiaria had acquired many powers and faculties which held good outside the confessional, and in public.[5] Even in the Penitentiaria, however, some of the offices had become open to sale,[6] and in this way

[1] *" La Dataria non fa più un quattrino, perchè le compositioni sono levate del tutto, et quelli emolumenti, che detta Dataria solea portare alli altri pontefici." Avviso di Roma of October 26, 1566, p. 312b, Vatican Library.

[2] *Avviso of December 8, 1571, *ibid.* 1042, p. 150b.

[3] *Avviso of August 16, 1570, *ibid.* 1041, p. 327.

[4] GÖLLER, I., 1, 75 *seqq.*, 81. For the old archives of the Penitentieria see GÖLLER in *Festschrift für A. de Waal*, Freiburg, 1913, I *seqq.*

[5] GÖLLER, I, 1, 1 *seqq.*

[6] GÖLLER, II., 2, 93 *seq.* 146.

the general blight had made its way into this, the holiest of the Roman tribunals.[1]

Attempts to bring about an improvement had not been wanting. All the Popes of the XVIth century except Pius III. had turned their attention to it, not even Alexander VI. and the three weeks' pontificate of Marcellus II. being exceptions.[2] The bull of Pius IV. of May 4th, 1562, marked a notable advance in the reform of the Penitentiaria,[3] which, however, it was left to Pius V. to set upon an entirely new basis.

A first step was taken at the end of 1566. With the object of obtaining dispensations from matrimonial impediments more easily some of the officials of the Penitentiaria had been making false statements in their supplicas ; this abuse was declared by the Pope to fall under the same penalties as forgery,[4] It was not long, however, before he set his hand to effecting a radical change in the whole department, at the suggestion, and with the advice of Cardinal Borromeo and his confidant, Ormaneto.[5] We again hear of reforms and projects of reform during 1567 ;[6] in the following year Cardinals were appointed to consider these projects,[7] and in 1569 definite

[1] It is therefore untrue that the fees demanded by the Curia were a payment for absolution ; they were nothing but the charges made for the drawing up of the documents. *Ibid.* 132 *seqq.*

[2] GÖLLER, II., 1, 101 *seqq.* For Paul III. and Paul IV. see also Vol. XI. of this work p. 197 ; Vol. XIV., p. 203.

[3] GÖLLER. II., 1, 126 *seqq. Cf.* Vol. XV. of this work, p. 411.

[4] Muto proprio of December 5, 1566, Bull. Rom., VII., 315. The date in LADERCHI, 1566, n. 88.

[5] Letter from Ormaneto to Borromeo, February 7, 1567, on the reform of the Penitentieria, Ambrosian Library, Milan, F. 38, Inf. p. 85–91b, with many other matters connected with this reform attached.

[6] The reform of the Grand Penitentiary and other court dignitaries is announced as complete in an *Avviso of August 9, 1567 (Urb. 1040, p. 413, Vatican Library) ; there is hardly any more business ; the employés can hardly support themselves. An *Avviso of August 9, 1567 (*ibid.* 427b) speaks of a Papal decree according to which all the employés must be clerics.

[7] *Arco, March 13, 1568, State Archives, Vienna.

action was taken. The Penitentiaria in its existing form was entirely suppressed with all its powers,[1] in order to come into being again in an entirely new form, in virtue of the bull of May 18th, 1569.[2] Except in a few cases, the new Penitentiaria only had powers of absolution and dispensation in the internal forum,[3] everything else being in the hands of the Dataria and Cancelleria. There was also a considerable change in the office of the Grand Penitentiary ; the clerks and procurators, who had previously numbered 27 and 24 respectively, were reduced to two, in each case, while the offices of referendaries, correctors and revisors, were abolished,[4] the superfluous clerks and procurators being employed in the Apostolic Cancelleria.[5] The Grand Penitentiary and all his subordinates were to exercise their office in person ;[6] the procurators were to be priests, or at least subdeacons,[7] and no fees were to be demanded for the issue of documents.[8] The sale of offices was entirely done away with.[9]

---

[1] *" Pubblicata la Bulla della penitentieria," and by this it is abolished, and there is no more business ; everything now goes to the Cancelleria and Dataria (*Avviso di Roma of March 5, 1569, Urb. 1041, p. 34, Vatican Library). Bull of April 23, 1569, in GÖLLER, II., 2, 98. As early as February 14, 1569 (Urb. 1041, p. 14) an *Avviso declares that the matrimonial dispensations of the Penitentiaria were suspended, because a dispensation had been granted, but that the Pope had refused it.

[2] Bull. Rom., VII., 746 seqq., 750 seqq.

[3] Ibid., 750 §2. In GÖLLER, II., 2, 15 seqq. there is a list of the faculties granted to the Grand Penitentiary by Pius V., and later on by Gregory XIII.

[4] Bull. Rom., VII., 747 § 3.

[5] Bull of May 19, 1569, ibid. 752.

[6] Ibid. 747, § 6 and 12.

[7] Ibid. § 10.

[8] Ibid. 749, § 17.

[9] " Illorumque omnium officiorum in ipso Poenitentiariae officio constitutorum venditionem, aut quamvis aLam voluntariam tacitam vel expressam ea dimittentium dispositionem expresse prohibemus," and this under pain of invalidity.

The college of penitentiaries who, by commission of the Grand
Penitentiary, were at the service of penitents in the three great
basilicas of Rome, were also subjected to new regulations.
According to the provisions of Pius IV., twelve of these so-
called " minor penitentiaries," drawn from various religious
orders and nationalities, were to work at S. Maria Maggiore ;
Pius V. halved the number and ordered that they should all
of them be drawn from the Roman province of the Dominican
Order, assigning to them a suitable house near S. Pudenziana,
and a sufficient revenue.[1] Eight Franciscan Observants
were to act as penitentiaries at the Lateran,[2] and twelve Jesuits
at St. Peter's, who also lived close by in a house of their own.[3]
The community life which he insisted upon for the penitentiaries was the reason for assigning this office to religious,
and it was also obviously suitable that those who thus lived
together should belong to the same Order ; at the same time,
the Pope left the selection of capable men to the Provincials
of the various Orders.[4]

The other Papal tribunals and courts did not escape the
zeal of the Pope, who was anxious to effect improvement
everywhere. On February 15th, 1566, the reform of the
Segnatura was effected,[5] and since the officials of the Apostolic
Camera had exercised their office with excessive strictness,

[1] Bulls of September 1 and 6, 1568, Bull. Rom., VII., 703 seqq.,
706 seqq.

[2] SACCHINI, P. III., 1, 6, n. 2.   S. Franciscus Borgia, V., 371.

[3] SACCHINI, n. 1–8. Circular of Francis Borgia to the provincials of the Jesuits, April 24, 1570, S. Franciscus Borgia, V.,
356 ; to the provincials of Spain, April 28, 1570, ibid. 371. Cf.
Cardinal Alciati to Fr. Borgia, July 8, 1569, ibid. 121 ; GÖLLER,
II., 1, 48 seq.

[4] SACCHINI, loc. cit. n. 2.   In GÖLLER, II., 2, 139 seq. a list,
dated March 16, 1568, of the sins withdrawn from the absolving
power of the penitentiaries.

[5] There only remained the four Cardinals, Reumano, Cicada,
Simoncelli, and Vitelli with 34 referendaries ; only 12 of the latter
had a consultative vote. *Cusano, February 16, 1566, State
Archives, Vienna.

the Pope took rigorous measures on May 29th, 1567.[1] It was rumoured in June, 1567, that the powers of the Camerlengo were to be limited.[2] The correctors of the Cancelleria were reformed on October 21st, 1569,[3] and after long discussion,[4] the auditors of the Camera, by a decree of November 20th, 1570.[5] Towards the end of 1568, it was reported in Rome that the Cancelleria had decided to meet only twice a week, on account of the reduction of its business.[6] Lastly, the reforming zeal of the Pope was turned to the improvement of the archives of the Curia, which had hitherto been very much neglected.[7]

The Council of Trent had entrusted the reform of the Church to the bishops ; it therefore seemed obvious to Pius V. that, as Bishop of Rome, he must set them an example in his own diocese.

The Council had laid it down that one of the principal duties of a bishop was to make a visitation of all the churches and of all the ministers of the sanctuary. The Pope therefore wished to fulfil this obligation of visitation in the Eternal City as far as he could in person.[8] He began on Sunday, May 12th, 1566, with the basilica of St. Peter's, in order to

---

[1] Bull. Rom. VII. 601 *seqq.* On the other hand, however, Pius V. protected the rights of the Camera ; *ibid.* 609, 641 *seq.*, 646, 690, 697, 894.

[2] *Avviso di Roma of June 14, 1567, Urb. 1040, p. 403, Vatican Library.

[3] Bull. Rom., VII., 785.

[4] *Avviso di Roma of August 16, 1570, Urb. 1041,. p. 327, Vatican Library.

[5] Bull. Rom., VII., 865. An *Avviso di Roma (Urb. 1041, p. 380, Vatican Library) reports on December 9, 1570, the publication of the bull.

[6] *Avviso di Roma of November 6, 1568, *ibid.* 1040, p. 597.

[7] Motu proprio of July 18, 1569, Bull. Rom., VII., 762. Order of August 19, 1568, for the registration of the documents belonging to the Apostolic Camera, for the search for those which had been lost, etc., *ibid.* 697.

[8] *Avviso di Roma of April 27, 1566, Urb. 1040, p. 218b, Vatican Library.

ascertain for himself if everything was in good order for the administration of the sacraments, and for the worthy celebration of divine worship. The baptismal font did not satisfy him, and he gave orders for a better one to be made, more in keeping with the dignity of the noblest temple of God on earth. In the sacristy he examined the reliquaries, the chalices, the sacred vessels and the vestments. After that, all laymen were excluded, the canons and other priests, including the bishops, knelt down, and the Cardinals formed a semi-circle on the right of the Pope, who then delivered a long discourse on the things necessary for the sacerdotal life, and the due performance of the divine worship.[1] After the visitation, the Pope turned to the Archpriest of St. Peter's Cardinal Farnese, and said to him that he hoped he would find all the other churches in as good a condition.[2] On July 1st, 1566, he visited the church and hospital of S. Spirito, and here again he satisfied himself minutely as to the custody of the Blessed Sacrament, the baptismal font, the chrism, the sacred vestments, the sacristy and the sacristans. He then went to see the sick in the hospital, " doing everything with all possible charity and love."[3] He also personally

---

[1] *[" Die dominica XII. maii (1566) hora 17 . . . ivit ad ecclesiam S^ti Petri] . . . ordinavit quod fieret fons [baptismalis] pulchrior, prout dicebat requirere nobilitatem et ecellentiam ecclesiae, quam dixit esse primam totius orbis. Vidit postea sacellum, reliquias sanctorum, calices, vasa sacra et omnia super magna credentia parata, etc. Deinde sedens super sede ibidem parata, emissis extra sacellum omnibus laicis, fecit longum sermonem canonicis et aliis presbiteris, omnibus genuflexis etiam episcopis, et male dico quoad episcopos ipsos, cardinalibus in circulum a dextro latere sedentibus ; et sermo fuit circa mores ipsorum et modum deserviendi in ecclesia et multa dixit de dignitate sacerdotali " (FIRMANUS, *Diarium, p. 87. Papal Secret Archives). Cf. *Cusano, May 18, 1566, State Archives, Vienna, *Avviso di Roma of May 18, 1566, Urb. 1040, p. 229b, and *report in Cod. Vatic. 5514, p. 1–15, Vatican Library.

[2] * Avviso di Roma of May 18, 1566, ibid.

[3] * Avviso di Roma of July 6, 1566, Urb. 1040, p. 251 seq., Vatican Library : " il che tutto con tanta carità e amore quanto dir si possa."

visited the other patriarchal churches,[1] going on July 10th, 1566, to the church and hospital of the Lateran,[2] and on September 30th to S. Maria Maggiore.[3] He had still further projects ; he wished to visit all the hospitals in Rome, as well as the convents of women and the prisons ;[4] he had a project of appointing a Cardinal to look after the prisoners, and expedite their trials.[5] " His Holiness," wrote the Imperial ambassador to the Holy See," is always working to reform the state of affairs in Rome, which is very distasteful to many people."[6]

Naturally the Pope had not the time to carry out all these visitations in person. In January, 1566, he had appointed a special congregation, composed of Cardinals Morone, Farnese, Savelli, Borromeo, Alciati and Paleotto, for the reform of the Roman clergy.[7] The Cardinal of Milan, who was undoubtedly the most important member of this congregation, soon left for his episcopal city, but in the middle of July the reform of the Roman clergy was committed to his intimate friend, Ormaneto,[8] who was in constant correspondence with the

---

[1] LADERCHI, 1566, n. 63.

[2] *" Il Papa è stato questa mattina a S. Giovanni a visitare la chiesa et l'hospitale et è andato per tempissimo et con pocchissime persone. A quest'hora ha visitato S. Pietro, S. Spirito et S. Giovanni." (Luzzara to the Duke of Mantua, July 10, 1566, Gonzaga Archives, Mantua). Cf. *Arco, July 13, 1566, State Archives, Vienna ; *Avviso di Roma of July 13, 1566, Urb. 1040, p. 243, Vatican Library.

[3] *Strozzi on October 5, 1566, State Archives, Vienna.

[4] *Arco, July 13, 1566, loc. cit. *Avviso di Roma of July 13, 1566, loc. cit.

[5] *Avviso di Roma of July 13, 1566, loc. cit. For the visitation of the prisons cf. Bull. Rom., VII., 688, 696, 801.

[6] *Arco, July 13, 1566, State Archives, Vienna.

[7] *Cusano, January 26, 1566, ibid.

[8] " Giovedi fu congregazione dell'Inquisizione et dopo pranzo del Concilio dove si trattò de riforma del clero di Roma, la qual cura è data a monsignor Ormaneto." Avviso di Roma of July 20, 1566, in BERTOLOTTI, Martiri, 37.

Cardinal,[1] and thus acted as an intermediary, by whose means the Archbishop of Milan continued his work of reform even in Rome.

The influence of Borromeo upon the renewal of the Roman church was universally recognized in other ways as well. The Pope, wrote Ciregiola, intends to hold a provincial synod, and to visit, either in person or by his deputies, all the churches in Rome, and it is thought that Borromeo will be recalled to Rome for that purpose, as he has had great experience in these matters.[2] When Bonhomini was expected in June, 1569, as a member of the reform commission, it was thought in Rome that he would bring with him a large volume of reform proposals from Cardinal Borromeo.[3] In December, 1566, Poggiani wrote that it was well known that the Roman reform was the offspring of that in Milan, and that its promoter had taken as his model a certain member of the Church.[4]

Under the presidency of Cardinal Savelli, Vicar of Rome, the reform commission held a series of sessions, at which Ormaneto, the Prior of Foligno, and Oliva di Perugia were

[1] Letters between the two are noted in *San Carlo*, indexed under Ormaneto.

[2] Letter to Cardinal Ferdinando de' Medici, June 19, 1566, State Archives, Florence. *Arco expected the return of Borromeo on account of the synod which was to be held in September (July 20, 1566, State Archives, Vienna); *Caligari thought his recall was certain that he might take part in the reform of the Church (to Commendone, August 3, 1566, Papal Secret Archives).

[3] *Avviso di Roma of June 11, 1569, Urb. 1041, p. 92, Vatican Library.

[4] " Non occorre, ch'io dica altro a V.S. ill. intorno alla stima, che si fa della sue constitutioni sinodali, vedendo ognuno, che la riforma romana è filgliuola della milanese, il che di giorno in giorno si va così dilatando, che cotesto membro entrarà in molto maggior riputatione, poichè da quello a un certo modo ha preso esempio il capo." To Borromeo in POGIANI Epist. II., xv.

also present.[1] One result of these meetings was certainly the edict of October 30th, 1566, which enjoined upon the Roman clergy the rules for leading a truly priestly life.[2] In August four visitors were charged to fulfil that duty in the Roman churches,[3] and a visitation of even the titular churches of the Cardinals was ordered in September.[4]

In the opinion of many members of the Curia, the visitors discharged their duties " very strictly."[5] One of them wrote in December to Florence that the Pope " has a very strict minister, who is Monsignor Ormaneto, who has no respect for anyone, since that is the wish of the Pope " ;[6] it was thought that a special motu proprio would permit him to take action and to inflict punishment without the usual legal procedure.[7] The Canons of St. Peter's sought to shield themselves from the reform by appealing to an ancient privi-

[1] Caligari to Commendone, June 18, 1566, Papal Secret Archives *Anal. Bolland.*, XXXIII. (1914), 195, n. 1. Oliva was afterwards Bishop of Chieti. The " Prior of Foligno " must be Tommaso Orfino (his name is Orfino, not Orsini or Ursinus as written by LADERCHI, 1566, n. 184 ; 1567, n. 64 and GAMS, p. 696, 928 ; *cf. infra* n. 3 ; UGHELLI, I., 773 ; IX., 733 ; MORONI, XXV., 141 ; LXX., 200, and in the index).

[2] LADERCHI, 1566, n. 58.

[3] *Arco, August 17, 1566, State Archives, Vienna. The names of the four visitors are in the letter in which Savelli announces the the visitation to each of the churches : " Vobis per praesentes denunciare decrevimus, qualiter die . . . ad vos vestramque ecclesiam Nos seu RR. PP. DD. Thomas Orphinus episcopus Stragulen., Alphonsus Binarius utriusque Signaturae referendarius vicesgerens noster, Nicolaus Ormannettus et Joannes Oliva visitatores a Nobis deputati veniemus seu venient, aut aliquis corum veniet." *Anal. iuris Pontif.*, I., Rome, 1855, 2734.

[4] Consistory of September 6, 1566, in LADERCHI, 1566, n. 63.

[5] *Ciregiola to Cardinal Ferdinando de' Medici, November 30, 1566, State Archives, Florence.

[6] *Avviso di Roma of December 8, 1566, Urb. 1040, p. 337b, Vatican Library : " Ha un rigoroso ministro che è mons. Ormaneto che non ha rispetto a niuno perchè così è la mente del Papa."

[7] *Avviso di Roma of September 25, 1568, *ibid.* 585b.

lege, according to which they could only be visited by the
Pope, but they only succeeded in getting their privileges
annulled, and a report from Rome states that they had been
visited, and were " in danger " of a startling reform.[1]   When
visiting S. Pietro in Montorio, Ormaneto and his colleague
Binarini found that the guardian had not complied with
the command to join the Observants of his Order ; he was
thereupon imprisoned, even though he had been the confessor
of Pius IV.[2]   Great discontent was caused among the canons
and beneficiaries of Rome by the fact that the commissioners
obliged them to officiate in their churches all through Lent,
whereas previously they had only been obliged to do so for
ten days in the month.[3]

Another regulation, which was undoubtedly just and
necessary, and which was made about the same time, could
not fail to increase the discontent in many quarters.   It
had for some time been rumoured that it was the Pope's
desire that all secular and regular priests should satisfy their
bishop as to their fitness to hear confessions.[4]   In March,

[1] *Avviso di Roma of October 19, 1566, *ibid*. 308.   LADERCHI,
1566, n. 62.   On November 30, 1566, Strozzi *wrote that they
wished to induce the Canons of St. Peter's to build themselves
near the basilica a house where they could lead a community life,
and constantly take part in the functions,and that Farnese as Archpriest was working against this proposal.   State Archives, Vienna.

[2] *Avviso di Roma of April 3, 1568, Urb. 1040, p. 499, Vatican
Library.   In his visitation of St. Gregorio, Ormaneto found grave
abuses in the matter of alms for masses, whereat the Pope was
much displeased.   *Avviso di Roma of October 1, 1569, *ibid*.
p. 159.

[3] *Avviso di Roma of March 8, 1567, *ibid*. 1040, p. 366.

[4] *" S'intende che vuole che tutti li confessori come preti come
frati vadino ad essaminarsi al vescovato, se sono idonei alla con-
fessione, altramente saranno privati del confessare trovandosi
inesperti."   (Avviso di Roma of November 16, 1566, Urb. 1040,
p. 321, Vatican Library).   Already in the consistory of January
23, 1566, Cardinals Borromeo, Savelli, Alciati and Sirleto had been
appointed commissaries for the examination of parish priests
in general.   *Arco, January 26, 1566, State Archives, Vienna.

1567, Pius V. had all the confessors of the Roman churches examined, and those who were unfit removed ;[1] at the beginning of 1571 the *approbatio* of the congregation of reform was required for all confessors.[2] An attempt was made to put difficulties in the way of unsuitable candidates receiving the priesthood, and it was ordered that for the future orders were not to be conferred unless the candidate had been examined before the Pope's Vicar a month previously.[3] Only by the express permission of the Pope could the Segnatura permit ordinations *extra tempora*, or the legitimatization of the illegitimate.[4] Even the Cardinals could no longer confer benefices in the churches of Rome, except on those who had been accepted as suitable by the vicar-general.[5]

With a view to creating a good spirit among the clergy the reform commission introduced sacerdotal conferences. All the parishes of Rome were divided into six districts, and the priests of each district had to meet once a week in one of the churches for the discussion of the needs of the parishes, as though in a little synod.[6]

The Pope also turned his attention to the exterior behaviour of the ecclesiastical body. In order to meet the evil custom by which even priests dressed as laymen, all clerics were obliged to wear the ecclesiastical dress ;[7] those who did not

[1] *Avviso di Roma of March 15, 1567, Urb. 1040, p. 370, Vatican Library.

[2] *Zibramonti, January 20, 1571, Gonzaga Archives, Mantua. *Cf.* *Avviso di Roma of January 20, 1571, Urb. 1042, p. 7, Vatican Library.

[3] *Avviso di Roma of May 12, 1571, Urb. 1042, p. 60, Vatican Library.

[4] Order to Capizuchi. *Avviso di Roma of January 29, 1569, *ibid.* 1041, p. 13.

[5] Bull. Rom., VII., 423. For the date see LADERCHI, 1566, n. 59.

[6] *Avviso di Roma of March 8, 1567, Urb. 1040, p. 366, Vatican Library.

[7] Edict of Cardinal Savelli of October 30, 1566, in LADERCHI, 1566, n. 58 ; *cf. ibid.* n. 63. *Strozzi, November 11, 1566, State Archives, Vienna.

comply with this regulation were to lose their benefices.[1] Doctors, physicians and jurists were ordered to give up wearing the biretta.[2]

With a view to putting the care of souls in a better state the Cardinal Vicar issued more detailed regulations for those churches which exercised parochial rights.[3] Since some of the parishes were too large to allow of the efficient discharge of their parochial duties, a motu proprio erected in these parishes eleven new vicariates, which were subject to the Cardinal Vicar,[4] while the Cardinals were exhorted to provide vicars for their titular churches.[5]

By order of the vicar-general all parish priests were to be in their churches for two or three hours on feast days to instruct the children in the fundamental truths of the Christian faith.[6] When many people had been struck down by the

[1] *Avviso di Roma of January 31, 1568, Urb. 1040, p. 381b, Vatican Library. For the preparation of the *bando* relating to this matter, *cf.* *Avviso di Roma of April 27, 1566, *ibid.* 218b.

[2] *Arco, November 1, 1566 ; *cf.* the *letters of April 27, 1566, November 1, 1567 and February 12, 1569. State Archives, Vienna ; *Avviso di Roma of October 19, 1566, Urb. 1040, p. 309, Vatican Library ; LADERCHI, 1567, n. 37. A general prescription on the dress of priests, laymen and women was issued on May 19, 1566, at the Capitol (*Avviso di Roma of May 25, 1566, Urb. 1040, p. 331b, Vatican Library) ; this was soon made less strict, but the household of the Pope and the Cardinals were obliged to observe it strictly (*Avviso di Roma of July 20, 1566, *ibid.* 255). *Zibramonti reports a further constitution on ecclesiastical dress on September 15, 1571, to the Duke of Mantua (Gonzaga Archives, Mantua). *Cf.* *Avviso di Roma of October 18, 1570 (*loc. cit.* 357). A prohibition to clerics to wear beards was proposed (*Avvisi di Roma of August 17 and September 7, 1566, *loc. cit.* 275, 282b ; *Arco, August 3, 1566, State Archives, Vienna.

[3] On September 13, 1569. DENGEL, Palast und Basilika S. Marco in Rom, Rome, 1913, 85.

[4] November 5, 1571, Bull. Rom., VII., 947.

[5] *Arco, September 7, 1566, State Archives, Vienna.

[6] *Avviso di Roma of July 17, 1568, Urb. 1040, p. 549, Vatican Library.

plague in the Borgo, the parish priests were urged to visit the sick, and then to make a report as to those in need, so that they might be provided for and helped.[1] They were told above all to look after the poor, to exhort them to lead Christian lives, and to give them the sacraments at due times.[2]

If the Eternal City was little by little to assume a new appearance in religious matters, it was necessary to purge if of many priests and prelates who, in forgetfulness of their duty, lived in Rome, far away from their dioceses and benefices. Even in the first weeks after his election, Pius V. ordered Cardinals Morone, Corgna and Rebiba to summon all the bishops living in Rome, and to send back to their dioceses all who were not excused for some urgent reason.[3] At the congregation he again repeated this order in the presence of the three Cardinals. The excuses which were made were received by the Pope with a bad grace (or at least so it was said in Rome) ; the bishops, he said, had no other duty than to repair to their dioceses, and to see to it that the reforms and decrees of the Council were enforced there.[4] The parish priests received similar orders to those which the Pope had already given to the bishops at an audience,[5] and in order that it might be taken seriously he ordered the auditor of the Apostolic Camera, Alessandro Riario, to take legal proceedings against those who disobeyed.[6] The penalty of se-

[1] *Avviso di Roma of August 14, 1568, *ibid.* 562b ; *cf. ibid.* 573. *Avviso di Roma of September 4, 1568.

[2] *Avviso di Roma of March 12, 1569, *ibid.* 1041, p. 40.

[3] *Avviso di Roma of January 26, 1566, *ibid.* 1040, p. 172. Acta consist. of January 23, 1566, in LADERCHI, 1566, n. 46 ; GUILIK-EUBEL, 47.

[4] *" Resideant, s'attenda alla riforma per mantener li decreti del Concilio." Avviso di Roma of February 16, 1566, Urb. 1040, p. 182, Vatican Library.

[5] *Avviso of February 24, 1566, *ibid.* 184b.

[6] Motu proprio of June 10, 1566, in LADERCHI, 1566, n. 46. Bull. Rom., VII., 464. Riario was instructed to take summary proceeding against all " tam in Urbe quam alibi et ubique locorum existentes et in propriis diocesibus non residentes."

questration was actually laid upon the diocese of Vaison,
because the bishop of that city never visited his diocese.[1]
The strict reformer did not give a thought to the fact that
by these orders his own court would be shorn of its splendours.
The Cardinals received orders to send back at once to their
posts those members of their households who held benefices
entailing the care of souls, and also to go themselves to their
own sees.[2] The Pope had already told a hundred Spaniards
at the court that they must go back to their benefices. The
correspondent who reports this fact was of opinion that very
soon the city would be half emptied of all important
personages.[3]

Naturally such expressions must not be taken quite literally. Even a Pius V. could not eradicate an inveterate habit
by words and exhortations alone, and accordingly in the
following year he began to take more stringent measures.
Five or six parish priests, who had no business in Rome,

---

[1] *Avviso of November 9, 1566, Urb. 1040, p. 318, Vatican
Library. According to a *report of Strozzi of the same date
(State Archives, Vienna) the bishop was deposed. The Bishop
of Vaison in 1566 was Giacomo Cortesi, Patriarch of Alexandria,
died 1570. His successor in the patriarchate was appointed
November 8, 1570 (MORONI, LVII., 173). In 1569, Chisholm,
the envoy of Mary Stuart, appears as Bishop of Vaison (GAMS,
648 ; Dictionary of National Biography, X., 262).

[2] Consistory of September 6, 1566, according to the Diarium
of Cardinal Farnese, in LADERCHI, 1566, n. 63. *" Die lunae
scilicet 13 ianuarii [1567] fuit consistorium sacretum, in quo
inter alia S^{mus} D.N. hortatus fuit cardinales, quod mitterent
eorum familiares habentes curam animarum ad earum curas
quanto citius, quia volebat, quod omnes episcopi et curati in-
differentur irent, etc. ; dixit etiam quod cardinales, qui poterant,
irent ad eorum ecclesias similiter " (FIRMANUS, Diarium, p. 152,
Papal Secret Archives). In the consistory of October 8, 1567,
all prelates were again bidden to return to their churches
(ibid.).

[3] *" Di modo che questa terra rimarrà mezza dissoluta d'huomini
di conditione." Avviso of December 8, 1566, Urb. 1040, p. 338,
Vatican Library.

were imprisoned,[1] and at the end of the year Binarini and Ormaneto received an order, which they were to carry into effect with all their power, to take proceedings against the bishops after having warned them, and against all other offenders without warning.[2] On Sunday, after the pontifical High Mass, the bishops were informed that the Pope did not intend any longer to exhort them to their duty,[3] and in the following year, 1568, the Pope made inquiries as to how many bishops, who had not resigned their sees, were still in Rome, and sent some of them to the Castle of St. Angelo.[4]

The question of residence made its appearance once more during the last years of Pius V. This time the man in whose hands was placed the carrying out of this difficult task was Carniglia. In virtue of a Papal edict, which bound all priests living in the Curia to furnish in writing their names, together with their benefices and their native land,[5] he drew up a list of all the possessors of benefices residing in Rome.[6] These then received orders to repair to their benefices,[7] and those who failed to obey were forced by Carniglia, acting under

[1] *Avviso di Roma of March 1, 1567, ibid. 365.

[2] *" S. Stà domenica ordinò a mons. Binarini et all Ormaneto che intimassero a tutti i vescovi che si trovano qui, la residenza et procedessero anco contro di loro, di maniera che a questo s'attende con ogni diligenza, et così anco per conto de curati, contra qualli prima si viene all' esecutione che a citatione come contumaci d' altre intimationi " (B. Pia to Luzzara, December 20, 1567, Gonzaga Archives, Mantua). Cf. *Arco, December 13, 1567, State Archives, Vienna.

[3] *Avviso of December 20, 1567, Urb. 1040, p. 164b, Vatican Library.

[4] *Avviso of March 20, 1568, ibid. 491. For the enforcement of the obligation of residence in 1568 cf. GRATIANI Epist., 366 ; for the bull of July 8, 1568, see infra, p. 217.

[5] *Avviso of February 8, 1570, Urb. 1041, p. 224b, Vatican Library. For a similar but earlier order cf. *Avviso of November 9, 1566, Urb. 1040, p. 318, ibid.

[6] *Avviso of December 30, 1570, Urb. 1041, p. 390, ibid.

[7] *Avviso of January 24, 1571, Urb. 1042, p. 12, ibid.

the Pope's instructions, to make restitution of the fruits.[1] Carniglia was also instructed to exhort all the Cardinals and prelates to send away all the members of their households who held benefices with a cure of souls,[2] similar instructions having been already sent to all Spaniards holding such offices.[3]

This renewal of religious life was naturally not limited to Rome. At the beginning of 1571 four bishops were appointed to make a visitation of the dioceses in the Papal States, namely Pietro de Lunel of Gaeta for the Marches, Giovanni Francesco Sormanni of Montefeltro for Umbria and the Patrimony, Paolo Maria della Rovere of Cagli for the Romagna and Lombardy, and Vincenzo Ercolano of Sarno for the Campagna.[4] They were to start at the beginning of Lent, and were especially to insist on the observance of the duty of residence, to regulate the granting of benefices, to see to the restoration of delapidated churches, and to examine into the proper distribution of revenues.[5] Four Jesuits were appointed to accompany them to preach to the people and to act as their advisers.[6] Sometimes the Pope himself acted

---

[1] *Avviso of January 27, 1571, *ibid.* 12b. A fresh warning to the bishops about residence : *Avviso of March 3, 1571, *ibid.* 25b.

[2] *Avviso of December 23, 1571, *ibid.* 168.

[3] *" Il Papa ha fatto intimare a tutti li Spagnoli che hanno beneficii curati, che debbano andare alle loro residenze." (Zibramonti to the Duke of Mantua, January 13, 1571, Gonzaga Archives, Mantua). *Cf.* *Avviso of January 13, 1571, Urb. 1042, p. 4, Vatican Library.

[4] *Avviso of January 6, 1571, Urb. 1042, p. 2, Vatican Library. The *briefs for the four bishops, of February 3, 1571, in the Archives of Briefs, Rome.

[5] *Avviso of January 24, 1571, Urb. 1042, p. 12, Vatican Library.

[6] *" S. Stà ha deputato quattro vescovi et quattro di questi padri del Giesù che vadino per lo State ecclesiastico visitando i vescovati. I vescovi visiteranno le città et quei padri visiteranno le diocesi et ordineranno quello che giudicheranno esser servitio di Dio, et a disordini a quali non potranno remediare, si remetteranno alla relatione che ne faranno a S. Stà, che poi riprenderanno quell' espeditione che le parerà più opportuna." (Zibramonti, January 6, 1571, to the Duke of Mantua, Gonzaga Archives, Mantua). It

as visitor in the neighbourhood of Rome. When he visited
Porto to see to the erection of fortifications against the cor-
sairs,[1] he also went to Ostia, and finding the church there
very much neglected, he bitterly reproached Cardinal Pisani
and took away 3,000 scudi from his revenues in order to make
good the damage.[2]

Besides all this, Pius V., first in the autumn of 1566, and
again in the following Lent, planned to hold a great provincial
synod of all the bishops of Italy, which was to lay down in
detail the line of reform to be adopted,[3] but as the provincial
synod of Milan held by Cardinal Borromeo had already
covered this ground, we may reasonably suppose that it was
on that account that the plan was allowed to lapse.[4]

would appear that only two of these bishops were actually accompanied by a Jesuit (SACCHINI, P. III., i. 7, n. 16). *Decree of
reform from Sormanni for Rimini in Cod. CP 5n. 24 of the Gambalunga Library, Rimini.

[1] LADERCHI, 1566. n. 63.

[2] *Ibid.* n. 64. *Strozzi, November 6, 1566, State Archives,
Vienna. *Avviso of November 16, 1566, Urb. 1040, p. 320b,
Vatican Library. The Pope also intended to visit Civitavecchia ;
ibid.

[3] See *supra*, p. 182, and *Avvisi of September 17 and December
8, 1566, Urb. 1040, p. 148b, 338b, Vatican Library.   *Strozzi,
December 7, 1566, State Archives, Vienna.

[4] How highly Pius V. appreciated the provincial synod of Milan
appears from a letter from Borromeo to the Bishop of Brescia
dated December 27, 1566 : La Santità di Nostro Signore per la
satisfatione che ha havuta di questro nostro concilio, et per il
desiderio che ha di vider la riforma incamminata, ha fatto pro-
hibere a i tribunali di Roma che non faccino cosa alcuna contro a
i decreti del suddetto concilio." In SALA, Docum. II., 272.

CHAPTER V.

REFORM OF THE CHURCH ON THE BASIS OF THE TRIDENTINE DECREES.

IN all his work for ecclesiastical reform in Rome and the Papal States the Pope always kept before him as his guide and rule the decrees of the Council of Trent, which he wished to see carried into effect with the minutest exactitude, and above all other places in his own immediate surroundings. The activities of Pius V. for the reform of the universal Church were planned upon the same lines.

In the first place he set himself, in some sense, to complete the work of the Council by carrying to a happy issue some of those undertakings which the Fathers of Trent had handed over incomplete to the care of the Apostolic See. Already, under Pius IV., the Catechism, which it was the wish of the Council to make the basis of uniform instruction throughout the Church, had neared completion.[1] Now, after a final revision made under the supervision of Sirleto,[2] it was found possible, towards the end of 1566, to issue it at the press of Paulus Manutius in Rome in several Latin editions, as well as an Italian one, which had, by the Pope's orders, been prepared by the Dominican, Alessio Figliucci.[3] The Pope also interested himself personally in the preparation of versions in other tongues. He entrusted the Jesuit, Paul Hoffæus, with the translation of the Catechism into German, and Peter

---

[1] *Cf.* Vol. XVI. of this work, p 24 *seq.*

[2] " [Sirleto] modo incumbit negotio τοῦ κατηχισμοῦ cum archiepiscopo Lancianensi et magistro s. Palatii. Et spes est illorum cito editum iri typis Aldinis " (Lombardo to Hosius, April 1, 1566, in CYPRIANUS, 413). For the part taken by Sirleto, *cf.* POGIANI Epist., II., xxxviii.

[3] SKIBNIEWSKI, 58 *seq.*, 134. RENOUARD, Annales, II., 57 *seq.*

Canisius was ordered to assist him.[1] The work of Hoffaeus was published at Dillingen at the beginning of 1568, with an introduction by Cardinal Truchsess.[2] The Pope also entrusted to the Jesuits the French translation of the Catechism.[3] He placed the work of preparing the Polish version in the hands of Cardinal Hosius of Ermland,[4] at the same time warning him to avoid a notable defect in the first Latin edition, which defect was also avoided in the German translation ;[5] the first publishers had been careless in the matter of its division into chapters and sections. The Catechism met with difficulties in Spain. The permission which had already been given to print it there,[6] in spite of the privilege granted to Paulus Manutius, was withdrawn by the Pope[7] when certain Spanish theologians took it upon themselves to find fault with a certain equivocal passage in the Catechism.[8] Cardinal Espinosa had been charged with the preparation of a Spanish translation, which was made by Funtidueña, but the censors expressed the view that it would be wiser to give up all idea of any translation into the vernacular.[9]

[1] Polanco to Hoffaeus, September 3, 1566, CANISII Epist., V., 816.

[2] *Ibid.* VI., 667.

[3] SACCHINI, P. III., 1, 2 n. 6.

[4] Brief of September 28, 1566, in LADERCHI, 1566, n. 343.

[5] CANISII Epist., VI., 109, 121.

[6] Of April 18, 1567, Corresp. dipl., II., 85 n. The same permission was given for Dillingen (CANISII Epist., VI., 660 *seq.*), and Poland (LADERCHI, 1566, n. 343), etc.

[7] July 19, 1567, Corresp. dipl., II., 85 n.

[8] From P. II., c. 2, n. 17, it appeared, in their opinion, that the precept of baptism in Matth. XXVIII., 18, did not apply to those who were damned. Corresp. dipl., *loc. cit.*

[9] Corresp. dipl., II., 85 n. An opinion of February 14, 1570, unfavourable to the translation of the Catechism was found among the writings of Carranza ; from this it may be supposed that the Catechism of Carranza had given rise to this doubt. Besides this there were, especially in Spain, many who were very nervous about theological works in the vernacular. In a letter to Castagna Rusticucci, on October 8, 1571, expressed the desire that the translation by Funtidueña should be printed. Corresp. dipl., IV., 453.

The year 1568 saw the printing of the revised breviary, that is to say the book of prayers used in the recitation of the canonical hours.

The custom of the recitation by the clergy, at certain fixed hours, of prayers in the name of the whole Church, could be traced back to the first centuries of the Christian era, and in its original form consisted of certain passages from the Holy Scriptures.[1]   In course of time these hours of prayer had become seven, one for the night and six for the day, and the breviary was for the greater part made up of the psalms, arranged in such a way that the whole Psalter was recited from beginning to end once in a week, the psalms being interrupted, especially in the night hour, by lections from the Holy Scriptures, or, on the festivals of saints, by lections drawn from their lives.[2]

Ever since the beginning of the XVIth. century more and more complaints had been heard of the departure of the breviary from its traditional form.[3]   It was objected that, as a result of the multiplication of the feasts of the saints, which had proper psalms of their own, these few psalms were constantly being said, and that the recitation of the complete Psalter had become almost impossible ; it was also objected that not enough time was devoted to the lections from the Holy Scriptures, while those drawn from the lives of the saints contained many incredible things, and were, moreover, written in very barbarous Latin.[4]   Moreover, so many secondary, but obligatory prayers had been added to the breviary properly

[1] The prayer for example at the ninth hour in the Acts of the Apostles III., 1.

[2] *Cf.* S. BÄUMER, Geschichte des Breviers, Freiburg, 1895. BATTIFOL, Hist. du bréviare romain, Paris, 1911.

[3] JOS. SCHMID in *Theol. Quartalschr.*, LXVI, (1884), 467 *seq.*, 452 *seq.* 478 *seq.* ; BÄUMER 364 *seqq.*

[4] A Papal permission attributed to Julius II. allowed the use of special offices when they were not expressly prohibited by the Church or incompatible with the Roman rite.   Such a permission opened the way to all manner of vagaries.   *Cf.* MERCATI in RASSENGA GREGORIANA, II. (1903), 419.

so called, that, except on festival days, the recitation of the
Divine Office took an unreasonably long time. The directions,
moreover, for the prayers which were to be said each day
were not arranged in any clear way, but entailed prolonged
search in various parts of the breviary, and much loss of
time.

The breviary which Pius V., in continuation of the work of
his predecessor, brought forward for discussion,[1] and eventually
placed in the hands of the clergy, accompanied by a bull of
July 9th, 1568,[2] sought to obviate all these difficulties.[3] The
Psalter and the Holy Scriptures were restored to their proper
importance, and provision was made for due order and clear-
ness. The changes now made were principally in the direction
of a rearrangement of the breviary lections. Many things
that were spurious or incredible were expunged, thus giving
full recognition to the science of historical criticism which
had been inaugurated by humanism ; even certain feasts,
such as those of St. Anne and St. Joachim, and the Presentation of the Blessed Virgin in the Temple, were sacrificed out
of regard for similar considerations.[4] The passion of the time
for good latinity was taken into account in composing the
historical lections, the compilation of which was the work of
the first humanist of the day, Giulio Poggiani.[5] The efforts of

[1] Every Wednesday there were consultations on the reform
of the Breviary (*Strozzi, October 19, 1566, State Archives,
Vienna). For the purpose of these meetings on the breviary
Savelli proposed Sirleto to the Pope, but Pius V. made difficulties
about this, as Sirleto was bound by his duty of residence in his
own diocese (*Avviso di Roma of October 26, 1566, Urb. 1040,
p. 312, Vatican Library). *Cf.* TACCONE GALLUCCI, 40.

[2] Bull. Rom., VII., 685 *seq.* The bull was published on July 16
(*Avviso of July 17, 1568, sent by Cusano, State Archives, Vienna).
On August 17, 1568 Bonelli wrote to Castagna : " Si è dato fuori
il Breviario riformato." Corresp. dipl., II., 433.

[3] SCHMID, *loc. cit.*, 634. BÄUMER, 438.

[4] SCHMID, *loc. cit.*, 647, 649. BÄUMER, 441, 450.

[5] POGIANI Epist., II., xxiii. For the time being the hymns of
the Breviary remained untouched, though Seripando wished for
their correction (letter of Capilupi, January 13, 1563, in *Arch.*

Christian humanism to give the west the full benefit of the writings of the Greek Fathers were gloriously crowned with success by the fact that the breviary lections were now drawn from their works as well, and that now for the first time the four great Greek Doctors, Althanasius, Basil, Gregory Nazianzen and John Chrysostom were honoured by the Apostolic See with public cultus as teachers of the universal Church, and placed side by side with the four great Doctors of the west.[1]

Just as the Breviary of Pius V. was not a completely new work, but rather a restoration of the ancient usage of the Roman Church, with such changes as were called for by the times,[2] so the same thing may be said of his Missal, which was given the force of law by a bull of July 14th, 1570.[3] The introduction of this reform of Pius V. was made obligatory for all the churches of the west which had not possessed a liturgy of their own for at least 200 years.[4] It was of great benefit to the Church that any changes in these two liturgical books were reserved to the Apostolic See, for this put an end

---

stor. Lomb., 1893, 116).   For some of the hymns included at that time, see DELAPORTE in *Rassegna Gregoriana*, VI. (1907). 495 *seq.* ; *Rivista storica*, 1910, 329.

[1] This was shown for the first time by K. KELLNER in *Zeitschr. für kath. Theol.*, XL. (1916), 1 *seqq.*

[2] " I believe," wrote Sirleto on October 23, 1563, " that the first thing to be done is to remove all novelties, but in such a way that no further novelties are put in their place." MOLITOR, 4.

[3] Bull. Rom., VIII., 839 *seq. Cf.* J. WEALE in *Analecta liturgica*, I., (1888).   A *bull " super breviario et missali novo " of August 14, 1571 in the Archives of Briefs, Rome.   On March 11, 1571, all earlier versions of the office of the Madonna were forbidden, because they contained much that was superfluous and had been filled with superstitions through the covetousness of the printers.   Only the new and corrected edition was allowed and enjoined.   Bull. Rom., VII., 896 *seq.*

[4] Thus the breviary of Quinofies was especially superseded ; this, moreover, had already been prohibited by Paul IV. on August 8, 1558.   BROMATO, II., 493.

to the caprices of incompetent persons, who had introduced so many unsuitable things, even into the Mass itself.[1]

The liturgical reforms of Pius V. made rapid progress in almost every diocese. Even many of those churches which might have retained their ancient breviary, nevertheless, with Pope's permission, drew largely upon the new breviary and missal.[2] The reforms, however, were not carried into effect everywhere without meeting with great difficulties. In Spain they caused great excitement,[3] because there the churches used in the choir magnificently illuminated books of great size, which could only be replaced by new ones at great cost. The Spanish Hieronymites, who only fell short by six years of the 200 required by the bull of Pius V., declared that the change would cost them in Spain alone 200,000 ducats. The monopoly which gave Paulus Manutius the sole right to print the breviary, under pain of excommunication, gave rise to much complaint ; one single press, it was said, could not cope with the enormous demand, while the absence of competition led to both inferior printing and increased prices.[4] Pius V. very soon gave Spain leave to print the new breviary independently of Paulus Manutius.[5]

[1] *Cf.* A. FRANZ, Die Messe im deutschen Mittelalter, Freiburg, 1902.

[2] Jos. SCHMID in *Theol. Quartalschr.*, 1885, 468 *seqq.* ; BÄUMER, 457 *seqq.* Pius V. himself, however, allowed several exceptions to the obligation to use his Breviary, as for example to the Canons Regular of the Lateran (brief of December 18, 1570, Bull. Rom., VII., 875 *seq.*) and to the church of Toledo (brief of December 17, 1570, in MOLITOR, 294 ; *cf.* 15 *seq.*).

[3] " grandissimo moto " ; Castagna to Bonelli, October 1, 1568, Corresp. dipl., II,. 468. Pacheco had obtained leave from the Pope that only the second, corrected, edition of the breviary should be sent to Spain. *Arco, September 4, 1568, State Archives, Vienna.

[4] *Cf.* the memorial of Bandini to Clement VIII., published by MERCATI in *Rassegna Gregoriana*, V. (1906), 18 *seqq.*

[5] Bonelli to Castagna, November 3, 1569, Corresp. dipl., III., 187 ; *cf.* II., 468 ; III., 102, 142. Complaints of Manutius' printing monopoly in general were specially made in Germany. where

The bringing to perfection of the Roman Catechism, as well as of the two liturgical books was to a great extent due to the zeal and energy of Cardinal Borromeo.[1]   To the services which he had already rendered to the Church at the Council of Trent, he thus added the further one of having given effect, and that without any great delay, to a desire which the Fathers of the Council had expressed to the Holy See before they separated.[2]

It was more difficult to comply with another wish of the Council, namely the printing of an edition, which should be as far as possible free from errors, of the Holy Scriptures, and especially of the Latin version which had been in use in the Church from ancient times.   But Pius V. set to work with great zeal on this matter as well.[3]   For this purpose, in 1569, the Pope appointed a commission composed of Cardinals Colonna, Sirleto, Madruzzo, Souchier, Carafa, and Morone ;[4]

the Protestant printers paid no attention to such privileges and excommunications as the Catholic publishers had to do. CANISII Epist., V., 281, 282 ; BRAUNSBERGER, Pius V., 67.

[1] " Prius vero quam discederet [Roma], Catechismum, quam avunculi auctoritate iusserat inchoari, perficiendum, et Breviarium item, Missalemque librum restituendum curavit " (BASCAPÉ, I., 1, c. 9, p. 22).   In a letter to Sirleto of September 4, 1566, Borromeo urges him to hasten as much as possible the work on the breviary (JOS. SCHMID in Theol. Quartalschr., 1884, 654 ; cf. SALA, Docum., II., 244).   From Milan he also took steps to get Marini to compile a book of sermons (homiliarium) for the use of those having the care of souls.   SALA, II., 244, n. 3, 246, 258, n. 117 and 120.

[2] Sess. 25 contin.

[3] HÖPFL, 77–101.   C. VERCELLONE, Variae Lectiones, I., Rome, 1860, xx seqq.

[4] HÖPFL, 78.   Cf. *Avviso di Roma of March 12, 1569, Urb. 1041, p. 40, Vatican Library.   On November 11, 1568, Lombardo wrote to Hosius (Cyprianum 484) : " Manutius incumbit Breviario novo, et missale edetur in lucem in paschate. Marianus Rheatinus, Hieronymi scholiastes incumbit Bibliis, ut editio vulgata emendatior prodeat."   An *Avviso of April 16, 1569, sent to Vienna by Cusano, records the beginning of the labours of the Biblical commission.   State Archives, Vienna.

the commission set to work with the help of twelve consultors. Learned men were found, even outside Rome, who placed their talents at the service of the commission.   Thus the Benedictines of the Badia in Florence, at the command of the Pope, collated twelve Florentine codices, the monks of Montecassino thirty-four, while another member of the Cassinese Congregation, Ambrogio Ferrari, Abbot of S. Benigno at Genoa, furnished critical notes on certain passages of the Bible. The labours of the commission, however, made very slow progress ; thus Arias Montanus at Antwerp, produced more work on the Antwerp polyglot in a month than the Roman commission on the Vulgate in a whole year.[1]   In the opinion of Cardinal Colonna the reason for this was the diversity of views among the members of the commission, some of whom wished to change everything out of hand, while others wished to treat everything as authentic.[2]   However, the work on the Vulgate was never allowed to come to a complete standstill in the time of Pius V.

Steps were also taken in the time of Pius V. on the difficult task of preparing an authentic edition of the codex of Canon Law. The congregation set up in 1566 for the emendation of the decretals of Gratian was composed of Cardinals Colonna, Boncompagni, Sforza, Sirleto and Alciati, to whom Ferreri and Carafa were afterwards added ; these had at first twelve and afterwards fifteen lawyers to advise and assist them.[3]

[1] Colección de docum. inéd., XLI. (1862), 178.   HÖPFL, 101.

[2] Carafa to Salmeron, June 17, 1569, in HÖPFL, 308 seq.

[3] AUGUSTINI THEINER disquisitiones criticae in praecipuas canonum et decretalium collectiones, Rome, 1836, App. prima 3 seqq. A *brief of February 18, 1567 " pro cardinalibus deputatis ad correctionem decreti Gratiani : facultas recipiendi e bibliotheca Vaticana quoscunque libros opportunos facto chirographo bibliothecario de illis restituendis " in the Archives of Briefs, Rome, I., 2, 1867b. A *brief of March 26, 1568 to the Bishop of Plasencia renews the exhortation already sent to him under Pius IV. to send to Rome for the purpose of correcting the decretals of Gratian five unpublished councils of Toledo, and the most correct manuscripts in his possession, for those already printed

In this way, under Pius V., active measures were taken to lay new foundations in every direction, and to call into existence the groundwork for the uniform instruction of the people, for the worthy celebration of divine worhsip, as well as for the development of ecclesiastical jurisprudence and theology. A further ordinance of the zealous reforming pontiff was of importance for ecclesiastical science. When, in 1568, he issued his Breviary, not only were the four Greek Fathers declared Doctors of the Church, but a fifth was added in Thomas Aquinas, who had been raised to this dignity by a special bull of April 11th, 1567.[1] This honour conferred on the great theologian was also directly connected with the Council of Trent. During the long controversies of the XIVth and XVth centuries his teaching had stood all tests, and his victory was complete at the close of the Middle Ages ; at the Council of Trent the difficult task of formulating the doctrine of justification against the reformers had been solved by following St. Thomas,[2] while the sovereignty of the great Dominican theologian had been unquestioned at the Council

---

(*ibid*). At the Council of Trent (THEINER, Acta, II., 654) the desire had been expressed for the compilation of an entirely new ecclesiastical codex, a thing asked for by the Vatican Council, undertaken under Pius X., and completed under Benedict XV. by Cardinal Gasparri.

[1] Bull. Rom., VII., 564 *seq*. The complete edition of the works of St. Thomas which Pius V. caused to be prepared (see *supra* p. 130) was printed in an addition of only 1000 copies, so that the edition was already almost exhausted at the time of its appearance. Francis Borgia, October 28, 1569, in S. Franciscus Borgia, V., 223.

[2] Conc. Trid., sess. 6, c. 6 is taken from S. Thom., S. th. 3, q. 85, a. 5 ; sess. 6, c. 7 from 1, 2, q. 112, a. 4 and 2, 2, q. 24, a. 3. *Cf.* MANDONNET, Dictionn. de théol. cath., IV., 915. Pius V., in the above mentioned bull of April 11, 1567, says that thanks to the teaching of St. Thomas the errors which only made their appearance after his death were refuted " quod et antea saepe et liquido nuper in sacris Tridentini concilii decretis apparuit." Bull. Rom., VII., 564.

in other matters as well.[1] When, therefore, a Papal bull conferred upon him, the representative of scholasticism, an honour hitherto reserved for the mighty intellects of antiquity, not only did the Church herself take the science of the Middle Ages under her protection against the hostility of the Protestants and even of some Catholics, but she also recognized the teaching of Aquinas as the richest fruit of an earlier scientific evolution, and as an unperishable treasure, but at the same time she proclaimed that she recognized her own doctrines in those of the great schoolman.[2] At the same time

[1] In a speech made at the Council, delivered on March 7, 1563, the feast of St. Thomas, the speaker said that since the death of Thomas no council had been held without his help, and that this held good of the Council of Trent : " Vestra comitia perpendite. Ex plurimo eoque honorabili doctorum coetu quotusquisque consultor accedit, qui d. Thoma auctoritate veluti splendente gemma, suam sententiam non exornet ? At in consultissimo patrum recessu, doctor pic sententiam rogatus, frequentissime censet, ad quem ut ad Lydium lapidem, si quid ambiguitatis aut controversiæ fuerit exortum, communibus votis referendum existimetis, et qui eum sui placiti patronum obtinuerit, incertam indiciorum aleam non sit habiturus, quin secundum eum sententia ferenda sit." (Ioannis Gallio Burgensis Oratio in laudem ss. doctoris Thomae Aquin. in LE PLAT, I., 625). In a brief of November 3, 1593, to the Jesuits, Clement VIII. says that the Council of Trent approved and adopted the works of St. Thomas (ASTRAIN, III., 580). Cf. MANDONNET, loc. cit. ; FRANC. SYLVII Opera, V., Antwerp, 1698, 386.

[2] In the bull of July 29, 1570, Pius V. says : " [D. Thomae] doctrinam theologicam ab ecclesia receptam aliis magis tutam et securam existere." (Bull. Rom., VII., 481). In consequence of the ordinance of the Council (sess. 5, de ref. c. 1) that in every cathedral there should be a prebend for a teacher of theology, this bull assigns in perpetuity to the Master of the Sacred Palace a prebend at St. Peter's together with the obligation of expounding the doctrine of St. Thomas. Already in a consistory of March 6, 1566, Pius V. had manifested his devotion to St. Thomas by inviting the Cardinals to attend the High Mass on the following day at the Minerva, the feast of the saint. Consistorial Archives, in GULIK-EUBEL, 47.

the line for further theological development was clearly traced
out.   Just as the raising of the four principal Greek Fathers
to the dignity of Doctors of the Church signified ecclesiastical
approval of the efforts which had been made to spread the
knowledge of the Greek Fathers in the Latin Church, and to
place them side by side and on equal terms with those of the
west, so the conferring of the same honour on St. Thomas was
an ecclesiastical approval and a solemn confirmation of those
schools of theology which, ever since the beginning of the
century had made the writings of Aquinas the basis of all
theological teaching, and which, by following him, had paved
the way for a further development of ecclesiastical science.[1]

All scientific and literary activity found, generally speaking,
an intelligent patron in Pius V., a man himself of keen intellect.
Wherever in the world any useful scientific work was produced
by Catholics, the Pope was quick to help it with his encouragement and assistance.   He found time to praise the canon,
Martin Cromer, in far off Cracow,[2] and the Imperial councillor,
Georg Eder,[3] as well as the learned Augustinian, Panvinio,
and Girolamo Muzio, who were close at hand.   At the same
time the light of his favour did not shine only on the champions
of approved antiquity, or on behalf of those things which,
like dogma and canon law, interested him personally.   During
the XVIth century there was a great activity in the theological
sciences ; new branches of learning were springing up, and
Pius V. gladly extended his protection to the tender plants.
The name of his brother in religion, Sisto da Siena, the founder

---

[1] Modern scholasticism is distinguished from the old by the fact
of its adherence to Thomas Aquinas, and by its closer union of
positive with speculative theology (CHR. PESCH, Praelect. dogm.,
I[5], Freiburg in Breisg., 1915, 26).   These two things found expression in the raising of Thomas Aquinas and the four Greek Fathers
to the position of Doctors of the Church.

[2] *Brief of February 18, 1569, Brevia, Arm. 44, t. 40, p. 26,
Papal Secret Archives.   For what follows cf. supra p. 129 seqq.

[3] Brief of January 2, 1569, ibid. t. 13, p. 286, which is printed
in the beginning of the later editions of Eder's book.   N. PAULUS
in Hist.-polit. Blätter, CXV. (1895), 25.

of biblical criticism, is indissolubly linked with his own. He encouraged the efforts of the Cologne Carthusian, Surius, to lay the sound foundations of hagiography. Rudely awakened from its sleep by the Centuriators of Magdeburg, historical criticism began to attempt its first flights in reply, at the hands of Catholic writers, and here too it was Pius V. who, in answer to the request of Hosius, sought to organize this form of defence against Protestant attacks.[1]

Pius V. also had a share in another way in laying the solid foundations of the structure upon which, under the influence of the Council of Trent, the life of the Church was to be built anew. To the already existing cardinalitial congregations of the Inquisition and the Council, he added a third in the Congregation of the Index of prohibited books. The first and eighth Tridentine prescriptions on the Index had called for the correction of certain classes of books, but so far no inquisitor or bishop had taken any steps to comply with this demand. On November 9th, 1570, he gave instructions to Manriquez, the Master of the Sacred Palace, at the same time giving him the fullest powers to carry out his task.[2] This act in itself implied the power to form a special congregation of the Index, but the actual congregation of Cardinals was only appointed in the March of the following year, and held its first meeting on March 27th, 1571.[3] Yet another congregation,

---

[1] *Cf. supra* p. 129. EICHHORN, Hosius, II., 463. On December 16, 1567, Philip II. asked the Pope for permission to print the work of the Franciscan, Michele de Medina, against the Centuriators. Corresp. dipl., II., 273 *seq.*

[2] The motu proprio is printed in HILGERS, 510-513.

[3] SANTORI, Diario XXIII., 322 (March 5, 1571). Report of Antonio Posio, the first secretary of the Congregation of the Index, in HILGERS, 513. *Avviso di Roma of September 9, 1570, Urb. 1041, p. 338b, Vatican Library : the censorship of theological and philosophical books is no longer to be in the hands of the Cardinals, but of the Master of the Sacred Palace. *Avviso of October 13, 1571, Urb. 1042, p. 131b, *ibid. ;* the Pope has appointed four Cardinals to draw up a new Index ; Martial, Propertius, etc. " si leveranno via." On July 17, 1568 (State Archives,

that of the bishops, owed its origin to Pius V., who, in a brief
of February 13th, 1572,[1] charged Cardinals Ludovico Madruzzo,
Santori, Burali and Aldobrandini to examine the petitions
of the bishops, as well as any accusations brought against
them, and to submit their decisions to the Pope for approval.
This new congregation, however, had already held its first
meeting in the autumn of the previous year.[2]

The congregation which had been formed for the interpretation of the decrees of the Council was kept specially
busy with questions in the time of Pius V.[3]   These dealt for
the most part with practical questions concerning benefices,
the obligation of making contributions to the seminaries, the
education of girls in the convents of women despite the law
of enclosure and the like.   The French Calvinists gave
occasion for a decision of greater dogmatic importance.
According to Calvin baptism had not the power of taking away
original sin, and the French preachers, in consequence, made
it clear that in baptizing they had no intention of doing what
the Roman Church understood by baptism.   The Council
had declared that the baptism of heretics was only valid
if they intended to do what was intended by the Church of
Christ,[4] and the French Catholics therefore felt serious doubts

Vienna).   *Arco wrote that in accordance with the request of the
Duke of Florence Boccaccio was being reprinted at Padua after
the Roman Inquisition had purged it of its more scandalous
contents.   *Cf.* DEJOB, De l'influence du Concile de Trente, 167,
and Vol. XVI. of this work, p. 12.

[1] Published by J. HILGERS in *Pastor bonus*, XV. (1902-3), 238.
That the " congregatio episcoporum " still existed in the time of
Gregory XIII., see in *Anal. iuris Pontif.*, I., Rome 1855, 2257.

[2] " *Alli 22 di settembre [1571], di sabato, nelle quattro tempora,
intervenni alla prima congregazione della Consulta de' vescovi,
instituta da Sua Santità acciò i vescovi et anco i sudditi sapessero
a chi ricorrere, per non infestare sempre l' orecchi di Sua Beatitudine."   SANTORI, Autobiografia XII., 352.

[3] The decrees of the congregation, edited by Poggiani, have been
printed ;   between February 2, 1566 and September 25, 1568,
there were 257.   POGIANI Epist., I., 372-496.

[4] Sess. 7, de bapt. can. 4.

as to the validity of Calvinist baptisms.[1] The Congregation of the Council decided in favour of their validity, on the ground that, in spite of their errors as to the effects of baptism and the true Church of Christ, the preachers steadily maintained their intention of administering true Christian baptism, and of doing what the Christian Church had always done in conferring it.[2] This decision was confirmed by Pius V.[3]

In the same way other decisions of the Pope which touched more or less directly on questions of dogma were based for the most part on the Tridentine decrees. Thus, in conformity with what had been done at the Council, he forbade too heated discussions of the Immaculate Conception of the Mother of God.[4] With regard to the question of the chalice for the laity, which the Council had referred to the decision of the Apostolic See, he showed himself openly opposed to the attitude adopted by his predecessor, and when the Bishop of Passau addressed a question to him on the matter, he told him in the clearest terms that he was, under no circumstances, to allow the chalice in his diocese.[5] Some of his decrees on

---

[1] *Cf.* the letters of the Jesuit, Joan. Maldonatus of June 28, 1567, and October 5, 1568, to Cardinal Hosius, in CYPRIANUS, 442 *seq.*, 469 *seqq.*; J. M. PRAT, Maldonat et l' université de Paris au XVIe siècle, Paris, 1856, 202 *seq.*; MALDONATI Disputationum et controversiarum, tom. I., Lyons, 1614, 62 *seqq.*

[2] P. FAGNANUS in *I Decretalium*, I., Cologne 1704, 133. BENEDICT XIV, De synodo dioec. 1. 7, c. 6, n. 9 (Opera, XI., Bassani, 1767, 128). BELLARMINE, De sacram. in genere, I., 1, c. 27 (Opera, III., Venice, 1721, 50).

[3] Sanctissimus auditis votis dixit, non esse rebaptizandos. Decree of the Inquisition of March 5, 1606 in *Annal. eccles.*, II., 140, MIRBT, Quellen³, (1911) 311 *seq.*

[4] Decrees of August 7 and November 30, 1570, Bull. Rom., VII., 845 *seq.*, 872 *seq.* *Avviso of September 23, 1570, Urb. 1041, p. 347b, Vatican Library.

[5] Brief of May 26, 1568, in GOUBAU, 83 *seq.* It states, in reply to the bishop's observations : " in eadem sententia mansimus, in qua etiam tum, cum a praedecessore nostro ea licentia efflagitata atque expressa fuit, fueramus." *Cf.* WIEDEMANN, Reformation, I., 315 *seqq.* Already on February 2, 1566, Polanco had written

matters dealing with the rate of exchange[1] and the payment of interest,[2] have no relation to the decrees of the Council, and still less was this the case with his renewal of the constitution of Paul IV., directed against those who denied the doctrine of the Most Holy Trinity and the principal truths of Christology.[3]

The Council itself had recognized the right of the Holy See to interpret, or where there was any doubt to define more clearly, the decrees of the assembly, and Pius exercised this right with regard to certain matrimonial impediments which had been formulated at Trent, the meaning and scope of which he now determined more exactly in special decrees.[4]

Several other questions which had been mooted at Trent, but which for various reasons had not been settled, were subsequently approved and sanctioned by the Apostolic See. Several Spanish bishops, for example, had proposed to the Council the prohibition of bull-fights,[5] but in the time of Pius IV. it had been considered very doubtful in Rome

to Hosius : " Non est, quod de coniugio sacerdotum, de calice vel aliis huiusmodi multum timeamus " (in CYPRIANUS, 405 ; cf. BRAUNSBERGER, Pius V., 41). Phillip II., however, in a letter to Cardinal Ricci of June 11, 1568 thought it opportune to take steps even with Pius V. to prevent the concession of the marriage of priests in Germany : *" Dovendo D. Pietro di Avila trattare con S. S^(tà) da mia parte sopra vari affari e pregarla in primo logo di non accordare il matrimonio ai sacerdoti di Germania secondo l' istanza fattane per esser un affare della più grande importanza, gli ho commandato ancora di participarvi tutto.   Ricci Archives, Rome.

[1] Bull of January 28, 1571, Bull. Rom., VII., 884 seq.

[2] Decrees of January 19, 1569, and June 10, 1570, ibid. 736, 738 ; cf. LADERCHI, 1570, n. 164.

[3] Bull of October 1, 1568, Bull. Rom., VII., 722 seq.

[4] The impediments of spiritual relationship and affinity (sess. 24, de matr. c. 2 and 4) in a brief of August 20 1566, and that of public honesty (ibid. c. 3) in a brief of July 1, 1568.   Bull. Rom., VII., 476, 678.

[5] ŠUSTA, II., 117, n. 53 seq.

whether such a decree would meet with any success.[1]   Pius V.
showed greater courage.   After, as had already been done
by Thomas of Villanova,[2] the Council of Toledo in 1566[3] had
expressed itself against this popular sport, which was so dear
to the Spaniards, Pius V., through his nuncio in Madrid,
begged the king to abolish a custom which the Pope had
already done away with in the Papal States.[4]   Philip II.
resisted this proposal on the score of the great irritation and
discontent which it would cause in Spain.[5]   On the other hand
Pius V. was of opinion that if the Council had forbidden duels,
it was all the more necessary to combat the abuse of bull-
fights,[6] and, acting on the advice of Francis Borgia, on November 1st, 1567, he issued a bull which strictly prohibited these
spectacles " which were more suited to devils than to men."[7]
Although the Papal nuncio was at pains to see that the Papal
prohibition was made known far and wide by the Lenten
preachers, the Spanish bishops had not the courage formally
to publish the bull.[8]   The king begged that the old custom
might be allowed to continue, at least under certain conditions ;[9] it was maintained that as the bull-fighters were

[1] " Placerent [this and another proposal] nisi essent difficilis
observationis." so it was said in Rome.   *Ibid.*

[2] Opera, Venice, 1740, 627.   *Cf. Stimmen aus Maria-Laach*,
LXV., 246.

[3] Conc. Tolet. of 1566, n. 26, in HARDOUIN, X., 1169.

[4] Bonelli to Castagna, January 31, 1567, Corresp. dipl., II., 31.

[5] " grandissimo disturbio et discontento di tutti li popoli."
Castagna to Bonelli, June 17, 1566, *ibid.*, 137.

[6] Bonelli to Castagna, July 11, 1567, *ibid.*, 155.

[7] Bull. Rom., VII., 630.   That this bull was obtained through
the influence of Francis Borgia, see Borgia to Polanco, November
19, 1567 (S. Franciscus Borgia, IV., 551).   Borgia had been led
to take this step by Juan Quirós de Sosa (his letter to Borgia of
August 17, 1567, *ibid.*, 517 *seqq.*) and Pietro Camaiani, Bishop of
Ascoli (Borgia to the latter, November 22, 1567, *ibid.*, 552 ; *cf.*
155).   For the attitude of the Jesuits towards bull-fights, *cf.*
NADAL, Epist., IV., 390. *seq.*

[8] Castagna to Bonelli, May 14, 1568, Corresp. dipl., II., 366.

[9] Castagna to Bonelli, June 16, 1568, *ibid.*, 323.

mounted on horses there was no danger.[1]   In the end all that
Pius V. obtained was that the bull-fights were forbidden for a
time, on the pretext of the mourning in which the nation was
plunged on account of the imprisonment of Don Carlos ;[2]
otherwise the bull had no effect in Spain, and Gregory XIII.
found himself obliged to remove the penalty of excommunication inflicted by his predecessor.[3]

A warning of the Council may perhaps have lent strength
to the intention of Pius V. to prohibit the use of figured music
in divine worship, and to allow nothing but the Gregorian
chant.[4]   A brief directed against a kind of Church music
which provoked sensuality rather than piety was issued by
him a few years later, on the authority of what had been said
at the Council, to the Bishop of Lucca, in whose city the
musical performances during Holy Week occasioned all
manner of scandals among the young people of both sexes,
who flocked to them in great numbers.[5]   A prohibition of
burials in the churches was also the outcome of a proposal

[1] *Ibid.* 366.

[2] *Ibid.* 323.

[3] THEINER, Annales, II., 122, 590.

[4] *Avviso of July 5, 1567, Urb. 1040, p. 413, Vatican Library.
Perhaps the legend of the threat to figured music in Rome, and how
it was saved by Palestrina, sprang from this statement and a
confusion of Pius V. with his predecessor.   It was in this same
year 1567 that Palestrina thought of leaving Rome and entering
the service of the Emperor :   *" Il cantore Giov. di Palestrina si
contenta di venir a servire la M^{tà} V^{ra} per quattrocento scudi
d' oro l' anno ; io ho fatto quanto ho potuto per ridurlo ancora a
meno, ma non ho potuto ottener più.   Adesso aspetterò che la
M^{tà} V^{ra} mi commandi quello ho a fare circa quest' huomo, il quale
mi vien lodato da molti " (Arco, November 8, 1567, State Archives,
Vienna).   *" Con Giov. di Palestrina non passerò più innanzi."
(Arco, January 3, 1568, *ibid.*).

[5] Brief of April 4, 1571, in LADERCHI, 1571, n. 165.   In this,
as the Council had done, Pius V. censured the " lascivia " of these
performances.   Two other briefs, of April 2, 1570, on ecclesiastical
music in Mexico, *ibid.* 1570, n. 417.

which had been put forward at Trent,[1] and for the future
only the bodies of the saints were to find a resting place in the
churches.[2]

If Pius V. was careful to observe the instructions of the
Council in such secondary matters, much more did he prove
himself its champion and defender the moment the more
essential matters on which the assembly had built up its
scheme of reform were called in question.

In 1566 the Bishop of Córdova wrote to Pius V.[3] that after
the Council of Trent one hope alone remained to the adversaries of a radical reform of the Church, namely that more
attention would be paid to its practical application than to
its wishes, and that Rome would be quick to dispense its
stricter ordinances.   But even this last hope met with bitter
disappointment under a Pope of whom it had been foretold
that he would be quite inexorable in all that concerned the
Council,[4] and who, at the beginning of the second year of
his reign could write that he thought his zeal for the carrying
out of the Council was known to all the world, and that
the office of the man who was entrusted with the care of the
whole Church called for as much zeal as responsibility, since
the decrees of a Council were useless unless they were carried
into effect by the Pope and the bishops.[5]

Pius V. had certainly taken care that nobody should be
left in the dark as to his own zeal for the Council.   He continued with all his energies that ordinance of his predecessor

[1] Theiner, ANNALES, II., 590.   *Cf. supra* p. 86, n. 3, and Vol.
XVI. of this work, p. 441 n.

[2] Bull of April 1, 1566, §5, Bull. Rom., VII., 436.   *Bandi, V.,
7, p. 2-3, Papal Secret Archives.   PECCI, Storia di Siena, II., 70.

[3] In THEINER, Bildungsanstalten, 112.

[4] *" In le cose di concilio, religione a iustitia sarà inesorabile "
(Serristori, February 15, 1566, State Archives, Florence).   On
January 12, 1566 *Camiani wrote to the Duke of Modena (State
Archives, Modena) that the Pope intended that the Council should
be carried out in every respect.

[5] To the Archbishop of Cambrai, January 26, 1567, in GOUBAU,
23.

which enacted that the bishops-elect and the university
professors in particular must swear to the Tridentine profession of faith.[1] He perseveringly did all in his power to
have the decrees of Trent accepted and recognized everywhere.[2] He sent the decrees of the Council together with the
announcement of his accession to the throne to the ends of
the earth, as for example to the archbishops and bishops of
Mexico, Guatemala, Honduras and Venezuela, as well as to
Goa.[3] He at once caused an exhortation to observe them
to be sent to Spain,[4] as well as to Hungary and Poland,[5]
at the same time repeatedly expressing his conviction that

---

[1] *To the rector of the university of Macerata, January 5, 1569 ;
the ordinance of Pius IV. was not observed there, and the Pope
sends copies of the profession of faith (Brevia, Arm. 44, t. 13,
p. 287b, Papal Secret Archives).   Similar *briefs to Bologna and
Perugia of the same date (*ibid.* p. 228b, 289b) ; to the Archbishop
of Cologne, Frederick von Wied, of June 13, 1566, in LADERCHI,
1566, n. 269 ; to the university of Cologne in 1571, in HANSEN,
Rheinische Akten, 596 *seq. ; cf.* 589, n. 1, 638, n. 1 ; to the Bishop
of Eichstätt for the university of Ingolstadt on January 29, 1568,
in MEDERER, IV., 319 *seqq.*, 322. *Cf.* BRAUNSBERGER, Pius V.,
12-19 ; SACCHINI, P. III., 1. 4 n., 130.   Also an Arabic version
of the Tridentine profession of faith was printed in Arabic char-
acters *Romae iussu SS. D. N. Pii V. in colleg. soc. Iesu anno* 1566 ;
see ZENKER, Bibliotheca orientalis, I., 191.

[2] *Cf. supra*, p. 192 *seqq.*

[3] *Cf.* in LADERCHI, 1566, n. 500 the letter to the Archbishop of
S. Domingo of February 3, 1566 ; *ibid.* n. 501 the list (incomplete)
of the American bishops to whom similar letters were sent.   The
two letters to the Archbishops of Goa and Mexico, of October 7,
1567, in GOUBAU, 41 *seq.*, 45 *seq.*

[4] GOUBAU, 2 *seqq.*   Collección de docum. inéd., IX., 395.

[5] To the Archbishop of Gran, February 11, 1566, in GOUBAU, 6 ;
to the Archbishop of Gnesen and the Bishop of Cracow, January 17,
1569, *ibid.* 125 *seq.*, 129 *seq. ;* to the diocesan synod of Freising,
February 28, 1567, *ibid.* 31 ; to the Archbishop of Prague,
July 23, 1568, *ibid.* 93 ; to the Bishop of Ajaccio, May 4,
1569, *ibid.* 177 ; to the legate of Avignon, June 25, 1569, *ibid.*
185.

the observance of the Tridentine decrees was the one and only cure for the wounds of the Church.[1]

If he exacted obedience from the bishops for all the precepts of the Council, there was one in particular which he insisted upon in their regard, which was fully in accordance with the wishes of the assembly, namely the establishment of seminaries for the education of the future clergy.[2] He frequently wrote that among all the ordinances of the Council none was so useful or so much in keeping with the needs of the times as the decree about seminaries.[3] It is true that in more than one diocese there was a long delay before the establishment of a seminary was brought about ; Pius V. therefore found himself obliged to send pressing exhortations to many of the bishops,[4] and to others, especially the ordinaries

[1] " Ad has igitur, quibus afflicta laborat ecclesia, tot tantasque plagas utcunque sanandas et ad iram Dei aliquo modo avertendam atque placandam unicum nobis remedium superest, diligens videlicet ss. oecumenici concilii Tridentini decretorum custodia." (Christophoro episcopo Palentino, on February 1, 1566, in GOUBAU 3). " Nullum enim occurrit nobis, mentem nostram huc et illuc versantibus, aliud remedium ad ecclesiam ipsam in commodiorem et tranquilliorem statum redigendam, quam ut s. generale concilium Tridentinum . . . utique servetur " (to the Archbishop of Gran, February 11, 1566, *ibid.* 6).

[2] " Districte praecipimus ut ipsum concilium . . . observes ac praeter cetera illud de seminario in unaquaque ecclesia instituendo saluberrimum laudatissimumque decretum primo quoque tempore exequaris," (to the Bishop of Würzburg, January 23, 1566, in LADERCHI, 1566 n. 223). " Obtestamur, ut officii vestri memores, cum alia, quae . . . in ipso concilio statuta fuerunt, debita obedientia observare curetis, tum illud de clericorum seminario in unaquaque ecclesia instituendo," (to the Archbishop of Gran, February 11, 1566, in GOUBAU 7).

[3] " Quo nihil utilius, nihil his temporibus ecclesiis opportunius neque accommodatius statui potuit " (GOUBAU 7). " Res ipsa declarat, nihil a concilio Tridentino providentius et utilius statutum fuisse," (to the Archbishop of Prague, July 23, 1568, *ibid.* 95).

[4] *Cf.* the briefs to Prague and Gran already cited. *Exhortation on October 26, 1570, to the Grand Master of the Teutonic Order

and chapters of Portugal,[1] stern rebukes. On the whole,
however, the Council met with willing obedience. As the
Pope himself recognized, in many places similar institutions
had already been set up, while new ones were coming into
existence every day.[2] The Congregation of the Council had
to answer many questions,[3] especially from Italy, as to the

to found a seminary, as he had many parishes under his care, in
Brevia, Arm. 44, t. 15, p. 238, Papal Secret Archives. *Praise
for the Bishop of Breslau for having erected a seminary ; ibid.
t. 13, p. 187.

[1] Briefs to the Bishops of Guarda, Evora, Portalegre and Viseu
of July 26 and 27, 1569, in LADERCHI, 1569. n. 318, 321 ; to their
respective chapters, ibid. n. 322-325 ; two of these letters are also
in GOUBAU, 193 seq., 200 seq. ; letters to the Bishops of Portalegre,
Porto and Leiria, of July 27, August 9, and September 1, 1569,
Corpo dipl. Portug., X., 331, 335, 339.

[2] " Et in aliis locis quam plurimis huiusmodi seminaria instituta fuerunt quotidie instituuntur," (to the Archbishop of
Prague in GOUBAU, 95.)

[3] e.g. in 1566 : at Gravina (POGIANI Epist., I., 382), at Reggio
(ibid. 394), at Turin (403) ; in 1567 : at Casale (404), Imola
(405, 445), Nocera (411, 441), Marsico (414), Como (417, 428, 435),
Naples (419, 450 seq.), Majorca (433), Benevento (430), Braga
(439), Milan (439), Trani (440), Nicastro (441), Brescia (448, 462).
Venice (453) ; in 1568 (up to September 25) : at Milan (454, 490),
Cremona (445), Ravenna, " cardinali Urbinatensi " (460), Padua
(461), Catanzaro (463, 465), Perugia (460), Nicastro (466), Naples
(463, 480 seq., 488), Portugal, " cardinali Infanti " (467, seqq.,
470, 489, 491 seq.), Braga (471), Coimbra (471), Rimini (472 477),
Salerno (475), Gerace (476), Savona (484), S. Angelo de' Lombardi
(495). The list in THEINER, Bildungsansalten 118 seq., is incomplete, and Bergamo, Messina (and Polizio) are wanting. *Exhortation to Antonio, Bishop of Como, to found a seminary,
April 24, 1567, in the Archives of Briefs, Rome. Ibid. *bulls of
August 6 and December 8, 1567, for the seminaries of Eichstätt
and Naples *Praise to the Bishop of Saint-Omer for the erection
of a seminary, ibid. According to SIEBENGARTNER (p. 87) the
earliest seminaries were set up at Rieti and Eichstätt in 1564, at
Milan in 1565, at Benevento, Verona and Larino in Sicily in 1564,
at Brixen (? certainly Brescia) in 1568 ; in the meantime France

duty of contributing to the seminaries. At first Germany rather lagged behind in the establishment of these institutes ;[1]

lagged behind ; in Spain the earliest seminaries are those of Mondoñedo and Tarragona (1570). In the Low Countries the proposal of the council of Malines in 1570 to set up a seminary met with opposition because the three existing " convitti " were in accordance with the prescriptions of the Council. A. DEGERT (Histoire des séminaires français jusqu'à la révolution, Paris, 1912) mentions as the earliest seminaries those of Rieti 1564, Rome 1565, Milan 1566, Imola and Ravenna 1567, Rimini and Bologna 1568. In Italy the seminary of Orvieto dates from 1566 (PARDI, Guida di Orvieto, 100), Bonomi erected that of Spoleto in 1567 (COLOMBO, Vita di Bonomi, Turin, 1879, 15), Cardinal Giulio della Rovere that of Ravenna in 1567 (*Manuscript in the Seminary Archives there), and Cardinal G. Paleotto that of Bologna (GUIDICINI, Miscellanea Bologn., 52 ; MASINI, III., 219 ; Omaggio del seminario di Bologna all'arciv. Giac. della Chiesa, Bologna, 1908), Bishop Valerio that of Verona (cf. *Costituzioni fatte per il Ag. Valiero et il capitolo sopra la schola degli accoliti 1571, Capitular Library, Verona). In 1571 a seminary was also established at Padua ; see (L. TODESCO and SEB. SERENA) Il seminario di Padova, Padua, 1911. FRANC. LANZONI (La fondazione del seminario di Faenza e S. Carlo Borromeo, Faenza, 1896, 41) places the date of the foundation of all the seminaries in the Romagna as follows : Imola, January 1, 1567, Ravenna, May 25, 1567 (or 1568), Rimini, May 18, 1568, Bologna, June 27, 1568, Faenza, July 15, 1576, Ferrara, 1584, Sarsina 1646, Folri, May 29, 1659, Bertinoro (apparently) 1708, Cervia 1827 (there is no definite information as to a small earlier seminary), Cesena 1570, Comacchio 1779 (these last two dates from information courteously supplied by Lanzoni). A brief of Pius V. of August 23, 1566, placed Swiss youths in the seminaries of Milan, Cremona, Pavia, Parma and Modena ; see WIRZ, Materialen zur Schweizergesch., n. 405, p. 386 seq. For the foundation of the seminaries cf. MICHAELIS THOMASII, Disputationes ecclesiasticae, Rome, 1565, 151 seqq.; De variis collegiis ad utilitatem publicam constituendis ; p. 192 seqq.; De seminario puellorum Deo dicandorum.

[1] " For the most part the German bishops sent their clerics to the rapidly developing Jesuit schools, which were generally united to establishments for poor students. Such were soon set up at Graz, Olmütz, Vienna, Innsbruck, Linz, Komotau, Dillingen,

the Bishops of Augsburg, Eichstadt, and a few more were willing to set them up, but they were rather hampered than helped by their cathedral chapters.[1]

A pontifical brief to the Bishop of Breslau added to praise for the foundation of a seminary, congratulations on the synod held there for the purpose of promulgating the Tridentine decrees.[2] A seminary and a synod were also the things which above all recommended to the Archbishop of Prague, in a letter which was sent to him by the Pope.[3] What real importance the Pope attached to the holding of synods everywhere, in accordance with the decrees of Trent, is shown by a letter to the Archbishop of Salerno, who sought to excuse himself in Rome for having twice postponed his promised provincial synod. The Pope rebuked him for his delay, saying that the excuses which he had put forward were worthless, that the archbishop must pay no attention to the discontent of some of the bishops and lay judges, but go forward quietly with the work and that he, the Pope, now that the deliberations of the Council had at last, after such great labours and difficulties, and so many delays, been brought to a happy issue, was fully resolved to carry them into effect.[4]

Ingolstadt, Munich, Trêves, Mayence. The bishops also sought to secure free places in the Papal seminaries. The synods of Augsburg 1566, Constance, 1567, Salzburg, 1569 . . . and others, had, however, decided upon the establishment of seminaries. Similar decisions were actually carried out, though on a very modest scale, at Eichstätt in 1564, at Würzburg in 1570, and at Breslau in 1571." (SIEBENGARTNER, *loc. cit.*). The Bishop of Würzburg on August 7, 1566, expressed to the Congregation of the Council his readiness to found a seminary. *Cf.* the reply of the Congregation of March 25, 1567, in POGIANI Epist., I., 412.

[1] To Francis Borgia, April 5, 1568, CANISII Epist., VI., 181.

[2] *Brief of May 14, 1568, Brevia, Arm. 44, t. 13, p. 186, Papal Secret Archives.

[3] Brief of June 23, 1568, *loc. cit.* p. 216, printed in GOUBAU 93, with the date July 23.

[4] Brief of May 24, 1566, in LADERCHI, 1566, n. 182, where is also the letter of the archbishop. The provincial synod was held at Salerno in 1566, diocesan synods in 1565 and 1567. LADERCHI 1566, n. 183. *Cf. ibid.* 341 the exhortations to the Archbishop of Gnesen.

It would appear, however, that for the most part no special exhortations from the Pope were necessary in this matter, and that during his pontificate many provincial and diocesan synods were held without any difficulties being made.[1] The

[1] CALENZIO (Documenti, 577 *seqq.*) gives the following list of synods from 1564 (provincial synods in italics) :

1564 : *Rheims,* Haarlem, Milan, Orvieto, Parma, Perugia, Sebenico.

1565 : *Braga, Cambrai, Compostella, Evora, Granada, Mexico, Milan, Prague, Saragossa, Toledo, Valencia, Utrecht,* Modena, Naples, Ermland.

1566 : Lucca, Pavia, Tarragona, Toledo, Valencia, Vicenza, Cambrai.

1567 : *Benevento, Manfredonia, Otranto,* Augsburg, Cambrai, Constance, Naples, Narni and Terni.

1568 : *Ravenna,* Luni, Sarzana, Milan, Olmütz, Utrecht, Orvieto.

1569 : *Capua, Milan, Salzburg, Urbino,* Faenza.

1570 : *Malines,* Arras, Leeuwarden, Namur, Osnabrück, Piacenza, Ravenna, Roermond, Salamanca, Trêves.

1571 : *Benevento, Besancon,* Bruges, Bois-le-duc, Foligno, Ghent, Haarlem, Lucca, Osnabrück, Siguenza.

1572 : Granada, Malaga, Milan, Seville, Vercelli.

The list only includes councils of which Calenzio knew of the printed acta, either separately or in collections ; it is nevertheless incomplete. Thus synods were held at Tarragona in 1564, 1565, 1566, 1567, 1569 (GAMS, Series episc.). According to information kindly supplied by Canon Lanzoni ten diocesan synods were held at Faenza between 1569 and 1580, of which those of February, 1565, October 1569, and July 1571, come during the pontificate of Pius V. The Capitular Library, Verona, possesses the *acta of the Paduan synod of August 17, 1566, and the *decrees of the synod of Mantua of 1567 (Cod. DCCXC., Io. Iac. Dionisii Collactanea, p. 262 *seq.*, 267 *seq.*). In the archiepiscopal archives at Ravenna are *notices of the diocesan synods held there in 1564, 1567 and 1571. A synod of Lucca in 1570 in Sinodi Lucchesi (Memorie e documenti per . . . Lucca, VII.), Lucca, 1834, 167 ; one of Bologna, 1567, in LE BRET, IX., 560, at Terni in 1567 in POGIANI Epist., II., xxxi. GAMS (*loc. çit.*) records the Portuguese synods of Braga 1566, Guarda 1565 and 1570, the two provincial

most important was the provincial synod held at Milan in
1569 by Cardinal Borromeo, which, like that held in 1565,
in the reign of Pius IV., was confirmed by a brief from the
Pope.[1]

Another matter upon which Pius V. was insistent with the
bishops was one which had so far been urged both by the
Council and by recent Popes without much effect, namely
the obligation, both of residing in person amid their flocks,
and of exacting the same residence from priests in charge of
souls.   A great step was taken towards this important reform
when Pius V., by a series of ordinances, made the Eternal
City, the favourite place of refuge, extremely uncomfortable

councils of Lisbon in 1566 and Goa in 1567, the synod of Lima in
1567, that of Syracuse in 1567, Lyons in 1568, and Avignon in
1569.   LADERCHI records synods in Belgium : 1566, n. 440, 469 ;
1570, n. 284 seq. ; those in Portugal and Spain ; 1566, 488 seqq.,
those of Goa ; 1567, n. 249 ; 1570, n. 429 ; the synod at Urbino :
1569, n. 346 ; those of Salzburg, Lucca, Naples : 1571, n. 66, 165,
478.   The synod of Ravenna, ibid. 1568, n. 47 (the acta printed
in app. to t. XXXVI. of MANSI, Paris, 1882, 289), the confirmation
of the council of Milan, 1566, n. 51, of that of Valencia, 1567, n.
268.   For the synod of Salerno, see supra, p. 214, n. 1, for
that of Manfredonia 1567 cf. TÖRNE, Pt. Gallio 42 seq.   For the
synod of Constance 1567 cf. LÜTOLF, in Kathol. Schweizerblättern,
X. (1894), 453 seqq. ; SAMBETH in Freiburger Diözesanarchiv,
XXI. (1890), 50 seqq.   *" Dis veneris 28 maii [1568] in sero rever-
sus fuit ad Urbem rev. cardinalis Moronus, qui visitavit ecclesiam
suam Mutinensem et fuerat in concilio synodali sive provinciali
facto per rev. dominum et protectorem meum cardinalem Urbin-
atensem in civitate Ravennatensi."   (Frimanus, Diarium. p. 240b,
Papal Secret Archives).   An *Avviso di Roma of December 20,
1567, Urb. 1040, p. 164b, announces that after Lent the Cardinals
(Morone, Farnese, Sforza) would set out for their churches in
order to hold provincial synods there, Vatican Library.

[1] Briefs of June 6, 1566 and May 12, 1570, Bull. Rom., VII.,
458, 819.   The latter brief corrects some decrees of the synod,
as was also done by the brief of November 4, 1567, in the case of
the synod of Valencia (ibid.) 631).   Cf. the decrees on the synods
of Rheims of October 27, 1566, and of Valencia of November 11,
1567, in POGIANI Epist., I., 393, 442.

for the prelates and priests who were bound to residence.[1]
A further edict took away from those who were still neglectful
of their duty the last hiding places and refuges which the
Council had been obliged to leave to them. In those cases
where there was no recognized episcopal authority, the bishops
were given power to act as the representatives of the Apostolic
See, and there was to be no appeal from their sentence in the
matter of residence, while all the existing Papal dispensations
were revoked.[2] These general ordinances were followed
by particular Papal directions addressed to individual bishops.
Thus, immediately after he had ascended the throne, Pius V.
charged the Bishop of Verona, in a special brief, to carry out,
by force if necessary, the decree of the Council as to residence,
it having come to his ears that this matter was somewhat
neglected in Verona.[3] The Archbishop of Candia, who only
found four of his nine suffragans in their dioceses, was ordered
to confiscate their revenues and apply them to the restoration
of churches.[4] The Emperor himself, when he asked that one
of his councillors might be excused from the duty of residence,
had to be content with a refusal.[5]

[1] *Cf. supra* p. 187.

[2] Bull of July 8, 1568, Bull. Rom., VIII., 683 *seqq. ; cf.* *Bandi V.
11, p. 94, Papal Secret Archives. Concerning a general monitor-
ium threatening the loss of benefices to non-resident bishops and
parish priests, see *Avviso di Roma of April 3, 1568, Urb. 1040,
p. 496, Vatican Library. " All must go into residence ; those
who wished to be excused must renounce the revenues they had
already received." *Avviso of August 28, 1568, *ibid.* 565b.

[3] *Brief of March 14, 1566, Brevia, Arm. 44, t. 12, n. 36, Papal
Secret Archives.

[4] *Brief of August 3, 1569, *ibid.* t. 14, p. 165. In the Archives
of the Sacred Congregation of the Council at the Vatican are
preserved the *acta* of the visitations made by Lunel, Bishop of
Gaeta, at Città di Castello, Norcia and Narni (3 vols.) ; there
are also four vols. for the visitation of Rimini and Cesena made by
G. Fr. Sormanni, Bishop of Montefeltro, in 1572, and one volume
for the visitation at Camerino made in the same year.

[5] Brief of July 16, 1569, in LADERCHI, 1569 n. 217. An *exhortation of June 27, 1571, to the King of France to order the

This personal presence of the bishop in his diocese was naturally desired both by the Council and by the head of the Church principally in order that the pastor might make himself acquainted with the state of his flock by frequent visitations, and wherever good bishops were found they manifested their zeal in this way.[1] Above all others, that great champion of reform, Cardinal Borromeo, gave a splendid example in this respect, especially by his laborious visitation of the Swiss portion of his diocese. By means of the visitation of the Roman churches, which Pius V. began in person,[2] he aimed at inciting all the bishops to imitate him, while he also tried in every way to make their fulfilment of this duty of their office easy for them. In the case of parish churches no obstacles were to be put in the way of their examination and intervention into everything, even on the plea of Papal exemptions ; if their episcopal faculties were not wide enough, they were to make their inquiries as the representatives of the Apostolic See.[3]

In practice, however, the Pope found so few signs of the zeal he looked for in the discharge of this duty among the

bishop " Ventiarum " (Vence) to go into residence and to provide for the lack of priests, in Brevia, Arm. 44, t. 16, p. 170b, Papal Secret Archives.   *Brief of March 15, 1571, " Angelo [Giustiniani] Gebennensi " on account of his long absence from his church, which had given rise to scandal and harm, ibid. p. 35b.

[1] *Thus Cardinal Giulio Feltre della Rovere, Archbishop of Ravenna, visited his city in 1566 and again in 1571, and his diocese in 1567 (Archiepiscopal Archives, Ravenna). *Visitatio Veronensis diocesis sub. Aug. Valerio ep. Veronesni ab a. 1565 ad a. 1573, in the episcopal archives, Verona, XIII. *Fragment of the acta of a visitation made by the " episcopus Feltriensis anno 1569," in Cod. Regin., 377, p. 105-108, Vatican Library. Abbot Bonhomini of Nonantola visited his district : COLOMBO, Vita di M.G.F. Bonomi, 15.

[2] Cf. supra p. 179 seq.

[3] Cf. the bull of September 22, 1571, Bull. Rom., VII., 943 ; LADERCHI, 1571, n. 166, on the visitation of the parishes belonging to the Gerosolimitani.

bishops of Italy, that he decided to send apostolic visitors to all the Italian dioceses to demand an account of the bishops and chapters as to how they fulfilled their duties.[1] He began with the Kingdom of Naples, a Papal fief, which was to be visited by Tommaso Orfino, Bishop of Strongoli. Declaring that if the Archbishop of Naples had the right of visitation in all the dioceses under his jurisdiction without the royal *exequatur*, the Pope, as the head of the bishops, had the same right in a higher degree, Pius V. brushed aside the difficulties raised by the Viceroy of Naples in claiming that the royal *exequatur* was necessary for the apostolic visitor.[2] Orfino was therefore able to carry out the task imposed on him in the churches of Calabria, at Otranto and Bari and the neighbouring districts, and even in Naples itself.[3] A similar duty to that which had been laid on Orfino for the south, was entrusted to the distinguished Dominican bishop,Lionardo Marini, in north and central Italy. In the autumn of 1566 Pius V. appointed Marini Bishop of Alba in Monferrato, and empowered him to make on his way there a visitation of 24 churches in northern Italy.[4] Marini did not altogether come up to the hopes of the zealous Pope, and two years later he rebuked him because he had not as yet visited all the places in his district.[5] We have proof that during 1571 and 1572 apostolic visitors were sent to several of the cities

[1] LADERCHI, 1566. n. 184.

[2] *Ibid.* 1567, n. 64. *Cf.* Bonelli to Cristoforo Rodriguez, S.J. (who was to accompany Orfino), December 30, 1566, S. FRANC. BORGIA, IV., 691 ; Bonelli to Orfino, December, 1566, *ibid.* 692 ; Rodriguez to Pius V., January 7, 1567, *ibid.* 693 ; Salmeron to Rodriguez, August 18, 1566, SALMERON Epist., II., 95 *seqq.* For the name of Orfino, *cf. supra* p. 183, n. 1.

[3] LADERCHI, 1567, n. 65.

[4] Namely Sulmona, Marsi, Chieti, Penne and Atri, Ascoli, Ancona, Sinigaglia, Fano, Pesaro, Rimini, Cesena, Forlì, Bertinoro, Faenza, Imola, Modena, Reggio, Mantua, Lodi, Vigevano, Casale, Asti, Acqui. Brief of October 24, 1566, in UGHELLI, IV., 422.

[5] Brief of August 19, 1568 in LADERCHI, 1568, n. 43.

of Italy.[1] Commendone made a visitation of the monasteries of South Germany in 1569 as Papal legate,[2] while Bartolomeo Porzia did the same in the diocese of Aquileia, with the consent of the Archduke, Charles of Austria.[3] The Pope intended to extend to Spain,[4] and even to the whole Church,[5] the visitation which he had ordered for Italy.

The unfortunate experience which Pius V. had had of some of his episcopal brethren made him seek with all the more anxiety for means of excluding unworthy candidates from the episcopate, at least for the future. In a secret consistory on April 18th, 1567, he enacted that henceforth every Italian bishop must be examined in Rome by a commission.[6] On May 3rd three archbishops were charged with the duty of examining all those who were proposed in consistory for bishoprics and abbacies.[7] As far as he could,

---

[1] *Decreta a rev. D. visitatore apostolico facta de anno 1571 pro ecclesia parochiali S. Michaelis de Arimino : Barb. L 152, Vatican Library.   *Appunti e decreti della sacra visita di Pietro de Lunel vescovo di Gaeta deputato del Papa come legato apostolico a visitare le diocesi di Spoleto : Cancellaria arcivescov. at Spoleto. Cf. SORDINI in Bollet. per l'Umbria XIII. (1908).

[2] LADERCHI, 1568, n. 90. M. MAYR in Studien u. Mitteil. aus dem Benediktiner-und Zizterzienserorden, XIV. (1893), 385 seqq. A. STARZER in Blätter des Vereins für Landeskunde von Niederösterreich, 1892, 156 seq.

[3] LADERCHI, 1569, n. 222. A *command to the Archbishop of Avignon, of July 17 1569, to begin the visitation of the legation as soon as possible, in Brevia, Arm. 44. Papal Secret Archives.

[4] Requesens to Philip II., February 1, 1567, Corresp. dipl., II., 31.

[5] Letter from the Cardinal of Portugal to Francis Borgia, of October 25, 1569, S. FRANC. BORGIA, V., 222.

[6] *B. Pia to the Duke of Mantua, April 19, 1567, Gonzaga Archives, Mantua. *Arco, on the same date, State Archives, Vienna.

[7] *" Furono deputati tre arcivescovi sopra l' esamine di quelli che da qui innanzi havranno da esser proposti in concistorio a vescovadi et abbadie, et sono l'arcivescovo Maffeo, l'arcivescovo S. Severina et l'arcivescovo Feruffina " (B. Pia to the Duke of

Pius V. also took strong measures against unworthy prelates,[1] though he knew well, at the same time, how to find words of comfort and encouragement whenever a good bishop was in danger of losing heart under the stress of the difficult conditions of the time and the weight of his responsibilities.[2] He was never sparing of letters of exhortation and encouragement to the bishops of the whole world.[3]   It was with manifest joy that he bestowed his praise on the Bishop of Verdun, the Premonstratensian, Nicholas Pseaume, for his loyalty to the Catholic religion and the Holy See, saying that Pseaume, almost alone among the bishops, had kept his flock free from the heresy which surrounded it on all sides, and that God

---

Mantua, May 3, 1567, *loc. cit.*).   For the part taken by Santori in the examination of bishops see his Autobiografia, XII., 350, and *Audienze del card. Santorio from 1566 to 1579, Papal Secret Archives, Arm. LII., 17, where there is a list of " persone di consideratione " suited to fill episcopal sees.

[1] The Bishop of Rimini ended his days in the Castle of St. Angelo in 1569 for immorality, and the Bishop of Bovino for simony (RODOCANACHI, St. Ange, 175).   *Zibramonti, February 2, 1572 : action taken against Archbishop Verallo for immorality. Gonzaga Archives, Mantua.   For the action taken by Pius V. against the Archbishop of Besançon, Claude de la Baume, see FEBVRE, Philippe II. et la Franche-Comté, Paris, 1911, 580 *seq.*, 590 *seq.*   De la Baume had to pledge himself to the publication of the Tridentine decrees, and to follow this by putting the Catholic reforms into force.   *Cf. ibid.* 584 *seq.*, the attempt to introduce the Roman Inquisition into Besançon.

[2] Letter of September 21, 1569, to Juan de Ribera, Archbishop of Valencia, who wished to resign " ob praesentium temporum calamitates episcoporumque ignaviam " in LADERCHI, 1569, n 316 ; GOUBAU, 227 *seq.*   In LADERCHI, 1571, n. 146, intervention by Pius V. on behalf of the Bishop of Lausanne.

[3] *Exhortation to the Spanish and French bishops in Brevia, Arm. 44, t. 12, n. 24.   *Ibid.* t. 16, p. 66b : " Episcopo Coriensi." of April 23, 1571 : he is praised because he has published the decrees of the Council, and had improved the morals of his clergy : he is exhorted to persevere, and not to overlook the Zwinglian part of his diocese.   Papal Secret Archives.

had shown by this how much can be accomplished by a good pastor who, without any human help, and armed only with his own zeal, is ready to expose his life to all risks, to shoulder every burden, and who will not admit into his city even royal officials, if they are objects of suspicion.[1] When he bestowed the title of patriarch of Antioch on the distinguished Juan de Ribera, who had been Bishop of Badajoz since 1562, and Archbishop of Valencia since 1568, Pius V. used even stronger terms of eulogy, styling him the " light of all Spain " and a model of sanctity, before whose humility and strictness of life the Pope felt himself quite ashamed ; he recalls the way in which Ribera himself took the sacraments to the sick, and states that he led the life of a monk rather than of a bishop, and that his example had been a mighty influence for good upon many of the Spanish bishops.[2]

By his regulations concerning examination for orders and parochial office,[3] and on the choice of parish priests,[4] Pius V. had seen to it that the bishops should have good priests to assist them in the care of souls. In his capacity as Bishop of Rome he issued a series of ordinances on the sacerdotal manner of life for those holding office in the Eternal City,[5] but he left it to the bishops to make their own provision for this elsewhere ; very few constitutions of the kind which

[1] *Brief of May 7, 1569, Brevia, Arm. 44, t. 14, p. 107b, Papal Secret Archives. Cf. brief of July 5, 1569, in LADERCHI, 1569, n. 193. Praise for Valeriano Protaszewicz, Bishop of Vilna, September 6, 1567, in the Archives of Briefs, Rome.

[2] In NIC. ANTONIO, Bibliotheca Hisp. nova, Madrid, 1783, 767. Pius VI. beatified Ribera (died 1611) on August 13, 1796 (BARBÉRI, Bull. Rom. contin., X., Rome, 1845, 34) ; the Jesuit Francesco Escriva wrote his life, Valencia, 1612. He was the son of the Viceroy of Naples, Pedro Afan de Ribera.

[3] See supra, p. 184 seq.

[4] Editti of March 18 and August 19, 1567, Bull. Rom., VII., 555, 605. Cf. *Avviso di Roma of May 17, 1567, Urb. 1040, p. 396b, Vatican Library.

[5] Cf. supra, p. 183.

were applicable to the whole Church were issued in the reign of Pius V.[1]

Pius V. interested himself greatly in the religious instruction of the people, and in their edification by means of the worthy celebration of divine worship. A custom had already grown up by which, on Sundays and festivals, even pious laymen gathered together the children of the poor in the churches and instructed them in the fundamental truths of Christianity. Now, in accordance with a recommendation of the Council of Trent,[2] Pius V. exhorted the bishops to promote and encourage this pious custom, and to set up confraternities of Christian Doctrine, to the members of which he granted an indulgence.[3] Such confraternities had been formed at Milan about 1560 by a simple hat-maker, Marco Sudi, and had spread rapidly, as far as Rome, where they received a great impetus from the protection extended to them by the Pope.[4] Even for the island of Corsica, which was in such a low moral state, Pius V. urged with great insistence, as one of the principal remedies to be adopted, the instruction of the children and young people in the fundamental truths of religion, Christian doctrine, and a catechism in the vernacular.[5] He addressed a similar exhortation to Avignon,

---

[1] On August 30, 1567, Pius V. confirmed the ordinance of Pius IV. of November 9, 1560, that all that a cleric might have gained by illicit trading should pass to the Apostolic Camera (*Anal. iuris Pont.*, VIII., 1430, *seq.*). He declared null (*ibid.* 1799) the wills made by clerics in favour of their natural children. *Cf.*
* B. Pia to the Duke of Mantua ; *Avvisi di Roma of January 31, 1568, and March 3, 1571, Urb. 1040, p. 481b ; 1042, p. 25b, Vatican Library. According to the *Avviso of November 2, 1566 (*ibid.* 1040, p. 313) on that date a bull was issued on the reform of priests in accordance with the Tridentine decrees.

[2] Sess. 24, de ref. c. 4.

[3] Bull of October 6, 1571, Bull. Rom., VII., 945 *seq.*

[4] LADERCHI, 1571, n. 170 *seq.*

[5] " Omnibus viribus ac diligentia eniti debes, ut instituendorum in tua dioecesi puerorum . . . quam maximam curam suscipias." To the Bishop of Ajaccio, May 4, 1569, in GOUBAU, 178.

where heresy was threatening to take a stronger and stronger hold.[1]

Pius V. watched with special care over all that pertained to the proper celebration of divine worship. An abuse had crept in in Rome by which the churches and their porticoes were disfigured by all kinds of buildings, by the setting aside for dwelling purposes of the more remote parts of the churches themselves, and by the opening of windows from the adjoining houses which looked into the interiors of the churches. An edict of the Cardinal Vicar, Savelli, on November 28th, 1566, ordered the removal of all such constructions within fourteen days ; at the same time a stop was put to all burials under the pavements of the churches.[2] The Romans at that time were far from strict in their behaviour in church and during the services,[3] and Pius V. found himself obliged to order by a bull, that which is generally taken for granted among good Christians, namely, that they should go to church modestly and reverently, speak in a low voice, pay attention to the services, and always bend the knee before the Blessed Sacrament. If we may judge from another prohibition contained in the bull, disturbances and quarrels, and even acts of violence were by no means uncommon in the churches ; very often ladies of ill fame held their court there with their admirers, amid much chattering and laughter, while beggars pestered the worshippers during the functions and sermons ; the courts, too, made use of the precincts of the churches for their business.[4] For example, the disputations with which the judges who were entering upon their term of office, were accustomed to prove their worth were usually held in the church of Sant'Eustachio.[5] Festival days were profaned in all sorts of ways by servile work, markets, etc.[6] Hitherto,

[1] May 18, 1569, *ibid.* 179.

[2] LADERCHI, 1566, n. 68.

[3] *Cf.* TACCHI VENTURI, I., 177 *seqq.*

[4] Bull of April 1, 1566, Bull. Rom., VII., 435 *seq.*

[5] *Strozzi, December 21, 1566, State Archives, Vienna. LADERCHI, 1566, n. 66.

[6] Bull. Rom., VII., 436. *Avviso di Roma of November 2, 1566 Urb. 1040 p. 315 Vatican Library.

from the vigil of All Saints onwards, the church of S. Maria ad Martyres, the ancient Pantheon, had remained open all night for the purpose of gaining an indulgence, giving rise to grave scandals.[1] Both the ecclesiastical and the civil authorities had already on previous occasions issued ordinances against the profanation of the House of God,[2] but no one set himself against it with so much resoluteness or with such grave threats as Pius V.,[3] who found a powerful ally in the reformed Orders, whose churches were for the most part only frequented by those people to whom piety was a matter of deep reality.[4] In his fight against superstition the new Pope was again helped by Ormaneto who, for example, caused to be cut off from the Chair of St. Peter the cords which some women, probably from superstitious motives, had tied to it.[5] It is clear that almost all these ordinances were suggested by the decrees of the Council of Trent on the worthy celebration of mass.[6]

In the diocese of Calahorra, a remarkable exhibition of the proverbial Spanish class feeling had led to disturbances and damage even in the churches. There were two parties, the *hidalgos*, who were exempt from taxes, and the *pecheros*, who were not thus exempt. The *hidalgos* claimed precedence over the others and the first places, even in the churches, at mass, at the reception of the sacraments, and in processions. This gave rise to endless strife and quarrels, and in the little city of Osio, during the procession of Corpus Domini, the mayor

[1] LADERCHI 1566. n. 65. *Avviso di Roma *loc. cit.*

[2] TACCHI VENTURI I., 184.

[3] In the bull already cited.

[4] TACCHI VENTURI, I., 186.

[5] *Avviso di Roma of January 24, 1568, Urb. 1040, p. 479, Vatican Library.

[6] Sess. 22, " de observandis et evitandis in celebratione Missae." This decree is supported by the ordinance that Mass is to be celebrated at a suitable time, and by a motuproprio forbidding its celebration during the evening hours of the day preceding the midnight mass of Christmas, and of the early morning mass of Easter. Published March 29, 1566, Bull. Rom., VII., 433.

and others were killed, and several persons severely injured. The provincial synod of Saragossa in 1565 attempted to suppress the evil, but in vain. The intervention of the civil authority, which divided the churches into two, lengthways, assigning the right half to the *hidalgos* and the left to the *pecheros*, only made matters worse, and embittered the state of feeling. Pius V. then intervened with all his energy against these exhibitions of an " Indian spirit of caste " ; he revoked the decision of the civil authorities as inadequate, and declared that anyone who claimed a special place in church would incur excommunication.[1]

The Pope also addressed a severe rebuke to the priests of many dioceses in Spain, who were wanting in respect for the Blessed Sacrament especially during the celebration of the divine mysteries.[2] On the other hand, Pius V. did all he could to keep alive among both priests and people reverence for the Most Holy Sacrament. When it was carried through the streets of Rome to the sick, the Pope ordered that even the Cardinals who met It must get off their horses, or from their carriages and accompany It, as the King of Spain and other princes were accustomed to do.[3] The Franciscans

---

[1] Brief of February 14, 1571, in LADERCHI, 1571, n. 168.

[2] To the Archbishop of Tarragona, January 8, 1571, *ibid.* n. 167. Briefs to the same effect sent to eight other Spanish bishops, *ibid.* n. 168.

[3] *" In consistoro lunedì S. S^{tà} ordinò doppo un longo esordio che sempre che serà portato per Roma il s^{mo} sacramento per communione tutti quelli che lo incontrano anco cardenali o altri signori personaggi smontino di cocchio o cavalli dove si trovino et vadino ad accompagnare il s^{mo} sacramento, lasciando da canto ogni negotio, et allegò in questo proposito quello che il re cattolico et altri principi religiosissimamente hanno usato di fare." (B. Pia to Luzzara, July 10, 1568, Gonzaga Archives, Mantua). *Cf.* consistorial acta of Cardinal Farnese, in LADERCHI, 1568, n. 19. Ormaneto thought of issuing an ordinance that during the procession of *Corpus Domini* made by the Pope, women should not stand at their windows, but should take part in the procession. *Avviso di Roma of June 12, 1568, Urb. 1040, p. 534, Vatican Library.

obtained the privilege of venerating the Blessed Sacrament during the recitation of the breviary.[1] A sacrilege committed against the Blessed Sacrament by a Protestant who had broken into a Catholic parish church at Tarvis in Carinthia, led to a special brief from the Pope to the Archduke Charles, asking for the condign punishment of the offender.[2] On the other hand, he refused his approval to the custom existing in some districts of refusing to give the Blessed Sacrament, through a mistaken sense of reverence, to those. condemned to death.[3] In accordance with the decrees of Trent,[4] Pius V. sought to promote the frequentation of the sacraments, especially among the clergy. Clerics in minor orders were to go to confession and communion at least once a month, and those in major orders twice a month ; priests were to say mass at least once a week, even those who had no care of souls.[5]

Pious bodies for the encouragement of prayer and works of charity, especially those which originated from the Dominican Order, found a strong protector in Pius V. ; such were the Confraternity of the Rosary,[6] that of the Name of God for the healing of feuds,[7] that of the Beheading of St. John the Baptist, which took charge of those condemned to death,[8] the

---

[1] Brief of January 8, 1568, Bull. Rom., VII., 647 seq.

[2] Brief of January 21, 1568, in GOUBAU, 66.

[3] To Castagna, January 25, 1568, ibid. 68 seq. LADERCHI, 1568, n. 200. For the immediate occasion of the brief, cf. SACCHINI, P. III., I., 1, n. 22. The brief, it is true, caused much displeasure to the King of Spain and his counsellors " per essere cosa molto nova in questi regni " (Castagna to Bonelli, March 8, 1568, Corresp. dipl., II., 321). Later on Philip II. ordered that in every prison there should be a chapel where those who were condemned to death could receive communion. SACCHINI, loc. cit

[4] Sess. 23, de ref., c. 11, 13, 14.

[5] To the chapter of Valence, October 14, 1569, in GOUBAU, 234 seq.; cf. Polanco, October 21, 1566, Anal. Bolland., VII., 66.

[6] Brief of September 17, 1569, Bull. Rom., VII., 774.

[7] Briefs of September 20, 1569, and June 21, 1571, ibid., 777, 921.

[8] Brief, without date, ibid., 768.

Confraternity of the Most Holy Trinity, founded in 1549 by Philip Neri, which housed poor pilgrims for three days, and gave assistance to those who were dismissed from the hospitals, until they were recovered,[1] and that of the Annunciation of Mary established at the Minerva to give dowries to poor girls.[2] The Pope personally took part in this last named good work, which saved so many girls in danger of dishonour. On April 5th, 1567, he went to the church of his Order and gave dowries to 80 poor girls ;[3] the Imperial ambassador wrote that the Pope intended to spend as much as 10,000 scudi for this purpose.[4] Pius V. also showed his high esteem for virginity and the honour of women by the care which he took of the convent of S. Caterina della Rosa for the education of the daughters of the poorer classes who were exposed to risk,[5] as well as by the severity with which he proceeded against offenders in this respect.[6] He strove with special zeal against blasphemy, which at that time had become almost habitual.[7] and sent to the bishops a bull which, among other things, visited this offence with heavy penalties, begging them to call in the help of the secular arm in carrying it out.[8] When Benevento made difficulties about accepting the bull, the Pope called upon the assistance of the Neapolitan troops, under the command of Hannibal von Hohenems, against the city.[9] As he had done in the

[1] Brief of March 21, 1571, *ibid.*, 901. LADERCHI, 1571, n. 172.

[2] Without date, Bull. Rom., VII., 962.

[3] *Arco, April 5 and 12, 1567, State Archives, Vienna.

[4] *Arco, March 8, 1567, *ibid.*

[5] Brief of February 10, 1568, Bull. Rom., VII., 655.

[6] Strict action against a concubinist taken " in flagranti " : *Avviso di Roma of October 19, 1566, Urb. 1040, p. 307, Vatican Library. A very strict bull against concubinists : *Avviso di Roma of May 14, 1569, Urb. 1041, p. 76, *ibid.*

[7] " Blasphemiae scelus (quod nunc) supra modum invaluit." Bull of April 1, 1566, Bull. Rom., VII., 437. *Cf.* *Bandi, V., 7, p. 2 *seq.*, Papal Secret Archives.

[8] Brief of April 16, 1566, to the Duke of Ferrara, in sending him the bull of April 1, 1566, to be carried out with the help of the secular arm. LADERCHI, 1566, n. 84.

[9] *Arco, August 3, 1566, State Archives, Vienna.

case of blasphemy, so did the Pope take action against slander
among the Romans.   Defamatory pamphlets against princes,
prelates, officials, and anyone else were prohibited under grave
penalties, as being a source of hatred and feuds, which sometimes even led to murder.   The first beginnings of the Roman
newspapers also fell under this ban, namely, those " Avvisi "
which were spread abroad in manuscript, at least when the
good name of anybody was attacked, or any matter which
was being dealt with by the Pope in private was divulged.[1]
By the advice of Ormaneto Pius V. contemplated throwing
the statues of Pasquino and Marforio into the Tiber.[2]

Just as he sought to strengthen religious feeling everywhere,
and thus renew the life of the Church from within, so did this
zealous reformer who was now seated on the chair of Peter
set himself to remove all those things which hitherto had
done harm to the Church, and had given her enemies cause
for accusations and calumnies.   He therefore inaugurated
a ruthless war against every kind of simony.   From the first
Pius had displayed an almost morbid fear of soiling his hands
with money, and could hardly bring himself to discuss financial questions.   When Grassi, a cleric in the Apostolic Camera,
wished to lay before him a scheme for adding to the Papal
revenues without burdening the people, the Pope replied
that he had no wish to amass wealth, and that Grassi would
do better to devise some means of bringing back to the Church
the nations that had broken away from her.[3]   He condoned
in the case of the Archbishop of Trêves the payment of an-
nates, with the exception of a fifth part, and it would seem
that he would have liked to condone them altogether in the
case of the Archbishop of Cologne, and contrary to all custom
the bulls were issued before the money was paid.[4]   When
the Archbishop of Naples received the pallium the question
was urgently raised as to whether it was lawful in such cases

[1] Brief of March 17, 1572, Bull. Rom., VII., 969.
[2] *Cusano, July 17, 1568, State Archives, Vienna.
[3] *Cusano, July 6, 1566, *ibid.*
[4] BRAUNSBERGER, Pius V., 12.

to demand the fees which had hitherto been paid for the support of the officials of the Curia. Paul IV. had wished that it should be done gratuitously, and accordingly Pius V. had the question examined anew by Cardinals Morone, Corgna and Dolera. When these Cardinals reported that some fee should be demanded, Pius V. was not satisfied with their opinion, and in the consistory he spoke in severe terms of such payments as an abuse which has long been tolerated, but which he forbade for the future ; henceforth the consistorial advocates were not to receive more than four scudi from an archbishop who asked for the pallium.[1] In Poland, where the clergy had a bad name for being covetous of money, the inter-nuncio Vincenzo Portico was ordered to grant Papal dispensations entirely gratuitously ; he must recieve no payment whatever for the drawing up of the documents.[2] The Pope had granted an indulgence in favour of Philip II. to all those who assisted the king with money in his warlike undertakings against the Moors and Turks, but he firmly rejected the proposal to keep part of the funds raised in this way for the needs of the Holy See, and this he did so as to avoid any appearance of having made the concession in his own interests.[3] Pius V. entirely abolished the faculty of sending out preachers of indulgences which had belonged to certain churches and hospitals, a thing which had given, and still gave, occasion for many justifiable complaints.[4]

[1] *Arco, February and April 6, 1566, State Archives, Vienna. Consistorial acta of February 15 and April 26, 1566, in GULIK-EUBEL, II., 47 n. LADERCHI, 1566, n. 44.

[2] LADERCHI, 1569, n. 24, from Gabutius.

[3] LADERCHI, 1566, n. 72.

[4] Bull of February 8, 1567, Bull. Rom., VII., 535. *" N.S. ha rivocato tutte le indulgenze si può dir del mondo che la Spagna con essa revocatione havrà gran negotio." (B. Pia to the Duke of Mantua, sending him the bull, February 22, 1567, Gonzaga Archives, Mantua). LADERCHI, 1567, n. 25. Bull of January 2, 1569 against unauthorized letters of confession and indulgences of Spanish bishops, in Bull. Rom., VII., 735. The prescriptions of the Council concerning preachers of indulgences, see in sess. 21, c. 9 ; sess. 25, de indulg.

In accordance with the warning of the Council, the Pope was very cautious in granting new indulgences.[1]

The zealous reformer fought with special vigour against the so-called " confidential simony," by which a benefice was taken in charge (*confidentia*), generally by a bishop or a Cardinal, on behalf of somebody else, either because the latter had not yet reached the canonical age, and was perhaps still a child, who could only obtain the actual possession (*accessus*) of the benefice much later, or else because he intended at a later date to resume the benefice (*regressus*) which he had to all appearance resigned. These " confidenze " made it possible for certain bishoprics and benefices to become practically hereditary in families, passing from one relative to another, and as often as not were in quite unworthy hands. The Council of Trent and Paul IV. had prohibited this abuse ;[2] Pius V. expressly declared that before everything else, and more than anything else, he had from the first had at heart a determination to root it out.[3] Nobody but the Pope was in a position to act with the necessary authority against this plague, because the principle delinquents, the so-called " custodini " were for the most part Cardinals and bishops, against whom it was not easy to take judicial proceedings.[4] For this reason Pius V., as a first step, reserved to himself the decision of all disputes which had arisen on the subject of " confidenze."[5] There then followed a careful investigation

[1] *" Non concede più indulgentie plenarie di colpa et di pena, ma solo concede indulgentie per 7 anni, per un giorno solo." Avviso di Roma of March 1, 1567, Urb. 1040, p. 364b, Vatican Library.

[2] Sess. 25, de ref., c. 7. For Paul IV. see Vol. XIV. of this work, p. 197 *seq.*

[3] Motuproprio published on January 5, 1567, §5, Bull. Rom. 510. LADERCHI (1568, n. 11) wrongly assigns the edict to 1568. As early as May, 1566 the Pope declared that on account of the bull of Paul IV. forbidding further " regressi," those granted by Pius IV. could not be allowed. *Arco, May 18, 1566, State Archives, Vienna.

[4] Motuproprio of January 5, 1567, §4.

[5] *Ibid.* §5.

of every case in which confidential simony was proved ;[1] next came an express declaration that even the Cardinals were included in the prohibition which had already been issued,[2] and lastly the revocation of all the " confidenze " which had so far been allowed, and a prohibition of any being allowed in the future.[3] After this the Council's prohibition of the reservation of any part of the revenues when a benefice was granted, was renewed.[4] Outside Rome, it would seem that confidential simony was especially prevalent in the Low Countries, for which reason a severe rebuke was addressed to the bishops there by the Apostolic See as early as 1568.[5]

The prohibition of " confidenze," and even more, the restrictions in the matter of renunciations, cut off a rich source of revenue from the Apostolic Camera, and struck a severe blow at the Papal finances. But though the Pope was often urged to relieve his pecuniary straits by once more allowing the *regressi*,[6] it was impossible to induce him to do so. On

---

[1] On June 1, 1569, Bull. Rom., VII., 754. Here are adduced some of the reasons why certain persons were unwilling to take immediate possession of their benefices : some do so because they do not wish to be forced to take orders, or to go into residence, or to wear ecclesiastical dress, others because they are thinking of taking part in war, or having recourse to lawsuits, and others again because they have not yet obtained absolution from crimes, etc. (*ibid.*, 755).

[2] November 14, 1569, *ibid.*, 758.

[3] September 12, 1571, *ibid.*, 939. He issued the bull " volentes omnem haereditariam beneficiorum ecclesiasticorum successionem de ecclesia Dei tollere " and to facilitate the free conferring of benefices on worthy persons. *Cf.* *Avviso di Roma of September 8, 1571, Urb. 1042, p. 115, Vatican Library.

[4] June 1, 1570, Bull. Rom., VII., 827 ; *cf.* Conc. Trid., sess. 24, de ref. c 14.

[5] To the Archbishops of Malines, Cambrai, and Utrecht, to the Bishops of Bois-le-duc, Ypres, Middelburg, Haarlem, Tournai, Arras, Saint-Omer and Namur, July 5, 1568, in GOUBAU, 91 *seq.*

[6] Letter of November 16, 1566, in LADERCHI, 1566, n. 59. *Avissi di Roma of April 19, 1570, and July 25, 1571, Urb. 1041, p. 267b ; 1042, p. 95, Vatican Library.

one occasion it was said to him that his strictness in the granting of benefices was ruining the Curia, but he replied that it was better that the Curia should be ruined than that the service of God and the very existence of Christianity should suffer the same fate.

Very often the " confidenze " were nothing but a device to alienate ecclesiastical property from its original purpose ; the benefice was placed in custody with the condition that the fruits should be given over to a layman.[1]   There were many such devices. In these latter days, so runs a complaint in one of the bulls of Pius V., " in these latter days, the making over of ecclesiastical property to the laity has come to such a pass that little by little the better part is being devoured by strangers ; what was intended for the maintenance and training of the ministers of the Church, for the establishment of seminaries, the assistance of the poor and the sick, the building of churches, the restoration of buildings that are falling down, the education of good and learned men—all that is being appropriated by hordes of laymen."[2]   Naturally it was out of the question to eliminate at a single blow so widespread and deeply rooted an evil, but Pius V. issued a series of special regulations which at least limited it and prevented its further growth.[3]

A constitution of Pius V. concerning the sale of places and territories in the Papal States is specially important.[4]   In this we read : Previous Popes had forbidden the alienation of ecclesiastical goods by declaring it invalid, but people who

[1] Bull. Rom., VII., 755.

[2] Bull of September 9, 1568, *ibid.* 709.

[3] Revocation of certain privileges of officials of the Curia, etc. *ibid. ;* protection of the rights of the Apostolic Camera over the inheritance of ecclesiastics ; edict of January 5, 1568, *ibid.* 646. In controversies concerning prebends the fruits must be deposited with some trustworthy person named by the judge ; brief of March 30, 1568, *ibid.* 663.   During the vacancy of bishoprics all the benefices are reserved to the Pope : brief of March 9, 1568, *ibid.* 659.

[4] Bull of March 29, 1567, *ibid.* 560 *seq.*

were ambitious and greedy of power had under all manner of pretexts suggested to the Popes that it was more advantageous to the Church that certain cities, territories and fortresses in the Papal States should be held either permanently or temporarily in fief. Several Popes had consented to this, but since the inviolable loyalty towards the Holy See of the cities and territories of the Papal States was of great importance in these days, he intended to put an end to such alienations ; this was his definite intention for the period of his reign, and he wished at any rate to prove to his successors that he could not consider it right to look upon such things as lawful, and he hoped that they would remember that the Popes must render an account of their administration before the tribunal of Jesus Christ. He wished also, as far as possible, to remove even the occasion of such alienations, and he accordingly declared that all the territories of the Papal States, including those which had hitherto been held in fief, were now, in virtue of this his present declaration, incorporated in the Apostolic See and restored to it, and he ordered that in future no one must even propose to make a fief of any city or territory in the Papal States under pain of excommunication and treason. Gregory XIII., Sixtus V., Innocent IX. and Clement VIII. confirmed and amplified these prescriptions. It was in virtue of this constitution that the Duchy of Ferrara was restored to the Apostolic See under Clement VIII., and that of Urbino under Urban VIII.[1]

As had been the case with Church property, so several of the preceding Popes had proved themselves too easy-going with other ecclesiastical rights. Specially harmful had been the concession to the civil princes of the right of presentation to several bishoprics and important benefices. In the election capitulation drawn up after the death of Paul IV., the decision that the future Pope should only grant such rights with the consent of two-thirds of the Cardinals had been expressly accepted and sworn to by all the Cardinals, but Pius IV. had thought himself at liberty to dispense himself from the oath in a number of cases. Pius V. thought very differently. At

[1] LADERCHI, 1567, n. 12.

the very beginning of his pontificate he publicly called attention to this principle of the election capitulation,[1] and a short time afterwards took away from the Duke of Mantua the right of presentation to the bishopric of that city which had been granted to him by Pius IV.,[2] and later on he extended the same thing to all the rights of presentation which had been granted by his predecessors, except such as had really received the required consent of the Cardinals.[3] It was in vain that the princes protested. The Mantuan agent in Rome wrote to the Duke that the Pope was so determined in his opposition to such rights of patronage that he did not even dare to speak to him on the subject ; there was no hope whatever of making him change his mind, where the liberties of the Church were concerned.[4] The Pope courteously but firmly rejected all the complaints of the princes.[5]

[1] Bull. Rom., VII., 427.

[2] Acta consist. card. Gambarae, July 19 and December 23, 1566, in LADERCHI, 1566, n. 197 seqq.

[3] *" Aspetti V. S. R^ma di veder presto bolle di riforme di molte cose, le quali N. S. vuol dar fuori. Ha fra l'altre rivocato tutti li iuspatronati, etiam ducum et regum, che sono ex privilegio, onde il re di Portogallo havrà qui che fare." (B. Pia to the Bishop of Mantua, September 17, 1567, Gonzaga Archives, Mantua). *The Pope has abolished all rights of patronage except those " ex fundatione et dotatione " (Arco, December 13, 1567, State Archives Vienna). *Abolition of the Portuguese right of patronage by a brief of February 7, 1567, Corp. dipl. Portug., X., 237. *Arco, August 23, 1567, State Archives, Vienna ; cf. *Arco, March 23 and 29, 1567, ibid. See also Acta consist. card. Farnes, February 7, 1567, in LADERCHI, 1567, n. 14.

[4] *" Il card^le mi replicò ch' egli credeva che tutto questo fosse vero et che averebbe anco fatto opera di farne capace N. S., ma che sapesse certo che S. S^tà stava tanto mal disposta contra questi iuspatronati che restava offeso solo a sentirne parlare, et che difficilissima cosa, per non dire impossibile, pareva a lui che fosse il sperare di poter vincere il Papa in queste materie ne le quali si tratta de la libertà de la chiesa." Luzzara to the Duke of Mantua, June 12, 1566, Gonzaga Archives, Mantua.

[5] Two letters to the Cardinal of Lorraine and his mother

It was doubly fortunate for the Church that she should have found at her head so wise and vigorous a leader in the way towards a complete renewal of her life, and that that leader should have presented himself just at the right moment. In the time of Adrian VI. even such an eagle as Pius V. would certainly have found his wings clipped, but now the way lay open before him, and this was especially owing to the labours and sacrifices of those great men who, by their foundation of the great reforming Orders had found a way of multiplying themselves, and producing innumerable more or less faithful copies of themselves.   Besides this, the great reforming Pope found among his own contemporaries many men of a like stamp with himself.   Philip Neri with his band of disciples was working close at hand for the moral regeneration of the Eternal City.[1]   In north Italy it was under Pius V. that the great Archbishop of Milan began by means of his provincial councils to become the disciplinary law-giver for the whole Church.   Germany had its Peter Canisius and France at least its Cardinal of Lorraine and its Possevino.   These men formed the mountain tops, which, visible to the eyes of all the world, shed their light far and wide, but the historian, if he looks a little deeper, can see that they were neither isolated nor alone, but only the highest peaks of a whole mountain range, yet showing at the same time that side by side with these heights of sacrifice and energy there were still to be found the lowest depths of decadence and immorality.

According to the saying of Borromeo,[2] in the XVIth century it was the clergy of Spain who especially proved themselves the " nerve centre of Christianity."[3]   Among them must be

---

Christina, of October 16, 1567, in LADERCHI, 1567, n. 15 seq. ; two others to King Sebastian and Cardinal Henry of Portugal, of October 27, 1567, ibid., n. 17 seq.

[1] Further particulars in Vol. XIX. of this work.

[2] " Il clero . . . di Spagna che è il nervo di tutta la christ-ianità."   Borromeo, August 18, 1565, in STEINHERZ, IV., 436.

[3] The following Spaniards of the XVIth century were deemed worthy of canonization : John of God (died 1550), Francis Xavier (died 1552), Thomas of Villanova (died 1555), Ignatius of Loyola

numbered that simple priest who, before the time of Pius V., had for forty years travelled about in voluntary poverty, preaching from one city to another, and by his eloquence working miracles of moral regeneration ; this was Juan de Avila. His original intention had been to go as a missionary to America, but at Seville, whence he was preparing to set sail, the archbishop persuaded him to devote himself to his archdiocese. Avila's eloquence sprang from his very soul. His only preparation for his sermons consisted in spending the preceding night in meditation and prayer ; it was said of him that he studied on his knees ; when he was asked how to become a good preacher, his answer was that it was only necessary really to love God. His own discourses, to quote an eye-witness, kindled a fire in the hearts of his hearers ; not only did the common people flock to him, but noble lords and ladies gave up lives of sin, or dedicated themselves to lives of high perfection. In many ways his ideas coincided with those of Ignatius Loyola, whom he greatly venerated. Avila, too, realized that the true foundation for a lasting renewal of the Church was to be sought specially in the instruction of the young, and the training of good priests. The Apostle of Andalusia died at Montilla at the age of seventy, on May 10th, 1569.[1]

That thing which was so often manifested in the work of Avila, namely that a small impulse is sufficient to call into being a deep religious life, even in a community that is to all appearances quite depraved, was also proved by another great popular missionary, Alessandro Sauli, the Apostle of Corsica, in a much more neglected field of missionary labour.[2] Born

(died 1556), Peter of Alcantara (died 1562), Francis Borgia (died 1572), Louis Bertrand (died 1581), Teresa of Jesus (died 1582), John of the Cross (died 1591), Paschal Baylon (died 1592).

[1] Beatified by Leo XIII. in 1894. Louis of Granada wrote his life (Opere, VI., Madrid, 1787, 611 seqq.). Other special literature in *Kirchenlexikon of Freiburg*, I², 1766.

[2] Life by GABUTIUS in *Acta Sanct.*, October, V., 806-83 . *Cf.* S. Alessandro Sauli, Note e documenti, Milan, 1905. His correspondence with Bascapé was edited by PREMOLI in *Riv. di scienze storiche*, 1907 and 1908.

of a noble family at Milan, the fifteen year old Sauli knocked
one day, dressed in cloth of silver, at the doors of the Barnabite
convent in that city, and asked to be received into the Order.
In order to test his firmness of purpose, he was ordered to go
in broad daylight, with a cross upon his shoulders, to the
market place and there preach a sermon on penance. Sauli
did as he was told, and found men ready to listen to him, which
is certainly a striking proof that, in spite of all their licentious-
ness, a true Christian spirit was still to be found in the great
cities of Italy.   Ordained priest, this young man, who was so
full of talent, was first given a cure of souls at Pavia, where
he also taught philosophy and theology ; in 1567 he was
elected General of his Order, and in 1570 was made Bishop of
Aleria in Corsica by Pius V.[1]

Sauli found appalling conditions existing in the island.
After the insurrection of Sampieri (died 1567) the country
had become a desert, the people greatly reduced in numbers,
and in a state of absolute barbarism. Pestilence and famine,
too, were rife, agriculture was at a standstill, and men sub-
sisted on acorns and herbs.   Filippini, the historian of Corsica,
gives the names of sixty places which were laid waste and
entirely deserted ; within a period of thirty years 28,000
murders had been committed.[2]   After his arrival in the island
Sauli wrote to Borromeo that in his whole diocese he could
not find two habitable rooms, and that he had not the materials
to build even a Capuchin's cell.   In his episcopal city only
the walls of the cathedral and a fort were standing, everything
else had been destroyed by fire and pillaged. For the time
being, therefore, Sauli took up his residence at Corte, and
courageously began his episcopal labours. The means by
which he sought to repair the religious devastation were those
recommended by the Council of Trent. The first thing he
sought for was a supply of priests to instruct the people ; he
gathered them together in synods to instruct them in their

---

[1] By a bull dated " anno dell' incarnatione 1569, 4 id.
febr., i.e. February 10, 1570, printed in S. Alessandro Sauli, 110
seqq. Cf. PREMOLI, Barnabiti (1913), 231 seqq.

[2] F. GREGOROVIUS, Corsica, I., Stuttgart, 1854, 54-56.

duties, he established a seminary, urged catechetical instruction, and with incredible privations and labour carried out an episcopal visitation. Time after time he fell ill, as the result of his toil in that pestilent climate, but he persevered none the less. In the most desolate part of his diocese, at Argagliola, his fellow workers deserted him, and left him alone at his post. Besides the duties of his episcopal office he undertook all the labours of a simple priest ; in the seminary he himself delivered the lectures, and on his journeys he himself taught the catechism, visited the sick and heard confessions. His influence over the people was so great that, in the quarrels which were always breaking out, he dared to throw himself between the combatants, in order to prevent the shedding of blood, and thus to obviate those consequences which, on account of the appalling prevalence of the vendetta, followed upon a murder. He continued his unwearied activities for more than twenty years, until Gregory XIV. in 1591 translated him to the see of Pavia, where he died in the following year. Pius X. canonized him in 1904.

Pius V. had his part in the reform of Corsica by addressing briefs of encouragement to Alessandro Sauli and the other four bishops of the island, in which he strongly urged upon them above all things the religious instruction of the common people, the reform of the clergy, and the strict observance of the Tridentine decrees.[1] He exhorted the Republic of Genoa to assist the Corsican bishops in their laborious task.[2]

Just as Sauli, like the Pope himself, had come from a religious Order, so was it to fall to such bodies in the future to take an immense part in the renewal of ecclesiastical life. Pius V. fully realized the importance of this, and from this conviction sprang his anxiety to give back their full vigour to these valuable instruments of reform.

---

[1] Briefs of May 4, 1569, onwards, in LADERCHI, 1569, n. 81 *seq.* The Bishop of Sagona, Girolamo Leonio, received a special brief praising him for having worked with success for the establishment of peace. The other four briefs are in the same strain. For Blessed Burali and Ribera see *supra* pp. 165, 222.

[2] Brief of May 4, 1569, in LADERCHI, 1569, n. 83.

CHAPTER VI.

The Reform of the Religious Orders.

The Council of Trent also forms a landmark in the history of the religious Orders, which were able to raise themselves from the low state into which they had fallen, on the basis of its decrees. It is true that even in the first half of the XVIth century the monastic Orders still retained their important place in the Church ;[1] they still gave to her a number of good bishops, while they gave the Holy See its nuncios and Cardinals, and the universities their professors of theology ; at the Council of Trent they had been represented by distinguished and influential doctors and bishops. The Dominican Order in particular had distinguished itself in the years immediately preceding the Council by a band of men who were illustrious alike in ecclesiastical learning and administration, and in his many rescripts in favour of his own Order, Pius V. professed himself its grateful son and disciple, and one who owed everything to it.[2] Another proof that not everything in the monasteries was corrupt and spoilt is to be found in the many attempts made to awaken the old ideals to a new life by the formation of reformed congregations ; the whole of the XVth and XVIth centuries are filled with such attempts and foundations.[3]

But it is plain that, although individual members of the

[1] Tacchi Venturi, I., 43 seq.

[2] " Unde, licet imparibus meritis, Nos etiam tamquam ex fonte profluximus." Constitution on St. Thomas Aquinas, §2, Bull. Rom., VII., 564 ; cf. 801, 904.

[3] Tacchi Venturi, I., 45. Pius Schmieder in Studien und Mitteil. aus den Benediktiner-und Zisterzienserorden, XI. (1890), 580 seqq. ; XII. (1891), 54 seq. For the good convents in Germany see Braunsberger, Pius V., 70.

Orders could, if they so wished, keep themselves free from the general decadence, these shining exceptions could not disguise the fact that the decadence existed, and it was these very men who so eminently represented their Orders who made the fact clear.[1] To this matter the Council had set its hand. In its decrees on the reform of the religious, both men and women, it struck a mortal blow at the principal existing abuses, and wherever these decrees took effect and were carried out the Orders took on a new lease of life. In reality, during the century that followed the Council, all the ancient Orders were reformed, while some of them attained to a state of perfection such as had never been seen even in the best period of religious life.

In the case of several of the Orders the difficulties in the way of a renewal were so great as to seem almost insuperable, even with the best will in the world. By order of Pius V. in 1569 the procurator-general of the Cistercian Order, Nicholas Boucherat, and his companion, Dionigi de Laceronis, made a visitation of all their convents in south and central Italy, as well as in Sicily.[2] In the 27 Cistercian houses on the mainland they only found 56 Cistercians, distributed over

---

[1] Testimony of Musso, Seripandò, etc., in TACCHI VENTURI, I., 46 seq.

[2] Cf. A. POSTINA in Zisterzienser-Chronik, XIII. (1901), 193 seqq. Postina (p. 196, n.) attributes the report of the visitation to 1561, but it bears the date 1569, though in another hand ; moreover, the *brief giving faculties for the visitation is dated January 28, 1569 (Nicolao Boucherat, proc. gen. ord. Cist. de Recluso Trecensis dioec., ac Dionysio de Laceronis de Morimondo Mediolanensis dioec. Monasterii dicti ordinis Cist. prioribus commissariis : Archives of Briefs, Rome) ; lastly, in the bull of March 8, 1570, the visitation is spoken of as having taken place recently (recenti visitatione). Nor is any proof to the contrary furnished by the mention, made in the report, of Cardinal Taddeo Gaddi (died 1561), because it does not state that Gaddi was still alive. For the reform of the Cistercians at Florence, cf. GUILLAUME, L'abbaye de Cava, Cava de' Tirreni, 1877, 324. A brief of September 7, 1566, on the reform of the Cistercians in Tuscany in WADDING, XX., 429.

eleven centres, while the remaining abbeys and priories were either completely abandoned, or inhabited by monks of other Orders, and in some cases by a few secular priests in order to provide for the bare necessities of divine worship. The report of the visitation of the famous Abbey of Fossanova, says that the church indeed was very spacious, but was stripped of all adornment, that the ancient stalls of the choir had absolutely disappeared, that the roof of the church was full of holes, so that the rain came in everywhere, and the monks could not remain in choir near the altar. A fourth part of the house of the monks was in ruins, and here too the rain came in everywhere, so that what was left of the house was falling into ruin. The chapter-house was still intact, but the windows had no glass or protection of any kind, so that the cold and wind came in unchecked ; it was the same with the windows of the church, so that in the winter the monks could not sing office there, nor even say mass because of the danger of the wind blowing away the sacred host. The chapel and the room in which St. Thomas Aquinas had died were without a roof, and on the verge of falling down. In the dormitory the rain came in so badly that very often the monks had to leave their cells on account of the water that poured in, and move their beds to some other place. Things were no better in the other monasteries ; of some we are told that no one any longer dwelt within their tottering walls, and where we do hear of monks being in residence it is often added that they lacked the necessary means of support. Conditions were, comparatively speaking, best in the monastery of S. Maria del Sagittario, in the diocese of Anglona. There there were ten monks, says the report, but they had not the means to support and clothe themselves. The monastery was falling down and they had no refectory. The dormitory was still standing, however, and the church was intact and well equipped, but even this was due to the fact that the monks were for the most part carpenters by trade.

The seven Cistercian houses in the island of Sicily were in rather a better state. Some of them were still either completely or partially in a good state of repair, but taken altogether they only contained thirteen monks, and all of them lacked the books and vestments necessary for divine worship.

It is uncertain whether the monasteries in question had come to be held in commendam because they were ruined and deserted, or whether the commendatory abbots were responsible for the ruin, but so long as the revenues of the abbeys passed into alien hands it was impossible in every case to bring about a revival of their religious life ; even zealous and energetic men, who were likely to give them a new impetus, could not but feel but little inclination to enter half ruined monasteries. In these desperate circumstances Pius V. did all that he could. In a bull of reform for the Cistercians,[1] he not only assured them of his own sympathy, declaring that one of the most pressing of all his many pressing anxieties was that so many religious houses had been stripped of their rights and left to fall into ruin, but he also forced the commendatory abbots to leave a sufficient number of religious in the monasteries, to provide them with all that was necessary, and to restore the ruined buildings. He further gave the monks themselves a number of regulations, the observance of which was calculated to produce a revival of religious life. In the circumstances of the times Pius V. did not dare to abolish the system of commendams itself. This had become widespread, especially in France, where no less than 1040 monasteries were held in commendam,[2] but a conference in consistory on this deplorable state of affairs only resulted in everything being left as before.[3]

Pius V. had been asked for help by the Cistercian abbots, but in many cases he took action without waiting to be asked, driven thereto by the burning zeal which he felt for the restoration of the religious Orders. There is nothing in the Church

---

[1] Of March 8, 1570, Bull. Rom., VII., 813 *seqq.* On October 23, 1567, Pius V., had granted a brief of protection against the commendatory abbots ; *ibid.* 622.

[2] THEINER, Acta, II., 679.

[3] " Decretum est, nunc quidem nihil innovare." Consistory of December 11, 1570, in GULIK-EUBEL, II., 47.

of God, he wrote on one occasion,[1] which we consider more glorious and more useful than the flourishing of true discipline among those who, by the inspiration of the Holy Ghost, have dedicated themselves to the monastic life. In the case of those houses which through their own fault persisted in a state of decadence, he showed both his zeal and his ruthlessness, as was the case with the Abbey of Fonte Avellana in the diocese of Gubbio, once famous on account of St. Peter Damian. In the first instance the Pope sought, through the agency of the Archbishop of Ravenna, Cardinal Giulio della Rovere, to bring back the monks, who had fallen into a very bad state, to a better manner of life,[2] but when they rejected his reforms on the pretext that their vows only bound them to the more or less easy life then prevalent, Pius V. suppressed the abbey and gave it to the Camaldolese ; the former monks of Fonte Avellana were obliged either to join the latter or enter some other Order.[3]

The suppression of the Order of the Humiliati caused a greater stir.[4] This Order, which owed its origin to a body of men of noble birth who had been taken to Germany as hostages, and had there devoted themselves to a zealous religious life, had adopted as their form of manual labour the manufacture of cloth, and had in this way attained to a wealth which brought about their ruin. About the middle of the XVIth

[1] Bull of April 23, 1568 (for the Knights of the Cross), Bull. Rom., VII., 666.

[2] *Brief· to the Cardinal, March 26, 1568, Archives of Briefs, Rome.

[3] Bull of December 10, 1569, in LADERCHI, 1569, n. 52, and in Bull. Rom., VII., 788. *Cf.* ALB. GIBELLI, Monografia dell'antico monastero di S. Croce in Fonte Avellana, Faenza, 1896 ; MITTARELLI, Ann. Camaldul., VIII., Venice, 1764, 130 *seqq.*

[4] SALA, Documenti, I., 195 *seqq.*, 215 *seqq.*, 220 *seq.*, 237 *seqq.*, 248 *seqq.*, 254 *seqq.;* III., 339, 383 *seqq.* BASCAPÈ, 1, 2, c. 4 and 10, p. 34 *seqq.*, 44 *seqq.* SYLVAIN, II., 17 *seqq.* *De reformatione Humiliatorum in Cod. Ottob. 2519 (varia diversorum, t. XII. cardinalis Ludovisii) p. 146-156 ; *ibid.*, p. 152-154, sopra le cose de Frati Humiliati a Ms. Ormaneto, Vatican Library.

century it comprised less than 200 members,[1] who, living in magnificent palaces, and surrounded by servants, squandered the great possessions of the Order in banquets and worldly pleasures.[2] It needed some courage to interfere for their reform, because the nobles of Lombardy looked upon the rich houses of the Humiliati as places of retirement for the members of their families, and because the Order had at its command the influence of powerful friends and relatives.[4] Cardinal Borromeo, however, who had been Protector of the Humiliati since 1560,[4] possessed this courage.   He had already, in the time of Pius IV., made some attempts to reform them through the agency of Ormaneto, but in vain.   After the death of his uncle he went into the matter with Ormaneto and with the Pope himself, and asked for a brief ordering all the superiors to resign their office, limiting their term of office to a short period, placing in other hands the administration of the property, and obliging all the members to a true monastic and common life.[5]   Armed with this brief, in June, 1567, Borromeo took the Humiliati by surprise at their chapter at

[1] According to BASCAPÈ, 1, 2, c. 13, p. 54, in the 94 provostships, of which many were vacant, there were 174 monks, with revenues of 25,000 ducats ;   another 30,000 ducats of revenue were given in commendam.   In Milan alone the Humiliati possessed eight churches.   The bull of February 8, 1571, mentions only 84 priests and 17 lay brothers (Bull. Rom., VII., 891).   According to Tiraboschi (Vetera Humil. monumenta, I, Milan 1766, diis. VIII) the order in the middle of the XVIth century had 162 members, including the novices and lay brothers, 97 houses, of which 39 were commendams and 58 provostships, and 60,000 gold florins.   SALA, Dissertazioni e note (for the biography of Borromeo), 413, n. 3.

[2] Thus the bull of reform of May 1, 1567, in LADERCHI, 1567, n. 74.

[3] BASCAPÈ, 1, 2, c. 4, p. 35.

[4] SALA, Docum, I., 414.

[5] Brief of May 1, 1567, in LADERCHI, 1567, n. 74.   SALA, Docum. I., 195 *seqq*.   *Cf.* BASCAPÈ, *loc. cit.*   A *brief " Duci et dominio Venetiarum " of June 20, 1567, invites him to assist the Cardinal in the reform of the Humiliati.   State Archives, Venice, *Bolle.*

Cremona ; they had had no suspicion of what was impending when he declared the recently held election of a new General invalid, and in virtue of his plenary powers from the Pope[1] conferred that office on a more worthy man, who, under the influence of the Barnabites, had adopted a stricter manner of life.[2]

Borromeo had been quite prepared to have to secure the acceptance of the brief by force, but the Humiliati did not venture on armed resistance until it came to a question of imposing new superiors.[3] They maintained that the brief had been obtained by means of misrepresentations, and was therefore invalid ; they appealed to the Pope, and at the same time sought to secure the protection of the secular princes. These steps having proved unavailing,[4] and as Borromeo continued his efforts to impose the reform,[5] the exasperation of many of the members of the Order grew beyond all bounds. On the evening of October 26th, 1569, the Cardinal was taking part in some devotions in the little chapel of his palace when a shot was fired at him from a distance of some four or five paces. The ball struck him on the spine, but only penetrated his dress, and was afterwards found on the ground ; some small shot pierced his dress and reached the wall without doing any damage. In the midst of the general confusion Borromeo remained quite unmoved, and ordered that the function should be quietly proceeded with, a thing which facilitated the escape of the assassin.[6]

---

[1] Of May 10, 1567, in SALA, Docum., I., 201.

[2] For the latter see BASCAPÈ, 1, 2, c. 4, p. 36.

[3] *Cf.* the five letters of Borromeo of June 26, 1567, in SALA, Docum., III., 383 *seq*.

[4] Brief of June 28, 1567, *ibid.* I., 205.

[5] *Brief to Borromeo of September 10, 1568, with faculties for the reform (it includes the notice : '' S.D.N. mandavit fieri reformationem etiam per viros alterius ordinis a cardinali deputandos). Archives of Briefs, Rome. *Cf.* the *brief of May 22, 1567, to the General of the Humiliati, *ibid.*; BASCAPÈ, 1, 2, c. 10, p. 44 ; bull of July 23, 1568, Bull. Rom., VII., 695.

[6] Letter from Borromeo to Pius V., October 29, 1569, in *San Carlo Borromeo*, 366 (in GIUSSANO, 176 the letter has been altered

Soon afterwards the responsibility for this crime began to be attributed to the Humiliati. Before long Borromeo learned further particulars when a provost of the Humiliati, named Bartolomeo, struck with remorse, secretly informed the Cardinal that he had actually heard some of the Humiliati planning his assassination. If the matter had been dealt with in accordance with Borromeo's wishes, a judicial inquiry would have been held, but Pius V. was determined upon the punishment of the assassins. The bishop who was sent to try the case declared that all who did not inform him of what they knew about the matter were excommunicated. At this point Borromeo thought it a matter of conscience to urge Bartolomeo to comply with this demand. With the help of several confessions made before the Papal commissary, the full truth was at length discovered, namely that the affair had been carried out by one of the Humiliati, and had been planned by three dignitaries of the order, the provosts of Vercelli, Caravaggio and Verona.[1]

Pius V., who had previously had thoughts of abolishing the Order, now determined to expiate the crime by the suppression of the whole institute. At a consistory which he held on the subject on February 7th, 1570, none of the Cardinals spoke openly in favour of its continuance, and Pius V. declared that, with the exception of the General, he did not know of a single worthy man in the whole order.[2] A bull of February 7th, 1571, suppressed the Order,[3] and another of the following day

in style). Contemporary report in SALA, Docum., III., 418. *Cf.* BASCAPÈ, 1, 2, c. 12, p. 50 ; L. ANFOSSO, Storia dell' archibugiata tirata al card. Borromeo in Milano, 1569, Milan, 1913.

[1] BASCAPÈ, *loc. cit.*, p. 50 *seq.* A *brief of July 15, 1570, on the attempt in the Archives of Briefs, Rome.

[2] SANTORI, Diaro, 320 *seq.* For the steps taken by the General an behalf of his Order *Avvisi di Roma of September 23 and 27, 1570, Urb. 1041, p. 343, 348, Vatican Library. There was also on idea of incorporating the Humiliati with the Barnabites and thus helping their reform. *Cf.* SALA, Docum., I., 263 *seq.;* S. Alessandro Sauli, 104 *seqq.*

[3] Bull. Rom., VII., 885. On March 6 the bull was publicly posted : see *Avviso di Roma of March 7, 1571, Urb. 1042, p. 28, Vatican Library.

made over its possessions to various ecclesiastical purposes.[1]
The female branch of the Order, however, was allowed to
continue.[2]

In the case of some of the Orders, in order to simplify their
government, and thus conduce to their reform, Pius V.
reunited the various branches to their parent stock. For
example, with the original intention of reintroducing a stricter
monastic life, a special congregation of Servites had been
formed alongside the original Servite order, and in the same
way the Amadei, and to some extent the Clareni,[3] had sprung
up within the Franciscan Order, but with the lapse of time
decadence had crept into even these congregations, and Pius
V. therefore, in these two cases, did away with their separation
from the main Order.[4] Borromeo in particular worked for
the reform of these Franciscan congregations, though it was
only after a long time, and after having to overcome an

[1] Bull. Rom., VII., 888 ; cf. SALA, Docum., III., 248. Sums
were also distributed among the Cardinals : see *Avviso di Roma
of February 14, 1571, Urb. 1042, p. 22, Vatican Library. A
letter of August 5, 1573, on the punishment of the guilty Humiliati
in Arch. stor. Lomb., 1908, 187 seq. The brief of March 13, 1570,
which asks the Duke of Savoy to hand over the aggressor, in
LADERCHI, 1570, n. 156. For the use made of the Humiliati
houses of Lugano and Locarno cf. REINHARDT-STEFFENS, Doku-
mente, 21

[2] A *brief of July 6, 1571, to the Bishop of Verona approves his
plan of adding to the nuns of S. Cristoforo at Verona four experienced nuns, who would be able by their example to lead the
others to a better manner of life. The bishop received the
power to change at will the habit and office of the Humiliati
nuns. Brevia, Arm. 44, t. 16, p. 189 seq., Papal Secret
Archives.

[3] The Clareni began in 1294 ; the founder of the Amadeisti died
in 1482.

[4] Bull concerning the Servites, May 5, 1570, Bull. Rom., VII.,
817 ; on the Amadeisti, etc., January 23, 1568, ibid. 651. SALA,
Docum., I., 190 ; cf. HOLZAPFEL, 138 ; WADDING, XX., 445, 447,
461, 476.

obstinate resistance, that he succeeded in reuniting them with the Observants.[1]

Immediately after his election Pius V. displayed special anxiety in the case of the Spanish Orders. This was the result of representations laid before him by Philip II. Even before the Council of Trent had issued its decrees on religious communities, the Spanish king had had their reform under consideration. His particular object was to make the Orders in his kingdom independent of superiors residing abroad. The reasons which prompted this desire had their root in a genuine zeal for religion. In the case of the Order of Calatrava, for example, the superior was appointed by the Cistercian abbot of Morimond, and his choice almost always fell upon a Frenchman, who did not know Spanish, did not understand the conditions of his subjects, and who therefore could not remove the evils which had crept in. The French monasteries, moreover, were decadent in various ways, and in some cases were even infected with the ideas of the new religion, to such an extent that Philip very reasonably could not look for any good results from this close union with France. It must be admitted, however, that considerations of quite another kind also influenced the king. Some of the monasteries in Navarre and Aragon had to make contributions to the mother houses in France, which gave the French king an excuse for interference in Spanish affairs.[2]

In 1560 the king obtained from Pius IV. for the Order of Calatrava its independence from Morimond. He had similar plans for the Cistercians in Navarre and Aragon, and later, in 1564, for the Trinitarians, and in the same year for the Carmelites, who were all to be only nominally dependent upon their Generals in Italy. It was also the king's wish that the Grand Master of the Mercedarii should always be a Spaniard, though he was never to hold his office for life. When in 1563

---

[1] LADERCHI, 1568 n. 34. BASCAPÈ, 1, 2, c. 5, p. 36. Ioanni de Stronconio O. Min. on the reform of the Clareni, August 1, 1567, in WADDING, XX., 445.

[2] SERRANO in Corresp. dipl., IV., xxix.

the Cortes suggested a reform of the Order, Philip conceived
a far-reaching plan. His ambassador in Rome, Requesens,
was instructed to ask that the king might appoint visitors ;
until they had completed their work, and new rules had been
published for the Order, no more novices were to be accepted,
and after the visitation new superiors were to be appointed ;
it was also provided, as part of the proposed reform, which
was to be carried out under the supervision of the archbishops,
that all the small houses were to be suppressed, and the
superiors were only to remain in office for three years.[1]

All these proposals were shipwrecked, partly on account
of the protests of the French king, and partly because of the
opposition of the superiors of the Orders. When he went as
legate to Spain in 1565,[2] Cardinal Boncompagni took with him
briefs for the reform of the Trinitarians, Franciscans, Carmelites, Augustinians and Isidorians, but he made no use of
his powers because, at the death of Pius IV., which occurred
soon afterwards, he returned hurriedly to Italy.[3]

Better days for the reform of the Spanish Orders came with
the accession to the throne of Pius V. Even in the first days
of his reign the new Pope said to the Spanish ambassador that
in this matter he would grant the king more than he had asked
for ; let them send him from Madrid their proposals as to how
the necessary faculties should be drawn up, but let them at
the same time keep the matter secret, because in such cases
passions were likely to be sharply divided, and the Orders had
their agents everywhere.[4] In spite of this, however, the sending of the necessary briefs was delayed for a time. In Rome
they were convinced that the reform could never be carried
into effect without the co-operation of the civil power, but
at the same time it seemed dangerous to give such wide powers
over ecclesiastical affairs to the king and his nominees. Pius
V., moreover, did not wish to place the reform of the Orders

[1] *Ibid.* xxx *seq.* For Calatrava *cf. ibid.* I., 306.
[2] See Vol. XVI. of this work, p. 334.
[3] Corresp. dipl., IV., xxxiii ; *cf.* I., 9.
[4] Requesens to Philip II., January 25, 1566, *ibid.* I., 112.

in the hands of bishops who were not themselves religious, and had no experience of monastic affairs.[1]   For all these reasons the briefs had to be written and rewritten several times before they were thought to comply with all the existing requirements.[2]

The reforming zeal of the Pope specially had in view the Spanish Conventual Franciscans, who had a bad name with him ; the same thing applied to those other religious bodies which, following the example of the Franciscans, had divided into two branches, one more strict, and known as the Observants, and the other more mitigated, and called Conventuals. Pius V. now sought to counteract that tendency to decadence which followed upon the extension among the Spanish convents of the less strict branch, by putting an end altogether to this division in the Orders, and making them all Observants. The bull which was issued for this purpose on December 2nd, 1566,[3] complains in its preamble of the bad state of so many Orders which for a long time past had been drifting away from their original rule, and especially of the scandalous life of the Franciscan Conventuals, with regard to whom King Philip had asked for the intervention of the Pope.[4]   The Pope therefore ordains that the bishops, together with the Provincial of the Observants, and another religious of the stricter manner of life, shall introduce the reform into all their convents. Those who had hitherto been Conventuals must make over their houses to the Observants, and suffer themselves to be

[1] Requesens 13 (18 ?) September, 1566, *ibid.* 339.

[2] Requesens, December 8, 1566, *ibid.* 409.

[3] Bull. Rom., VII., 494.

[4] *Cf.* *Fragmento d' una lettera del Re di Espagna [d. d. 15 Nov. 1563] con un Memoriale circa gl' abusi de Regolari : Cod. Ottob. 2519 (Varia diversorum t. XII cardinalis Ludovisii) p. 200-209. The Memoriale *ibid.* 202b-204. *Ibid.* 204-205 : De reformatione regularium et conventualium (" Rex catholicus petit revocari omnia privilegia " etc.) ; p. 205-209 : Memoriale d' alcuni capi occurrenti sopra la reformatione di Espagna (" Che si representa a S. Sᵗᵃ la necessità che è di riformare nelli regni di Castiglia, Aragon, Valencia "). Vatican Library.

scattered among the various convents. For the future no
one was to be superior of a convent unless he belonged to the
stricter branch. What was thus ordered in the case of the
Franciscans was to apply equally to all the other Spanish
Orders which were divided into Conventuals and Observants,
such as the Canons Regular, the Benedictines, the Cistercians,
the Dominicans, the Augustinian Hermits, and the Carmelites.
Where more grave defects had occurred severe penalties
must be inflicted, and, in case of need, even condemnation
to the galleys and imprisonment for life. The convents
of nuns, which had hitherto been under the direction
of the Conventuals, must also be reformed by the bishop
and his colleagues, and placed under the care of the
Observants.[1]

Naturally the bishops were unable to visit all the houses of
their dioceses at the same time, and it was therefore possible
for the religious who were unwilling to change their manner
of life, to fly to another house of their Order before the arrival
of the commissioners and thus perpetually escape the notice
of the bishop. Several of the Conventual houses, moreover,
were not conveniently situated for the purposes of the
Observants, and could only with great difficulty be taken
over by them. As the result, therefore, of some representations made to him by the king, the Pope declared[2] that the
visitation could also be carried out by other persons commissioned for this purpose by the bishops and the provincial
superiors, and that the bishops and provincials might decide

[1] Edict of December 12, 1566. Bull. Rom., VII., 496 ; cf.
WADDING, XX., 435.

[2] April 16, 1567, *ibid.* 565 *seqq.* A *bull for the reform of the
Spanish nuns, July 15, 1567, in the Archives of Briefs, Roma ;
cf. LADERCHI, 1568, n. 38. In the Archives of Briefs, Rome, there
is another *bull of November 9, 1568, on the extension of the
reform of the convents of the Franciscans and Poor Clares to the
kingdoms of the crown of Aragon. A *brief of January 7, 1571,
to the Bishop of Urgel, who is unwilling to assist the provincial
in the reform of the recalcitrant nuns, in Brevia, Arm. 44, t. 15,
p. 286. Papal Secret Archives.

what was to be done with monastic houses which were not suitably situated for the Observants.[1]

In the same brief the Pope also made provision for those Orders which had no houses of the stricter observance, and which could not therefore be reformed by removing their members to such houses. Pius V. placed these under the care of other religious of a similar manner of life, as for example the Franciscan Conventuals of the Third Order under the Observants of the Premonstratensians, and the Hermits of St. Jerome under the Observants of the Order founded by the same saint.[2] The Carmelites, Trinitarians and Mercedarii were to be led to a better manner of life by the bishops, with the assistance of two Dominicans.[3]

The Franciscan Conventuals willingly submitted to the reform, and as early as November 5th, 1567, the Pope was able to express his satisfaction at what had been accomplished.[4] The attempt to subject the Spanish branch of the Premonstratensians to a reorganization met with greater difficulties. The Hieronymites were appointed as their visitors. Philip II. would have liked them to adopt the rules and habit of the visitors, and thus end their days in the Order which he himself favoured ;[5] a pontifical ordinance to this effect had already been issued,[6] but now, in response to the protests of the

[1] Edict of April 16, 1567, §3, 5, *loc. cit.*, 568 *seq.*

[2] *Ibid.* §6-7, *ibid.* 569. *Cf.* Requesens to Philip II., March 16, 1567, Corresp. dipl., II., 72. Castagna had called attention to the conditions existing among the Spanish Premonstratensians, in the Third Order, and in a branch of the Hieronymites : to Bonelli, January 2, 1567, *ibid.* 1 *seq.*

[3] Edict of April 16, 1567, §8, *loc. cit.*, 570.

[4] Corresp. dipl., IV., xxxiv, n.

[5] *Ibid.* xxxviii. As a reason for the suppression Philip II. brings out the fact that in the greater part of the 18 Spanish houses of the Premonstratensians there were not more than from four to eight religious, who were ignorant and not very edifying. Letter to Zuñiga of May 14, 1568, *Coleccion de docum. inéd.*, VII., 531.

[6] Corresp. dipl., IV., xxxix : " Mandamus, quod dicti fratres Praemonstratenses ad observantiam fratrum s. Hieronymi de observantia Hispaniarum cum effectu reducantur."

Premonstratensians, Pius V. revoked his brief and turned in great displeasure on the Hieronymites because, it would seem, they had begun to carry out the brief too literally,[1] but though he no longer contemplated the total suppression of the Order, the Pope did not cease to insist upon the reform, and fresh briefs, drawn up by Ormaneto,[2] were dispatched, which were very strict, and aimed at the removal of the existing disorders. The nuncio was ordered to examine the acts of the visitations and to proceed against the more serious abuses with the greatest severity. A reform bull from the Pope then sought to secure a better state of affairs for the future.[3]

The reform of the Franciscan convents of the Third Order met with similar difficulties. These were true religious, because the inmates of these houses for the most part took true vows, but their manner of life was so far from edifying that the Pope thought of suppressing them. At first, as the result of insufficient information, Pius V. had looked upon them as people living in the world, and had arranged for the total destruction of their communities. On the representation of the Provincial, Gordillo, he withdrew this ordinance and substituted for it an exhortation to embrace the rule of the Franciscan Observants, placing at the disposal of those who did not wish to do so certain convents where they could end their days, but without the right of taking novices. This arrangement of the Pope's did not please Philip II., and he endeavoured to postpone its execution in the hope that he

[1] To Castagna, March 18, 1568, Bull. Rom., VII., 661 seq. Philip II. said that the acts of violence of the Hieronymites against the Premonstratensians referred to in §2 of this brief were an invention. To Zuñiga May 14, 1568 : Bull. Rom., VII., 530 ; cf. Corresp. dipl., II., 270, 382, 416, 450.

[2] From December 8, 1569, to January 4, 1570, Corresp. dipl., III., 234 n.

[3] Cf. Corresp. dipl., IV., xxxviii-xli. For the reform of the other Orders cf. *brief of July 13, 1568, on the Augustinians in Aragon, of November 3, 1569, to the Bishops of Valencia and Segovia on the convent of nuns of Las Huelgas in the diocese of Burgos, etc. Archives of Briefs, Rome.

might eventually succeed in winning over the Pope to the total suppression of the *Tercerones*, but Pius V. would not give way, and at last, after many negotiations, the affair was settled in accordance with his plan.[1]

Although he had himself asked for the Pope's intervention in the case of the Spanish Orders, Philip II. was far from satisfied with all the Papal provisions. Thus, in a letter to Zuñiga, his ambassador in Rome, he bitterly complained that the Pope had given neither him nor the ambassador any previous notice of the briefs concerning the Premonstratensians.[2] nor did he approve of the Carmelites, Trinitarians and Mercedarri being brought back to better ways by the Dominicans. Pius V., however, adhered to his arrangement on the ground that the bishops already had enough to do in the administration of their dioceses, and that, moreover, they knew nothing of the religious life or rule.[3] When, too, the king reverted to his former wish that the Spanish Cistercians should be separated from the main body of the Order and formed into a special congregation, the Pope would not agree to this.[4] In other matters as well there was good reason for complaint in Rome as to the excessive and usurping interference of Philip in the affairs of the Orders ; he had, for example, sent a layman to preside at the provincial chapter of the Mercedarii, a proceeding which Pius V. was not slow to censure.[5]

The arrangements which Pius V. had made for the Third Order and the Conventuals in Spain soon came into force for the Low Countries as well.[6] In Portugal, too, at the request

[1] Corresp. dipl., IV., xli-xlv ; *cf.* WADDING, XX., 459, 467, 469.

[2] Letter to Zuñiga from Cordova, March 30, 1570, *ibid.* III., 283.

[3] Bonelli to Castagna, December 16, 1569, *ibid.* 201 ; *cf.* 262, 323.

[4] Bonelli to Castagna, April 29, 1570, *ibid.* 263. Attempts had already been made in the time of Pius IV. to separate the Spanish Cistercians from Morimond ; *ibid.* I., 305.

[5] Bonelli to Castagna, September 6, 1569, *ibid.* III., 138.

[6] The Bull. Rom., VII., 624, n. mentions the brief of November 2, 1567 (Angelo Aversano). A *brief on the reform of the Observants (to the same) of October 23, 1567, in Archives of Briefs, Rome.

of King Sebastian, the same prescriptions were made binding in 1567.[1]   In the preceding year a request had been addressed to the Pope in the name of the king that he would unite all the Benedictine houses in Portugal after the manner of the Castilian and Cassinese congregations.   Archbishop Bartolomeo a Martyribus, the Bishop of Oporto, and two Benedictines of the congregation of Valladolid, had introduced this reform, which Pius V. confirmed on April 30th, 1566.[2]   He also united the Cistercians in Portugal to the congregation of Alcobaça in 1567.[3]   Immediately after this an exhortation was sent to Cardinal Henry to bring back the monks and nuns of the order of Vallombrosa to a true religious life.[4]

The care which Pius V. had shown for the Franciscan Conventuals in the Iberian peninsula was soon afterwards extended to the whole Conventual Order.   At the beginning of June, 1568, he released them from the direction of the nuns of their Order,[5] and set himself to revive the full severity of the Franciscan ideal of poverty by forbidding them once more the possession of private property.[6]   This ordinance on poverty found a ready welcome among the Conventuals, and the Order of its own accord began to set about the work of reform.   A

---

[1] Brief of October 30, 1567, Bull. Rom., VII., 624 ; *brief on the reform of convents, May 28, 1568, to Gasparo, Bishop of Leiria in the Archives of Briefs, Rome.   *Brief of December 13, 1569, regretting that the king has entrusted the visitation of a convent to a young cleric, in Brevia, Arm. 44, t. 14, p. 301, Papal Secret Archives.   The reform had already been begun under Pius IV. : *letter from King Sebastian of Portugal to Cardinal Ricci of February 20, 1565, Ricci Archives, Rome.

[2] The brief was repeated in an edict of Gregory XIII., Bull. Rom., VIII., 3.   Cf. Corpo dipl. Portug., X. (1891), 208 seq.; SCHMIEDER in Studien und Mitteil. aus dem Benediktiner-und Zisterzienserorden, XII. (1891), 73.

[3] SCHMIEDER, loc. cit.

[4] *Brief of July 4, 1568, Archives of Briefs, Rome.

[5] June 3, 1568, Bull. Rom., VII., 674.   The reform had already begun under Pius IV. ; cf. HOLZAPFEL, 589, and supra p. 251.

[6] June 8, 1568. Bull. Rom., VII., 676 ; WADDING, XX., 474, 481.

general reform was inaugurated at the general chapter of 1568, and this was, in accordance with the wishes of the Pope, made more strict and comprehensive by the General and Provincials, and then confirmed by a bull.[1] The Pope charged the Protector of the Order, Cardinal Borromeo,[2] with its execution, and the latter took great pains with the introduction of community life among the Conventuals of his diocese.[3] In Borromeo's name, and through the agency of the visitors and the commissary-general, Girolamo Curti, of Milan, the new constitution was also accepted in Germany by the chapter of the Order at Ueberlingen in 1572. The zealous Provincial of the Franciscan Conventuals in Upper Germany, Jodocus Schlüssler, had already, previously to this, been appointed apostolic visitor by Papal brief ; in 1571 a chapter, also held at Ueberlingen, had introduced several useful reforms, especially one which provided that in future no one should have the office of superior conferred upon him by the civil power.[4]

The Congregation of the Third Order of St. Francis was also committed to the care of Borromeo. Before this, Cardinal Carpi had already worked on behalf of the Order, and on April 28th, 1569, he had issued some ordinances for its use, which aimed at the revival of its religious life, which had fallen into a lax state.[5] The success which these provisions

[1] July 23, 1568, *ibid.* 691 *seqq.*

[2] *Ibid.* §3.

[3] BASCAPÈ, I, 2, c. 5, p. 36.

[4] K. EUBEL, Gesch. der oberdeutschen (Strassburger) Minoritenprovinz, Würzburg, 1886, 118. For the part played by the future Sixtus V. in the reform of his Order *cf.* TEMPESTI, I., 70 *seqq.* and Corresp. dipl., I., 113. *Brief to the senators of Savoy and the Bishop of Geneva, January 7, 1570, on the reform of the Franciscans at Chambéry and of the Augustinians of the convent of S. Pietro de Albignaco, in Brevia, Arm. 44, t. 14, p. 327b, Papal Secret Archives.

[5] Bull of July 3, 1568, Bull. Rom., VII., 679. On November 15, 1567, a *brief was sent to the Observant, Angelo da Stronconio, on the reform of the Brothers and Sisters of the Third Order in Italy. Archives of Briefs, Rome.

met with, however, was but small. Pius V. himself then
intervened with so much severity that it was said in Spain
that he wished to make an end of the Third Order. This
report was declared to be false in a special letter from the Pope,[1]
but the prescriptions of the Papal bull, later on mitigated by
Sixtus V., were certainly very drastic. The government of
the congregation was regulated, private property was prohibited, enclosure was enforced, and obedience to the ordinances of Carpi was prescribed.[2]

Similar exhortations and ordinances were sent under Pius V.
to a number of religious communities. Such were the Knights
of the Cross, who had fallen into a bad state on account of
the system of commendams,[3] and the Canons Regular of San
Salvatore, to whom a new General, visitor and procurator-
general were given.[4] Two Dominicans were sent to the
Camaldolese to satisfy themselves as to the conditions prevailing in the order, and to take what steps were necessary ;[5]
new statutes, which paid special attention to the matter of
studies, received the Papal approval in 1571.[6] Pius recommended the monks of Vallombrosa to the care of Cardinals
Ricci and Bobba.[7] Even the Cassinese congregation of the

[1] To Castagna, July 15, 1568, in LADERCHI, 1568, n. 36.

[2] Bull of July 3, 1568, *loc. cit.*

[3] April 23, 1568, Bull. Rom., VII., 666.

[4] Edict of December 7, 1571, *ibid.* 953. Bull. Congr. S. Salvatoris, I., 139 *seq.*

[5] *Briefs " Archangelo de Tonsis de Soncino O. Praed." of
March 8, 1568, and " Eliseo Veneto Ord. Praed." of May 3 1568,
the latter on reform in the Veneto (Archives of Briefs, Rome).
Mittarelli, Ann. Camald., VIII., 128.

[6] MITTARELLI, *loc. cit.*, 134 *seq.* SCHMIEDER in *Studien und
Mitteil. aus dem Benediktiner- und Zisterzienserorden*, XII., 69.
The Pope ordered them to resume the monastic habit ; hitherto
they had worn the dress of secular priests (*Avviso di Roma of
June 18, 1569, Urb. 1041, p. 96 Vatican Library). Suppression
of the Camaldolese Conventuals, May 26, 1569 : MITTARELLI, *loc.
cit.* 135.

[7] *To Cardinal Ricci, April 10, 1568, to Cardinal Bobba for the
reform of the convent of Pinerolo, June 30, 1568, Archives of

Benedictines, which on the whole was able to point to many
worthy members,[1] received an exhortation to restore their
former purity of observance, since, through the neglect of
superiors, the Order had fallen away from its former eminence.[2]
The Pope addressed a similar reproof to the General of the
Carthusians, saying that he had learned with great sorrow
that even there there was reason to fear the loss of discipline,
unless attention was paid at once to repairing the damage
done, and that holy men must be placed at the head of their
houses, whose whole care must be devoted to the maintenance
rather than the weakening of discipline.[3] Pius V. was
specially dissatisfied with the Carthusians in Spain.[4]

Several apostolic letters were sent to Portugal complaining
of the state of affairs in the military Orders there. The
struggle with the Moors, on account of which these bodies
had been founded and endowed with property and ecclesiastical
privileges, had lost its importance as far as Europe was concerned, but Pius V. could not understand how the heirs of
those heroes of the Moorish wars could live in ease on their

Briefs, Rome. *Brief of March 10, 1570, " Nicolao praesidenti
generali congregationis Vallumbrosae," with powers to carry out
a reform, *ibid.*

[1] SCHMIEDER, *loc. cit.* 69.

[2] *Brief of April 7, 1571, " Capitulo generali Congregationis
S. Iustinae de Padua O.S.B." in Brevia, Arm. 44, t. 16, p. 23.
*" Memoriale ad Pium V. pro reformatione congregationis Casin-
ensis " in Archives of S. Angelo, Arm. 12, caps, 4, n. 10, Papal
Secret Archives. A brief with faculties to absolve, June 13, 1571,
in Bull. Rom., VII., 919.

[3] *Brief of March 19, 1571, Brevia, Arm. 44, t. 16, p. 40, Papal
Secret Archives.

[4] LADERCHI 1568, n. 28. *Brief of June 11, 1571, to Basilio
d'Urbino, on the reform of the Certosa of Pisa, Archives of Briefs,
Rome. *Brief to the King of Poland, July 5, 1568, against his interference in the administration of the Certosa "Paradisus Mariae,"
in Brevia, Arm. 44, t. 13, p. 225, Papal Secret Archives. For the
reform of the Augustinians see *Avvisi di Roma of September 27,
1570, and April 14, 1571, Urb. 1041, p. 343 ; 1042, p. 47b, Vatican
Library.

rich benefices and in the enjoyment of their ecclesiastical privileges, without ever drawing a sword. If they could no longer win laurels on Portuguese soil, let the Knights go to Africa and there measure themselves against the infidel in warfare in defence of the Christian faith. It would seem that his first exhortation to this effect, addressed to the Order of Christ,[1] did not fall on deaf ears.[2] When similar appeals to the Orders of S. Giacomo della Spada and di Avis[3] had no effect, Pius V. withdrew from them their ecclesiastical privileges,[4] and ordered that no one be allowed to put on the habit of the Knights of these Orders unless they had served for three years in the wars in Africa, and that the offices which had a revenue of more than 100,000 reals should not be conferred on account of seniority, but solely for merit. A seminary must also be established for the training of the young Knights in Africa.

Pius V.'s anxiety for the revival of the religious life was by no means exhausted with the ordinances already mentioned. On July 3rd, 1568, he wrote[5] that in virtue of his office it was his duty to exact from the religious Orders, even more than from any other part of the Church, that they should keep themselves in a high state of efficiency, or return to it, and to this end, especially in the years 1567 and 1568, he issued a number of ordinances aimed at removing abuses in the Orders.[6]

---

[1] Of May   29, 1566, Corpo dipl. Portug., X., 214.

[2] In a brief of June 28, 1569, it is held up as an example to the other military Orders. LADERCHI, 1569, n. 330.

[3] Of June 28, 1569, which mentions another of September 13, 1568 ; *ibid.*

[4] August 28, 1570, in LADERCHI, 1570, n. 135.   *Cf.* Corpo dipl. Portug., X., 355. For the reform of the Order of St. Lazarus *cf.* bull of January 26, 1567, Bull. Rom., VII., 516-533 ; LADERCHI, 1567, n. 26.

[5] Bull. Rom., VII., 679.

[6] Many such letters e.g. in WADDING, XX. (= W.) and specially in the Archives of Briefs, Rome. Thus, in addition to those already quoted or to be quoted later on, we find :—

For 1567 : *January 15, to the Capuchin nuns at Naples concerning the wise administration of their convent ; *January

The ambassador of the Duke of Modena had just arrived when, on February 20th, 1566, the Pope again wrote that in matters

24, to the Cardinal of Lorraine : faculties to reform the nuns in the dioceses of Metz and Verdun ; *February 15, to Cardinal Giulio della Rovere for the reform of the Poor Clares at Ravenna ; *March 7, to Carafa, Archbishop of Naples : " there must not be a greater number of nuns in a convent than the revenues can support " ; *March 11, bull concerning the direction of the convents of women at Milan ; *March 13, to Cardinal Savelli, Archbishop of Benevento, on the visitation of convents ; *April 12, to the Bishop of Tournai on the reform of the Benedictines ; May 10, to the Minister-General of the Observants concerning the reform at Ragusa (W. 443) ; May 22, to the Bishop of Assisi : " youths under 16 not to be allowed in the convents " (W. 444) ; *May 28, to Cesare Gambara, Bishop of Tortona ; *June 11, to Cardinal Bobba, on the Augustinian nuns of the convent of S. Caterina at Aosta in the province of Tarantaise ; *July 2, to the Bishop of Mileto on a convent at Squillace ; *July 8, to the Bishop of Tournai ; August 1, to the Observant, Paolo Ariguccio, Provincial of Tuscany (W. 447) ; *August 6, to the Bishop of Montefeltro : " he must make a visitation of the abbey Castri Durantis."

For 1568 : *January 19, to Federico [Cornaro], Bishop of Bergamo : reform of nuns ; *January 28, on the enclosure of the Carthusians in France ; February 2, to Cardinal Giulio della Rovere on reform at Ravenna (W. 464) ; *April 8, to Cardinal Morone on the Hieronimites of the rule of St. Augustine ; *May 28, to the convent of St. Ursula at Louvain : " let them keep the enclosure " ; July 14, reform of the convent of Cuneo, in the diocese of Mondovì (W. 474) ; *July 17, to the General of the Franciscans : " they are to send some monks from Lombardy to reform the Poor Clares of Naples " ; *July 21, to the Dominican, Dom. della Rovere (Astensis dioecesis) : reform of nuns ; *July 27, to the Bishop of Sulmona ; *August 10, to the Cassinese abbot on the nuns at Capua ; *August 11, to Bonelli (Autograph of the Pope) ; *September 1, to the nuncio, Vincenzo Portico : reform of the convents in Poland ; *September 10, to Giov. Franc. Bonhomini, a cleric of Verona : faculty for the visitation of his monastery at Nonantola ; *October 1, to Cardinal Borromeo ; *October 15, to the Cardinal of Aragon on the visitation of the

of religion, and in all that concerned friars and priests, there

convents in his diocese of Mileto ;   *December 7. to Federico,
Bishop of Bergamo : he is to make a visitation of churches and
monasteries.

For 1569 : *June 10, to the Bishop of Fiesole ; *June 18, bull
for the reform of the convent of the Observants, S. Montani at
Gaeta.

For 1570 : April 4, to Stefano Molina, Franciscan Observant,
on the reform of the Poor Clares at Naples (W. 495) ; *April 12,
to Tommaso (Orfino), Bishop of Foligno, on the reform of the
Benedictines ; *July 14, to Cardinal Borromeo ; *July 15, to the
Archbishop of Prague ; *December 4, " Ruffino Campaniae
archipresbytero ecclesiae Veronensis, commissario nostro," on a
scandal in the convent of nuns, of the Carmenino at Mantua ;
*December 8, to Stefano Molina : " he is to transfer 4 nuns from
Aquila to the convent of the Augustinian nuns of S. Maddalena
at Naples, in order to reform it " ; *December 15, " episcopo
Mazariensi " on the nuns of Trapani.

For 1571 : *January 25, Bonifacio [de Stephanis], episcopo
Stagnensi on the Observants in Bosnia ; *February 8 and March
10, to Niccolò [Ormaneto], Bishop of Padua ; *February 13, to
[Boldrino Gregorio], Bishop of Mantua, on the enclosure of nuns ;
*March 10, to Cardinal Borromeo ; *May 28, bull on the Francis-
cans ; *June 12, to the Bishop of Padua on apostates ; *July 2,
to the archpriest, Ruffino, on the punishment of nuns in the
convent del Carmenino at Mantua ; *July 2, " Episcopo Carthaginensi " on the reform of nuns ; *August 15, to the King of
France : " may God help in the reform of the Dominicans at
Paris " ; *August 22, to the Archduke Charles on the reform of
convents ; *September 8, to Cardinal Borromeo on the Cluniac
nuns of the convent of S. Maria de' Cantuani ; *to Cardinal
Morone on the reform of S. Chiara at Mantua ; *September 17,
to the Cardinal of Vercelli, G. Ferreri, on a Benedictine monastery
" nullius dioecesis " ; *September 18, to [Antonio Altoviti],
Archbishop of Florence, to the Prior of the Ospedale degli Inno-
centi there, and to the Provincial of the Franciscans of the province
of Tuscany, on the reform of the nuns in the diocese of Volterra ;
*November 10, to [Pietro de Lunel], Bishop of Gaeta, on the
reform of the nuns of S. Chiara at Montefalco ; *November 29
" Episcopo Carthaginensi " on the reform of nuns.

was no need to press him, and that there, if anywhere, he must act with extreme care.[1]

In all his enactments concerning the Orders the Pope adhered strictly to the prescriptions on which the Council of Trent had built up its legislation for monastic life.[2] Like the Council[3] he started with the principle that their preservation as well as the guarantee of new life was not to be sought in new expedients, but in a return to the manner of life traced out for the Orders by their founders ; therefore all his ordinances were carefully adapted to the peculiar character of each congregation. The great stress which Pius V. laid upon the vow of poverty as the foundation stone of the Orders was quite in keeping with the spirit of the Council.[4] In vigorous terms he condemned the abuse which had crept in in so many ways, which allowed to individual monks and nuns a kind of private possession and thus undermined the community life, and destroyed the sense of homogeneity among the members of a religious house ; this abuse, he said, is the root of all evils in any convent where it has crept in, and not even the

For 1572 : *February 8, to the abbot of the Cassinese congregation : he must reform the Benedictines at Capua ; *March 12, to the Prior-General of the Carmelites, Giov. Batt. de Rubeis : faculties to reform the convent at Mantua ; *April 12, to the Archbishop of Palermo [Iacopo Lomellini] ; he is to excommunicate those who have seized the property of the monastery of S. Martino (State Archives, Palermo). L. Iacobilli, *Croniche di Foligno, in the possession of Mgr. Faloci Pulignani at Foligno, relates the reform of the Dominican convent at Foligno in 1566-1567. For the " Constitutioni delle venerabili monache convertite di Napoli " which were corrected by Pius V. himself, see PADIGLIONE, La Biblioteca del Museo Nazionale nella Certosa di S. Martino in Napoli, Naples, 1876, 110 *seq.*

[1] *" Nelle cose della religione, delli frati e delli preti non bisogna toccarli et averli tutti li rispetti possibili si mai s' ebbero." Rosetti to the Duke of Modena, State Archives, Modena.

[2] Sess. 25, de regularibus et monialibus.

[3] *Ibid*, c. 1.

[4] Sess. 25 de reg. et mon. c. 2-3.

holiest monastic rule can prevent its ruin.[1] The Tridentine
decrees had carefully sought to prevent the government of
monastic houses falling into improper hands, and quite a third
part of its reform prescriptions is devoted to this very matter.[2]
In this, too, Pius V. showed himself in complete agreement
with the views of the Council. Who does not know, he wrote
to the Carthusians, that the neglect of superiors is the ruin of
their subjects ?[3] In order that those who had no claims
should not insinuate themselves into the office of superior,
Pius V. threatened severe penalties against all intrigues of
this kind.[4] He further limited the tenure of office by superiors
in most cases to a few years,[5] and obliged them to share in
the common life of their subjects, while as regards their rooms,
table and dress they were to be in no way different from the
others.[6] By this he secured two further points : if the superiors of religious houses no longer made their appearance as
great nobles, their office would no longer offer such attractions
for ambitious men, and this in its turn was bound to produce
a reaction in the direction of a rule that was tempered by
humility and charity.

A crying evil throughout the Church were those monks who,
under the pretext that they had only taken the vows of religion
out of fear, or while they were still boys, and without fully
realizing what they were doing, had surreptitiously obtained

---

[1] " Omnium malorum radix, ubicunque gliscit, omne bonum in
regula quamvis bene instituta pervertit " (to the Cistercians § 19,
Bull. Rom., VII., 816) : " cum omnis religio privatae proprietatis
usa labefactetur et corruat " (to the Servites, § 1, *ibid*. 821). *Cf.*
ibid. 693, § 16 (to the Conventuals), 671, § 19 (to the Knights of
the Cross), etc.

[2] *Loc. cit.* c. 6 *seqq.*

[3] **" Quis enim nescit, negligentiam praepositorum esse sub-
ditorum ruinam ? " *brief of March 19, 1571, Brevia, Arm. 44,
t. 16, p. 40, Papal Secret Archives.

[4] Bull. Rom.. VII., 677, § 8 and 693, § 24 (for the Conventuals),
823, § 5 (for the Servites), 670, § 18 (for the Knights of the Cross).

[5] *Ibid*. 692, § 10, 824, § 17, 669, § 15.

[6] *Ibid*. 677, § 4, 693, § 17, 824, § 22.

permission from the Penitentieria to lay aside their habit, and had then obtained a cure of souls. Italy was full of such, and they provided heresy with its ablest preachers.[1] The Council had set up a barrier against this fatal tendency by making it very difficult to leave an Order, and by declaring that for the future all vows of religion taken before the age of sixteen were invalid.[2] The Pope carried the matter a step further by fixing the age of nineteen as that necessary for religious profession in several Orders.[3] Paul IV. and Pius IV. had already issued ordinances against monks living out of their monasteries, and it only remained for their successor to put these laws into force, a thing which Pius V. proceeded to do in the first months of his reign.[4] He also removed another abuse which had in various ways given occasion for apostasy from the religious life. It often happened that monks, on the pretext of seeking a higher state of perfection, passed to another Order, and then easily obtained permission to live outside their monastery, when they began to lead an unsettled life, and even to put aside the religious habit altogether. The Council of Trent had already taken steps against this abuse, but several superiors of Orders, on the strength of certain pretended privileges, continued to accept such monks who had left their monasteries. Pius V. put an end to this by declaring all such privileges invalid.[5]

In the case of the convents of nuns, the decrees of Trent, besides securing freedom of entry into an Order, had strongly insisted upon enclosure, by which no nun, once she had taken her vows, could leave her convent, and no stranger could enter

---

[1] *Cf. infra*, p. 299.

[2] Sess. 25, de reg. et mon., c. 15 and 19.

[3] Bull. Rom., VII., 692, § 5 (for the Conventuals), 825, § 23 (for the Servites : " youths under 15 must be sent back from their convents to their home.")

[4] *Avvisi di Roma of March 23 and December 8, 1566, Urb. 1040, p. 197b, 337b, Vatican Library.

[5] Bull of October 14, 1569, Bull. Rom., VII., 783 *seqq.*, issued on December 2, 1569. *Avviso di Roma of December 3, 1569, Urb. 1041, 193b, Vatican Library.

it without the permission of the bishop. Pius V. strengthened this law in both respects, ordering that the enclosure must be set up even when this had not been contemplated in the rule, or had not been observed from time immemorial.[1] It was Borromeo and Ormaneto who had asked for this bull.[2] A further edict declared that abbesses and prioresses came under the law of enclosure, even when they were of royal blood.[3] The Pope adhered strictly to what he had laid down,[4] and it was only with great difficulty that Serristori was able to obtain leave for the Duchess of Florence to be admitted to convents with two or three ladies when she was travelling in places where she could not find a lodging elsewhere.[5]

Since the co-operation of the secular arm was necessary for the enforcement of his bull on the enclosure, Pius V. addressed briefs on the subject to several of the Italian princes.[6] In Rome Ormaneto and the other reformers began at once to make strict use of their powers.[7] The nuns were obliged to set up the enclosure, and small convents were united to large ones ;[8] thus, for example, five convents were

[1] Bull of May 29, 1566, Bull. Rom., VII., 447. *Cf.* *Avviso di Roma of May 25, 1566, Urb. 1040, p. 231b, Vatican Library.

[2] BASCAPÈ, I, 2, c. I, p. 26.

[3] Of January 24, 1570, Bull. Rom., VII., 808 ; *cf.* 450. B. Pia *reports a new bull to enforce the enclosure on April 29, 1570, Gonzaga Archives, Mantua.

[4] Examples in Corresp. dipl., II., 105, n. 2.

[5] Serristori on September 29, 1568, Legaz. di Serristori, 455.

[6] *Arco, July 12, 1567, State Archives, Vienna.

[7] *" Attendono hora li riformatori a voler serrar le monache." (*Avviso di Roma of June 7, 1567, Urb. 1040, p. 399b, Vatican Library). *" Alphonso Binarino vicepres. vicarii almae arbis et Nitolao Ormaneto notaria nostro et Ioanni Olivae et Leoni Carpano commissariis nostris " November 12, 1567, on the visitation and reform of the religious women in Rome ; *brief of January 20, 1568, on the reform of S. Maria di Campo Marzo, *ibid.* *of July 7, 1568, and February 22, 1570, on the convent of Poor Clares at S. Silvestro in Rome, *ibid.*

[8] *Avviso di Roma of March 8, 1567, Urb. 1040, p. 366, Vatican Library.

formed of the eleven belonging to the Franciscan nuns of the Third Order, and the Dominican and Augustinian nuns were treated in a like manner.[1]   In order to cultivate a better spirit in the convents the Pope caused some of the older sisters from other cities to be transferred to the houses in Rome.[2]   Naturally such a method was only of use where there was already good will, and where the only cause of trouble had been the lack of knowledge, but too often this good will was wanting ; it was said in Rome that some of the nuns had poisoned themselves at the prospect of reform at the hands of Carniglia.[3]

As had been the case in the Eternal City, the enclosure was enforced in the Papal States,[4] and in the rest of Italy and in Spain.[5]   A beginning had already been made under Pius IV. ; the correspondence of Cardinal Borromeo gives some idea of the difficulties which had to be overcome.[6]   At Milan the law of enclosure had been so completely lost sight of that even dances were held in the convents ; the nobles of the city would not hear of the shutting up of the religious houses because they did not wish for any interference with their intercourse with their relatives who were nuns, while the religious themselves looked upon the enclosure as a mark of want of confidence. Cardinal Borromeo had to send long letters to the three sisters

[1] *Avviso di Roma of May 3, 1567, ibid. 390b.

[2] "They are expecting eight experienced nuns from Perugia for the reform of the Roman convents," says an *Avviso di Roma of March 16, 1571, Urb. 1042, p. 37, ibid.

[3] *Avviso di Roma of February 7, 1571, ibid. 46.   For the corruption in the convents of women see TAMASSIA, Famiglie italiane, Milan, 1910, 322 seq. (for the years 1554 and 1555).

[4] Reform of the convents of women in the Roman province of the Dominicans : *brief of May 15, 1568, Brevia, Arm. 44, t. 13, p. 189, Papal Secret Archives ; enforcement of the enclosure at Perugia in 1571 ; PELLINI, Storia di Perugia, II., 807.

[5] *Avviso di Roma of June 5, 1568, on the reform of the Conventual women, State Archives, Naples, C. Farnes., VI., 1.   Brief to Spain of January 15, 1568, in LADERCHI, 1568, n. 38.

[6] SYLVAIN, I., 267 seqq.   Cf. S. Aless. Sauli, Note e documenti, 81.

of Pius IV., who had taken the veil at Milan, in order to overcome their opposition to the law of enclosure.

Pius V. was also responsible for the first Papal law of universal obligation forbidding women to enter the monasteries of men,[1] and abolishing all contrary privileges which had hitherto been granted. This law was issued in response to a request of the Carthusians, and later on was published in greater detail by Pius V. at the request of the Benedictine congregation of Monte Vergine.[2] In Germany, however, it was found difficult to carry the law into effect immediately or everywhere.[3]

Before long various objections and disagreements made themselves felt with regard to some of the Tridentine decrees. The Council had based the reform of the Church principally upon the authority of the bishops,[4] who were to have full power in their own dioceses, and in ordinary circumstances had all matters in their own hands. But the whole organization of the great Orders, which extended, under their own superiors, over many dioceses, rested upon the principle that in some respects they must form an exception to this rule ; to such religious bodies as the Dominicans, the Franciscans, and the Jesuits it would have been fatal if they were to be broken up into as many divisions as there were dioceses, and if each of these divisions were to be placed under independent superiors. Differences of opinion were therefore both possible and even probable, nor in practice were they wanting. Even a man like Cardinal Borromeo thought that he was acting entirely in accordance with the spirit of the Council when he disposed of the regular clergy of Milan with a greater freedom than even a Philip Neri was willing to allow, and for that reason he himself founded a special congregation of priests, the Oblates of St. Ambrose, who were to be absolutely under obedience to the Archbishop of Milan.[5] The so-called " men-

---

[1] Brief of October 24, 1566, Bull. Rom., VII., 487.

[2] Brief of July 16, 1570, *ibid.* 488.

[3] BRAUNSBERGER, Pius V., 73 *seq.; cf.* 100.

[4] *Cf.* Vol. XV. of this work, p. 337.

[1] *San Carlo,* 76.   VAN ORTROY in *Anal. Bolland.,* XXIX. (1910), 373.

dicant" orders found themselves in a specially difficult position ; these were those religious bodies which were devoted to the care of souls, and which, according to their original constitution, could not possess property, though more than one such Order had been dispensed in that respect. Several of the bishops, after the Council, were unwilling any longer to recognize the existing privileges of these congregations. The result was that the Mendicants could no longer preach even in their own churches in virtue of the mere approbation of their own superiors, while several bishops would no longer give them permission to do so gratuitously, and even in some cases unreasonably prohibited this or that member of an Order from preaching at all. Other bishops would not allow their flock to receive communion in the churches of the Mendicants, or else publicly declared that all who assisted at Mass except in their own parish churches were excommunicated. Others, again, claimed for themselves, either wholly or in part, the legacies made to the Mendicants ; in a word, as the Pope said' they laboured with might and main to subject the Mendicants to themselves, and were of opinion that the care of souls was not the concern of religious, but belonged only to the secular clergy.[1] Since almost all these infringements of rights which had been guaranteed by the Church were based upon ill-understood passages in the decrees of the Council of Trent, the Pope in a bull dealing with the subject, gave an explanation of 26 such passages, which had given occasion for as many interpretations which were prejudicial to the Mendicants.[2] The prescriptions of this bull were later on extended to a number of other Orders,[3] while the Dominicans were once more specially protected against certain infringements of their

[1] Bull of May 16, 1567, Bull. Rom., VII., 573 *seqq*.

[2] *Ibid.*

[3] To the Canons of the Lateran, of S. Salvatore, and of S. Croce di Olimbria, to the Cassinese, the Olivetans, the Vallombrosans, the Cistercians, the Carthusians, the Spanish Hieronymites, the Camaldolese and the " Fratres Militiae Iesu Christi reformati " in Portugal. Bull of August 16, 1567, Bull. Rom., VII., 584.

rights.[1] In one respect, however, the Pope afterwards adopted a stricter attitude towards the Mendicant Orders ; he had declared that their members could be authorized to hear confessions by their own superiors without the approbation of the bishops,[2] but as the result of some unfortunate experiences he withdrew this privilege.[3]

It might have been supposed that the ancient privileges of the Mendicant Orders, which Pius V. himself added to,[4] had been fully defined and explained by these bulls, but suddenly a fresh difficulty arose. The Council, it was said, had granted to all the Orders, with the exception of the Capuchins and the Franciscan Observants, the right to possess real estate ; the result of this, it was claimed, was that, except for these two bodies, there were no longer any Mendicant Orders, and that the erstwhile Mendicants were bound to contribute to the seminaries. Pius V. accordingly declared[5] that the aforesaid dispensation of the Council had in no way altered the character of those orders, and that the Dominicans, Franciscans, Augustinian Hermits, and Carmelites, to whom he added the Servites, must be considered to be Mendicant Orders as before ; that the noviciates of these Orders were nurseries for capable preachers and confessors, and were deserving of the name of seminaries no less than those which were established by the bishops, and must therefore be held to be exempt from contributions to the episcopal seminaries.[6] Once this bull had expressly placed the Servites on the same footing as the four older Mendicant Orders, the same privilege could no longer be withheld from other Orders, and the Minims of St. Francis of Paula,[7] the Gesuati[8], and the Jesuits,[9] obtained a declaration

[1] Bull of September 23, 1567, *ibid.* 586.

[2] *Ibid.* 574.

[3] Bull of August 6, 1571, *ibid.* 938 *seq.*

[4] Bull of July 29, 1566, *ibid.* 468 *seq.*

[5] October 3, 1567, *ibid.* 614 *seq.*

[6] ' eorumque domos, non minus quam ea, quae per ordinarios erecta sunt, seminaria vocari posse." Bull. Rom., VII., 614, § 2.

[7] November 9, 1567, *ibid.* 633.

[8] November 18, 1567, *ibid.* 636.

[9] July 7, 1571, *ibid.* 923.

that they were true Mendicant Orders and shared in their privileges. Other bodies as well obtained a share in these privileges, even though they were not by their constitution Mendicant Orders ; such were the Congregation of S. Giorgio in Alga, near Venice,[1] and the Hermits of St. Jerome[2], but in these cases the concession extended only to spiritual and not to temporal privileges.[3]

In several of these bulls the Pope expressed his satisfaction at the work being done by the Mendicant Orders. He speaks of " the rich fruits which they daily produce in the vineyard of the Lord " and of " the purity of their zeal for religion and their voluntary poverty, by means of which they devotedly serve the Most High in a spirit of true humility," and he therefore exempts them from imposts, and from the obligation of supporting the troops that pass their way.[4] He bestows special praise on the Franciscan Observants, which Order, he says, is " founded on humility, and on joy in the midst of sorrow," and which hitherto " has produced such abundant fruit, and continues to produce it in full measure day by day."[6]

[1] September 11, 1569, *ibid.* 772.

[2] March 30, 1571, *ibid.* 908.

[3] Brief of July 30, 1570, *ibid.* 837. The Knights of St. John to some extent shared in certain exemptions of the Mendicants from taxes : November 29, 1568, *ibid.* 726 *seq.*

[5] Bull of July 20, 1566, Bull. Rom., VII., 468. On exemption from military charges *cf. ibid.* 507, 971. The abolition of the " gabelle " for the Mendicant Orders was under consideration from the beginning of 1567 ; when the Pope was told that they brought in 15,000 scudi, he replied that in spite of that he was abolishing them in order to give a good example to the princes. *Avviso di Roma of January 18, 1567, Urb. 1040, p. 349, Vatican Library.

[6] Bull of May 28, 1571, Bull. Rom., VII., 917. For the privileges granted by Pius V. to the orders *cf.* ANT. MARIA BONUCCI, Compendio delle grazie e favori, conferiti dalla somma beneficenza dell' ottimo, e massimo Pontefice San Pio Quinto agli ordini e specialmente alla Compagnia di Gesù, Rome, 1713. For the rights of precedence of the Canons of the Lateran and the Canons of S. Giorgio in Alga, *cf.* Bull. Rom., VII., 877, 915.

The great degeneracy of many Orders, which is blamed in the strongest terms in the edicts of Pius V., was not of universal application. If the Pope spoke in words of bitter reproach of the Spanish convents of the Conventuals, a testimony to the generally healthy state of the Observants is to be found in the fact that he was able to call upon them to reform the more mitigated branch of their Order.[1] In Italy, at any rate, the Franciscan Conventuals were, according to the testimony of Pius IV., " learned and zealous."[2] Pius V. expressly praised the stricter Hieronymites,[3] and if King Sebastian of Portugal could not speak well of the Benedictines in his kingdom, the Papal bull of reform repeats the eulogies pronounced by the king on the congregations of Montecassino and Valla-dolid.[4] The briefs issued by the Pope in favour of the Order to which he himself belonged are very numerous ; these documents do not give the impression that he found much to find fault with or to reform in the Dominican Order ; the paternal love which, as he himself often confessed, he felt for his Order,[5] moved him, not to find fault, but rather to grant new favours and privileges.[6] He sought above all to keep the

[1] See *supra.* p. 251.

[2] " sabios y celosos en Italia . . . no asi in España," Corresp. dipl., I., 112 n.

[3] " ubi [in Spain] multa et insignia sunt monasteria ipsorum fratrum s. Hieronymi, qui sub segulari observantia et religiosa vita degentes devotum Altissimo famulatam continuo exhibent " (Bull. Rom., VII., 569). Castagna wrote to Bonelli on October 11, 1568 : " Los Jerónimos tienen muy buena fama en España y los distingue el Rey." Corresp. dipl., II., 416 n.

[4] Bull. Rom., VIII., 3.   [5] *Ibid.* VII., 801, 904.

[6] Edict of February 14, 1567, Bull. Rom., VII., 544 (for Majorca) ; of February 16, 1567, *ibid.* 546 (for the Irish province) ; of August 27, 1568, *ibid.* 699 (since they were the first confirmed by the Pope, the Dominicans have precedence over the other Mendicant orders) ; of September 1, 1568, *ibid.* 703 (on the penitentiaries of S. Maria Maggiore) ; of September 23, 1568, *ibid.* 714 (for the college of recently converted Moors at Tortosa) ; of January 18, 1570, *ibid.* 801 (on the privileges of the whole Order) ; of June 27, 1570, *ibid.* 833 (the same) ; of July 21, 1571, *ibid.* 931 (of the

Dominicans in the front rank in the matter of learning ; he therefore ordered in the case of the Dominicans of Aragon that no one should take a bachelor's degree unless he had taught theology and philosophy for four years, and that no one should attain the degree of master unless he had been appointed by the General of the Order or the chapter-general to interpret Peter Lombard, had taught for four years, and had been proposed for the dignity by the provincial chapter.[1]

The prescription of the Council of Trent which ordered the grouping into congregations of those monasteries which were isolated and independent of the bishops was of great importance to the Benedictines. The fresh impulse which that Order experienced during the post-Tridentine period coincided with the formation of such groups, as had already been the case in the XVth century and even earlier. The grouping of five abbeys in Flanders into the Congregation of the Exempts of Belgium (1569) took place in the time of Pius V.[2] Before the close of the century two of its abbots had been appointed Bishops of Cambrai and St. Omer respectively, while the Society of Jesus owed various colleges to it.[3] The day of the

faculty for absolution of the " bolla crociata ") ; of March 21, 1571, ibid. 904 (superiors may nominate their subjects as notaries). Pius V. issued several bulls of reform for the female branch of the Order, as well as one for the Dominicans of Paris ; see supra p. 267 ; in Spain he abolished the Dominican Conventuals; see supra. p.252.

[1] Edict of July 7, 1569, Bull. Rom., VII., 760.

[2] Cf. SCHMIEDER in Studien und Mitteilungen aus dem Benedictiner- und Zisterzienserorden, XII., 78.

[3] The abbot of Saint-Bertin as Bishop of St. Omer set up a college there " e pecunia, quam sacerdotali frugalitate ac parsimonia ad alendos pauperes studiosos seposuerat." SACCHINI, P. III., 1, 3, n. 151. Brief of Pius V. of November 3, 1569, on the college at Douai, ibid. 1, 4. n. 208 (with wrong date 1568 ; of. Brevia, Arm. 44, t. 14, n. 276b, Papal Secret Archives) : " Collegium vestrae Societatis sumptibus monasterii Aquicinctensis [Anchin] eiusque abbatis [Jean Lentailleur] nuper illic institutum esse cognoscentes . . . et monachorum eorum, qui in opere tam egregio perficiendo de religione quam optime meruerunt, pietatem caritatem devotionem vehementer in Domino commendavimus."

election of Pius V. saw the death of the celebrated ascetic
Louis of Blois (Blosius), who had brought his abbey of Liessies
in Hainault[1] to a very flourishing condition, and who was
himself a zealous supporter of the Jesuits and their work.[2]
The union of the Benedictine abbeys in the diocese of Constance
was decided upon at a meeting of the abbots at Ravensburg
in 1568, but at first had to endure much opposition from the
bishops.[3] In Switzerland the abbeys gradually began to
recover from the injuries inflicted upon them by the religious
innovations ; at Einsiedeln, Abbot Eichhorn won for himself
the name of second founder of that ancient centre of learning
by his services to the economic improvement of the abbey,
and his zeal for monastic discipline.[4] At St. Gall, where
Protestantism had even made its way among the monks,
Cardinal Borromeo, when he visited it in 1570, found in the
abbot, Othmar Kunz, a man who was full of good intentions
to bring about a better state of affairs ;[5] Pius V. sent him a
brief to encourage him and urge him forward.[6] The abbot

---

[1] Opera omnia, Louvain, 1568, Antwerp, 1632 (in the latter at
p. xxxvii-lxxxvi his biography). *Cf.* ZIEGELBAUER, IV., 144 ;
HURTER, Nomenclator, III[3]., 133 *seqq.*

[2] O. MANAREI de rebus Soc. Iesu commentarius, 18.

[3] SCHMIEDER, *loc. cit.*, 81. For the visitation of convents made
by Commendone *cf.* Vol. XVIII. of this work.

[4] MEIER VON KNONAU in *Allgem. Deutsche Biographie*, V., 730.

[5] Borromeo, September 30, 1570, in REINHARDT-STEFFENS,
Doc. I., 12.

[6] SCHMIEDER, *loc. cit.*, 82. MAYER, Konzil von Trient, II., 155.
How much he had it at heart that the Benedictines should be
united in a congregation appears from the attitude of Pius V.
towards the monastery of Farfa and the German monks there.
Cf. SCHMIDLIN in *Hist. Jahrbuch*, XXIV. (1903), 258 *seqq.* Already
under Julius III. a reform had been attempted at Farfa by the
Jesuit Bobadilla (a thing which has escaped the notice of Schmidlin). For the state of the monastery *cf.* POLANCO, Vita Ignatii,
IV., 133 : " Fere viginti monachi germani ibi versabantur, qui
et vivebant, et ut ipse [Bobadilla] scribit, bibebant germanice ;
et eos ad arctiorem vitae rationem traducere nihil alius esse, quam
vel sepelire eos, vel dimittere." Cardinal Alessandro Farnese on

of Dissentis, Christian von Kastelberg, both as head of his venerable monastery, and as leader of the League of the Grisons, laboured in all things " in accordance with the spirit of Borromeo."[1]

While among the Benedictines the congregations were formed by the grouping of several independent abbeys, in other Orders a similar formation of congregations took place owing to the fact that members of different monasteries, who were desirous of a stricter manner of life, joined together within the Order, generally under a provincial of their own. Since the middle of the XVIth century quite a number of these congregations testified to the formation of a stricter party, which subsequently stood for the reform section of each order. It was above all the rule of St. Francis of Assisi, which, over and above what was strictly enjoined, contained so much that was only a matter of counsel and represented an ideal, which opened the way to the formation of such special congregations. One such had come into being in the houses of the so-called Recollects, whither those friars who aimed at a stricter manner of life could betake themselves. Pius V. gave encouragement to these establishments by enjoining that in each province of the Franciscan Observants there must be two such houses.[2]

One Franciscan congregation of extreme severity began to take a wider extension under Pius V. Its founder was Peter of Alcantara, who imitated the penance and poverty of St. Francis so literally that he himself did not advise it in the case of others, and which seems almost inconceivable.[3] According to the account of St. Teresa,[4] who knew him personally, for

July 19, 1566, asked for two German Jesuits for the reform of Farfa (S. Franc. Borgia, IV., 285 seq.), and got them (Borgia to Farnese, July 27, 1566, ibid. 291).

[1] WYMANN, 241. MAYER, loc. cit. 166.

[2] March 9, 1569, Bull. Rom., VII., 742.

[3] Acta Sanct., October VIII., 623 seqq.

[4] Autobiografia, c. 27 and 30 (Oeuvres, éd. M. BOUIX, I., Paris, 1859, 330 seq., 364; German translation, Aachen, 1868, 358 seq., 394). Cf. RENÉ DE NANTES in Études franciscaines, X. (1903), 162 seqq.

forty years he never slept for more than an hour and a half a day, and that standing with his head leaning on a piece of wood fastened to the wall ; he could not lie down because his cell was only four and a half feet in length ; often he ate only once in three days, and " when I expressed my wonder at this," says St. Teresa, " he said that it was very easy once he had got accustomed to it ; his body was in consequence extremely emaciated." With all his sanctity, he was very gracious, he only spoke when he was spoken to, but then the holiness and grace of his soul gave to his words an irresistible power and attractiveness. His whole life was one unbroken prayer, in which he attained to the highest degree of mystical contemplation.

When he was a student of 16 at the University of Salamanca in 1515 Peter entered an already very strict congregation of Franciscan Observants, which had come into existence in the time of Alexander VI., and had one so-called *custodia* in Spain, and another in Portugal. Peter himself and his whole life is an eloquent witness to the spirit which prevailed in this body. In spite of his overwhelming austerity he was elected guardian, and in 1538 provincial of his *custodia*, which had by this time been formed into a province. His constitutions, in which he still further increased strictness to its utmost limits, were immediately accepted in 1540 by the chapter-general at Plasencia. Soon afterwards Peter was called to Portugal to introduce his reform there. There, too, disciples flocked to him, so that it was possible to form a new *custodia*, that of Arabida, which in 1560 became a province. He was able at last to satisfy his desire of leading a life given over entirely to meditation in a lonely convent, but once again he felt himself irresistibly drawn to the foundation of a manner of life of even greater severity and self-denial. Since this time he met with opposition, he travelled bare-foot to Rome, in 1555, and after many difficulties won over Julius III. to his plan, and then founded at Pedrosa, near Plasencia, a convent in accordance with his ideals. In spite of its severity the new life met with such success that in 1561 an entire province of the Order followed its example, and after the death of the

founder in 1562, it gradually spread through no less than 20
provinces of the order. Clement IX. proclaimed Peter of
Alcantara a saint in 1669.

A little later than the Spanish Franciscans, a reformed congregation was set up among the Carmelites in Spain. The
convents of women in that Order contained many members,
but there was hardly any enclosure and their manner of life
was far from strict. Yet it was precisely there that the fire
was smouldering beneath the ashes ; when Teresa de Ahumeda,
a Carmelite nun of great ability in the convent of the Incarnation at Avila, went with four sisters of like mind with
herself to a small house at Avila, in order to devote herself,
in complete segregation from the distractions of the world,
entirely to prayer and penance, the enthusiasm for a like
life of sacrifice spread rapidly. In 1567 Teresa began to found
other convents of a like spirit in other places, while by means
of the Carmelite friar, John of the Cross, the movement spread
to the male branch of the Order, and became of great importance to the Church in the centuries which followed.[1] Both
Peter of Alcantara and Teresa were guided in the exercise of
prayer and self-denial by the desire to make atonement, after
the example of Christ crucified, for the sins of the world, and
to sacrifice themselves for the salvation of others and the
reform of the Church. Looked at in this light, the congregations which they founded belong to the period of Catholic
restoration ; they differ from the contemporary Orders which
were devoted to the care of souls only in the means which
they adopted, and not in the end they had in view.

If Pius V. restored their religious life to many of the Orders,
in others he reformed the rule itself, or for the first time gave
them a rule and constitution. The congregation of the Canons
Regular of S. Giorgio in Alga, near Venice, the Hermits of
St. Jerome, and in general all those religious bodies which
led a community life, and were distinguished by their dress
from the secular clergy, but which had hitherto retained their
property and taken no vows, were now obliged to take the

[1] Particulars in Vol. XIX. of this work.

three solemn vows of religion, and adopt a definite religious rule, and were forced to expel those of their number who would not agree to this.[1] Of no less vital importance for the religious without solemn vows was another regulation concerning ordination to the priesthood. In order that priests, to the lowering of their dignity, should not have to beg for alms publicly, or provide for their support in some other undignified way, the Council of Trent had ordered that in the case of the secular clergy only those should receive priests' orders who either possessed a benefice or were able to live upon their own patrimony.[2] Pius V. now extended this order to all religious who had not taken solemn vows.[3] Solemn vows are distinguished from simple ones by their almost indissoluble character ; dispensation from the simple vows of religion can be easily obtained, but solemn vows, on the other hand, are hardly ever dispensed, not even if a person leaves his Order. Moreover, certain special canonical effects are attached to solemn vows ; marriage, for example, is invalid in the case of those bound by them, whereas, *in se* and *per se*, it is only illicit for those who have taken simple vows. The ancient monasticism did not recognize the solemnity of vows, but St. Thomas Aquinas considers them an essential part of the religious state.

That Pius V. did not look with favour upon religious with only simple vows is made clear by the bulls already spoken of, and still more by his attempts to change the constitution of the Society of Jesus.

Ignatius of Loyola and his first companions had all passed through the complete course of philosophy and theology at Paris, at that time the first university in the world, and had obtained the degree of master. When they gave their hitherto free company the form of a religious Order with solemn vows, they aimed at maintaining the high standard of learning which they had thus attained, and they therefore decided

---

[1] Bull of November 17, 1568, Bull. Rom., VII., 725 *seq.*
[2] Sess. 23, de ref. c. 2.
[3] October 14, 1568, Bull. Rom., VII., 723.

that only those should become members of the Society of Jesus who had in like manner proved their capacity for learning by means of searching examinations. Since, however, the number of the members would have to remain very small as the result of this decision, and it would be impossible to carry on their work on any large scale, they also admitted other capable priests, but only as *coadiutori*, that is to say as fellow-labourers with the Society properly so-called. The *coadiutori* only took the simple vows of religion ; they could fill almost all the offices in the Order, but were not represented in its legislative assemble, the General Congregation, and thus could not pass laws which would have lowered the scholarly status of the Order.

Since a sufficient number of fully qualified priests did not enter the Order, and Ignatius had in consequence decided to receive youths and educate them in the Society, he only granted solemn vows to those who had given proof of possessing sufficient learning, and that only after a long noviciate, generally of sixteen years. Until then these young religious on their part, were only bound to the Order by simple vows, while the Order, on its part, was not bound to them at all ; should they show themselves unsuited to the purposes of the Society of Jesus, the General could dispense their vows and dismiss them.

The bulls of Paul III. and Julius III. had approved this arrangement, but Pius V. thought that there was a certain want of equity in the fact that with these simple vows the Order was not bound in the same degree as were those who entered it.[1] He did not, however, interfere immediately, but in 1567 he ordered the Jesuits to lay before the Congregation of the Council a justification of these simple vows for the scholastics ; at the same time he once again reverted to the intention of Paul IV. of forcing the Jesuits to adopt the use of prayer in choir ; the memorial which he now asked for was to deal with that matter as well.

The arguments put forward by the Jesuits did not meet

---

[1] SACCHINI P. III., 1, 3, n. 1 *seqq.* ASTRAIN, II, 317 *seqq.*

with complete success ;[1] with regard to the simple vows of
the scholastics the Pope declared himself satisfied, nor did he
insist any further on this point ; the reasons adduced also
convinced him that solemn office sung in choir was not com-
patible with the active work of the Jesuits in their care of
souls, but he felt that it was his duty to hold them to prayer
in choir, though without singing, and allowing the students
and colleges to be exempt ; in the case of the other churches of
the Order he said that he would be satisfied if, in the case of
necessity, the choir was formed of two persons only.[2] Even
this obligation was only imposed orally, without any formal
annulment of the earlier Papal concessions, and with a further
grant of a delay pending the publication of the new breviary.[3]
In the professed house in Rome the choir was commenced in
1568,[4] but did not continue for long, since Pius V.'s successor,
Gregory XIII., revoked the order of his predecessor.

A much deeper blow was struck at the constitution of the
Society of Jesus by the decree of October 14th, 1568, which
made solemn vows a necessary condition for sacerdotal ordination in the case of religious.   This decree had been in readiness
for some time ; as early as the Christmas of 1566 the Pope had
ordered his vicar-general not to admit to the priesthood any
religious who had only taken simple vows. The General of
the Jesuits, Francis Borgia, accordingly had recourse to the
Congregation of Cardinals to ask whether the Society of Jesus
was affected by this order notwithstanding the bulls of Paul III.
and Julius III. The Congregation replied that the Jesuits
might continue to do as they had hitherto done, but that if a
priest was dismissed from the Order and found himself in
need, they must provide for his support. Neither the Jesuits
nor the Pope were satisfied with this reply ; Pius V. ordered
the congregation to re-examine the question, and when it had
decided to abide by its decision, he still thought it better that

---

[1] Extract in SACCHINI P. III., 1, 3, n. 1-22 ; of. ASTRAIN, II.,
318 seq.

[2] SACCHINI, loc. cit., n. 23.

[3] Ibid.

[4] Ibid. 1, 4, n. 144.

in the case of the Jesuits as well, sacerdotal ordination should only be allowed after the taking of solemn vows.[1] On May 26th, 1567, Cardinal Alciati informed the General of the order of the Pope's decision, which was to apply, not only to Rome, but to the whole Order.[2] The decree of the following October revoked all contrary privileges possessed by the Jesuits.

With this act one of the essential fundamental principles of the Jesuit Order, as hitherto constituted, was destroyed, and the Society of Jesus, as conceived by Ignatius of Loyola, was bound to disappear within a few years. The long period of probation before definite admission into the Order could no longer be retained, since ordination could not be put off for so long, and Loyola's principle of strict selection of those to be accepted became impracticable for the future.

In these circumstances Borgia addressed a circular to the provincials and the more eminent Jesuits, asking them how it would be possible to adhere to the constitutions of the Order without in any way failing in obedience to the Pope.[3] At last recourse was had to the expedient of making all without exception to take the vows of religion solemnly before ordination, but reserving the right to take part in the General Congregation to those who were subsequently admitted to the fourth solemn vow of obedience to the Pope.

Even so, the change which Pius V. had introduced into the constitutions gave rise to disturbances within and hostility without. Ignatius had introduced many things into his Order which later on proved their wisdom, but which at that time seemed altogether novel. Hitherto, in reply to the difficulties which might arise, it could be answered that these

---

[1] Borgia to Nadal, June 7, 1567, in NADAL, Epist., III., 480 *seqq.;* SACCHINI P. III., 1, 3, n. 26 *seqq.;* ASTRAIN, II., 321 *seqq.*

[2] SACCHINI, *loc. cit.*

[3] CANISII Epist., V., 487. SACCHINI, *loc. cit.* n. 38. The letter to Nadal in his Epist., III., 480 *seqq.* The reply of Nadal from Liège, August 14, 1567. *ibid.* 521 *seqq.* The reply of Salmeron of June 22, 1567, in his Epist., II., 121. *Cf.* SACCHINI P. III., 1, 4, n. 122 *seqq.*

things had received the approval of the Popes, and rested
upon the authority which Ignatius enjoyed among his followers as a saint and a man enlightened by God, but now these
two pillars on which the Order rested had been severely shaken
when Pius V. withdrew the concessions of his predecessors,
and declared an essential point in the conception of the founder
to have been a mistake.[1]   The enemies of the Order made
the most of this reform of Pius V. ;   the Pope, so they said, is
opposed to the Jesuits, he intends to change the Order completely, or to suppress it,[2] etc.

In reality Pius V. was in no sense hostile to the Society
of Jesus.   He valued their services,[3] endowed their colleges
with revenues,[4] added to their privileges,[5] and helped them in

[1] " Infirmantur in fide instituti animi omnium, quotquot ad
hanc religionem vocati sumus ; si enim duas illius partes videmus
abrogatas, quo pacto poterimus reliquis confidere ? "   Nadal in
his memorial to Gregory XIII., in NADAL, Epist. IV., 171.

[2] Cf. a letter of the Jesuit, Gonzáles Dávila, of December 18,
1567, in S. Franciscus Borgia, IV., 576 n.   Borgia sent a letter to
Spain on March 7, 1568 in answer to these insinuations ; ibid.
575 seqq.

[3] Cf. the account in SACCHINI P. III., 1, 2, n. 4 seqq.; ASTRAIN,
II., 326 seq.

[4] (DELPLACE) Synopsis Actorum S. Sedis in causa Societatis
Iesu 1540-1605, Florence, 1887, 44-58 (52 numbers, for the most
part permissions for colleges).   *Motuproprio di S. Pio V sotto il
dì 26 febbr. 1566 con cui concede la facoltà al collegio dei Gesuiti
di Roma di poter ricevere la rassegna di 120 luoghi del monte
Giulio e Pio detti del soccorso di Avignone, o tutti di un solo
monte, o il prezzo per la compra dei medesimi e di tenerli per lo
spazio di 10 anni, il quale terminato possano rendere, transferire e
dovendo reprindere la primiera loro istituzione di vacabili (Estratti
de libri instrument. esistenti nell' arch. segreto Vatic. 1374 seqq.
Serie 4 dell' Inventario, p. 122, State Archives, Rome).   *Brief
of April 22, 1567, for the college of Olmütz (handing over of a
Conventual convent), Archives of Briefs, Rome.   Cf. Gregory
XIII., January 22, 1572, in Synopsis, 63.

[5] Institutum Societatis Iesu. I : Bullarium, Florence, 1892,
38-49.

their difficulties with letters of recommendation. The Order he wrote to Toulouse in 1566, is doing so useful a work in the Church by its colleges that anyone who loves and supports it thereby proves himself a true and pious Catholic.[1] He exhorted the University of Cologne[2] to put no obstacles in the way of the Jesuits, for their colleges were nurseries of Catholic doctrine and of a life led in the Christian spirit, and had been called into existence by the providence of God ; he himself embraced with paternal love the colleges and all the priests of the said Order. In another edict Pius V. speaks of the incalculable fruits produced in the Christian world by the Society of Jesus, which had trained such teachers, preachers, and missionaries, men distinguished alike for learning and piety, and for their exemplary life and holiness.[3] He paid another equally glowing tribute to the Jesuits in the last year of his life, when he spoke of them as men who had truly renounced the attractions of the world, and who, despising earthly riches, had united themselves so closely to their Saviour that, girt about with poverty and humility, they

---

[1] *" ut qui illam diligunt et fovent, plane ostendant, vere se pios esse et catholicos et utilitatis publicae studiosos." Ordini civium nobilium Tolosae (s.d.), Brevia, Arm. 44, t. 12, n. 132, Papal Secret Archives.

[2] " Societatis Iesu collegia, quae quasi quaedam catholicae doctrinae christianorumque morum seminaria Dei providentia per diversas orbis provincias calamitosis hisce . . . temporibus excitavit, atque adeo Patres omnes praedictae Societatis ea benevolentia paterna prosequimur etc." Brief of July 3, 1570, in REIFFENBERG, I.: Mantissa, p. 50.

[3] " Innumerabiles fructus, quos benedicente Domino christiano orbi Societas Iesu, viros litterarum praecipue sacrarum scientia, religione, vita exemplari morumque sanctimonia perspicuos, multorum religiosissimos praeceptores at verbi divini etiam apud longinquas et barbaras illas nationes, quae Deum penitus non noverant, optimos praedicatores et interpretes producendo, felicissime haetenus attulit." Brief of April 29, 1568, Bull. Soc. Iesu, 42.

went to the very end of the world to preach the Gospel at
the peril of their lives [1]

If the decree making solemn vows a condition for sacerdotal
ordination was a blow to the Jesuits, it was an advantage to
the Somaschi, founded by Jerome Emilian. This Order had
not as yet fully worked out its constitutions, and the Pope's
decree put an end to several canonical uncertainties. The
Order now adopted the rule of St. Augustine.[2]

As far as the other Orders were concerned Ormaneto laid
before the Pope proposals for the reform of the Capuchins.[3]
The Theatines were confirmed in their former privileges, and
received new ones.[4] So far the Barnabites had not spread
very widely, and in 1552 and 1559 steps had been taken to
merge the Order into that of the Jesuits.[5] Under Pius V.,
however, the Order received a new life owing to the merits
of the man who may be considered its second founder,
Alessandro Sauli.[6]

Pius V. gave its first Papal approbation to a religious congregation which had only recently come into existence, and
thus greatly assisted its progress towards becoming a true

[1] Brief of July 7, 1571, Bull. Rom., VII., 923. The Venetian
ambassador wrote on April 12, 1567, that the Pope favoured the
Roman Jesuits, who devoted themselves zealously to the service
of God and the instruction of youth ; they have four houses in
Rome, their churches are always full, and many receive the sacraments there. MUTINELLI, I., 72.

[2] Brief of December 6, 1568, Bull. Rom., VII., 729 *seqq.*

[3] *Avviso di Roma of February 2, 1569, Urb. 1041, p. 25,
Vatican Library ; *cf.* *Avviso of June 14, 1570, *ibid.* 290b. Prohibition of passing from the Capuchins to the Minims and vice
versa : brief of October 6, 1567, Bull. Rom., VII., 617.

[4] February 13, 1568 (year of the Incarnation 1567), Bull. Rom.,
VII., 537 ; *cf.* LADERCHI, 1568 n. 17. *Motu proprio of July 12,
1566, which grants exemption from " gabelle " to the Clerks
Regular of S. Silvestro in Rome, in Estratti de libri instrument.
esistenti nell' arch. segreto Vatic. 1374-1557, serie 4 dell' Inventario, State Archives, Rome.

[5] *Arch. stor. Lomb.*, XXXVIII. (1911), 152 *seq.*

[6] *Ibid.* PREMOLI, Barnabiti, 206. *Cf. supra,* p. 237 *seq.*

religious Order ; this was the congregation of the Fatebenefratelli. After a long life spent as a shepherd and as a soldier,
its founder, John of God, had been suddenly filled with the
deepest sorrow for his past life by a sermon of the Apostle of
Andalusia, John of Avila. By Avila's advice he began to
devote himself to the service of the sick. He first established
a small house at Granada, and then a large hospital, of which
he took charge with a few companions until his death in 1550.[1]

Most likely John of God had no thought of founding a new
Order ; he and his companions, however, wore a special dress,
but they took no vows of religion, and thus remained seculars.
They only adopted a definite rule through the efforts of
Rodrigo de Siguenza, who also had been a soldier, and had
then devoted himself to the service of the sick in the hospital
at Granada, and was soon afterwards elected Superior of the
little company. Rodrigo then sent his predecessor in that
office, Sebastian Arias, to Rome, to obtain from the Pope his
approval of their pious fraternity, and leave to wear a religious
habit, which could not then be worn by others, since the one
which they had hitherto used had been made use of by im-
postors in order to obtain alms. The bull in which the Pope
granted this request, and placed the brotherhood under the
Augustinian rule,[2] gives some particulars as to the extent and
activities of the congregation. In the hospital at Granada
more than 400 incurables, lunatics, cripples and aged persons
were maintained. The annual cost was more than 16,000
ducats, gathered by the Brothers as voluntary alms. Besides
the one at Granada, the congregation had similar hospitals
at Côrdova, Madrid, Toledo and Lucena. The bull of Pius V.
did not as yet give the Fatebenefratelli the right to elect a
superior for the whole congregation, nor did it oblige them to
take the three vows of religion.

Pius V. had only a short span of life left to him when he
signed the bull in favour of the Fatebenefratelli, but at the
close of his days he could truly say that the work of reform

---

[1] Cf. Vol. XI. of this work, p. 529 seq.
[2] Of January 1, 1572, Bull. Rom., VII., 959.

of the Church in its head and in its members had been substantially accomplished.

If we attempt to form a general idea of the reforming
activities of Pius V. we can only wonder that he should have
been able to accomplish so much in his comparatively short
pontificate.. In versatility and zeal he surpasses all the reforming Popes of the XVIth century. It was characteristic of him
that he was never satisfied with what he had done. The
Imperial ambassador wrote that when the Pope was entering
upon the second year of his pontificate, it seemed that his
Holiness had become " terrible," and was stricter and more
fixed in his purpose, and without consideration for any of the
princes. Only now, so he himself said, was he beginning to be
Pope and to understand all that that implied.[1] A year later
the Pope declared in consistory that he had not done his duty
completely, that he begged God to pardon him for his neglect,
and promised that he would be more full of zeal henceforward.[2]
At the beginning of March, 1571, the Romans were expecting
in terror from hour to hour a reform which, as a news-sheet
that was secretly passed from hand to hand put it, would be
" terrible."[3]

Yet how unfavourably had the secular ambassadors,
especially those of the King of Spain, expressed themselves
as to the goodwill of the Roman court in the matter of the
carrying out of the decrees of the Council ! It is the special
glory of Pius V. that he gave the lie to these doubts and fears.
By his unflagging zeal the dead letter of the Council gradually
became a living force and changed the whole appearance of

---

[1] *" che sia divenuta [S. S^{tà}] terribile e più dura e pertinace
nelle sue oppinioni senza haver rispetto a principe alcuno et ha
detto c' hora comincia a esser papa e a conoscerlo." Strozzi,
January 25, 1567, State Archives, Vienna.

[2] *" conoscer di non haver fatto tutto quello gli conveniva con
tutto ciò ch' haveva fatto molte riforme, però pregava Dio a
perdonarci, perchè da qui innanzi sarebbe più diligente." Arco,
January 24, 1568, *ibid*.

[3] *Avviso di Roma of March 1, 1571, Urb. 1041, p. 23b, Vatican
Library.

the Church.   It is with deep emotion that one may see to-day in the church of S. Maria Maggiore, among the relics of the great Pope, the printed copy of the Tridentine decrees which he used.[1]   This little book became in his hands the lever by means of which he uprooted from its bed a whole world of disorders.

[1] Venice, 1565.

CHAPTER VII.

The Roman Inquisition preserves Religious Unity in Italy.

The wish that his works might be buried together with the great champion of the tribunals of the faith had found expression at the time of the death of Paul IV. in the destruction of the Palace of the Inquisition. But the futility and impracticability of any such idea was manifest to all when the former Grand Inquisitor of Paul IV., as soon as he had ascended the throne of St. Peter under the name of Pius V. proceeded to build a new and even more secure home for the Holy Office. On May 18th, 1566, the palace of the deceased Cardinal Lorenzo Pucci, situated in the Leonine City, close to the German cemetery, passed, mainly by purchase, into the hands of Pius V., and the building, where the Inquisition was already carrying on its business, was made over to it as its permanent abode.[1] In the July of that year we find it stated that the Pope was thinking of erecting a new building, that three plans had been prepared, and that 50,000 scudi had been assigned for the purpose from the Papal treasury. In the opinion of the architect, Pino, however, this sum was insufficient. The projected palace would have to be very large, must have room for the prisons in its upper storeys, and must be built in such a way as to be safe from attacks such as that which had taken place at the death of Paul IV.[2]

[1] Bull. Rom., VII., 445 *seqq.; cf.* Fontana in *Arch. Rom.*, XV· (1892), 462. A *bull " Cum nos " of August 15, 1567, contains the " confirmatio emptionis palatii ipsius inquisitionis." Archives of Briefs, Rome.

[2] *Ciregiola to Cardinal Medici, Rome, July 19, 1566, State Archives, Florence, Medic. 5096. *Arco on August 10, 1566, wrote to Vienna that the money for the building had been taken

The Pope, our informant adds, is occupying himself on the subject of the Inquisition more anxiously than anything else.[1]

On September 2nd, 1566, the first stone of the new building was laid with great solemnity, amid salvos of cannon from the Castle of St. Angelo,[2] and then was pushed forward with all speed. The builders of St. Peter's were instructed to interrupt their labours on the basilica, and assist with the building of the new palace of the Holy Office.[3] In July, 1567, the Pope paid a visit to the building,[4] but it was not until 1569 that he was able to place over the iron doors of the completed edifice his own coat of arms, together with those of Cardinals Pacheco, Rebiba, Gambara and Chiesa, with an inscription proclaiming that the palace was to be used for the warfare against heresy, and the spread of the Catholic religion.[5] Even before the first stone was laid the Pope

from the revenues of St. Peter's (State Archives, Vienna). The *Diarium of C. Firmanus on July 1, 1566, gives as the names of the architects " domini " Pino and Sallustio. Papal Secret Archives.

[1] * " A niuna cosa più attende S. Stà che all' inquisizione." Ciregiola, loc. cit.

[2] *Avviso di Roma of September 7, 1566, Urb. 1040, p. 282, Vatican Library.

[3] * " La fabrica della Inquisizione tuttavia si sollicita, et per formarla presto, hanno levato li muratori et scarpellini di S. Pietro, nel qual hora si fa niente." (Avviso di Roma of October 5, 1566, loc. cit. 295). The Imperial secretary, Francesco Strozzi, also *wrote on October 26, 1566, to Maximilian II. that in spite of his poverty and niggardliness (towards the Emperor) the Pope was pushing forward " gagliardamente " the building of the palace of the Inquisition ; all the builders in Rome had been made to assist and it was becoming like a fortress. State Archives, Vienna.

[4] *Report of B. Pia of July 19, 1567, Gonzaga Archives, Mantua.

[5] " Pius V. P.M. Congregationis sanctae inquisitionis domum hanc qua haereticae pravitatis sectatores cautius coercerentur a fundamentis in augmentum catholicae religionis erexit anno 1569." (CIACONIUS, III., 992. BUCHELIUS, Iter Italicum [1587-1588], in Arch. d. Soc. Rom., XXIII. [1900], 49). For the palace of the Inquisition cf. LANCIANI, IV., 21-23.

had taken steps for the formation of well-arranged archives
in the new building, ordering all that the minutes of the trials
of the Inquisition should be collected and placed in the Holy
Office, and that they were only to be made use of there.[1]
Pius V. then took steps to provide the necessary revenues
for the Roman tribunal of the faith.[2]

If Pius IV. had imitated the mildness of Paul III. and
Julius III. in his administration of the Inquisition, it was only
natural that one who was so stern and so zealous for the purity
of the faith as was Pius V., should once more adopt the policy
of Paul IV.   It was an expression of his holy zeal when,
making use of the very words of Paul IV., he declared that
questions of faith must take precedence of all other business,
since the faith is the substance and groundwork of Christianity,[3] and he stated in a solemn constitution that it would
be his first care to see that heresies, false doctrines, and errors
were removed and banished as far away as possible, for that

---

[1] Decree of January 31, 1566, n. 102 ; PASTOR, Dekrete, 28 seq.

[2] On April 3, 1566, the tenure of Conca (as to this see TOMAS-
SETTI, Campagna, II., 387 seqq.; ABBATE, Provincia di Roma, II.
[1894], 215), hitherto belonging to Grottaferrata, was assigned in
consistory to the Holy Office (Diarium of Cardinal Farnese, in
LADERCHI, 1566, n. 94.   *Bulla dismembrationis tenutae Conchae
etc., tertio nonas April, 1566, registered on May 20, Arm. 52,
t. 5, p. 1 seqq., Papal Secret Archives.   Cf. Bull. O. Praed., V.,
124 ; LANCIANI, IV., 23).   An *Avviso di Roma of July 7, 1571
(Urb. 1042, p. 84, Vatican Library) announces that the Pope in
spite of his financial straits has assigned 12,000 scudi to the
Inquisition from the sale of the property of Pallantieri.   *" Notifi-
catio facta S.D.N.P. et consensus Suae S^{tis}, quod scuta 3000
partis palatii s. Inquisitionis exponantur seu investiantur in tot
locis montis fidei per M. Lor. Puccio," of July 27, 1569, Arm. 52,
t. 3, p. 198, Papal Secret Archives.   A *mandate of January 11,
1570, assigns a salt mine " pro usu familiae et pauperum car-
ceratorum " in the palace of the Inquisition ; ibid. Arm. 29, t. 242,
p. 189.   A *mandate of November 19, 1567, orders that the
exemption of the Inquisition from taxes is to be strictly observed ;
ibid. t. 232, p. 11.

[3] Bull. Rom., VII., 422.   Cf. Paul IV. in PASTOR, Dekrete 16.

only thus could security and peace be restored to the Church.[1]

After an audience with Pius V., the Inquisitor of Brescia gave it as his opinion in March, 1566, that in all that concerned the tribunal of the faith the Pope stood in need of the bit rather than the spur ;[2] a short time afterwards the Venetian ambassador, Tiepolo, wrote that nothing lay so near the heart of the Pope as the Inquisition.[3] Under his government all appearance of any readiness to offend against it or to favour heresy had to be carefully avoided. Cardinal Sirleto, a few weeks after the election of Pius V., thought it advisable to send a special warning to Commendone on the subject. The Pope, so he wrote by Caligari, is very scrupulous in matters of faith ; Commendone must be on his guard against having any private conversation with the heretics, or, like Cardinal Este at Poissy, attending their sermons, for Pius V. would take any such act very ill.[4] When, in the last year of the Pope's life, the case of the Count of Cajazzo was being considered by the Holy Office, Cardinal Rambouillet dared to say a word on his behalf, but Pius V. silenced him abruptly, saying that it ill beseemed one who wore the Cardinal's robes to speak on behalf of anyone accused by the Inquisition.[5]

[1] Bull of December 21, 1566, Bull. Rom., VII., 499.

[2] Tiepolo on March 9, 1566, in MUTINELLI, I., 37. For Pius V.'s great strictness in all that concerned religion, see also the *report of the Este ambassador of February 23, 1566, State Archives, Modena.

[3] Tiepolo on July 20, 1566, in MUTINELLI, I., 50. In like manner *Arco, June 29, 1566, State Archives, Vienna.

[4] *" che Nostro Signore è molto scrupuloso nelle cose della fede. . . . Nostro Signore haveria malissimo e quì sono molti osservatori delle sue attioni." Caligari to Commendone, February 2, 1566, Lett. d. princ., XXIII., Papal Secret Archives.

[5] *" Mal vi si conviene, Monsignore, a parlare in difesa d' uno inquisito havendo l'habito che havete." (Avviso di Roma of January 31, 1571, Urb. 1042, p. 15, Vatican Library). Cajazzo, however, after a " canonical purgation " was dismissed by the Inquisition (*Avvisi di Roma of September 15 and 27, 1571, ibid. 120, 123). On September 8, 1571, Arco *announces that his liberation was imminent. State Archives, Vienna.

From the first no one expected anything else from Pius V. The new Pope, so wrote Cardinal Cicada in announcing the election to the Republic of Genoa, will be a distinguished pastor, who will above all things set his heel upon the heretics and the enemies of the faith.[1] As early as the beginning of February, 1566, the Imperial ambassador Arco wrote that there was talk of reorganising the tribunals of the Inquisition ;[2] a few days later he speaks of the reform as an accomplished fact ; an entirely new congregation had been set up for the administration of the Inquisition, composed of the four Cardinals, Scotti, Pacheco, Rebiba and Gambara[3] In a motu proprio the Pope justified this step by saying that he wished to facilitate a more speedy decision of the trials then pending before the Holy Office, and that the nine members of the old commission were too busy with other matters ; the ordinance of Pius IV. held good in the case of the new

[1] " Bonissimo pastore, el quale sopra tutto sarà acerrimo persecutore delli heretici et altri nemici della nostra fede." Cicada, January 11, 1566, in Rosi, Riforma in Liguria, 63.

[2] * Arco, February 2, 1566, State Archives, Vienna.

[3] * Arco, February, 1566, State Archives, Vienna. *Serristori, February 6, 1566, State Archives, Florence. The names of the same four Cardinals are given as Inquisitors on the occasion of the autodafè in Rome on June 23, 1566 (FIRMANUS, *Diarium, p. 101b, Papal Secret Archives ; cf. App. nn. 35-47) as well as in an edict of July 4, 1567, in HILGERS, Index, 504. On the death of Scotti in 1568, Chiesa took his place (*Arco, April 3, 1568, loc. cit.; a list of the Cardinals of the Inquisition in FIRMANUS, *Diarium, on November 30, 1568, loc. cit., 272 ; cf. supra, p. 289). On February 28, 1568, the *Avvisi di Roma (Urb. 1040, p. 484 Vatican Library) report that Borromeo as well was to be summoned to the Inquisition. Santori was appointed consultor to the Inquisition ; see his *notes on his audience with the Pope on February 5, 1566, Papal Secret Archives, Arm. LII., 17, and his Autobiografia, XII., 340. " Arcangelus Blancus, episc. Theanensis," became " commissarius generalis Inquisitionis " in 1566 ; Brevia, Arm. 29, t. 224, p. 7b, Papal Secret Archives. For the important services of Gambara to the Inquisition cf. ALBÈRI, II., 4, 186 ; Corresp. dipl., II., 76.

commission, namely that the consensus of even two of its number gave legal force to its decisions.[1]

About the middle of February, 1566, it was feared in Rome that in the administration of the Inquisition the new Pope would follow in the footsteps of Paul IV., the more so as the procurator-fiscal of the tribunal had taken up his abode at the Vatican, and held long consultations with the head of the Church.[2] It was a fact that the Pope, following the example of Paul IV., was frequently present at the meetings of the Inquisition, and that in his decrees on matters concerning the tribunal of the faith he closely imitated those of the Carafa Pope.[3] A decree of July 28th, 1569, according to which an accused person, once he had been convicted of heresy or had confessed to it, was to be forced to fuller confession by means of torture, is directly reminiscent of Paul IV.[4] When he enacted that all the decisions arrived at at a meeting of the Inquisition were to be issued in the name of the Cardinal Inquisitors, even though they resulted from a Papal order,[5] or when he laid it down that participation in the acts of the tribunal of the faith carried with it no sort of irregularity,[6] or that heresy involved the immediate forfeiture of all ecclesiastical benefices,[7] Pius V. was using the very words of the edicts of Paul IV. An edict of Pius V.

[1] Motu proprio " Cum felicis " (without date), Bull, Rom., VII., 502.

[2] *Cusano, February 16, 1566, State Archives, Vienna.

[3] The contrast with Pius IV. is shown in the decrees which I have published, even as regards their exterior form. While those issued under Pius IV. all appear under the names of the Inquisitors, of the 14 issued under Pius V., 7 bear the name of the Pope at their head ; see PASTOR, Dekrete, 28.

[4] *Ibid.* 31. DIANA, 580.

[5] Decree of March 14, 1566, in PASTOR, *loc. cit.*, 29 ; it is in literal conformity with that of Paul IV. of May 28, 1556 ; *ibid.* 19.

[6] Decree of December 9, 1567, *ibid.* 30 ; *cf.* the decree of Paul IV. of April 29, 1557, *ibid.* 21.

[7] The corresponding decree of Paul IV. of June 17, 1556, *ibid.* 19 (in DIANA, 178, with the date July 18, 1556) was renewed by Pius V. (DIANA, 579 ; *cf.* PASTOR, *loc. cit.* 23, n. 2).

of June 6th, 1566,[1] is merely a fuller statement of the ideas of Paul IV. ; this edict is an exhortation to the princes, and a command to all other Christians to obey the Cardinals of the Holy Office in all that concerns the Inquisition, and it gives the Inquisition precedence over all other tribunals in its right to pronounce judgment on offenders.   The opening words of the decree in which Pius V. orders that matters concerning the faith, which is the substance and basis of Christianity, must take precedence of all other matters, are copied literally from the decree of Paul IV.   The obligation of secrecy concerning all matters treated of by the tribunal, which had been imposed by his two predecessors, was insisted upon even more strictly by Pius V. ; any infringement of this secrecy was to be considered as a personal affront to the Pope.[2]   The advice of the consultors was taken under Pius V. with regard to the old custom of not making known to one who was accused before the Inquisition the names of the witnesses, and of taking precautions against their becoming known ; as the result of their advice the existing custom was retained.[3]

Probably the contrast between Pius V. and his predecessor comes out most clearly in a constitution upon the procedure of the Inquisition which he issued towards the end of the first year of his reign.[4]   He appeals in the first place to his

---

[1] Bull. Rom., VII., 422, without date ; with date in Cod. Barb. Lat. 5195, p. 100b-101b, Vatican Library.   The decree was only issued at the beginning of October, 1566 (*Avviso di Roma of October 5, 1566, where the decree is also assigned to June ; Urb. 1040, p. 294, Vatican Library).   *Cf.* the decree of Paul IV. of October 1, 1555, in PASTOR, *loc. cit.* 15 *seq.*

[2] Decree of January 31, 1566, in PASTOR, *loc. cit.* 28 *seq. ;* LADERCHI, 1566, n. 2.   On June 10, 1569, Pius IV's prohibition of making copies of the acta of the Inquisition was renewed (see Vol. XVI. of this work, p. 315).   PASTOR, *loc. cit.* 31.

[3] Decree of March 14, 1566, in PASTOR, *loc. cit.* 29 ; DIANA, 579 ; AMABILE, I., 291.   *Cf.* HINSCHIUS, VI., 346, n. 10.

[4] Of December 21, 1566, Bull. Rom., VII., 499 *seqq.; cf.* LADERCHI, 1566, n. 95.

own long experience as Grand Inquisitor ; this had shown
him that many of those summoned before the tribunal of
the faith brought false witnesses to speak for them, and that
in their depositions accused persons helped each other, and
by means of cunningly devised excuses and artifices deceived
their judges and even the Popes.[1] Several accused persons
had even succeeded in obtaining from the tribunals of the
faith and from the Popes documents in their own favour,
as for example certificates in which they were declared to be
good Catholics, both in their life and their beliefs, or else
Papal briefs and consistorial decrees which ensured to them
the protection of the Pope, and prevented the Inquisition
from taking any further action against them. Their former
errors were thus maintained and even more widely spread
under the aegis of such declarations. In order to obviate
this abuse Pius V. then proceeds to give the Inquisition a
free hand to take steps against heretics in spite of such documents, especially when they had given fresh signs of heresy.
Even when a trial had been decided by the authority of the
Council of Trent itself, the Inquisition has the right to reopen
the case and re-examine it. Finally, the Pope renews the
bull of Paul IV. of February 15th, 1558, against heretics and
schismatics.[2] It is obvious to whom the Pope refers when he
complains that even some of the Popes had been deceived by
the heretics.

Some of the decrees of the Cardinal Inquisitors form a
corollary to this stern edict. It was certainly in order to
foil the intrigues of the prisoners of the Inquisition in the matter of mutual assistance, that it was enacted that except
when they were making their defence, those who were imprisoned might only confer with other persons, or read or
write, with the permission of the Inquisitors. Anyone who
broke this rule might be subjected to torture. Even the

[1] The printed version of the bull in Bull. Rom., VII., 499 is
very much mutilated at this point ; it may be completed from the
text in Laderchi.

[2] For this bull see Vol. XIV. of this work, p. 303.

governor of the prison could only visit a prisoner if he was accompanied by somebody else.[1]

If Pius V. sought to put an end to cunning intrigues against the Inquisition, he also took steps to protect his officials from violence. Acts of hostility and actual violence against the Inquisitors were not unknown in the XVIth century. On August 27th, 1561, Pius IV. complained that, from fear of the heretics, few persons offered their services as notaries for the tribunal of the faith,[2] and that at Avignon nobody dared to take action against the heretics from fear of the consequences.[3] Pius V. had learned by his own experiences of early days that it needed courage to be an Inquisitor.[4] In a constitution of April 1st, 1569,[5] he complains of the influence which was daily being gained by wicked men, who sought in every way to overwhelm the Inquisition and to obstruct the labours of its officials ; the very gravest penalties were accordingly to be inflicted upon anyone who should kill, maltreat or intimidate an Inquisitor, or any of his assessors and assistants, as well as those who should attack, set fire to, or rob the churches, houses, or property of the Inquisition and its officials, or burn, steal or disturb the docu-

---

[1] Decrees of June 7th, 1567, July 13 and October 26, 1569, in PASTOR, *loc. cit.* 29, 31.

[2] Bull. Rom., VII., 138.

[3] *Ibid.* 146.

[4] CATENA, 7 *seq.*, 10. For another case of violence, against Santori at Naples, see the latter's Autobiografia, XII., 335, 337 and *supra* p. 166. *cf.* FUMI, L'Inquisizione, 204.

[5] Bull. Rom., VII., 744 *seqq.* *Cf.* the *Avviso di Roma of May 7, 1569 (Urb. 1041, p. 68b, Vatican Library) and the *report of Arco of the same date, State Archives, Vienna. For the probable occasion of this constitution (a decree for the Grisons, which, on account of the arrest of the heretic Cellaria, had set a reward on the head of the Inquisitor, Pietro Angelo Casanova) *cf.* LADERCHI, 1569, n. 57. The proposed publication of the bull at Naples proved to be unnecessary ; *ibid.* n. 76. Another *bull of 1569 contra molestantes ministros S^{tae} Inquisitionis," in Arm. 8, caps. 4, n. 1, Papal Secret Archives.

ments belonging to the Holy Office, or should abet such offences ; and lastly those who should forcibly break into the prisons of the Inquisition, set free its prisoners, or rescue the imprisoned from their gaolers, or give them sanctuary. Anyone who was guilty of such acts of violence at once incurred excommunication, was held guilty of high treason, forfeited his benefices and property, and was to be handed over to the secular arm. A special brief, on the other hand, again confirmed in its privileges a confraternity which, since the middle ages, had undertaken the defence of the Inquisition.[1] Another edict was specially directed to the safeguarding from molestation of those religious who had recourse to the tribunal of the faith or were cited by it as witnesses.[2]

Pius V. appealed to his own long experience as Inquisitor in justification of his stern measures against the followers of the new religion. If we may judge from his decrees it certainly cannot be held that his experience had given him any respect for the Protestant movement in Italy. Judging from what he says in these decrees the Italian Protestants were in his opinion a sect which was groping in the dark ; they had sufficient courage to spread their doctrines secretly and unseen, but once they were discovered and brought to judgment, in the great majority of cases their boldness miserably crumbled away, at the very moment when it was called upon to prove that the movement really inspired constancy of opinion and the courage that makes martyrs ; on the contrary, they denied their Protestantism and recanted. For this reason, as he often said, in his opinion sternness was the

---

[1] Brief in favour of the " cruce signati " of October 13, 1570, Bull, Rom., VII., 860. In his early activities as Inquisitor Ghislieri had been helped by a member of the Compagnia della Croce against the heretics in the Swiss part of the diocese of Como (CATENA, 6). For the Crocesegnati cf. FUMI, L'Inquisizione, 19–26. The Duke of Florence quickly dissolved a confraternity of Crocesegnati which was set up in Siena in 1569. CANTÙ, Eretici, II., 452.

[2] Decree of August 7, 1567, in PASTOR, Dekrete, 30 ; DIANA, 580.

true remedy for heresy.[1] If they did not hesitate to inflict the severest penalties in a few cases, Italy would be saved from a civil war, which, as had already happened in France,[2] would drown the country in blood, while the religious divisions would only grow worse ; whereas by acting as he suggested the punishments with which God would otherwise visit the world would be averted.[3]

The Pope's views of justice, however, afforded the heretic some excuse, even though they did not justify them ; he often recognized that the low state of morals among the clergy, a thing which he fought against with all his strength, was the starting point and foundation from which the Protestant movement drew its force.[4] This, however, was far from giving the

[1] " Omai l'esperienza, che in caso di erectici si è fatta anche in altre città d'Italia, mostra, giusta l'opinione del Pontefice, che il rigore sia la vera medicina di questa peste." (Cardinal Cicada to the Doge of Genoa, June 4, 1568, in ROSI, Riforma in Liguria, 90). " Quo lenius cum illis [Hugonottis] agitur, eo magis eorum corroboratur audacia " (Pius V. to Catherine de' Medici, June 27, 1566, in LADERCHI, 1566, n. 423).

[2] CATENA, 68 seq.

[3] So wrote Pius V. to Charles IX. on April 13, 1569, after having enumerated the crimes of the Huguenots : " nam si qualibet inductus causa (quod non putamus) ea de quibus Deus offenditur insectari atque ulcisci distuleris, certe ad irascendum eius patientiam provocabis, qui quo tecum egit benignius, eo debes acrius illius iniurias vindicare." GOUBAU, 166 ; cf. 163.

[4] " che il principio e origine delle eresie nella maggior parte era stato il mal esempio che avevano dato gli ecclesiastici ; però li confortava [i cardinali] e pregava al ben vivere." (Pius V. in the consistory of January 12, 1566, in Serristori, Legaz. 420 ; cf. GOUBAU, 2, 12, 24, 28, 109, 127 seq., 132, 143, etc.). The principal objection which he had met with from the Italian Protestants when he was Inquisitor was the " scandalo delle meretrici di Roma " and, in connection with that, the corrupt life of clergy and laity, whereas it was Rome which should have set an example to the world (CATENA, 49). For moral and religious conditions in Italy cf. the picture drawn by H. BÖHMER, Studien zur Geschicte der Gesellschaft Jesu, Bonn, 1914, 177 seqq.

reformers any right to undertake the foundation of an entirely new Church. There has always been on earth, so Pius V. wrote, only one true religion, and there can be only one which is the religion which the Apostles preached, which the early martyrs attested by their blood, and which has been handed down from the time of the Apostle Peter to later times by means of his successors.[1] In the opinion of the Pope, therefore, it is obvious where the true Church of Christ is to be found, and if the new believers still resist it after they have been sufficiently instructed, their conduct could only be looked upon as obstinacy and pride.

In Italy, Protestantism did not come forward, as it did in Germany, more or less openly, but made use of underground ways to propagate its doctrines. From his own experience in this matter, Pius V. was borne out in his view as to the altogether treacherous character of the religious innovators. Books containing the new doctrines were secretly disseminated ;[2] preachers of the new " Gospel " travelled about the country disguised as merchants or in other ways,[3] and, what was worse, ecclesiastics who had secretly lapsed from the faith appeared in Catholic pulpits, dressed as Catholic priests, and covertly spread the opinions of Luther and Calvin under the

---

[1] To Sigismund Augustus of Poland, December 17, 1568, in GOUBAU, 114 seq.

[2] "Ho inteso dire che gli eretici hanno consertato di mano in mano tra di loro di fare ogni opera adesso per infettare Italia con mandarvi homini secreti con libri et con ogni sorta d'industria " (Castagna' June 5, 1568, Corresp. dipl. II. 381). " Ha çerca de un año que el Papa fué avisado por el Duque de Florentia y por otras personas que estuviesse sobre aviso ; que de Alemania, Flandes y Francia y otras partes donde ay hereges se embiavan cartas y libros contaminados a muchas personas de Italia, donde avia artas dañadas en lo de la fee." The Pope charged Cardinal Gambara with the task of watching over heretical books (Requesens to Philip II., March 16, 1567, ibid. 76).

[3] ROSI, Riforma in Liguria, 68.

guise of Catholic doctrine.[1]   The honesty of a Pius V. could
only see in such folk dishonest hypocrites and traitors to
the Church.

It would then have needed outstanding instances of the
courage that makes martyrs, as well as deep religious con-
victions, and what is more, many such instances, to have led
the Pope to have formed a higher opinion of Italian Protestantism, but any such examples of strength of character
were altogether lacking during his pontificate.   The new
believers almost all made their abjuration at the sight of
the stake, or in any case returned to their allegiance to the
Church at the last moment.[2]

The first autodafé took place on June 23rd, 1566, at the
Church of S. Maria sopra Minerva,[3] when fifteen sentences
were pronounced, and fourteen of the condemned were
present, seven of whom were sentenced by false witness to
scourging and the galleys, and seven made their abjuration.
Two of these were specially notorious.   One, a heretic whose
name is not known, had had himself circumcised in order
to be able to marry a Jewess, although he already had a wife
in Spain.   The other, Pompeo de'Monti, a Neapolitan noble,
and a relative of Cardinal Colonna, was handed over to the
secular arm as a relapsed heretic.   As we learn from the
sentence,[4] Pompeo, since his relapse was well known,   had

[1] TACCHI VENTURI, I., 330 *seqq.* The first preachers of the
reformation in Italy, Fra Galateo, Fra Bartolomeo Fonzio, and
Fra Ubaldo Lupetino, were all apostate monks. BENRATH in
Real-Enzyklopädie of Herzog, IX[3]., 529 *seq.* Examples from
the time of Pius V. see *infra* 301, 306, 311 *seq.*

[2] Attempts to effect conversions were not wanting at this time.
Cf. Cod. Vatic., 6317 : *FRA LATTANTIO ARTURO, Raggionamento
fatto ad un carcerato inquisito d'heresia (on the worship of the
saints), 1570, Vatican Library.

[3] Tiepolo on June 29, 1566, in MUTINELLI, I., 48 ; FIRMANUS,
*Diarium, see App. nn. 35-47. Corresp. dipl., I., 288. *Arco,
June 29, 1566, State Archives, Vienna. SANTORI, Autobiografia,
XII., 342.

[4] Preserved in Dublin, and published by BENRATH in *Rivista
cristiana*, VII. (1879), 503–505, and in *Allg. Zeitung*, 1877, n. 76,
Beilage.

spontaneously given himself up to the Inquisition. At first he denied that he had ever held or abjured heretical opinions, and then, in spite of all the proofs to the contrary, he maintained that at any rate after his abjuration he had not again fallen into heretical opinions, but under torture his courage proved unequal to further denials. After his abjuration Pompeo de'Monti was beheaded and burned on July 4th, 1566 ; he died with every sign of repentance.[1]

In the time of Pius V. the autodafés were conducted with greater solemnity than under previous Popes ;[2] the Cardinals and all the Papal court attended, and a great concourse of people assembled, especially when some one who had hitherto been held in high repute had been discovered to be a secret heretic and had been condemned as such. On account of the great crowd the Cardinals could hardly obtain seats at the first autodafé of 1567, which took place at the Minerva on February 24th ; among those who made their abjuration there was a well known preacher who, in the previous year, had set up his pulpit amid great crowds in Florence and even in Rome, and had been condemned to imprisonment in his convent as a convicted heretic.[3] The second autodafé of the same year, on June 22nd, caused a similar demonstration, when the distinguished Neapolitan noble, Mario Galeota, made his abjuration with nine others.[4]

---

[1] FIRMANUS, *Diarium, see App. nn. 35–47. SANTORI, loc. cit. ORANO, 15. BERTOLOTTI (Martiri, 36) quite wrongly and without any proof says that he was burned alive. Cf. the information from the Archives of S. Giovanni Decollato in AMABILE I. 296 : ibid. 297 seq. for the sending of heretics from Naples to Rome.

[2] Requesens, July 4, 1566, Corresp. dipl., I., 288.

[3] FIRMANUS, *Diarium, see App. nn. 35–47. An *Avviso di Roma of September 21, 1566 (Urb. 1040, p. 287, Vatican Library) is able to tell us that the preacher in question (Basilio) had admitted his heresy. Cf. *Avviso di Roma, without date, sent by Arco with his letter of March 1, 1567. State Archives, Vienna.

[4] FIRMANUS, *Diarium see App. nn. 35–47. B. Pia in BERTOLOTTI, Martiri, 43. For particulars as to the relapsed heretic

Even greater excitement was caused by the autodafé of September 21st, 1567.[1] Among the seventeen condemned there was a prelate who was a well-known figure in Rome, the protonotary-apostolic, Pietro Carnesecchi,[2] at one time principal private secretary to Clement VII., and held in high esteem by the Duke of Florence and the Queen-Mother of France. After having been brought several times before the Inquisition, Carnesecchi had, in the time of Pius IV., obtained a discharge,[3] but Pius V., in consequence of fresh signs of

mentioned by Pia, who was condemned and burned on the following day, see *Avviso di Roma of June 28, 1567, Urb. 1040, p. 410, Vatican Library. *Cf.* SCIPIONE VOLPICELLA, Mario Galeota letterato Napoletano del secolo XVI. (Memoria letta all'Accademis di Archeologia, lettere e belle arti), Naples, 1877, and Appendice alla mem. su M. Galesta. BENRATH in *Hist. Taschenbuch*, VI. (1885), 169–196. An apostate Dominican, Perini, who had married and become a professor in Calabria, made his abjuration as a relapsed heretic (*Avviso di Roma of June 28, 1567, Urb. 1040, p. 410, *loc. cit.*). The Bishop of Policastro made his abjuration before the Pope (*ibid.* and *Arco, June 21, 1567, State Archives, Vienna).

[1] FIRMANUS, *Diarium see App. nn. 35–47. *Avviso di Roma of September 27, 1567, Urb. 1040, p. 442, Vatican Library. Report of B. Pia in DAVARI in *Arch. stor. Lomb.*, VI. (1879), 795. BERTOLOTTI, Martiri, 38–43.

[2] L. WITTE, Pietro Carnesecchi, Ein Bild aus der italienschen Martyrergeschichte, Halle, 1883. LEON. BRUNI, Cosimo I de' Medici e il processo d'eresia del Carnessecchi, Turin, 1891. A. AGOSTINI, Pietro Carnesecchi e il movimento valdesiano, Florence, 1889 (cf. *Arch. stor. Ital.*, Ser. 5, XXVI., 1900, 325 *seq.*). A. DAL CANTO, Pietro Carnesecchi, Rome, 1911. MUTINELLI, I., 52, 73. PALANDRI, 116. GIAC. MANZONI, Estratto del processo di Pietro Carnesecchi (*Miscellanea di Stor. Ital.*, X), Turin, 1870. HASE in *Jahrb. für protest. Theol.*, 1877, 148. 189. CANTÙ, Eretici, II., 422–434 and *Arch. stor. Ital.*, Ser. 3, XIII. (1871), 303 *seq.* *Arco, September and October 4, 1567, State Archives, Vienna. *Cf. Rivista stor.*, 1912, 41 ; 1913, 187. For the proceedings against Carnesecchi, see also, AMABILE, I., 148.

[3] See Vol. XVI. of this work, p. 308 *seq.*

heresy, had had his case reopened.[1] Cosimo de' Medici
did not dare to refuse to hand over his protégé.[2] Confidence
in his powerful patron encouraged the inconstant man in the
mad idea of trying to save himself again on this occasion by
an obstinate denial of the charge. The Florentine ambassador
in Rome soon learned that for this very reason, and in spite
of all the efforts of the Duke of Florence and other powerful
friends, the trial was taking a very ugly turn.[3] Carnesecchi
had to appear at the autodafé on September 21, 1567, and
receive sentence.

The reading of the minutes of his trial lasted for two hours,
and with increasing surprise the hearers learned how a man,
who had always, as far as outward appearances went, been a
minister of the Church, and who had apparently without any
scruple enjoyed the richest ecclesiastical benefices, had had
secret relations with almost all the heretics, had accepted a
number of doctrines contrary to the faith, and had succeeded
by impudent lies and subterfuges in deceiving his judges.[4]

The Florentine and Mantuan envoys describe the impression
made by the reading of the acts of the trial by speaking of him
as " a very wicked man " and " the most loathsome and villan-

[1] A letter of Carnesecchi found among the papers of Giulia
Gonzaga gave the excuse (*Arco, June 29, 1566, State Archives,
Vienna). On May 15, 1566, Camillo Luzzara wrote to the Duke
of Mantua that it was said at the court that many people would
have to do with the Inquisition, " massime quelli che hebbero
stretta practica con la S. Donna Giulia, contro la quale vogliono
che si sian de male cose, et che se fosse viva che dovesse essere
chiamata a Roma infallibilmente. L'arcivescovo d'Otranto fu
molto amico suo." Gonzaga Archives, Mantua.

[2] For his handing over *cf.* LADERCHI, 1566, n. 195 *seq.* (briefs
of June 20 and August 1, 1566).

[3] " Risposemi [Cardinal Pacheco] che le cose del Carnesecchi
erano in mal termine . . ., e mi tornò a dire che non ha cervello,
ed essersi governato molto male, e che portava gran pericolo della
vita non si mostrando penitente. . . . Crede il cardinale che la
speranza ch'egli ha havuto nell' EE. VV. gli abbia nociuto."
Serristori, May 16, 1567, Legazioni 435 *seq.*

[4] A list of his heretical opinions in LADERCHI, 1567, n. 54.

ous heretic " who had been heard of for many years.[1]   His behaviour during the autodafé was not calculated to help popular
opinion in favour of the unhappy man.   At first Carnesecchi,
relying on his powerful patrons, listened to the accusation with
a lofty air, but he suddenly collapsed when, contrary to his
expectations, he was condemned to be handed over to the
secular arm.   On his return to his prison he sought consolation
from the Capuchin, Pistoja, who was wont to care for the
unhappy sinners.[2]   Once more the Pope postponed the carrying out of the sentence for ten days, in order to give the blinded
man an opportunity for the contrite confession of his errors,
which would have saved his life.[3]   On October 1st, he,
together with another, was beheaded and burned, but to the
end he was so vague and confused in his statements that, as he
himself had said, neither the Catholics nor the heretics could
feel satisfied about him.[4]

---

[1] " Gl'inquisitori e tutti dicono essere malissimo uomo (Serristori
September 21, 1567, Legaz. di Serristori 441).   In ristretto non
fu udito da molti anni in qua il più brutto, il più scelerato heretico
di costui. . . . Ogniuno di passo in passo stupiva d'udir tanta
scelerato heretico di costui. . . . Ogniuno di passo in passo stupiva
d'udir tanta sceleragine " (B. Pia to the Duke of Mantua in
BERTOLOTTI, Martiri 39).

[2] B. Pia, *loc. cit.*   For Pistoja *cf. Arch. Rom.*, XIII., 156.

[3] Legaz. di Serristori, 443.

[4] " Egli medesimo in ultimo confessò non aver satisfatto nè
alli eretici, nè alli cattolici " (Tiepolo, September 27, 1567, in
CANTÙ, Eretici, II., 434).   Giov. Antonio de Taxis wrote on
October 11, 1567 : " Il Carneseccha se confesso et comunico il dì
inanzi, pero con tutto questo dicono che mori non del tutto
repentito " (in LASSEN, Briefe des Masius, 396).   It may be supposed that Taxis confused Carnesecchi with his companion, who
was really converted.   But Firmanus (*Diarium p. 195, Papal
Secret Archives : see App. nn. 35–47) on October 1, 1567, says
of the *two* victims :   " Isti die praeterita acceperant ss. sacramentum Eucharistiae " although he calls him " *impoenitens* " (that is,
impenitent while there was still time).   *Arco on September 29,
1567, writes of Carnesecchi : " Esso mostra curar poco di vita o
di morte " (State Archives, Vienna).   On October 4 he *relates

It must be pointed out that in 1568, among more than sixty persons condemned by the Inquisition, we find only two who persisted in their opinions until death. At the first autodafé in that year, on January 4th, all the twenty-two who were summoned made their abjuration.[1] On May 9th, five out of the twenty-five who had to appear at the solemn autodafé were handed over to the secular arm ; three of these, who had been condemned to the stake as relapsed heretics, showed themselves repentant and were exempted from the death penalty. Among them was an old man of seventy who, taking his stand under the gallows, delivered a truly Christian discourse to the people, so that all who were present were much moved. Two, however, who were quite impenitent, remained firm in their opinions, and perished at the stake.[2] At the third autodafé of this year, on November 30th, sixteen of the accused recanted ; three, who had relapsed, were handed over

that Carnesecchi was burned on the Wednesday, and with him a Minorite ; it is doubted whether he repented, since before he was beheaded he wished to make a speech, but was not allowed to do so. The friar died repentant (*ibid.*).

[1] FIRMANUS, *Diarium, see App. nn. 35–47. According to the *Avviso di Roma of January 10, 1568 (Urb. 1040, p. 473, Vatican Library) there were 23. Among them was Niccolò Orsini, Count of Pitigliano, who had occasioned doubts as to his Christian faith by keeping a harem of Jewesses (LITTA, Famiglie celebri Italiane, Fam. Orsini, tav. XVIII) : he was condemned to pay a thousand scudi and to do penance for a time with the " Theatines." (i.e. according to EDUARDO FUGGER, Arch. stor. Ital., Ser. 5, XLII. [1908], 371, the Jesuits). *Cf.* *Avvisi, *loc. cit.* ; LADERCHI, 1567, n. 89 ; Corresp. dipl., II., 108 *seqq.* His safe conduct of June 14, 1566, in FONTANA in *Arch. d. Soc. Rom.*, XV. (1892), 466 *seqq.* The baron Bernarcedo of Naples was condemned to perpetual imprisonment (*Avvisi, *loc. cit.*).

[2] *Avviso di Roma of May 15, 1568, Urb. 1040, p. 517b, Vatican Library. *Arco to Maximilian II. on the same day, State Archives, Vienna. ORANO, 23–25 (where only the names of those who died penitent are given).

to the secular arm, but died on December 6th with every sign of repentance.[1]

The following year, 1569, produced just as few obstinate heretics. On February 28 an " obstinate Lutheran " was executed by hanging ; it was found impossible to the end to induce him to return to the Church.[2] Another solemn autodafé took place on May 22nd ;[3] four of the ten who were sentenced were handed over to the secular arm ; of these only one, Bartolomeo Bartoccio, remained steadfast in his opinions even to the terrible death at the stake.[4] One of his companions in misfortune, a rich man of noble birth, and a skilled lawyer, who had several times previously been brought before the Inquisition, but had recanted, seemed likely on this occasion to display a greater firmness of purpose at the autodafé. When his sentence had been read he attempted to make a discourse to the people, but was prevented by a gag.[5] Before his execution he too confessed " with great devotion, and in the Catholic way "[6] One of the four who were condemned, who was not a relapsed heretic, received a pardon, of which,

---

[1] FIRMANUS, *Diarium, see App. nn. 35–47.　*Avviso di Roma of December 4, 1568, Urb. 1040, p. 612, *loc. cit.*　For the execution of the repentant see ORANO, 27–9 ;　B. Pia in BERTOLOTTI, Martiri, 50 ; *Arco, December 8, 1568, *loc. cit.*

[2] ORANO, 30.

[3] *Cf.* the printed copy of the Avvisi of May 27 and 28, 1569, in BERTOLOTTI, Martiri, 54 ; *Avviso di Roma of May 25, 1569, Urb. 1041, p. 83, Vatican Library. " Domani si farà nella Minerva una grossa abiuratione, dove saranno da sei o otto comburendi." (B. Pia to Luzzara, May 21, 1569, Gonzaga Archives, Mantua, in BERTOLOTTI, Martiri, 49, printed with the doubly erroneous date of May 27, 1568). Tiepolo, May 28, 1569, in MUTINELLI, I., 80.

[4] M. ROSI, La riforma religiosa in Liguria e l'eretico umbro Bartolomeo Bartocci, Genoa, 1894. A. FALCHI, Un eretico Castellano (Bart. Bartoccio) bruciato in Roma, Città di Castello, 1908.

[5] BERTOLOTTI, *loc. cit.* and *Avviso di Roma of May 25, 1569, *loc. cit.*

[6] ORANO, 30 ; *cf.* ROSI, *loc. cit.*, 171.

however, he was not informed until he was actually on the gallows, and there showed himself to be steadfast in his protestations of repentance.[1]

Much more notorious than Carnesecchi and Bartoccio was Antonio della Paglia da Veroli, or as he preferred to call himself in ancient Greek form Aonio Paleario, a professor of belles lettres at Siena, Lucca, and after 1555 at Milan, who, especially at a later date, was held up as a martyr and a saint of the Protestant faith.[2] The works of Paleario, a didactic poem on the immortality of the soul, and various discourses and letters, show him to have been a talented humanist ; a satirical work against the Papacy, which was only printed after his death, but had been sent to Germany by Paleario in 1566, belongs to the time while he was still at Siena, and proves that he had then thrown himself headlong into the cause of

---

[1] BERTOLOTTI, *loc. cit.* The apostate Franciscan and protestant preacher Cellaria was executed at this time ; he had already recanted in 1557, and before his death became a Catholic. For his " ex abdito Archivo " see LADERCHI, 1569, n. 57 *seqq.* Guido Zanetti da Fano, a heretic of long standing, but not relapsed was condemned to imprisonment ; *ibid.* n. 66 *seqq.*

[2] GURLITT, Leben des Aonio Paleario, eines Martyers der Wahrheit, Hamburg, 1805. Later biographies by M. YOUNG (pseudonym of the authoress), London, 1860 ; J. BONNET, Paris, 1862, trans. into German by Merschmann. Hamburg, s.a. (1863) ; DES MARAIS (Marchese Bisleti in Veroli), Rome, 1885 ; G. MORPURGO, Un umanista martire, Città di Castello, 1912. For the appointment of Paleario as professor at Lucca *cf.* GIOV. SFORZA in *Giorn. stor. d. lett. Ital.*, XIV. (1889), 50-71 ; for his family and his relations with them LEON. DINI in *Arch. stor. Ital.*, Ser. 5, XX. (1897), 1 *seqq.; cf. ibid.* Ser. 5, XXIV. (1899), 352. An extract from his trial at Rome published by FONTANA in *Arch. della Soc. Rom.*, XIX. (1896), 151-175. A. RONCHINI, Due lettere inedite di A. Paleario in *Atti e Memorie della Deputazione di storia patria per le provincie Moden. e Parm.*, VII., 4, Modena, 1874. *Cf.* CANTÙ, Eretici, II., 452-462.; BENRATH in *Real-Enzyklopädie of Herzog*, XIV.[3], 602 *seqq.;* REUMONT, Bibliografia, 98 *seqq.*, 307. A portrait of Paleario in the episcopal seminary at Veroli.

the religious innovators.[1]   The year 1542 saw him summoned
before the Inquisition at Siena, the principal matter of accusation being a small work in Italian on the Passion of Christ.[2]
Paleario replied to the questions that were put to him, mainly
concerning the power of the Pope, to the satisfaction of the
judge, so that he was released without condemnation.[3]   Undoubtedly in order to remove the bad impression caused by
his summons, Paleario then published a letter to a friend, and
more especially an apologia to his judges, in which, however,
the true facts are quite differently stated.[4]   The clever humanist later on himself confessed that his discourse had never
been delivered, and that he had made use therein of statements
that were quite fictitious.[5]   By the advice of Sadoleto Paleario

---

[1] For the time of his apostasy from the Church (1535) cf.
STÄHELIN, Briefe aus der Reformationzeit (Schriften der Universität Basel, 1887), 35 seq., where other sources concerning Paleario
are given.

[2] Later confused with the treatise ' De beneficio Christi " ;
cf. Vol. XII of this work, 496.

[3] " Ad singula respondit recte, quamvis in aliquibus capitibus
not satis clare."   FONTANA, 164.

[4] BONNET-MERSCHMANN, 128-150.

[5] " Haec oratio non fuit habita, sed scripta, et multa sunt
efficta, imo vero pene omnia in peroratione, neque enim concursus
ille tot civium senensium verus fuit ulla ex parte, etc."   Thus
Paleario himself at his trial in Rome, FONTANA, 175.   It is strange
therefore that BENRATH, loc. cit. IX.[3], 603, acquits the humanist
on the strength of that very speech !   With all its pathetic statements and its obvious evasions of the matter in question, Bonnet
takes it as true gold.   The conscientious historian on the other
hand can only attach importance to the stern coldness of the acta
of the Roman trial.   It is true that Paleario in his discourse
declares that he could not attain a happier lot than martyrdom,
and that " in times like ours I believe that no Christian ought to
die in his bed," etc.   (BONNET-MERSCHMANN, 141), but Paleario's
actual behaviour before his judges makes it quite impossible to
attach the full meaning to these and other such high-sounding
phrases.   For the trial at Siena cf. GROTTANELLI DE' SANTI in
Miscell. stor. Senesi, II., (1894).

then abstained for a time from all theological discussion.[1]

In 1559, however, Paleario was again accused, this time before the Inquisition at Milan ; he voluntarily appeared before the judge, and on January 23rd, 1560, was able to obtain an acquittal.[2] In spite of this, in 1567 the Milanese tribunal had once more to inquire into his opinions, the matter of the accusation this time being his Sienese apologia, which had now been printed.[3] In the following year, by order of the Pope, his trial was transferred to Rome.[4] At the Roman inquiry, the excitable but vague and credulous rhetorician cut a sorry figure. He maintained in all seriousness that the reigning Pope had bought the Papacy by a gift of 30,000 and 8,000 scudi. He saw a serious fault on the part of Pius V. in the fact that the new edition of the Roman breviary no longer contained an office of the Holy Name of Jesus which had been approved by Clement VII. and Paul III., and for this " grave public sin " as well as on account of the strictness of the Pope against the heretics, he maintained that Pius V. was not the true Pope, and that anyone who lives in grave public sin cannot be the Vicar of Christ. But on the other hand he was so far from being a true Protestant that he accepted the authority of the Fathers, especially St. Augustine, and of the Council of Trent.[5] He refused from the first to admit any

---

[1] BONNET-MERSCHMANN, 151. FONTANA, 175.

[2] FONTANA, 165 seq.

[3] FONTANA, 166. For the other charges against Paleario cf. LADERCHI, 1568, n. 40 seqq. Laderchi had at his disposal the acta of the Roman Inquisition.

[4] F. GABOTTO in La Cultura, 1891, tries to prove from a letter of Paleario of May 17, 1568, " non esser vero che da questa città [Milan] il Paleario fosse tratto a forza." This letter, with the date May 11, 1568, was already published by CANTÙ in Arch. stor. Lomb., VI. (1879), 481, n.

[5] " Subscripsi mea manu quod dictaverunt mihi theologi . . ., qui allatis codicibus divi Augustini [perhaps this refers to the passages on the punishment of heretics] ostenderunt mihi multa quae ignorabam et propterea fuimus concordes. Item, allatis concilii Tridentini decretis, sententiis Patrum, a quibus mens mea numquam soluit dissentire, ut dixi in primo meo responso etc."

formal error on his part, saying that there could be no error in the love of one's neighbour and of the honour of Christ ;[1] he again renewed his often expressed assurance that he was ready to die " for Christ "[2] but at the same time he subscribed to a retraction, proposed to him by the Jesuit Ledesma, in which he accepted the Council of Trent, and the faith of the " holy, Catholic, and Roman Church," and retracted his views as to the unlawfulness of punishing heretics, and the forfeiture of the Papal power on account of grave sin.[3] The sentence of the Inquisition only took the form of making him promise no longer to appear in the dress of a heretic. When he refused to accept this Paleario was treated as impenitent and was handed over to the secular arm.[4] He was strangled, and his body was consigned to the flames on July 3rd, 1570 ; before he died he confessed, invoked the Madonna and the saints, and made a profession of the faith of the " holy Roman Church."[5]

(FONTANA, 174). For the reassembly of the Council of Trent under Pius IV. Paleario had composed an " Epistola de concilio universali et libero " (republished by ILLGEN, Programm der Leipziger Universität, 1832).

[1] FONTANA, 172.

[2] LADERCHI, 1568, n. 42.

[3] Published by DAUNOU, Essai historique sur la puissance temporelle des Papes, II., Paris, 1818, 278. An extract in FONTANA 172 : " Credo et confiteor, quidquid s. concilium Tridentinum definivit et quidquid sancta Ecclesia catholica Romana credit et confitetur."

[4] FONTANA, 175.

[5] Thus the register of the Confraternity of S. Giovanni Decollato (in ORANO, 38 seq.; FONTANA, 158), which took charge of those condemned to death. The notice of Paleario, published for the first time by Lagomarsini (Pogiani Epist., II., 188), was called in question or rejected by protestant writers, as for example by BONNET-MERSCHMANN, 265 n., by MENDHAM, Life of Pius V., 117, by MacCRIE, etc. But it is incontestibly genuine (see ORANO, 38 seq., and FONTANA, 158), nor is it possible to see why the book of the confraternity should have invented it. In that book obstinate heretics are either not mentioned at all or else are entered

Although during 1567 the autodafé was held three times in
Rome, and the same number of times in the following year,
during the second half of the pontificate of Pius V. we only
have records of two such solemn spectacles.[1]   After the above

as such.   BENRATH (loc. cit. 605) is right in saying : " this retractation was not in any case made officially," but the register of
the confraternity does not claim that there was any retractation
before the tribunal, and only speaks of a simple declaration made
before his death, as occurs in many other instances : such a
belated repentance would at the utmost only entail that the death
by fire was changed to strangulation, with the subsequent burning
of the body, but not a pardon : " it is proper to bear in mind that
repentance after sentence was of use for the salvation of the soul,
but made no difference for the saving of the body " (FONTANA,
159).   It is quite impossible to see how the last letters of Paleario
to his family, which were entrusted to the said confraternity for
transmission, prove the report to be a falsehood (as BONNET,
loc. cit. claims).   For that matter Paleario lived quite cut off
from his strictly Catholic family, and it would appear that this
separation was not merely local. (DINI in Arch. stor. Ital., Ser.
5, XX., 1897, 16).   Thanks to De Thou the view got about that
Paleario died the true death of burning which was reserved for
heretics.   Cf. LADERCHI, 1569, n. 71 seqq.

[1] As neither the Avvisi di Roma nor the reports of the embassy
to Vienna mention any solemn autodafés for the years 1570 and
1571, and no information is to be found in the lists of the confraternity of S. Giovanni Decollato, it may be concluded that
there were none.   For 1570 Orano (p. 36-40) besides Palearic
mentions as being executed for religion a certain Porroni of Rome,
who was in the prisons of the Inquisition, but, it is expressly
stated, not as a heretic (" non come luterano "), and also the poet
Niccolò Franco, who according to a false entry in the book of the
confraternity was executed for heresy, and according to three
other witnesses (BERTOLOTTI, Martiri, 51) for libel (cf. Scritti in
onore di A. d'Ancona, 1901, 543 seq.; CANTÙ, Eretici, II., 435),
and lastly a Frenchman, whom Orano himself does not dare
definitely to call a heretic.   For 1571 Orano (p. 40) has nothing in
particular to report and Bertolotti (p. 57-60) has no executions to
report.   The *Avviso of July 8th, 1570, says that Altinio Paltoni
was burned on that date ; he had been a lector at Pavia. Urb. 1041,
p. 307, Vatican Library.

mentioned autodafé of May 22nd, 1569, the Cardinals and
prelates did not assemble again in any numbers at the Minerva
until February 3rd, 1572, in order to assist at the abjuration
of thirteen heretics, one of whom was handed over to the
secular arm and was burned on February 9th, together with
four women ; all five were reconciled before they died.[1]
During 1571 it is true that the abjuration of five of the common
people took place on February 18th, but this occasion was not
published in advance, and took place without any solemnity
in the Sistine Chapel, it being feared that the fact that even
members of the lower classes had been condemned on so grave
a charge might give scandal.[2] It would seem that heresy
among the true Romans was looked upon as something
extraordinary ; the records of the Confraternity of the
S. Giovanni Decollato do not number a single person of Roman
birth among the heretics who were put to death up to the time
of the death of Pius V. and even later.[3]

Among the cities of the Papal States none was called upon
to send more of its inhabitants for judgment before the Roman
Inquisition than Faenza.[4] It is reported in April, 1567, that
many persons had been arrested there and taken to Rome
on the suspicion of heresy together with a Servite preacher,
and that at the same time the bishop was called upon to give

---

[1] *Avviso di Roma of February 9th, 1572 (Urb. 1053, p. 31,
ibid.). *Arco, February 9, 1572, State Archives, Vienna. BER-
TOLOTTI, Martiri, 61 *seq.* ORANO, 40-44. See also AMABILE, I.,
315 *seq.* The four women, according to the *Avviso already
quoted, were " streghe." ORANO (p. 45-52) mentions four other
executions in 1572, on February 22, March 15, and July 19, but
in all four cases the reason for the capital punishment is not
sufficiently clear.

[2] BERTOLOTTI, Martiri, 58.

[3] *Cf.* the lists of those who abjured in *Arch. d. Soc. Rom.* XII.
(1889), 342 ; BERTOLOTTI, Martiri, 45, 55. That the " Porroni
romano " of Orano (p. 36) is wrongly included among the heretics,
see *supra* 311, n. 1.

[4] *Cf.* ORANO, 25–27, 30, 32 ; BERTOLOTTI, Martiri, 41, 55.

an explanation of his negligence.[1] At Faenza, so states a report of the following year, thirty-seven heretics had recently been imprisoned, and the whole district had been infected by a teacher who had now fled to Geneva, and that probably the only remedy was the free use of the stake.[2] In September, 1568, Tiepolo reported that at Amandola, a small town in the Marches, brigands and escaped monks had set fire to the churches and destroyed the sacred images, and that the Pope intended to take severe measures with Amandola and the neighbouring S. Ginese, since he had heard that there were many heretics there. No place in the Papal States, however, had a worse name in this respect than Faenza ; the Pope even thought of destroying the city and transferring its inhabitants elsewhere ; many persons from that city had recently been handed over to the Roman Inquisition.[3]

The Pope, who had already had experience of that place as Inquisitor, set up there a commissariate-general of the Inquisition, whose jurisdiction extended over the dioceses of Faenza, Ravenna, Imola, Cervia, Cesena, Bertinoro and Sarsina.[4] The choice of the first commissary-general, however, was not a happy one ; this was Angelo Gazini da Lugo. The Inquisitor was too severe ; a chronicler wrote that even the stones trembled before his terrible rigour. A contemporary

[1] *" In Faenza sono stati presi molte persone havute per heretiche con un frate de Servi predicatore che si conducono qui, et il vescovo è chiamato per la negligenza usata." B. Pia to Luzzana, April 12, 1567, Gonzaga Archives, Mantua.

[2] *" . . . et si scuopre quella terra tutta infetta per opera di un maestro di scuola che se n'è poi fuggito a Genevra che si dubita che non bisogni andarvi col fuoco." Cipriano Saracinello to Cardinal Farnese, February 28, 1568, State Archives, Naples C. Farnes, 763.

[3] Tiepolo, September 25, 1568, in MUTINELLI, I., 79. Cf. CANTÙ, Eretici, II., 408 ; *Avviso di Roma of September 17, 1568, among the correspondence of Cusano, State Archives, Vienna.

[4] What follows is taken from the kind information of Prof. Giuseppe Donati of Florence, who is preparing a work on the Riforma e Contrariforma a Faenza nel sec. XVI.

names 115 persons who had been accused of heresy, and even so the list was not complete. About half the accused had to be released for lack of proof, but the others were visited with the severest penalties, such as death, the galleys, and imprisonment. A painter named Giovanni Battista Bertucci was sent to prison merely for having said that indulgences which had been bought with money were of no value.[1] It would seem that at first Pius V. was well pleased with the Inquisitor of Faenza, for on November 20th, 1570, he made him Bishop of Polignano in Apulia. But this satisfaction of the Pope had been based upon false information, and quickly evaporated when he was better informed. A contemporary writer says that if Gazini had not died the Pope would have ignominiously deprived him of his bishopric.

In spite of the wide extent which the Protestant movement seemed likely to attain at Faenza, it was soon evident that even there, as in the rest of Italy, it had taken no real root among the masses of the people. In a great fire which had broken out in the city an image of the Madonna remained unharmed amid the flames. Everyone saw a miracle in this occurrence, and at once the daily diatribes of the Protestant preachers against the worship of the saints and of their images failed to have any effect. The clergy, the city council and the populace ran to witness the miracle ; pilgrimages came in great number from the surrounding country to the miraculous image ; startling cures were effected to the amazement of the physicians ; a little church was erected by popular subscription to contain the image, and finally Pius V. in a brief which gave the city the assurance of the Pope's forgiveness, approved the religious celebrations which were held in celebration of the event. Later on Gregory XIII. condoned, in the case of those persons who had been condemned by Gazini, those penalties which had not already been complied

[1] From Donati. *Cf.* P. BELTRAMI, L'atto d'abiura dell'eretico faentino G. B. Bertucci (1564) in *Romagna*, II., 6 *seq.* According to Marcello Valgimigli, *Notizie storiche, for the year 1567, 200 persons were condemned at Faenza under Pius V. Library, Faenza.

with. Gazini's successor administered the inquisition with so great mildness that none of the records have anything to say about his activities. Protestantism at Faenza was practically at an end.[1]

On July 20th, 1566, Tiepolo tells us how, during the previous conclave a casket containing notes for the Inquisition had been stolen from Cardinal Ghislieri, the reigning Pope ; this was later on recovered, to his great satisfaction, because it would have entailed many imprisonments, both in and out of Rome.[2] This casket may have been a fiction of the popular imagination, but it is at any rate a fact that the Pope watched with the greatest care for every sign of heresy, especially in Italy, and his vigilance extended even further than that. It was said, so Arco wrote after the Pope had read to him a letter received from Germany, which stated that the government in Austria was composed of ten Protestants and two Catholics, that the Pope had his spies everywhere ;[3] that if the former Grand Inquisitor had eyes and ears even beyond the Alps, in his own country he did not altogether trust to the vigilance of the tribunals in the various cities ; that when he did not receive information from any place concerning heretical tendencies he thought that the

---

[1] There were also heretics in other parts of the Papal States. *Cf.* Tiepolo, September 25, 1568 (MUTINELLI, I., 79), for the disturbances and destruction of the sacred images at Amandola ; CANTÙ, Eretici, III., 719, for the heretics executed at Bologna in 1567 and 1568 ; BERTOLOTTI, Martiri, 41, for the heretics from Bologna and Forlì condemned in Rome in 1567 ; *cf.* WACHLER, G. Rehdiger und seine Buchersammlung in Breslau (1828), 14 ; *brief of February 2, 1569 " Thomae de Arimino O. Praed. deputato in inquisitorem in Arimin., Pisaur. et Fanens. civitatibus," Archives of Briefs, Rome.

[2] MUTINELLI, I., 49.

[3] " *Mi vien ancora detto, che ha non solo in Italia, ma anco fuori d'Italia per tutti i regni et stati spie, che gli danno minuto raguaglio della vita et costumi de'principi, de ministri loro, et di quelli che sono loro appresso." Arco, July 13, 1566, State Archives, Vienna.

Inquisitor there was not doing his duty.[1] In such cases, and more especially when the said tribunals found themselves opposed by apparently insuperable difficulties, he was wont to intervene directly ; more than one of the haughty princes and nobles of Italy had in the end to yield to the undaunted resolution and persistence of this man, who was universally venerated as a saint.

Venice in particular was looked upon as the starting point and refuge of heresy in northern Italy. The Venetian ambassador in Rome exerted himself to convince the Pope that in spite of isolated cases of heresy in his native place all was well in Venice, and that Rome could rely upon the vigilance of the Council of Ten,[2] but Pius V., who had had distressing experiences as Inquisitor in Venetian territory, did not trust the Republic.[3] During the first months of his pontificate he sent as nuncio to the city of the lagoons Giovanni Antonio Facchinetti, the future Innocent IX., to labour there for the reform of the clergy and the convents of nuns, and against the new religionists.[4] However unwillingly the Venetians accepted this supervision of their own Inquisition, and however much they disliked the zeal of Facchinetti,[5] they did not quite dare to oppose the will of the Pope ; while, during the pontificate of Pius IV. only forty-one trials concerning questions of faith had taken place in Venice, we have record of eighty-two during the reign of his successor.[6] It caused

[1] Tiepolo in ALBÈRI, II., 4, 172.

[2] Tiepolo, March 2 and 9, and April 27, 1566, in MUTINELLI, I., 35, 37, 41 seq. ; cf. CANTÙ, Eretici, III., 140.

[3] Cf. the report of Tiepolo for 1569, in ALBÈRI, II., 4, 191.

[4] Tiepolo, March 2, 1566, in MUTINELLI, I., 35.

[5] *The Florentine ambassador to Venice, Cosimo Bartoli, to Cosimo I., August 2, 1567, State Archives, Florence, Medic. 2978.

[6] Cf. COMBA, Elenco generale degli accusati di eresia dinanzi il Sant' Uffizio della inquisizione di Venezia A. 1541–1600, in Rivista Cristiana, III. (1875), 28 seqq., 71, 100 seq., 158, 207, 235, 297, 326, 366 seq., 411 seq., 447. The list is arranged according to the native places of the accused. Vicenza heads the list with 23 names. Particulars in BENRATH, Gesch. der Reformation in

great excitement when the Pope demanded—a thing that
often occurred in the time of Pius V., when it was hoped that
such a course would yield fuller information as to the spread
of the Protestant movement—that a heretic, Guido da Fano,
should be handed over to the Roman Inquisition. At first
the Senate refused its consent absolutely and repeatedly,
saying that Venice was not accustomed to send its accused
before foreign tribunals, but in spite of this Pius V. remained
immovable in his demand, and in the end the proud Signoria
had to yield him the victory ; by the end of August, 1566,
Guido had arrived in Rome.[1]

As was the case with Venice, the Pope also distrusted
the Republics of Lucca and Genoa, both of which were brought
into contact with the Calvinists by their commercial relations
with Lyons and Geneva.[2]

Hitherto the Genoese had shown themselves quite docile

Venedig, Halle, 1887, 70 *seqq.* *Cf.* also L. G. PÉLISSIER, Les
archives des inquisiteurs d'état à Venise, Besançon, 1899. See
also the learned dissertation by P. PASCHINI Una umanista,
disgraziato nel Cinquecento, Publio Francesco Spinola (executed
on January 31, 1567), Venice, 1919.

[1] BENRATH, *loc. cit.* 68 *seq.* " El papa los ha apretado de
manera que se resolvieron en embiarle " wrote Requesens to
Philip II. on September 18, 1566. Corresp. dipl., I., 347. LADER-
CHI, 1566, n. 194. *Arco, August 3, 1566, State Archives, Vienna.
Pius V. had already made it a condition for his receiving the
Venetian embassy for the " obedientia " that Niccolò da Ponte,
who had been withdrawn from the Roman Inquisition, should be
handed over. *Cusano, February 2, 1566, State Archives,
Vienna. The two letters to the Doge and the nuncio in Venice,
dated July 27, 1566 (Nunziat. de Venezia 17, 10 and 11, Papal
Secret Archives), in which Pius V. asked for the handing over of
Guido Zanetti da Fano, belong to the so-called " Lettere di
proprio pugno." Different from these are the completely
autograph letters of Pius V., at the head of which the
Pope placed the name of Jesus. *Some of these are preserved,
though unimportant as to their contents, in the State Archives,
Florence.

[2] Tieplo in ALBÈRI, II., 4, 190.

to the spiritual authority,[1] but their obedience was put to a
hard test when, in October, 1567, Bartolomeo Bartoccio was
imprisoned at Genoa, when he was passing through the city,
as a propagator of Protestant doctrines in Italy.[2] Cardinal
Cicada demanded the handling over of the heretic to the
Roman Inquisition,[3] but the Senate of Geneva, where Bartoccio had resided for twelve years, threatened to break off
commercial relations if the prisoner were not set at liberty.[4]
A long correspondence ensued, both with the Swiss republics
of Geneva and Berne, and with Cardinal Cicada.   In Rome
Genoa pointed out that all its trade with Flanders and Germany passed through Switzerland, and that the people in
the latter country were " but little versed in the usages of
civilisation ";[5] that Berne had already kept back 24,000
scudi of Genoese money ;[6] Rome should at least allow them
to pacify the irritation of this barbarous people.[7] but Pius
V. would not suffer himself to be turned from this purpose
by any of these considerations, and at length induced the
mercantile Ligurian republic to bend to his will, even in a
matter that so much concerned their trade and finances,
and Bartoccio was tried in Rome.[8]

Soon after Bartoccio had been taken away fresh difficulties
for the Senate of Genoa made their appearance.   It would
seem that the Eucharist had been celebrated in Genoa according to the Calvinist rite for the first time, and the mildness
with which the Inquisitor had dealt with the case had caused
surprise and even consternation in Rome.   It availed the

----

[1] Rosi, Riforma, 17 *seqq.*   From 1540 to 1583 there were 366
trials before the Inquisition at Genoa, which, however, must not
be counted as cases of heresy ; *ibid.* 43.

[2] *Ibid.* 68 *seq.*

[2] *Ibid.* 70.

[4] *Ibid.* 73.

[5] " Per la Svizzera, dove habita una nazione assai incolta di
costumi civili " ; *ibid.* 74.

[6] *Ibid.* 75.

[7] *Ibid.* 74.

[8] See *supra*, p. 306.

Senate nothing that it sought to show that the matter was of no real importance ; the Pope sent Bianchi, Bishop of Teano, as judge-extraordinary, and when the latter proceeded with the utmost rigour, condemned some of the offenders to the galleys and insisted on their making a public recantation in penitential dress, contrary to all previous usage in Genoa, of just as little avail were the protests which were made, to the effect that it would be better to spare such Spanish pro-cedure in a city which was " all zeal, good-will, and piety " and that the very publicity of the recantation only served to call attention to the heresy. The Senate resigned itself to what had been done when the Pope paid tribute in a brief to Genoa as a city of long proved Catholic loyalty, but went on to show that for that very reason the city ought not to take exception to the wiping out of the recent stain upon its honour by means of the same penalties as were used in Florence, Venice, Rome and elsewhere.[1] Two years later Pius V. himself, in answer to a request from the Senate, mitigated the penalties which had been inflicted as far as possible.[2]

Immediately after receiving news of the election of Pius V., the Republic of Lucca had hastened to renew its edicts against any dealings with the exiles from Lucca at Lyons.[3] and thus, even before paying its homage to the new Pope, the city had met his wishes. In the following year all dealings with their exiled fellow-citizens at Lyons were even more strictly prohibited.[4] But in spite of all its loyalty to the Holy See, the Republic, in its instructions for the paying of homage had charged its representative to do all he could in Rome

---

[1] Brief of June 5, 1568, in LADERCHI, 1568, n. 44. ROSI, *loc. cit.* 158 *seq.*

[2] Brief of October 27, 1570, in ROSI, 159 *seq.*

[3] See Vol. XVI. of this work, p. 347.

[4] Edicts of January 11 and 15, and March 27, 1566, 1567 and 1568, given by EUG. LAZZARESCHI, Le relaziono fra S. Pio V. e la repubblica di Lucca, Florence, 1911, 6–8. The Pope soon lost his distrust of Lucca, Requesens to Philip II., November 21, 1567, Corresp. dipl., II., 262 *seq.* ; *cf.* 158.

to prevent the Pope from introducing the Inquisition into Lucca.[1]

Similar fears were also felt in other cities of northern Italy in the time of Pius V., at any rate of that form of the Inquisition which was customary in Spain. At Milan where, only a short time before, such strong and heated opposition had been offered to the introduction of the Spanish Inquisition,[2] the Papal bull against irreverence in church, simony, sodomy and concubinage,[3] once more caused anxiety lest this edict should pave the way for the introduction of Spanish methods.[4] This time it was the archbishop himself, Cardinal Borromeo, who laid before the Pope the fears of the city. Nothing is left undone in Milan, so he wrote, in the matter of the punishment of the guilty, but the bull allows judicial proceedings to be taken on the strength of a mere secret accusation,[5] whereas, according to the Imperial code, secret accusations are not permitted. The real cause, however, of all the anxiety which is felt is to be found in the suspicion that it is intended to introduce the Inquisition on the Spanish model, not so much out of love for religion, as for political reasons, and because some of the municipal authorities wish to enrich themselves at the expense of the citizens. All attempts to remove this fear from the minds of the Milanese are vain ; they tell me that the Pope himself is guided by the purest motives, but that in practice the ordinances of the bull can be interpreted by the officials in their own way, and that thus all kinds of novelties will be introduced by degrees.[6]

[1] Lazzareschi, *loc. cit.* 7 n. 1.

[2] *Cf.* Vol. XVI. of this work, p. 336 *seq.*

[3] Of April 1, 1566, Bull. Rom., VII., 501 *seqq.*

[4] VERGA, 30 *seqq.*

[5] ' Ut praemissorum delictorum . . . notitia facilius habeatur, volumus quod in singulis casibus, non solum per accusationem et inquisitionem, sed etiam ad simplicem et secretam denuntiationem procedatur." Bull. Rom. V.. 437, § 13.

[6] " Et accioch è N. S. sappia una volta la radice ed il fondamento ove s'appoggiano tutte queste difficoltà, bisogna che habbia questo per una massima verissima, che in questo popolo è universale

The same bull of Pius V. met with similar opposition at Mantua as well ; it was thought by the priests and monks that it would lead to malicious accusations, and pave the way for the Inquisition. The publication of the Latin text occasioned a great deal of murmuring, and efforts were made to induce the Duke to protest against the proposed Italian version.[1]

At that time Duke William was already annoyed with Rome because the Pope was disputing the right of presentation to the bishopric of Mantua which had been granted to him by Pius IV., and which had been finally taken away from him by a decree of December 23rd, 1566.[2] The Pope had gone so far as to send the Duke a citation ; when, subsequently the citation was taken away from the envoy together with his

suspicione che si cerchi di mettere in questo stato l'inquisizione alla foggia di Spagna, non tanto per zelo di religione quanto per interessi di stato et per voracità di qualche ministro o consigliere che per questa via disegnasse di arricchirsi colle facoltà di questi gentilhuomini e cittadini " (in VERGA 31). At Milan there were hardly any condemnations to the stake for Lutheranism. FUMI, L'inquisizione Romana, 301.

[1] STEFANO DAVARI in *Arch. stor. Lomb.*, VI. (1879), 773 *seqq.*, 787 *seqq.* The Spanish Inquisition was feared and hated at that time not only in Italy. When in 1569 the Jesuit, Antonio Possevino, returned to Rome from a journey to Avignon, the report that he had been charged by the Pope to introduce the Spanish Inquisition there caused a riot and an attack on the Jesuit college (LADERCHI, 1569, n. 180 *seq.* SACCHINI, P. III., i. 5, n. 139 *seq.* FOUQUERAY, I., 443–446). The energetic measures taken by the Pope, however, were successful in keeping Avignon safe from Protestantism in spite of the dangerous proximity of Orange (LADERCHI, 1566, n. 414 *seqq.* ; 1567, n. 163 ; 1568, n. 171 ; 1569, n. 176 *seqq.* ; GOUBAU, 133, 135, 169, 179, 184, 217). The Pope himself in a letter to Philip II. of October 26, 1569 (Corresp. dipl., III., 168 *seqq.*) had to defend himself against the charge that he did not pay enough respect to the privileges of the Spanish Inquisition.

[2] LADERCHI, 1566, n. 197 ; *cf.* 1567, n. 22. Tiepolo in ALBÈRI, II., 4, 180, 190.

ambassadorial credentials, the Pope thought of forcing the
Duke to present himself personally in Rome, and of deposing
him if he did not appear.[1] In Mantua the Inquisition had
to bear the brunt of the displeasure of the prince, whose
irritation was shared by the whole city. When in 1567 the
Inquisition imprisoned some Mantuan citizens, the Duke's
representative, Francesco di Novellara, made a protest
against any further action being taken by the tribunal until
the prince had had satisfaction.[2]

Pius V. had no intention of quietly allowing any such
violation of recognized ecclesiastical rights. On May 31st
he had recourse to the Duke with a request that, for the
sake of peace and quiet, he would refrain from any such
usurpations of the rights of the Church, and would allow the
guilty parties to be punished. He informed him at the same
time that he had removed the Inquisitor, Ambrogio Aldegati,
as being too easy-going, and had appointed in his place the
Dominican, Camillo Campeggio.[3]

The irritation felt both at the court and in the city
was by no means allayed by this appointment, the more so as
Campeggio made some further arrests, and arranged autodafés for August 3rd and October 26th, at which several
persons made their abjuration.[4] Besides this, several of the

[1] Requesens to Philip II., September 18, 1566, Corresp. dipl.,
I., 346 ; cf. 388.

[2] DAVARI, loc. cit. 774, 788.

[3] Ibid. 775. The *brief of nomination, May 31, 1567, in the
Archives of Briefs, Rome.

[4] " Si dice che hoggi i frati de S. Domenico doppo il vespero
fanno abiurare dieci di quelli loro prigioneri et che si faranno
salire in pulpito imitrati a chiamarsi in colpa " (L. Rogna, August
3, 1567, Gonzaga Archives, Mantua). So runs the text, as I am
assured by the keeper of the Archives, A. Luzio. Davari, who
published it, loc. cit. 790, besides unimportant changes, has read
abbrucciare instead of abiurare ! On October 26, 1567, L. Rogna
wrote : " Oggi su un palco eminente fatto in S. Domenico si
abiureranno alquanti di quelli reputati eretici." Even here Davari,
loc. cit. has changed abiureranno into abbruciarono. According to
the records that have so far come to light no heretic died at the
stake in Mantua.

Duke's counsellors were themselves heretics,[1] and heresy had assumed a revolutionary and political character at Mantua.[2] A canon of Mantua, whom Pius V. demanded should be sent to Rome on October 31st, 1567,[3] openly maintained that the human soul perished with the body.[4] The convent of the Dominicans was violently assaulted,[5] and the Duke summoned the Inquisitor before him and rebuked him for having imprisoned respectable citizens without the knowledge of the prince.[6] An attempt to obtain from Rome, by means of a special envoy, the recall of the Inquisitor, was rendered hopeless by a fresh act of violence which occurred immediately after the departure of the envoy. On Christmas night, two brothers of the Third Order, who were on their way to the midnight service, were killed in the public streets.[7] As was only to be expected Pius V. refused the request of the envoy, saying that if the Duke persisted in his leniency towards the heretics, he would witness even worse crimes ; that the Pope could not allow himself to be frightened or turned aside from his course of action against the heretics even if all the Dominicans were cut to pieces.[8] The envoy returned home in January, 1568, without having accomplished his purpose. All that he had obtained was that the Inquisitor was to make his excuses to the Duke.[9]

In order to put an end to this state of confusion, Pius V.,

---

[1] " Qui [a Roma] si sa molto bene . . . che l'Ecc. V. è male consigliata et ingannata, e che ha tre o quattro consiglieri heretici marci." The Count of S. Giorgio to Mantua, December 24, 1567, in DAVARI, 793.

[2] Campeggio, October 14, 1567, *ibid.* 791.

[3] See the *brief to the Duke of Mantua in the Gonzaga Archives, Mantua.

[4] BERTOLOTTI, Martiri, 45. He was an Averroist or follower of Pomponazzo.

[5] DAVARI, 776.

[6] *Ibid.*

[7] *Ibid.* 792.

[8] *Ibid.* 777 ; *cf.* 793.

[9] *Ibid.* 777 *seq.* ; 795.

at the beginning of 1568, sent the Archbishop of Milan, Cardinal Borromeo, to Mantua.[1] What a serious view the Cardinal took of his difficult task is shown by the fact that in order to obtain a happy issue he ordered continuous prayers by day and night in all the churches and convents of Milan, arranged in such a way that as the hour of prayer ended in one church, it was taken up in another.[2] As a matter of fact Borromeo's skill and prudence were successful in February, 1568, in appeasing the Duke and restoring the authority of the Inquisition. The more important offenders were to make their abjuration in private, and on April 4th a public auto-dafé took place, at which three natives of Verona were handed over to the secular arm, and on April 12th were beheaded and burned.[3] The reconciliation with the head of the Church was completed by a brief of April 21st, in which the Pope returns thanks for a communication which the Duke had addressed to him concerning the public autodafé.[4]

At the end of 1567 Cardinal Correggio had written to the Duke that those who made light of the old religion were also the enemies of their hereditary prince, quoting as an example the machinations of the French Protestants.[5] Events at

---

[1] BASCAPÈ, I. 2, c. 6, p. 37.

[2] In this way Borromeo was the first to order the so-called perpetual prayer, a thing which he often employed later on. BASCAPÈ, *loc. cit.*

[3] Letter from Capilupi and Amigone in DAVARI, 796.

[4] Gonzaga Archives, Mantua : see App. n. 48. Already on March 8, 1568, the Pope had praised the Duke for his devotion, and for doing what he had promised Borromeo (*Brevia, Arm. 44, t. 13, p. 164, Papal Secret Archives). Rome continued to keep a close watch on Mantua after this, sending warnings as to heretical tendencies, and asking for the handing over of those who, in any specially dangerous degree, were propagating them. *Cf.* the letters from Rebiba to Mantua of September 11 and November 6, 1568, and of June 16, 1571, in BERTOLOTTI, Martiri, 48 *seq.*, 58.

[5] " nè hanno altro fine che di fare in ogni luogo quello che hanno fatto et fan del continuo in Francia " Correggio, December 20, 1567 in DAVARI 791.

Mantua seemed to bear out the Cardinal's words ; the sending
to Rome of one of the Mantuan heretics led to a conspiracy
against the sovereign.   Pius V. gave the Duke all the help
he could in the investigation of the plot.   The Bishop of
Casale was given the necessary powers to imprison and examine
even the clergy, and when a certain Flaminio Paleologo
appealed from the bishop to his privileges as a Knight of
the Order of Santiago, Pius V. had a letter written to the
King of Spain to beg him not to extend his protection to the
criminal.[1] Speaking generally, the new religion at Mantua
did not fight with religious weapons only.   In March, 1568,
manifestos were discovered which held up as meritorious acts
before God and man the murder of Cardinal Borromeo, the
bishop and the Dominicans.[2] A preacher who had leanings
towards the innovators dared to condemn from a public
pulpit the methods of procedure adopted by the Inquisition, but the Pope had him summoned to Rome and
punished.[3]

Revolutionary ideas were also disseminated by the innovators in the district of Tenda in the Maritime Alps.   Many of
their adherents no longer believed in one God, while others
held that any acts of violence against clergy who possessed
property were lawful.   In 1566 a widespread insurrection
against Count Honoratus II. broke out, but this was easily

[1] Brief to Philip II. of June 28 1569 in LADERCHI, 1569, n. 64.
Bonelli to Castagna, June 29, 1569, Corresp. dipl., III., 94.
F. VALERANI, Prigionia e morte di Fl. Paleologo, 1568–1571,
Alessandria, 1912 (Extract from *Rivista di storia ed arte della
provincia d'Alessandria*).

[2] *Arco, March 29, 1568, State Archives, Vienna.   Cardinal
Rebiba in a letter to the Bishop of Mantua of March 27, 1568, in
BERTOLOTTI, Martiri, 46, mentions a " bando " which the Duke
" ha fatto fare per trovare et castigare gli autori di quei cartelli
contro il santo offitio."

[3] Roberto Novella da Evoli.   *Cf.* BERTOLOTTI, *loc. cit.* 51 *seqq.*
and the trial of Paleario in *Arch. d. Soc. Rom.*, 1896, 171, 173 *seq.* ;
*Avviso di Roma of June 17, 1570 (his removal to the prison of
Ostia), Urb. 1041, p. 295, Vatican Library.

suppressed.[1] It was not only Protestant errors, properly
so called, which had to be dealt with in Italy at that time.
In 1568 sixteen heretics, who among other things had revived
monothelism,[2] were arrested at Ferrara, and condemned to
the galleys and quarries, while at Naples a sect made its
appearance in 1567 which had adopted the rites of Judaism.[3]
Moreover, a great number of the Italian Protestants belonged
to that purely rationalistic sect known as the Anabaptists,[4]
not because its condemnation of infant baptism was its principal
doctrine, but because in the eyes of the world at that time,
that was their most monstrous belief.   From time immemorial
men had been admitted into the Church by baptism almost
exclusively as infants ; if the sacrament had been administered to such invalidly, it followed that for many centuries
there had been no Christians and no Church, and that the
foundation of Christ had long since disappeared.   This explains the great horror that was felt for the Anabaptists.

Rome kept a watchful eye upon all these many forms of
heresy. At the beginning of his reign Pius V. formed the
project of sending to all the Inquisitors of Italy orders to
furnish reports to Rome of all who were suspected of heresy.[5]

[1] Report of the Franciscan Conventual, Bojero of Nice, who by
the orders of the Bishop of Ventimiglia gave missions in Tenda in
1566 (GIOFFREDO, Storia delle Alpi marittime, V., Turin, 1839,
ad an. 1566. Cf. P. DEGIOVANNI, Gli eretici di Tenda-Briga-
Sospello nei secoli xv. e xvi. Florence, 1881, 9 seq., extract from
Rivista crist.).   In a *brief of August 7, 1566, Pius V. praises
the zeal of the Count for the repression of heresy, Brevia, Arm. 44,
t. 12, p. 99, Papal Secret Archives.

[2] CANTÙ, Eretici, II., 98.

[3] Ibid. 332. Laderchi 1567, n. 61. Little is known of the
heretics in Sicily (cf. V. LA MANTIA, Origini e vicende dell'Inquisizione in Sicilia in Riv. stor. Ital., 1886, 481 seq.) ; in 1568 and
1569 an autodafé took place at Palermo (Arch. stor. Sicil.,
XXXVIII., 1914, 306, 309. For the heretics at Verona cf.
Riv. stor. Ital., 1912, 241.

[4] Cf. BENRATH in Studien und Kritiken, 1885, 1 seqq.

[5] Babbi, the Tuscan envoy to Rome, July 2, 1566, in CANTÙ,
II., 431.

Even though it is true that such reports arrived in great numbers, the Inquisitors in the various Italian provinces had to submit to constant admonitions and even to deposition when they were negligent in fulfilling their duty.[1] A whole series of letters was addressed to the secular princes on behalf of the Inquisition, either to recommend to them a new Inquisitor,[2] or to demand the handing over of some specially dangerous heretic,[3] or to threaten punishment to the princes

[1] *Cf. supra* p. 322.

[2] Camillo Campeggio, appointed Inquisitor at Mantua (see *supra* p. 322) was, by a *brief of May 31, 1567, also recommended to the Duke of Ferrara for his dominions, on the ground that there were heretics there, who were causing the Pope much anxiety.   Archives of Briefs, Rome, and State Archives, Modena.

[3] Brief of March 30, 1566, to the Duke of Ferrara, in FONTANA, Arch. d. Soc. Rom., XV. (1892), 461. *Brief to Luigi Birago, Governor of Saluzzo, of December 29, 1567.   Archives of Briefs ; a brief of June 3, 1566, to the same, urging him to drive out the Huguenots, who were wont to escape from Piedmont to Saluzzo, in FONTANA, *loc. cit.* 463 ; to Lelio Orsini, Lord of Ceri, May 9, 1566 : he is to hand over to the bearer of the brief his agent Baldo Fabii, in order that he may take him to the Roman Inquisition, *ibid.* 461 *seq. ;* to the Count of Tenda, December 30, 1569, with a request to hand over to the Bishop of Ventimiglia two heretics, in LADERCHI, 1569, n. 74 ; FONTANA, *loc. cit.* 473 ; *cf.* LADERCHI, 1570, n. 145 *seq.*; to the Duke of Savoy, April 29, 1570, on a similar occasion, in LADERCHI, 1570, n. 143 ; FONTANA, 474.   In a *brief of August 30, 1567, Lodovico Pico Count of Mirandola is asked to deal with the imprisoned heretic Lanzoni as the Inquisitor, Campeggio, shall order (Archives of Briefs).   By order of the Pope, Cardinal Rebiba wrote on September 11, 1568, to the Duke of Mantua that a heretic who had already been condemned by the Inquisitor was continuing his activities in the Duke's territory : he must be handed over to the Inquisitor, and the officials must be told that the Duke intends to be obeyed in these matters. There was a further admonition on November 6, 1568, on account of certain heretics who thought themselves safe at Pavia and Monferrato under the protection of certain influential persons (BERTOLOTTI, Martiri, 48 *seq.*) ; in like manner on June 16,

themselves in the case of undue interference. Ercole, Lord
of Sassuolo, in the Duchy of Modena, who had allowed two
heretics into his territory, was placed in the Castle of St.
Angelo, until he had caused both of them to be delivered to
the Roman Inquisition.[1] When he had on his own authority
mitigated the punishment of a relapsed but repentant heretic,
Pius V. threatened the Duke of Savoy with excommunication,

September 15, and December 8, 1571, concerning a heretic who
lodged at Monferrato and Leghorn, and who was finally captured
by brigands, who sought to obtain their pardon on the score of
this capture (*ibid.* 58 *seq.*). Cardinal Bonelli wrote by the Pope's
command on April 26, 1566, to the Duke of Savoy, concerning a
school master who had already been condemned, but who was
continuing to spread his doctrines, and whom the civic officials
would not hand over to the Inquisitor (*ibid.* 34). On January 30,
1570, on February 13 and April 24, 1571, Cardinal Bobba had
recourse to the Duke for the handing over of a Franciscan heretic,
who had spontaneously surrendered to the Inquisition at Turin
(*ibid.* 56 ; *cf.* 57). For the vigilance of the Roman Inquisition *cf.*
also the information in BATTISTELLA, Il S. Officio e la riforma
religiosa in Bologna, Bologna 1905, 65, *seq. ; ibid.* 97 *seq.*, 100
seq., 105, for the execution of heretics at Bologna in 1567, 1568,
1570.

[1] " *La cosa, ch'io scrissi a V. S. Illma, che Nostro Signore
haveva intentione di mandar un commissario a Modena per le
cose della inquisitione, non essendo quella città la più netta del
mundo pare che si vada credendo et crescendo perche a questi
giorni N^{ro} Sig^{re} fece mettere qui in castello il sig^r Hercole de li
signori di Sassuolo per havere, come dicono, tollerato dui heretici
Modenesi, un Rangone et uno Castelvetro, in detta terra sua.   Ma
perche scrisse subito questo signore a'suoi agenti che prendessero
questi tali et li consegnassero a chi ordinava Sua Santità, è stato
rilassato con segurtà di presentarsi et fare ogni sforza perche
questi tali effettualmente siano dati nelle forze di Sua Beat^{ne}
Tutta questa istoria dicono che dà molto di pensare a Morone, et
però il povero signore ha una chiera molto afflitta, o sia per il male
passato del corpo o per l'infirmità presente dell'animo."   Caligari
to Commendone, June 29, 1566, Lett. di princ. XXIII. 270, Papal
Secret Archives. *Cf.* *Arco, June 22, 1566, State Archives,
Vienna.

and the Duke had to give way.[1] The Duke of Florence showed himself most favourable to the Roman Inquisition,[2] but on the other hand, Alfonso, Duke of Ferrara, the son of that Rénée of France who had Protestant leanings, behaved very differently.[3] Under the influence of his wife, Emanuele Filiberto of Savoy had more and more tolerated the Protestants.[4] Again and again Pius V. urged him to take steps against the religious innovators,[5] and at last had the satisfaction of seeing the Duke turn definitely against them, so that about 1570 they were driven out from Cuneo and Caraglio, the two principal centres of their activities, and in this way their power was broken.[6]

[1] Letter from Rome of January 22, 1567, in BERTOLOTTI, Martiri, 34 seq.

[2] " Es grande essecutor de lo que se ordena en la Inquisicion de Roma " (Zuñiga to Philip II., September 17, 1568, Corresp. dipl., II., 460). Cf. Bollett. Senese, XVII., 160, 197. At Siena as well the Florentine government was very vigilant against the heretics (ibid. 171) ; for the trials of heretics held there, ibid. 171 and CANTÙ, III., 449 seqq.; for the Sienese heretic Benvoglienti summoned to Rome on March 10, 1569, CANTÙ, 450 and Bollett. Senese, XVII., 183. In 1569 Pius V. still entertained suspicions of heresy at Siena.

[3] ALBÈRI, II., 2, 415. Bibl. in Archiv für osterr. Geschichte, CIII. (1913), 26.

[4] Zuñiga wrote on April 7, 1568, that in the opinion of the Duke of Florence a descent of the French heretics upon Italy would not meet with much opposition in Savoy " o porque no querria declararse contra Francia porque le governava su muger, la qual no acogeria de mala gana los hereges." Corresp. dipl., II., 339. Cf. ALBÈRI, II., 4, 189, and Vol. XVI. of this work, p. 351.

[5] Cf. the report of the " abbate di S. Solutore " to the Duke, Rome, December 9, 1566, in CIBRARIO, Lettere inedite di Santi, Papi, Principi, Turin, 1861, 394 seq. In Cod. K. 20 of the Vallicella Library, Rome, there are accounts *" de comprehensione Ioh. Honorati Marini haeretici opera Pii V. a duce Sabaudiae permissa eiusque causa in Taurinensi Inquisitione agitata 1566."

[6] A. PASCAL, Storia della riforma protestante a Cuneo nel sec. XVI., Pinerolo, 1913.

The edicts addressed by Rome to the provincial Inquisitors, however, did not always contain exhortations to greater activity. When complaints reached Rome about the Inquisitor at Pavia, Fra Pietro da Quintiano, who had imprisoned a certain Miliavacca, the Roman Inquisition had the minutes of the trial sent to it, and as a result, on October 18th, 1568, ordered the Inquisition of Pavia to acquit and release the condemned man from his imprisonment.[1] The unjust Inquisitor was informed that the Cardinal Inquisitors had been very much astonished at the trial, that the witnesses were not worthy of credence, that their depositions were negligible, and in no way proved the charge of heresy, and that it had been suggested to the witnesses, by the way in which the questions had been put, what answers they were to make.[2] The Cardinal Inquisitors sought to lay the principal blame on Fra Pietro's subordinates,[3] but he had nevertheless to resign his office.[4]

The German students at the University of Padua, many of whom were Protestants, remained for the most part undisturbed, so long as they did not rouse the hostility of the

---

[1] The decree (of Cardinal Ribiba) is printed by ETTORE ROTA in *Bollett. della Soc. Pavese di storia patria*, VII. (1907), 27-29.

[2] " Questi signori miei sono restati molto scandalezzati di detto processo, e gli è parso che si sia dato a' testimoni esaminati più fede di quello che conveneva, attenta maximamente la qualità loro e detti suoi, e l'interessi ch'havevano con il Miliavacha; oltrache, la maggior parte delle cose che dicono sono frivole, et anco non pertinenti alla heresia, et in quella che potevano toccarla, poco verisimili ; sono stati interrogati di mal modo et con interrogatori suggestivi ; et il mettere prigione quel testimonio et fare alli altri precetti penale pecuniarii in simil caso non è stato laudato, et in somma non s' è proceduto con quella saldezza e gravità che conviene a tanto tribunale." Although Miliavacca may not be the best man in the world, the Inquisition must nevertheless confine itself to inquiring into heresy, or at least into those offences which smack of heresy. *Bollett. Pavese, loc. cit.* 27 seq.

[3] *Ibid.* 28.

[4] *Ibid.* The gravest accusations of abuse of his office were also brought against him (*ibid.* 23 seqq.).

people by provocative behaviour in the churches and by making fun of Catholic things.[1] An exception to this general tolerance occurred in the time of Pius V. when, in 1570, the German professor, Weydecker, was brought before the Inquisition, and only released when he had abjured Protestantism.[2] At Padua they contrived to evade the making of the Tridentine profession of faith, which Pius IV. had made a necessary condition for taking a doctor's degree, by conferring the academic degrees without any public ceremony, at the hands of the so-called Counts-Palatine,[3] a right which Pius V. took away from the said Counts as far as he could.[4]

According to Arco two things especially occupied the Pope in the middle of the first year of his pontificate,[5] namely, his care for the Inquisition, and his struggle against " that terrible sin on account of which the dreadful judgment of God burned the cities that were infected by it "—sodomy.[6] On April 1st, 1566, he gave orders that those guilty of sodomy were to be handed over to the secular arm,[7] and under Pius V. there was

[1] BIAGIO BRUNI in *Atti del R. Istituto Veneto di scienze, lettere ed arti,* Ser. 7, V. (1893-94). 1015-1033. Between 1550 and 1599, 5083 German students of law, and 977 of philosophy (" artisti ") were lodged at Padua ; *ibid.* 1016.

[2] *Cf.* A. LUSCHIN VON EBENGREUTH in *Zeitschrift für allgem. Geschichte*, III. (1886), 805-817.

[3] BRUNI, *loc. cit.* 1030 *seqq.* It is also related of the students at Pisa in 1567 that they made vile mockery of the Catholic religion (CANTU, Eretlci, II., 437). At Siena, in April, 1566, the making of a profession of faith was demanded of the students (*Bollett. Senese*, XVII, 167). The governing body there kept a special watch on the German students (*ibid.* 167, 189 *seqq.*, 195).

[4] Edict of June 1, 1568, Bull. Rom., VII., 673. *Avviso di Roma of July 17, 1568, Urb. 1040, p. 549, Vatican Library. As early as March 20, 1568, the *Avvisi (*ibid.* 491) report that it had been decided " che tutti che si vogliono addottorare passino per ignem et aquam."

[5] *Arco, July 20, 1566, State Archives, Vienna.

[6] Pius V. in a brief of August 30, 1568, Bull. Rom., VII., 702 *seq.*

[7] Bull. Rom., VII., 43 ; among the *Editti, 205, there is one against blasphemy and sodomy, dated 6 Kal. apr. 1566, Casanatense Library, Rome.

no fear of such a bull remaining a dead letter.   A number of
imprisonments for sodomy[1] during July, 1566, filled Rome
with fear, especially the nobles, who well knew that the Pope
would apply his law in the case of great and small alike ;[2]
it is a fact that the punishment of burning was used in cases
of crimes against nature all through the reign of Pius V.[3]
In October, 1571, the complaint made by a preacher in the
Apostolic palace, that justice was only employed against the
poor and not against the rich, called forth a Papal edict ordering the strict enforcement of the laws against sodomy.[4]   A
brief had already been issued by which clerics who were guilty
of that offence lost all their benefices, dignities and revenues,
and, after degradation, were to be handed over to the secular
arm.[5]

Since the Inquisition had the power to deal with crimes
against nature, as giving ground for the suspicion of incredulity
and heresy, the same thing held good, and for the same reason,
of attempts to invoke the assistance of the evil spirits for any

---

[1] Tiepolo, July 20, 1566, in MUTINELLI, I., 50.

[2] *' che fa giusticia anco per i grandi '' (Arco, July 20, 1566,
State Archives, Vienna).   An *Avviso di Roma of July 20, 156
(Urb. 1040, p. 255, Vatican Library) states : '' Roma è quasi
tutta sbigottita per le gagliarde provisioni et essecutioni, che si
fanno contro li maledetti sodomiti nè si guarda in faccia a
persona.''

[3] Cf. the *Avvisi di Roma of April 2, 1569 : '' a sodomite was
burned,'' September 3, 1569 : '' the servant of a sodomite was
actually burned, and his master, who had fled, in effigy '' ; May 13,
1570 : '' a man was burned for bestiality '' ; October 6, 1571 :
'' to-day four sodomites were burned '' (Urb. 1041, p. 51, 143,
274 ; 1042, p. 129, Vatican Library).   Cf. MUTINELLI, I., 50 ;
Bollett. Pavese, IV., 591 seq.

[4] *Avviso of October 20, 1571, Urb. 1042, p. 135, loc.
cit.

[5] August 30, 1568, Bull. Rom., VII., 702 seq.   A *brief of
March 15, 1569, to the vicar of the Archbishop of Tarragona,
which orders the carrying out of this edict, in Brevia Arm. 44,
t. 14, p. 33, Papal Secret Archives.

purpose whatever.[1]   During the humanist period, when the
study of the occult played so great a part,[2] this side of the
activities of the Inquisition must have been specially important, but we know very little about it.   In 1568 the tribunal of
the faith at Pavia was engaged upon the case of a magician
who, by means of astrology, divination and alchemy, claimed
to be able to discover hidden treasure, and was engaged in
compiling, together with other people, a manual of magic.
In that same year five other persons were accused before the
Inquisition of witchcraft.[3]   During the reign of Pius V.
several witches were condemned in Rome,[4] Milan,[5] and elsewhere.[6]

[1] It is evident from various sources that even under Pius V.
the Inquisition did not confine itself to questions of faith alone.
Ciregiola on September 1c, 1568, *wrote to Cardinal F. de' Medici
that the Cardinal Inquisitors had persuaded Pius V. that it was
his duty to undertake some far-reaching enterprise against the
Huguenots, and to add some new saints to the Breviary (State
Archives, Florence).   An *Avviso di Roma of April 1, 1570 (Urb.
1041, p. 251, Vatican Library) tells of a meeting of the Inquisition
on account of the Emperor's protest.   An adulterer was handed
over to the Inquisition : *Cusano, March 2, 1566, State Archives,
Vienna.

[2] FUMI, L' Inquisizione, 72 *seqq.*

[3] ETTORE ROTA in *Bollett. Pavese*, VII. (1907), 20 *seq.*

[4] See *supra* p. 312, n. 1.   A sorceress was imprisoned by the Roman
Inquisition in 1569 for having foretold to the Pope his coming
death and to Cardinal Mula the tiara (*Avviso di Roma of December 24, 1569, Urb. 1041, p. 206b, Vatican Library).   *" Frustrate
5 vecchie in Roma fattucchiate " (August 6, 1569, *ibid.* 116b).

[5] *Brief of September 10, 1569, to the Senate of Milan concerning
witches condemned by the archiepiscopal tribunal.   Brevia, Arm.
44, t.14, p. 224, Papal Secret Archives.

[6] A woman was accused of witchcraft at Cocconato in Piedmont
on August 31, 1569 : " Margaritam Allamanam . . . deviasse a
fide Christi catholicaque religione et ministeriis sacrosanctae
ecclesiaè, retro post satanam conversam daemonum illusionibus et
fantasmatibus seductam eius iussionibus obedire, ad eiusque
servitium revocari ad cursum ; et publice vociferatur, ut vulgo
dicitur, eam esse mascham." (FERD. GABOTTO, Valdesi, Catari e

A bull of Pius V., dated February 26th, 1569, expressly states the fact that the Jews, in particular, made use of " divination, conjuring, magic arts, and witchcraft," and led many persons to believe that by such means it was possible to foretell the future, trace thieves, discover hidden treasure, and in general obtain knowledge otherwise beyond the reach of mankind.[1]   It is well known that Juvenal, in his 14th satire, speaks of the divination practised by the Jews in Rome. The Jews often appear as magicians and wizards during the period of the Renaissance.   In Ariosto's comedy, *Il Negromante*, the hero is a Jew who had been driven out of Spain, who makes use of his magic arts at the expense of disappointed or infatuated lovers.[2]

The same bull accuses the Jews of many other crimes, as well as of dabbling in magic.   It states that they are usurers and are bleeding needy Christians.   They afford a refuge to robbers and brigands, and enable them to dispose of their

streghe in Piemonte dal sec. XIV. al XVI., Extract from n. 18 of the *Bulletin de la Soc. d' hist. Vaudoise di Torre Pellice*, Pinerolo, 1900, 17).   A trial for witchcraft in 1567 is related by BERTOLOTTI in *Rivista Europea*, XXIII. (1883), 625.

[1] Bull. Rom., VII., 740.   Several examples are given by the *Avvisi di Roma.   Gabriele Pianer, dean of the pontifical chap-lains, was imprisoned with a Jew because they were making calculations as to the length of the Pope's life, the Jew making use of a phial, in which devils were shut up ;   he was condemned to the punishment of scourging (*Avvisi of June 12 and July 31, 1568, Urb. 1040, p. 533, 556, Vatican Library : *cf.* *Arco, June 12, 1568, State Archives, Vienna).   A Jew was imprisoned, who made predictions with the " bolla de' spiriti " about the Pope's life. (*Avviso of July 23, 1569, Urb. 1041, p. 117, *loc. cit.*).   For the " Processi per ebraismo in Napoli " see AMABILE I., 306 *seq.*

[2] *Cf.* BURCKHARDT, Renaissance, II.[10], 268, 275 *seq.*, 373. See also the example in the time of Paul III., mentioned in Vol. XIII. of this work, p. 215.   GREGOROVIUS (Wanderjahre in Italien, 1[2]., Leipzig 1864, 75) in explaining the bull of Pius V. mentions the fact that " oggi pure donne ebree a Roma portano segretamente nelle case arti magiche e filtri amaforii."

booty as receivers of stolen goods. Going about the city
in the guise of itinerant pedlars, they act as procurers, and
have thus brought about the ruin of many innocent women.
In general, they hate the name of Christian, and seek treacher-
ously to ruin all who bear it.[1]

Several of the edicts of Pius V. against the Jews are more
easily understood, both as regards their occasion and their
purpose, if the above-mentioned accusations are borne in
mind. When, in 1569, Cardinal Bonelli caused all their books
to be confiscated in order that a better idea might be formed
of their privileges in the matter of demanding interest,[2] and
when, a year later, these privileges were declared void and the
Jews were subjected to the ordinary laws concerning usury.[3]
these measures speak for themselves, and it is equally obvious
why the Jews were forbidden to enter the houses of prostitutes,
or to admit them to their houses, shops, or work-rooms,[4]
and why licenses to ply the trade of pedlar were only to be
granted for the future to Jews whose moral character was
above suspicion.[5] It is also plain that it was useless to expect
from the Jews a conscientious observance of the ecclesiastical

---

[1] Bull. Rom., VII., 740.

[2] *Avviso di Roma of January 15, 1569, Urb. 1041, p. 4b,
Vatican Library. Decrees of Cardinals Saraceni and Sirleto of
October 11 and 16, 1567, in RIEGER, II., 167.

[3] *Avviso di Roma of September 20, 1570, *loc. cit.* 342 *seq.* A
Papal decree of October 8, 1566, allowed them an interest, which
according to our reckoning would be 12 %. (VERNET in *Université
catholique*, 1895, II., 108 n.). For the enormous charges for
interest among the Jews in the XVth and XVIth centuries *cf.*
ERLER in *Archiv für kathol. kirchenrecht*, LIII. (1885), 5, 11, 37.
Even in 1569 the profits averaged 20 % (RIEGER, II., 167). The
Jews, says Sadolet, in 1539, are the masters of the Christians
and every day take away from them their property and force them
to emigrate (ERLER, *loc. cit.* 41).

[4] FERRARIS, Prompta Bibliotheca, IV., s. v. ' Hebraeus ''
n. 25. ERLER, *loc. cit.* 52.

[5] *Avviso di Roma of August 17, 1566, Urb. 1040, p. 275b,
Vatican Library.

laws as to books, and accordingly they were only allowed to buy and sell books by special license.[1]

The strict laws of Paul IV., according to which the Jews were not allowed to live among the Christians, to go about without a distinctive mark, to acquire landed property, or keep Christian servants,[2] had been almost entirely repealed by Pius IV. on February 27th, 1562,[3] as being a source of trial and vexation to the hated children of Israel. Pius V., it is true, caused the Governor of Rome, Pallantieri, to publish an edict on April 10th, 1566, which ordered that any offence committed against the Jews should be punished by flogging,[4] but in other respects he reverted to the laws of Paul IV. In the middle of February it was reported that the wall surrounding the Ghetto had been restored, and that those who were forced to remain within vainly attempted to obtain the enlargement of the space allotted to them for their habitation.[5] They were all forced to go to the Ghetto, nor was any attention

---

[1] Edict of the " Magister s. Palatii " Tommaso Manriquez of January 19, 1566, printed in HILGERS, Index, 501 ; cf. LADERCHI, 1566, n. 28 ; ERLER, loc. cit. 52 ; CATENA, 51. RIEGER (II., 164) without any justification limits this prohibition to buying and selling Jewish books.

[2] Cf. Vol. XIV. of this work, p. 272.

[3] Bull. Rom., VII., 167 seqq. For Pius IV.'s indulgence towards the Jews cf. ERLER, loc. cit., 49 ; VERNET, loc. cit., 1891, II., 642 seq. *" Sono molto travagliato per conto degli Hebrei i quali hanno grandissimi favori per ritornare le cose loro nel stato che erano innanzi la bolla di Paolo IV." (T. Cospi, January 18, 1561, State Archives, Bologna). Even Cardinal Borromeo showed himself very indulgent towards the Jews (LANCIANI, IV., 16).

[4] LADERCHI, 1566, n. 107. *Avviso di Roma of April 13, 1566, Urb. 1040, p. 210, Vatican Library. ERLER, loc. cit. 52.

[5] *Avviso di Roma of February 16, 1566, loc. cit. 182. With reference to the consistory of January 23, 1566, Arco announces : *" Vuole S.S^{tà} che li Giudei ritornino tutti nel seraglio deputato loro al tempo di Paulo quarto " (State Archives, Vienna). Under Pius IV., as *Cusano writes on February 2, 1566, the Jews were scattered all over the city, having paid many ducats to the Pope for that permission (ibid.).

paid to their request to be allowed to wear a red distinctive mark instead of the yellow one which had been ordered for the Jews.[1] A little later on the Pope forbade them to take part in the market hitherto held on Wednesdays—that day having been chosen for their sake—and transferred it to the Saturday.[2]

By April 19th, 1566, all the prescriptions of Paul IV.'s bull concerning the Jews had been renewed, and extended to the whole Church, while Pius IV.'s mitigation of it had been expressly revoked.[3] Since the Jews evaded the prohibition of possessing landed property by means of fictitious sales, a new ordinance was issued according to which all such property which had not been actually handed over within a fixed time reverted to the house of catechumens and the Monte di Pietà.[4] On the strength of certain briefs of Paul III. and Pius IV., however, an exception was made in the case of the Jews of Ancona.[5]

It was not to be expected of the Jews of the Middle Ages or of the modern era that was just beginning that they should grow up side by side with a Christian nation, or look upon a Christian land as their home. Staff in hand, they constantly wandered from one Christian country to another, and were

---

[1] *Avviso di Roma of April 13, 1566, Urb. 1040, p. 210, Vatican Library. LADERCHI, 1566, n. 112. Even in this respect Pius IV. had been more lenient with them (LANCIANI in *Arch. d. Soc. Rom.*, XVII. [1894], 229 *seqq.*).

[2] *Cusano, May 11, 1566, State Archives, Vienna.

[3] Bull. Rom., VII., 439. The *brief of May 17, 1566, with which it was sent to Cardinal Borromeo, says that the bull had become necessary because of the intolerable freedom allowed to the Jews. Borromeo must publish it, and as at that time the Christians at Milan were oppressed by the usury of the Jews, let him enact that no other interest is to be demanded but such as is customary in the Papal States, and never compound interest. Brevia, Arm. 44, t. 12, n. 79, Papal Secret Archives.

[4] Motuproprio of January 19, 1567, Bull. Rom., VII., 514.

[5] Brief of April 5, 1567, Bull. Rom., VII., 32 (in the bull of Gregory XIII. of February 23, 1573).

convinced, deeply hating the Christians as they did, that they could make use of their knowledge of Christian affairs for felonious purposes among the Turks and infidels.[1] It was said as early as July, 1566, that the Jews felt that under the stern regime of Pius V. it was no longer any use for them to remain in the Papal States.[2] A year later 300 Jews from Rome actually accepted the invitation of a renegade who claimed to have obtained from the Sultan the city of Tiberias and certain islands of the Archipelago for the purpose of colonizing them with members of the chosen people.[3] It was reported in Rome in April, 1567, that the Pope intended to drive the " Hebrews," as they were called, from his dominions.[4] In a bull of February 26th, 1569,[5] Pius V. actually took this extreme step, which had previously been taken by Ferdinand the Catholic in 1492, and by Charles V. in Naples in 1539. In this edict the Pope first sets forth the grievances against the Jews.[6] Since the gravity of their offences was increasing every day, to the injury of the state, and since the Jews contributed nothing of importance to the common good, they

[1] LADERCHI, 1569, n. 78. Erler *loc. cit.* 36.

[2] *Avviso di Roma of July 20, 1566, Urb. 1040, p. 255b, Vatican Library. *Arco wrote on July 20, 1566, that the Pope wished that the Christians should not in any way help the Jews, for which reason some had themselves baptized and others went away. State Archives, Vienna.

[3] *Avviso di Roma of July 5, 1567, Urb. 1040, p. 413, Vatican Library. *B. Pia wrote on July 19, 1567, that every day Jews were leaving for Tiberias, which had been given to them (State Archives, Mantua). On July 5, 1567, *Arco reports that more than 40 Jewish families had left for Tiberias during that week State Archives, Vienna.

[4] *Avviso di Roma of April 19, 1567, Urb. 1040, p. 382b, Vatican Library.

[5] Bull. Rom., VII., 740. An *Avviso di Roma of February 14, 1569, reports that the bull had been " spedita " (Urb. 1041, p. 14b, Vatican Library). *Cusano speaks of it on March 5, 1569, State Archives, Vienna.

[6] *Cf. supra* p. 334.

must within three months leave the whole of the Papal States, with the exception of Rome and Ancona ; if any of them, after that period, were found within Papal territory, they were to forfeit their possessions and become the serfs of the Roman Church. The Jews left the Papal States in May, and went for the most part to Asia Minor.[1]

Feliciano, the Archbishop of Avignon, had the courage, in a letter of April 6th, 1569, to intercede for the Jews in his diocese, on the ground that they had lent money to the Catholics in the war against the Huguenots, and that their exile would lead to disturbances. The Pope replied that, according to the testimony of the Bishop of Carpentras, no decree had given so much satisfaction in the Venaissin for many years as the bull against the Jews.[2] At the request of the syndics, however, he extended the time fixed for their departure until

---

[1] ERLER, loc. cit. 54. RIEGER, III., 168. According to the *Avviso di Roma of March 19, 1569, they asked for a delay in their departure in order that they might collect the debts owing to them (Urb. 1041, p. 18b, Vatican Library). In various places the bull was either not obeyed at all or only for a short time ; see FABRETTI, Sulla condizione degli ebrei in Perugia, Turin, 1891, 9 seqq. Of the Jews in Rome it is stated in May, 1569 : *" Si dice che S.S. vuole che li Hebrei vadino ad habitare al Coliseo, onde per le quotidiane restrintioni questi poveri se ne vanno più tosto che obligarsi a così dure novità " (*Avviso di Roma of May 14, 1569, loc. cit. 76). At Bologna, where the Jews were enclosed in the Ghetto in 1566 (GIUDICINI, Miscell. Bologn., 56), several pious foundations were trying to get the house of catechumens left to them, on the ground that with the departure of the Jews there was no longer any need for it ; against this the governing body of the house pointed out in a *petition on April 13, 1569, that it was just the time when many Jews would be converted (Cod. Vatic. lat. 6184, p. 82, Vatican Library). In a *brief of March 26, 1568, Pius V. had given the catechumens of Bologna a synagogue which had come into the possession of the Apostolic Camera. Archives of Briefs, Rome.

[2] Brief of May 3, 1569, in LADERCHI, 1569, n. 187. In this brief we read : " Scimus perversissimam hanc gentem omnium fere haeresum causam seminariumque semper fuisse."

August 15th.[1] Venice, too, thought of banishing the Jews in 1569, on account of their felonious relations with the Turks.[2]

Notwithstanding all these strict ordinances, Pius V. had a certain feeling of kindliness for this unhappy people; above all, he sought as far as possible to win them to Christianity, nor, as he himself says, were his efforts altogether unsuccessful. Many Jews and Jewesses were baptized; whenever any of the more eminent among the Roman Jews showed themselves ready for conversion, the Pope performed the sacred rite with his own hands, and in this way many were led to follow their example. At the end of November, 1566, the house of catechumens, built by Paul III., was almost quite full, and about the same time, the convent of the Annunziata, where recently-converted Jewish girls could take the veil, was found to be too small for the numbers that entered, so that the convent had to be transferred to a larger house.[3] Pius V. also furnished revenues for the catechumenate, which he placed under the spiritual care of the Jesuits.[4] He soon gave up his idea of purchasing a special palace for the use of the converted Jews,[5] and later on he thought it better not to have

[1] Brief to Cardinal Armagnac on May 4, 1569, in LADERCHI' 1569, n. 190. According to the *Avviso of July 26, 1570 (Urb. 1040, p. 312, Vatican Library) the Jews at Avignon vainly offered large sums of money to the Pope to be allowed to remain. According to CHARPENNE, Avignon, II., 453, the Jews of that place nevertheless succeeded in remaining.

[2] LADERCHI, 1569, n. 78.

[3] Bull of November 29, 1566, Bull. Rom., VII., 489.

[4] LADERCHI, 1566, n. 109. SACCHINI P. III., 1, 2, n. 70. The Jesuits very soon gave up the house of catechumens.

[5] Negotiations were made for the palace of the former abbreviator, Chirinotto, " che é sotto la Trinità " (*Avviso di Roma of August 31, 1566, Urb. 1040, p. 278b, Vatican Library). Pius V. abandoned the plan because he feared to be cheated in the price (*ibid. 301, October 12). A *" Bulla pro domo catechumenorum Urbis," of August 28, 1568, is in the Archives of Briefs, Rome. According to the *report of Strozzi on January 18, 1567, the Pope gave the catechumens 10,000 scudi (State Archives, Vienna).

any special place for the catechumens, preferring to place the sons of the converts either in the houses of craftsmen or in seminaries.[1]

Among the more notable Jewish converts mentioned above, whom the Pope baptized with his own hands, the place of honour belongs to the seventy-year-old president of the synagogue, Elias, and his three sons. They received the sacrament with great solemnity, in the presence of the Cardinals, and a great crowd of people, including many Jews, in St. Peter's, on the third day of Pentecost, June 4th, 1566.[2] " Moved by the great pity, goodness, and holiness which they daily saw in the life of the Pope," in August, 1566, twenty-six Jews, and twelve more in October, of the same year, followed the example of Elias.[3] In each case it was arranged that baptism should be conferred with great solemnity by a Cardinal.[4]

Cod. Vatic. lat. 6792, 1, 94 *seq.* contains an estimate of the *" Intrata tanto ordinaria quanto extraordinaria della casa di catecomini " from January to April, 1568, Vatican Library.

[1] *Avviso di Roma of May 28, 1569, Urb. 1041, p. 84b, Vatican Library. An *Avviso of August 16, 1567 (*ibid.* 1040, p. 431b) speaks of 10 catechumens who wished to escape to Tiberias in order to return to Judaism. The Pope had them arrested. *Arco, August 16, 1568, tells the same tale (State Archives, Vienna).

[2] LADERCHI, 1566, n. 108. *Avviso di Roma of June 8, 1566, Urb. 1040, p. 135, Vatican Library. *Avviso di Roma of June 8, 1566, State Archives, Vienna. Description of the ceremonies of the baptism in Firmanus, Diarium, published in RIEGER, II., 423 *seqq.*

[3] *Avvisi di Roma of August 17 (the baptism is announced for the following day) and October 19, 1566, Urb. 1040, p. 274b, 306b, Vatican Library. Baptism of a learned Jew : *ibid.* 225, July 20, 1566. " Arbitror " wrote Poggiani to Otto Truchsess on September 21, 1566, " hoc pontifice, amplius centum iudaeos homines Iesu Christo nomen dedisse, et ex illis ditissimum et doctissimum quemque. Transeunt ad christianam religionem viri cum coniugibus et liberis, neque urbani modo, sed provinciales et externi." (Epist., IV., 121).

[4] *Avvisi di Roma of August 17 and October 19, 1566, *loc. cit.* There was a case of a Jew who had himself baptized twice over, and was therefore burned (*Avviso of November 26, 1569, *ibid.* 1041, p. 190b, Vatican Library.

The sermons, too, which after the beginning of 1568 were preached for the Jews on all feast days,[1] led to several conversions.[2] In the middle of 1569, twenty-seven Jews asked for Baptism at Benevento.[3]

The attraction exercised by Judaism in Spain, even in the XVIth century, is shown in a remarkable way by a brief of Pius V., of September 6th, 1567. In this brief the Pope says that he has already conferred on Cardinal Espinosa, the Spanish Grand Inquisitor, faculties to absolve from their sin those Christians who had made use of Jewish religious rites ; he goes on to declare that in the case of priests and clerics who had been guilty of such things, it was not possible to remove all the canonical consequences of such an act. The Grand Inquisitor must no longer allow anyone who, having received any ecclesiastical order, had taken part in Jewish rites, to enjoy ecclesiastical benefices ; he must not advance them to a higher order, nor must he under any circumstances allow priests who had been guilty of that offence to say mass.[4]

The Pope took part in person in all the many activities of the Inquisition. If we have constant record of his activity in this respect during the first months of his pontificate,[5] the same thing is true of the whole of the first half of his reign. On June 14th, 1567, Bernardino Pia wrote to Mantua that it was not possible to give greater pleasure to the Pope than by helping him in things concerning the Inquisition.[6] A little later, the Imperial ambassador, Arco, was of the opinion that Pius V. was more full of zeal against the heretics than

---

[1] *Avviso of January 17, 1568, *ibid.* 1040, p. 477.

[2] *Avviso of May 7, 1569, *ibid.* 1041, p. 68b, (4 conversions).

[3] Petition from the " consoli et città di Benevento " June 29, 1569, that a jubilee might be granted to all who were present at the baptism, in Cod. Vatic. lat. 6184, p. 14, Vatican Library.

[4] To Didacus de Spinosa, Cod. Barb. 1502, p. 221 *seqq.* ; 1503, p. 120 *seqq.* Vatican Library.

[5] See *supra* p. 170, 291.

[6] *A. Luzzara, Gonzaga Archives, Mantua.

against the Turks ;[1] the prisons, he says, are full of them,[2] so that they are far too small,[3] and again in September Arco repeats that the Pope is extremely scrupulous about all that concerns the Inquisition.[4] The Spanish ambassador, Requesens, also wrote in July, 1566, that the Pope had not so far been absent from a single session of the Inquisition,[5] although these were held at least once a week, and sometimes two or three times ;[6] moreover, the Pope's view is always most practical and severe,[7] and carries the day even against the votes of all the Cardinals.[8]   It was said in Rome in February, 1568, that the Pope was thinking of following the example of Paul IV. by appointing a Grand Inquisitor ;[9] during Lent he would not hold consistories in order that an extra session of the Inquisition might be held each week. These extraordinary sessions had been called for by the case of the unhappy Archbishop of Toledo, Bartolomè Carranza,[10] whose trial Pius V. had called to Rome.

[1] *Arco, October 13, 1567, State Archives, Vienna.

[2] *ibid. May 10, 1567.

[3] *ibid. November 22, 1567,

[4] " *scrupolosissimo " ; ibid.   September 11, 1568.

[5] To Philip II., July 4, 1566, Corresp. dipl., I., 288.

[6] To Philip II., September 18, 1566, ibid. 350.

[7] Ibid.   See also the following note.

[8] " En las cosas de Inquisicion se haze siempre lo que el Papa vota aunque sea contra el parecer de los cardenales, y el voto de S.S. diz que es el mejor y mas riguroso que ninguno de los otros." To Philip II., May 17, 1567, Corresp. dipl. II. 115.

[9] *Avviso di Roma of February 14, 1568, Urb. 1040, p. 487, Vatican Library.

[10] Ibid.   On June 7, 1567 *B. Pia wrote to Luzzara : " Due congregationi si fanno hora ogni settimana inanzi a N. S. di ordinario per la S^ma Inquisitione.   Il lunedi et questa sola per la causa de l'arcivescovo di Toledo.   Il giovedi l'ordinaria, non si potria dire con quanta ansia et diligenza S. B^na attenda a questo." (State Archives, Mantua). Cf. *Serristori, February 13, 1567.   State Archives, Florence, Medic. 3287.

CHAPTER VIII.

The Trial of the Archbishop of Toledo, Bartolomè Carranza. The Condemnation of Baius.

THE removal of Carranza to the Eternal City is certainly one of the most striking proofs of the great impression which the personality of Pius V. had made even upon the greatest men of his time. It had been in vain for Pius IV. to attempt to intervene in the discussion of the case of the disgraced archbishop.[1] King Philip was of opinion that the authority of the Spanish Inquisition would suffer if a trial were to be removed from its jurisdiction, and perhaps decided in a contrary sense by the Papal tribunals, while he was convinced that he could not do without the help of the Inquisition in the government of his kingdom.[2] He had therefore strained every nerve, even with Pius V., to keep the trial of the Archbishop of Toledo in the hands of the Spanish Inquisition. But when the Pope persisted, the apparently impossible took place, and the mighty Spaniard gave way. To the amazement of all Spain, on December 5th, 1566, the archbishop left Valladolid in the litter which was to convey him to Cartagena. There he had to wait until April 1567, for the Duke of Alba, who was to

---

[1] See Vol. XVI of this work, 370 seq..

[2] SERRANO in Corresp. dipl. II. xi : " El secreto de toda la resistencia de Felipe II. en este asunto, estaba en hallarse convencido . . ., que yendo la causa à Roma sufría un golpe mortal la autoridad de la Inquisición Española." Requesens pointed out to the Pope that it was the conviction of Philip, " que non podia guardar sus reinos en la religion y obediencia de la Sede Apostolica, non conservando la autoridad del Santo Officio, a quien seria gran nota no confiar S. B. dél este negocio." To Philip II. June 1, 1566, ibid. I. 256 ; cf. II. xi. seq.

convey him to Rome, so that it was only on May 28th, that Carranza reached the Eternal City.[1]

The Spanish Inquisition had a bad name with the Roman people.[2] The archbishop was universally looked upon as innocent,[3] and it was commonly said that the trial would be over in a few weeks, and that Carranza would go back to Spain a Cardinal. His supporters hoped that he would have entered Rome amid popular acclamations, and would be received by the Pope before the trial commenced. In reality, the day after the arrival of Carranza at Civitavecchia, the Spanish ambassador, Requesens, set out to go there to receive him accompanied by two companies of cavalry under the command of Paolo Ghislieri, but the latter had had orders to receive the archbishop merely in the name of the Spanish king, and not of the Pope, and when on the return journey the cavalcade neared the gates of Rome the great crowd of people sought in vain for the archbishop. Requesens took him secretly, accompanied only by a few horsemen, in a litter as far as the gates of the Castle of St. Angelo, where, to Carranza's disgust, his former jailor, Lope de Avellaneda, took charge of him in Rome as he had done in Spain.[4]

In the composition of the tribunal the Pope had every consideration for the Spanish king. If among the assessors of the four Cardinal Inquisitors there were to be found the Master of the Sacred Palace, Tommaso Manriquez, and other declared friends of Carranza, there were also Giulio Santori

---

[1] Corresp. dipl., II., vi, xviii. POGIANI Epist., IV., 262.

[2] " Todo el pueblo està mal con la Inquisición de Espana de gracia, ó por mejor decir, malicia ó de falta de celo de la fé y religión." Dr. Simancas to Busto de Villegas, November 5, 1568, Corresp. dipl., IV., vi.

[3] Zuñiga to Philip II., March 9, 1568, ibid. v.

[4] Requesens to Philip II., May 31, 1567, Corresp. dipl., II., 124 seqq., cf. xix. seq. *B. Pia, May 31 and June 4, 1567, Gonzaga Archives, Mantua. Cf. also the volumes, from the legacy left by Santori, bearing the title " Processus in causa Toletana," in Miscell. Arm. X., 1–4, Papal Secret Archives, the use of which would be of value for a special work on the subject.

and Felice Peretti who, as Neapolitan bishops, acknowledged Philip as their sovereign. Among the Cardinals of the Inquisition, Pacheco was a Spaniard and devoted to the king. Philip, too, was allowed to nominate as many persons as he chose as auditors and assessors.[1]

The tribunal began its work at the beginning of June, 1567 ; at least one meeting was held every week to deal with the case of Carranza.[2] First of all the minutes of the Spanish trial were read, which drove the Italians to desperation by their endless prolixity.[3] Very soon the Spanish acta were set aside, and they devoted themselves entirely to the writings of the accused man, in so far as they did not feel satisfied in Rome with the verdict of the Spanish theologians as to his doctrine ; many of the propositions which in Carranza's own country had been stigmatized as heretical or at least suspect of heresy, seemed to learned men in Rome to be quite harmless.[4] The Pope himself formed an unfavourable opinion of the views of the Spanish theologians.[5] Moreover, he found fault with the fact that so few questions had been put to the archbishop, so that he might have had the opportunity of explaining in what sense he had meant statements which might seem erroneous when spoken or written. That is not just, he said to the Spanish ambassador, when he tried to justify the proceedings of the Spanish Inquisition, because heresy lies in the intellect

[1] List of the members of the tribunal in Corresp. dipl., II., xxi. *seq.*

[2] According to the *Avviso di Roma of August 2, 1567, every Monday. Urb. 1040, p. 425b, Vatican Library.

[3] Corresp. dipl., II., xxiii.

[4] Cardinals Pacheco and Gambara told Zuñiga : " Muchas de las proposiciones que allá [in Spain] se dieron por heréticas y sospechosas, se ha declarado aqui de comun consentimiento de todos los teólogos de esta congregación y de ortos que eran católicas." Zuñiga to Philip II., April 29, 1570, Corresp. dipl. IV., xvi.

[5] " Dijome [the Pope] mucho mal de las calificaciones que se habian hecho en España." Zuñiga to Philip II., Corresp. dipl., IV., xiv.

and in obstinacy, and not in words or letters.[1] The Pope had
assumed control of the trial with the idea that the accusations
made against Carranza were only too well founded, but when
he came to examine the matter at first hand he realized that
several of the accusations were groundless ; he began to
hesitate,[2] and remained undecided to the end. Not even his
friends, however, were able to clear the ground from all the
charges against the archbishop. Carranza's zealous advocate,
the distinguished moral theologian Azpilcueta, who had come
to Rome to defend him in spite of his age and weak state of
health,[3] considered that the charge of heresy against his client
was without foundation, but admitted that the Inquisition
had only done its duty in imprisoning him.[4] Cardinal Chiesa,
to whose opinion Pius V. attached much importance, thought

[1] " que agora havia sido menester tornarle a examinar, porque
en España hubo en esto gran descuydo, porque dixo que quisieron
hacer mucho caso de lo que se hallava dicho y scripto del arçobispo,
y no trataron tanto de saber dél como entendía y estava en todas
aquellas materias en que parescia que habia errado. . . . Dixome
que no se havia de hacer assy, porque la heresia estava en el
entendimiento y en la pertinacia y no en la escripto." Zuñiga to
Philip II., August 17, 1568, Corresp. dipl. II., 439 *seq.*

[2] Dixo [the Pope] que ante que viesse el processo del arçobispo
lo tenia por muy culpado ; que despues havia stado algo suspenso,
porque havia visto que no se verificaban algunas cosas de las que
le havian referido (Zuñiga to Philip II., July 13, 1571, Corresp.
dipl., IV., 388). Just then Zuñiga had reproached the Pope
for having come to the trial with the conviction of the innocence
of Carranza (*ibid. ; cf.* the letter to Philip II. of October 21, 1569,
ibid., viii.).

[3] Corresp. dipl., IV., vii.

[4] " Concebí, creí, y confirmé muchas veces dos cosas, la una que
el dicho Reverendísimo estaba bien preso ; y al cabo, los que le
prendieron quedar ian honrados por haber hecho su deber contra
un tan gran varón." (Memorial á Felipe II., in *Ciencia Tomista*
VII., 407 ; Serrano in Corresp. dipl. II., xxix.). Azpilcueta came
to Rome on October 21, 1567. A very laudatory letter of recommendation of him from the nuncio in Spain, in Corresp. dip., II.,
94.

that a strong suspicion of heresy attached to Carranza's name.[1] The same view was expressed by the Jesuit, Toledo, who had a great reputation for learning in Rome,[2] and who, in January, 1570, was called in to assist at the discussions, and often had interviews with the Pope on the subject.[3] The archbishop's friends could only set against this that the erroneous proposi- tions had been corrected elsewhere in his writings.[4] If Carranza had been willing to ask pardon for his imprudent propositions, it would certainly have been granted, but he continued to make complaints of his opponents and to attempt to justify himself, so that the Pope sent him a severe rebuke.[5]

In the meantime opinions and rumours, both for and against the accused, were making themselves heard in Rome. Often enough, says an eye-witness, one can in a single day see the wind blowing from all four quarters in this matter.[6] For the most part, however, public opinion favoured Carranza. In July, 1567, it was rumoured that the case was almost settled in his favour, and that very soon the task of passing a judgment on his doctrines would be referred to the ordinary Roman courts, and that the archbishop would be given quarters in one of the monasteries of Rome instead of in the Castle of St. Angelo. When none of these things came to pass a fresh rumour was current that a decision would be arrived at before Christmas.[7] while similar reports recurred again and again during the years that followed.[8] The Pope himself wrote to

[1] *Ibid.* IV., xvi.

[2] *Ibid.* xvii., n.

[3] *Ibid.* xiii, xxi. Zuñiga thought that Toledo, and the Jesuits generally were predisposed in favour of Carranza ; *ibid.* xiii.

[4] Zuñiga to Philip II., July 13, 1571, *ibid.* 389.

[5] Corresp. dipl., IV., ix., n.

[6] *Ibid.* viii.

[7] See the extracts from the Avvisi di Roma, *ibid.* II., xxiv.

[8] For 1568 *cf. ibid.* xxvi. According to the *Avviso di Roma of August 17, 1569 (Urb. 1041, p. 133, Vatican Library) the Spanish ambassador went to Carranza to congratulate him on his release. On September 24, 1569 (*ibid.* 146b) we are told that the decision had been come to. On December 10, 1569 (*ibid.* 195) it is again

the chapter of Toledo on July 20th, 1567, that the trial would end " very soon."[1]

As a matter of fact, however, the decision was by no means at hand. On November 7th, 1567, the tribunal asked to be allowed first to examine the writings of Carranza which had been left in Spain. On March 27th, 1568, it wrote to Spain for further information as to the various statements of the archbishop. On August 2nd in the same year, the Pope, in a brief to the Cardinal Espinosa, asked to have the writings of Carranza on the Epistles of St. Paul, and his sermons which were in the possession of private individuals.[2] The case had not really been ripe for judgment when it had been transferred to Rome. On December 31st, 1564, the day when the Papal demand to take over the case took effect, the trial in Spain had been abruptly stopped and no further steps had been taken there to continue it.[3] About the middle of 1569, however, the deliberations were so advanced that everyone was of opinion that a decision was imminent. In October the sessions and deliberations of the commission came to an end, the Pope took possession of the minutes of the trial, and together with Cardinals Peretti and Aldobrandini subjected them to a close examination in order that he might form his own opinion on the matter. It was thought that the final judgment would be pronounced about Easter, 1570.[4]

This time, too, the general expectation was at fault ; events

stated that the archbishop will soon be set at liberty. On August 12, 1570 (*ibid.* 318) it is reported that the end of the case had been proposed, but very secretly, at a meeting of the Inquisition. On July 18, 1571 (Urb. 1042, p. 89b, *loc. cit.*) it is stated that the case s very near its end.

[1] Pogiani Epist., IV., 260 *seq.*

[2] Corresp. dipl., II., xxiv. *Cf.* Zuñiga to Philip II., August 17, 1567, *ibid.* 439 *seqq.* ; Philip II., October 11, 1568, on the appointment of further Spanish assessors, *ibid.* 474 *seq.* The *brief of November 7, 1567, to Cardinal Espinosa in Brevia, Arm. 44, t.13, p. 60b, Papal Secret Archives.

[3] Corresp. dipl., II., xxvii.

[4] *Ibid.* IV., x., xiv.

were tending in the direction of trying to find further reasons for putting off the decision to the Greek Kalends. For a long time it had been no secret that the Pope's decision would not be in accordance with that of the Spanish Inquisition, and this gave rise to great excitement in Madrid as well as at the Spanish embassy in Rome. If the Apostolic See should decide against the Inquisition, and Carranza had to return to Toledo, and resume his former position as first bishop of the kingdom a terrible blow would, in the opinion of Philip, have been struck at the Inquisition, and this its royal protector wished at all costs to avoid.[1] Thus the controversy as to Carranza's guilt or innocence had developed into a struggle between the cesaropapalism of Madrid and the interference of Rome, and also into a struggle between the Roman and Spanish schools of theology. If in the Eternal City an unfavourable judgment were passed upon the captious pedantry of the Spanish view of Carranza, then the Roman theologians would find themselves overwhelmed with reproaches, with the object of showing that the self-opinionated Spaniards knew better than Rome itself what was Catholic and what was not. The letters of the Spanish ambassador, Zuñiga, in 1569, are filled with complaints of the Roman judges. According to these letters the Pope was prejudiced in favour of the archbishop, and let himself be influenced by his friends. The officials who had charge of the trial were all suspected by Zuñiga ; they had allowed themselves to break through the proper procedure, and had not the necessary learning to enable them to pronounce on theological questions. Things would have gone very differently if a greater number of theologians had been sent from Spain to act as assessors, and the Romans would not have been able to forget the respect due to the Spanish Inquisition. Let new opinions on Carranza's writings be prepared in his own country, so that men might be able to form a truer judgment as to the meaning and consequences of his propositions.[2]

[1] *Cf. supra* p. 344, n. 2.
[2] Corresp. dipl. II., ix.

As far back as July 28th, 1568, in an autograph letter to the Pope, Philip II. had made complaints of the direction in which the discussions of Carranza's case had seemed at that time to be tending.[1] He now renewed his protests in a stronger form. His letter of October 26th, 1569,[2] addressed to the Spanish ambassador in Rome, but really intended for the Pope, to whom it was to be presented, bears at its head the name of the king, but it is really the Inquisition which is speaking by the mouth of the king, and its language, as though conscious of its power even against the head of Christianity, is in striking contrast to the reverence otherwise shown to the Vicar of Christ. In the first place we find enumerated the departures from the usual procedure which had been allowed in Rome, in order to favour Carranza and to keep from the Pope a full understanding of his errors, and this, moreover, in an affair which had become " the spectacle of all the nations." Trials of bishops in Spain had always come before the Inquisition, and the exception made for Carranza " contrary to the privileges and authority of the Holy Office " had been founded upon the firm confidence that the prudence, secrecy and due order to which they were accustomed in Spain would be observed in his case.[3] In a covering letter[4] the ambassador had further supplementary instructions. In this we read : Carry out the task with all the diligence and zeal which I⋅look for in you, and which the nature of the case, as you will see for yourself, demands ; you must ask the Pope to listen to you attentively and without interruption, as the nature of the communication demands. He was then to point out that no one ought to favour the Inquisition or strive so much for the preservation of religion in the Spanish dominions as the Pope, in obedience to whom that realm had been kept by the Inquisition and by true religion ; that the Pope's attitude had ruined the Holy Office,

[1] *Ibid.* vii.

[2] Extract, *ibid.* xi. This important document, however, is not given in its context.

[3] " la cautela, secreto y orden acostumbrados en España ' *ibid.*

[4] Extract, *ibid.* xii.

but that as far as the king was concerned, he could not and
would not cease to favour the Inquisition, as he had done
all his life.

At first Zuñiga did not dare to comminicate these rebukes
and threats to the Pope ; Cardinal Pacheco, too, as well as
Simancas, the Bishop of Badajoz, and later on Cardinal
Granvelle, dissuaded him from doing so.[1] Now that Philip
—so ran the opinion of Granvelle—has handed over the archbishop and his trial to the Roman tribunals, and the Pope
has examined the acta so carefully, he will not be able to
persuade the world that the royal tribunals, which do not
possess the complete acta and have not heard all the parties,
can still be better informed as to the true state of the case.
As far as he personally was concerned, Granvelle adds, he
would never have given his approval to the king's allowing
the case to be taken out of Spanish territory. This had
proved a serious blow to the Inquisition, and it afforded very
good grounds for a breach of relations if the Pope did not mend
his ways ; such a breach would compel him to do so.   Zuñiga
did not dare to take Granvelle's advice and urge violent
measures. He wrote to the king that as soon as he heard
that there must be no question of Carranza's going back to
Spain, he would endeavour to win over the judges to consent
to that.[2]

When, a little after Easter, 1570, the decision of Carranza's
trial was thought to be imminent, Zuñiga thought that the
time had come to inform the Pope of the principal points in
the royal instructions. In questions of smaller moment
Pius V. had often felt it right to resist, even with considerable
heat, the demands of the princes, but now the strong-willed
man remained outwardly calm. With characteristic brevity
he assured Philip in a few stiff autograph lines, that he was
always glad to receive the observations of the ambassador and the king concerning the trial, and that if his office
permitted even greater concessions in the case of trials of
bishops he would have been quick to make them. The

---

[1] *Ibid.*   [2] *Ibid.* IV., xiii.

king, however, must remember that his warnings concerned matters which either formed part of the trial or did not ; if they did not, they could not influence the decision, while if they did, they were quite well known to the Pope.[1]

Some time after Zuñiga had thus communicated to the Pope the principal points of the king's memorial, he read to him the complete document. This time, too, the Pope remained perfectly calm. He even condescended to reply to the accusations : some of the complaints, he said, rested on a false basis while others were of no importance. Then Zuñiga touched upon the matter which had specially wounded the sensibilities of the Spaniards, namely that the opinions of their theologians had been set aside in Rome. With regard to this, Pius V. openly told the ambassador that he did not think very highly of those opinions, and that in the matter of Carranza's Catechism, which had been so violently attacked, the book indeed contained many things that were not suited for the populace, and that for that reason it had quite rightly been prohibited, but he let it be understood that he considered it quite orthodox as far as its doctrine was concerned. God knows, he said, that there was no pre-disposition in favour of the archbishop on his part. If Carranza were guilty he could not have fallen into worse hands. The king might rest assured that the Pope would be guided by the dictates of justice alone. If the archbishop should be reinstated, that would not prevent the king from banishing him if he feared disturbances for his kingdom from his return. The Pope would consent to this if the fear were shown to be well grounded. Zuñiga replied that the king did not fear disturbances, but was only afraid of the scandal that would be caused by Carranza's return, and that his fear sprang from his zeal for religion.[2]

While the ambassador was doing his best in Rome to avert

[1] " que si las advertencias que de allà pueden venir son fuera del proçesso de la causa, que no pueden servir a la determinacion della ; y que si están eo el proçesso, nos son notissimas." Letter of April 19, 1570, ibid. III., 295.

[2] Corresp. dipl., IV., xiv. seq.

the dreaded blow, they were not inactive in Spain. The Inquisition sought in the Orders and universities, and among the bishops, for learned men to examine the doctrines of Carranza anew.[1] and opinion after opinion was sent to Rome.[2] Many suggestions were submitted to the king as to how he could evade a final decision by the Pope. Zuñiga advised definite resistance ; let the king declare that he would only accept the Papal decision if it were expressed in such and such terms, and be in accordance with the views of the Spanish theologians ; if this could not be obtained, let him apply for the right to decide the case in Spanish territory.[3] The Bishop of Badajoz was more moderate ; he advised that the Papal decision be accepted, but that the archbishop be induced to resign.[4] The secret Council of State, on the other hand, held that the best course would be to obtain, with the Pope's approval, the appointment of a reliable administrator of the archdiocese with the right of succession,[5] as this would prevent Carranza from returning with his former power. The strangest advice was that given by the supreme council of the Inquisition ; the Pope must be given to understand that the King could not co-operate with him in letting the hands of justice be tied, and still less in allowing the archbishop to return, or to receive the revenues of the bishopric in his absence.[6] The Holy Office apparently claimed the right of surveillance even over the Vicar of Christ. It is true, however, that it only looked upon its own proposal as an extreme step, to be taken if the Pope refused to accept the representations of the king. In the meantime let fresh

[1] List of the names suggested to Cardinal Espinosa, February 3, 1570, *ibid.* xvi., n. 2.

[2] The first in June, 1570, *ibid.*, xvii, *cf.* 385 ; others on May 11, June 14 and 29, 1571, *ibid.* xxiv, n. 4.

[3] *Ibid.* xx. *seq.*

[4] *Ibid.* xxi.

[5] *Ibid.* and Castagna to Rusticucci, November 2, 1570, *ibid.* 68.

[6] *Ibid.* xxi. ; " no podia el Rey dar lugar que se deje de hacer justicia."

consultors be sent to Rome, and steps be taken to see that the Pope listened to them.

The letters of Philip II. to his ambassador as well as to the Pope himself bring out clearly the pretensions of the Spanish supremacy. To the few lines in his own hand which Pius V. had addressed to the king about Easter, 1570, in answer to the communications made to him by Zuñiga,[1] the ambassador was instructed to reply by a long defence of the Spanish condemnation of Carranza ;[2] eminent men of learning, of unblemished reputation and great authority, had expressed themselves as to his case, above all the two Dominicans, Domingo de Soto and Melchior Cano ;[3] on the other hand the learned Romans were quite unknown in Spain, while Manriquez was looked upon as the declared friend of the archbishop, and as for Toledo, every sort of report was current concerning him ;[4] if the archbishop were reinstated and came back to Spain, he would be able to teach and preach as he liked with greater authority than ever, so that it would have been better never to have taken any proceedings against him.[5] If Pius V. had written to the king saying that he must leave the question of Carranza's guilt to his, the Pope's, conscience, Zuñiga must, by the king's orders, inform the Pope in return that Philip's conscience with regard to his royal duty was not satisfied to do so. The ambassador must then put forward two demands : in the first place the decision must be left to men of knowledge and experience, and they must be in sufficient numbers, and secondly the final sentence

[1] See *supra* p. 352.

[2] Philip II. to Zuñiga, Ubeda, June 6, 1570, Corresp. dipl., III., 383-386.

[3] It is significant of the attitude of Pius V. that in his eyes the eccentric Cano was no authority, notwithstanding his learning : " que él [Pius V.] tenía en ruin opinión á Melchor Cano," Zuñiga, July 23, 1570, *ibid*. IV., xix.

[4] They maintained that he was of Jewish origin : " Si es verdad que es confeso, como algunos piensan, tengolo por de mucho inconveniente." Zuñiga wrote on October 21, 1569 ; *ibid*. xiii., n.

[5] *Ibid*. III., 384 *seq*.

must be submitted to the king before it was published.   If
it should happen that " extraneous considerations and private
ends " entered into the trial, the king would be " constrained "
for the safeguarding of the " common good " to remedy this
by " the means best suited to prevent a scandal."[1]

The same ideas and demands recur several times in other
letters from Spain.   What was bound to hurt the Pope most
was the fact that, notwithstanding his assurances, both
Zuñiga and the king persisted in making out that he was
predisposed in Carranza's favour, and that he was not allowing justice to take its course.[2]   Nor were threats wanting.
Zuñiga openly declared that his master found himself constrained for the safeguarding of the common goood to take
steps to prevent the return of Carranza, as, for example,
by calling together a conference of prelates to consider the
matter, on the plea that in Spain, as in other countries,
princes who were strongly Catholic, and most obedient to
the Holy See, had not infrequently held such conferences in
order to obviate difficulties which were feared as the result of
certain Roman ordinances, and which might have disturbed
the peace of their countries.[3]

[1] " Advirtiendo a S. B. que si entendieremos que se tiene
consideracion a otros respectos y fines particulares, nos seria
forçado . . . acudir al remedio por el beneficio universal por
los mejores medios que conviniesse para el buen exemplo."   Ibid.
38.

[2] Zuñiga to Philip II., July 13 1571 (report of his audience
with Pius V.), ibid. IV., 388 : " Dixele que en el modo que havia
procedido, havia dado muchas occasiones a que V. M. tuviesse en
esta parte alguna sombra ; y que Su Santidad havia entrado a ver
esta causa con opinion que el Arçobispo stava siu culpa, y habia
nombrado consultores muy apasionados y sospechosos, etc."
Cf. Zuñiga to Philip II., October 12, 1571, ibid. 472.

[3] " Como seria hacer junta de prelados sopra esta causa, pues
en estos reinos y en otros han acostumbrado principes muy
católicos, y muy obedientes á esta Santa Sede hacer semejantes
juntas para resistir á los inconvenientes de algunas cosas de las
que en Roma se han proveido, que parecian podrian disturbar la
quiete de sus estados."   Zuñiga, July 23, 1570, ibid. IV., xix.

In this way a complete net-work—in which the web was the national sense of superiority, and the woof specious maxims, rebukes and threats—enfolded the Pope more and more, so as to tie his hands completely and remove the decision to Madrid. Very characteristic is an autograph letter of May 11th, 1571,[1] in which the king " the devoted and loving son " of the Pope, sought to deprive him of all freedom of action. First Philip lauds his own zeal in the affair of Carranza, a zeal which he says befits " his own duty to the service of Our Lord, the defence of his Catholic faith, his Church and his religion." He has not been able to forego taking the steps he has taken, or undertaking the course in which he still persists, that is to say his determination to set his hand to the measures best suited to ensure that the world, which is watching the affair so closely, shall realize and understand his intention. This intention is nothing but the wish and the aim that justice shall be done on the basis of the manifest truth. Since the unhappy business has dragged on so long, it has seemed good to Philip, as the devoted and loving son of the Pope, to warn him that his authority and good name would be greatly jeopardized if the idea got about that His Holiness intended to reinstate the archbishop out of any considerations of favouritism or affection ; at present, however, as the ambassador has already, by the king's orders, pointed out to the Pope, the methods and procedure of the Roman trial seemed to suggest that that was the case.[2] He therefore implores the Pope to treat an affair of so great importance with the care, freedom of judgment and zeal which men looked for in him, taking counsel with learned men who were inspired with zeal for religion,

[1] *Ibid.* 273 *seq.*

[2] " Me ha parecido como devoto hijo de V. S. y que tanto amor le tiene, advertirle quanta autoridad y reputacion aventuraria V. S. en que se pensase, que de algun genero de pasion o aficion queria librar al Arzobispo, como lo ha dado a entender en el modo y orden con que se ha procedido como de my parte se lo ha referido my embaxador " (Corresp. dipl., IV., 274). The ambassador renewed this complaint again later on ; see *supra* p. 356, n. 2.

and above suspicion that they would suffer themselves to be guided by anything but the love of truth and justice. In saying this the king was but complying with his duty of serving His Holiness, and he does so in order that the Pope may realize that other duty which, should the matter turn out otherwise, the king would feel bound to perform. " May Our Lord preserve the sacred person of your Holiness, as is so necessary for us. Aranjuez, May 11th, 1571. Your Holiness' very humble son : the King."

It certainly called for all Pius V.'s command of himself to reply, not only gravely and firmly, but also with dignified gentleness, to a document which almost in every line concealed a sharp pin-prick. In his reply he assures the king that the archbishop is not being judged with any partiality other than that which is due to the love of the truth ; he is at peace in the consciousness that God has given him this grace. The interpretation which the king sets upon the Pope's conduct he gladly attributes to his praiseworthy zeal, but at the same time he gives him a paternal exhortation not to lend his ear to those who would make him presume to attribute the supernatural jurisdiction of the one true Judge to his own tribunal or to any other. In reference to Philip's words which claimed that zeal for the faith, the Church, and religion was what had guided his actions, he points out that it is not possible to fight for the Church if one's hand is raised against the Church, and still less for religion and the faith, if one takes up a position opposed to religion and faith.[1] For the rest the Pope re-

---

[1] " La torniamo di nuovo paternamente ad avertire a non prestar mai boni orecchi a chi volesse estendere questo suo buon zelo a presumere di volere alligare al suo nè ad altro iuditio la soprannatural giuridittione del judice proprio, nè a chi tentasse perniciosamente insinuare che si potesse pugnare per la Chiesa contra Chiesa, nè per religione contra religione, nè per la fede contra la fede." Letter of August 12, 1571, Corresp. dipl., IV., 408. The king's letter of May 11 did not reach the Pope until July 31 (ibid.) ; Philip's autograph reply of September 10, 1571 (ibid. 437) sought to justify and excuse the attitude which he had taken up ; if he thinks for the peace of his kingdom and makes

fers him to the replies which he had already made to the same accusations.

It was true that the Pope " with all the moderation that was possible in dealing with such a document,"[1] had given a full reply to the complaints of Philip II. on June 6th, 1570.[2] As for the trust which the king put in the theological opinions which were supposed to make Carranza's guilt clear, the Pope repled that if the archbishop were guilty, His Holiness firmly hopeid that the mercy of God would not allow him to be deceived against his will ; in other words, if Carranza is guilty, let the king rest assured that he will be condemned. But if the appeal to the Spanish opinions is to be taken as meaning that a Roman decision which did not agree with them would not meet with the obedience and respect due to it, then the counsellors who suggested such an idea to the king must remember that the Church of God has but one head on earth ; such a view would be clearly at variance with the sense of that dogma ; in a word it would mean that they were setting up a rule and measure for the decisions of the Holy See in matters concerning which it belonged to it alone to judge.[3]

A second matter of complaint was contained in the demand that more learned theologians should be consulted, and in greater number. To this it was replied that, although Philip had a high opinion of the Spanish theologians, the Pope thought just as highly of the other members of the com-

---

complaints to the Pope, it is by no means his intention to act in any way against the obedience which he owes to the Pope as a loyal son.

[1] " con quella maggior temperantia che i sensi di detta scrittura permettono." Corresp. dipl., III., 386.

[2] *Ibid.* 386-388.

[3] " Si risponde con lacrime di charità, che lasciando hora da parte la causa del arcivescovo, s' attenda bene a chi suggerisse questi pensieri a S. M.; che la Chiesa di Dio non ha in terra senon un capo, et che questo sinistro concetto offenderebbe molto la integrità di questo articolo, perchè questo sarebbe in effetto volersi far regola dei iuditii di questa Santa Sede nelle cause che a lei sola toccano di giudicare." *Ibid.* 386.

mission, which, with the Cardinals, comprised sixteen persons,
a quite sufficient number.[1]

The complaint that was most offensive to the Apostolic See
was Philip's hint that other points of view which were not
objective, as well as private ends, might influence the decision.[2]
Once more the reply to this is indeed severe, but at the same
time very restrained. The Pope is willing, we read, to put
an indulgent interpretation on this assertion, and to ascribe it
to the king's zeal, but with all love he would have him reflect
that the zeal of a son must never go to the length of hurting
his father. If Philip had seen fit to threaten " suitable
remedies " on account of these " inapplicable considerations
and private ends " he now received the reply : let the counsellor who has led the king into a stream that is so full of shoals
remember " that God had provided His Church with sound
remedies with which to deal with bad ones."[3]

The Pope gave no definite answer to the other two demands
of the king, namely, that the final decision should be communicated to Madrid before it was published, and that the
Pope should first take into consideration the new opinions
sent by the Spanish theologians ; with regard to the latter it
is courteously, but quite clearly pointed out that it is not the
king's business to try and teach the Roman See with unsought
theological opinions, or to anticipate the final sentence. Let
Philip remember, the reply runs, what happened in the Old
Testament to King Ozias[4] when he tried to offer incense,
thereby taking upon himself a function which belonged to the
priest alone.[5]

The last part of the document brings out the extreme care
with which Carranza's case had been dealt with in Rome.
The Pope had been present in person during the whole of the

---

[1] *Ibid.* 386 *seq.*

[2] See *supra* p. 356.

[3] " che contra caltivi rimedii Dio ha provisto nella sua chiesa
di rimedii buoni " (This was certainly a threat of excommunication). Corresp. dipl., III., 387.

[4] Paral., xxvi., 16 *seqq.*

[5] Corresp. dipl., III., 387.

reading of the minutes, and when it was seen that the archbishop had not been sufficiently fully examined in Spain, he
had appointed Spanish and Italian consultors, who had
diligently questioned Carranza on all the more important
points during more than two months. Besides this the Pope
had several times sent to Spain to seek for information and to
investigate the archbishop's writings ;[1] several matters had
been gone into in Rome which had either been passed over in
Spain or were unknown there. As to the procedure adopted
in the deliberations, the Pope caused all present to give their
opinions ; the controverted points were discussed by all,
and the Pope made everyone give his opinion on each single
point, and finally had himself gone personally into the whole
in his own study. Three years had been spent in this, and he
hoped therefore that the final decision would be a just one,
not only before God, but even in the eyes of men.[2]

In spite of this crushing retort Philip II. remained fixed in
his ideas. Zuñiga was instructed to make a public protest
if the final decision should take the form of the acquittal of
Carranza, or if it should not be submitted to the king before
it was published.[3] In Philip's eyes Pius V. was still prejudiced
in favour of the archbishop.[4] Zuñiga was instructed to go on
making the former Spanish demands, and to do all he could
to make the Pope look favourably upon them ; he even one
day said to him that he must not let the stain rest upon his
good name of having had a man like Morone acquitted by him
as Cardinal, and the Archbishop of Toledo similarly set free
by him as Pope. This remark was not without a calculated
sting, for Zuñiga knew that the Pope's conscience was not quite
easy about the acquittal of Morone.[5]

[1] See *supra* p. 349.

[2] Corresp. dipl., III., 387 *seq.*

[3] *Ibid.* IV., xxii., xxiv., n.

[4] Zuñiga, July 13, and October 12, 1571, *ibid.* 388, 472.

[5] " que no dexasse tal memoria de si como seria que fuese
absuelto, siendo cardenal, un hombre como el Cardenal Moron,
y siendo pontifice, el Arçbispo de Toledo. Muevele en gran
manera la conscientia de aver absuelto a Moron. . . ." Zuñiga
to Philip II., July 13, 1571, *ibid.* 389.

In several respects the Pope met the king's wishes. He did not, it is true, give in to the frequently repeated proposal that a larger number of theologians should be allowed to take part in the discussions, and when the ambassador protested he replied that if that were to be done, they would not get through in ten days what was now accomplished in an hour ;[1] when Zuñiga expressed the wish that the Pope would at any rate summon to Rome the authors of the most recent opinions in order to hear their explanations, Pius was very angry, and answered that he would not do so, and that Zuñiga wanted the case to drag on for ever.[2]

Pius V. was willing to make some concession in the case of Philip's other demand, namely that the final sentence should be sent to Madrid before it was published.[3] On the other hand he gave a ready consent to a third wish expressed by the king, declaring that he was quite ready to examine the opinions which had recently been submitted by the Spanish theologians. As a matter of fact these last opinions satisfied him as little as had the previous ones, and the nuncio, Castagna, was told to inform the king[4] that these opinions concerned themselves only with words, and did not take into consideration the sense which the author attached to the words ; to understand the sense it was necessary to keep before one's mind the whole sense of the writings. The method adopted by the Spanish theologians would make heretics of St. Augustine and other perfectly orthodox doctors, by divorcing their words from their context. It must also be remembered that the archbishop had written previous to the decrees of the Council of Trent, and that where errors or heresies were discovered in his writings it was very difficult to say that he must on that account be held a heretic, and whether the final decision should be left to the canonists or the theologians.[5] This last

[1] Zuñiga to Philip II., October 12, 1571, ibid. 470.

[2] Ibid. 473.

[3] Zuñiga, January 30, 1571, ibid. xxiii.

[4] Rusticucci to Castagna, August 20, 1570, ibid. III., 514 seq.

[5] " Le dica liberamente [to the King] che le censure atte sopra il scritti che qua si chiamano scartafacci, sono più presto censure

remark was certainly added because Zuñiga had attributed the divergence between the Spanish views of Carranza to the fact that the learned men in Rome were canonists and not theologians.[1] According to the view held in Rome it was certainly the business of the theologians to decide whether a proposition were orthodox or not, but whether a man was to be considered a heretic because of an heretical statement was the business of the canonists. Zuñiga also had to hear from the Pope's own lips that the authors of these opinions were not fit to form a judgment, because they paid attention only to the words used, and did not take into consideration the context or the meaning of the writer ;[2] these much discussed writings undoubtedly contained real heresies.[3]

The Spanish opinions, however, were not without their effect on Pius V. He became perplexed, and had the opinions carefully examined, with the result that the final decision was again postponed. Such was Zuñiga's account of the situation in April, 1571,[4] and in July of the same year the Pope himself

delle parole che di quello che habbia inteso per quelle parole l'autore o scrittore ; e che a voler vedere il senso dell'autore convien ponderare la scrittura precedente et subsequente ; perchè in quella maniera che hanno censurato quelle si potrebbe censurare ancora S. Agostino et altri Santi Catt. Dottori, prendendo le lor parole troncate." Corresp. dipl. III. 514.

[1] *Ibid.* IV., xvi.

[2] " Dixo que no saben qualificar los theologos que las [the qualifications] han hecho, porque hechan mano de las palabras y no del sentido que se puede collegir que tuvo el author en toda la obra." Zuñiga to Philip II., July 13, 1571, *ibid.* 388. " Todo el fundamento de lo que se allega por parte del Arçobispo consiste en decir que si bien se hallan en el Catecismo y en sus cartapacios muchas opiniones hereticas, que en estas mismas obras se verá que donde trattó de proposito cada materia, la declaró catholicamente, y que esto prueva el buen animo del author." *Ibid.* 389.

[3] *Ibid.* 473.

[4] " que le aperitan mucho las calificaciones que de allá se embiaron, que las hace ver con diligentia, y así la resolucion irá mas á la larga de lo que se pensaba." Zuñiga, April 20, 1571, *ibid.* xxii.

told him that he had not been able yet to come to a decision ;[1] when in October the ambassador insisted on knowing when the matter would be settled, Pius answered him on oath that he himself did not know.[2] The Pope was almost continually occupied with the acta of the trial, and had not yet completed his examination of them, in spite of the assistance given him by Cardinals Montalto and Aldobrandini.[3]

In this way the whole of 1571 went by. In the first months of 1572 the state of the Pope's health did not allow of his dealing with important business,[4] with the result that when his death occurred on May 1st, 1572, the trial of Carranza was not yet finished. One determination alone had remained clearly before the mind of this conscientious judge, amid all the vicissitudes of the discussions ; he was determined not to give the judgment of a Pilate, but to decide according to the dictates of justice alone, even though the whole world should fall in ruins.[5] There can be no doubt that the wearisome business had entailed for him a whole world of anxieties and troubles ; the unwearied perseverance with which he had always assisted in person at the endless discussions aroused the wonder of his contemporaries.[6] On February 24th, 1568, Bernardino Pia wrote to Mantua that he had been unable to get through his business because of the constant meetings which were held over the affair of the archbishop.[7]

[1] Zuñiga, July 13, 1571, *ibid.* 388.

[2] " Preguntéle quando pensava acabar este negocio, Juróme que no lo sabia." Zuñiga, October 12, 1571, *ibid.* 471.

[3] *Ibid.* 470, 474.

[4] *Ibid.*

[5] " Confesóme el Papa, que era verdad que habia dicho á Alvaro de Lugo que si el Arcobispo estaba innocente, que él no haria la sentencia de Pilatos, que por temor del alboroto del pueblo condenó á Nuestro Redentor conociendo que no tenia culpa." Zuñiga, July 4, 1571, *ibid.* xxiv. " Però S.S. non è mai per deviare del retto guiditio, nè da quello che concerne la giustitia, se bene ruinasse il mondo." Rusticucci to Castagna, August 25, 1570, *ibid.* III., 515.

[6] *Ibid.* II., xxiii.

[7] Gonzaga Archives, Mantua.

The Imperial agent, Cusano, was of opinion that the wearisome trial was one of the causes which hastened the death of
the Pope. On the one hand, Cusano says, he had realized
the innocence of the archbishop, and considered it his duty
to acquit him, but on the other there was reason to fear nothing
short of a breach with Spain if he were to annul the sentence
of the Spanish Inquisition. Cusano also bears witness that
Philip II. had expressed himself quite definitely on this point,
for the reason that there would be great scandal and much
harm done in Spain if the Inquisition should fall under the
suspicion of having made use of its power for the furtherance
of the private vengeance of any of its officials. The constant
anxiety and uneasiness of conscience, the difficulty of steering
a course between these two reefs was, says Cusano, the real
commencement of his incurable malady, the stone, which
brought about his death.[1]

It would be quite unjust to look upon the zeal of Pius V.
for the Inquisition and for the punishment of the guilty as a
sign of any natural hardness of character. In the advice
which he sent to the princes and bishops as to the way in which
they should treat heretics, he clearly expressed the ideas which
governed his conduct towards the followers of the new religion.
In the first place, he was convinced that the first duty of a ruler
is the administration of justice, and justice demands the
punishment, and the severe punishment, of the guilty as much
as the protection of the innocent, while apostasy from the
Church was in his eyes a grave crime.[2] Moreover, he was
firmly convinced that it was precisely by stern measures against
the sectarians of the time that he could prevent much shedding
of blood, while, on the contrary, tolerance and half measures
could only lead to greater evils.[3] Hence came his warning to

[1] *Cusano, May 24, 1572.

[2] " Mali vitiorum poenam, boni virtutum praemium, sibi a te
expectandum esse intelligant. Haereticorum venena ne gregem
tuam inficiant, quanta potes diligentia contende." To the Bishop
of Agram, August 11, 1569, in GOUBAU, 203.

[3] " Habes, carissime Fili, recens exemplum sceleris, furoris,
audaciae haereticorum. Vides, quam noceat cum iis molliter

Catherine de' Medici, which at first sight gives a wrong impression : " in no way and for no reason must you show mercy to the enemies of God ; you must use all rigour with men who will show no mercy either to God or your sons."[1] He himself acted on this principle, not out of harshness but from a sense of duty.

It is, however, clear that in the second half of his reign the Pope did not attach to the repression of heresy the same predominating importance which he did at first ; the fact that from 1569 to 1572 there were only two autodafés in Rome points to this.[2] At the beginning of 1570 the Capuchin, Pistoja, who was highly esteemed by Pius V., remarked to him that he saw every day manifest examples of the Pope's zeal for the administration of justice, but the Pope ought to bear in mind that for one passage in the Sacred Scriptures where God is called just, there are ten which bring out His mercy. Let the Vicar of Christ then take care to perform works of mercy instead of justice on the heretics, since the unhappy souls which were being sent to perdition through the power of the Turks afforded him every opportunity of exercising the former virtue.[3] The zeal with which Pius V., from that time forward, worked for the formation of a league

agere quibus impunitas auget audaciam, patientia furorem, clementia feritatem. Intelligere potes, quam inutile sit eorum consilium, qui suadent, ut differas et procrastines, etc." To Charles IX., June 16, 1566, in LADERCHI, 1566, n. 423. " Si superiores reges Franciae dissimulando et tolerando id malum crescere non fuissent, facile extirpare haereses et regni sui paci et quieti consulere potuissent ; neglectis praedecessorum nostrorum paternis hortationibus, dum istiusmodi carnis prudentia nituntur, sublata pace, quae sine unico rectae veraeque religionis cultu manere non potest, regnum illud . . . in extremum periculum adduxerunt." To Sigismund of Poland, March 26, 1568, in GOUBAU, 73.

[1] March 28, 1569, *ibid*. 155.

[2] See *supra* p. 312.

[3] The Venetian ambassador, April 15, 1570, in CANTÙ, Eretici, II., 410.

against the Turks, may really to a great extent afford an explanation of the fact of the cooling of his zeal for the punishment of the new believers. Peter Canisius, too, when he was in Rome, had successfully urged him to show moderation towards those prelates in the north whose faith was so feeble.[1]

While Protestantism had undoubtedly received a mortal blow in Italy, it was every day becoming clearer that a new form of heresy was springing up in the north under a Catholic disguise. The news of this was received with all the more anxiety in Rome because the Low Countries, already so much endangered on the score of religion, threatened to become the centre of the new movement, and especially the long celebrated University of Louvain, which had hitherto been the staunch opponent of Luther.

For a long time past Protestant doctrines had been an incentive for Catholic theologians to maintain the opposing doctrines of the Catholic Church, to go into them more deeply and to develop them scientifically. The untiring zeal with which the followers of the new religion sought to spread their ideas by means of books and writings, broadsheets and ballads, explains the way in which Protestant ideas had obtained a hold upon public opinion, and had acquired a greater influence even with many Catholics than they themselves suspected. The fact that Luther's fundamental and principal doctrine had found a reflection in the theory of justification held by Contarini, Pole and Gropper had been of far less importance. On the other hand, a fatal influence which was to last for many centuries had been introduced into Catholic thought and life by the Protestant teaching as to grace and free-will as the outcome of the system which was founded at Louvain after the middle of the XVIth century by Baius, and which was carried to completion in the following century by·the Jansenists.

Baius (Michael du Bay)[2] who had occupied the royal chair

[1] Canisii Epist., VI ., 583.

[2] X. Le Bachelet, Dictionnaire de théologie catholique, II., Paris, 1905, 38–111. M. Scheeben in Kirchenlex. of Freiburg, I², 1852–1862. F. X. Linsenmann, Michael Bajus und die Grundlegung des Jansenismus, Tübingen, 1867 ; also Scheeben

of Sacred Scripture at Louvain since 1552 directed his studies, as he wrote to Cardinal Simonetta in a letter of 1569, to the attempt to reconcile the followers of the new beliefs with true Catholic doctrine.   Since the Protestants, so he wrote, attach no value to anything outside the Sacred Scriptures and the most ancient Fathers of the Church, I have tried to reduce theology to the study of the sacred books and of those Fathers who are still of weight among the Protestants, such as Cyprian, Prosper, Leo, and the four western Doctors.[1]   But when Baius tried to set aside the intellectual labours of the medieval theologians his doing so was not inspired only by his wish to conciliate the exponents of the new faith, but rather by his opinion that in the Middle Ages theology had degenerated, and had got on to the wrong lines by mixing itself up with Aristotelian philosophy, and that it ought to be brought back to the earlier Fathers, among whom he looks to St. Augustine as his master above all others.

This breach with medieval tradition was at once shown to be fatal by his treatment of the fundamental question of the whole of Baianism, the original state of man.   If, according to the teaching of the Holy Scriptures, Adam was from the first not only the servant but the son of God, if the movements of concupiscence were restrained in him and made subject to reason, theologians had hitherto seen in these and other gifts of the first man nothing but free and gratuitous gifts of God.   Since human nature could have no claim whatever to these gifts as things necessary or due to it, such gifts of grace were called supernatural ; if God had left the first man in a state in which he lacked all these graces, nothing would have been wanting to his nature of the things that

in *Katholik*, 1868, I., 281 *seqq*. M. Baii . . . Opera omnia, cum bullis Pontificum et aliis ipsius causam spectantibus . . . studio A.P., Colon., 1696 (due to the labours of the Jansenist Gerberon ; the second part contains under the title *Baiana* the documents relating to the controversy). The Library of the Anima, Rome, contains in MS Preuckiana Collectanea ms.   C 43, p. 5–36, several *documents on Baianism.

[1] LE BACHELET, II., 38.

belonged to it, and his state would have been in no way abnormal.

But Baius rejected this idea of natural and supernatural gifts in the first man as a manifest error, for which philosophy by its interference in matters of faith was responsible. If, according to Baius, Adam's sonship of God and his freedom from the rebellion of concupiscence are a necessary part of human nature, the absence of such an equipment in the state of fallen man to-day must be a defect, an alteration of human nature which, according to the Louvain theologian, had been absolutely spoiled and evil since the time of the Fall, and the virtues which are related of the heroes of classical antiquity are really only vices, having the appearance of virtues. Concupiscence, such as now exists in man, is according to him nothing but original sin. At this point the question at once arises as to how movements in man independent of his will can be looked upon as personal sin. Baius replies that the concept of liberty only excludes external violence, but not interior necessity. Thus Baius, from the starting point of his fundamental error, proceeds to its further consequences, and builds up a whole theological system on grace and redemption, on sin and merit, and on the love of God and justification. In his teaching on sin in general and original sin in particular, " he scarcely distinguishes his views on both questions from the terrifying doctrine of the reformers of the enslavement of human nature by the devil which was brought about by sin."[1]

In 1563 Baius began to make his views public by means of small works written in clear and precise terms, in which for the most part he makes use of the words of St. Augustine, but, taking the sentences of Augustine out of their historical setting, the Pelagian controversy, he often gives them an entirely new meaning.

Long before he had begun to write, he and his disciple Hessels had maintained their views at the university, and had met with so much support there that the Chancellor of the

---

[1] SCHEEBEN in Kirchenlexikon of Freiburg, I.[3], 1861.

university, Ruard Tapper, when he returned to Louvain from
the Council of Trent in 1552, was quite amazed at the change
which had taken place there during his absence. Although
he was Inquisitor General of Flanders he tried at first to resist
the new movement by methods of persuasion, but his efforts
met with no success, while even a warning from Granvelle
which Tapper obtained was only able to check the movement
for a short time.   The struggle began to break out when the
guardians of the Franciscan convents of Ath and Nivelle
sought to put an end to Baianism among their subjects by
obtaining from the Paris faculty, on June 27th, 1560, a condemnation of 18 propositions drawn from the new teaching.
At this point Baius thought that the time had come to defend
himself ; his supporters formed the plan of printing the works
of St. Prosper, in order to show that the Louvain professors
were only putting forward the doctrines of ancient Christianity.
Their adversaries, however, were not silent, and they had
recourse to Granvelle with a memorial.   The Cardinal, who
found the controversy exceedingly inopportune at that
moment of unrest in Flanders, tried to smother it by obtaining
a brief from Pius IV. imposing silence on both parties.   Philip
II. approved the step taken by his representative in a letter
of November 17th, 1561.[1]

It had been realized in Rome since the end of 1560 that all
was not well in the University of Louvain.   For a long time
past an order had been in force there that every student,
before he was admitted, should take an oath that he would
remain in the Catholic Church, of which the Pope was the
head.   Now, however, there was a movement in favour of
doing away with this oath, as being an obstacle to the free
coming of students.   Pius IV. issued two briefs on this subject,
one on January 29th, 1561, to Granvelle, and one on February
5th to the university, in the latter case threatening excommunication to anyone who opposed the oath.[2]   The prudence
of the legate Commendone, who had been sent to invite the

---

[1] LE BACHELET, II., 40.
[2] ŠUSTA, Kurie, I., 49.   RAYNALDUS, 1561, n. 42.

prelates of Lower Germany to the Council, and who arrived
in Flanders in May, 1561, was successful in adjusting the matter
in a peaceful manner.[1]

Commendone, however, had to report many disturbing
things as to the state of affairs at Louvain. The party of
Baius and Hessels, so he wrote on June 9th, 1561, is very
strong; a great number of the graduates, and about half the
professors, favour the innovators ; since three of the representatives of the old regime have recently been promoted to
the episcopate, none but Baians remain in the faculty, and they
have everything in their own hands. It is not possible,
however, to take severe measures against this new movement,
since that might drive Baius and Hessels into apostasy, a
thing which would have the gravest consequences on account
of the great esteem in which they are held on account of their
learning and their irreproachable lives. The assembly of
the Council causes special difficulty as Baius and Hessels wish
to be sent to it as the representatives of the university, and
there is a disposition at Louvain to grant their request. If
however, so Commendone thought, these two men were allowed
freely to express their views at the Council, there would be
disturbances in Germany, while if they were not, a pretext
would be afforded to the Protestants to complain of the
absence of free speech at the Council. There was also danger
to be feared from the imprudence of the opposing party ; very
soon the General Chapter of the Franciscans would be held,
at which the theological controversy would be discussed. It
was quite possible that on that occasion the small fire might
develop into a great conflagration.[1]

While he was at Louvain Commendone tried by every means,
on May 24th, 1561, to reconcile the contending parties. But
the legate learned how tenaciously the innovators stood by
their contention that Baius was only defending the ancient
teaching of the Church from a letter addressed to him by

---

[1] RAYNALDUS, *loc. cit.*

[1] *Miscell. di storia Ital.*, VI., 162. RAYNALDUS, 1561, n. 44.
PALLAVICINI, 15, 7, 7.

Hessels on May 27th, 1561.[1]   In his letter to the legates of the
Council Commendone proposed, as the best way to avert the
threatened storm, that the Pope should summon the case
before himself, impose silence on the Franciscans, and in his
own name suggest the sending of Baius and Hessels to the
Council.[2]   This advice, however, which the legates referred
to Rome together with their own proposals,[3] arrived too late.
Cardinal Borromeo replied to them on July 6th, 1561, that he
had already had information on the subject from Granvelle,
and that the Pope had decided to send the latter a brief
imposing silence, on his own initiative, even under censures
and penalties, until either the Council or the Pope had decided
the question.[4]   Pius IV. had come to this decision so hastily
that there was no possibility of awaiting the fuller report
which the legates of the Council had promised to make upon
the controversy and the proposals of Commendone.[5]   The
latter, who continued to insist upon Baius and Hessels being
summoned to the Council,[6] received a reply in a letter from
Cardinal Gonzaga on August 31st, that the Pope had already
made up his mind.[7]   It was not until two years later that
Baius and Hessels were sent to Trent by Margaret of Parma as
royal theologians,[8] and assisted at the last three sessions of
the Council, which afforded them no opportunity of explaining

[1] In Šusta, Kurie, I., 192. " Nobis " we read " praecipue
incumbere putamus, ut studendo, docendo, disputando ex anti-
quissimis et solidissimis nostrae religionis fundamentis studeamus
nostri temporis erroribus occurrere."

[2] Letter of June 9, 1561, *ibid.* 36.

[3] June 30, 1561, *ibid.* 34 *seq.*

[4] Borromeo to the legates, 6 July, 1561, *ibid.* 49 : " Hoggi ha
risoluto di scriver al detto cardinale un breve, dove gli commette,
che *imponat silentium sub censuris et penis* sin'a le determinatione
del concilio oche espongano a S. S^{tà} le lor differenti."   *Cf.*
Borromeo to the legates, 12 July, 1561, *ibid.* 58.

[5] *Ibid.* 50 ; *cf.* 36.

[6] From Lübeck, July 24, 1561.   *Miscell. di storia Ital.*, IV.,
200.   Pallavicini, 15, 7, 10.

[7] In Šusta, *loc. cit.*

[8] Raynaldus, 1561, n. 46.

their views. Their private statements, and the writings of
Baius occasioned much scandal, but in their capacity as royal
theologians, and on account of the speedy closing of the
Council, they escaped condemnation.[1]

Although Granvelle had forbidden the two professors any
further exposition of their doctrines under pain of excommunication, Baius nevertheless allowed himself to be persuaded
to the false step, after his return from Trent, of publishing
some further writings on the controverted points, and of
reprinting his earlier works. His principal adversary in the
university, Joss de Ravestein, known as Tiletanus, then
had recourse to the Augustinian Hermit, Lorenzo de Villavincentio, who was highly esteemed by Philip II. Lorenzo
wrote to the king from Brussels on November 21st, 1564,[2]
with the result that the Universities of Alcalà and Salamanca
condemned a series of the propositions of Baius.[3] At the same
time Philip II. appealed for a definite decision of the controversy to the Pope, to whom Tiletanus also made a report
of the case.[4]

Baius was not known in Rome. Granvelle, who had had to
take proceedings against him, but who was otherwise favourably disposed towards him, was at that time in the Eternal
City. As Grand Inquisitor, Pius V. had had to deal with
Baianism in the time of his predecessor, and had a good
recollection of the case when Granvelle represented to him
that Baius was a learned and cultured man, and a priest of
irreproachable life, who could do a great deal for the Church,
and in any case had a right to be treated with every consideration.[5] The Pope was very ready to take this point of view.
Learned men of various nationalities were charged to give

---

[1] Morillon to Granvelle, June 20, 1568, in POULLET, III., 279.

[2] GACHARD, Corresp. de Philippe II., II., xx.

[3] LE BACHELET, II., 41, 47. No particulars of this condemnation are known.

[4] *Ibid.* 48. *Cf.* the letter of Villavincentio of 1571 in GACHARD,
loc. cit. 174.

[5] Granvelle to Morillon, November 13, 1567, in POULLET, III.,
106.

their opinions of the writings which were submitted to them for examination, and the prudent step was taken of giving them copies without a title page, so that they might not know who was the author. The bull in which, on October 1st, 1567, as the result of these opinions, Pius V. condemned 76, or according to a later estimate, 79 propositions,[1] does not name Baius or Hessels, and where mention is made of the supporters of the condemned propositions they are spoken of in terms of respect. It was certainly out of consideration for them that the propositions were enumerated without any mention of the censures which they individually deserve, and it is only at the end of the list that it is stated that they are proscribed as a whole as heretical or erroneous, suspect, etc., but it is not stated which of them are heretical, erroneous, etc.[2] Moreover the bull was not printed or publicly posted, and the Pope left its execution to Cardinal Granvelle, who was told to proceed with all possible moderation.[3]

Granvelle did not like to have the bull solemnly published in Louvain, and he entrusted its execution to his vicar-general, Maximilian Morillon. Hessels had died in November, 1566, and Morillon was to summon Baius before him and show him the bull. If necessary the vicar-general was to communicate it also to the theological faculty, and to insist that no attempt be made in any way to defend the condemned propositions, since, as he wrote to him, Granvelle could assure him that everything possible had been done to interpret them in an orthodox sense, and that the Pope had gone into the matter as carefully as if he had been concerned with the salvation of the whole world.[4]

[1] The bull itself does not give the number of the propositions.

[2] " Quas quidem sententias . . . haereticas, erroneas, suspectas, temerarias, scandalosas et in pias aures offensionem immittentes respective damnamus."

[3] POULLET, III., 106 seq. LE BACHELET, II., 48.

[4] " Car je vous puis asseurer que, pour les saulver, l' on a faict tout ce qui a esté possible, et qu' en cest affaire Sa Saincteté a usé d'une diligence que, si ce fut esté pour gaigner tout le monde, l'on n'eust sçeu faire plus." POULLET, III., 107.

The letter to Morillon, in which Granvelle gave him full instructions on all these matters, was fated to come under the notice of Baius himself. In another letter, also addressed to Morillon, Granvelle expressed his fears for the future, because learned men like Baius have a love for their books like the love of a father for his son. He takes the opportunity of urging all possible gentleness in the execution of the bull.[1]

At first it seemed as though Granvelle's fears would not be justified. On December 29th, 1567, Morillon informed the dean and the eight professors of theology of the bull, and all of them, not excepting Baius himself, declared their readiness to submit to it.[2] The commissary of the Flemish province of the Franciscans also received orders to forbid to his subjects the use of the condemned propositions.[3] The Franciscans obeyed,[4] and in 1568 Cornelius Janssen the elder, Bishop of Ghent, bore witness concerning Baius that he considered him a man worthy of all respect, who said mass every day and was definitely opposed to the sectarians; that as a teacher he was as capable as could be desired, while in his lectures he never touched upon his new doctrines, nor had he acted otherwise for three years previous to the Papal condemnation; Janssen adds that he would never have thought it possible that the new doctrines should have disappeared so completely; in the schools there is as little thought of them as if they had never existed, while Baius himself, when there had been a question of putting them forward once more, would not agree to do so. Among some of the most learned graduates they are now held in as great horror as once they were esteemed.[5]

Baianism thus seemed to be dead, but this was only in appearance. Baius did not abide by his first resolution of simple obedience to the decision of the Church. In June,

---

[1] Granvelle to Morillon, November 13, 1567, *ibid.* 104 *seq.*

[2] LE BACHELET, II., 49. Morillon wrote to Granvelle on December 21, 1567, that he would have Baius brought before him on the following day. POULLET, III., 153.

[3] Morillon to Granvelle, January 11, 1568, in POULLET, III., 169.

[4] Morillon to Granvelle, June 20, 1568, *ibid.* 282.

[5] *Ibid.* 281.

1568, Morillon wrote that he found him greatly changed. Baius was complaining that he had been condemned without being heard ; he maintained that some of the condemned propositions were not to be found in his books, while others were wrongly stated ; that points had been decided which hitherto had been open, and that it might well be that some day he would write a book against the bull.[1] Morillon did not fail to reply to this, and advised him specially to refrain from publishing anything against the bull, because neither the Pope nor the king would suffer it, and that Baius would only do himself harm by so acting.[2] Baius then calmed down, and at last gave a clear assurance that it was his intention to persevere in obedience to the Pope ; Morillon must excuse his irritation on account of the great pain which the Pope's condemnation had given him, which had been aggravated by his enemies' refusal to keep silence. It was true that Tiletanus had sent the bull to the Bishop of Ypres, the University of Douai, and to several monasteries.[3]

In spite of all his promises, however, Baius tried to defend the condemned propositions in writing. On January 9th, 1569, he sent an apologia to the Pope, in which he acknowledged 30 of the propositions which had been condemned in Rome, but maintained that they contained nothing but what had been taught in the Holy Scriptures and by the Fathers of the Church. In a covering letter he said that the honour of the Pope had suffered by the bull being published so widely, firstly because of the obvious calumnies which it contained, and secondly because it was opposed to the words and ideas of the Fathers of the Church. It was a scandal to many learned men in the north, who on account of their struggle with the heretics were wont to lean more upon the teaching of the Sacred Scriptures and the Fathers than were the medieval theologians, and who might get the idea that zeal for scholasticism had led to the condemnation of the Fathers

[1] Morillon to Granvelle, June 20, 1568, in POULLET, III., 278.
[2] *Ibid.* 279.
[3] *Ibid.* 280.

themselves. That was why he was presenting this apologia ; the Pope must decide whether the bull had not been fraudulently obtained. On March 16th, 1569, Baius sent a similar letter to Cardinal Simonetta, who, however, was already dead by the time it arrived.[1]

It was very obvious what the consequences of this must be. Some of the Franciscans in Flanders, it is true, encouraged the mad idea that the Pope was inclined to withdraw the bull,[2] whereas in fact a Papal brief of May 13th, 1569, declared that even if the bull had never been issued, it would have to be now ; the Pope now confirmed it, and imposed perpetual silence upon all who approved the propositions condemned. Morillon received from Granvelle the difficult task of inducing the hot-headed scholar to recant, and then to absolve him from the ecclesiastical censure under which he had fallen.

On June 20th, 1569, Morillon set himself to discharge this duty. At first Baius was surprised that he should have brought down ecclesiastical penalties upon himself by his remonstrances to the Pope ; but he then knelt down to ask for absolution. When, however, Morillon insisted that he must first recant, he rose to his feet and declared that he must first receive a copy of the bull, because the latter itself admitted that some of the condemned propositions could be defended " *in rigore* and according to the strict sense of the words."[3]

---

[1] LE BACHELET, II., 50.

[2] Morillon to Granvelle, March 20-21, 1569, in POULLET, III., 521.

[3] In reality the bull does not admit this, but says that the propositions are " rejected " according to the tenor of the words and in the sense in which they had been maintained by their defender " Quas quidem sententias . . . quanquam nonnullae aliquo pacto sustineri possent in rigore et proprio verborum sensu ad assertoribus intento haereticas, etc., damnamus." The bull is written without punctuation marks and Baius placed a comma after " intento " although it should obviously come after " possent " so that the " in rigore " etc., refers to " damnamus." The controversy concerning the " Comma Pianum " is still being carried on.

Morillon replied that the bull could not be given either to him or to his opponents, because the Pope intended to put a stop to the whole controversy. Baius replied that he was very glad to hear that, but regretted that the condemned propositions should have been so freely made known to his adversaries. After a long discussion Baius at length agreed to make his recantation.[1] The Provincial of the Franciscans in Flanders, too, among whom the celebrated Louvain professor always had a number of adherents,[2] obliged the guardians of the province, by a decree of September 1st, 1569, to give currency to the abjuration which he had made.[3]

In spite of this, however, the new doctrines were not yet entirely crushed. It took Baius a long time to overcome the interior struggle between his obedience to the Pope and his attachment to his ideas, which he looked upon as the teaching of St. Augustine, nor did he always keep his feelings to himself. The Franciscan, Godfredus of Liège, thought it necessary to preach against Baianism, and theologians like Cunerus Petri and the youthful Bellarmine, at that time a professor in the Jesuit college at Louvain, wrote refutations of it,[4] for the new doctrines still found many followers.[5] It must be added that in 1570, after the death of Tiletanus, Baius had become dean of the faculty, and the college of professors was composed entirely of his disciples. Under these circumstances, some of the bishops of Flanders thought it right to demand of Baius a public statement of his attitude towards the condemned propositions.[6]

Morillon had long been of the opinion that the fault of Baius lay in his want of knowledge of scholasticism, and in

---

[1] Morillon to Granvelle, June 20, 1569, in POULLET, III., 607 seqq.

[2] Morillon, September 26, 1568, ibid. 369.

[3] LE BACHELET, II., 51.

[4] LE BACHELET, Auctarium Bellarminianum, Paris, 1913, 314-338.

[5] " Advertens non deesse multos, quibus hae opiniones placerent" Autobiography of Bellarmine edited by LE BACHELET, 452.

[6] Cf. LADERCHI, 1570, n. 292.

his lack of judgment, remarking that he had for a long time past noticed the latter defect in the celebrated professor.[1] Baius gave further proof of this by the way in which he complied with the demand of the bishops. In his lectures on April 17th and 19th, 1570, he set forth his attitude towards the bull, substantially reiterating the point of view, apparently long since set aside, which he had adopted in his apologias to Pius V. and Cardinal Simonetta.

This settled the fate of Baius. The Duke of Alba intervened and demanded of the provincial council, then assembled at Malines, in June, 1570, that the bull should be solemnly published at Louvain, and subscribed by all the professors. The bishops had the courtesy to inform Baius privately of what was about to be done, and found him ready to accept it. On November 16th the bull was published by Morillon at Louvain, in the presence of Baius, the professors and the students. The doctors then had to swear to the bull, a thing which drew tears from Baius.[2] In the evening the rector of the university sent each of the doctors a formula, in which they had to declare that they accepted the condemnation of the 76 propositions, and that they would act in accordance with their acceptance. No signatures, however, were received to this formula, for when Morillon had gone it was rumoured that he had carried out the publication of the bull on his own authority without the order of the bishops, and the latter had to defend him against this charge in a special letter.[3]

Later on, however, after further pressure on the part of the Pope and the Duke of Alba, the doctors decided on April 17th, 1571, that they must look upon the 76 propositions as condemned, and take away from the students all the books which contained them. Yielding to further pressure on the part of Alba the doctors on August 29th promised the fullest

---

[1] To Granvelle, June 4, 1569, in POULLET, III., 596 : " Tout le mal est que, comme jugent par delà les sçavantz de luy, qu'il n'est d'érudition fondée en scholastique ny de bon jugement, et il y at longtemps que je m'apperceois de ce dernier poinct."

[2] LADERCHI, 1570, p. 292.

[3] Of December 23, 1570, *ibid.* n. 293.

submission. Baius had to declare that he accepted the bull with all reverence, that he considered it to have been sufficiently promulgated, that he submitted to it unreservedly, and that if the Pope wished for anything further he would do it.[1] The Louvain controversy then remained quiescent until the death of Pius V.

With the exception of his bull against Baius, Pius V. only issued one other decree in direct defence of doctrine ; on October 1st, 1568, he renewed the constitution of Paul IV. against that form of Protestantism which denied the Trinity and the Divinity of Jesus Christ, His miraculous conception and the satisfactory value of His death, and the virginity of His Mother,[2] thus almost completely depriving Christianity of its supernatural character. By this decree Pius V. dealt his final blow in the struggle against Italian Protestantism, since it was Italians, the Sienese Lelio and Fausto Socinus, who maintained these opinions in their fullest form, and it was the Italian form of Protestantism from which Socinianism sprang. From the first Protestantism in Italy was strongly infected by infidelity,[3] and it was at the hands of Italians that the transformation of believing Protestantism into complete infidelity received its first impulse and its subsequent development.

But how disappointed had been the hopes of the Italian

---

[1] Le Bachelet, II., 52.

[2] Bull. Rom., VII., 722.

[3] Ochino " in his later writings shows himself involved in a volte-face from the positive rigorist view . . . towards those ideas of which Seb. Castellio and Lelio Socinus are the representatives. . . . The Geneva theologians themselves complained of the Italian exiles as ' academic sceptics ' . . . but how little the course taken by the Italian reformation had followed these developments . . . a broader examination of the question can hardly be said to give the lie to the above mentioned theologians of Geneva, when they recognized in these men a specifically Italian form of scepticism." This is the view of K. Benrath : " Über die Quellen der italienischen Reformationsgeschichte, Bonn, 1876, 11 seq.

religious innovators !   Italy, so thought Curione in 1550, makes
progress from day to day, and the time of the harvest is now
at hand.[1]   Shortly after the election of Pius V., a Protestant
of Valtellina wrote to a co-religionist at Trent that at Valtellina
the Papacy was more and more discredited ; that there was
reason to hope that the " diabolical mass " would soon be
abolished in the Grisons, that the preaching of the " Gospel "
was spreading in France, and that the " cursed mass " was
altogether stamped out in Scotland and England ; it was
reported that " Christian liberty " was taking root in Poland
and other countries ; that he and those who shared his
opinions hoped that ere long they would hear of great things,
and especially of the complete destruction of the kingdom
of the Roman Antichrist.[1] But by the middle of the reign
of Pius V. the doom of Protestantism was sealed at least in
Italy.

If in these modern times, with their hostility to all restraint
of freedom of thought, the method of procedure by violence
adopted by Pius V. could not be tolerated, it was undoubtedly
a blessing for Italy in its results.   It was not in vain that the
Pope so often called for vigilance, and so insistently pointed
to the horrors of the Huguenot wars.   He knew his fellow

[1] TACCHI VENTURI, I., 350.

[1] " *De le nuove di qua in circa la religione per la gratia del
Signore son molto buone et prima qui in Valtelina ogni giorno
si va distruggendo il Papato et speremo in breve che i signori
Grisoni habbia[n] a mandare a spassa la diabolica messa. Di poi
si dice per cosa certa che la Francia ha levato via del tutto la
persecutione et è posto ognuno ne la libertà de la fede talmente
che la religione ogni dì va crescendo et cominciasi a predicare
l'evangelio e farsi le congregazioni in publico.   La Scocia e
l' Ingalterra ha [sic !] levato via del tutto la maledetta messa.   Si
dice anchora di Polonia et di molti altri regni esser venuti ne la
libertà christiana et percio speriamo in curto tempo de sentir gran
cose et massime l' ultima ruina del gran regno d' Antichristo
Romano." Letter of Giov. Ant. Zurleto to Leonardo Columbino
to Trent from Tirano, April 13, 1566, original in Cod. Mazzetti,
616, p. 21, Municipal Library, Trent.

countrymen, and he well understood that if the new ideas took strong root in their easily heated imagination there was every reason to fear that the sword and dagger would soon be drawn by citizen against citizen, and by city against city, and the struggles of Guelph and Ghibelline would be renewed with all their horrors and with redoubled fury.[1] It can hardly be doubted that the victory of Protestantism would have given to Italy as well its Thirty Years' War. The country-side would have become a wilderness, and the lover of art can only think with horror of the fate that would have overtaken the masterpieces of Raphael and Michelangelo if a war against sacred images had broken loose in the privileged sanctuary of the arts. The resoluteness and energy of Pius V. saved his country from being bathed in streams of blood. Politically, Italy was broken up, but he preserved to her one bond of union, her common religious thought and outlook. At the same time he preserved to her—a thing which in the absence of political importance was her strength—the unchallenged glory of being and remaining the supreme school of the arts in Europe.

[1] Through the Bishop of Narni he invited the Italian princes to help Charles IX. against the Huguenots in the following terms : " Potersi mentre i tumulti son lontani, i principi de sudditi lor prevalere : ma quando s'aventassero questi mostri in Italia, quale infermità, et difficultà patiscano gli stati col mezzo dell' heresie proverebbero. La cui pestilenza pur troppo sparsa per l' Italia poco più vi ponesse piè, esser facil cosa da imaginare quel fuoco fosse per accendere ne cervelli Italiani." CATENA, 69.

APPENDIX.

PRELIMINARY NOTICE.

THE following documents are intended to confirm and complete the text of my book ; it has formed no part of my plan to provide a true and full collection of documents. In every case the place where the document was found is given with the greatest possible exactitude. As far as the text is concerned, I have, as a rule, preserved intact the wording of the documents or letters, which for the most part I have had before me in the original ; there is no need for me to justify the changes I have made in the matter of capital letters and punctuation. Where I have ventured on alterations I have always noted the fact, though small mistakes and obvious copyist's errors have not been specially noted. The additions which I have made are enclosed in square brackets, while unintelligible or doubtful passages are marked by a note of interrogation or by the word " *sic.*" Those passages which I have omitted, either when copying the documents or in preparing them for the Press, and which were not essential or unnecessary for my purpose, are marked by dots (. . .).

I. THE CONCLAVE OF PIUS V. ACCORDING TO THE DIARY OF CORNELIUS FIRMANUS.[1]

Ea nocte [sequenti diem 23^{am} decembris 1565] omnes rev^{mi} vigilarunt facientes praticas pro electione novi pontificia : erant enim multi qui quaerebant et totis viribus instabant quod eligeretur in pontificem rev^{mus} Moronus, alii erant qui ipsius exclusionem quaerebant : fiebantque praticae et conventiculae tanta cum celeritate, strepitu, rumore ac concursu quod vix credi possent ; aliqui rev^{mi} ibant fere currentes portantes de per se busias cum luminibus absque aliquibus ex eorum conclavistis, alii sine luminibus nec omnino vestiti, adeoque videbatur maximus conflictus. Sed si illa nocte

---

¹ See *supra*, p. 27, n. 5.

ducebatur in capellam praedictus rev^mus Moronus, erat certe pontifex ; nam ipsius adversarii erant perterriti et habebant facies albas prout pannus lineus est, nec sciebant a principio quid facerent ; sed quoniam habuerant tempus procurandi exclusionem, vel quia sic erat Dei voluntas, cuius secreta non est nostrum scire, seu quia adhuc non venerat hora eius, antequam fieret scrutinium, fecerunt perfectam et securam exclusionem. In mane autem antequam lucesceret dies, ceperunt cardinales pontificem eligere, cupientes magna cum celeritate venire versus capellam ut concluderetur negocium ; qui maxime infestarunt me ut cito pulsarem campanellam pro missa ut citius fieret scrutinium ; et deputati ex capitibus ordinum mandabant quod pulsarem hora solita et consueta, prout feci et forsan prius, ut utrique parti ut melius possem complacere. Fuit dicta missa ex more et factum deinde scrutinium, in quo praedictus rev^mus Moronus habuit 26 vota et tres accessus, quos dederunt rev^mi Sforzia, Ursinus et Vercellensis.

Erant tunc in conclavi 51 rev^mi, videlicet Pisanus, Moronus, Tridentinus, Farnesius, Crispus, de Perusio, Saracenus, Sancti Vitalis, S^ti Clementis, de Pisis, Reumanus, Capisucus, Alexandrinus, de Araceli, Sabellus, S^ti Georgii, Cornarius, Salviatus, Simoneta, Pacecus, Amulius, Corrigiensis, de Gambara Borromeus, Altaemps, Gesualdus, de Sermoneta, Ferrariensis Mantua, de Aragonia, Colunna, Novocomensis, Patavinus, Delphinus, Bobba, Sforzia, Ursinus, Vercellensis, Lomellinus, Crassus, Sirletus, Urbinas, de Monte, Simoncellus, Vitellius, Estensis, Madrutius, Medices, Alciatus, Paleotus [et Castiglione] : adeoque pro perfecta pontificis electione requirebantur 34 vota, de quibus quinque defuerunt ; sed certe fuit maximus conquassus, strepitus ac rumor in nocte : nullus enim cardinalis quievit, et multi ipsorum fere currebant per conclave praesertim rev^mus Estensis, qui laboravit pro decem hominibus et aperto marte quaerebat exclusionem. Similiter fecerunt etiam rev^mi de Sermoneta, Urbinas et nonnulli alii. Visi fuerunt multi rev^mi perterriti et quasi flentes, qui, licet inviti, ibant tamen ad capellam ad consentiendum electioni fiendae, considerantes non posse ipsam electionem aliquo pacto impedire. Nunquam vidi tam magnam in alicuius rev^mi favorem frequentiam, quae tamen nil profuit, quia sic datum erat desuper. Credo equidem quod optimus fuisset pontifex et bene gubernasset Romanam Ecclesiam.

.Illo sero [diei 30] fuerunt visae multae conventiculae et
praticae cardinalium quaerentium creare pontificem rev^{mum}
S^{ti} Vitalis. Nil tamen factum fuit ; nam rev^{mus} Borromeus
(qui habebat in posse suo magnam ·votorum quantitatem)
nolebat accedere, licet quidam de suis libenter accessissent.
Dictus vero Borromeus cupiebat creare rev^{mum} de Araceli ;
sed· rev^{mus} de Altaemps non erat contentus. et sic fuit diu
praticatum et laboratum in vanum.

Die 5^a summo mane hora XII^a fuit inceptus magnus
rumor pro creando in pontificem rev^{mum} cardinalem Sirletum,
et duravit, maxima cum multorum rev^{morum} acceleratione
et concursu usque ad horam 15 ; nam aliqui ex parte rev^{mi}
Borromei adiuvabant dictam electionem, multi etiam faventes
rev^{mo} S^{ti} Vitalis quaerebant exclusionem. Illo interim
rev^{mus} Sforzia publice in aula Regum dixit rev^{mo} Borromeo
quod nolebat aliquo pacto ire ad rev^{mum} Sirletum, quia nunquam in tota nocte aliquid de eo sibi dixerat, cum honestum
ipsi videretur quod omnia debuisset scire et replicavit nunquam
nisi coactum iturum dicta ex causa, licet ipsum rev^{mum} sum-
mopere diligeret et pontificia dignitate dignum cognosceret.
Cumque videret rev^{mus} Borromeus firmo ac determinato animo
ea dici, rogavit rev^{mum} Sfortiam quod saltem permitteret ire
rev^{mum} de Medicibus : cui respondit se nunquam prohibi-
turum, immo eum rogaturum ut iret in eius praesentia ; et
exinde omnia ref igescere ceperunt, licet rumor in totum non
cessaret.

Illo mane ceperunt magistratum triduanum rev^{mi} Pisanus,
Reomanus et Madrutius.

Dum fieret rumor pro eligendo rev^{mum} Sirletum in pontificem
rev^{mus} Vitellius camerarius ivit ad cameram rev^{mi} de Medicibus, cui dixit pontificem iam fuisse creatum et quod propterea
ipse etiam iret et cum aliis interveniret, qui tumultuanter
incepit dicere quod non per terrorem et metum fiebant pontificum electiones et quod nolebat ire, et iratus exivit a sua cella
sive camera, tertio eidem replicando. Deinde fecerunt circulum circa 15 cardinales in capite aulae regiae ante cameram
rev^{mi} Reumani, ubi Borromeus et quidam alii rev^{mi} satis
rogarunt rev^{mum} Farnesium ut secum iret ad ducendum
rev^{mum} Sirletum ad capellam ut eum pontificem crearent ; qui
respondit quod sibi non displicebat et bene sciebat eum fore
dignum pontificatu, sed tamen nolebat iri nisi audita intentione et voluntate suorum consociorum et quod cito respon-

deret ; interim autem bene factum putabat fieri scrutinium, in quo forsan Deus inspirasset quid foret agendum ; et sic factum fuit. Nec praetermittam quod dum fierent praticae supradictae, rev^{mus} Sirletus, qui divum Jeronimum repraesentare videbatur, flebat continuo et rogabat rev^{mos} ipsius fautores quod desisterent ab incepto nec quaererent ipsum in pontificem eligere, quia sciebat se non fore sufficientem ad sustinendum tam grave pondus et habendum gubernium tanti momenti, genuflexusque in lecto (in quo infirmus iacebat) indesinenter flebat et rogabat eius familiares ut Deum deprecarentur supliciter quod non succederet ipsum eligi in pontificem ; et credo certissime quod supra dicta ex toto corde agebat, nam semper fuit vir exemplaris, amator paupertatis et in minimis contentus, absque superbia, dulcissimae, conversationis et denique sanctissimae vitae.

Illo sero fuerunt factae praticae pro rev^{mo} cardinali Tridentino, credo potius ad honorandum eum quam quod aliqua esset intentio ipsum creandi pontificem.

Die 6^a ianuarii, quae erat dies Epiphaniae, celebrarunt omnes infrascripti rev^{mi}, videlicet Moronus, Farnesius, Crispus, Saracenus, S^{ti} Vitalis, Pisarum, Reumanus, Alexandrinus, Sabellus, Simonetta, Pacecus, Amulius, Corrigiensis, de Gambara, Borromeus, Gesualdus, de Sermoneta.

Illa die post prandium fuit aliqualis rumor in conclave et visae fuerunt quaedam praticae multorum rev^{rum} pontificem diversimode creare quaerentium, in vanum tamen, quia nondum venerat hora.

Illa die inter horam 21^{mam} et 22^{mam} omnes rev^{mi} iverunt ad cameram rev^{mi} cardinalis Alexandrini, quem quasi invitum et per vim duxerunt ad capellam Paulinam, et cum vellent eum eligere in pontificem, tanta erat confusio quod nesciebant quomodo illud agere deberent : aliqui enim petebant fabas ut per vota fieret, alii dicebant quod portarentur scabella et alia consueta pro scrutiniis, alii etiam, meliorem viam ac magis expeditam eligentes, dicebant quod publica voce danda essent vota per quemlibet cardinalem, et ita fieri deberet electio ; prout, sedato clamore ac magno strepitu, factum fuit. Nam omnes sederunt in solitis eorum locis et tunc rev^{mus} decanus stans dixit : Ego Franciscus cardinalis Pisanus, sacri collegii decanus, eligo in summum pontificem rev^{mum} dominum meum Michaelem cardinalem Alexandrinum nuncupatum. Post eum rev^{mus} Moronus similibus verbis

elegit eundem, deinde rev^mi omnes infrascripti similiter
elegerunt, videlicet Tridentinus, Farnesius, Crispus, de
Perusia, Saracenus, S^ti Vitalis, S^ti Clementis, Pisarum,
Reumanus, Capisuccus, de Araceli, Sabellus, S^ti Georgii,
Cornarius, Salviatus, Simonetta, Paceccus, Amulius, Corri-
giensis, Gambara, Borromeus, de Altaemps, Gesualdus, de
Sermoneta, de Aragonia, Colunna, Novocomensis, Nicolinus,
Patavinus, Delphinus, Boba, Sforzia, Ursinus, Castellionensis,
Vercellensis, qui etiam tulit votum descripium rev^mi cardinalis
Ferrerii patrui sui qui erat podogra impeditus et nomine etiam
ipsius elegit, Lomellinus, Crassus, Sirletus, Urbinas, de Monte,
Simoncellus, Vitellius, Estensis, qui etiam elegit nomine rev^mi
cardinalis Ferrariensis patrui sui infirmi, Madrutius, Medices,
Alciatus, Paleotus. Quo facto, licet scrutininium fieri debuisset
etiam sine praeiudicio electionis, tamen eo omisso omnes rev^mi
surrexerunt et iverunt versus dictum rev^mum Alexandrinum,
qui surgens, fuit per rev^mum decanum interrogatus an acceptaret
electionem de se factam per sacrum collegium ; qui stetit
aliquantulum nolens respondere, tandem, sollicitatus per
multos rev^mos, dixit haec propria verba : Mi contento su.
Et nos clerici cerimoniarum fuimus rogati tam de electione
quam acceptatione.

[Copy, Papal Secret Archives, XII., 31 p. 25 *seq.*]

2. FRANCESCO TOSABEZZO TO THE DUKE OF MANTUA.[1]

1565, December 15, Rome.

. . . Mon ^r Illmo nostro che come saggio et prudente ha
scoperto un gran paese nel particolare della creatione del
nuovo Pontefice, ha voluto secondo l'amorevolezza di che è
verso V. Ecc^a ch' ella sappia il termine in che si trovano le
cose, che fin adesso più tosto si ha da temere che sperare
d'haver cosa che sia in nostra sodisfatione. Dice dunque S. S.
Illma che ci sono tre soggetti che vanno per li tavoglieri, li
quali fanno più strepito d'ogni altro, l'uno è Morone et questo
è tanto inanzi che Borromeo non desidera alcuno più di lui,
onde se non si dà tempo alli Francesi di venire el al card^le di
Ferrara di fargli l'esclusione, va a pericolo di riuscire Papa
subito. Per rimedio di che ha pensato S. S. Illma di persuadere
a Borromeo che voglia aspettare le sue creature, cioè Buoncompagno, Crivello et Comendone, et così vedere di fuggire
questa borasca, non essendo come V. Ecc. sa Morone buono ne

---

[1] See *supra*, p. 23, n. 2.

per noi, ne per li mondo. L'altro è Farnese il quale de ha anch'egli buono, non perchè non sia conosciuto, ma perchè il collegio è tanto povero che quando li card^li vedranno di havere a distribuire fra loro ottanta mila scudi d'entrata, dubita che non si risolvi. Tuttavia il S. Card^le nostro spera di tenere saldo Borromeo et Alt'Emps, con tutto che ad Altemps sia stata offerta la vicecancelleria. Il terzo soggetto è Ferrero, il quale è desiderato da Borromeo, ma il collegio vecchio l'ha per un da poco et un ignorante, però la sforza di Borromeo fa ch'egli ne habbia buono, et il S. Card^le nostro confessando la cosa come la sta, dice, che quanto sie per lui non gli spia-cerebbe, perchè è suo amico, come è anco il ca d^le Vercelli suo nipote, oltre che sa per essere lui un da poco, serebbe forse più largo che non fu Papa Pio. Ma vi è questo oggetto della gelosia che si ha da havere dello stato di Monferrato per conto di Savoia, et però il Card^le nostro non concorrerà in questo soggetto se non in caso che non possa fare di manco, ante-ponendo sempre l'utile et interesse particolare di V. Ecc^a al suo proprio. Farnese propone Alessandrino non perchè riesca Papa conciosia che è difficile cosa, ma si bene per fare l'adito più facile a se stesso. Di Ferrara non vi è speranza, fin qui, non ci volendo concorrere Borromeo in alcun conto laonde bisogna aspettare aiuto di Franza et vedere di straccare con lungo tempo Borromeo, nel qual caso Ferrara potria havere anch'egli buono, ma a questo ci vuol tempo et per ciò bisogna sapere schrinire bene. Araceli è cosa che sia Papa, con tutto che Firenza l'aiuti et maggiormente Trani, con tutto che Farnese lo favorisca, il qual Farnese fa questo acciò che riu-scendo Papa habbia da vivere poco et da fargli una promotione di card^li a suo modo, col mezzo dei quali possa poi al sicuro et in breve entrare Papa in conclavio ad un altra sede vacante, et la causa che questi due ne hanno poco buono è che la Sta di Pio nanti la morte sua lasciò ordine alli nepoti card^li che non facciano Papa Theatino alcuno et manco creatura di Paulo quarto. Amulio sarebbe aiutato da Borromeo, ma è in malissima opinione di tutto il collegio, di modo che ha da sperare poco al papato. Fiorenza favorisce Montepulciano Araceli et Nicolino, ma vorria piutosto Nicolino et pur vede che Montepulciano è più riuscibile et l'aiuta, non vorria ne Morone ne Farnese. Hora per vedere d'impedire che uno de soggetti amico alla casa non succeda Papa si procurerà per una delle creature di Borromeo, cioè per Buoncompagno, per

Comendone et per il Crivello, ma si dubita che sieno difficili
tutti. Borromeo lauda più Comendone, ma Buoncompagno
seria più a proposito per la casa, et questo è appunto disiderato
da Fiorenza, venendosi però al particolare delle creature,
Montepulciano sarebbe Papa, se Borromeo lo volesse, ma lo
abhorrisce come la peste, però si conchiude che ogni cosa è in
grandissimo disordine, ne si sa vedere altro che imbarazzi et
travagli. . . .

      [Orig. Gonzaga Archives, Mantua.]

3. Avviso di Roma of 12 January, 1566.[1]

. . . Si vede veramente, che è stata opera del Spiritu Santo,
perchè il Papa si mostra tutto buono, tutto santo et tutto sin-
ciero, pieno d' humanità et d' affabilità senza veruna hipocresia.
Dice messa ogni dì, detto la messa fa collatione, 1 panata et
2 ovi con mezzo bicchiero di vino, poi dà audienza fino alla
sera, che cena a 24 hore con poco di carne. Discorre spesso
con cardinali quali tiene per fratelli; dice haver parenti
nepoti, figliuoli di una figlia di sua sorella, quali dice voler
lasciar in modo c e non siano mendichi, ma non li vuolene
duchi ne marchesi ne conti, et un parente frate, che stava a
Perugia, che l'ha mandato a chiamare, et lo farà cardinale,
et ha anco chiamato uno di quelli della casa di Gislieri di
Bologna, che dice lui esser di quella casa, et si crede che lo
farà general della chiesa. Non vuol cosa alcuna da prencipi,
ne per se ne per i suoi, che a essi prencipi farà tutte le gratie
che potrà. Non vole ne gabelle ne dacii straordinarii, che
viverià con quel poco che ha, et che la sua panata con li suoi
2 ovi li bastano. Ha levato la bottega della Dataria, et fatto
Datario il vescovo Maffei, ne vuol più compositioni, et ha fatto
castellano l'arcivescovo di Napoli, et confirmato governatore
di Roma il Palentieri. Vuole che i cardinali servino il grado
loro, non gli vuole ne Theatini ne frati ne Giesuiti, che i ricchi
tenghino il grado loro et che a i poveri darà di quello che vaca
a ciascuno la parte sua. Quando gli viene raccordato qualche
fatto di qualcuno, è solito a dire, che sa d'esser posto alla
cura d'huomini e non d'angeli. Raccoglie humanamente
non solo tutti quelli che mai lo servirno, ma ciascuno che mai
lo conobbe; fa gratie et incita le persone a chiederle. Piglia
et abraccia tutte le creature di Paulo IV.; si dice che fa venir

[1] See *supra*, pp. 54 n. 4, 66 n. 2, 68 n. 3, 72 n. 2, 77 n. 1, 84 n. 3.

Don Antonio Caraffa et il figliuolo del duca di Paliano et anco
sig. Matteo Stendardo, ai quali dice volersi mostrar grato.
Quelli che governano hora sono Farnese, Vitelli, Pisa et
Reumano. Fa venir anco a Roma il duca Ottavio per dar
grandezze alle cose. He has made Vitelli governor of the
Borgo, the brother of the Cardinal and General of the Knights
of Orsino, " in somma grandissima liberalità " ; he has
restored his apartments to Cardinal Urbino, and given him
the bishopric of Montefeltro, he has given 40 poor Cardinals
500 scudi, and 100 scudi a month to each, 10 scudi to the
conclavists, 4 to his servants. 50 to Count Hannibal d'Altemps,
and 200 to each Auditor of the Rota. He has given Farnese
the direction of the Segnatura, and will assign to him the
" stanze di Torre Borgia." He is retaining some of the
" famiglia " of Pius IV., and is replacing many by creatures
of Paul IV., a thing which makes others, especially Marcantonio Colonna, jealous, since the Carafa have been recalled,
but this is a vain fear " perchè non si mostra vendicativo sin
hora. Vuol pagare tutti i debiti di Paolo IV et vol fornir la
fortificatione di Borgo, et questa mattina si ha cominciato a
lavorare et anco finirà le fabriche di Belvedere." This morning there was a General Congregation " per consolar i cardinali " : he listened to each of them and granted all the
favours asked for so long as they were not to the disadvantage
of third parties ; he then caused all to go out except the
Cardinals, whom he thanked saying to them, " che non li
vuole tener per servitori ma per fratelli ; " and published the
day of St. Antony, his birthday (in his 62nd year) as the day
of his coronation. " Da tutti questi indicii si raccoglie che
siamo per haver un buon Papa, et dove la nova della sua
creatione spaventò tutta Roma, per esser frate et di
S. Domenico, così le sue attioni fanno giubilar tutti et ciascun
li prega longa vita et sanità, della quale ha bisogno patendo
di renella grandemente, et essendo mal complessionato."
Ha perdonato a Morone, che adorandolo poi avrebbe detto :
" Dimitte nobis debita nostra, gli rispose in generalibus "
e lo ha benedetto. " Ha trovato l'introito molto felice,
essendo da conferir in beneficii più di 200^m sc. et trovato in
Castello da 800^m. Ha detto di voler deputar 3 cardinali,
quali habbino a conferir tutti li beneficii vacati et che vacar-
anno, sicome era a tempo di Paulo IV, et alle cose temporali
vuole deputar alcuni altri cardinali, volendo lu solo attendere

alla conservatione della religione. Il comendator di Castello vorrebbe dar a credere, che lui fosse stato quello che havesse fatto il Papa, ma è stato veramente il Spiritu Santo."

[Orig. Urb. 1040, p. 163, Vatican Library].

4. CORNELIUS FIRMANUS ON THE CORONATION OF PIUS V.[1]

17 January, 1566.

GATTICUS has published (p. 342) some passages from the long description given by Firmanus of the Coronation of Pius V. The following, hitherto unpublished, description of the *Forma suggesti pro coronatione papae facti,* is of interest :

" . . . Erat in primo arcu a dextris dictae sedis depicta mulier magnae staturae, quae dextra tenebat flammam, sinistra vero securem cum tallio ab utroque latere, super cuisus capite erat scriptum : Abundantia, status temporis, et ad pedes : Iustitia. In secundo arcu prope praedictum, per quem intrabatur in sugesto per eos qui veniebant a Sancto Petro, erat alia mulier ut supra depicta, quae prope dextrum crurem [sic] habebat scabellum cum calice desuper, et dicta mulier tenebat pateram in dextra super calicem tanquam si voluisset aliquid in eum immittere, manum sinistram tenebat spalmatam et ab eodem latere puer nudus amplectebatur eius crurem [sic] ; super eius capite erat scriptum : Amor, Charitas, Clementia ; ad pedes autem : Charitas. In angulo erat mulier, quae super manum dextram tenebat ecclesiam et brachio sinistro amplectebatur tabulam cum quibusdam litteris quae legi non poterant ; super cuius capite erat scriptum : Felicitas animi Tranquillitas ; ad pedes autem : Religio. In primo arcu ad sinistram sedis erat depicta mulier respiciens caelum, devote manibus iunctis tenens tres rosas, super cuius capite erat scriptum : Existimatio bona gloria ; ad pedes vero : Spes. In alio arcu prope praedictum erat mulier, quae dextra tenebat bilanciam et brachio sinistro amplexa fuerat cornu abundantiae ; supra caput erat scriptum : Facultas copia status temporis ; ad pedes vero : Aequitas. In pariete respiciente domum archipresbiteratus S[ti] Petri erat mulier, quas dextro brachio tenebat organum, et sinistra habens brachium extensum tenebat calicem, cum inscriptione tali supra caput, videlicet : Charitas nominis bona fama laus ; ad pedes autem : Fides.

[Copy, Miscell. Arm. XII, 31, p. 43, Papal Secret Archives.]

[1] See *supra,* p. 70 n. 1.

5. NICCOLÒ CUSANO TO THE EMPEROR MAXIMILIAN II.[1]

1566, February 2, Rome.

L'ultimo del passato mese il Papa fece castellano di Castello S. Angelo di Roma un certo Francesco Bastone[2] ch'è del Bosco sua patria, il quale si dice l'ha fatto per render a lui la gratitudine del obligo haveva al padre del detto Bastone perche dicono lo levò da guardare le peccore ove la madre sua l'haveva mandato non havendo altro modo miglior da notrirlo essendo in estrema povertà et l'aiutò ad imparare lettere mandandolo alla scola col figliolo dalli frati che stavono nel Bosco sua patria, i quali visto che'l era per riuscire nelle lettere lo fecero frate, ove continuò li studii in modo che divenne dottore in theologia. Accade che fu data querella alla Inquisitione di Roma d'alcuni di questi frati di non so che d'heresia, i quali lo mandarono a Roma a giustificarli, il che gli reuscì così bene che l'Inquisitor vedendolo cosi dotto et di buona vita lo ritenne seco dandolo in mano tutte le cose della Inquisitione, le quali trattò con tanta sodisfattione del card.le di Chieti che essendo Papa lo fece morendo il suo padrone Inquisitore et poi vescovo et cardinale per il ch'è hora venuto Papa onde di minimo et povero guardiano di peccore è venuto pastor generale sopra tutti li pastori del grege di Christo ch'è de miracoli di questa corte.

[Orig. State Archives, Vienna.]

6. JOHANNES SAMBUCUS[3] TO CARDINAL G. SIRLETO.[4]

1566, February 20, Vienna.

Cum, ut scis, aliquoties hunc pontificem familiarissime ante 3 annos accessissem atque de studiis et vetustis codicibus edendis admonerem, quorum copia tanta apud nos delitescit, memini illum mihi aliquoties respondisse : ' Mi Sambuce, utinam per me staret : ego ederem optimos quosque libros graecos, neque hic eos tineis absumendos paterer. Sed sum pauper fraterculus ; in meis viribus id situm non est.' Utinam, mi optime atque illustrissime Schirlette, hanc vocem illi aliquis repeteret atque ad sanctos literatosque conatus ex-

[1] See *supra*, pp. 46 n. 4, 71 n. 1.
[2] The *Diarium of Cornelius Firmanus announces on October 13th, 1568 the death of " Franc. Bastonus (senex) " ; his successor as castellan of S. Angelo was his son Albert. Papal Secret Archives.
[3] Polyhistor ; historiograph to Maximilian II. and Rudolph II., born 1531, died 1584 ; see *Allg. Deutsche Biographie*, XXX., 307 *seq*.
[4] See *supra*, p. 129 n. 3.

citaret, quod non dubito sponte ipsum ac prolixe facturum.
Vale.

Viennae X kalendas martii MDLXVI.

[Orig. Vatic. 6792, p. 127. Vatican Library.]

7–8. CAMILLO LUZZARA TO THE DUKE OF MANTUA.[1]

Rome 27 March, 1566.

Il Papa continua nel levare la mattina per tempissimo et
subito dice la messa et sta un poco ritirato, poi fa colatione
et dopo dà audienza, et questa dura tutto il di, se non viene
interrotta o da consistorii o da le congregationi o da le segna-
ture che si fanno ad ogni settimana. Di queste le congregationi sono le più continue, perchè sono sopra le cose del
concilio, de la inquisitione et de lo stato de la chiesa, et in
queste comincia ad intravenire il S. card^{le} Alessandrino il
quale comincia ad havere tutte le facende o poco manco,
et già qualche card^{le} come Aragona, che so io, piglia l'hora
de l'audienza del Papa col mezo di lui, et ricerca che sia
presente a quanto ha da trattare, et di questo card^{le} d'Aragona altro non so io che dire, se non che è assai caro al Papa . .

. . . . Nella corte passano hora poche novità che diano materia
d^{i} ragionare, perchè questo Papa se ne passa con una maniera
di vivere assai quieta et ritirata, nè in Palazzo si fanno più
quei ridotti che al tempo degli altri papi vi si solevan fare
d'ogni conditione di cortigiano. Banchi anch'esso in questa
parte non è quel che solea essere già, di modo che a volere
sapere vovelle della corte conviene andare per le case de card^{li}
et de ambasciatori, et a questo ci vuole otio et commodità
grande, il che non posso havere io che ho da spendere il tempo
in altro come ben sa l'Ecc. V., la quale si degnarà di scusarmi
hora se in questa parte io non supplissi al mio debito et al
desiderio che forse ella haverà di sapere le minutie di tutta
questa corte.

[Orig. Gonzaga Archives, Mantua.]

9. AVVISO DI ROMA OF 13 APRIL, 1566.[2]

Il Papa andò lunedì alle 7 chiese con pochissima compagnia
di gente et solo il card. Alessandrino e Savello, e con molta
devotione ; et fa ogni giorno opera con intelligentie, reforma
et bandi, perchè si viva più christianamente che sia possibile,

---

[1] See *supra*, p. 52 n. 1.   [2] See *supra*, pp. 58 n. 2, 61 n. 1.

et sin hora riesce giusto et santo principe, et se ne spera tuttavia de bene in meglio, et è essemplarissimo in tutte le sue attioni et di tanta bona mente quanto si può desiderare. E stato tutta questa settimana santa alle funcioni della Capella et il venerdì santo comandò, che non si cocesce cosa alcuna in casa sua, et non solo ha fatto la quaresima, ma l'ha degiunata tutta non ostante alcuni difetti d'infirmità et la vecchiezza, così sia pregato Iddio che la mantenghi et prosperi lungamente.

[Orig. Urb. 1040, p. 210. Vatic. Library.]

10–15. Buildings of Pius V. at Bosco.[1]

1. Avviso di Roma of 23 March, 1566.

The Pope intends to employ for the construction of the church at Bosco the 20,000 scudi deposited at Milan by Pius IV. for the Swiss League.

[Orig. Urb. 1040, p. 197. Vatic. Library.]

2. Avviso di Roma of 14 June, 1567.

S. S. fa fabricare al Bosco un monasterio dell'ordine suo, per il qual s'intagliano qui le porte, balursti et finestre de preciosissimi marmi, li quali poi si mandaranno. Expenditure 200^m Scudi, for 30–40 frati who shall live in the convent, et si fa far una superbissima sepultura, perchè là vol essler sepolto, et ha mandato per via del mare l'altr'hieri a quela fabrica molte colonne de serpentini et porfidi, et la solicita, come s'havesse a morir fra un mese.

[Orig. Urb. 1040, p. 407. Vatic. Library.]

3. Avviso di Roma of 19 July, 1567.

On Tuesday the Pope received from Cardinal Ricci " una pietra nera lunga una canna," which will be sent to Bosco.

[Orig. Urb. 1040, p. 421. Vatic. Library.]

4. Avviso di Roma of 23 July, 1569.

Il Papa sollecita la sua sepultura che fa lavorare nella casetta del Bosco, la quale è di marmo bianco con statue e con la sua persona ritratta di naturale con gli habiti alla

---

[1] See *supra*, p. 124 n. 1.

pontificiale ingenocchiato avanti un crucifisso con un breve
in mano aperto, che sarà di gran valuta, et finita la manderà
al Bosco alla chiesa che fa fabricare.

[Orig. Urb. 1041, p. 117^b. Vatic. Library.]

5. Avviso di Roma of 5 December, 1570.

P. Serafino (Grindelli ; see BRUZZONE in Riv. Alessandria,
XI., 8 [1903], 7 *seq.*) reports to the Pope about the fabric of the
convent at Bosco.

(Orig. Urb. 1041, p. 376. Vatic. Library.]

6. Brief of 17 October, 1571, to the Governor of Milan.

" Mittimus dil. fil. Iacobum de la Porta architectum ad
nostrum monasterium Boschi." Please help him.

[Archives of Briefs, Rome.]

On June 21, 1567, Arco* reports that the Pope " andò
a vedere certe colonne che manda alla chiesa del Bosco " ;
(State Archives, Vienna). *Ibid.* an * Avviso di Roma of
March 2, 1569, concerning the sending of rich vestments to
Bosco ; for the tomb of St. Dominic at Bologna " fa anco
fare di molti ricchi acconci da porre sul altare et sopra l'arca."

16–25. PURIFICATION OF MORALS IN ROME, 1566.[1]

1. Bando.

" che non si vada la notte accompagnato con donne di mala
vita per Roma, che dette donne non tenghino arme in casa
ne nissuno vi vadi in casa con arme etc.", 12 maggio 1566.

[Editti V, 60, p. 204. Papal Secret Archives.]

2. Avviso di Roma of 25 May, 1566.

An order will shortly be issued " che le cortegiane stiano
in una o due parte della Città come seria in Trastevere o
verso il Popolo."

(Orig. Urb. 1040, p. 231^b, Vatican Library.]

3. Avviso di Roma of 1 June, 1566.

Difficulty about the order concerning the" cortegiane" ;
perhaps they will now receive a sign.

[Orig. *Ibid.* 220^b.]

[1]See *supra*, p. 90, n. 2.

4. Avviso di Roma of 29 June, 1566.

" Hiersera a forza de sbirri le meretrici sgombrorno Borgo et li conservatori s'affaticarno per trovar luoco da serrarle."

[Orig. *Ibid*. 248.]

So reports Arco on June 29, 1566 (original in State Archives, Vienna).

5. Avviso di Roma of 27 July, 1566.

By order of the Pope, the Vicar on Monday issued the following order against prostitutes : " che se ne vadino molte cioè le più scandalose, et l'altre vadino in Transtevere. Ma li habitanti di quel luoco in numero di più di 400 con il loro caprione andorno dal card. Morone, che vi habita, pregandolo, che fosse loro protettore appresso il Papa, accio esse cortegiane non vi fossero poste, et mercordì andò da S. S., nè con molte raggioni che dicesse non pote ottener altro, se non che per adesso non si poteva far altro. Il senatore, conservatore et il popolo tutto di Roma hanno poi fatto officio, che solo si levino dalle strade maestre et d'appresso le chiese monasterii et dalle case di gentildonne et che le lascia habitar nelle altre strade men publiche di Roma, nè anco l'hanno potuto ottenere, ma solo s'è contentato, che possino habitar tutta strada Giulia. da Ponte S. Angelo a Ponte Sisto, nondimeno sin hora non si vede, che vadano, nè in uno nè in l'altro loco."[1]

[Orig. Urb. 1040, p. 260b. Vatic. Library.]

6. Avviso di Roma of 3 August, 1566.

Questi dì li Romani fecero consiglio contra le mutationi delle meretrici et 40 di loro con li conservatori andorno a supplicare il Papa, che non le voglia mandar in Trastevere ; hebbero in risposta : Tutta questa matina havete sonato il vostro campanozzo in congregarvi a far che per conservarvi l'infamia, che noi per debito nostro, honor nostro et commune satisfatione cercamo di levarvi, nè è bene comportar, che dalle meretrici siano habitate le più belle strade di Roma santa, ove è sparso il sangue di tanti santi martiri, ove sono tante reliquie, tante devotioni, ove è la Sede Apostolica et tanta

---

[1] *Cf.* the letter of C. Luzzara of 27 July, 1566, in BERTOLOTTI, Repressioni, 8 (wrong date, the 22nd) ; report of Tiepolo of 26 July, 1566, in MUTINELLI I.. 51 *seq.* letter of Arco of 27 July, 1566 (State Archives, Vienna), and especially the *report of Aless. Mola to Card. Ferd. de' Medici, dated Rome, 25 July, 1566 (State Archives Florence, Medic. 5096).

religione : città, che per specchio del mondo tutta doverà esser monda da vicii et peccati a confusione d'infideli et heretici, in fine non conoscete il ben vostro : con che se gli levò davanti.

[Orig. Urb. 1040, p. 264. Vatic. Library.]

A similar Avviso in BERTOLOTTI, Repressioni, 9 ; see *ibid.* 8, the report of Luzzara. *Cf.* Tiepolo in MUTINELLI, I., 53 *seq.* According to Firmanus, Diarium (Papal Secret Archives) the deputation was received on July 24, 1566. On Augu t 3, 1566, Arco reports that the Pope replied : " O volete le meretrici o moi ; se volete esse, noi partiremo di Roma, se volete noi lasciate che obediscano." (State Archives, Vienna).

7. Avviso di Roma of 10 August, 1566.

Questi dì li conservatori di Roma a nome del popolo presentorno una littera con molte informationi delle meretrici, et di scacciarle, allegando molte ragioni, per conservation della Città, dell' honore delle donne maritate et delle citelle ; hebbero in risposta : Noi lo vederemo, consideraremo et se sarà bene, l'abrazzaremo ; et hoc interim per causa del monitorio sono già partite più di 300 meretrici delle principali di Roma, et tuttavia vanno fuori, per questa causa, molte ritornate in se si sono maritate, retirate et convertite, et le triste non trovano, chi comprinoi le loro robbe con tutto il buon precio, parendole quelle di mal acquisto. Li patroni delle case restano mal contenti, che non le pono affittare se non assai manco, et di questo beneffetto ne gode più il publico, se ben i Romani se ne becano il cervello con voler impedire. Anco la pragmatica del vestire va inanzi, ne s'ha rispetto a persona, et contra alcuni contrafacenti si procede hora con farli pagar assai grande penne. Si publicarà quest'altra senttimana una terribil bolla contra li adulteri et un bando contra tavernarii et hosti per non supportare tanto gran numero di forfanti, che si sono posti alla poltronaria in quei luochi. S'aspetta anco una bolla et generale riforma di tutto questo clero oltra la corte, il popolo et la città tutta, la quale purgata di tante et tante imondicie portà ben farsi chiamar Roma santa. Hieri havemmo un bando rigorosissimo dell'arme."

Orig. Urb. 1040, p. 270, Biblioteca Vatican Library.]

Cf. the AVVISO of 17 August, in BERTOLOTTI, 9.

8. Avviso di Roma of 17 August, 1566.

The *doganieri* of Rome complained to the Pope of the loss occasioned by the " dogane per la partenza delle meretrici et delli hebrei. Il Papa gli ha detto di volerli osservar li loro capitoli, nelli quali crede non esser mentione dì queste cose, et che però anco farà in modo, che essi non ne patirano in alcun modo ne vuol comportare, che li sia fatto torto nè dalla Camera nè da altro. Tuttavia le meretrici sono stemate assai, et quelle che tante restano, sono come sbigotite et disperse, et ne sono state amazzate alcune, che si dice per esser avenuto per opera di quelli che tengono le loro robbe in salvo, nondimeno non è certo, altri credono che venga da loro parenti ; alla fine la loro remotione et gli tanti romori di mandarle in Trastevere, N. S. doppo la informatione si è risoluto di lasciare, che il popolo con gli conservatori le accomoda in luoco, che stia bene, et come saranno comodate tutte nella parte di Campo Marzo dall'Arco di Portugallo in qui verso il Populo, però fuori delle strade grande come nelle traverse verso la Trinità, si come già è dato principio."

[Orig. Urb. 1040, p. 275[b].   Biblioteca Vatican Library.]

9. Avviso di Roma of 7 September, 1566.

" Bando del card. Savelli " published " giovedi " (Urb. 1040, p. 282[b], in Vatican Library ; edited BERTOLOTTI, Repressioni 10).   This " Bando contro le meretrici " was printed in Rome in 1566 by Ant. Blado.   Very rare as is also the " Bando sopra le meretrici," published in " Bologna l'ult. di gennaro et reiterato il 1[o] di febraio 1568," Bologna, Benaci, 1568.

10. Avvisi di Roma of the 2 and 7 November, 1566.

Printed by BERTOLOTTI, *loc. cit.* 10-11.   *Cf.* POLANCI *Epist.* in *Anal. Bolland.* VII.. 69.

26. BERNARDINO PIA TO CAMILLO LUZZARA.[1]

Rome 22 January, 1567.

Dominica qui si diede licenza al popolo di mascherarsi, pero huomini et non donne ne religiosi et furon prohibite le caccie de tori et simile spettacoli et ordinati che i palii, che si solevano correre per Banchi et per Borgo si corrano dalla vigna di Julio

[1] See *supra*, p. 88 n. 5.

fin a S. Marco non essendo fatione conveniente da farsi sotto
le stanze de S. St^{à}.[1]

(Orig. Gonzaga Archives, Mantua.]

27. Pope Pius V. to the Governor of the Campagna and Marittima.[2]

With a view to taking steps to provide for the safety from
robbers of those who come to the city, and since the " Algidi "
forest is, on account of its marshy character and size, very
convenient for robbers, we command you to open out the road
on both sides by cutting down the trees, and " graviter ferimus"
that through neglect this has not been done. " Quia vero
latrociniis in ea silva committ solitis occurri omnino
volumis," we ordered you to have the trees cut down by the
population in such a way that the road shall be safe, and
where it is necessary, to protect it, and to burn the trees,
taking care that they shall not spring up again ; it is our
will that the ancient road, which was once paved with stones,
shall be repaired and restored to its former width.

[Arm. 44 t. 13, p. 105, Papal Secret Archives.]

28-34. Avvisi concerning the Purification of Morals in Rome in 1567.[3]

March 15 : This morning " 3 meretrici Venetiane frustate " ; a sheet of paper fastened to their breast showed
the reason. Orig. Urb. 1040, p. 370b, Vatican Library.[4]

April 3 : " 3 meretrici frustate," because they had " uscite
dai luoghi deputati," ibid. 376.

[1] Note. With the Avvisi di Roma of January 18, February 8, and 14, 1567
(see Clementi, 216 seq.), cf. the *report of Arco of February 9, 1566 (Non ha
voluto S.Stà dar licenza di far maschere se non con condizione che le donne
[i.e. the prostitutes] non possino andarvi), the *report of Cusano of March 2,
1566 (prohibition of bull-fights), and *that of Strozzi of January 18, 1567
(prohibition of the carnival in the Borgo, " where the priests live "), State
Archives, Vienna. Ibid. a *report of Arco of February 21, 1568, concerning
the strict enforcement of these orders. Cf. also the *Avviso di Roma of
January 29, 1569, Urb. 1041, p. 11, Vatican Library.
[2] See supra, p. 102 n. 3.
[3] Cf. supra, p. 92 n. 1.
[4] See Firmanus, *Diarium : " Die sabbati XV. dicti mensis [martii 1567] ante
ecclesiam Sti Ambrosii et per stratas omnes circumcirca fuerunt a carnifice
fustigatae tres meretrices quoniam non paruerant ordinibus et edictis vicarii
Smi Domini Nostri, inter quas fuit quaedam Armeria Veneta, pulcherrima
iuvenis et absque dubio puchrior omnibus aliis meretricibus Urbis : fuit etiam
quaedam Nina de Prato, et elia dicta Isabella ; et prosit." (Papal Secret
Archives). Cf. also the *report of Arco of March 29, 1566, State Archives,
Vienna.

April 14 : " 3 meretrici " placed in the " Convertite," *ibid.* 382.

May 17 : " Si fa hora una generale rassegna delle publice meretrici per darli occasione o di conversione o di sgombrare il paese," *ibid.* 396b.

July 19 : Banishment of " 60 meretrici " (see BERT LOTTI, Repressioni, 11) ; the Romans are discontented, " il gonimedi desperati et sarano il resto come li Hebrei," *ibid.* 421a

August 2 : Pius V. ordered six noble ladies of ma.ture age to go to the prostitutes and exhort them with many promises to give up their sinful life, *ibid.* 426.

August 30 : The " meretrice Buggiardina " condemned to perpetual imprisonment (murata). *Ibid.* 434b.

35–47. EXTRACTS FROM THE " DIARIUM " OF CORNELIUS
FIRMANUS CONCERNING THE ACTIVITY OF THE ROMAN
INQUISITION, 1566-1568.[1]

[1566] Die dominica 23 dicti mensis [iunii] fuerunt 24 cardinales in ecclesia beatae Mariae supra Minervam, ubi fuerunt reconciliati et absoluti quidam haeretici et falsi testes ; et quoad penas corporales diversimode condemnati, et fere maior pars ad triremas, et eorum unus nobilis propter reincidentiam fuit traditus curiae saeculari tamquam incorrigibilis, et alius ultra multas opiniones haereticas fassus fuerat quod in civitate Ferrariensi fecit se circumcidi more iudaeorum, ut haberet in uxorem quandam Sarram iudaeam, licet in Hispania aliam teneret uxorem. Septem testes falsi fuerunt condemnati ad fustigationem et ad triremes, diversimode quoad tempus, et ad reficiendas expensas calumniatis : et fuit late sententia contra quendam fratrem ordinis minorum Conventualium absentem et eius figmentum tentum super sugesto cum cappa sui ordinis, cum descriptione nominis. Et inquisitores erant rev^mi Tranensis, Pisarum, Paceccus et Gambara. Alii viginti cardinales fuere : ego casu interfui et Deus voluit, nam erat magnum impicciatorium bancorum et nil erat ad propositum aptatum.

[1566] Illa die [25 iunii] vidi septem falsos testes, per deputatos inquisitionis (ut dixi supra) condemnatos, qui fustigabantur per Urbem, et ducti fuerunt ad Capitolium

[1] *Cf. supra*, pp. 292 n. 3, 301 n. 1, 302 n. 1, 305 n. 1.

cum quatuor haereticis sequentibus eos cum crucibus rubeis in parvo zagulo ; qui omnes deinde missi fuerunt ad triremes.

[1566] Die iovis quarta dicti mensis [iulii] quidam don Pompeius de Monte fuit decapitatus, deinde conbustus in Ponte, quoniam fuerat haereticus et pluries relapsus. Homo erat aetatis 50 annorum incirca, magnus et pulcherrimi aspectus. Ivit ad mortem satis contritus et ego vidi.

[1566] Die sabati 6ª eiusdem mensis [iulii] fuerunt suspensi quatuor in Ponte, de quibus unus fuit combustus propter sodomiam.

[1567] Dicta die [lunae 24 februarii] hora 20ª, fuerunt ducti ad ecclesiam Bᵗᵃᵉ Mariae supra Minervam decem haeratici, qui eorum pravas opiniones abiurarunt et diversimode fuerunt condemnati. Fuit inter alios quidam dominus Basilius de Cremona canonicus regularis, qui de anno praeterito publice praedicaverat in ecclesia Sᵗⁱ Ioannis Baptistae Florentinorum cum maximo populi concursu et alias etiam in diversis ecclesiis Urbis praedicaverat habitusque erat excellens in arte praedicandi. Iste illa die confessus fuit multas pravitates haereticas, et fuit condemnatus ad perpetuos carceres. Duo equites custodiae Suae Sᵗ ˢ, quoniam dederant litteras et receperant a quibusdam in officio sᵐᵃᵉ inquisitionis carceratis, fuerunt condemnati ad triremes, unus quia fuit confessus errorem suum, pro quinque annis alter, qui fuerat per testes convictus, ad vitam. Interfuere 25 cardinales cum eorum cappis violaceis, sed quoniam maxima venerat hominum multitudo ad videndum praedictum dominum Basilium, vix cardinales potuerunt sedere in locis suis ; et ego passus fui magnum laborem ut ipsos accommodarem.

[1567) Die dominica 22 dicti mensis [iunii] in ecclesia beatae Mariae supra Minervam fuerunt iuxta morem factae abiurationes per decem inquisitos propter enormissimum crimen haeresis, quorum unus fuit quidam Marius Paleottus baro Neapolitanus, quidam ex ipsis, quia alias abiuraverat ef fuerat relapsus, traditus fuerat curiae saeculari et die lunae sequenti suspensus in Ponte et eius corpus combustum, qui multa in furcis dixit de fide catholica. Fuit lectus processus eodem die cuiusdam Simonis absentis, cuius effigies delata fuit in suggesto. Interfuere 22 cardinales et populus infinitus. Plures fuerunt condemnati ad varias et diversas penas triremium et carcerationum et similium et bene merito.

[1567] Die dominica 21 septembris. Fuerunt ducti ad ecclesiam B^tae Mariae supra Minervam 17 haeretici, inter quos fuit quidam dominusi Petrus Carnesicca Florentinus, qui alias fuit secretarius intimus fe. re. Clementis septimi, prothonotarius apostolicus ex privilegio, et erat abbas habebatque de redditibus ecclesiae quatuor millia ducatos, ut dicebatur. Infelix iste pluries et per multos annos tenuerat infinitas haereticas opiniones maximi momenti, et pluries fuerat misericordiam consequutus et sententias habuerat absolutorias, et tamen quotidie peior effectus fuerat, et sic per rev^mos deputatos s^mi officii inquisitionis fuit sententiatum quod effectualiter degradaretur, et curiae saeculari eum tradiderunt tanquam relapsum et impenitentem; et cum primum fuit sibi impositum vestitellum cum flammis depictis et satellites duxerunt eum ad carceres rev^mi gubernatoris. Poterat praedictus dominus Petrus esse aetatis sexaginta annorum; pulcherrimus erat aspectu et magnum nobilitatis signum ostendebat.

Fuit etiam frater ordinis fratrum minorum conventualium S^ti Francisci, praedicator, pulcherrimi aspectus et senex, qui fuit similiter traditus curiae saeculari, et mandatum per rev^mos deputatos quod degradaretur. Fuerunt quatuor bononienses ex quibus duo fratres germani erant nobiles de familia de Luparis, et alter similiter nobilis de familia de Ludovicis, alius bononiensis de Fioravantibus non tamen nobilis, alius doctor legum dictus Philippus Caputdurus; quidam magister scholae Mutinensis et alius librarius Ferrariensis habitator in civitate Bononiae. Fuerunt tres Faventini, unus presbiter, alius diaconus et alter hortulanus; et quidam alii. In totum fuere 17 haeretica pravitate deturpati, qui, exceptis duobus primis supradictis, fuerunt diversimode variis penis condennati: aliqui enim quod murarentur in perpetuum, alii ad perpetuos carceres et alii ad triremes ad tempus.[1] Interfuere dictae abiurationi 23 cardinales, quorum seniores steterunt ante sugestum haereticorum versus columnam, ut melius possent videre ac intelligere, et sic iuniores steterunt versus altare maius; et idem fecerunt officiales et iudices in alio sugesto, nam steterunt digniores versus columnam prope pulpitum, in quo erat dominus Matthias cantor capellae, qui legebat processus. Gubernator Urbis non interfuit, sed bene auditor camerae, qui sedit supra senatorem Urbis iuxta

Exact list of the 17, with the penalties is in BERTOLOTTI, Martiri 41.

facultates sibi traditas in emptione sui offici per quas debet semper esse post gubernatorem.

[1567] Die mercurii prima octobris summo mane decapitati fuerunt dominus Petrus Carnesicca haereticus impenitens et quidam frater ordinis minorum conventualium S^{ti} Francisci relapsus, qui in ecclesia B^{tae} Mariae supra Minervam fuerant traditi curiae saeculari, et deinde fuerunt combusta eorum corpora. Isti die praeterita acceperant s^{mum} sacramentum eucharistiae. Praedictus dominus Petrus non fuisset decapitatus, si confiteri voluisset suos errores, nam regina Franciae, dux Florentiae et infiniti alii nobiles supplicabant pro vita ipsius ; sed quia (ut dixi), licet ivisset convictus, noluit unquam confiteri et ostendere signum penitentiae fuit punitus : et antequam abscideretur sibi caput, nihil dixit, et quia ferrum mannare non abscidit collum nisi usque ad medium, carnifex cum gladio abscidit reliquum. Frater autem fecit sermonem antea devotissime de fide Christi, dixit Credo et multa alia et postquam caput fuit abscissum, semper per dictum unius Paternoster aperuit os, prope quod frater capuccinus, dictus il Pistoia vulgariter, tenuit tabellam cum figura Christi : et crediterunt omnes optime de ipso.

[1568] Die dominica quarta dicti mensis [ianuarii] abiurationem fecerunt in ecclesia beatae Mariae supra Minervam 22 homines diversarum conditionum, qui in variis penis fuerunt condemnati. Interfuerunt 22 cardinales.

[1568] Dicta die [dominica 9^a maii] hora 18^a fuerunt ducti ad ecclesiam B^{tae} Mariae supra Minervam 25 haeretici, inter quos ivere novem de terra S^{ti} Genesii provintiae Marchiae Anconitanae. Quinque ex dictis 25 haereticis traditi fuerunt curiae saeculari, quorum duo erant impenitentes et tres relapsi ; alii omnes diversis penis condemnati fuerunt. Interfuere illa die 16 cardinales.

[1568] Die lunae 10 dicti mensis [maii] tres haeretici relapsi ut supra fuerunt suspensi in Ponte, deinde combusti, quorum unus senex LXX. annorum fecit sermonem christianissimum antequam se deiiceret a furca, et omnes audientes commovit. Duo autem impenitentes, negantes ultra alia auctoritatem pontificis, post infinitas exhortationes, absque cruce et cum mitris zagulis, in quibus erant depicti diaboli eorum domini et protectores, ducti fuere prope praedictos et vivi in falsis opinionibus persistentes combusti fuerunt.

[1568] Die ultima novembris, in festo S^{ti} Andreae hora 19^a

fuit incepta abiuratio haereticorum in ecclesia B^{ae} Mariae
supra Minervam, pro qua S^{mus} D^{mus} N^r concesserat interes-
sentibus septem annos indulgentiarum. Fuerunt haeretici
impenitentes et relapsi tres, qui fuerunt dati curiae saeculari et
consignati gubernatori Urbis praesenti ; sexdecim penitentes
fecerunt abiurationem ; qui diversimode fuerunt condemnati
et ut plurimum ad triremes vel in perpetuum vel ad tempus.
Quorum unus, cum aduisset se esse condemnatum per decen-
nium ad triremes, cepit alta voce flere et acclamare quod erat
infirmus et nolebat ire ad triremes, sed potius mori vel com-
buri ; et ideo rev^{mi} domini cardinales inquisitores, videlicet
Pisarum, Pacechus, Gambara et Ab Ecclesia, mandarunt
quod duceretur ad carceres ita ut neminem alloqui posset ; et
sic factum fuit. Fuerunt etiam quatuor regnicoli, qui deposue-
rant falsum contra quosdam inquisitos, qui similiter ad triremes
ad tempus fuerunt condemnati.

[1568] Die lunae 6 decembris, in festo S^{ti} Nicolai fuerunt
suspensi in Ponte tres haeretici relapsi ; qui fuerunt traditi
curiae saeculari, et supra dixi in abiuratione facta in festa
S^{ti} Andreae, et fuerunt combusti. Ostenderunt (ut mihi
relatum fuit) maximam contritionem.

(Copy, Papal Secret Archives, XII., 31.]

48. Pope Pius V. to the Duke of Mantua.[1]

1568, April 21, Rome.

Dilecti fili nobilis vir salutem et apostolicam benedictionem.
Le nostre occupationi ordinarie et i giorni santi che sopravenero
sono stati causa che non havemo potuto rispondere fin qui alla
lettera di V. Ecc^a de V de questo, la quale ci ha veramente
data consolation grande per l' aviso che conteneva dell' abiura-
tion successa quietamente, ancorche per lettere di mons^r
Borromeo et del r. Inquisitore l'havessimo inteso più distinta-
mente. Di che ne ringratiamo il Sr Dio, e ne laudamo insieme il zelo et la prudenza di lei, la quale può esser sicura
con questi mezzi d'indurre i popoli suoi a vivere come si conviene nel timore di S. D. M^{tá}, mossi necessariamente dall'
esempio di V. Ecc^a, onde noi l'esortiamo a perseverare in
questo suo fermo proposito per honore et gloria del S. Dio
et per stabilimento insieme dello stato suo, si come havemo
detto più a longo ancora a mons^{re} Capilupo al quale ci rimet-

---

[1] See *supra*, p. 324 n. 4.

tiamo, et per fine di questo le mandiamo la beneditione nostra ch'il S^{re} Dio gliela conceda sempre.

[Orig. Gonzaga Archives, Mantua.]

49. AVVISO DI ROMA OF MAY 29, 1568.[1]

Cardinal Bonelli wishes " ridurre alla moderna " the Palace of the Knights of Malta in the Borgo. " Li preti del Jesù di Roma hanno cominciato a dar principio alla chiesa che vogliono fare, ma per quanto s'intende la faranno la maggior parte alle spese del card. Farnese etc."

An *Avviso di Roma of June 3, informs us, in completion of this, that Cardinal Farnese had placed several hundred bronze medals with the effigy of Pius V. in the foundations of the Gesù, to the " fabbrica " of which he gave annually 5000 scudi, up to the sum of 20,000.[2]

[Orig. State Archives, Vienna : Romana.]

50. BERNARDINO PIA TO CAMILLO LUZZARA.[3]

1568, July 10, Rome.

Prohibi ad ogni sorte di persone anco card^{li} il far portar o buttar mondicie in fiume, ma che si portino a luoghi deputati, et questo per proveder all' aria et al acqua del fiume che si beve. Impose una gabella di tre giulii al mese a tutti i cocchi di Roma et di ogni sorte di persone per poter soccorrere al matonare o selcaire la città con manco dispendio de possessori et padroni delle case che spendevano et spendono grossamente.

[Orig. Gonzaga Archives, Mantua.]

51. DEATH OF CARDINAL VINC. VITELLI (19 NOVEMBER, 1568).[4]

Dicta die [veneris 19^a novembris] Card. Vitelli died. Iste cardinalis potest dici vere quod omnia scivit et nihil ignoravit ; nam fuit semper studiosissimus et perscrutator rerum antiquarum, et habebat infinitos libros manuscriptos, non solum in Urbe sed etiam in civitate Avinionensi et aliis multis in locis magno labore et expensis perquisitos et transcriptos ; et inter alias suas virtutes voluit etiam scire cerimoniarum pro-

---

[1] See *supra*, p. 123 n. 3.

[2] See RONCHINI in *Atti Mod.* II, 372 *seq.*, VII., 19 *seq.* KRAUS-SAUER, III., 657, 667 ; ANGELI in *Arte decorat.* XV., 3 *seq.* Milan, 1906 ; Mem. intorno a J. Barozzi, Vignola, 1908, 67, 155 ; GIOVANNONI in *Arte*, 1912 *seq.*

[3] See *supra*, p. 108 n. 5.

[4] See *supra*, p. 160 n. 3. For Card. Vitelli and his collection of codices, RANKE, Fürsten und Völker, I. (1827), x. *seq.* and Vol. XIV. of this work, p. 201 n. 4.

fessionem et tantum in ea profecit quod magister merito dici poterat.[1]

[Diarium of C. Firmanus XII. 31, p. 265ᵇ.   Papal Secret Archives.]

52. NICCOLÒ CUSANO TO THE EMPEROR MAXIMILIAN II.[2]

1568, December 18, Rome.

Pius V. is irritated with Card. d'Este on account of his quarrel with the people of Tivoli,[3] " ove ha fabricato un palazzo regio pieno d' infinite dilitie et di rarissime fontane che li costa più di cento milia ducati et certo io vedo non ne sia un altro in tutta la cristianità."[4]

[Orig. State Archives, Vienna, Romana.]

53–57. AVVISI CONCERNING THE PURIFICATION OF MORALS IN ROME IN 1568.[5]

June 5 : Beginning of the reform of the " camere locande " in Rome, so that they shall not be let to prostitutes.   Urb. 1040, p. 524b, Vatican Library.[6]

August 21 : On Wednesday a young man was burned on account of " brutezze " : in consequence the order was given for the closure at night of many " porte false."   The " donne pubbliche " are to be watched over like the Jews. " Si vererano altre riforme più strette e più rigorose." *Ibid.* 567.

September 4 : " Questi di frustata una bellissima cortegiana," who was imprisoned : she tried to commit suicide. *Ibid.* 573.

September 25 : Noble Roman ladies condemned to imprisonment for life for adultery. *Ibid.* 585.

October 20 : " Ogni giorno și frusta qualche meretrice uscendo del seraglio et si fanno altre giustitie rigorose per ogni piccolo delitto et tutti vivono con timore." *Ibid.* 589.

---

[1] In the margin is the following remark : " Fuit legatus Campaniae : fecerat scribi in diversis professionibus libros 280 pulcherrimos, quos voliut Papa habere, eo mortuo, in sua guardaroba."
[2] See *supra*, p. 115 n.
[3] After his disagreement with the Pope, Card. d'Este withdrew to Tivoli ; see WINNEFELD, Die Villa Hadrians bei Tivoli, Berlin, 1895, 5.
[4] See *report of B. Pia, from Rome, 10 June, 1570 (Gonzaga Archives, Mantua).
[5] See *supra*, p. 92 n. 1.
[6] Also in the Carte Farnes. of the State Archives, Naples.

58. NICCOLÒ CUSANO TO THE EMPEROR MAXIMILIAN II.[1]

Rome, 26 March, 1569.

"Dicono che il Papa è entrato in humor di far rovinar il theatro che fece Pio quarto in Belveder, cosa rara et bellissima come cosa ch'habbi della gintilitia et che non sic onvenghi nel luogo, ove residero i pontefici et vicarii di N. Sr Jesu Chrısto." Cardinal Ricci is concerning himself greatly on behalf of the building, but neither his proposal to erect a winter garden there, nor his warning that its removal would shake the foundations of the palace, can divert the Pope from his purpose ; he only gets more excited. It is feared that he will begin this very day. "Intendo ha in oltre gran' caprizzo, di far guastar l'Anfiteatro, chiamato volgarmente il Colisseo et alcuni archi trionfali, che sono le più belle et rare antichità di Roma sotto pretesto che sono cose gintili et per levarne a fatto la memoria et l'occasione siano viste da quelli che vengono a Roma più per vedere le dette cose che per visitar limina Petri et andar alle sette chiese et a vedere le reliquie de' martiri et santi di Dio, il che si legge fu già fatto da papa Gregorio XI., il quale diede principio a far rovinar il detto Colisseo et ancora fece romper di molte statove di marmo et ne fece far salcina per murrar et riparar le chiese rovinate di questa città."

[Orig. State Archives, Vienna.]

59. AVVISO DI ROMA OF 2 APRIL, 1569.[2]

Si ragiona chel Papa voglia guastar il theatro di Belvedere come cosa di gentilità et fatto a posta per farvi spettacoli publici cosa poco conveniente a pontefici, et anco che vuol ridure tutte le altre antiquità in servitio di religione et culto divino, acciò quelli verrano a Roma, habbino d'andare a veder le 7 chiese e non l'antiquità profana.

[Orig. Urb. 1041, p. 51. Biblioteca Vaticana.]

60–65. AVVISI CONCERNING THE PURIFICATION OF MORALS IN ROME IN 1569.[3]

April 30 : To-day a prostitute was whipped because she conducted a gambling hell. Urb. 1041, p. 74, Vatican Library.

June 14 : Great excitement was caused, and it is not to be put into force by the " bando," that all married women who had been prostitutes were to leave Rome within two months. *Ibid.* 90.

---

[1] See *supra*, p. 113 n. 3. Similar report in Avviso of 2 April, 1569.
[2] See *supra*, p. 113 n. 3. [3] See *supra*, p. 92 nn. 1, 2.

August 13 : " Non si lascia di proveder contra le donne maritate che fanno cativa vita et ultimamente ne sono state carcerate sette." *Ibid.* 131.

August 17 : A " cortegiana " died, who had been married, and left 4000 ducats to the Compagnia dei SS. Apostoli. *Ibid.* 133.

October 5 : " Si levano due strade principali alle meretrici et si restringono in vicoli strettissimi, sopra che mons. Ormanetto col governatore et molti altri deputati sono stati in fatto a consegnarli il luogo chiamato delli otto cantoni." *Ibid.* 158b.

October 17 : Commencement of the " fondamenti all' Hortacci " (on the Ripetta near the Mausoleum of Augustus) " per restringer le cortegiane." *Ibid.* 180.

For the progress of this work from October to November, see LANCIANI, IV. 21 ; *cf.* also the *Avviso di Roma of February 4, 1570, Urb. 1041, p. 231b, Vatican Library.

66. FOR THE HISTORY OF THE CHURCH OF ST. PETER'S UNDER PIUS V.[1]

I. Avvisi di Roma on St. Peter's.
1568.

May 22 : " Quella bella Madonna di marmo fatta di mano di Michel Angelo si messe in S. Pietro nella capella di Sisto."[2] Urb. 1040, p. 520. Vatican Library.

1570.

March 4 : A bull that all ecclesiastical goods, " male alienati " are to come to the " fabbrica di S. Pietro. Urb. 1041, p. 239. Vatican Library.

August 16 : On Sunday Cardinal Morone and the deputies of the fabbrica of St. Peter's were for two hours with the Pope for the adjustment of the ecclesiastical goods which were alienated by the Apostolic Commission which had been given full judicial powers in this matter against the bishops. The " fabbrica " obtained from the Pope many favours, including that of " componere super bonis alienatis et fructibus indebite perceptis." *Ibid.* 327.

September 27 : The commissaries " super bonis male

---

[1] See *supra*, p. 122 n. 3.
[2] For this under Gregory XIII., see ORBAAN in *Jahrb. der Preuss. Kunstsamml.*, XXXIX., (1919), part 79.

alienatis " are so strict that many are complaining of them. The Pope has ordered a mitigation. *Ibid.* 343.

October 18 : The bull concerning the " fabrica di S. Pietro " has greatly restricted the powers of the commissaries. *Ibid.* 357.

1571.

January 6 : On Wednesday lightning struck the campanile of St. Peter's and did a great deal of damage. Urb. 1042, p. 2.

II. Discoveries during the building of St. Peter's.

Cf. as to these ARMELLINI, 281 and LANCIANI, IV., 7. As to the tiles of the church of St. Peter's bearing the arms and name of Pius V., see *Mél. d'archéol.*, VIII., 454.

67. CARDINAL SANTORI AND HIS AUDIENCES WITH PIUS V.[1]

There are few Cardinals of the XVIth century concerning whose lives we have such detailed information as of Giulio Antonio Santori, who was born at Caserta in 1532, and was for the most part known as the Cardinal of Santa Severina (also as Sanseverino) from his archiepiscopal see in Calabria.[2] Held in high esteem by all his contemporaries on account of his holy life, his zeal for the cause of the Church, and his widespread activities, Santori has nevertheless so far found no biographer. This eminent Prince of the Church, who was buried in the Lateran basilica, is in every way deserving of a special monograph : if his early life is of interest, this is still more the case with his cardinalate of 32 years (1570 to 1602), during which he took part in six conclaves, and on two occasions came near to attaining to the supreme dignity.

Santori, who was the friend and counsellor of seven Popes, has himself described in great detail a great part of his life. His autobiography is marked by its great detail and its love of the truth. He does not conceal the defects of his own period of crisis, and he describes with touching simplicity his permanent return to a genuinely Christian life. Some passages will remain indelibly fixed in the mind of every reader, e.g. his description of his first departure from Rome,[3] and the expression of his sentiments when he had to give up

---

[1] See *supra*, p. 107 n. 3.
[2] SICKEL (Berichte, I., 12) treats of Santori and Sanseverino as two distinct persons.
[3] Autobiografia, XII., 232 *seq.*

hopes of the tiara, to which he had been so near.[1] From some of the passages which RANKE (Päpste, I., 302 ; III., 86* *seqq.*) and GNOLI (Vittoria Accoramboni, 245) have quoted from the autobiography of Santori, it is possible to form an estimate of his importance. Very valuable therefore was the publication of the complete work by CUGNONI in the *Archivio della Societa Romana*, XII. and XIII., based upon two copies in the Corsini Library, Rome. In these the biography only goes as far as 1592. Whether the codex of the Albani Library which was used by RANKE contained more cannot be gathered from the data given by the Berlin historian, nor can the question now be decided, since the Albani Library perished in a storm, together with the vessel which was conveying it to Prussia. Another copy of the autobiography, to which my attention was called by my deceased friend, Prof. A. PIEPER, is to be found in the Altieri Library, Rome, Cod. 22–C–13. but this copy too ends with 1592. Fortunately we have at our disposal various other sources for the ten missing years; of some of these we shall treat in the next volume. Here we can only take into consideration those which belong to the time of Pius V. These are in the first place detailed and valuable notes on the consistories in which Santori took part. This " Diario consistoriale " of Santori was edited by TACCHI VENTURI in Studi e documenti XXIII.–XXV., and is characterized by so great accuracy that it is sufficient here to refer to the notes of that distinguished historian. It has escaped the notice of TACCHI VENTURI that there is also a copy of the " Acta Concistoriali descripta ab em. Santorio Sanseverino," given by Cardinal Siciliano di Rende, Archbishop of Benevento. Cf. CARINI, Atti Concistoriali dal 20 maggio 1570 al 18 dicembre, 1604, Rome, 1893. A passage which is there included on p. 9, on the consistory of March 17, 1572, is missing in TACCHI VENTURI.

In his autobiography (XIII., 153) Santori also mentions his " Libri delle mie private udienze." I have found this hitherto unknown source in the Papal Secret Archives, where it is to be seen in Arm. 52, t. 17 *seqq.* I give here the more important passages concerning the audiences of Santori with Pius V.

1566.

February 5 : The Pope informed me that he had appointed

---

[1] See *ibid.* XIII., 202 *seqq.*

me to the Inquisition . . . Gli parlai di collocar il corpo
di S. Giov. Chrisostomo in loco honorifico. Gli parlai anco
di vescòvi non residenti, disse che ne desse nota. Gli parlai
delle donne dishoneste travestite da homini et a cavallo, che
non le comportasse nel suo pontenicato ne dandosi licentia
di mascare, disse che l'ordinarà.

April 3 : Ho parlato a N.S. . . . dei capi della riforma dei
regolari, quali l'hebbe S.S. . . ., capi della riforma del clero
Romano. . . .

April 30 : Dei balli dell'hosterie di meretrici nelle feste :
volse sapere i particolari.

May 5 : Del card. di Napoli e della giustificatione da farsi :
che desse memoriale a S. S. nella S. Congr. giovedì.

May (no day) : De erroribus Graecorum : Addidit de secta
alia mortuos viventes putantium nisi eorum cadavera de-
coxerint vel confosserint.

May (no day) : Degli maleficii di Roma e del stato ecc^{co} . . .

May (no day) : De gratiarum actione pro sepultura card.
Neapolitani : Ingemuit.

May 27 (or 28) : Di schiavi battezzati di Napoli e lunga
servitu per evitar i scandali : quod non possunt, cum bap-
tismus non liberet a servitute.

August 14 (ante consist.) : Locuti sumus de visitatoribus
. . ., de desiderio bene regendae ecclesiae aut ex hac vita
discedendi . . ., de reformatione fratrum convent. ex fr.
Ambrosio Salvio.

September 14 : Ho parlato a N. S. de predicando infidelibus
et de eorum speciebus, de Chiis factis captivis, de episc.
Naxiensi, etc.

September 30 : Instruttioni per il governo, ch'io le facci·
e dia per gli avisi del governo.

December 13 : Del monasterio di S. Pietro a Maiella di
Nap. e della religione di Celestini : Che tutta la religione è
corrotta, e che non si può, ma bisogna mandare a visitar tutta
la religione per huomini versati.

December 28 : De panibus tactis in mensa Domini : quod
ignorabat prohibitionem nec sibi videtur superstitio.

1567.

January 12 : Quoad sacerdotes pauperes exercentes rustica
opera : illorum pauperati compatiendum esse, sed potius
in ignorantiam omnia convertendum esse quam in hoc. Ego

dixi de iure illis licere rusticari . . . De tradendis curiae
saeculari processibus vel revelandis : Minime ; quod ego ex
specul. affirmavi (appellando a Borromeo di Milano).

March 25 : Sulla festa di S. Vincenzo. " Hic plura de S.
Vincentii laudibus utrinque dictum est, et doctrina et sanc-
titate. Dixit quod pars estiva habet doctiores sermones,
in quibus gravia exponit et multa explicat ex S. Thoma satis
condite, sed quod in hyemali parte loquitur simplicius, at-
tendens fructui spirituali et simplicitati."

1568.

March 28 : Del successo dele cose di Napoli circa la Capece
monica : iratus est in facinus et in vicarium illum.

May 20 ; Delle suppressioni di monasterii di Celestini del
regno : quod non supprimentur, sed unientur ad reparationem
religionis.

November 1 : Qui disse del card. Carrafa parole molto
efficaci.

1571.

December 4 : Di molte cose, della guerra contra Turchi.
Della vittoria[1] seguita, e prevista da molti servi di Dio : e
S. S. anco disse dell'altre cose e dei putti d'Otranto, che grida-
vano vittoria quel dì, che passò la galea, che partava la nova,
sul monte, per lettere d'un Cappucino.

December 10 : Della riforma del vicario del Papa e del
dubbio che io sentivo contra la cognitione della giurisditione
contra laici nelle cause profane : S. S. venne nel medemo
parere, sebene causava confusione o maggior occupatione nelle
cose secolari.

1572.

January 27 : Dei schiavi christiani e di quei Turchi, che
se vogliono battezzare : disse che facessero instruire etc.
e parlò di quello, che diceva : felice cattività, per la quale
io mi salvo l'anima, e che la cosa di Mammetto sempre l'haveva
tenuta per una pazzaria.

February 5 : S. S. mostrò una moneta d'oro di Giustiniano
imperatore, che era di thesori che si trovavano, ch'egli ne
vorrebbe, che si trovasse tanto, che per 10 anni potesse per
mare e per terra fare essercito contra il Turco. . . . Dar a

[1] See Vol· XVIII. of this work.

S. S. quelli avvertimenti per togliere i disordini e vitii dalle galee dell'Armata christiana : Se diede e li lesse quasi tutti, ma per la carestia del tempo dissi più volte, che S. S. i leggesse e considerasse poi maturamente.

[Orig. Arm. 50 t. 17 (Audien iae annorum 1566-1579) Papal Secret Archives.]

68. The Briefs of Pius V. and the Archives of Briefs.

The briefs of Pius V. in the Papal Secret Archives (Arm 39, t. 64 and 65, Arm. 42, t. 25–27 ; Arm. 44. t. 12–20, 26, 31 ; Arm. 45, t. 41, and in a special Armarium the Epistolae or Brevia ad principes) are substantially completed by the collection in the Archives of Briefs. The latter, however, was for a long time almost inaccessible, and that as a result of the fate that befel them. During the time of the Papal dominion they were in the Palazzo della Consulta. After the end of the temporal power in 1870 they were placed for safety at the Anima. They were then taken to the Palazzo Altemps because the Secretariate of Briefs had its private chancery there ; later on they were transferred to the ground floor of the magnificent Palazzo della Cancelleria, where I was able to avail myself of them during a long period of time. When, as a result of the constitution *Sapienti consilio*, of June 29, 1908, the Secretariate of Secret Briefs became part of the Secretariate of State, Pius X. ordered the incorporation of the archives at the Cancelleria into the Papal Secret Archives. The acta were transferred during the summer of 1908, finding their final home in the premises near the Specola of Gregory XIII., which had at one time served as the pontifical armoury. Very opportunely, the Consistorial Archives, which had hitherto been housed in altogether inadequate premises on the ground floor of the Cortile di S. Damaso[1] were also placed close to them in a room near the Cortile di Belvedere. It was only when they were united to the Papal Secret Archives that these two archives became conveniently accessible to historical research. Thus, as he had done in other ways in carrying on the traditions of Leo XIII. in promoting archival research, Pius X. conferred a lasting benefit upon historical science.

[1] See Vol. II. of this work, p. 203.

With the exception of certain fragments belonging to an earlier time, the archives of the Secretariate of Secret Briefs contain nothing but acta from the time of Pius V. down to that of Pius IX., 1566–1846. They are divided into six series, comprising about 7,000 volumes. The first and principal series contains, together with the secret briefs, consistorial documents and marriage dispensations, amounting in all to 5,074 volumes. The other series contain briefs concerning indulgences, honours granted to corporations, to ecclesiastics and laymen, dispensations from canonical prescriptions, grants of privileged altars, etc.[1] A catalogue has been begun,[2] but it has not yet been completed. Many will be glad to have a short account of the first series in so far as it relates to Pius V. For this purpose I have made use of the notes of Prof. Dr. HANS HIRSCH, who, as a member of the Austrian Historical Institute in 1903, made a detailed study of the collection, principally for the purpose of his edition of the Nuntiaturberichte. The codices have a twofold signature ; one is written upon the volumes in ink, and is given below in Column I., and alongside it a second numeration in pencil, which is later than the first since it gives the same numeration to the volumes of minutes and to the copies, adding in the latter case an " a." This second enumeration is given below in Column II. Finally, the codices which are bound in red leather have a title in gold lettering, and on the back of the volumes in white vellum a sign is written in ink. The note " fait " which is borne by many of the volumes, means that those volumes were taken to Paris in the time of Napoleon. The volumes are not all of the same character ; with some of the volumes of minutes there are also volumes of later copies, as well as volumes of registers of briefs, similar to the collection of the Papal Secret Archives. If WIRZ (Quellen zur schweiz. Gesch. XXI., xxvii.) only found two volumes to his purpose in the Archives of Briefs, this must not lead us to the conclusion that those archives are wanting in importance ; on the contrary, they contain much valuable material, especially as regards the internal affars of the Church.[3]

---

[1] See *Corriere d' Italia*, 27 August, 1908.
[2] See MERGENTHEIM, Die quinquennalfakultäten pro foro externo, I., 88, Stuttgart, 1908.
[3] See Catalogue of the available Archives.

I. II.

1. 1. " 1554 [sic] Bullarium. Pius V.," bound in red leather.
2. 2. " 1561/67 Pii IV. et V. cedol.," bound in red leather.
3. 3. " 1566 Pii V. Brevia lib. I.," bound in red leather, " fait."
4. 4. " Pius V. Originalia usque ad Junium 1567," parchment binding.
5. 4a. " 1567 Pius V. lib. I.," bound in red leather.
6. 5. " Pius V. 1567 Originalia usque ad decemb. 1567," parchment binding.
7. 5a. " 1567 Pius V. lib. II.," bound in red leather, " fait."
8. 6. " 1567 Pius V. lib. III.," bound in red leather ; " fait."
9. 7. " 1568 Pius V. lib. I."
10. 8. " 1568 Pius V. Brevia lib. II.," bound in red leather ; " fait." (Original minutes from January to June, 1568.)
11. 9. " 1568 Pius V. lib. III.," bound in red leather ; " fait." (Original minutes from July to December 1568.)
12. 10. " 1569 Pius V," bound in red leather. (Original minutes for the whole year 1569.)
13. 11. " 1570 Pius V. lib. I.," bound in red leather. (Copies.)
14. 12. " Pius V. 1570 Originalia," parchment binding. (Original minutes for the year 1570.)
15. 12a. " 1570 Pius V. lib. II.," bound in red leather. (Copy of the above.)
16. 13. " Pius V. 1571," parchment binding.
17. 13a. " 1571 Pius V. lib. I." (I. to III. corrected), bound in red leather.
18. 14. " Pius V. 1566–1572 Originalia diversorum lib. I.," parchment binding.
19. 15. " 1577 [Corr. in 1567] Pius V.," bound in red leather ; " fait." (Original minutes for the years 1567 and 1568 to September.)
20. 16. " 1571 Pius V. lib. II.," bound in red leather. (Copies, 1571 and 1572 to March.)
22. 18. " Pius V. 1569 " (1569 erased and then marked in pencil : 1566–72), parchment bound. (Copies, Matrimonial Briefs for the years 1568–1569, other fragments for 1569–1572.)
23. 18a. " 1566 Pius V., lib. II." (lib. II. erased), bound in red leather ; " fait." (Copy of above.)

24. 19. " 1566, 1567. Matrimonialia Pius V.," bound in red leather. (Concept.)

25. 20. " Pius V. Matrimonialia lib. II.," parchment bind-ing. (Concept.)

26. 20a. " 1568 lib II. Pius V. Matrimonialia," bound in red leather. (Copy of above.)

26. 17. " 1571 Pius V. lib. I.," (I. with ink erased, and in III. altered), bound in red leather. (Original concept of September, 1571, to March 1572.)

The original minutes of the briefs of Pius V. are also in the collection of the Papal Secret Archives.[1] Two volumes of the original minutes have been taken away from Rome ; one is to be found in the British Museum, London, the other in a private Italian library. Since these codices have hitherto been entirely overlooked, it will not be out of place to give a short account of them here.

(1). British Museum, London. Additional 26,865[2] (Presented by G. J. Payne, Esq., 29 July, 1865), 597 sheets, original minutes of the briefs of Pius V. from January 8, 1566 to January 30, 1567, commencing with the brief of Pius V. to the Emperor Maximilian II., printed by Schwarz 1 *seq.* from the original in Vienna. As is often the case, the date here is different : the original has January 9, the minute January 8.

p. 51 : Minute of the brief for " Io. Bapt. archiepisc. Ros-sanen. [Castagna], nostro et apost, sedis nuncio in Hispaniarum regnis : te nostrum et apost, sedi nuntium in Hispaniarum regnis confirmamus et si opus sit de integro constituimus et deputamus eodem modo, quo istuc a proedecessore nostro . . . missus fuisti. 24 January, 1566."

p. 65 : Minute of the confirmation of " Iulius Rogerius, apost. sedis notarius," sent by Pius IV. as nuncio to Poland. 2 March, 1566.

p. 118 : Minute of the brief for " Iulius archiepisc. Sur-rentinus : Cum te nuper ad chariss. in Christo filium nostrum Maximilianum Roman. Imperatorem electum nostrum et apost. sedis nuncium certis facultatibus concessis et cum potestate legati de latere deputaverimus, cumque gravissimis postea animum nostrum moventibus te prius in Burgundiam, Flandriam et Brabantiam mittendum duxerimus," he sends him thither " eadem potestate." 21 March, 1566.

---

[1] SCHWARZ, Briefwechsel Maximilians II. mit Papst Pius V., S. vii. *seq.*
[2] In Addit. 27870, " Epilogus brevium beati Pii V."

p. 141 : Minute of the brief to the Emperor Maximilian II.[1] " Venerabilem fratrem Iulium archiepiscopum Surrentinum istuc misimus, ut cum peractis comitiis Augustanis dilectus filius noster cardinal s Commendonus, sedis apost. de latere legatus istuc discesserit maneat ipse apud Maiestatem Tuam et nostri atque eiusdem sedis nuncii munere fungatur." 1 March, 1566.

p. 173 : Minutes of the brief to Charles IX. of France : " Cum ad te mittere statuissemus praelatum nostri et sedis apostolicae nuncii apud Maiestatem Tuam officio functurum, qui et nobis putatissimus esset et tibi futurus esset merito acceptus, delegimus ad hoc munus venerabilem fratrem Michaelem episcopum Cenatensem. Etenim cum eodem officio apud clarae memoriae Henricum patrem tuum ita functum fuisse sciamus etc." 25 March, 1566. (There follows many credential briefs for the nuncio.)

On p. 469 is to be found the original minute of the brief to Castagna, on July 30, 1566, which was drawn up secretly and mentioned in Vol. XVIII. of this work, Chap. I., concerning Carranza with the following autograph postscript " Pius p.p. V. ita mandavit expediri. Ant. Florebellus Lavellinus."

On p. 496 : to the Archduke Ernest : minute of the credentials brief for " Alexander Casalis, cubiculi nostri magist.," of September 12, 1566.

On p. 506 : to Philip II. : minute of the credentials brief for Camaiani who was to treat of matters which had already for some time past been treated of by means of letters and the ordinary nuncio. September 27, 1566.

(2). The " Catalogue des livres, manuscrits, etc., composant la Bibliothèque de Horace de Landau, I., Florence, 1895, has a list of the autograph letters of Pius V. This library is now in the possession of Madame Finaly at the Villa alla Pietra near Florence. At the request of His Excellency Prince Franz von Liechtenstein and the librarian Ulrich Schmid in 1909, the use of the codex in question was, as a great exception, made over into the hands of the Austrian Historical Institute in Rome. The codex in question bears the mark 1176–1401, and on the back in leather bears the title " Schediasmata autographa epistolarum divi Pii V." A subsequent preliminary notice (p. 46) informs us of the origin of the codex as follows : " Il volume originale sudetto fu casualmente trovato

---

[1] Erroneously in SCHWARZ, Briefwechsel.

dal Dr. Lodovico Coltellini infrascripto la sera del dì 7 novembre 1771 in una bottega di un droghiere in Cortona, dal qual droghiere era stato comprato per cartaccia a peso e si era già cominciato a stracciarlo per involtarvi il pepe e lo zucchero." The volume of 225 pages is a miscellany put together later on, containing almost entirely rough copies, minutes for briefs of Pius V. in the hand of Ant. Florebellus Lavellinus, from March, 1566, to September, 1568 ; only from p. 24–36b, 85–94, and here and there haphazard, are the sheets registers of briefs ; at the end (p. 248 *seqq.*) there are various matters of another kind.

The Landau codex contains no brief which is to be found in the series of the true and proper archives of briefs, and that because it, as well as that in the British Museum, formed part of the aforesaid archives. A careful examination made by Prof. Pogatscher, to whom I here take the opportunity of expressing my gratitude for the help he has given me, showed that only a part of the minutes contained in this volume found their way into the registers of briefs in the Papal Secret Archives. It was upon these latter registers of briefs that the secretary of the Spanish Embassy, Fr. Goubau, drew up his well known collection of the Epistolae Pii V. in 1640. As is the case with the other volumes of minutes, so a comparison of the passages printed in Goubau with the minutes in the Landau Codex reveals a number of variations, which are of interest as showing the orgin of each document. Very often these corrections are only a question of style, but sometimes are worthy of attention by reason of their matter.

For example, in the brief to the Bavarian Chancellor, Simon Thaddeus Eck, of Feb. 14, 1567, printed in Goubau 24–26, after " segregare " in the Codex Landau, p. 133, we read the following words : " Vere ostendis to esse fratrem Ioannis illius Echi qui nascenti haeresum pesti tanta pietate sese primus opposuit et catholicam veritatem tam acriter constanterque defendit."

In the brief to the Emperor Maximilian II. of May 15, 1568, in Goubau 81–83, after the words " ab eo talia tentari," in the Codex Landau p. 208, we read : " Qui enim talia agunt et spretis censuris ecclesiasticis ecclesiarum bonis manus admovere non dubitant, ii nimis famae suae prodigi sunt et salutis.[1] Si tamen in bonis eius ecclesiae temporalibus ius

---

[1] Originally : " ii nimis officii et salutis suae immemores sunt."

se aliquod habere existimat, polliciti fuimus aliquem idoneum iudicem ipsi dare, qui eam rem cognoscat et servata aequitate iudicet aut per compositionem transigat. Quod si eum iudicem a M^{te} tua dari maluerit, eo quoque contenti erimus, sicut ei scripsimus. Quocirca M^{tem} tuam, etc." Whereas in the brief to Eck the addition is not cancelled, here the whole of the phrase down to " ei scripsimus " is cancelled, and instead there is placed in the margin that which is printed in GOUBAU. Further, after " Quocirca Maiestatem tuam " there followed : " cuius officium est ut ecclesias et ecclesiarum iura tueatur, defendat et protegat " which was afterwards cancelled. That the text in GOUBAU is not always correct is shown by another variation : on p. 82, l. 6 from the top, instead of " iure peti " should be read " vi peti " thus runs not only the minute in the Codex Landau, but also the volume of the register of briefs in the Papal Secret Archives, Arm. 44, t. 13.

The words after " debet " in GOUBAU 82, l. 5-7 from the bottom, in the Codex Landau read : " ne bona temporalia illius ecclesiae contra ius et de facto, ut dicitur, occupentur."

Of general interest is an addition in the brief to the Bishop of Passau, of May 26, 1568, concerning the prohibition of communion under both kinds (GOUBAU 83-85 ; cf. supra p. 205, n 5). Here too it would seem that GOUBAU has not followed exactly the volumes of registers of briefs, since in Arm. 44, t. 13, as well as in the Codex Landau, p. 210 seq., in this place after " habendos " (GOUBAU 84, 1.1 from the bottom), there is a long passage, which has not been cancelled, and which runs as follows : " Sed ne praedecessoris quidem nostri concessione quisquam moveri debet. Primum enim is tanta in re minus quam decuit et oportuit diligentem et maturam deliberationem habuit. Non enim ad sacrum collegium cardinalium, ut debuit et ut mos est, de tanta re rettulit, quod si fecisset et nos qui tum de eorum numero eramus et multo maior ac sanior ut presumitur . . . [illegible word] cardinalium pars nihil temere[1] innovandum esscensuissemus. Consuluit ille duos aut tres solum de tanto collegio et eos potissimum quos sibi facile assensuros esse putavit. Ea tamen in re Spiritus Sancti gratia illi manifesto affuit, quod ab iis, qui communicare sub utraque specie

---

[1] In the register-volume of Briefs in the Papal Secret Archives is the anomalous reading : " et nos et maior cardinalium pars nihil temere."

cuperent, talem fidei confessionem exegit, quam si vere et
ex animo facturi essent, fortasse ne nos quidem tantopere
eam concessionem improbaremum.   Quamobrem, etc."

69. THE BIOGRAPHERS OF PIUS V.

The earliest " Vita di Pio V.," preserved in Varia polit. XVII.
of the Papal Secret Archives, and composed immediately
after the death of the Pope by TOMMASO PORCACCHI, remained
for a very long time unpublished, and it was only in 1914
that VAN ORTROY published it in *Anal. Bolland.* XXXIII.,
207-217.   This life is a very reliable work ; it also provides
fresh particulars, and has only the one defect of being too
short.

The first full biography of Pius V. which was printed was
that published in Rome in the summer of 1586[1] by GIROLAMO
CATENA.[2]   Catena, who came from Norcia, had known Pius
V. personally.   He had been in the first place in the household
of Cardinal Dolera who died at the beginning of 1568, then
from 1568 to 1571 he was secretary to Cardinal Girolamo
da Correggio,[3] and later on held the same post with Cardinal
Bonelli.[4]   Catena enjoyed a great reputation in the Curia ;
Sixtus V. was especially well disposed towards him, and called
him his " Consulta."   It was to this Pope who had a great
admiration for Pius V., that Catena dedicated his work.[5]
Sixtus V. acknowledged the tribute, ordered that it should be

---

[1] See the *report of the Venetian ambassador of June 7, 1586 State Archives,
Venice.

[2] Reprinted in Rome, 1587, 1647, and 1712 (*cf. Arch. d. Soc. Rom.*, XXXIII.,
291).   According to an *Avviso di Roma, of August 5, 1584, the life by Catena
was already prepared at that time, and was to be printed in a Spanish translation.   Urb. 1052, p. 339b, Vatican Library.

[3] *Cf.* BIGI, Vita del card. G. da Correggio, Milan, 1864.

[4] The *Lettere di G. CATENA, scritte in nome del card. di Correggio 1568–
1569 in the Cod. Barb., LXII., 57 ; Item 1569-1571, *ibid.*, LXII., 25 ; Item
scritte in nome del card. Alessandrino 1571–1572, *ibid.* LXII., 26, e scritte in
nome del card. Alessandrino 1575–1577, *ibid.*, LXII., 56.   From his printed
correspondence it appears that at the end of 1572 Catena became secretary
to Bonelli : Delle lettere di G. CATENA, Primo volume, Roma, 1589, 312. The
second volume of this collection does not follow.   In 1577 there appeared at
Pavia H. CATENAE Academici Affidati Latina Monumenta, containing letters
and minor writings.   The *Genealogia della famiglia Bonelli Ghisliera by
CATENA is in Cod. Barber., LXII., 27, Vatican Lbrary.   CATENA also wrote :
Della beretta rossa da darsi a cardinali, Discorso, Roma, 1592, and De magno
obelisco Circensi circoque maximo. Epist. et Carmen, Romae, 1587.   Still
unpublished is the *Risposta alle ragioni allegate da gli aversarii contra la
potestà et diretto dominio temporale universale del Papa a favore dell'Imperatore et altri principi temporali, fatta dal Signor G. CATENA, in Cod. D. 29,
p. 287–369, of the Library at Carlsruhe.   CATENA also tried his hand at poetry,
though not very successfully ; see CIACONIUS, III., 1000, 1002 ; *cf.* Carmina
illustr. poet., III., 316 *seq.*

[5] See the dedication by Catena prefixed to the life.   For the decision of the
municipal authorities in Rome concerning the printing of Catena's life of Pius V.
see RODOCANACHI, Capitole, 122.

printed,[1] and later on rewarded Catena with a gift of 100 scudi.[2]

Catena began to collect his materials immediately after the death of Pius V. In his dedication to Sixtus V., he himself says as to this : " Tutto quello, che in questa carte scrivo, parte ho preso da gli originali delle lettere, da Nuncii, et da Principi stessi scritte, et dalle instruttioni, et scritture del medesimo papa, le quali son venute in poter mio, parte dalla relatione in iscritto di coloro che trattato hanno in negocii, altre ho vedute io stesso, et intese dalla bocca del Pontefice." It can be established from many passages in his work that Catena made good use of his material. His statements are almost always reliable, and it is only in the dates that some inaccuracies are to be found.[3] On the other hand real penetration is wanting, as well as the working out of the materials which he had collected, and a clear arrangement. Catena s biography is rather a collection of facts, which, however, is of considerable value to-day on account of its full character. This explains why it has served as the basis for all the later biographies of the Pope.[4]

The necessary critical sense, however, has not been used in making use of it, and this is all the more obvious when compared with the work of Catena himself, since in the circumstances under which he wrote, it was almost inevitable that he should have fallen into the error of over-estimating the achievements of his hero. In this respect he has sinned less by making statements directly false, than by his tendency to exaggerate the successes of Pius V. and to keep silent about his failures. If we read the account which Catena gives of the relations between the Pope and Spain, France and Germany, we must come to the conclusion that with regard to those countries Pius V. *completely* carried out his plans and

[1] CATENA states this expressly in his Lettere 60.
[2] See *Avviso di Roma of July 16, 1586, Urb. 1054, p. 287, Vatican Library.
[3] The letter to the Archbishop of Seville (Catena, 21), corresponds with the original in Cod. Barber., 3618. Of the " Informatione " on Pius V. good use is made on p. 28 (cf. p. 34), on p. 58 seq. of the instructions for Torre, on p. 77 seq. of those for Commendone on p. 93 seq. of the " Provedimenti " for the West Indies, etc. The letter of Philip II. about Don Carlos is well translated on p. 84 seq., and only the date is changed from 20 to 22. In the appendix of letters on p. 225, March 5 is substituted for 8 (according to GOUBAU, 302 seq.). Cf. also MENDHAM, 46, n.
[4] RANKE (Papste, I.) as well relies principally on Catena, but he also makes use of at least some manuscript sources. The figure of Pius V. as represented so brilliantly in the Venetian reports interested him very much : " I have reports of him which describe him to the life. A pious man : simple as a child, yet the most rigid inquisitor and persecutor of the Protestants." E. GUGLIA, L. v. Ranke, Leipzig, 1893, 62.

met with nothing but success. To some extent Catena is
not responsible for these defects, because, immediately after
the appearance of his " Vita di Pio V." Philip II. managed
to get the author to change, in a new edition, some of those
passages which seemed to him harmful to himself and other
princes. Thus we can hardly be surprised if, in dealing with
the relations between Philip II. and Pius V., it is not made
sufficiently clear (p. 85 *seq.*) that the Spanish king adhered
inflexibly to his cesaropapalism.[1] In the same way the
relations of the Pope with Venice are dealt with too favourably (p. 112 *seq.*). The success of Commendone with the
Emperor Maximilian in 1568 is set forth as a reality (p. 99)
while nothing whatever is said of the deceit which the Emperor practised at the expense of the Holy See in this matter.
Nor is the conferring of the title of Grand Duke upon Cosimo
I. well treated of (p. 119). Very characteristic of the way
in which Catena exaggerated the good in Pius V. is his statement that in order to promote the cloth industry the Pope
expended 100,000 scudi, whereas in reality it was only 10,000.[2]

As to the directly false statements into which Catena, in
his wish to exalt the fame of his hero, allowed himself to be
drawn,[3] the most surprising are those concerning France.
After speaking of the very proper deposition of the heretical
French bishops, Catena says : " Pio fece publicare in Francia
la detta sentenza si che i vescovi furono levati et posti in
lor vece i cattolici " (p. 60), which is in direct contradiction
of the truth. And Catena says nothing of the protection
which Châtillon, who had been deposed from the cardinalitial
dignity, received from the French government. With regard
to the breaking of the concordat he maintains (p. 61) that on
account of the remonstrances of Pius V. the French sovereigns
withdrew from their position.

TÜRKE (p. 27 *seq.*) has also shown how incredible is the

---

[1] Catena may also be excused by the difficulties with which historians at
that time had to contend, and which affected these very matters : indeed,
his life of Pius V. was absolutely prohibited in the Spanish dominions. With
FUMI, L'Inquisizione, 271, *cf.* the *Report of M. Brumani from Rome, September 10, 1588, Gonzaga Archives, Mantua, and HUBNER, Sixte-Quint, Paris,
1870, II., 30. See also CATENA, Lettere, 19 *seq.*, 60 *seq.*, and *Bibliofilo*, X.
(1889), 2 *seq.*

[2] See *supra*, p. 108. Catena (p. 71) adds another 600 men to the auxiliary
Papal troops sent to France in 1569.

[3] Such as the statement that during the mortal illness of the Pope in Rome
" il tutto passato con ordine et quiete " (p. 112) from which the conclusion is
drawn that this was a proof of the " ottimo governo " of Pius V. That, on
the contrary, the traditional disturbances were not altogether wanting is
expressly stated in the Vita di Pio V. in *Anal. Bolland.*, XXXIII., 202.

account given by Catena (p. 171) of the promises which Charles IX. made in 1571 to Cardinal Bonelli, informing the Pope that he was arranging the marriage of his sister with Navarre with the sole purpose of being able the more easily to destroy the leaders of the Huguenots, and further making the advice of the Pope responsible for this plan.

In a much more cautious and reserved way are these matters dealt with by the second biographer of Pius V., GIOV. ANTONIO GABUZIO, rector of the Barnabite College in Rome, in his work, " De vita et rebus gestis Pii V.," which was first published in Rome in 1605, and dedicated to Paul V. Here there is no mention at all of the statements of Catena concerning the assurance given by Charles IX. that the marriage of his sister to Navarre had the sole purpose of giving the Huguenots in Paris a sense of security, and that he decided on taking action against the " traitors " principally from love of the Pope. On the other hand, Gabuzio expressly states that the king had declared that he could no longer conceal his intentions, and that Bonelli had gone away without having obtained anything.

If Gabuzio is in this matter the more reliable informant, this is explained by the fact that he was helped by Cardinal Bonelli in the composition of his work much more than Catena. As Gabuzio relates in the dedication of his work to Paul V., it was that Cardinal who persuaded him to compose it, and furnished him with the materials. The difference here mentioned is all the more important in that in other matters Gabuzio follows Catena closely, and further, as TÜRKE rightly points out (p. 29), shows a tendency to embellish and exaggerate his accounts. It is only in details that Gabuzio gives any new information ; it is not easy to distinguish them because Gabuzio treads so closely in the footsteps of Catena,[1] whom, strangely enough, he does not name, that his text in many places reads like a translation.[2]

If Gabuzio met with a much wider success than Catena, so much so that THEINER (Annal. eccles., 1572, n. 12) wrongly

---

[1] Thus for example concerning the success of the action taken by Pius V. against the French heretical bishops, he says : " Eam damnationem in Galliam promulgandam iisque de sede deiectis alios catholicos subrogandos Pius curavit." (II. c. 3).

[2] In the preface he merely says that his work was " cum ex aliis multis ac probatis auctoribus, tum ex variis ac certis, quae idem cardinalis [M. Bonelli] ceterique multi locupletes et oculati testes mihi suppeditarunt, monumentis ac testimoniis bona fide collectum." The severe blame of MENDHAM (p. x.-xi.), for his not having made mention of Catena, is fully deserved.

speaks of him as the principal writer on Pius V. and recently PREMOLI (Barnabiti, I., 332) describes his life as the best, this is due to his better and more skilful arrangement of his matter and to his good latinity. It added a great deal to the popularity of Gabuzio's biography that the Bollandists included only his account in the Acta Sanctorum, since it was suited to that purpose as having more definitely the character of a saint's life than that of Catena.[1]

All the later biographies of Pius V. have tended in that direction. Without any pretence to absolute completeness, we here given in chronological order the best known of these works :

1. ARCHANGELUS CARACCIA DE RIPALTA O. Pr., Brevis enarratio gestorum S. P. Pii P. V ex processibus et probatis authoribus digesta, Romae 1629. Substantially this is only a reproduction of the " Epistolæ " mentioned on p. 62, n. 1, from the edition of Cologne; 1567. Equally insignificant is the Vita Pii V. by CARACCIA publ. in 1615.

2. L. JACOBILLI, Vite del SS. Pio V. etc., Todi, 1661.

3. P. FATICA, Vita del glor. P. Pio V, Reggio, 1664.

4. AGAZIO DI SOMMA.[2] Vita del S. P. S. Pio V, dedicated to Pope Alexander VII. Original in the Chigi Library, Rome, I–III–69 ; many copies, e.g. Rome, nell' Archivio Papal Secret Archives, Miscell. Arm. XI, 60 ; Barberini Library, 3 copies in Cod. LIV, 23, 24 e 37 ; Corsini Library, Cod. 39-C-8 ; National Library, Paris, 5571. A second copy at Paris cited by MARSAND, II., 179, who greatly over esti-mates its worth, does not substantially contain anything new. The original Italian was not printed, it is found in a French version in the work of FÉLIBIEN, Vie de Pie V. par A. DI SOMMA, Paris, 1672 ; cf. ECHARD, Script. O. II., 220.

5. A. BZOVIUS, Pius V. Romanus Pontifex sive annalium eccles. tomus ultimus 1566-1572, Romae, 1672.

6. AMBROS. RAMDING, Beatus Pius V P. M. delineatus, Aug. Vindel., 1672.

7. A. M. MONTI, Ristretto d. vita e miracoli del b. Pio V, Bologna, 1672.

---

[1] Even before Gabutius a work was issued, which he has quoted in one place, by A. FUENMAYOR, Vida y hechos de Pio V., Madrid, 1595, which, however, is almost entirely based upon Catena ; see MENDHAM, viii. ; cf. 93.

[2] There also exists by the same author a *discorso della prefettura di Roma, in Cod. X. V. 30, p. 247 seq. of the Casanatense Library, Rome, and in the Barberini Library, LVI., 108. For Agazio di Somma cf. also BELLONI, Seicento, 89, 149.

8. *Kurtzer Entwurff und Inhalt dess wunderthätigen Lebens Pii dess V.*, Würtzburg, 1673. The first biography in German ; see BRAUNSBERGER, Pius V. 108, n. 7.

9. P. A. MAFFEI, Vita di S. Pio V S. P., Roma, 1712.[1]

10. SAMAYO, Compendio de vida del glor. P. S. Pio V, Roma, 1728.

11. J. LADERCHI, Annales, ecclesiastici, 3 voll. Romae, 1728-1737.

12. GIAC. ANT. TAGLIAPIEDRA, *Mem. stor. di 50 cardinali dell'ordine de' predic., Cod. Ital. 89 of the Court Library, Monaco (compiled in 1774) : II, 259-401 su Pio V.

13. P. M. GHISLIERI [O. Pr.], Elogio storico di S. Pio V, Assisi, 1797, dedicated to Pius VI.

14. J. MENDHAM, The life and pontificate of Saint Pius the Fifth, London, 1832.

15. FALLOUX, Histoire de St. Pie V, 2 voll., Paris, 1846 ; reprinted Liège, 1852 ; 3. éd. 1858 ; in German, Regensburg, 1873. See *Stimmen aus Maria-Laach*, IV., 504 ss. ; *Literar. Handweiser*, 1873, 102 s.

16. T. M. GRANELLO, Fra Michele Gislieri, I e II, Bologna, 1877-1878.

17. V. DE BROGNOLI, Studi storici sul règno di S. Pio V, 2 voll., Roma, 1883.

18. CH. A. JOYAU, Saint Pie V, pape du rosaire, Poitiers [1892].

19. FR. FABERI, S. Pio V. Studio storico [Siena, 1893]. See *Literar. Rundschau*, 1893, 331.

20. P. FARACHON, Lépante. St. Pie V, Paris, 1894.

21. C. DELL' ACQUA, Di S. Pio V., Milano, 1904.

22. COSMOS ILLUSTRATO, Roma, 1904, January–February (illustrated).

23. P. SPEIZI, Pio V, Roma, 1905. *Cf.* H. Bihlmeyer in *Hagiograph. Jahresbericht*, 1904 6, Kempten, 1908, 257.

24. P. DESLANDRES, St. Pie V, Paris, 1911. *Cf. Hist. Jahrb.*, XXXII., 398.

25. C. M. ANTONY, St. Pius V, Pope of the holy Rosary, London, 1911.

26. G. GRENTE, St. Pie V. (Les Saints), Paris, 1914.

True biographies, however, are not wanting, but all these works are based upon Catena and Gabuzio, and are not strictly scientific works which attempt to separate legend from

[1] *Cf.* MENDHAM, xv.

history.   Besides LADERCHI,[1] only BROGNOLI has made much
use of original unpublished sources.   It is true that GRENTE
claims to have made wide archival researches, but the unpublished sources which he quotes are so scanty as hardly to
deserve consideration.[2]   There thus remains still a rich
harvest in the archives,[3] from which to build up from the
original sources a strictly critical and historical account, in
which the figure of Pius V. will stand out more true to nature
and far more effectively than is the case with the usual
panegyrics.[4]

[1] A part of the original letters collected by LADERCHI in the Barberini
Library, Rome ; see Corresp. dipl., I., xxix.

[2] Cf. my list in *Histor. Jahrbuch*, XXIX. (1919), 801 *seq.*

[3] SERRANO has recently in Corresp. dipl., I., xv., shown how little the pontificate of Pius V. has as yet been studied in the original sources.   BALZANI
(Sisto V., Genoa, 1913, 13) points out that so far no historian has done justice
to Pius V.

[4] With regard to this I must record that three years ago I wrote : " It is
time that the pedantic period of the lives of the saints came to an end.   They
do not stand in need of pious inventions ; they can bear the full light of historical criticism, and moreover, cannot fail to draw advantage from it."   (*Zeitschrift fur kathol. Theol.*, 1898, 147.)

INDEX OF NAMES IN VOL. XVII.

ADRIAN VI., Pope, 113, 116, 236.

Agreda, Petrus de (Bishop of Venezuela), 210.

Alba, Duke of, 344, 379.

Albani, Giov. Girol., Cardinal, 167.

Albano, Jo. Bapt. (poet), 129,

Albert V. (Duke of Bavaria). 116 n. 1.

Albert the Great (O.P.), 119.

Alcalà, Duke of (Viceroy of Naples), 219.

Alcantara, see Peter of Alcantara.

Alciati, Cardinal, 7, 39, 71, 81, 110, 181, 184 n. 4, 199, 280 seq.

Alçolaras, Joannes de (Bishop of San Domingo), 210 n. 3.

Aldegati, Ambrogio (Bishop of Casale, inquisitor at Mantua), 322, 325.

Aldobrandini, Giovanni (Bishop of Imola, grand-penitentiary), Cardinal, 156 n. 1, 168, 204, 349, 364.

Aldobrandini, Tommaso (secretary of briefs), 74 n. 2.

Aldrovandi, Cico, 67 n. 1.

Alessandrino, Cardinal, see Bonelli, Michele.

Alessi, Galeazzo (architect), 125 n.

Alexander VI., Pope, 171 n. 5, 176, 276.

Altemps, see Hohenems.

Altovito, Antonio (Archbishop of Florence), 262 n.

Amadori, Giovanni, 22.

Amalterio, Cornelio (poet), 128 n. 3.

Amalterio, Girolamo (poet), 128 n. 3.

Angelico, Fra (painter), 116.

Anjou, see Henry of Anjou.

Anna, Giov. Domenico de (Bishop of Bovino), 221 n. 1.

Anspach, Joh. (Bavarian humanist), 128 n. 2.

Antoniano, Silvio (latinist, professor at the Roman university), 134.

Aquaviva, Giulio, Cardinal, 168.

Aquaviva, Orazio (O. Cist., Bishop), 168.

Aquaviva, Ottavio, Cardinal, 168 seq.

Aquaviva, Ridolfo (S.J., martyr), 168.

Araceli, Cardinal, see Dolera.

Aragon, Cardinal of, see Avalos.

Arco (Imperial envoy in Rome), 3, 10 seq., 55 n. 2, 162, 173 n. 3, 292, 315, 331, 342 seq.

Arias Montanus, 199.

Arias, Sebastian, 285.

Ariguccio, Paolo (Provincial of the Observants), 261 n.

Arimini, Thomas of (O.P., Inquisitor), 315 n. 1.

Athanasius, St., 196.

Attaide, Georg. de (Bishop of Viseu), 212 n. 1.

Augustine, St., 362, 368 seq.

Avalos, Iñigo de (of Aragon), Cardinal (administrator of the bishopric of Mileto), 7, 261 n.

Avellaneda, Lope de (jailor of Carranza), 345.

Avellino, Andrew (Theatine), 165.

Avila, see John of Avila.

Avila, Pedro de (Spanish envoy in Rome), 17, 206 n.

427

Azpilcueta (theologian), 347.

BAIUS, Michael (professor at Louvain), 367–380.

Balduini, Martin (Bishop of Ypres), 232 n. 5, 376.

Bandini, Franc. (Archbishop of Siena), 197 n. 5.

Bartoccio, Bartolomeo (heretic), 306 seq., 318.

Bartolomeo (provost of the Humiliati), 247.

Bascapè (biographer of Charles Borromeo), 43, 237 n.

Basil, St., 196.

Basilio (heretical preacher), 300 n. 3, 401.

Basilio d'Urbino (Carthusian), 259 n. 4.

Bastone, Albert (friend of the Ghislieri family), 46, 71, 392 n. 2.

Bastone, Francesco, 46, 392.

Beatrizet (engraver), 52 n. 1.

Bellarmine, R. (S.J.), 378.

Belo, Lorenzo, 131.

Beltran, see Bertrand.

Bencio, Trifone (Papal secretary), 74 n. 2.

Benedetto, P. (preacher), 60 n. 2.

Benedict XV., Pope, 200 n.

Benvoglienti (heretic), 329 n. 2.

Bernarcedo (heretic), 305 n. 1.

Bernardi, Giov. B. (Bishop of Ajaccio), 223 n. 5.

Bernardine, St., 47.

Bernieri, Paolo Emilio (Ferrarese envoy), 9.

Bertrand [Beltran], Louis (O.P.), St., 237 n.

Bertucci, Giov. Batt. (painter, heretic), 314.

Bianchi, Arcangelo (O.P., commissary-general of the Inquisition, Bishop of Teano), Cardinal, 165, 292 n. 3, 319.

Binarini, Alfonso (Bishop of Camerino), 148 n. 1, 183 n. 3, 184, 189 n. 2.

Birago, Luigi (governor of Saluzzo), 327 n. 3.

Blosius (Louis of Blois), 274.

Bobadilla (S.J.), 274 n. 6.

Bobba, Cardinal, 7, 149 n. 1, 258, 261 n., 328 n.

Boccacio, 204 n

Boccapaduli, family of the, 135.

Bojero (Franciscan), 326 n. 1.

Boldrino, Gregorio (Bishop of Mantua), 235 n. 3, 262 n.

Bonaventure, St., 129.

Boncompagni, Cardinal, 3 seq., 11, 21, 23 seq., 27, 35, 51 n. 2, 199, 250.

Bonelli, Family of the, 76 n. 3.

Bonelli, Domenica (niece to Pius V., mother of Cardinal Bonelli), 76, 84.

Bonelli, Gardina (sister to Pius V.), 76.

Bonelli, Michele (O.P., nephew to Pius V.), Cardinal [Alessandrino], 51 n. 2, 63 n. 1, 74 n. 3, 77–84, 110, 117, 146, 150, 155, 157, 195 n. 2, 197 n. 3, 207 nn., 328 n., 335.

Bonhomini [Bonomi], Giov. Franc. (abbot of Nonantola), 170, 182, 218 n. 1.

Boniface VIII., Pope, 152.

Borgia, Francis (S.J.), St., 19 n. 4, 83, 207, 237 n., 280.

Borromeo, Camillo, 138 n. 2, 140 n. 5.

Borromeo, Cesare, 138 n. 2, 140 n. 5.

Borromeo, Charles, Cardinal, 1, 3 n. 5, 4 seq., 17–31, 33–39, 42 seq., 58 n. 7, 71, 89, 137 n. 2, 138 seqq., 142 n. 2, 144 seq., 150, 152, 158 seq., 165, 170, 176, 181 seq., 184 n. 4, 191, 198, 213 n., 216, 218, 236, 238, 245–248, 257, 261 n., 266 seqq., 274, 292 n. 3, 320, 324 seq., 336 n. 3, 337 n. 3, 372.

Boucherat, Nicolas (procurator-general of the Cistercians), 241.

Broccardo, Count, 2.

Brocchi, Fr., 132 n. 3.

Brus von Müglitz, Anton (Archbishop of Prague), 209, 211 n. 2, 214.

Buccia, Doctor (court-jester of Pius IV), 70.

Burali, Paolo (Theatine, Bishop of Piacenza), Cardinal, 156 n. 1, 161, 165 seq., 204, 239 n. 1.

Bussoti, Bartolomeo (treasurer to Pius V.), 104 n. 7.

Buzi, Gianantonio (sculptor), 124.

Cajazzo, Count of, 291.

Caligari, Andrea (auditor to Commendone), 3 seq., 29 n., 44, 86, 182 n. 2, 291.

Callixtus III., Pope, 171.

Camaiani, Nosti (Florentine agent in Rome), 4, 10.

Camaiani, Pietro (Bishop of Fiesole, then of Ascoli, Spanish nuncio), 207 n. 7.

Campeggio, Camillo (inquisitor at Mantua), 322, 327 n. 2.

Canisius, Peter (S.J.), 129, 156 n. 1, 161 n. 1, 193, 236, 367.

Cano, Melchior (O.P.), 355.

Capitone, Feliciano (Archbishop of Avignon), 220 n. 3, 339.

Capizuchi, Cardinal, 7, 41 n. 2, 73, 81, 131 n. 3.

Capua, Pietro Antonio di (Archbishop of Otranto), 303 n. 1.

Carafa, family of the, 99.

Carafa, Alfonso, Cardinal, 123.

Carafa, Antonio, Cardinal, 156, 159, 166, 198 seq.

Carafa, Gian Pietro (Paul IV.), 48.

Carafa, Mario (Archbishop of Naples), 219, 229, 261 n.

Cardano, G., 132 n. 1.

Carlos, Don. (son of Philip II.), 208.

Carnesecchi, Pietro (heretic), 302 seqq., 307, 402.

Carniglia, Bernardino, 141 n. 2, 189 seq.

Carnevale, Domenico (painter), 117.

Caro, Annibale (poet), 128 n. 6.

Carpano, Leone (Papal commissary), 266 n. 7.

Carpi, Pio Rodolfo, Cardinal, 12, 14, 17, 123, 257.

Carranza, Bartolomé (Archbishop of Toledo), 164, 193 n. 9, 343–364.

Casale, Alessandro (Papal envoy), 123 n. 2, 137.

Casanova, Pietro Angelo (inquisitor), 296 n. 5.

Castagna, Giov. Batt. (Archbishop of Rossano, Nuncio), 193 n. 9, 195 n. 2, 197 n. 3, 207 nn., 253, 362.

Castellet, Pedro de (Bishop of Urgel), 252 n. 2.

Castellini (Bavarian agent in Rome), 116 n. 1.

Castellio, Seb. (heretic), 380 n. 3.

Castelvetro (heretic), 328 n. 1.

Castiglione, Cardinal, 7.

Castro, Nicol. de (Bishop of Middelburg), 232 n. 5.

Cataneo, Federigo (Mantuan envoy), 2 n. 3, 20 n. 1.

Catena, Girolamo (biographer of Pius V.), 127, 128 n 3, 129 n. 1, 420 seqq.

Catherine de' Medici (Queen-regent of France), 12, 22, 298 n. 1, 302, 366.

Cavani, Ludovico (poet), 125 n. 2, 128 n. 3, 129 n. 1.

Cecone da S. Lupidio (chief of banditti), 102 n. 1.

Cellaria (heretic), 307 n. 1.

Cervantes, Gaspar (Archbishop of Salerno, then of Tarragona), Cardinal, 164, 169, 214, 226 n. 2.

Cesarini, Cardinal, 38 n. 2.

Cesi, Pietro Donato (Bishop of Narni), Cardinal, 110 n. 4, 156 n. 1, 161 n. 1, 168, 382 n. 1.

Charles (archduke of Austria), 227, 262 n.

Charles V., the Emperor, 338.

Charles IX. (King of France), 158, 163 seq., 298 n. 1, 366 n., 382 n. 1.

Chiesa, Giov. Paolo della, Cardinal, 81, 110, 156, 159, 213 n., 289, 292 n. 3, 347.

Chigi, Family of the, 121 n. 1.

Chirinotto (abbreviator), 340 n. 5.

Chisholm, William (Bishop of Dumblane), 188 n. 1.

Chrysostom, John, St., 196.

Cicada, Cardinal, 4, 7, 11, 14 seq., 29 n., 30, 160, 178 n. 5, 292, 298 n. 1, 318.

Ciregiola, 182, 333 n. 1.

Cirillo, Bernardo (master of the household to Pius V.), 55, 137 n. 2, 141.

Clement VII., Pope, 302, 309.

Clement VIII., Pope, 159, 197 n. 4, 201 n. 1, 234.

Clovio, Giulio (artist), 116.

Colonna, Cardinal, 7, 113 n. 1, 129, 198 seq., 300.

Colonna, Marcantonio, 32, 33 n. 1, 69.

Commendone, Cardinal. 4, 21, 24, 81, seq. 86, 149 n. 3, 220, 291, 371 seq.

Conca, 290 n. 2.

Concini, Bartolomeo (Florentine agent in Rome), 10.

Conosciuti, Lionardo, 4 n. 5, 21 n. 3.

Contarini, 367.

Conti, Torquato, 103 n. 1, 127.

Corgna, Cardinal, 4, 7, 14, 30, 187, 230.

Cornaro, Federigo (Bishop of Bergamo), 261 n., 262 n.

Cornaro, Luigi, Cardinal, 7.

Correa, Tommaso (poet), 128 n. 3, 129 n. 1.

Correggio, Cardinal, 7, 15, 17, 137 n. 2, 324.

Cortesi, Giacomo (Bishop of Vaison), 188.

Cosimo I. (Grand-duke of Tuscany), 3, 9 seq., 16, 20, 22, 24, 29, 45 n. 1, 151, 174, 204 n., 297 n. 1. 299 n. 2, 302 seq., 329.

Covarrubias, Didac. de (Bishop of Segovia, canonist), 254 n. 3.

Crescenzi, Cardinal, 114 n. 4.

Crispi, Cardinal, 7, 29 n., 40.

Crivelli, Cardinal, 3 seq., 7 n. 5, 24, 35.

Cromer, Martin (administrator of bishopric of Ermland), 202.

Curione, 381.

Curti, Girolamo (commis. gen. of the Franciscans), 257.

Cusano, Galeazzo (Imperial agent in Rome), 33, 51 n. 2, 62, 80, 111 n. 1, 113, 140 n. 3, 141, 148 n. 2, 198 n. 4, 336 n. 5, 365.

Delfino, Zaccaria, Cardinal, 7, 10, 24, 29 n., 149 n. 3.

Diaceto, Angelo (O.P., Bishop of Fiesole), 262 n.

Dolera, Cardinal [Araceli], 3, 7, 11, 13 seqq., 17, 20 seq., 24, 30, 33 seq., 39, 81, 149 n. 1, 160, 230.

Doria, Gian Andrea (admiral), 107 n. 3.

Drascovich, Georg. (Bishop of Agram), 365 n. 2.

Eder, Georg (Imperial councillor), 130, 202.

Eichhorn, Joachim (abbot of Einsiedeln), 274.

Eisengrein, Martin, 130 n. 6.

Eisengrein, William, 129 n. 5, 132 n. 5.

Elias (chief of synagogue), 341.

Elizabeth (Queen of Spain), 12.

Eltz, Jakob von (Archbishop of Trêves), 229.

Emmanuele Filiberto (Duke of Savoy), 4 n. 3, 11, 35, 248 n. 1, 328 seq.

Ercolano, Vincenzo (Bishop of Sarno), 190.

Ercole, Lord of Sassuolo, 328.

Ernest of Bavaria (administrator of bishopric of Freising), 174.

Esparcho, Ant. (Greek humanist), 131.

Espinosa, Diego de, Cardinal (Spanish grand-Inquisitor), 156 seqq., 193, 342, 349, 354 n. 1.

Este, Family of the, 34.

Este, Alfonso d' (Duke of Ferrara and Modena), 9, 228 n. 8, 261, 327 n. 2, 329.

Este, Ippolito d', Cardinal, 2 seq., 5, 7, 11, 13, 15, 18, 21–25, 27 seq., 30, 40, 43, 79 n. 1, 154, 291.

Este, Luigi, Cardinal, 7, 9, 12, 28, 40.

FABII, Baldo (agent of Lelio Orsini), 327 n. 3.

Facchinetti, Giov. Ant. (nuncio to Venice, later Pope Innocent IX.), 316.

Farnese, Alessandro (Cardinal), 7, 11, 13, 15 seq., 18 21 23, 27 seq., 30–39, 43, 73, 75, 78, 80, 82, 103 n. 2, 111 n. 1, 123, 137, 149 n. 3, 180 seq., 184 n. 1, 216 n.

Ferdinand, The Catholic, 338.

Ferdinand II. (Archduke of the Tyrol), 127 n. 4.

Ferrari, Ambrogio (abbot of S. Benigno in Genoa), 199.

Ferreri, Guido, Cardinal, 4, 7, 28, 40, 262 n.

Ferreri [the elder], Pier Francesco, Cardinal, 3 seq., 7, 11, 23 seqq., 34 seqq., 40, 199.

Figliucci, Alessio (O.P.), 192.

Filippini (historian), 238.

Floribello, Antonio (secretary of briefs), 74 n. 2, 137 n. 2.

Firmanus, Cornelius, 27, 38, 304 n. 4.

Folieta (historian), 131 n. 4.

Fonzio, Bartolomeo (protestant preacher), 300 n. 1.

Franco, Niccoló (poet), 311 n. 1.

Francis II. (King of France), 128 n. 4.

Francis of Assisi, St., 275.

Francis Xavier (S.J.), St., 236 n. 3.

Funtidueña (Spanish theologian), 193.

GABRIELLI, Giulio, 96 n. 4.

Gaddi, Taddeo, Cardinal, 241 n. 2.

Gaetani, Cardinal, 7.

Galateo, Fra (protestant preacher), 300 n. 1.

Galeota, Mario (heretic), 301, 302 n.

Galli, Tolomeo, Cardinal, 6 n, 7, 74.

Gallina, Bartolomeo (2nd husband of Gardina Ghislieri), 76 n. 3.

Gallio, Giov., 201 n. 1.

Gambara, Cesare (Bishop of Tortona), 137 n. 2, 261 n.

Gambara, Giov. Francesco, Cardinal, 7, 73, 81 n. 3, 137 n. 2, 146, 289, 292, 299 n. 2, 346 n. 4.

Gasparo (Bishop of Leiria), 212 n. 1, 256 n. 1.

Gazini, Angelo (commissary-general of the Inquisition at Faenza, Bishop of Polignano), 313 seqq.

Gerberon (O.S.B., Jansenist), 368 n.

Geri, Filippo (Bishop of Assisi), 261 n.

Gesualdo, Cardinal, 7.

Ghislieri, Family of the, 46, 84 n. 3.

Ghislieri, Domenica Augeria (mother of Pius V.), 46.

Ghislieri, Francesco (governor of Ascoli), 101 n. 4.

Ghislieri, Gardina (sister of Pius V.), 76.

Ghislieri, Girolamo (nephew of Pius V., governor of the Borgo), 50 n. 2, 84 n. 3.

Ghislieri, Paolo (father of Pius V.), 46.

Ghislieri, Paolo (nephew of Pius V., commander of the Papal guard), 84 seq., 345.

Giberti, Matteo, 139.

Ginnasi, Francesco, 134.

Giustiniani, Angelo (Bishop of Geneva), 218 n

Giustiniani, Vincenzo. (General of the Dominicans), Cardinal, 129, 156 n. 1, 165.

Gloriero, Cesare (secretary of briefs), 74 n. 2.

Godfredus of Liège (Franciscan), 378.

Gonzaga, Family of the, 24, 34.

Gonzaga, Cesare (brother-in-law to Card. C. Borromeo), 22.

Gonzaga, Ercole, Cardinal, 372.

Gonzaga, Ferrante (governor of Milan), 48.

Gonzaga, Francesco, Cardinal, 7, 11 n. 2, 23 seq., 34.

Gonzaga, Gianvincenzo (Prior of Barletta), 162 seq.

Gonzaga, Giulia, 303 n. 1.

Gonzaga, William (Duke of Mantua), 11 n. 2, 23, 235, 321 seqq.

Gordillo (provincial of Spanish Franciscans), 254.

Gorrevod, Ant. de (Bishop of Lausanne), 221 n. 2.

Granvelle, Cardinal (viceroy of Naples), 15 seq., 36, 45 n. 1, 62 n. 4, 81 seq., 137, 232 n. 5, 352, 370–375.

Grassi (cleric in the Apostolic Camera), 229.

Grassis, Carlo de (Bishop of Montefiascone and Corneto, governor of Rome), Cardinal, 168.

Grasso, Francesco, Cardinal, 3, 7, 11.

Gregory of Nazianzen, St., 196.

Gregory XIII., Pope, 51 n. 2, 177 n. 3, 208, 234, 256 n. 2, 280, 314.

Gregory XIV., Pope, 239.

Grimaldi, Carlo (Bishop of Ventimiglia), 326 n. 1, 327 n. 3.

Grimaldi, Louis (Bishop of Vence), 218 n.

Gropper, 367.

Gualtiero, Sebastian (Bishop of Viterbo, nuncio in France), 4.

Guarini, Francesco (Bishop of Imola, governor of Rome), 2.

Guasco, Cesare (architect), 126.

Guidiccioni, Alessandro (Archbishop of Lucca), 208.

Guido da Fano, see Zanetti.

Guise, Charles de, Cardinal of Lorraine, 4, 158, 235 n. 5, 236, 261 n.

Guise, Mary of (Queen of Scotland), 164.

Hamericourt, Gérard de (Bishop of Saint-Omer), 212 n. 3, 232 n. 5, 273.

Havet, Ant. (Bishop of Namur), 232 n. 5.

Henry (Infante of Portugal), Cardinal, 212 n. 3, 220 n. 5, 256.

Henry II. (King of France), 158, 164.

Hessels (Louvain theologian), 369–372.

Hoffäus, Paul (S.J.), 192 seq.

Hohenems, Hannibal von, Count, 1, 6, 67, 228.

Hohenems, Mark Sittich von [Card. Altemps], 4, 16 seq., 20, 22 n. 4, 23, 30, 33, 41, 99 n. 1.

Honoratus II. (Count of Tenda), 325, 327 n. 3.

Hosius, Stanislaus, Cardinal, 114 n. 4, 129, 158, 193, 203.

Hülsen, F. Van (engraver), 52 n. 1.

Ignatius of Loyola, St., 236 n. 3, 237, 278 seq., 281.

Innocent VIII., Pope, 70.

Innocent IX., Pope, 234.

Janssen [Jansenius], Cornelius (the elder, Bishop of Ghent), 375.

John of Austria, Don, 85 n. 5.

John of Avila, 237.

John of God, St., 236 n. 3, 285.

John of The Cross, St., 237 n., 277, 285.

Julius II., Pope, 171.

Julius III., Pope, 7, 49, 99 seq., 113, 134, 150, 274 n. 6, 276, 279.

Kastelberg, Christian von (abbot of Disentis), 275.

Khuen–Belasy, Joh. Jakob von (Archbishop of Salzburg), 156 n. 1, 161 n. 1.

Kunz, Othmar (abbot of St. Gall), 274.

Labacco, Ant. (artist), 1 n. 2.

La Baume, Claude de (Archbp. of Besançon) 221 n. 1.

Laceronis, Dionys. de (Cistercian), 241.

Ladrone, Ferrata di, Count, 174 n.

Lando, Pietro (Archbishop of Candia), 217.

Lanfranc, Mark Ant., 131 n. 2.

Lanzoni (heretic), 327 n. 3.

Lasso, Diego, 69.

Ledesma (S.J.), 310.

Lentailleur, John (abbot of Anchin), 273 n. 3.

Leo X., Pope, 7, 134, 171.

Leonio, Girolamo (Bishop of Sagona), 239 n. 1.

Logau, Kaspar von (Bishop of Breslau), 212 n. 1, 214.

Lombardo, Gianfrancesco, 97 n., 198 n. 4.

Lomellini, Benedetto, Cardinal, 7.

Lomellini, Jacopo (Archbishop of Palermo), 263 n.

Longus, Andreas (Bishop of Honduras), 210.

Lorraine, Cardinal of, see Guise, Charles de.

Louis of Blois, see Blosius.

Louis of Granada, 237 n. 1.

Lugo, Alvaro de, 364 n. 5.

Lunel, Pietro de (Bishop of Gaeta), 190, 217 n. 4, 220 n. 1, 262 n.

Lupetino, Ubaldo (protestant preacher), 300 n. 1.

Luzzara, Camillo (Mantuan Ambassador in Rome), 8 n. 4, 18, 140 n. 5, 143, 172, n. 6, 235, 303.

Madruzzo, Cristoforo, Cardinal [of Trent], 3, 7, 11, 14 seq., 30, 35 n. 6, 162, 198.

Madruzzo, Luigi, Cardinal, 7, 204.

Maffei, Marcantonio (Archbishop of Chieti), Cardinal, 73, 82, 129, 137 n. 2, 161 n. 1, 168, 172, 220 n. 7.

Maggi, Ottaviano (Venetian poet), 129 n. 1.

Magnus, Olaus (Archbishop of Upsala), 114 n. 4.

Maldonatus, J., 205 n. 1.

Manlio, Marcantonio (first husband of Gardina Ghislieri), 76 n. 3.

Manriquez, Tommaso (O.P.), 130, 203, 336 n. 1, 345, 355.

Manutius, Paulus (printer), 67, 69, 131, 132 n. 1, 192 seq., 197, 198 n. 4.

Marcellus II., Pope, 49, 176.

Margaret of Parma, 372.

Margarita da Allamana (a witch), 333 n. 6.

Mariano of Rieti, 198 n. 4.

Marini, Giov. Onorato (heretic), 329 n. 5.

Marini, Lionardo (O.P., Bishop of Alba, Archbishop of Lanciano), 198 n. 1, 219.

Martial, 203 n. 3.

Martyribus, Bartol. de (Archbishop of Braga), 256.

Matuliani, Vincenzo, 65 n.

Maximilian II., Emperor, 6 n., 9 seqq., 25, 45 n. 1, 68, 112, 163, 217, 289 n. 3, 333 n. 1.

Mazzoni, Giulio (painter), 119.

Medici, see Catherine ; Cosimo.

Medici, Ferdinando de' (son of Cosimo I.), Cardinal, 7, 10, 37, 146 n. 3, 333 n. 1.

Medici, Francesco de' (son of Cosimo I.), 113.

Medina, Michael de (Franciscan), 203 n. 1.

Melchiori (Bishop of Macerata), 156 n. 1, 161 n. 1.

Mercati, Michele (physician to Pius V., director of the botanical garden at the Vatican), 114.

Mercurian, Girolamo (doctor), 107 n. 1.

Messanella, Niccolò Francesco di (Bishop of Policastro), 302 n.

Miani, Girolamo (Founder of the Somaschi), 284.

Michelangelo, 123, 382.

Miliavacca (heretic), 330.

Minale (Papal treasurer), 101 n.

Molina, Stefano (Observant), 262 n.

Moncornet (engraver), 52 n. 1.

Montalto, Felice Peretti da, Cardinal (later Pope Sixtus V.), 110 n. 4, 129, 156 n. 1, 165, 346, 349, 364.

Monte, Innocenzo del, Cardinal, 7 *seq.*, 70, 150 *seq.*

Montepulciano, Cardinal, *see* Ricci.

Monti, Pompeo de' (heretic), 300 *seq.*, 401.

Montufar, Afons. de (O.P., Bishop of Mexico), 210.

Morillon, Maximilian (Vicar-general to Card. Granvelle), 374–379.

Morone, Cardinal, 3 *seq.*, 5 n., 7, 10–13, 15 *seq.*, 20, 23–29, 35 *seq.*, 40, 42, 81 *seq.*, 147, 181, 187, 198, 216 n., 230, 261 n., 328 n. 1, 361, 408.

Mucanzio (master of ceremonies), 160.

Mula, Cardinal, 3, 7, 11, 15, 21, 24, 26 *seq.*, 81 *seq.*, 149 n. 1, 156, 160, 333 n. 4.

Muratori, Dom. (painter), 53 n.

Muret, Marc Antoine (latinist), 128 n. 4, 134.

Muzio, Girolamo, 132 n. 2, 202.

NACCHIANTI, Jacopo (O.P., Biblical critic), 130.

Navagero (Bishop of Verona), 139.

Nelli, Niccolò (engraver), 52 n. 1.

Neri, Philip, St., 60, 165, 228, 236, 268.

Niccolini, Cardinal, 7, 10 *seq.*, 24. 73. 137 n. 2.

Nicholas V. Pope, 120.

Niëulant, Nic. (Bishop of Haarlem), 232 n. 5.

Noronha, Andrea de (Bishop of Portalegre), 212 n. 1.

Novella da Evoli, Roberto (preacher), 325 n. 3.

Novellara, Francesco di (delegate of the Duke of Mantua), 322.

OCHINO, 380 n. 3.

Odescalchi, Bernardo, 48

Ognies, Gilbert d' (Bishop of Tournai), 232 n. 5, 261 n.

Olaus, Nic. (Archbp. of Gran), 211 n. 2.

Oliva, Giovanni (Archbishop of Chieti), 82, 182, 183 n. 1, 261 n., 266 n. 7.

Oltramari, Girolamo (Modenese envoy), 1 n. 5.

Orfino, Tommaso (Prior of Foligno, Bishop of Strongoli), 182, 183 n. 1, 219, 262 n.

Ormaneto, Niccolò, 82, 139, 141–144, 148 n. 1, 176, 181–184, 189 n. 2, 225, 226 n. 3, 229, 245, 254, 262 n., 266, 284.

Orsini, Flavio, Cardinal, 7, 28, 34.

Orsini, Fulvio (humanist), 115 n.

Orsini, Giulio, 94 n. 6.

Orsini, Lelio (Lord of Ceri), 327 n. 3.

Orsini, Niccolò (Count of Pitigliano), 305 n. 1.

PACHECO, Francisco, Cardinal, 2 n. 4, 5, 7 *seq*, 12 n. 5, 16–21, 30 *seq.*, 41, 146, 197 n. 3, 289, 292, 303 n. 3, 346, 352.

Paciotti (architect), 127.

Padniewski, Phil. (Bishop of Cracow), 214 n. 5.

Paleario, Aonio [Antonio della Paglia] (heretic), 307–311.

Paleologo, Flaminio (heretic), 325.

Paleotto, Gabriel, Cardinal, 4, 7, 34, 110, 181, 213 n.

Paleotto, Mario (heretic), 401.

Palestrina, Pier Luigi da, 208 n. 4.

Pallantieri, Alessandro (governor of Rome and of the March of Ancona), 2, 100, 103 n. 1, 290 n. 2, 336.

Paltoni, Altinio (heretic), 311 n. 1.

Panvinio, Onofrio, 52 n. 1, 131, 202.

Parisani, Giulio (Bishop of Rimini), 221 n. 1.

Pariseti, Girolamo (jurist), 134.

Paschal Baylon, St., 237 n.

Paul III., Pope, 5, 7, 39, 131, 279, 290, 309, 337, 340.

Paul IV., Pope, 1, 7, 14 *seq.*, 22, 24, 28, 40, 49 *seq.*, 63, 66 *seq.*, 100, 123, 131, 143, 154, 159, 164, 206, 230 *seq.*, 234, 265, 279, 288, 290, 293 *seqq.*, 336 *seq.*

Paul of Arezzo, *see* Burali

Pavesi, Stefano (O.P., Archbishop of Sorrento), 156 n. 1.

Pellevé, Nicolas de (Bishop of Amiens), Cardinal, 156 n. 1, 161 n. 1, 164.

Peretti, *see* Montalto.

Perini (heretic), 302 n.

Petri, Cunerus (theologian), 378.

Peter of Alcantara, St., 237 n., 275, 277.

Peter Damian, St., 244.

Philip II. (King of Spain), 2 n. 4, 9, 12 *seq.*, 15 *seqq.*, 21 *seq.*, 31, 36 *seq.*, 42, 79, 157, 159, 161, 207, 226, 227 n. 3, 249–255, 286, 325, 344 *seqq.*, 350 *seqq.*, 355–362, 370, 373.

Pia, Bernardino, 342, 365.

Pianer, Gabriel (dean of the Papal chaplains), 334 n. 1.

Pico, Lodovico (Count of Mirandola), 327 n. 3.

Pietro da Quintiano, Fra (Inquisitor at Pavia), 330.

Pinelli, Dom., 123 n. 2.

Pinheiro, Rodrigo (Bishop of Oporto), 212 n. 1, 256.

Pino (architect), 289 n.

Pisani, Francesco, Cardinal, 3, 5 n., 7, 11, 14, 30, 40, 137 n. 2.

Pisani, Luigi, Cardinal, 7.

Pistoja, Girolamo da (Capuchin), 304, 366.

Pistone, Giov. Batt. (fiscale), 137 n. 2.

Pius III., Pope, 176.

Pius IV., Pope, 2–9, 11 *seqq.*, 15 *seqq.*, 19 *seqq.*, 23 *seq.*, 26, 33, 39, 42, 50 *seq.*, 66 *seqq.*, 70, 72 *seqq.*, 99, 101, 103, 110 *seqq.*, 120, 131, 133, 143, 150, 154, 159, 176, 178, 184, 192, 199 n. 3, 206, 210 n. 1, 216, 234 *seq.*, 245, 249, 265, 267, 272, 290, 292, 302, 316, 331, 336 *seq.*, 344, 370.

Pius V., Pope, Vol. XVII.

Pius X., Pope, 200 n., 239.

Platina (historian), 131.

Plauto, Camillo (jurist), 134.

Poggiano, Giulio (humanist), 74 n. 2, 128 n. 4, 182, 204 n. 3, 341 n. 3.

Polanco (S.J.), 205 n. 5.

Pole, Reginald, Cardinal, 139, 367.

Ponce de Léon, Pedro (Bishop of Plasencia), 199 n. 3.

Ponte, Niccolò da (heretic), 317 n. 1.

Pontius, Petrus, 131 n. 1.

Porroni (prisoner of the Inquisition), 311 n. 1, 312 n. 3.

Porta, Beatus a (Bishop of Coire), 221 n. 3.

Porta, Guglielmo della (painter), 113 n. 1, 118.

Portico, Vincenzo de (nuncio to Poland), 230, 261 n.

Porzia, Bartolomeo (apostolic visitor), 220.

Posio, Antonio (secretary to Congregation of the Index), 203 n. 3.

Possevino, Antonio (S.J.), 236, 321 n. 1.

Propertius, 203 n. 3.

Protaszeiwiez, Valerian (Bishop of Wilna), 222 n. 1.

Pseaume, Nicolas (Bishop of Verdun), 221.

Pucci, Alessandro, 174.

Pucci, Lorenzo, Cardinal, 288, 290 n. 2.

Pulzone, Scipione (painter), 53 n., 77 n. 3.

Puteo, Cardinal, 12.

QUINOÑES, Cardinal, 196 n. 4.
Quirós de Sosa, Juan, 207 n. 7.

RAMBOUILLET, Charles d'Angennes de (Bishop of Le
Mans), Cardinal, 163, 291
Rangone (heretic), 329 n. 1.
Ravestein [Tiletanus], Josse de
(Louvain professor), 373,
376.
Rebiba Cardinal, 7, 14, 73, 80
seq., 172, 187, 289, 292,
327 n. 3.
Reinoso, Franc. de (majordomo to Pius V.), 82 n. 4.
Requesens, Luis de (Spanish
envoy in Rome), 8 n. 4,
11–18, 29, 31 seqq., 36 seq.,
40, 62, 65, 69, 77, 116, 137,
250, 343, 344 n. 2, 345
seq.
Reumano, Cardinal, 3, 7, 12,
73, 75, 78, 80, 137 n. 2, 160,
172, 178 n. 5.
Riario, Alessandro (auditor of
the Apostolic Chamber),
123 n. 2, 187.
Ribera, Juan de (Bishop of
Badajoz, Archbishop of
Valencia, patriarch of Antioch), 221 n. 2, 222, 239
n. 1, 254 n. 3.
Ribera, Pedro Afan de (viceroy of Naples), 222 n. 2.
Ricasoli, Giov. Batt. (Bishop
of Pistoja), 174.
Ricci, Cardinal [of Montepul-
ciano], 3, 7, 11, 13, 15, 17,
20 seqq., 24, 30, 33 seqq.,
37, 39, 41, 114 n. 5, 116,
125 n. 1, 147, 206 n., 258.
Richardot, Franc. (Bishop of
Arras), 232 n. 5.
Rodriguez (S.J.), 150 n. 5.
Román, Alonso (S.J.), 164.
Rosetti (Modenese envoy in
Rome), 263 n. 1.
Rossi, Giov. Ant. (artist), 127
n. 4.
Rovere, Dom. de (O.P.), 261 n.
Rovere, Giulio della, Cardinal
[of Urbino], 7, 28, 70, 162,
212 n. 3, 218 n. 1, 244,
261 n.

Rovere, Guidobaldo della (Duke
of Urbino), 11, 117, 131.
Rovere, Paolo Maria della
(Bishop of Cagli), 190.
Roxas y Sandoval, Chr. (Bishop
of Cordova), 209.
Rubeis, Joh. Bapt. de (general-
prior of the Carmelites),
263 n.
Rucellai, Annibale (Spanish envoy in Rome), 156.
Ruffino (archpriest at Verona),
262 n.
Rusticucci, Girolamo (private
secretary to Pius V.), Cardinal, 74, 82, 156 n. 1, 167,
193 n. 9.

SADOLET, Giov. (Cardinal), 308,
335 n. 3.
Sadolet, Paul (Bishop of Car-
pentras), 339.
Sallustio (architect), 289 n.
Salviano, Ippolito (physician),
134.
Salviati, Bernardo, Cardinal, 3,
7, 122 n. 2.
Sampieri (Corsican rebel), 238.
Sandizell, Moritz von (Bishop
of Freising), 174.
Sanseverino, Cardinal, see San-
tori.
Sansovino, Pandolfo, 131.
Santa Croce, Cardinal, 6 n. 2,
149 n. 1, 152 n. 4.
Santa Fiora, see Sforza.
Sante of Padua (O.P., Inquisi-
tor), 47.
Santori, Giulio Antonio, Car-
dinal [of Sanseverino], 149
n. 3, 161, 166 seq., 204,
220 n. 7, 292 n. 3, 345.
Saraceni, Cardinal, 3, 7, 29, n.,
30, 335 n. 2.
Saracinello, Cipriano, 117 n. 1.
Sarzana, Lionardo da (sculptor),
53 n.
Sauli, Alessandro, St. (Barnabite, Bishop of Aleria and
Pavia), 237 seqq.
Savelli, Cardinal (Vicar-general
of Rome), 7, 71, 137 n. 2,
181, 182, 184 n. 4, 185 n.
7, 186, 195 n. 1, 224, 261 n.

Scappi, Bartolomeo (cook to Pius V.), 58 n. 1.
Schaumburg, Martin von (Bishop of Eichstätt), 210 n. 1, 214.
Schenk, Fred. V. (Archbp. of Utrecht), 232 n. 5.
Schüssler, Jodocus (Provincial of the German Franciscans), 257.
Scotti (Bishop of Trani and Piacenza), Cardinal, 3, 24, 35, 39, 73, 75 n. 2, 81, 137 n. 2, 160, 166, 172, 292.
Sebastian (King of Portugal), 256, 272.
Selvago, G., 132 n. 3.
Serbelloni, Gabrio (captain of the Papal guards), 6.
Serbelloni, Gian Antonio, Cardinal, 7, 16.
Sergiusti, Niccolò, 131 n. 3.
Seripando, Girolamo, Cardinal, 195 n. 5.
Sermoneta, Cardinal, 28 seq.
Serristori (Florentine ambassador in Rome), 10, 36 n. 1, 57, 65 n. 1, 144 n. 2, 266, 303.
Sforza, Alessandro, Cardinal, 7, 11, 22, 28, 37, 199, 216 n.
Sighicelli, Giov. Batt. (Bishop of Faenza), 313 n. 1.
Sigismund Augustus (King of Poland), 128 n. 4, 299.
Siguenza, Rodrigo de, 285.
Simancas, Didaco de (Bishop of Badajoz), 345 n. 2, 352, 354.
Simoncelli, Cardinal, 7, 178 n. 5.
Simonetta, Cardinal, 4, 7, 24, 29 n, 81, 368, 377, 379.
Sirleto, Cardinal, 3 seq., 7, 27, 37 seq., 43 n., 71, 81, 129, 132, 159, 184 n. 4, 192, 195 n. 1, 196 n. 2, 198 seq., 291, 335 n. 2.
Sixtus of Siena (Biblical critic), 130.
Sixtus IV., Pope, 171.
Sixtus V., Pope, 159, 234, 257 n. 4, 258.
Socinus, Fausto, 380.
Socinus, Lelio, 380.

Soius [Soye], Philip (engraver), 52 n. 1.
Soriano, Michele (Venetian envoy), 64.
Sormani, Giov. Franc. (Bishop of Montefeltro), 190, 217 n. 4, 261 n.
Soto, Dom. de (O.P.), 355.
Souchier, Jerôme (Abbot-general of the Cistercians), Cardinal, 156, 158 seq., 198.
Spinola, Publio Franc. (heretic), 317 n.
Sprenger, Bartholomew (painter), 127.
Stephanis, Bonif. de (Bishop of Stagno), 262 n.
Stronconio, Angelus de (Observant), 257 n. 5.
Strozzi (Imperial agent), 87 nn., 146, 169, 289 n. 3.
Stuerdo, Carlo (envoy from Parma), 87 n. 4.
Sudi, Marco (hat-maker), 223.
Surius (hagiographer), 203.

Tapper, Ruard (chancellor of Louvain university), 370.
Taxis, Giov. Ant. de, 304 n. 4.
Temudo, George (Archbp. of Goa), 210.
Teresa, St., 237 n., 275 seqq.
Terranuova, Duke of, 159.
Thomas Aquinas, St., 119, 129, 165, 200 seq., 242, 278.
Thomas of Villanova, 207, 236 n. 3.
Tiepolo, Paolo (Venetian envoy), 41 n. 5, 52 n. 1, 96 nn., 101, 169, 291, 313, 315.
Tiletanus, see Ravestein.
Toledo (S.J.), 348.
Torre, Michele della (Bishop of Ceneda, nuncio), 161 n. 1.
Torrentius, Lavinius (poet), 130 n. 7.
Tosabezzo, Franc. (Mantuan ambassador in Rome), 2 n. 5.
Trani, Cardinal, see Scotti.
Trennbach, Urban von (Bishop of Passau), 205.

Trinità, Della, Count, 48.
Truchsess, Otto (Bishop of Augsburg), Cardinal, 162, 193, 214, 341 n. 3.

Uchanzki, Jac. (Archbp. of Gnesen), 214 n. 4.
Urban VIII., Pope, 234.
Urbino, Cardinal, see Rovere, Giulio della.
Urfinus, see Orfino.

Valiero, Agostino (Bishop of Verona), 217, 218 n. 1, 248 n. 2.
Valtodano, Christophorus, F. de (Bishop of Palencia), 211 n. 1.
Vargas (Spanish ambassador), 18.
Vasari, Giorgio (painter, art-historian), 118 seq., 122, 127.
Vecchi (banker at Rome and Siena), 94.
Velde, Franc. van den (Bishop of Bois-le-Duc), 232 n. 5.
Veles, Marquis de, 174 n.
Verallo, Archbishop, 221 n. 1.
Vettori, P., 132 n. 3.
Vignola, Giacinto (painter), 123.
Vignola, Giac. Barozzi da (artist), 1 n. 2.
Vignola, Jacopo (architect), 123, 125 n.
Villalpanda, Bern. de (Bishop of Guatemala), 210.
Villavincentio, Lorenzo de (Augustinian hermit), 373.

Vincent of Beauvais, 119.
Vitelli, Vincenzo, Cardinal, 7, 15, 22, 30, 32, 35, 73, 75, 78 seqq., 83, 133, 137 n. 2, 153, 178 n. 5.
Volpi, Giov. Ant. (Bishop of Como), 212 n. 3.
Volterra, Daniele da (painter), 120.
Volterra, Ulisse da, 127 n. 4.

Walhain, Max de (Archbp. of Cambrai), 209 n. 5, 232 n. 5, 273.
Weydecker (protestant in Padua), 331.
Wied, Frederick von (Archbp. of Cologne), 210 n. 1, 229.
Wirsberg, Friedrich von (Bishop of Würzburg), 211 n. 2, 214 n.

Zambeccari, Pompeius (Bishop of Sulmona), 261 n.
Zanetti, Guido, da Fano (heretic), 307 n. 1, 317.
Zoppio, Hieron. (poet), 129 n. 1.
Zuccaro, Taddeo (painter), 127 n. 4.
Zucchi (pupil of Vasari), 118 n. 1.
Zuñiga, Juan de (Spanish envoy in Rome), 161 n. 1, 162 seq., 168 seq., 255, 347 n. 2, 348 n. 3, 350, 352–356, 361 seqq.
Zuñiga Avellaneda, Gaspar de, Cardinal, 161 n. 1, 164.